# Understanding Research

## A Consumer's Guide

**Vicki L. Plano Clark**
*University of Nebraska–Lincoln*

**John W. Creswell**
*University of Nebraska–Lincoln*

**Merrill**
Boston Columbus Indianapolis New York San Francisco Upper Saddle River
Amsterdam Cape Town Dubai London Madrid Milan Munich Paris Montreal Toronto
Delhi Mexico City Sao Paulo Sydney Hong Kong Seoul Singapore Taipei Tokyo

**Vice President and Editor in Chief:** Jeffery W. Johnston
**Publisher:** Kevin M. Davis
**Development Editor:** Christina Robb
**Editorial Assistant:** Lauren Carlson
**Vice President, Director of Sales and Marketing:** Quinn Perkson
**Marketing Manager:** Jared Brueckner
**Marketing Assistant:** Brian Mounts
**Senior Managing Editor:** Pameia D. Bennett
**Senior Project Manager:** Mary Harlan
**Senior Operations Supervisor:** Matthew Ottenweller
**Operations Specialist:** Laura Messerly
**Senior Art Director:** Diane Lorenzo
**Cover Designer:** Jeff Vanik
**Cover Art:** Jupiter Images
**Media Producer:** Autumn Benson
**Media Project Manager:** Rebecca Norsic
**Full-Service Project Management:** Aptara
**Composition:** Aptara
**Printer/Binder:** Edwards Brothers Malloy
**Cover Printer:** Phoenix Color Corp.
**Text Font:** Meridien Roman

Credits and acknowledgments borrowed from other sources and reproduced, with permission, in this textbook appear on appropriate page within text.

Every effort has been made to provide accurate and current Internet information in this book. However, the Internet and information posted on it are constantly changing, so it is inevitable that some of the Internet addresses listed in this textbook will change.

---



**Library of Congress Cataloging-in-Publication Data**
Plano Clark, Vicki L.
Understanding research : a consumer's guide/Vicki L. Plano Clark, John W. Creswell.
p. cm.
Includes bibliographical references and index.
ISBN-13: 978-0-13-158389-4
ISBN-10: 0-13-158389-1
1. Research--Methodology. I. Creswell, John W. II. Title.
Q180.55.M4P58 2010
001.4--dc22

2008052732

**Merrill**
is an imprint of

www.pearsonhighered.com

10 9 8 7 6 5 4
ISBN-13: 978-0-13-158389-4
ISBN-10: 0-13-158389-1

*To my parents, Jack C. and Ellen L. Plano, for all their support and encouragement and in recognition of their many scholarly accomplishments that showed me such a gratifying path to follow.*

*—Vicki*

*This text is dedicated to all of the students in my educational research classes at the University of Nebraska–Lincoln, and to all of the staff and graduate students who have devoted hours of time to projects in the research Office of Qualitative and Mixed Methods Research at the University of Nebraska–Lincoln.*

*—John*

# ABOUT THE AUTHORS

**Vicki L. Plano Clark** (Ph.D., University of Nebraska–Lincoln) is Director of the Office of Qualitative and Mixed Methods Research, a service and research unit that provides methodological support for proposal development and funded projects at the University of Nebraska–Lincoln (UNL). She is also a Research Associate Professor in the Quantitative, Qualitative, and Psychometric Methods program housed in UNL's Department of Educational Psychology. She teaches research methods courses, including foundations of educational research, qualitative research, and mixed methods research. She has authored and co-authored over 25 articles, chapters, and student manuals, including the books *Designing and Conducting Mixed Methods Research* (Sage, 2007) and the *Mixed Methods Reader* (Sage, 2008) with John W. Creswell. Her writings include methodological discussions about qualitative and mixed methods approaches, as well as empirical studies using these approaches in the areas of education, family research, counseling psychology, and family medicine. Prior to focusing on research methods, she served 12 years as Laboratory Manager in UNL's Department of Physics and Astronomy, working with the Research in Physics Education Group to develop innovative curricular materials to help students understand introductory physics concepts. In her spare time, she is currently working to develop her own understanding of quilt making and the game of golf, and she and her husband, Mark, take many walks with their little terrier mutt, Kona.

**John W. Creswell** (Ph.D., University of Iowa) is a Professor of Educational Psychology and teaches courses and writes about mixed methods research, qualitative methodology, and general research design. He has been at the University of Nebraska–Lincoln for 30 years, and teaches in the graduate program of Quantitative, Qualitative, and Psychometrics Methods (QQPM). He has authored or coauthored 12 books, many of which focus on types of research designs, comparisons of different qualitative methodologies, and the nature and use of mixed methods research. His books are read around the world by audiences in the social sciences, education, and the health sciences. In addition, he has co-directed for the last five years the Office of Qualitative and Mixed Methods Research at Nebraska that provides support for scholars incorporating qualitative and mixed methods research into projects for extramural funding. He serves as the founding coeditor for the Sage journal, *Journal of Mixed Methods Research*, and he has been an Adjunct Professor of Family Medicine at the University of Michigan and assisted investigators in the health sciences on the research methodology for their projects. He is a Senior Fulbright Scholar to South Africa and lectured during October 2008 on mixed methods and qualitative research at five universities to faculty in education and the health sciences.

# PREFACE

Welcome to *Understanding Research: A Consumer's Guide*! This title captures four perspectives that guided the development of this text.

First, this is a text about ***research***. We view research as a process of interconnected activities that individuals use to address important concerns or issues in fields, such as education, social work, and health. Individuals practicing research follow a general set of steps from the initial identification of a research problem to ultimately disseminating their conclusions so others can read and evaluate their work. Understanding this process is central to our thinking about research. We also recognize that researchers today have a large toolbox of approaches for conducting studies, including quantitative, qualitative, mixed methods, and action research. Each of these approaches is legitimate and appropriate for addressing certain types of research situations. This text provides a familiarity with these diverse research tools to meet the needs of today's students, practitioners, and researchers.

Second, this text is written specifically for ***consumers***. Consumers use research in their jobs. Consumers include anyone who uses the results and implications of research studies to enhance their knowledge and improve their practice. Practitioners such as teachers, school administrators, counselors, social workers, nurses, and therapists can all benefit from becoming competent consumers of research. In order to use the research, consumers need to know how to read and critique the research. This text's content and approach have been conceptualized to meet the needs of this important consumer audience.

Third, fitting the needs of a consumer audience, the focus of this text is on ***understanding*** research, not conducting research. Specifically this text addresses the skills, knowledge and strategies needed to read and interpret research reports and to evaluate the quality of such reports. This focus is reflected in the overarching organization of the content, which is based on the major sections of a research article. After an introduction to research in Part I, Parts II–VI present chapters related to understanding the introductions, methods and results, and conclusions of research articles using the different approaches.

Finally, this text has been written as a ***guide*** that offers readers practical advice and strategies for learning to understand research. Throughout this text we relate the process of research to the process of taking a journey. When travelers take journeys, they use travel guides to navigate new places, to identify special attractions and sights, and to develop an appreciation for local customs. Likewise, this guide to understanding research aims to help consumers navigate the major sections of research reports, identify key elements when reading each section, and develop an appreciation for how different types of research are conducted and ultimately reported.

Keep in mind that this is not an advanced text, and it does not discuss all of the approaches to inquiry that are available. In addition, this text does not provide an exhaustive treatment of the research process, as it does not present details that are necessary for research producers, such as how to conduct statistical calculations. This is an introductory text focused on helping students who plan to be research consumers learn to understand research.

## Key Features

This text is a comprehensive introduction to research that is conceptualized from the perspective of helping students learn how to read research articles. In developing the content and writing style, we have attempted to consider the concerns and experiences of a consumer audience by developing a text that is engaging to read, includes up-to-date content, and has a strong applied focus. The following key features highlight the approach of this text:

- It helps students learn to read and evaluate research articles.
- It provides a balanced coverage of diverse approaches to research.
- It includes extensive activities and examples to engage students with the content.

Let's examine these in detail to see how each can help instructors and students achieve their course objectives.

## Helps Students Learn to Read and Evaluate Research Articles

This text emphasizes helping students become competent and critical readers of research articles. To this end, we offer guides throughout the text for reading and evaluating research articles. The text also provides many features to further help students become more skilled at interpreting and evaluating research including:

- An organization built around the major sections one typically finds when reading research articles and reports: introduction, method, results, and conclusions.
- *Tips for Reading Research* suggesting practical advice for applying concepts when students read actual studies.
- Eight full-text research articles. The articles are introduced with a *Walk-Through* that focuses readers' attention on the main points of the major sections of the article. Each article is annotated to help readers recognize the major sections of the report, the steps of the research process, and the characteristics of the research approach. The articles also serve as the context for applying each chapter's content in the *Practicing Your Skills* application exercises.
- Criteria for evaluating published studies provided in a checklist for each chapter that students can use to evaluate a study of their choice or a study assigned by the instructor.

## Balances Coverage of Diverse Approaches to Research

This text provides balanced coverage of all types of research design. This provides readers with a complete picture of educational, social science, and health science research, as it is currently practiced. The text begins with an overview of the process of research and then guides the reader through understanding how this process is presented within the major sections of a research report. The content describes and compares four major approaches to research: quantitative, qualitative, mixed methods, and action research. Keeping with the balanced coverage, the full-text articles represent 3 quantitative, 3 qualitative, 1 mixed methods, and 1 action research study.

The text also encourages readers to go beyond the general approach to recognizing and evaluating specific designs commonly used to implement each of the major approaches. The research designs are introduced as important considerations for understanding the methods and results of research reports. The highlighted research designs include:

- experimental, quasi-experimental, single-subject, correlational, and survey quantitative research designs;
- narrative, phenomenological, grounded theory, case study, and ethnographic qualitative research designs;
- triangulation, explanatory, exploratory, and embedded mixed methods research designs; and
- practical and participatory action research designs.

## Includes Extensive Activities and Examples to Engage Students with the Content

Learning to understand research is not easy. For most students, research reports represent new vocabulary, new concepts, and new ways of thinking critically about information. This text incorporates many features to help students engage directly with the content so that they can better develop their understanding and skills. Examples of these features include:

- Consumer-focused objectives that indicate concrete goals for what students will be able to do after learning the chapter content.
- Topics that are often perplexing to consumers new to learning about research, such as how to identify examples of research in the literature and why reading research is relevant for practitioners.
- Practical examples from students' own experiences to help explain research concepts.
- Extensive in-text examples from recently published research articles to illustrate the topics discussed. Note that citations included within example excerpts are not included in the text reference list.
- *What Do You Think?* exercises with *Check Your Understanding* feedback help students engage with the new content as they are reading.
- *Tips for Applying Research* that offer students advice for applying chapter content to their own practice situations.
- *Practicing Your Skills* application questions with suggested answers (in the Appendix) to help students apply chapter content to published research reports.
- Key terms bolded within the text and defined in the glossary to provide easy reference.

## SUPPLEMENTARY MATERIALS

### MyEducationalResearchLab

For practice recognizing the information presented within the major sections of a research article, go to the *Building Research Skills* section under the topic "Introduction to Educational Research" in MyEducational-ResearchLab, located at www.myeducationlab.com. Complete the exercise "Identifying the Major Sections of a Research Article" and use the provided feedback to further develop your skills for reading research articles.

*MyEducationalResearchLab* is a dynamic online learning environment for students located at www.myeducationlab.com that helps students master course content. **MyEducationalResearchLab** is easy to use. Wherever the MyEducationalResearchLab logo appears in the margins (see example in the shaded margin box to the left), readers can follow the simple instructions to access the MyEducationalResearchLab resource that corresponds with the chapter content.

You will find two types of activities in the MyEducationalResearchLab materials:

- **Activities and Applications:** Give students opportunities to understand the content of *Understanding Research* more deeply and to practice applying content. Instructors may choose to assign these activities as homework or use them in class. Feedback for these activities is available only to instructors.
- **Building Research Skills activities:** Give students scaffolded practice to strengthen skills that are essential for understanding research. Feedback is provided to help students further develop skills for reading research articles.

The following online supplements to the textbook are available for download on www.pearsonhighered.com. Simply click on "Educators," enter the author, title, or ISBN and select this textbook. Click on the "Resources" tab to view and download the available supplements.

### Online Instructor's Manual with Test Bank (0-13-158397-2)

Crafted by Vicki L. Plano Clark, this supplement provides instructors with opportunities to support, enrich, expand upon, and assess chapter material. For each chapter in the book, this manual provides lecture notes that summarize important concepts requiring review and reinforcement, strategies for teaching chapter content, and suggestions for when and how to use the supplements with the text. The test bank contains various types of items—multiple-choice, matching, short essay, and fill-in-the-blank—for each chapter. Questions ask students to identify and describe research processes and design characteristics they have learned about and to classify and evaluate quantitative, qualitative, and combined studies and research situations.

## Online TestGen (0-13-158390-5)

This computerized test bank software allows instructors to create and customize exams. TestGen is available in both Macintosh and PC/Windows versions.

## Online Course Cartridges

The online course cartridges contain the content of the Test Bank for both Blackboard (0-13-158393-X) and WebCT (0-13-158392-1).

## Acknowledgments

This book is a culmination of our collective experiences in the classroom, working with colleagues and students and writing about research methods. We could not have written it without the assistance of and support from many individuals. Our thinking about teaching and writing about research methods, including many ideas that helped to shape this text, has benefited from our colleagues in the Office of Qualitative and Mixed Methods Research. In particular we thank Dr. Ronald J. Shope, Dr. Denise Green, Amanda Garrett, Dr. Kimberly Galt, Sherry Wang, and Alex Morales for their insightful discussions and reactions to draft materials. We also appreciate the support we have received for our research and teaching efforts from faculty and students in our Quantitative, Qualitative, and Psychometric Methods graduate program. We are also grateful for the expertise and feedback from Amanda Garrett, Courtney Haines, and Timothy Gaskill.

In addition, VPC personally thanks John W. Creswell and Robert G. Fuller who, through their mentoring and collaboration, have profoundly shaped her professional writings and educational practices. VPC also acknowledges the amazing support and encouragement she has received throughout this project from family and friends. She is deeply grateful to Mark W. Plano Clark, Ellen L. Plano, and Diandra Leslie-Pelecky.

We are also indebted to Kevin Davis at Pearson/Merrill for initiating this book and providing the vision to develop a text for the research consumer audience. Christina Robb, our great development editor at Pearson/Merrill, provided patience, support, and numerous insightful reactions throughout the development process. We also thank our production team, including production editor Mary Harlan, project manager Kelly Ricci, and copy editor Kelly Tavares, for their detailed work. Finally, we thank the reviewers who helped shape this book with their feedback and attention to detail: Lynn Ahlgrim-Delzell, University of North Carolina–Charlotte; Pamela H. Baker, George Mason University; Robert Barcikowski, Ohio University; Kathleen Gee, California State University–Sacramento; Nancy Mansberger, Western Michigan University; Pamela Murphy, Virginia Tech University; Deborah Oh, California State University–Los Angeles; and Colleen Willard-Holt, Pennsylvania State University–Harrisburg.

# BRIEF CONTENTS

To start using My Educational ResearchLab activate the access code packaged with your book. If you do not have an access code go to www.myeducationlab.com to purchase access to this wonderful resource.

# CONTENTS

## PART FOUR Understanding the Methods and Results of Qualitative Research Reports 231

# PART ONE

# An Introduction to Research

Discussions of research are all around us. You see research reported in the local newspaper, hear about recent findings from your physician, and may even consider it when deciding which new dishwasher to buy. Research also plays an important role for us as professionals. Research justifies new policies and forms the basis for new materials and practice guidelines. Learning to understand research is not always easy. Researchers have developed a specialized process and language for conducting and reporting their studies, and you need to learn how to interpret the vocabulary and steps as you read research reports. By developing your skills for understanding research, however, you will open up resources and knowledge that can help you become better informed about topics important to you personally and professionally.

Your first step is to develop a big picture of what research is. When a researcher conducts a study and writes up a report, it's like a traveler taking a journey to a new destination and putting together a scrapbook of their travels. Travelers use road maps to find their way along unfamiliar highways and researchers use the process of research to complete their research "journeys." In Chapter 1 you will be introduced to the steps in the process of research that guide research studies. This will provide you with a general research "road map" for navigating research reports. Travelers also take different types of journeys to reach their destinations—some use specific routes planned from the start, whereas others allow routes to unfold in order to explore unexpected places. Likewise, researchers conduct different types of studies to cover the "terrain" of interest. In Chapter 2, we will focus on two major types of research—quantitative and qualitative—and learn how to understand research articles reporting these different types of "journeys" using the same general map. Let's get started!

# CHAPTER 1 The Process of Research: Learning How Research Is Done

*We have written this book to help you learn how to read and make sense of research reports. To understand research reports, however, you first need to know a little about what research is and how researchers conduct and report it. By learning how research is done, you can better recognize and evaluate the information that researchers include in their reports. We begin this chapter by first considering the question: What is research? After presenting a definition, we discuss where you can find research and reasons for reading research studies. We also provide an overview of the steps researchers use to conduct studies, suggest criteria for identifying research studies, and introduce the major sections of research articles used to report studies.*

## BY THE END OF THIS CHAPTER, YOU SHOULD BE ABLE TO:

- State your definition of research.
- Name different formats where you can find reports of research.
- Identify your reasons for wanting to read research.
- Name the seven steps that researchers undertake when they conduct research studies.
- Use the definition of research to assess whether a journal article reports a research study or some other type of scholarly work.
- Identify the major sections that appear in a typical research report.
- Know where to look for the steps of the research process that are reported within the major sections of a research report.

Let's begin by taking a moment to welcome you to this endeavor of learning to read and understand research reports. Whether you are a student just starting your career or an experienced professional enhancing your knowledge, we hope you will find learning about research a rewarding experience. Whatever your profession—teacher, principal, school counselor, social worker, nurse, service provider or other practitioner—you can find information that is useful for your practice from research studies. For example, perhaps you work in a school where teachers, counselors, and administrators want to increase the involvement of parents. Some personnel think that a new program should be started to encourage parents to get more involved. Other personnel are not convinced that such a program will be the best use of resources. In addition, no one in the school knows what types of programs are possible, what benefits the programs can have, or which type will work best within the school's community.

This is a perfect situation where you could read research on an important issue, such as parent involvement in schools. Although you may have personal experience related to this issue, you may not be familiar with reading research. Therefore, to help you develop skills for understanding research reports, let's begin by examining what research is. We'll start by considering the questions: What is research? Where do you find it? Why should you read it?

## What Is Research?

Before going any further, let's consider a definition of research. **Research** is a process of steps used to collect and analyze information in order to increase our understanding of a topic or issue. At a general level, research consists of three steps:

1. Posing a question.
2. Collecting data to answer the question.
3. Presenting an answer to the question.

This should be a familiar process. You engage in solving problems every day: You start with a question, collect some information, and then form an answer. Although there are a few more steps when researchers conduct formal studies, this is the overall framework for research. As we examine how research is conducted and reported, you will find these three parts as the core elements of any research study.

## Where Do You Find Research?

You can find individuals using the research process and reporting what they learned in many different venues. For example, as a student, you may have conducted a research project and reported what you learned in a class paper. Many graduate students also complete research projects as part of their master's theses or dissertations. As a practitioner, you may find research discussed when you read reports prepared to help determine policies. In addition to these different formats, researchers working at universities report their studies in places where many different audiences including other researchers and practitioners can read them. The most common way that researchers report their studies is by publishing their reports as journal articles. Because of their importance and prevalence, this book will focus on understanding research studies reported in journal articles, but keep in mind that the same process applies to research reported in many different forms.

## Why Should You Read Research?

Whether you are a teacher, counselor, administrator, nurse, special educator, social worker, parent, or other practitioner, the knowledge base of your profession is continually advancing. The primary way that new knowledge is gained is by scholars conducting research on issues that are important to our practice. Researchers are much like bricklayers who build a wall brick by brick with each study. They continually add to the wall by conducting studies and, in the process, create a stronger structure or understanding. Therefore, you need to read research in order to take advantage of the new knowledge that is generated for your own knowledge base, position in policy debates, and practices.

### Read Research to Add to Your Professional Knowledge

No matter how experienced you are in your practices, new problems continue to rise. For example, today we face problems such as increased violence in our schools, the increased use of technology by students, and rising rates of childhood obesity. You can be better equipped to develop potential solutions for problems such as these if you remain up to date in your field and continue to add to your knowledge. Research can play a vital role in our understanding of problems by studying questions to which the answers are previously unknown. For example, you can better understand the problem of school violence with knowledge about the extent of violence in schools, the factors that encourage and discourage violence, and the meaning that school violence has for individuals. By reading what researchers have learned, you can add to your own knowledge about a topic.

*Here's a Tip for Applying Research!*

When you want to learn about a problem related to your practice, read recent research studies in addition to books about the topic to learn the most up-to-date information in your profession.

## Read Research to Inform Your Position in Policy Debates

Research creates conversations about important policy issues. We are all aware of pressing issues being debated today, such as the integration of AIDS education into the school curriculum or the use of high-stakes testing. Policy makers range from federal government employees and state workers to local school board members, school committee members, and administrators. These individuals take positions on issues important to constituencies. For these individuals, research offers results that can help them weigh various perspectives. By reading research on issues related to policies, you become informed about current debates and stances taken by other public officials. For example, research useful to policy makers might examine the alternatives on welfare and its effect on children's schooling among lower income families or the arguments proposed by the opponents and proponents of school choice.

## Read Research to Improve Your Practice

The third reason that it is important to read research is to improve your practice—that is, to improve your ability to do your job effectively. Armed with research results, practitioners become professionals that are more effective, and this effectiveness translates into better outcomes, such as better children's learning. Today there is a push for practitioners across disciplines to use evidence-based practices. **Evidence-based practices** are personal and professional practices that have been shown to be effective through research. This means that individuals are encouraged to use practices for which there is support from research (the evidence) and not rely solely on practices that have been done in the past. Here are three ways that research can influence your practices:

> *Here's a Tip for Applying Research!*
>
> When reading a research study, look for recommendations for how the results apply to practice. These suggestions are usually listed near the end of the *Conclusion* section and may be found under a heading such as *Implications for Practice*.

- ***Research can suggest improvements for your practice.*** When researchers conduct studies to add to our knowledge about a topic, this new knowledge may result in specific suggestions for how your practice can be improved. You can learn about these suggestions by reading research reports and looking for statements at the end of the report where the authors explain the implications of the results for your practice. For example, at the end of a study about youth literacy habits (Nippold, Duthie, & Larsen, 2005), the authors suggested numerous programs that could be initiated by speech-language pathologists to promote youth reading habits for all students, including those with language disorders, based on the study's results.
- ***Research can help you improve practice by offering new ideas to consider.*** You can learn about new practices that have been tried in other settings or situations by reading research. For example, a high school counselor concerned about the smoking rates of students placed at risk may read about a peer-counseling program reported from a different location that helps adolescent smokers successfully quit smoking.
- ***Research can help you learn about and evaluate alternative approaches to use.*** Sometimes the available research suggests several possible approaches for practice and you can choose the best approach from among the alternatives. Consider using the following process to sift through available research studies to learn about different approaches and determine which will be most useful for your situation. The process is demonstrated in Figure 1.1, which focuses on three steps that a teacher might use to select a new strategy to implement in the classroom (Connelly & Dukacz, 1980).

As shown in the figure, a reading teacher decides to incorporate more information about cultural perspectives into the classroom and wants to find the best strategy to use. By reading research on the topic, this teacher learns about four lines of research that suggest alternative strategies that could be used. Research suggests that incorporating diverse cultural perspectives may be done with classroom interactions by inviting speakers to the room (line A) or by having the children consider and think (cognitively) about different cultural perspectives by talking with individuals

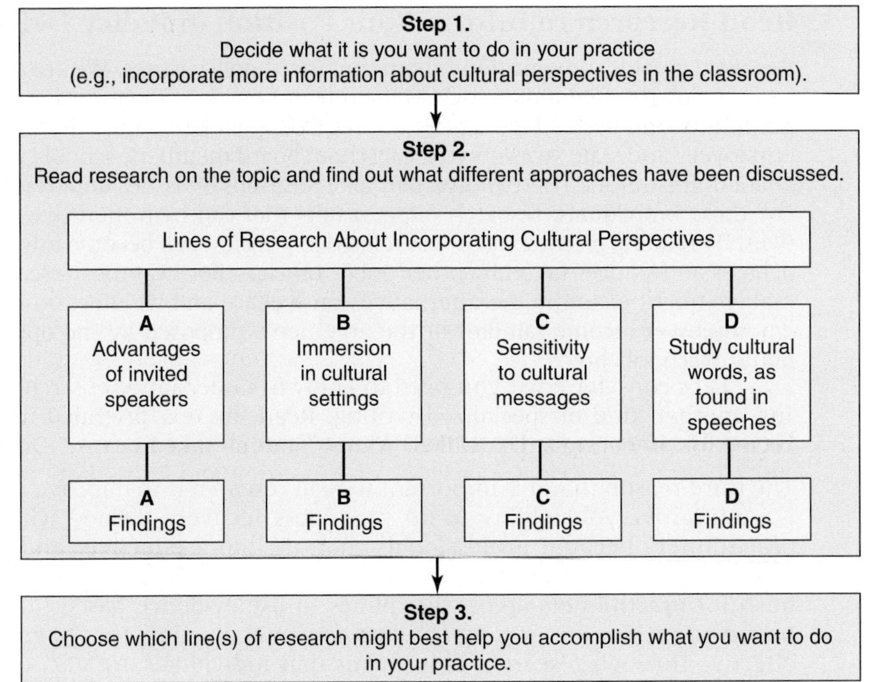


**FIGURE 1.1 Using Lines of Research to Evaluate Alternative Approaches to Practice**

*Source:* Adapted from Connelly & Dukacz, 1980, p. 29.

at a local cultural center (line B). It may also be accomplished by having the children inquire into cultural messages embedded within advertisements (line C) or identify the cultural subject matter of speeches of famous Americans (line D). This teacher can use this information to select a strategy to implement in the classroom to accomplish the goal of including more information about cultural perspectives.

## What Do You Think?

Consider the scenario introduced at the start of this chapter in which school personnel are thinking about starting a program to get parents more involved at school. What are three reasons why you should read research about parent involvement if you worked at this school?

### Check Your Understanding

There are many possible reasons why you would want to read research about parent involvement. Researchers conduct and report research studies to add to the knowledge about a topic. Therefore, you can read research about parent involvement to learn what the overall state of knowledge is about this topic. You should also read research studies to inform your position in the debate at the school whether to initiate a policy for a new parent involvement program. Finally, you could read research to inform your practices. By reading different lines of research about parent involvement, you could learn about approaches for involving parents in their children's education, such as using the Web to share information on what is done in class each day, starting a parents' club for parents wanting information on sending their children to college, or designing homework assignments that encourage students to involve their parents.

Did you come up with similar reasons? Now consider some reasons why you want to read research on a topic of your choice.

## What Do You Need to Know to Read Research Articles?

Hopefully you are convinced that it is important for you to read research articles to learn about the current state of knowledge about a topic, to understand different sides of an issue, and to improve practice. You may also be worrying that reading research is difficult and you are not sure how to understand the information presented in a research article. Reading research can be challenging, particularly when you are new to it. This is because the process of conducting research is a specialized activity and researchers use a specialized type of writing when they report their work in research articles. Therefore, to be a critical consumer of research articles, you first need a basic understanding of this process and the way that authors report it.

Let's consider what you need to know to understand research articles by examining another kind of specialized writing. Read the text provided in Figure 1.2. It is a recipe for preparing a dish called "Mom's famous baked beans." Does it make sense to you? If you have prior experience with cooking and know how recipes are reported, then you can easily understand the information in the figure. However, imagine that you have never seen a recipe before, you do not have any experience with cooking, and you have never eaten baked beans. Wouldn't this information seem strange and confusing? In order to understand this recipe, you need to know some basic information. First, you need to know what recipes are and a little about the process of cooking foods. Next, you need to know how recipes are reported and the types of information given in each section (a short description, the required ingredients, the directions for preparing, and the directions for cooking). You also need to know the special language used in recipes, from directions like "chop" or "bake" to abbreviated measures such as "tsp." for teaspoon. Finally, you need to know how to evaluate a given recipe (e.g., do you really have to bake the beans for exactly 45 minutes?). If you know this key information, then this recipe for baked beans becomes easy to understand.

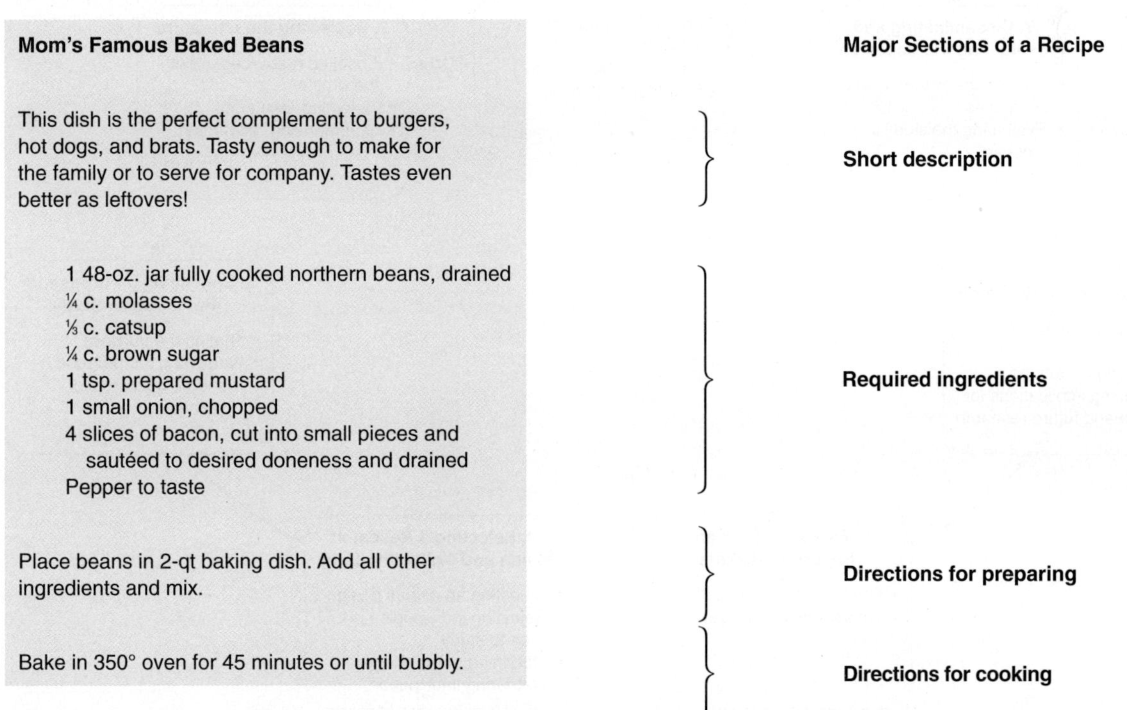


**FIGURE 1.2 Recipe for Mom's Famous Baked Beans**

*Source:* Reprinted with permission of Ellen L. Plano.

Just as is the case with reading recipes, learning to read and understand research requires knowing important background information.

- First, you need to know what research is and a little about the process used by researchers.
- Next, you need to know how researchers report their research and what type of information is given in each of the major sections of a research article.
- Finally, you need to learn the language of research and how to evaluate research.

These skills are introduced in the following sections and will be addressed in more detail throughout this book.

## What Steps Does a Researcher Take When Conducting a Study?

When researchers conduct a study, they follow a distinct set of steps. These steps were first identified as the "scientific method" based on the procedures used to conduct research in the physical sciences. Using a "scientific method," researchers pose a question, make a prediction, gather relevant data, analyze the data to test the prediction, and interpret the result to see if it resolves the question that initiated the research.

These steps provide the foundation for educational and social research today. Although not all studies include predictions, researchers use a process of steps whenever they undertake a research study. As shown in Figure 1.3, the **process of research** consists of seven steps:

- identifying a research problem
- reviewing the literature
- specifying a purpose for the research

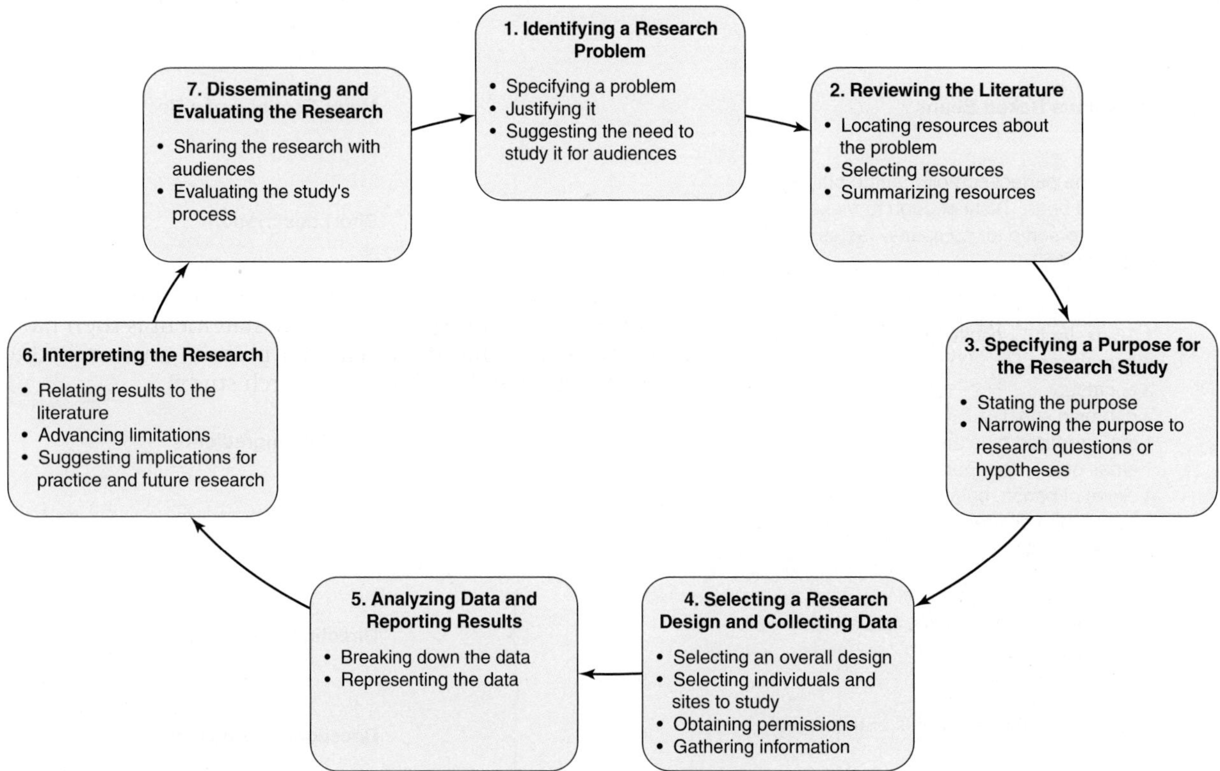


FIGURE 1.3 The Steps of the Process of Research

- selecting a research design and collecting data
- analyzing data and reporting results
- interpreting the research
- disseminating and evaluating the research

These steps provide a framework describing how researchers conduct their studies. In practice, these steps do not occur in a neat and orderly way during a study. In many cases two or more steps may be going on at the same time. Even so, these seven steps represent the major activities involved in any research study.

### Step 1—Identifying a Research Problem

Researchers begin conducting a study by identifying a topic to study—typically an issue or problem in education or society that needs to be resolved. **Identifying a research problem** consists of the researcher specifying an issue to study, developing a justification for studying it, and suggesting the importance of the study for select audiences that will read the report. By specifying a problem, the researcher limits the subject matter and focuses attention on an important aspect of the topic. Some examples of research problems include the increasing violence in high schools, the distractions caused by middle school students' cell phone use, and the difficulty of finding adequate foster parents.

### Step 2—Reviewing the Literature

It is important that researchers know what others have learned by studying the research problem they plan to examine. Researchers need to verify that their planned study does not repeat something that has already been done. They also need to ensure that their study builds on and adds to the accumulated knowledge about the topic. Because of these concerns, reviewing the literature is an important step in the research process. **Reviewing the literature** means that researchers locate summaries, books, and journal articles on a topic; choose which literature to include in their review; and then summarize the literature in their written report. The literature review conveys what is and is not known about the topic of the research study.

### Step 3—Specifying a Purpose for the Research

Researchers start by identifying a broad research problem that they want to address with their research, but they need to focus this problem to a specific intent for their study. **Specifying the purpose for research** consists of identifying the major intent or objective for a study and narrowing it into specific research questions or hypotheses. Researchers write a purpose statement that indicates the major focus of the study, the participants, and the location or site of the inquiry. This purpose statement is then narrowed to research questions or predictions that the researcher plans to answer in the research study. This step sets the direction and goals for a research study.

### Step 4—Selecting a Design and Collecting Data

An essential aspect of any research study is the collection of evidence to serve as the basis for answering the research questions and hypotheses. To get these answers, researchers identify an overall approach to the study's design and engage in the step of collecting or gathering data. The researcher **selects a research design** based on the specified purpose for the study. The research design provides the overall plan for collecting data, analyzing data, and reporting the results. **Collecting data** means selecting settings and individuals for a study, obtaining necessary permissions to study them, and gathering information by asking people questions or observing their behaviors. Of paramount concern in this process is the need to obtain accurate data from individuals in an ethical manner. This step produces a collection of numbers (e.g., test scores or frequency of behaviors) or words (e.g., responses, opinions, or quotes). The researcher collects these data to answer the research questions of the study.

### Step 5—Analyzing the Data and Reporting Results

Once researchers collect data, they next have to make sense of the information supplied by the individuals in the study. While **analyzing the data**, the researcher takes the data apart to determine individual responses and then puts the data together to summarize the information. **Reporting results** involves representing the results in tables, figures, and discussions to summarize patterns in the data and the results obtained from the data. This step produces the results and findings of a research study.

### Step 6—Interpreting the Research

Researchers end their studies by interpreting what they have learned. **Interpreting the research** means drawing conclusions about the results and explaining how they provide answers to the research questions. This interpretation can include summarizing the major results, comparing these results to predictions or other research studies, and suggesting implications of the results for audiences. Researchers also discuss the limitations of their studies and suggest implications of the results for practice and future research. This interpretation provides the conclusion to a research study.

### Step 7—Disseminating and Evaluating the Research

As a final step to research, researchers are expected to share their work publicly. This is called **disseminating the research.** After conducting the research, researchers develop a written report and distribute it to audiences (such as teachers, administrators, parents, or other researchers) that can use the information. It is by disseminating research that studies can make a difference for the problems in society that need to be addressed.

Researchers also share their research so other researchers and practitioners can evaluate it. **Evaluating research** involves assessing the quality of a research study. For example, most research journals use a process called "peer review" where experts in the field independently evaluate each study to determine whether it is worthy of being published within the journal. Different audiences use their own standards for judging the quality and utility of a research study. Researchers evaluate a study based on the quality of its literature, methods, and procedures. Practitioners consider the procedures, but focus on how useful they find the implications for their practice. Disseminating and evaluating research are an essential part of the research process so that studies and new knowledge are continually examined and critiqued by the larger community of researchers and practitioners interested in the study's topic.

> *Here's a Tip for Applying Research!*
>
> By reading and evaluating published research reports, you actively participate in the research process by assisting with the dissemination and evaluation of research studies.

## How Can You Identify Documents That Report Research Studies?

Researchers are expected to share their research studies in reports as part of the final step of any research study so others can evaluate it and learn from it. Therefore, when you read published documents, you need to be able to identify ones that report actual research studies. But how can you tell whether an article is a research study? Just as you can identify recipes by their list of ingredients and directions for preparing and cooking, articles reporting research studies also have key features that you can recognize.

### Look for Evidence of the Steps of the Research Process

Researchers engage in each of the steps in the process of research when conducting research studies. They also provide information about the first six steps when they disseminate their research in reports. Therefore, when you are reading reports and articles from the literature, you can use the definition of research and your knowledge of these steps to identify articles that report research. Examine the checklist for identifying a report as a *research study* provided in Figure 1.4. Research studies must include the collection of data from individuals (or some other social unit such as families or schools) and the analysis of that data.

Examine the study's title, abstract, and "method" section. Use the following list of questions to evaluate whether a written report is a research study. For each question, indicate the following ratings:

+ Your answer to the question is "yes."
− Your answer to the question is "no."

In addition to your rating, make notes about each element when you apply this checklist to an actual published study. You should be able to answer "yes" to all three questions for a research report.

| In a report of a research study, the author... | Your Rating | Your Notes |
|---|---|---|
| 1. Uses terms that identify the report as research, such as "study," "investigation," "empirical research," or "original research." | | |
| 2. Describes collecting data. | | |
| 3. Describes analyzing the collected data and reports results. | | |

**FIGURE 1.4 A Checklist for Determining Whether an Article Reports a Research Study**

When confronted with a new journal article, we first examine the article's title for clues as to whether it reports a research study. Words such as *research, study of,* or *investigation of* are often good clues. Then we turn to the abstract to look for evidence of data collection and analysis. An **abstract** is a one-paragraph summary of the article's content written by the article's author and placed at the very beginning of the article. Because they are so short (often 150 words or less), authors may not include good details about their studies in the abstracts. If the abstract does not satisfy the checklist in Figure 1.4, then we examine the article to see whether the author reports the collection and analysis of data.

## Watch for Articles That Present Other Types of Scholarly Writing

A common pitfall for those new to research is to assume that all journal articles represent research studies. In fact, there are many different types of scholarly writing that are published in professional journals. These writings may include thought papers, reviews of the existing literature, or descriptions of innovative practices. In most cases, these different types of scholarly writing may discuss problems, review the literature, and have a purpose, but they will not report the collection and analysis of data. Therefore, focus on the collection and analysis of data as the key indication that a document is reporting a research study.

With these ideas in mind, let's apply the checklist in Figure 1.4 to two example abstracts taken from articles found in the literature.

***Example 1—Identifying an article that is a research study***
This qualitative study investigated the perceptions of friendship faced by teenagers diagnosed with Asperger syndrome. This research aimed to provide teachers with an insight into the social world of Asperger syndrome from a student perspective. A multiple–case study approach was used to collect data from 5 secondary school students in Australia. Data were collected through the use of semistructured interviews. An inductive approach to data analysis resulted in a number of broad themes in the data: (a) understanding of concepts or language regarding friendships, (b) description of what is a friend, (c) description of what is not a friend, (d) description of an acquaintance, and (e) using masquerading to cope with social deficits. The insights provided by the participants in this study are valuable for teachers, parents, and anyone else involved in inclusive education. *(Carrington, Templeton, & Papinczak, 2003, p. 211)*

Using the checklist in Figure 1.4, we can conclude that this article is describing a research study. Notice how the authors used key words in the first few sentences including "study," "investigated," and "research," when referring to their work. This abstract also clearly satisfies items 2 and 3 on the checklist because the authors indicate that they collected data ("through the use of semistructured interviews") and analyzed the data (using "an inductive approach to data analysis").

***Example 2—Identifying an article that is NOT a research study***
This article presents an overview of a research-informed family resilience framework, developed as a conceptual map to guide school counselors' preventive and interventive efforts with students and their families. Key processes that characterize children's and families' resilience are outlined along with recommendations for how school counselors might apply this family resilience framework in their work. *(Amatea, Smith-Adcock, & Villares, 2006, p. 177)*

This article presents an interesting and scholarly discussion of issues and theories related to family resiliency and the implications for school counselors. Although the article may be very useful, and it discusses research conducted by others, this article does not indicate that the authors collected or analyzed data themselves. Therefore, this article is not an example of research, but is an example of a theoretical or thought paper.

### What Do You Think?

Consider the following abstract from an article about a vocabulary instruction program. Does this article report a research study?

> The author examined the effectiveness of a vocabulary intervention that employed structured, supplemental story read-alouds and related oral-language activities. Within each of 7 Title I schools across 2 sites, 15 third-grade teachers were randomly assigned to either use the intervention (treatment condition) or continue their usual practice (control condition). Trained test examiners administered oral and sight vocabulary pre- and posttests and reading achievement posttests. At 1 site, students in treatment, compared with control, classrooms performed significantly higher in vocabulary and reading achievement. In the other site, the intervention was not more effective. Contextual factors and student characteristics appeared to affect the results. *(Apthorp, 2006, p. 67)*

#### Check Your Understanding

From this abstract, we can conclude that this article is reporting a research study. The author did not use the word study, but she notes that she "examined" an issue. We also have direct evidence that the author collected data ("oral and sight vocabulary pre- and posttests and reading achievement posttests"). Clues that these data were also analyzed are found because two groups of students were compared, and different types of results from the analysis are reported (e.g., students in the treatment classrooms performed significantly higher).

## What Steps Do You Expect to Find Reported in a Research Article?

Now that you are familiar with the steps of the process of research and can identify a research article, we can consider how to read a research study. The steps of the research process are illustrated as a cycle in Figure 1.3 so you can see the interpretation, dissemination, and evaluation of one study often leads to the identification of a new problem, which starts the cycle for the next study. Consequently, researchers tend to keep cycling through these steps. In general, however, each research article reports only *one* cycle of the research process. In other words, most research articles disseminate information about six steps of the process as implemented for one study. These steps are recounted within the major sections of a research report.

## What Are the Major Sections of a Research Report?

Like most types of writing, researchers use sections to organize the information they report in a research article. As shown in the center of Figure 1.5, all research articles are typically divided into four major sections: introduction, method, results, and conclusion.

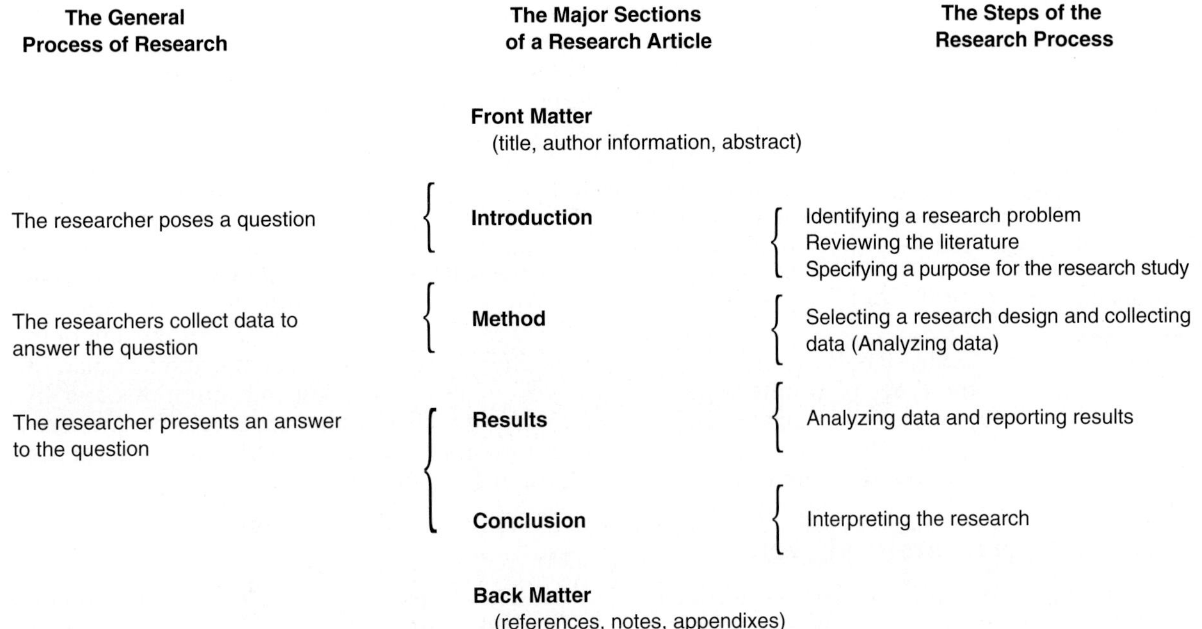


**FIGURE 1.5 The Major Sections of a Research Article and the Steps in the Process of Research**

*Note:* The final step of "disseminating and evaluating research" is represented by the entire published research article.

> For practice recognizing the information presented within the major sections of a research article, go to the *Building Research Skills* section under the topic "Introduction to Educational Research" in MyEducationalResearchLab, located at www.myeducationlab.com. Complete the exercise "Identifying the Major Sections of a Research Article" and use the provided feedback to further develop your skills for reading research articles.

In addition to these sections, authors also provide identifying information as **front matter** of the article (the title, information about the authors, and a short abstract) and supporting information as **back matter** at the article's end (a list of references, notes, and extra materials as appendices).

Figure 1.5 also indicates the general process of posing a question, gathering information, and answering the question on the left side of the figure to help you recognize the general process. It also shows where each of the more detailed steps of the research process is typically discussed within the four major sections. We do not list "disseminating and evaluating research" in the figure since the whole report represents this step. The four major sections provide an overall structure to articles reporting research studies. You can use them as landmarks to help you navigate through the information reported in articles. Each of these sections will be discussed in detail in Chapters 3 through 14, but we begin by introducing them to you here.

## The Introduction Section

Researchers generally begin their research articles with one or two introductory sections that introduce the study and provide background for the study being reported. These sections may be found under headings such as *Introduction, Problem Statement, Background for the Study, Conceptual Framework,* and *Literature Review.* In many studies, however, the text begins with no specific heading provided for the introduction section.

The researcher reports the first three steps of the research process in the **introduction section**.

- ***The introduction section begins by identifying the research problem.*** By identifying a research problem, the researcher provides a rationale for the importance of the topic and the study in a passage we call the "statement of the problem." Authors describe the topic and the problem and justify the importance of studying the problem for specific audiences such as teachers, administrators, or researchers

> *Here's a Tip for Reading Research!*
>
> Realize that the content of a research article is not written randomly, but it is organized using a definite structure. Use an article's major headings to understand the overall structure of the report and the information that is presented.

in this passage. You will learn how to read a statement of the problem passage in Chapter 3, "The Research Problem."

- ***The introduction section reports the review of the literature.*** The literature review may appear in the same section as the research problem or it may appear in its own separate section. In either case, the researcher reports information from articles and books to document what is already known about the problem that is being studied. You will gain an understanding of the steps involved in writing a formal summary of the literature about a topic in Chapter 4, "The Literature Review."
- ***The introduction section ends with the researcher specifying a purpose for the reported study.*** The statement of a study's purpose is the most important statement in a research study. It introduces the aim of the study, signals the procedures the researcher will use to collect data, and foreshadows the types of results expected. Researchers also report research questions and hypotheses that narrow the purpose to the specific questions that will be answered. Chapter 5, "The Purpose," provides information about identifying and interpreting purpose statements, research questions, and hypotheses.

## The Method Section

After the introductory sections set the context of the study, the researcher then reports how the study was actually conducted in the method section. This section almost always has a special heading such as *Method, Methods, Methodology,* or *Procedures.*

In the **method section**, the researcher describes the overall approach to the study, what we will discuss later as the study's research design, and then focuses on reporting the procedures used for data collection.

- ***The method section begins by identifying the study's research design.*** The researcher chooses an overall approach to the study based on the specified purpose. This approach guides decisions about the data collection, analysis, interpretation, and evaluation. You will be introduced to two overall approaches to research in Chapter 2, "Quantitative and Qualitative Research." In addition, Chapter 6, "Quantitative Research Designs," Chapter 9, "Qualitative Research Designs," and Part V, "Research Designs that Combine Quantitative and Qualitative Research," describe many different research designs within the approaches that researchers use in their studies.
- ***The method section reports the data collection.*** This section provides detailed, technical discussions about the procedures for collecting data. Describing the data collection means the researcher explains who participated in the study and the setting for the research, how permission to study these individuals was obtained, what data were collected, and how these data were gathered. Researchers can collect many different types of data such as asking participants to fill out forms or talking with them directly. Researchers need to provide clear descriptions of their procedures in their reports. Chapter 7, "Quantitative Data Collection," and Chapter 10, "Qualitative Data Collection," describe the procedures used for collecting data in research studies.
- ***The method section may describe the researcher's procedures for analyzing the data.*** After describing how the data were collected, researchers may briefly introduce the data analysis in the method section. The details of the analysis and subsequent results, however, are reported in the results section.

## The Results Section

The **results section** of an article represents the heart of the research study report. In fact, we have heard many students confess at the start of a course that they have only read the results section when reading research articles in the past. While the results may be of most interest, you can only really understand and interpret them within the context of the whole study and article. Researchers report their analysis of the data and the results in sections of a research report usually titled *Results* or *Findings.*

- ***The results section reports the details and products of the analysis.*** The data analysis process includes preparing the responses for analysis; implementing procedures to analyze the data; and reporting the results in paragraphs, tables, and figures. This is where you learn what the researchers found from their study. You will examine how different types of data are analyzed and reported in Chapter 8, "Quantitative Data Analysis and Results," and Chapter 11, "Qualitative Data Analysis and Results."

### The Conclusion Section

The final step discussed within a research report is the researcher's interpretation of the study. This interpretation appears within the **conclusion section** of a report, which is often called the *Conclusion* or *Discussion* of the article.

- ***The conclusion section reports the interpretation of the results of the study.*** Researchers summarize the major findings and interpret how the results answer the research questions stated earlier in the article. These interpretations include deciding whether the results confirm or disconfirm expected trends or predictions or examining the meaning of comments made by participants. They may also include comparing the results to those found in other published studies. In addition, researchers discuss the implications and limitations of the study. You will learn how to locate and understand these discussions in Chapter 14, "Interpreting the Research."

## Let's Apply the Research Process to Actual Studies

Let's start practicing your new skills by applying what you are learning to actual studies. In this book, we have included eight journal articles that apply the steps in the research process and give you examples of published journal articles reporting research studies.

At this time, read the two articles at the end of this chapter starting on pages 18 and 31. We will refer to the first one as the "quantitative parent involvement" study, and we will refer to the second one as the "qualitative parent role" study. As you read, note the marginal annotations that indicate (a) the major sections of the report and (b) the steps of the research process introduced in this chapter. Also, there are annotations that signal the major characteristics of quantitative and qualitative research to be discussed in Chapter 2. In Chapter 2 we will reflect back on these two articles frequently to demonstrate the authors' use of those characteristics.

While reading these articles, please bear in mind that they may seem difficult. Reading research studies will become easier in time as you learn to recognize the basic features of good research. For now, here are a few tips that will facilitate your reading:

- Look for cues about the major ideas by studying the headings and recalling Figure 1.5.
- Remember that research is a process consisting of several steps. Look for the major parts of the research process: problem, literature, purpose, data collection, data analysis and results, and interpretation.
- Look for the most important statement in the study—the purpose statement—which typically begins with phrase such as "The purpose of this study is," "The intent of the study is," or "The objective of this study is." This statement will help you understand what the study is trying to accomplish.

## Reviewing What We've Learned

- Recognize research is a process of posing a question, gathering information, and answering the question.
- Look for research reported in journal articles, books, school reports, policy reports, and student projects.
- Read research to learn new knowledge about topics, to become informed on policy debates, and to find suggestions for improving your practice.

- Expect formal research to use a seven-step process of identifying a problem, reviewing the literature, specifying a purpose, selecting a research design and collecting data, analyzing data and reporting results, interpreting the research, and disseminating and evaluating the study.
- Focus on the steps of collecting and analyzing data and reporting results as essential for identifying a report as a research study.
- Recognize that researchers report information about six steps in the research process within the major sections of a research article.
- When you read a research report, look for the introduction, method, results, and conclusion sections as the organizing framework for the information presented.

## Practicing Your Skills

Once you have read the quantitative parent involvement and the qualitative parent role studies at the end of this chapter, practice using your skills and knowledge of the content of this chapter by answering the following questions. Use the answers found in the Appendix to evaluate your progress.

1. Is the quantitative parent involvement report a research study? How do you know?
2. Is the qualitative parent role report a research study? How do you know?
3. Here is a list of the five major sections that appear in the quantitative parent involvement study. Which steps of the research process do you expect to find in each section?
   - The opening paragraphs (i.e., there is no heading for this section)
   - Influences on Parent Involvement
   - Method
   - Results
   - Discussion, Implications and Limitations, Conclusions
4. Assume that you are an educator interested in learning about parent involvement at school. Why might it be important for you to read these two research studies?

# The Quantitative Parent Involvement Study

Let's examine a published research study to practice the ideas we are learning. We will refer to this study as the "quantitative parent involvement" study. A formal reference for this study is:

> Deslandes, R., & Bertrand, R. (2005). Motivation of parent involvement in secondary-level schooling. *The Journal of Educational Research, 98*(3), 164–175.

This journal article reports a research study about parents' involvement in their children's education. The article begins by describing the importance of parent involvement along with different factors thought to predict their involvement. The authors conduct their study to explain the extent to which the different factors predict parent involvement at home and at school for parents with students in Grades 7–9 in the Quebec region of Canada. The researchers collect data from a large number of parents and analyze it to determine which factors are related to the two types of involvement. They conclude by interpreting the different models of parent involvement that they found.

As you read this article, note the marginal annotations that indicate (a) the major sections of the report and (b) the steps of the research process introduced in this chapter. Also, there are annotations that signal the major characteristics of quantitative research to be discussed in Chapter 2.

# Motivation of Parent Involvement in Secondary-Level Schooling

ROLLANDE DESLANDES
Université du Québec à Trois-Rivières, Canada

RICHARD BERTRAND
Université Laval, Quebec, Canada

Specifying a purpose for the research

ABSTRACT Inspired by K. V. Hoover-Dempsey and H. M. Sandler's (1995, 1997) model of the parent involvement process, the authors examined 4 psychological constructs of parent involvement: (a) relative strength of parents' role construction, (b) parents' self-efficacy for helping adolescents succeed in school, (c) parents' perceptions of teacher invitations to become involved, and (d) parents' perceptions of students' invitations to become involved. The authors obtained survey responses from 770 parents of adolescents in 5 Quebec secondary schools—354 parents of 7th graders, 231 parents of 8th graders, and 185 parents of 9th graders. Results emphasize that it is important that researchers distinguish parent involvement at home and at school when examining the predictive power of the 4 psychological constructs. Findings also provide evidence of grade-level differences in the predictive models of parent involvement at home and at school. Parents' perceptions of students' invitations was the most powerful predictor of parent involvement at home models across the 3 grade levels. Parents' role construction made important contributions to the prediction of their involvement at Grades 7 and 9; parents' perceptions of teacher invitations were associated with parent involvement at school across the 3 grade levels. Whether at home or at school, parents became involved if they perceived that teachers and students expected or desired their involvement.

Key words: parent involvement, parent motivation, secondary schools

**Introduction Section**

Identifying a research problem

01 In past decades, a wealth of studies showed that parent involvement is essential in children's educational process and outcomes (Henderson & Mapp, 2002). Parent involvement refers to parents' roles in educating their children at home and in school (Christenson & Sheridan, 2001). Involvement can take different forms, including discussions about school, help with homework, or volunteering at school. Parent involvement appears to have lasting benefits even through high school. When parents are involved, secondary students tend to earn higher grades (Deslandes, Royer, Turcotte, & Bertrand, 1997; Dornbusch & Ritter, 1988; Lee, 1994; Steinberg, Lamborn, Dornbusch, & Darling, 1992), show higher aspirations (Trusty, 1996), and have fewer disciplinary problems (Deslandes & Royer, 1997; Eccles, Early, Frasier, Belansky, & McCarthy, 1997).

A problem that calls for explanation

Reviewing the literature

A deficiency in the knowledge

02 Even though the benefits associated with parent involvement at the secondary level seem to be well understood, educators still know little about what factors lead parents to decide to become involved in their adolescents' schooling. In the present study, we explored how the psychological constructs, as defined in Hoover-Dempsey and Sandler's model (1995, 1997), influence the parent involvement process at the secondary level, and more precisely, at the first three grade levels in Quebec secondary schools. We addressed the following research question: What are the relative contributions of parents' (a) role construction, (b) self-efficacy, (c) perception of teacher invitations, and (d) perception of adolescent invitations to predict parent involvement at home and at school in Grades 7, 8, and 9? (Because the invitation for parents to become involved is presented by teachers and students, we considered, as did Walker, Hoover-Dempsey, Reed, and Jones [2000], teacher invitations and student invitations as two difference constructs, thus leading to four psychological constructs related to parent involvement.) Previous research on the evolution of adolescents' autonomy and parent involvement in secondary schools led us to expect some differences across grade levels in the predictive models of parent involvement at home and at school (Deslandes, 2003).

The quantitative purpose statement and research questions are narrow and specific

The literature specifies the direction of the quantitative study

## Influences on Parent Involvement

03 Jordan, Orozco, and Averett (2001) identified factors that influence levels and aspects of parent involvement. Family (e.g., education level, family structure, family size, parent gender, work outside the home) and child characteristics (e.g., age, gender, grade level, academic performance) are of particular relevance in this study. Research has shown that undereducated parents and single parents are less involved in certain types of involvement activities. For instance, Deslandes, Potvin, and Leclerc (1999) found that

*Address correspondence to Rollande Deslandes, Education Department, Université du Québec à Trois-Rivières, C.P. 500, Trois-Rivières, Québec, Canada, G9A 5H7. (E-mail: Rollande_Deslandes@uqtr.ca)*

adolescents from traditional families and well-educated parents report more affective support (parent encouragement and praise, help with homework, frequent discussions about school, and attendence at school performances or sports events) than do adolescents from nontraditional families and less educated parents. Astone and McLanahan (1991) also indicated that adolescents who live with single parents or stepparents report that their homework is monitored less than the homework of adolescents from traditional families. Deslandes and Cloutier (2000) reported that mothers are more involved with homework than are fathers. Dauber and Epstein (1989) argued that well-educated parents and those who do not work outside the home (Eccles & Harold, 1996) are more likely to be involved at school. Eccles and Harold concluded that parents with fewer children provide more help with homework than do parents with more children.

**04** Child characteristics also may influence parent involvement. For example, Deslandes and Potvin (1999) observed that mothers of adolescent boys communicated with teachers more often than did mothers of adolescent girls. Parents tend to become more involved when their children experience their first learning or behavior difficulties. According to Eccles and Harold (1996), parents of high-achieving children tend to participate more in school activities than do parents of low-achieving children. Epstein (2001) showed that parent involvement decreases dramatically as children move into secondary school. When Deslandes (2003) compared parent involvement in Grades 8, 9, and 10, he found a steady decline in parent involvement, but a steady increase in adolescent autonomy.

*Parents' Role Construction*

**05** Parents need to understand their roles because that understanding identifies the activities that they believe are necessary and part of their responsibilities as parents. In other words, parents are more likely to become involved if they view their participation as a requirement of parenting. Hoover-Dempsey, Jones, and Reed (1999) hypothesized three components of role construction, depending on whether parents focused responsibility for children's education on themselves as parents, on the school, or on parent–school partnerships.

*Parents' Self-efficacy for Helping Children Succeed in School*

**06** Parent self-efficacy is rooted in Bandura's (1997) self-efficacy theory and suggests that parents are more likely to be involved if they believe that they have the skills and knowledge to help their children. In other words, parents become involved if they believe that their actions will improve learning and academic performance (Hoover-Dempsey, Bassler, & Brissie, 1992; Stevenson, Chen, & Uttal, 1990). Prior research has indicated that parents believe that they will have more influence over their children's schooling when their children are in the elementary grades than they will when their children are in the upper grades (Freedman-Doan, Arbreton, Harold, & Eccles, 1993). In general, the stronger their self-efficacy, the more persistence parents exhibit in their involvement (Hoover-Dempsey et al., 2001).

*Parents' Perceptions of Teacher Invitations*

**07** Research also has shown that teachers' demands and opportunities for involvement, coupled with an inviting school climate, are related significantly to level of parent involvement (Comer & Haynes, 1991; Dauber & Epstein, 1993; Eccles & Harrold, 1996; Epstein, 1986). Parents tend to be more involved if they perceive that teachers and students both want and expect their involvement (Hoover-Dempsey et al., 2001).

The literature plays a major role

*Parents' Perceptions of Student Invitations*

**08** Parents will become involved if they perceive that their young children or adolescents want them to do so. Students' invitations are either implicit or explicit and emerge as a function of their age, their press for independence, and their performance level (Hoover-Dempsey et al., 2001; Walker & Hoover-Dempsey, 2001; Walker et al., 2000). For instance, when young children or adolescents ask for help with homework, they are expressing explicit invitations. On the other hand, if they express the desire to work alone, parents might respond by reducing their involvement. If children bring a poor report card home, they might be conveying implicit invitations. Seeking parental help does not necessarily mean that young children or adolescents are having academic difficulties. For example, Zimmerman and Martinez-Pons (1986) found that high-achieving students wanted more parental assistance than did low-achieving students.

**09** Reflecting on three of the four psychological constructs to involvement cited in the preceding paragraphs (i.e., parents' role construction, self-efficacy, and perceptions of teacher invitations), Reed, Jones, Walker, and Hoover-Dempsey (2000) found that parents' role construction, self-efficacy for helping the child succeed in school, and perceptions of teacher invitations represent motivators of parents' involvement in their children's education at the elementary level. Role construction was the first predictor of parent involvement; perception of teachers' invitations was the second predictor. Parent self-efficacy seemed less influential. The authors suggested that role construction may be a mediator of efficacy's influence on involvement (Reed et al.).

**10** In a study that compared 5th, 8th, and 11th graders' self-reported invitations to parent involvement in homework, Walker and Hoover-Dempsey (2001) revealed decreased levels of parent homework involvement across adolescence. Across the three age groups, students' invitations for parents' homework involvement was steady, but the

A deficiency in the knowledge

authors found that parents of younger students tend to help without being asked.

**11** Investigations are needed to better understand what motivates parents to become involved in their young children's education and, more particularly, in their adolescents' educational process. Researchers need to examine differences in parents' motivation to become involved across secondary-grade levels. To our knowledge, no study has yet examined the individual and combined contributions of Hoover-Dempsey and Sandler's (1995, 1997) four psychological constructs to predict parent involvement decisions across secondary-grade levels.

**12** We targeted adolescents in the first 3 years of secondary school in Quebec (equivalent to Grades 7, 8, and 9 in the American school system). Prior work (Deslandes, 2003) showed that parent involvement is significantly lower, and adolescent autonomy level is significantly higher, in the fourth year of secondary school in Quebec (Grade 10 in the American school system) than in the second and third years of secondary school).

**13** To examine how the four psychological constructs influence parent-involvement decisions across the three secondary grade levels, we posed the following research question: What are the relative contributions of parents' role construction, self-efficacy, perceptions of teacher invitations, and perceptions of adolescent invitations to predict parent involvement at home and at school in Grades 7, 8, and 9?

Method Section

Quantitative researchers include a large number of participants

## Method

*Participants*

Selecting a research design and collecting data

**14** Participants were 770 parents of secondary-level students attending five public schools located in urban and rural areas in the Mauricie and Centre du Quebec and Monteregie regions. The regions are representative of the general Quebec population. Forty-six percent (354) of the participants were parents of Secondary I students (equivalent to Grade 7 students in the American school system), 30% (231) were parents of Secondary II students (equivalent to Grade 8 students in the American system), and 24% (185) were parents of Secondary III students (equivalent to Grade 9 students in the American system). Nearly 51% of the students were girls and 49% were boys. Forty-seven percent of the students were first born in their family, 37% second born, 13% third born, and 3% fourth and fifth born, respectively.

**15** The demographics of the sample were as follows: Approximately 84% of the respondents were mothers, and 13% were fathers. The other respondents were either stepmothers or stepfathers, or others. Seventy percent of the participants were employed outside of the home. Seventy percent lived in a traditional family, and 30% lived in a nontraditional one, which corresponds exactly to what is being reported in the Quebec population in general (Quebec Statistics Institute, 2001). The majority of the families (37%) had two children, 25% had one child, 21% had three children, and the remainder of the sample (17%) had four or more children. About 3% of the respondents had less than a high school education, 65% had a high school diploma or a secondary-level trade formation, and 32% had a college or university education. Seventy-two percent of the participants had a job outside the home environment. Table 1 presents the characteristics of the whole sample and of the three subsamples.

Quantitative researchers select participants that are representative

The quantitative purpose statement and research questions call for observable and measurable data

*Measures*

**16** Among the eight constructs that we used, parents' role construction, self-efficacy, perception of teacher invitations, and reports of parent practices of involvement were adapted from the Sharing the Dream! Parent Questionnaire (Jones, Gould, Brown, Young, & The Peabody Family School Partnership Lab of Vanderbilt University, 2000). They are grounded in Hoover-Dempsey and Sandler's (1995, 1997) model of the parent-involvement process. The parents' perceptions of student invitations and their reports of involvement activities include items from questionnaires designed by Epstein and her colleagues (Epstein, Connors, & Salinas, 1993; Epstein, Connors-Tadros, Horsey, & Simon, 1996). The items have been translated in French, adapted in the Quebec context, and used in previous studies on the basis of adolescents' perceptions (Deslandes, 2000; Deslandes & Cloutier, 2002; Deslandes et al., 1997; Deslandes & Potvin, 1999).

**17** We used classical item analysis and factor analysis to evaluate the psychometric properties of the eight constructs (see the list of constructs presented as the predictors and the outcomes with the control variables in Table 2). The final decision of keeping or rejecting some of the items was based mostly on the eigenvalues greater than 1 criterion and on the scree test. For all the analyses, we used only those items loaded at least .30 on the factor to interpret the factors. We computed Cronbach's alpha reliability coefficient for each scale. We obtained all scores by calculating the mean score of the items of the same constructs, which are described in the following paragraphs.

Quantitative researchers use strategies to ensure the reliability and validity of instruments

**18** *Parents' role construction.* This construct measured the extent to which parents believed that it is their responsibility to help the school educate their adolescent (Hoover-Dempsey & Sandler, 1995, 1997). We based the construct on Hoover-Dempsey's work that suggests three types of parent role construction: parent focused (six items), school focused (five items), and partnership focused (six items; Hoover-Dempsey et al., 1999; Reed et al., 2000). Principal axis factor analysis revealed a single-factor solution that corresponded to a combination of the three types of role construction with a predominance of items related to the partnership-focused role construction. We used a construct that comprised 10 items ($\alpha = .72$) that measure behaviors that are parent focused, school focused, and

Quantitative researchers collect information in the form of numbers

**TABLE 1. Demographic Characteristics of the Sample and Subsamples (in Percentages)**

| Characteristic | *N* | Grade 7 | Grade 8 | Grade 9 |
|---|---|---|---|---|
| Adolescent gender | Female (51) | Female (44) | Female (52) | Female (60) |
| | Male (49) | Male (56) | Male (48) | Male (40) |
| Rank in family | 1 (47) | 1 (46) | 1 (46) | 1 (49) |
| | 2 (37) | 2 (36) | 2 (39) | 2 (36) |
| | 3 (13) | 3 (13) | 3 (13) | 3 (12) |
| | Others (3) | Others (5) | Others (2) | Others (3) |
| Participant gender | Mothers (84) | Mothers (84) | Mothers (83) | Mothers (87) |
| | Fathers (13) | Fathers (12) | Fathers (15) | Fathers (13) |
| | Others (3) | Others (4) | Others (2) | Others (0) |
| Participant education level | | | | |
| Primary level | 3 | 2 | 2 | 3 |
| High school or equivalent | 65 | 63 | 68 | 65 |
| College or university | 32 | 35 | 30 | 32 |
| Participant outside work | Yes (73) | Yes (76) | Yes (69) | Yes (69) |
| | No (27) | No (24) | No (31) | No (31) |
| Family structure | | | | |
| Traditional | 70 | 68 | 71 | 74 |
| Nontraditional | 30 | 32 | 29 | 26 |
| Family size | | | | |
| One child | 25 | 31 | 26 | 27 |
| Two children | 37 | 33 | 37 | 43 |
| Three children | 21 | 23 | 23 | 17 |
| Four or more children | 17 | 13 | 15 | 13 |

**TABLE 2. Control Variables, Predictors, and Outcome Measures**

| Control variable | Predictor | Outcome |
|---|---|---|
| Participant gender | Parents' role constructions | Parent involvement at home |
| Participant outside work | Parents' self-efficacy for helping adolescents succeed in school | Parent involvement at school |
| Participant education level | Relative parent influence | |
| Family size | Impact of parent efforts | |
| Family structure | Parents' perceptions of teacher invitations | |
| Adolescent gender | Parents' perceptions of adolescent invitations | |
| Rank in family | Invitations in academic domain | |
| Results in French | Invitations in social domain | |

The quantitative purpose statement and research questions call for observable and measurable data

mainly partnership focused in accordance with the adolescents' education. The parents had to respond to items, for exmple, "It's important that I let someone at school know about things that concern my teenager," and "I make it my business to stay on top of things at school") by using a 6-point, Likert-type scale that ranged from (1) *disagree very strongly* to (6) *agree very strongly*. One possible explanation for obtaining only one scale instead of three could be a cultural one. Another explanation could be associated with the fact that Hoover-Dempsey and her colleagues developed the constructs on the basis of pilot work with a small sample of 50 parents of elementary school children, reported in Reed et al. (2000).

**19** *Parents' self-efficacy for helping adolescents succeed in school.* We assessed this construct with Hoover-Dempsey and colleagues' scale after adaptations for parents of high school students (Jones et al., 2000). Factor analysis revealed a two-factor solution that accounted for 49% of the total variance in parents' self-efficacy for helping adolescents succeed in school. The first factor, relative parent

Quantitative researchers ask participants close-ended questions influence, contained four items (α = .68) and measured the extent to which parents believed that they could help their adolescent succeed in school compared with other sources of influence (e.g., "Other adolescents have more influence on my adolescent's motivation to do well in school than I do"). The second factor, impact of parent efforts, estimated the level of influence that parents' perceptions had on their adolescents' education. We assessed perceptions with five items (α = .63; e.g., "I feel successful about my efforts to help my adolescent learn"). Participants used a 6-point, Likert-type scale that ranged from 1 (*disagree very strongly*) to 6 (*agree very strongly*).

20 *Parents' perceptions of teacher invitations.* This construct provided an assessment of parents' perceptions of teacher invitations to become involved in their adolescents' schooling at home. We based the measure on an eight-item scale created by Hoover-Dempsey and her colleagues (Jones et al., 2000; Reed et al., 2000). In the present study, principal axis factoring analysis yielded a one-factor solution that was composed of four items (α = .70; e.g., "One or more of my teenager's teachers has spoken with me about homework"). We asked parents to rate the frequency of teachers' invitations on a 6-point, Likert-type scale that ranged from 1 (*never*) to 6 (*once or more per week*).

21 *Parents' perceptions of student invitations.* This construct is a modification of a similar construct for adolescents (Deslandes & Cloutier, 2002) that we derived from Epstein et al., (1993) and Epstein et al. (1996). Principal axis factor analysis revealed the presence of two factors that explained 50% of the total variance in parents' perceptions of student invitations. The first factor, invitations in the academic domain, included five items (α = .79; e.g., "My adolescent has asked me to . . . listen to him/her read something he/she wrote"). The second factor, invitations in the social domain, consisted of four items (α = .71; e.g., "My adolescent has asked me to . . . talk with me about current events"). All items were answered on a 6-point, Likert-type scale that ranged from 1 (*disagree very strongly*) to 6 (*agree very strongly*).

22 *Parent reports of involvement activities.* This measure was a modified version of the questionnaires elaborated by Epstein and colleagues (1993; 1996) and used in prior studies on the basis of adolescents' perceptions (e.g., Deslandes, 2000; Deslandes & Cloutier, 2002; Deslandes et al., 1997) and those designed by Hoover-Dempsey and her colleagues (e.g., Jones et al., 2000). Principal axis factoring analysis followed by varimax rotation revealed a two-factor solution that accounted for 35% of the total variance. The first factor, parent involvement at home, was composed of 16 items and assessed how often parents get involved in educational activities at home with their adolescents (α = .87; sample items: ". . . encourage my adolescent about school," ". . . help my adolescent study before a test"). The second factor, parent involvement in school, included eight items and measured how often parents were at school and how often they interacted with their adolescents at school and with the teachers (α = .67; sample items: ". . . go to school to attend an extracurricular event," ". . . have a conference with one or more of my adolescent's teachers"). Parents were asked to answer on a 6-point, Likert-type scale that ranged from 1 (*never*) to 6 (*once or more per week*).

23 *Demographics.* We collected information on family and student individual characteristics from the parents. Participants reported on their gender (mother, father, or other), education level (primary, secondary, college or university levels), family structure (traditional, nontraditional), family size (number of children living at home), and outside work (yes/no). They also provided information on their adolescents' gender (female, male), rank in the family, grade level (7, 8, or 9), and grades in French, their mother tongue, as reported in the last report card (see Table 2).

*Procedures*

24 We collected all the data from survey respondents by means of questionnaires in late spring 2001. Following the school principals' acceptance to participate in the study, we mailed nearly 2,560 parent questionnaires to the schools. Forty-five classroom teachers from five schools volunteered to send the questionnaires to 1,500 parents via the students. The package included a letter that explained the purpose of the study and requested voluntary participation. The participation rate was approximately 51% (770 parents accepted from the 1,500 questionnaires that were sent home). The classroom council received a token payment of thanks ($1) for each returned questionnaire, and the classroom teachers received a token payment of thanks ($10) for their collaboration and support. (The token payments were considered as costs associated with the collaboration and were paid through the research grant.)

## Results

Results Section

*Predicting Parent Involvement*

25 The primary question in the study focused on the relative strength of parents' role construction, self-efficacy, and perceived teacher and student invitation measures for predicting parent involvement at home and at school. We performed separate stepwise regression analyses to examine the best predictive models at Grades 7, 8, and 9 in Quebec secondary schools. We computed Mallow's C(P) statistic[1] for each final model and grade level. Descriptive statistics of the measures are illustrated in Table 3.

Quantitative researchers use statistical analyses to describe trends, relate variables, and compare groups

*Parent Involvement at Home for Seventh-Grade Students*

26 First, eight family and individual adolescent characteristics,[2] used as control variables, were introduced as a block and forced into the regression equation. Together, the control variables explained 4% of the variance in parent

Analyzing data and reporting results

involvement at home. After the introduction of the control variables, the analyses yielded a final five-variable model that explained an additional 42% (total $R^2 = 46\%$; total $R^2$ adj. = 42.5%) of the variance in parent involvement at home, $F(13, 232) = 15.47, p < .001$ (see Table 4). The variable corresponding to parents' perception of student invitations in the academic domain was the best predictor of parent involvement in schooling at home, $\Delta R^2 = .28$; $\beta = .31$, $p < .001$. The variable was followed by parents' role construction, $\Delta R^2 = .07$; $\beta = .18$, $p < .001$, parents' perceptions of student invitations in the social domain, $\Delta R^2 = .04$; $\beta = .25$, $p < .001$, and parents' self-efficacy, that is, perceived impact of efforts, $\Delta R^2 = .02$; $\beta = .15$, $p < .01$, and perceived relative influence $\Delta R^2 = .01$; $\beta = .12$, $p < .05$.

Quantitative findings include inferential statistics

**TABLE 3. Means and Standard Deviations for all Predictors and Outcome Measures**

| Variable | Grade 7 ($n$ = 246) *M* | *SD* | Grade 8 ($n$ = 156) *M* | *SD* | Grade 9 ($n$ = 112) *M* | *SD* |
|---|---|---|---|---|---|---|
| Parents' role constructions | 4.52 | .56 | 4.40 | .59 | 4.30 | .67 |
| Parents' self-efficacy for helping adolescents succeed in school | | | | | | |
| Relative parent influence | 4.14 | .87 | 4.13 | .94 | 4.14 | .90 |
| Impact of parent efforts | 4.41 | .66 | 4.32 | .71 | 4.19 | .73 |
| Parents' perceptions of teacher invitations | 1.55 | .61 | 1.40 | .52 | 1.31 | .48 |
| Parents' perceptions of adolescent invitations | | | | | | |
| Invitations in academic domain | 3.96 | 1.06 | 3.82 | 1.04 | 3.39 | 1.04 |
| Invitations in social domain | 3.80 | 1.06 | 3.61 | 1.0 | 3.65 | 1.0 |
| Parent involvement at home | 4.67 | .73 | 4.45 | .83 | 4.13 | .87 |
| Parent involvement at school | 2.28 | .70 | 2.12 | .71 | 2.00 | .66 |

Quantitative findings include descriptive statistics

**TABLE 4. Final Regression Models for Each Grade Level Predicting Parent Involvement at Home**

| Variable | $\Delta R^2$ | $\beta$ |
|---|---|---|
| Grade 7 | | |
| Control variables | .04 | |
| Parents' perceptions of adolescent invitations in the academic domain | .28 | .31*** |
| Parents' role constructions | .07 | .18*** |
| Parents' perceptions of adolescent invitations in the social domain | .04 | .25*** |
| Parents' self-efficacy | | |
| Impact of parent efforts | .02 | .15** |
| Impact of parent influence | .01 | .12* |
| Grade 8 | | |
| Control variables | .10 | |
| Parents' perceptions of adolescent invitations in social domain | .28 | .35*** |
| Parents' perceptions of adolescent invitations in academic domain | .07 | .26** |
| Parents' self-efficacy | | |
| Impact of parent efforts | .03 | .19** |
| Grade 9 | | |
| Control variables | .11 | |
| Parents' perceptions of student invitations in academic domain | .26 | .44*** |
| Parents' perceptions of student invitations in social domain | .03 | .20* |

*Note.* $\Delta R^2 = R^2$ change. Grade 7: Mallow's C(P) = 14.385; P = 14 (independent variables, including constant); Grade 8; Mallow's C(P) = 10.335; P = 12 (independent variables, including constant); Grade 9: Mallow's C(P) = 9.769; P = 11 (independent variables, including constant).
$*p < .05$. $**p < .01$. $***p < .001$.

The quantitative researcher represents results in figures and tables

*Parent Involvement at Home for Eighth-Grade Students*

**27** We observed a somewhat different pattern of relations in analyses conducted at the eighth-grade level; control variables explained 10% of the variance. Regression analysis revealed a three-variable model that accounted for an additional 38% of the total variance (total $R^2$ = 48%; total $R^2$ adj. = 43%) in the level of parent involvement at home, $F(11, 144) = 11.69$, $p < .001$. Parents' perceptions of students' invitations in the social domain was the most powerful predictor; it accounted for an additional 28% of the variance ($\beta = .35$, $p < .001$). Parents' perceptions of student invitation in the academic domain was the second strongest predictor, $\Delta R^2 = .07$; $\beta = .26$, $p < .01$, followed by parents' self-efficacy, that is, impact of efforts ($\Delta R^2 = .03$; $\beta = .19$, $p < .01$).

*Parent Involvement at Home for Ninth-Grade Students*

**28** The control variables accounted for 11% of the variance in the first step. A two-variable model explained an additional 30% of the variance (total $R^2$ = 41%; total $R^2$ adj. = 34%) in the level of parent involvement at home, $F(10, 101) = 6.81$, $p < .001$. Parents' perceptions of student invitations in the academic domain emerged as the first predictor in the final model, accounting for 26% of the variance ($\beta = .44$, $p < .001$); parents' perception of student invitation in the social domain was the second predictor, explaining 3% of the variance ($\beta = .20$, $p < .05$).

*Parent Involvement at School for Seventh-Grade Students*

**29** As shown in Table 5, control variables explained 9% of the variance in parent involvement at school. A three-variable model explained an additional 17% of the variance (total $R^2$ = 26%; total $R^2$ adj. = 23%) for level of parent involvement at school, $F(11, 234) = 7.51$, $p < .001$. Parents' role construction explained the greatest part of the variance, $\Delta R^2 = .13$, $\beta = .31$, $p < .001$. Parents' perceptions of teacher invitations ($\beta = .14$, $p < .05$) and parents' perceptions of student invitations in the social domain explained an additional 2% of the variance ($\beta = .15$, $p < .01$).

*Parent Involvement at School for Eighth-Grade Students*

**30** For eighth-grade students, introducing the demographic variables resulted in a small contribution to the model ($\Delta R^2 = .05$). Parents' perceptions of teacher invitations ($\Delta R^2 = .12$; $\beta = .31$, $p < .001$), and parents' perceptions of student invitations in the social domain, $\Delta sR^2 = .08$; $\beta = .29$, $p < .001$, added significance to the final model (total $R^2$ = 25%; total $R^2$ adj. = 19%), $F(10, 145) = 4.61$, $p < .001$.

*Parent Involvement at School for Ninth-Grade Students*

**31** For ninth-grade students, the control variables first introduced explained 9% of the variance in parent involvement at school. Subsequently, parents' role construction appeared as the stronger predictor of parent involvement at school (b = .36, p < .001), accounting for 22% of the variance. The second predictor was parents' perceptions of teacher invitations, explaining an additional 8% of the variance, which resulted in a final model (total $R^2$ = 39%; total $R^2$ adj. = 33%), $F(10, 101) = 6.48$, $p < .001$.

**Discussion** ← **Conclusion Section**

**32** We investigated the contribution of Hoover-Dempsey and Sandler's (1995, 1997) four psychological constructs—parents' role construction, self-efficacy, perceived student invitations, and perceived teacher invitations—to predict parent involvement at home and at school. We addressed whether predictive models might differ across the first three grade levels in Quebec secondary schools. The following paragraphs summarize the overall results.

**33** Of great importance were our findings that extended beyond family and adolescent characteristics—two different models that predicted secondary-level parent involvement at home and parent involvement at school. In similar research conducted with 1,227 parents of elementary students, Deslandes and Bertrand (2003) also reported two different parent involvement models—a home-based model and a school-based model.

Quantitative researchers compare results to predictions

*Parent Involvement at Home*

**34** With respect to seventh-grade students, after we controlled for family and individual characteristics, our findings showed that parents decided to become involved at home mostly because of their adolescents' specific academic invitations, such as asking (a) for ideas for a story or a project, (b) that a parent listen to the student read an original writing, (c) that a parent observe something learned or done well, or (d) for help to study or practice for a test. When personally invited by the adolescents, parents tended to perceive their involvement as expected and desired. Also predictive at a much lesser degree were parent beliefs that their responsibility was, for example, to closely watch their adolescents' progress and to keep abreast of activities at school (parents' role construction). Similarly, adolescents' personal invitations in the social domain, like talking with a parent about a TV show or current events or interviewing a parent for information or opinions, contributed to parent involvement at home. Contributing to a much lesser extent were significant parents' beliefs that their involvement could make a difference in their adolescents' school performance and that their help was better than any other sources of influence (parents' self-efficacy). Parents subsequently responded with high levels of involvement at home manifested by their help with homework when asked, discussions about school, future plans, course options, and so forth. Findings at the seventh-grade level supported a five-variable,

Interpreting the research

**TABLE 5. Final Regression Models for Each Grade Level Predicting Parent Involvement at School**

| Variable | $\Delta R^2$ | β |
|---|---|---|
| Grade 7 | | |
| Control variables | .09 | |
| Parents' role constructions | .13 | .31*** |
| Parents' perceptions of teacher invitations | .02 | .14* |
| Parents' perceptions of student invitations in the social domain | .02 | .15** |
| Grade 8 | | |
| Control variables | .05 | |
| Parents' perceptions of teacher invitations | .12 | .31*** |
| Parents' perceptions of student invitations in social domain | .08 | .29*** |
| Grade 9 | | |
| Control variables | .09 | |
| Parents' role constructions | .22 | .36*** |
| Parents' perceptions of teacher invitations | .08 | .31*** |

*Note.* $\Delta R^2 = R^2$ change. Grade 7: Mallow's C(P) = 12.199; P = 12 (independent variables, including constant); Grade 8: Mallow's C(P) = 12.845; P = 11 (independent variables, including constant); Grade 9: Mallow's C(P) = 8.138; P = 11 (independent variables, including constant).
$^*p < .05$. $^{**}p < .01$. $^{***}p < .001$.

predictive model of parent involvement at home that explained a significant portion of the variance (42.5%).

35 Concerning eighth-grade students, the full model comprised three variables that included, as the major predictors, (a) parents' perceptions of student invitations in the social domain (i.e., ask for opinion or information, discuss current events, exchange information on trends during parents' youth), (b) parents' perception of student invitations in the academic domain, and (c) parents' self-efficacy. One especially striking result in our prediction of parent involvement at home was the importance of adolescents' personal invitations in the social domain, such as talking with a parent about a TV show or current event or interviewing a parent for information or opinions. Those findings suggest that positive parent–adolescent interactions might contribute to adolescents' personal invitations to parents to become involved, which is related to subsequent parent involvement at home.

36 According to Belsky (1981) and Sameroff's (1975) transactional model, our results highlight the importance of reciprocal influences in the parent–adolescent relationship regarding schooling. Obviously, the quality of parent–adolescent relationships is key to a better understanding of parent involvement at home for secondary-level students. The quality of those relationships seems to be of paramount importance for eighth-grade students. The results are consistent with those of previous studies conducted in Quebec that provide evidence of the positive relation between authoritative parenting style characterized by high levels of warmth, supervision, and psychological autonomy (Steinberg, Elmen, & Mounts, 1989; Steinberg, Lamborn, Darling, Mounts, & Dornbusch, 1994), parent involvement in schooling (Epstein et al., 1993), perceived autonomy (Greenberger, Josselson, Knerr, & Knerr, 1975), and adolescent school grades (Deslandes et al., 1997; Deslandes, 2000; Deslandes & Potvin, 1999). Similarly, Deslandes and Cloutier (2002) found with a sample of 872 eighth-grade students in Quebec that specific invitations to involve parents requires that the adolescents are willing and open to work and exchange ideas with parents. The authors concluded that adolescents with a high level of autonomy, and more precisely, those who are highly work oriented and self-confident are more likely than adolescents without these traits to invite parent involvement.

The quantitative researcher compares results to prior research

37 Concerning ninth-grade students, analyses revealed a two-variable predictive model: (a) Parent perception of student invitations in the academic domain made the most significant contribution and (b) parent perception of student invitations in the social domain was a less powerful predictor. Whether parents believe that their involvement will have a positive impact on their adolescents' school performance is not significant at Grade 9. Rather, parents wait for their adolescents' invitations before they become involved at home. One possible explanation is that parents may consider that Grade 9 students have developed self-responsible behaviors toward school and schoolwork (see Xu & Corno, 2003). Consequently, parents rely on the adolescents to initiate the requests for parent involvement at home. That behavior somewhat reinforces the perspective that differences in adolescent autonomy modulate the degree of parent involvement at home (Deslandes, 2000).

*Parent Involvement at School*

**38** At the Grade 7 level, after the introduction of controlled variables, the addition of the four psychological constructs resulted in a three-variable model that predicted parent involvement at school. Across various family and individual characteristics, the more that parents of Grade 7 students believed their involvement was part of their parenting responsibilities (e.g., teacher conferences are helpful to parents; parents should call the school with concerns about their adolescents' progress), the more they perceived invitations from the teachers (e.g., one of the teachers spoke with them about homework; a school employee has asked the parents to have a conference about their adolescent), and the more they perceived invitations from their adolescents in the social domain (e.g., interview parents for information or opinions), the more they reported involvement at school (e.g., having a conference with one or more of their adolescents' teachers, attending an extracurricular event at school). Noteworthy is the more significant contribution of parents' role construction to the predictive model at the Grade 7 level. Parents reported that they would be more involved at school if they believed that it is their duty.

**39** Once we controlled for demographics, regression analyses yielded a two-variable predictive model at the Grade 8 level. Parents of Grade 8 students are involved at school if they perceive invitations from the teachers and from their adolescents in the social domain. The question of whether parents of Grade 8 students are involved at school seems to be primarily an issue of relations and parent–teacher and parent–adolescent relationships. We think of the development of trust in teachers (Adams & Christenson, 2000) and of positive parent–adolescent interactions as prerequisites to parents' decisions to become involved at school, and more important, at the Grade 8 level (see Christenson & Sheridan, 2001).

**40** For Grade 9, adding the four psychological constructs yielded a two-variable model that contributed significantly to the prediction of parent involvement at school. Parents' understanding that involvement at school is part of their responsibilities (parents' role construction) was by far the best predictor, followed by parents' perceptions of teacher invitations.

**41** To summarize, our findings clearly identify two categories of predictive models: (a) parent involvement at home and (b) parent involvement at school. Contrary to Hoover-Dempsey and Sandler's (1995) measures, parents' self-efficacy in its francophone version comprised two factors: (a) relative parent influence and (b) impact of parent efforts, whereas parents' role construction consisted of only one factor. Our findings confirmed the relevance of Hoover-Dempsey and Sandler's model mainly for the seventh graders' parent involvement at home model, in which perceived teacher invitations was the only missing construct (one of four). Parents' role construction contributed more significantly to seventh and ninth graders' parent involvement at school models. Parents' self-efficacy contributed significantly only in the seventh and eighth graders' parent involvement at home models, and its overall contribution was marginal.

Quantitative researchers take an objective approach

**42** Of major interest in this study is the powerful contribution exerted by parents' perception of student invitations in the models of parent involvement at home at the three secondary-grade levels. As adolescents mature, parent involvement at home becomes more a question of parent–adolescent relationships, which is particularly important at the eighth-grade level. Parents of students in Grades 7, 8, and 9 appear to be involved more proactively (e.g., in response to invitations) than reactively (e.g., in reaction to prior school grades, adolescent gender). The links between perceived adolescents' invitations and parent involvement at home are robust across various individual and family characteristics.

**43** Two notable patterns stand out in our results regarding parent involvement at school. The most outstanding pattern is the greater influence of parents' role construction. Parents must comprehend that parent involvement at school is part of their responsibilities before they decide to become involved. Also of interest in this study are the perceived invitations from the teachers to motivate parents to become involved at school.

**Implications and Limitations**

**44** The main implication derived from this study relates to the two identified categories of parent involvement predictive models. First, if the objective of the school interventions is to enhance parent involvement at home, the findings suggest the need to work directly with adolescents. That effort could be undertaken by (a) sensitizing adolescents to the importance of their inviting parents to become involved at home and by (b) coaching them on how to involve a family member in homework, discussions, or other tasks (Balli, Demo, & Wedman, 1998). For example, adolescents could ask their families to offer feedback about the assignments. Evidently, if parent involvement at home is the objective of school interventions, the involvement should focus on increased adolescent acceptance of and openness to developmentally appropriate parent involvement in schooling activities. Our findings also suggest that parent education programs should enhance parents' skills and self-efficacy. Parents should be aware of the importance of sustained parent–adolescent communication about schooling, and career and work planning over time. Parents could regularly attend workshops or meetings (e.g., parenting classes) to increase their parenting skills and their knowledge of different types of parent involvement, including less intensive involvement.

Quantitative researchers suggest implications for practice

**45** Second, if the objective is increased parent involvement at school, the implications are fairly straightforward: school interventions should first focus on individualized contacts

Quantitative researchers identify limitations in the study

that teachers initiate with parents. Our finding regarding perceived invitations involved specific requests from teachers, such as "One or more of my teenager's teachers has spoken with me about homework," ". . . has asked me to encourage my teenager to read," and so forth. Parents responded to teachers' specific invitations by attending an extracurricular event, by volunteering at school, and so forth. The findings call attention to the value of personal teacher–parent contacts for building trusting relationships that will be manifested subsequently by parent involvement activities at school and by other forms of parents' willingness to help. Those results suggest that preservice and inservice teachers could benefit from training programs that offer the opportunity to develop knowledge and skills needed to initiate first contacts with parents and foster parent involvement (Hiatt-Michael, 2001; Shartrand, Weiss, Kreider, & Lopez, 1997).

**46** There are limitations of this study that suggest directions for future investigations. First, the sample used in our investigation included only students in Grades 7, 8, and 9, and the subsamples were of various sizes. Future investigations need to expand across the secondary levels. We collected data only from parents of adolescents. Past research focused primarily on adolescents' perceptions; researchers should endeavor to use both adolescent and parent reports.

**47** Research findings indicate the need for further research on parent–adolescent and parent–teacher relationships to better understand parents' decision to become involved at home and at school. In addition, more research is needed on the relationship between parents' self-efficacy, role construction, and involvement. Some issues remain unclear. For instance, what is the explanation for the marginal contribution of parents' self-efficacy in the parent involvement at home model? As Hoover-Dempsey and colleagues (2000) suggested, is it possible that parents' self-efficacy is distal to parents' involvement decisions, whereas parents' role construction and perceived teacher and student invitations are more proximal? Researchers need to replicate this study in other settings by comparing different age categories to determine greater "generalizability" of the findings. Longitudinal research would help clarify the extent to which each of the studied psychological constructs changes over time and in different settings. To fully understand parents' motivation to become involved, educators need more qualitative studies that focus on the subject.

Quantitative researchers suggest future research

### Conclusions

**48** The results of this study highlight the importance of researchers considering parent involvement at home and parent involvement at school separately as opposed to their examining parent involvement in terms of global involvement. For example, parents' perception of student invitations in the academic domain made a significant contribution to the prediction of parent involvement at home but did not appear as a predictor of parent involvement at school. In addition, parents' perceived teacher invitations were associated with parent involvement at school, but not with parent involvement at home. Thus, the findings would have been missed had parent involvement been assessed in global terms. Obviously, the different models obtained in this study require more research that examines the influences on parent involvement at home and at school separately. In terms of practical implications, our research suggests that use of one of the psychological constructs should depend on whether parent involvement at home or parent involvement at school is the target. To enhance parent involvement at home, school administrators and teachers should work mainly with adolescents. To improve parent involvement at school, the results suggest the importance of sensitizing parents to their duties and responsibilities and of regarding the role of the school and the teachers when motivating parents to become involved.

**49** The results of this study provide evidence of grade-level differences in the predictive models of parent involvement at home and at school. For instance, at Grade 7, the parent involvement at home predictive model included three constructs: (a) perceived student invitations, (b) parents' role construction, and (c) parents' self-efficacy. At Grade 9, only one construct made a significant contribution—perceived student invitations. Regarding parent involvement at school, the predictive power of parents' role construction at Grade 9 was nearly twice as important as that at Grade 7. Overall, the pattern of results differs to some extent by grade levels. Analogous to those results, one might focus on the specific influences of each grade level that seem to be used in parents' involvement decisions. Further longitudinal research is needed to test changes in the models across all secondary grade levels.

### NOTES

This research was supported by grants to the first author from the Fonds québécois de la recherche sur la société et la culture (FQRSC) and to both authors from the Centre de Recherche et d'Intervention sur la Réussite Scolaire (CRIRES).

1. One can use Mallow's C(P) statistic to evaluate the amount of mean square error (bias and random error) in the model. We sought values of C(P) near or below *p* (number of independent variables in the model; Neter, Wasserman, & Kutner, 1990, p. 448). We obtained all statistics with SPSS 11.0 (e.g., the stepwise regression method and the SELECTION keyword [for the Mallow's statistic]).
2. Merging the 770 parents' file with the students' file totaled 514 cases.

### REFERENCES

Adams, K. S., & Christenson, S. L. (2000). Trust and the family-school relationship examination of parent-teacher differences in elementary and secondary grades. *Journal of School Psychology, 38*, 477–497.

Astone, N. M., & McLanahan, S. S. (1991). Family structure, parent practices and high school completion. *American Sociological Review, 56*, 309–320.

Balli, S. J., Demo, D. H., & Wedman, J. F. (1998). Family involvement with children's homework: An intervention in the middle grades. *Family Relations, 47*, 142–146.

Bandura, A. (1997). *Self-efficacy in changing societies*. New York: Freeman.

Belsky, J. (1981). Early human experience: A family perspective. *Developmental Psychology, 17*, 2–23.

Christenson, S. L., & Sheridan, S. M. (2001). *Schools and families: Creating essential connections for learning*. New York: Guilford Press.

Comer, J. P., & Haynes, N. M. (1991). Parent involvement in schools: An ecological approach. *The Elementary School Journal, 91*, 271–277.

Dauber, S. L., & Epstein, J. L. (1989). *Parents' attitudes and practices of involvement in inner-city elementary and middle schools* (CREMS Report 33). Baltimore: Johns Hopkins University, Center for Research on Elementary and Middle Schools.

Dauber, S. L., & Epstein, J. L. (1993). Parents' attitudes and practices of involvement in inner-city elementary and middle schools. In N. F. Chavkin (Ed.), *Families and schools in a pluralistic society* (pp. 53–71). Albany: State University of New York Press.

Deslandes, R. (2000, April). *Direction of influence between parenting style and parent involvement in schooling practices, and students autonomy: A short-term longitudinal design*. Paper presented at the 10th International Roundtable on School, Family, and Community Partnerships, New Orleans, LA. (ERIC Document Reproduction Service No. ED441586)

Deslandes, R. (2003). Evolution of parenting and parent involvement in schooling practices and Canadian adolescents' autonomy over a three-year span. In S. Castelli, M. Mendel, & B. Ravns (Eds.), *School, family, and community partnerships in a world of differences and change* (pp. 89–104). Poland: Gdansk University.

Deslandes, R., & Bertrand, R. (2003). *Raisons qui motivent les parents à participer au suivi scolaire de leur enfant du primaire*. [Reasons that motivate parents to be involved in their child's schooling at the elementary level]. Manuscript submitted for publication.

Deslandes, R., & Cloutier, R. (2000). Engagement parent dans l'accompagnement scolaire et réussite des adolescents à l'école.[Parent involvement in their adosescent's schooling and success in school]. *Bulletin de Psychologie Scolaire et d'Orientation, 2*, 1–21.

Deslandes, R., & Cloutier, R. (2002). Adolescents' perception of parent-school involvement. *School Psychology International, 23*(2), 220–232.

Deslandes, R., & Potvin, P. (1999, April). *Autonomy, parenting, parent involvement in schooling and school achievement: Perception of Quebec adolescents*. Paper presented at the annual meeting of the American Educational Research Association, Montreal, Canada. (ERIC Document Reproduction Service No. ED430697)

Deslandes, R., Potvin, P., & Leclerc, D. (1999). Family characteristics predictors of school achievement: Parent involvement as a mediator. *McGill Journal of Education, 34*(2), 133–151.

Deslandes, R., & Royer, É. (1997). Family-related variables and school disciplinary events at the secondary level. *Behavioral Disorders, 23*(1), 18–28.

Deslandes, R., Royer, E., Turcotte, D., & Bertrand, R. (1997). School achievement at the secondary level: Influence of parenting style and parent involvement in schooling. *McGill Journal of Education, 32*(3), 191–208.

Dornbusch, S. M., & Ritter, P. L. (1988). Parents of high school students: A neglected resource. *Educational Horizons, 66*(2), 75–77.

Eccles, J. S., Early, D., Frasier, K., Belansky, E., & McCarthy, K. (1997). The relation of connection, regulation, and support for autonomy to adolescents' functioning. *Journal of Adolescent Research, 12*, 263–286.

Eccles, J. S., & Harold, R. D. (1996). Family involvement in children's and adolescents' schooling. In A. Booth & J. Dunn (Eds.), *Family–school links: How do they affect educational outcomes?* Hillsdale, NJ: Erlbaum.

Epstein, J. L. (1986). Parents' reactions to teacher practices of parent involvement. *Elementary School Journal, 86*, 277–294.

Epstein, J. L. (2001). *School, family, and community partnerships: Preparing educators and improving schools*. Boulder, CO: Westview Press.

Epstein, J. L., Connors-Tadros, L., Horsey, C. S., & Simon, B. S. (1996). *A report from the School, Family & Community Partnership Project*. Baltimore: Johns Hopkins University, Center on Families, Communities, Schools and Children's Learning.

Epstein, J. L., Connors, L. J., & Salinas, K. C. (1993). *High school and family partnerships: Questionnaires for teachers, parents, and students*. Baltimore: Johns Hopkins University, Center on Families, Communities, Schools and Children's Learning.

Freedman-Doan, C., Arbreton, A. J., Harold, R. D., & Eccles, J. S. (1993). Looking forward to adolescence: Mothers' and fathers' expectations for affective and behavioral change. *Journal of Early Adolescence, 13*, 472–502.

Greenberger, E., Josselson, R., Knerr, C., & Knerr, B. (1975). The measurement and structure of psychosocial maturity. *Journal of Youth and Adolescence, 4*, 127–143.

Henderson, A. T., & Mapp, K. L. (2002). *A new wave of evidence. The impact of school, family, and community connections on student achievement. Annual synthesis*. Austin, TX: National Center for Family & Community Connections with Schools. Southwest Educational Development Laboratory. Retrieved from http://www.sedl.org/connections

Hiatt-Michael, D. (Ed). (2001). *Promising practices for family involvement in school*. Greenwich, CT: Information Age Publishing, Inc.

Hoover-Dempsey, K. V., Bassler, O. C., & Brissie, J. S. (1992). Explorations in parent–school relations. *The Journal of Educational Research, 85*, 287–294.

Hoover-Dempsey, K. V., Battiato, A. C., Walker, J. M. T., Reed, R. P., DeJong, J. M., & Jones, K. P. (2001). Parent involvement in homework. *Educational Psychologist, 36*, 195–209.

Hoover-Dempsey, K. V., Jones, K. P., & Reed, R. (1999, April). *"I wish I were a bird in the window": The voices of parents seeking children's school success*. Paper presented at the annual meeting of the American Educational Research Association, Montréal, Canada.

Hoover-Dempsey, K. V., & Sandler, H. M. (1995). Parent involvement in children's education: Why does it make a difference? *Teachers College Record, 95*, 310–331.

Hoover-Dempsey, K. V., & Sandler, H. M. (1997). Why do parents become involved in their children's education? *Review of Educational Research, 67*, 3–42.

Jones, K., Gould, D., Brown, A., Young, J., & The Peabody Family School Partnership Lab of Vanderbilt University. (2000). *"Sharing the dream" parent questionnaire*. Retrieved from http://www.Vanderbilt.edu/Peabody/family-school

Jordan, C., Orozco, E., & Averett, A. (2001). Emerging issues in school, family, & community connections. Austin, TX: National Center for Family & Community Connections with Schools. Southwest Educational Development Laboratory. Retrieved from http://www.sedl.org/connections

Lee, S. (1994). *Family-school connections and students' education: Continuity and change of family involvement from the middle grades to high school*. Unpublished doctoral dissertation, Johns Hopkins University, Baltimore, MD.

Neter, J., Wasserman, W., & Kutner, M. H. (1990). *Applied linear statistical models*. Homewood, IL: Irwin.

Quebec Statistics Institute. (2001). *Portrait social du Québec. Données et analyses*. Quebec, Canada: Publications gouvernementales du Québec.

Reed, R. P., Jones, K. P., Walker, J. M., & Hoover-Dempsey, K. V. (2000, April). *Parents' motivations for involvement in children's education: Testing a theoretical model*. Paper presented at the annual meeting of the American Educational Research Association, New Orleans, LA.

Sameroff, A. J. (1975). Early influences on development: Fact or fancy. *Merrill-Palmer Quarterly, 21*, 267–294.

Shartrand, A. M., Weiss, H. B. Kreider, H. M., & Lopez, M. E. (1997). *New skills for new schools: Preparing teachers in family involvement*. Harvard Family Research Project. Cambridge, MA: Harvard Graduate School of Education. Retrieved from http://www.ed.gov/pubs/New Skills

Steinberg, L., Elmen, J. D., & Mounts, N. S. (1989). Authoritative parenting, psychosocial maturity, and academic success among adolescents. *Child Development, 60*, 1424–1436.

Steinberg, L., Lamborn, S. D., Darling, N., Mounts, N. S., & Dornbusch, S. M. (1994). Over-time changes in adjustment and competence among adolescents from authoritative, authoritarian, indulgent, and neglectful families. *Child Development, 65*, 754–770.

Steinberg, L., Lamborn, S. D., Dornbusch, S. M., & Darling, N. (1992). Impact of parenting practices on adolescent achievement: Authoritative parenting, school involvement, and encouragement to succeed. *Child Development, 63*, 1266–1281.

Stevenson, H. W., Chen, C., & Uttal, D. H. (1990). Beliefs and achievement. A study of Black, White, and Hispanic children. *Child Development, 6*, 508–523.

Trusty, J. (1996). Relationship of parent involvement in teens' career development to teens' attitudes, perceptions, and behavior. *Journal of Research and Development in Education, 30*, 317–323.

Walker, J. M. T., & Hoover-Dempsey, K. V. (2001, April). *Age-related patterns in student invitations to parent involvement in homework*. Paper presented at the annual meeting of the American Educational Research Association, Seattle, WA.

Walker, J. M., Hoover-Dempsey, K. V., Reed, R. P., & Jones, K. P. (2000,

April). *"Can you help me with my homework?" Elementary school children's invitations and perspectives on parent involvement*. Paper presented at the annual meeting of the American Educational Research Association, New Orleans, LA.

Xu, J., & Corno, L. (2003). Family help and homework management reported by middle school students. *The Elementary School Journal, 103*, 503–536.

Zimmerman, B. J., & Martinez-Pons, M. P. (1986). Development of a structured interview for assessing student use of self-regulated learning strategies. *American Educational Research Journal, 23*, 614–628.

# The Qualitative Parent Role Study

Let's examine another research study to practice the ideas we are learning. We will refer to this study as the "qualitative parent role" study. A formal reference for this study is:

> Auerbach, S. (2007). From moral supporters to struggling advocates: Reconceptualizing parent roles in education through experience of working-class families of color. *Urban Education, 42*(3), 250–283.

This journal article reports a research study about the roles that working class parents of color create for being involved in their children's education. The article begins by describing that students of color are underrepresented in college and the importance of parent involvement on students' pursuit of a college education. The author conducts her study to explore the different roles that working-class parents of color create when their high school-age children want to go to college. She interviews a small number of parents participating in a college-access program and observes their behaviors at program meetings. From her data, she develops a typology of three different parent types based on their beliefs and actions. She concludes by interpreting the different parent roles and their implications for theory and for educators working with similar parents.

As you read this article, note the marginal annotations that indicate (a) the major sections of the report and (b) the steps of the research process introduced in this chapter. Also, there are annotations that signal the major characteristics of qualitative research to be discussed in Chapter 2.

Urban Education
Volume 42 Number 3
May 2007 250-283

10.1177/0042085907300433
http://uex.sagepub.com
hosted at
http://online.sagepub.com

# From Moral Supporters to Struggling Advocates

## Reconceptualizing Parent Roles in Education Through the Experience of Working-Class Families of Color

Susan Auerbach
*California State University, Northridge*

How do marginalized parents construct their role in promoting their children's access to educational opportunity? What lessons might their experience have for our understanding of parent involvement beyond the parameters of traditional models? This qualitative case study examined the beliefs, goals, and practices of 16 working-class African American and Latino parents whose children were in a college access program at a diverse metropolitan high school. It offers an alternative typology of parent roles, which reflects parents' contrasting social and cultural locations, biographies, and perceptions of—as well as relations with—their children and the school. With its highlighting of marginalized parents' voices at a critical juncture in student careers, this article contributes to a more inclusive discourse on families, schooling, and equity.

***Keywords:*** *parent involvement; college access; secondary education; high school; Latino education; educational equity*

Introduction Section

Identifying a research problem

A problem that calls for exploration

01 How do marginalized parents construct their role in promoting their children's access to educational opportunity, specifically college? This question is important in light of persistent patterns of underrepresentation of students of color in 4-year colleges, the well-documented influence of parents on students' aspirations and college pursuit, and calls for greater parent involvement in schooling (Gandara, 1995; Gandara & Bial, 1999; Hossler, Schmit, & Vesper, 1999; McDonough, 1997; Plank & Jordan, 1997). Indeed, parent roles can profoundly affect the extent to which low socioeconomic status (SES) students experience "conflict and challenge" on the pathway to college (Auerbach, 2001; McDonough, 1997).

A deficiency in the knowledge

02 Traditional parent involvement models of family-school partnerships, and the studies based on them, offer little insight into questions of access. In these works, consensus and cooperation are assumed; parent involvement is treated as a social fact on neutral terrain rather than as a socially constructed phenomenon on the contested terrain of schooling. Partnership models fail to acknowledge the ways in which parent roles in education, and the home-school relations in which they are embedded, are a reflection of broader social inequalities that affect students. The unequal distribution of economic, human, cultural, and social capital—in addition to schools' devaluing of the resources of lower SES families—constrain parents' involvement options, inclinations, and relations with schools (Auerbach, 2001; Lareau, 1989, 2003; Lareau & Horvat, 1999). Parents of color and schools often are separated by cultural divides as well as by legacies of racism, deficit thinking, and mutual distrust (Delgado-Gaitan, 1994b; Fine, 1993; Fordham, 1996). African American and Latino parents are more likely than those of the dominant culture to have a skeptical, ambivalent, and potentially adversarial stance toward school programs that have historically failed their communities (Lareau & Horvat, 1999; Olivos, 2003; Tillman, 2004). If the norm for students of color is underachievement in K-12 schools and underrepresentation in 4-year colleges, then parents of color with high educational aspirations for their children may need to take deliberate steps to ensure access and counter the tendencies of schools to reproduce inequality (Abrams & Gibbs, 2002; Auerbach, 2001; Delgado-Gaitan & Segura, 1989).

Qualitative researchers use research designs to plan their studies

Specifying a purpose for the research

The qualitative purpose statement and research questions explore a central phenomenon

03 This study draws on 3 years of ethnographic data to illustrate one of many possible alternative typologies of parent roles in the pursuit of educational access. What do parents of color without college experience think and do when they want their high school–age students to go to college? What shapes their beliefs, goals, and support strategies? Findings suggest that the involvement of working-class parents of color may be motivated by distinctive concerns linked to their social and cultural location, such as the need to help their students navigate barriers in the K-16 system or to transform family approaches to social mobility. Just as these parents' nontraditional strategies are often invisible to schools (Mehan, Villanueva, Hubbard, & Lintz, 1996), so too are their roles largely outside the partnership model. With its highlighting of marginalized parents' voices and the cultural logic behind their actions at a critical juncture in student careers, this article suggests directions for reconceptualizing parent roles in education and contributes to a more inclusive discourse on families, schooling, and equity.

Qualitative research recognizes the need to listen to participants' "voices"

## Mainstream and Critical Approaches to Parent Involvement

Reviewing the literature

**04** Far from being a self-evident social fact of schooling, parent involvement in education has been socially constructed to privilege White, middle-class norms and the expectations of educators (Auerbach, 2001; Jordan, Orozco, & Averett, 2002; Lareau, 1989). As López (2001) notes, "parent involvement has become a privileged domain signified by certain legitimate acts" (p. 417), such as helping with homework, attending Back to School Night, and chaperoning field trips. Because teachers place a high premium on school-based involvement and lower SES African American and Latino parents are less likely to come to the school than middle-class White parents (Gandara, 1995; Moles, 1993), teachers often assume that the former groups do not care about their children's schooling. Such assumptions, rooted in deficit thinking and the discourse on "at risk"-ness, perpetuate the myth of uninvolved minority parents (Valdés, 1996; Valencia & Black, 2002).

**05** Increasingly, scholarship has debunked this myth by documenting the many ways in which poor and minority parents value education, exhort their children to do well, have high educational aspirations, and respond to teachers' requests (see, e.g., Clark, 1983; Delgado-Gaitan, 1994a; López, 2001; Meyers, Dowdy, & Paterson, 2000; Reese, Gallimore, Goldenberg, & Balzano, 1995; Solórzano, 1992). Educators may be unaware or unappreciative of the invisible strategies that parents of color/low income use to support their children's education, such as making sacrifices so children can attend better schools or limiting children's chores to allow for study time (Mehan et al., 1996). For example, in describing how one migrant worker family "translated the lessons of working hard in the field into lessons for working hard in school" to their high-achieving children, López (2001) proposes that such transmission of sociocultural values be recognized as legitimate parent involvement and that schools build on such ways in which parents are already involved.

**06** For the past 20 years, parent involvement research, policy, and practice have been dominated by Epstein's (1990, 1995) model of family-school-community partnerships. This is based on the theory of overlapping spheres of home, school, and community influences that shape children's learning and development and a six-part typology of forms of parent involvement that schools should promote (basic obligations of parenting, home-school communication, volunteering at school, learning at home, school decision making, and community-school connections). Although useful for designing programs and survey research, this model places undue emphasis on school-based involvement, the priorities of educators, and cooperation that assumes shared goals and a level playing field for all (Auerbach, 2001). The partnership model and the mostly quantitative studies based on it fail to account for the needs and experience of many parents of color/low income as well as structural constraints on their actions and relations with schools. The partnership model, for instance, does not address the sense of exclusion that some parents feel at schools and their efforts to protect and advocate for their children in often insensitive bureaucracies (Auerbach, 2001; Fine, 1991; Lareau & Horvat, 1999; Olivos, 2003). Studies based on this model typically measure the effects of traditional forms of parent involvement on student achievement, discounting nontraditional strategies and status variables such as race and class (Epstein, 1990; Henderson & Mapp, 2002; Jordan et al., 2002; Mattingly, Prislin, McKenzie, Rodriguez, & Kayzar, 2002). In addition to being undertheorized and insufficiently rigorous in its methods (Baker & Soden, 1998; Mattingly et al., 2002), mainstream parent involvement research has stressed school-centered conceptions of parent roles with insufficient attention to "culturally appropriate definitions and family centered practices" among diverse populations (Jordan et al., 2001, p. viii), which call for more qualitative, naturalistic approaches.

**07** A smaller body of qualitative literature takes a more critical approach, examining parent involvement as socially constructed and politically contested through the lenses of race, class, culture, and gender (see, e.g., Abrams & Gibbs, 2002; Fine, 1993; Fordham, 1996; Lareau, 1989; López, 2001; Reese, Balzano, Gallimore, & Goldenberg, 1995; Useem, 1991; Valdés, 1996). Studies suggest that parents of higher SES often play a proactive role in managing and intervening in their children's K-12 careers, whereas parents of lower SES tend to provide indirect, behind-the-scenes support for education (Baker & Stevenson, 1986; Gandara, 1995; Lareau, 1989, 2003; McDonough, 1997; Mehan et al., 1996; Useem, 1991). In addition, middle-class and upper-middle-class parents exert considerably more influence over schools and decisions about their children's schooling, whereas poor and working-class parents have less power and more ambivalent relations with school staff (Olivos, 2003; Wells & Serna, 1996; Yonezawa, 1997). These class-based contrasts in parent involvement result in opportunities for a more "customized" education for higher SES children versus a more "generic" one for low SES children (Lareau, 1989). Race effects are closely tied to class in the literature, with parents of color less likely to have contact with schools, more likely to approach schools with wariness and mistrust, and more likely to encounter indifference and rebuff in their limited contact with educators (Fine, 1991; Fordham, 1996; Gandara, 1995; Lareau & Horvat, 1999; Yonezawa, 1997).

08 Building on the experience of marginalized parents, some researchers have proposed alternatives to mainstream conceptions of parent involvement. For example, Delgado-Gaitan (1994b) offers an empowerment model of family-school relations in which power is shared, influence is two-way between home and school, and parties are mutually accommodating, in contrast to the conventional one-way model dominated by the school's needs and expectations. López, Scribner, and Mahitivanichcha (2001) suggest that marginalized families need more home involvement by educators that addresses basic family needs and builds trusting relationships rather than more school involvement by parents.

09 This article uses a qualitative case study of how parents of color construct their role in promoting college access to suggest a reconceptualization of parent involvement. If research is to examine parent roles holistically within their social context and with a view to equity goals, it must draw from both mainstream and critical approaches to parent research. It must define parent involvement broadly beyond the six traditional types, highlighting the voices and beliefs of parents themselves. It must consider status variables, structural factors, and parents' lived experience along with process variables and individual psychosocial resources. In addition, researchers must recognize that the goal of parent involvement is not only raising student achievement but also enriching and expanding educational opportunity and equity for all students.

The literature describes a conceptual framework that informs the qualitative study; it does not direct the study

## Conceptual Framework

10 This study is grounded in a three-part, interdisciplinary theoretical framework as well as Hoover-Dempsey and Sandler's (1995, 1997) concept of parent role construction. I theorized that parent roles in education are fundamentally (a) socially structured by class and race but also (b) culturally mediated by particular cultural schemas and scripts as well as (c) psychosocially enacted according to individual psychosocial resources and relationships within families. Parent role construction occurs at the unique intersections of these three dimensions, which reflect a mediated system of structure, culture, and agency. I drew mainly on theories of cultural capital, social capital, and social networks in the work of Bourdieu (1973, 1979/1987), Lamont and Lareau (1988), Lareau (1989), and others to explain broad patterns in the data.

11 Social structure, as mirrored in the structure of schools, tends to disadvantage low SES/minority students and their families and reproduce inequality through mechanisms such as standardized testing and tracking (Lareau, 1989; MacLeod, 1995; Oakes, 1985). Working-class parents of color who aspire to college for their children have, on one hand, more systemic barriers to overcome and, on the other hand, fewer resources for the struggle, such as knowledge of the system. Culture, in the sense of a system of values and beliefs, mediates between individuals and their place in the social order by giving them various schemas for meaning-making (D'Andrade, 1992). Parents' home cultures may be at odds with dominant culture norms, leading to misunderstandings and tensions in family-school relations (Delgado-Gaitan, 1994b; Fordham, 1996; Valdés, 1996). Agency, or people's capacity for making a difference in the conditions of their lives, is typically experienced and enacted at the individual level. Parents' capacity for advocating for their children and proactively furthering educational goals such as college depends heavily on psychosocial processes and resources within the family (Eccles & Harold, 1993; Hoover-Dempsey & Sandler, 1997), making for variation within socially disadvantaged groups (Clark, 1983; Lareau & Horvat, 1999; Reese, Balzano, et al., 1995). With the three dimensions of structure, culture, and agency, parent roles can be examined from broad macrolevels to individual microlevels, with culture serving a bridging function.

12 Hoover-Dempsey and Sandler's (1995, 1997) model of parent involvement is useful for its attention to parent perspectives and elaboration of the concept of parent role construction or "parents' beliefs about the actions they should undertake for and with their children" (Hoover-Dempsey & Sandler, 1997, p. 11). Their four-part model theorizes that parent role construction is the key predictor in whether parents become actively engaged in their children's education. The next most important influence on involvement is parents' sense of self-efficacy about the likely impact of their efforts. The two less influential components of the model shaping parent roles are the child's invitations or demands for involvement and the school's or teacher's invitations or demands for involvement. Similar to other mainstream approaches, Hoover-Dempsey and Sandler operationalize high involvement in terms of conventional middle-class norms, such as parents providing direct instruction or reinforcing school-related behaviors—behaviors that may not be feasible for parents with limited formal education or English fluency. They also assume a level playing field of voluntary parent action, understating the constraints of class, race, culture, and school structure on what they term the involvement "choices" of marginalized

parents. Thus, the Hoover-Dempsey and Sandler model is highly generative but calls for adaptation when applied to working-class parents of color. Deslandes and Bertrand's (2005) test of the model with parents of Canadian secondary students found that the best predictor of parent involvement was parent perception of student invitations in the academic domain, suggesting that the model also may need adaptation to different levels and locales of schooling.

Method Section

## Research Setting and Methodology

Selecting a research design and collecting data

13 This study was conducted at a large, racially and socioeconomically mixed high school in the Los Angeles metropolitan area that was 46% Anglo, 34% Latino, 12% African American, and 8% Asian American. Pacific High had undergone some equity-based reforms to address race- and class-based divides in achievement and postsecondary outcomes between higher SES White and Asian students on one hand and lower SES Black and Latino students on the other. One such effort was the Futures Project, a partnership with the University of California, Los Angeles, that combined a small college access program with a study of the educational trajectories of 30 students of color. The Futures students were mostly average students with an interest in and (teacher) reported potential for 4-year university, who were recruited for the program from a ninth-grade Achievement through Individual Determination (AVID) college preparation class.

The qualitative researcher intentionally selects participants

14 A small, purposeful sample of parents of Futures students was selected to explore the role constructions of working-class parents of color who lack a college education but aspire to college for their children. Although not representative of Latino or African American parents at the school or generally, the sample reflects the preponderance of immigrant families in the project and variation on characteristics that could affect parent roles. The sample consisted of 16 working-class parents from 11 families, including 11 Mexican and Central American immigrants, 2 U.S.-born Chicanas, and 3 African Americans. Parents had a range of educational attainment, from no formal schooling to one semester of university, with about half having less than a high school diploma and half having completed high school or some community college. Parents varied in occupation (mostly skilled labor, sales, or clerical), English fluency (four with little fluency), marital status (six single), and child high school grade point average (GPA, from 1.7 to 3.8, average 2.6).

The qualitative researcher includes a small number of participants

15 Primary data was collected from in-depth, semistructured parent interviews in students' junior and senior years, a critical period for college

The qualitative researcher collects text and image data

preparation, search, and choice (Hossler et al., 1999). Open-ended questions and probes were designed to elicit stories and reflections on parents' goals, beliefs, practices, and knowledge regarding their role in their children's education and pathway to college. Six Spanish-dominant parents were interviewed in Spanish with the school's Latina community liaison. All interviews were taped and transcribed verbatim in English or Spanish, with Spanish translated by a native speaker assistant. Interview data were triangulated with field notes from 3 years of participant observation of Futures & Families parent meetings and other family-school interactions as well as student interviews from the Futures Project database, school staff interviews, academic transcripts, and school documents.

The qualitative researcher asks participants open-ended questions

**16** Topical, theoretical, and *en vivo* codes were used to identify emerging themes and patterns, with particular attention to how parents made meaning of their roles. Case summaries, data displays, and narrative analysis revealed further patterns and irregularities in the data and created an audit trail for findings. The extended period of fieldwork, use of thick description, and multiple methods helped strengthen validity and reliability according to current standards for qualitative research (Merriam, 2001). Validity also was enhanced by colleague checks, member checks, and analytical memos to monitor researcher subjectivity (Peshkin, 1988). As with other qualitative studies, findings are not meant to be generalized to populations but rather to inform theory building and promote insight into similar situations in what Yin (1993) calls "analytic generalizability." Thus, the role typology is not meant to apply universally to all working-class parents of color but to point to the need to refine mainstream theoretical frameworks.

The qualitative researcher codes the data to develop description and themes

**17** Given the centrality of the researcher as a qualitative research tool, it is essential to monitor the subjective factors that shape the research process (Lawrence-Lightfoot & Hoffman Davis, 1997; Peshkin, 1988). I assume that parents and educators often differ in their views of parent involvement and that the voices of parents have too often been silenced. Although my outsider positionality as a White, middle-class researcher may have blinded me to important cultural nuances, my experience as a parent of a struggling student and as an activist in urban schools provided some common ground. I also learned a great deal from parents at Futures meetings and social events throughout 3 years and from collaborating with colleagues of color, who generously shared their perspective and critiques. As the organizer of monthly Futures & Families meetings for parents about college access and planning, I may have influenced some parents' views, but given many parents' occasional attendance, that influence is likely to have been minimal.

Qualitative researchers take a reflexive and subjective approach

Results Section

## An Alternative Role Typology: From Moral Supporters to Struggling Advocates

Qualitative researchers use a flexible report format

Analyzing data and reporting results

**18** As anticipated for a within-group study of working-class parents, the data revealed considerable internal variation in how parents construct their roles. Parents spoke about their role in their child's education and college access in broad terms of support (in Spanish, *apoyo*) rather than the more narrowly conceived, often school-based parent involvement discussed in the mainstream literature. Support had multiple meanings for them, ranging from positive approval of the child's desire to go to college to specific forms of instrumental help. In data analysis, I experimented with placing parents along continua for specific traits or practices, such as knowledge of the K-16 system or contact with school staff, then combining these into an overarching continuum of support from less to more proactive forms. Noting where groups of parents clustered together, I then examined the possible characteristics that might unite each group. These differences are captured in an alternative typology of parent role orientations along a continuum of support (see Figure 1), which differs from Epstein's (1995) framework by emphasizing the constraints and struggles faced by marginalized parents and highlighting their stance as protectors and advocates. This typology is not comprehensive but rather indicative of the limitations of the well-known partnership model.

**19** At the less proactive end of the continuum were the Moral Supporters, who emphasized indirect, behind-the-scenes moral support for education at home (Auerbach, 2006). At the opposite end of the continuum were the Struggling Advocates, who provided more direct, instrumental support and monitoring at home along with advocacy at school. A third, unexpected category in between, the Ambivalent Companions, offered strong emotional support and occasional direct help but conveyed deeply ambivalent messages about schools and higher education. Similar to the first two categories, the Companions were moving toward college goals for their children but they diverged from the pathway toward other goals, suggesting their ambivalence. These contrasts and interruptions are represented schematically in Figure 1.

**20** The two extremes of the continuum resemble the spectrum of Chicana mothers' roles in Delgado-Gaitan and Segura (1989). Although all parents in that study offered their children moral and emotional support for schooling (Level I), a smaller number offered moral support in addition to direct help with school work (Level II), and the smallest number offered Level I and Level II support plus intervention with the school on their child's behalf

**Figure 1**
**Parents' Position on a Continuum of Support for College Pathways**

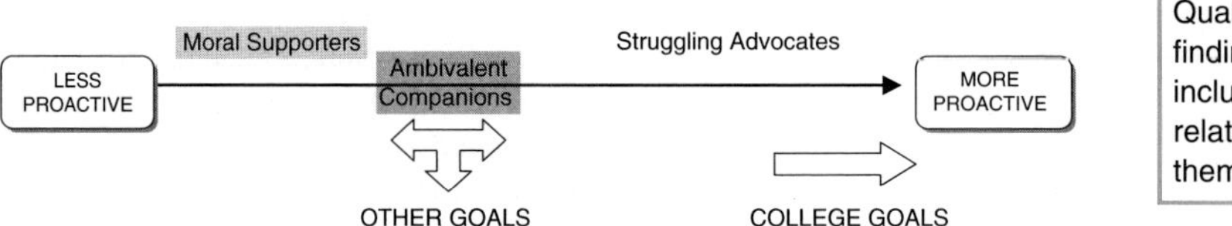


Qualitative findings include relating themes

(Level III). A similar trend was evident in my study, with the Moral Supporters comparable to Level I and Struggling Advocates to Level III but the Ambivalent Companions again in an ambiguous position. Unlike Delgado-Gaitan and Segura's (1989) neat schema, this study problematizes the contrasts and overlaps among parent role orientations and examines the influences that shaped them. Neither schema fit into traditional parent involvement frameworks, and these two typologies are not exhaustive of the possible roles of parents in education, thus begging the question of the need for more research in this area.

21 Characteristics of the three role orientations in this study are summarized in Table 1 below. Differences among the categories are symbolized in the metaphor of hands-off roles for the Supporters versus hands-on roles for the Advocates, with the Companions marked by a hands-up stance; demographic contrasts parallel these differences. The contrasting modes, locus, roots, and goals of support for the three categories suggest one possible alternative typology of parent role orientations compared to mainstream models.

22 In bringing the data into dialogue with sociological theories of cultural and social capital, I suggest alternative forms of capital that families bring to educational processes. Here, capital is conceptualized loosely as a resource that can be exchanged for some benefit or advantage—in this case, to promote a value and/or a goal with one's children. As we will see, parents in

**Table 1**
**An Alternative Typology of Parent Roles**

| | Moral Supporters | Struggling Advocates | Ambivalent Companions |
|---|---|---|---|
| Key quote | "I think that us *talking to her and stressing that she has to study* because she has to go to university— repeating that constantly—eventually it becomes something they can understand." | "I wanted to be ahead of the game. I knew *you have to take certain steps to be at a certain level*." | "For families like ours, where the parents didn't go to college, [our role] is *listening to our kids*; they'll get the information at school." |
| Metaphor | *Hands-off*; clearing the path, pointing the way from afar | *Hands-on*; pushing for progress, encountering rebuff | *Hands-up*; accompanying the journey, holding on to relationships |
| Mode of support | Approving, motivating, encouraging, indirect guidance (*consejos*) | Monitoring, advocating, seeking information, negotiating for access | Encouraging, communicating, protecting, occasional assisting on request |
| Locus of support | Home | Home and school | Mostly home |
| Root of support | Perception of child ability and motivation, trust in child, immigrant quest for mobility | Family mobility aspirations, distrust of system, belief that parents make a difference | Close relationship with child, wish to help her meet her goals and avoid the parent's struggles |
| Goal of support | Launch child for success, build resilience | Access opportunity, improve life chances | Bolster child's self-esteem, maintain relationship, keep safe |
| Frame of reference | Home culture, immigrant families | Middle-class college-goers | Extended family |
| Demographics in this study | Latino immigrants with lowest education levels, least college knowledge in sample | Black, Latino/a immigrant, and Chicano/a parents with mixed levels of education, greatest college knowledge | Black, Latina immigrant, and Chicana single mothers with some community college, sketchy college knowledge |

The qualitative researcher represents findings in figures and tables each role orientation have taken deliberate steps to develop their respective stores of what I call moral, navigational, and emotional capital. These resources can be seen metaphorically as yet another reflection of how parents believe they are supporting, or contributing to, their children's pursuit of educational opportunity.

## Moral Supporters: Pointing the Way, Clearing the Path

Qualitative findings include themes

23 The seven Moral Supporters (three couples and one father) were all married Latino immigrants who had the lowest educational attainment, least English fluency, and least K-16 knowledge in the sample. They offered moral and emotional support for college largely in the form of talking with their children, as in stressing the value of education, study, and hard work. These parents provided this support at home and rarely went to the school. Metaphorically, they took a hands-off stance, pointing the way toward a successful future and clearing the pathway when they could of impediments. They trusted their children to do well academically and take the steps they needed on their own to get to university. They also trusted the American school system, and Pacific High in particular, to prepare their children for college and provide superior educational opportunities.

24 These traits are evident in this translated excerpt from a portrait of José, an undocumented skilled craftsman and father of a high-achieving male student, compiled from juxtaposed quotes in the tradition of Lawrence Lightfoot and Hoffman Davis (1997):

> My son has always been very intelligent. When he was in kindergarten in Mexico, they let him out about four months early because there was nothing to teach him, nothing. The parent is the one who plants the seed. I tell him, "If you study, you are going to accomplish what you want. If you are going to let others [peers] guide you, forget it; things are going to go to hell." The parent's job is to motivate him so he continues his education so he becomes something (*llegar a ser algo*). And then the student has to go his own way. I think he sees that we [his parents] are nothing; he wants to become something. He takes the initiative himself. He makes all his own decisions. The student knows more than us. One simply advises him to investigate [college options]; one can't do more than that. If the student is good, let him fly.

There was striking agreement among the Supporters that the most important strategies for parents in promoting college-going were providing moral and emotional support, stressing the importance of education, and talking

262

**Table 2**
**Parents' Most Valued Support Strategies for Students' College Pathways**

| | Supporters | | | Advocates | | | | Companions | | | |
|---|---|---|---|---|---|---|---|---|---|---|---|
| Strategy | José & Blanca | Gabriel & Rosalia | Antonia & Jorge | Donna | Alicia & Luis | Manuel & Norma | Angela | Jolena | Joanne | Frances | Estelle |
| Provide emotional & moral support | | X | X | X | X | X | | X | X | X | |
| Stress hard work | | | | | | X | X | X | X | X | X |
| Talk with child about college and career | X | X | X | | X | | X | X | | | |
| Set limits on behavior | | | X | | | | X | | X | | X |
| Stress import of education | | X | | X | | | | | | | X |
| Seek info on financial aid | X | | | X | | | | | | X | |
| Save money | X | | | | | | | | | | |
| Talk with counselor about college | | | | | | X | | | | | |
| Talk with teacher about grades | | | | X | | | | | | | |
| Seek info about colleges | | | | | X | | | | | | |
| Attend school parent events | | | | | | X | | | | | |
| Ensure child takes SAT | | | | X | | | | | | | |

The qualitative researcher represents findings in figures and tables to children about university and careers, as well as setting limits on behavior (see Table 2). These priorities reflect several traditional Latino immigrant cultural values and modes of expression (Auerbach, 2006).

**25** First, the Supporters embraced the concept of *educación*—home-based training in morals and respect—as the foundation of academic and professional success as well as the source of parents' role as a motivator (Delgado-Gaitan, 1994a; Reese, Balzano, et al., 1995; Valdés, 1996). For example, José's wife Blanca, who had no formal schooling, said that sending children to school was not enough unless their parents had taught them to respect their elders and help those in need. Second, the Supporters emphasized the need for students to "study 100%" as "their only job," a reference to the traditional Latino *estudios* schema, in which the ticket to success is seen as diligent study and effort (Reese, Gallimore, et al., 1995). José modeled this for his son when the family first arrived in the United States by sitting with him every night with dictionary in hand to decipher his homework. The *estudios* schema can be seen as a variant of the immigrant work ethic applied to school tasks, as it was for the highly successful students in Gandara (1995) and López (2001).

**26** Third, the Supporters offered their own experience in cautionary tales designed to steer children away from their own example and motivate them to do well in school (Goldenberg & Gallimore, 1995; López, 2001). For example, Luis said that in talking to his son,

> I always use me as an example. Like, "Look at me. Do you want to work like me? You know, work hard and live like this? If you want to be more comfortable later, you have to work hard now, go to school." Couple times, I took him to my work [at a factory] just to let him see what kind of work I do and if he would like to do that for the rest of his life.

Parents often conveyed an ambivalent mix of regret, shame, and anger in talking about their missed educational opportunities, drawing a stark comparison between what they did versus what they hoped their children would do.

**27** The Supporters relied heavily on *consejos* (cultural narrative advice and teachings), a central form of Latino parent support for education (Delgado-Gaitan, 1994a; Gandara, 1995; Valdés, 1996; Villanueva, 1996). "Like I tell my son, success comes according to the *empeño* (dedication, commitment, effort) you invest in what you are doing," José explained. "If you are dedicated, then you can achieve whatever you want. If you don't put *ganas* (will, drive) into it, you become like us." Likewise, Gabriel was convinced that from an early age, "us talking to her and stressing that she has to study, has to get good grades because she has to go to university—repeating that constantly—has made the difference" in his daughter being a good student. Although most parents' *consejos* were in the form of general, often-repeated moral messages about the importance of education, some advice was more targeted, meant to fortify resilience in the face of obstacles. For example, Gabriel coached his child about speaking up for her rights at school as a Latina, and José taught his son to recognize opportunity whenever he could.

**28** In developing their role, the Supporters took their cue from their perceptions of their children as students. Seeing that their children were motivated to learn and *listo/a* (quick, smart) from an early age or diligent students in high school prompted parents to encourage their studies. Indeed, they portrayed their form of indirect support as best suited to self-motivated, efficacious students. "If the students do not have the *deseo* (desire) and *ganas* (will, ambition) to get to the university . . . you [as a parent] cannot do much to help them," according to Gabriel's wife, Rosalia; Gabriel thought his family might need to "change the strategy" for their low-achieving younger son. Similarly, Blanca believed that parent support should depend on the needs of each child. As Deslandes and Bertrand (2005) found, "differences in adolescent autonomy modulate the degree of parent involvement at home" (p. 171). Thus, child invitations for involvement—in the sense of parents' perception of the child's school performance, sense of responsibility, and receptivity to parents' support—were critical in shaping the nature of the Supporters' support.

**29** For their part, the two immigrant students of the Supporters were grateful for their parents' sacrifices and moral support. For years, these students had taken charge of their own school decisions, just as they had served as cultural brokers for the family. Both encouraged their parents to attend school meetings to learn more about college, but they did not expect direct parental help. "I wouldn't want them to be too involved because they'd be interfering with what I want," said Antonia's daughter, who refused to let her mother accompany her to Pacific High's College Fair. By contrast, the U.S.-born child of Gabriel and Rosalia was more impatient with her parents' limited college knowledge, similar to the Chicano/a high school students who felt "skepticism and resignation" about their parents' capacity to help them advance in Stanton-Salazar's (2001) study.

**30** The Supporters readily pointed to their limited knowledge base and school experience as a reason for not being more involved in their children's college pathway. Gabriel said,

> All the information we are seeing [through Futures & Families] is new because neither of us went to the university. We don't know what the process is like. It's very hard for an immigrant family to come [to meetings]; both parents have to work and you don't know the educational system. So there are barriers everywhere.

This limited college knowledge was tied not only to parents' educational histories but to their narrow information networks, in which families depended heavily on their children and on Futures & Families parent meetings for college information. Parents recounted with regret their own lack of educational opportunity and their parents' insufficient support or "push." Antonia, for instance, was determined to support her daughter's higher education precisely because her own parents had not allowed her to finish *secundaria* (junior high) in Mexico.

**31** The Supporters' role orientation corresponds to that of other immigrant parents who engage in invisible strategies and indirect guidance for education (Azmitia, Cooper, Garcia, & Dunbar, 1996; Mehan et al., 1996). These parents did not undertake conventional involvement strategies, such as homework monitoring or attendance at school events. Instead, given the constraints on their college-going cultural and social capital, they drew on inner resources of what may be termed "moral capital" to strengthen their children's resolve and academic focus (Auerbach, 2006; Azmitia et al., 1996; López, 2001; Reese, Balzano, et al., 1995; Treviño, 2004). Moral capital is related to the concepts of aspirational capital and familial capital in Yosso's (2005) model of "community cultural wealth" for marginalized students. Moral capital is distinct from traditional social capital in that it is not based in middle-class social networks, trust, or norms of reciprocity that lead to advantage; rather, it is tied to cultural values that are transmitted within the family and exchanged, indirectly, for advantage by promoting student persistence and resilience.

**32** Similar to the Latino parents in Stanton-Salazar (2001), the Supporters were noninterventionists who let their children plot their own pathways through high school. Yet similar to the immigrant parents in Mehan et al. (1996), they were not entirely passive; they made sacrifices and cleared the way of potential distractions, such as daily babysitting or the pressure to work, to facilitate their children's academics, and similar to the migrant parents in Treviño (2004), they urged their children to be proud, strong strivers in the face of barriers. Thus, the role of the Moral Supporters, though indirect and largely invisible to the school, was foundational to the success of children who were already on their way to college.

## Struggling Advocates: Pushing for Progress, Encountering Rebuff

33 At the opposite end of the continuum were the Struggling Advocates, who provided more direct, tangible support and monitoring at home along with advocacy at school. The five parents (one couple and three mothers) in this category were more mixed in race/ethnicity (three Latino immigrants, one U.S.-born Chicana, and one African American) and educational attainment (one with junior high school in Mexico, one with senior high school in Mexico, and three with U.S. community college experience). They had the most detailed college knowledge in the sample due to broader social networks with educators and college-educated people. These parents intervened with the school and initiated a greater number and variety of instrumental support strategies, such as talking to school counselors and monitoring homework. Metaphorically, the Advocates took a hands-on stance, pushing for progress as part of strong social mobility aspirations for both their children and themselves. They did not trust their children to succeed on their own, nor did they trust the school to guide them. Rather, they believed that parent action was necessary to give students the extra push that they needed to get ahead. These parents persisted in their efforts despite limited knowledge, frustration with the school, and resistance from their children.

34 The Advocates' stories reveal more direct efforts to help their children navigate the system mixed with considerable frustration in dealing with schools. This tension is evident in the following portrait of Donna, an African American school office manager with one semester of state college, whose son was an average student:

> I worked at a magnet [high] school. I did GPAs and transcripts and things for kids, worked with the college counselors. And it became very, very clear that we needed to make some changes in order to prepare Clarence for getting into college. I noticed that the colleges looked at the whole person. So he had to get it together: grades, SAT, community involvement in the school, and the whole thing. It's very important to keep track of what he's getting on these tests. I make him keep all his papers and I've found that over the years, he's gotten lower grades because the assignments weren't in that the teachers have overlooked. I came out and discussed it with [the teacher] and he was very apologetic. And then it happened again! They need these grades for colleges, for GPAs! We got him a real good teacher for Biology. You just kind of find out who the good teachers are from word of mouth from parents, and who's not really a jerk, excuse me, who you can kind of relate to. I should have been thinking about this [college] from day one. There's so many things I wish I had done.

Similar to other parents in the study, the Advocates acknowledged the importance of moral and emotional support for education. However, they were the only parents to consistently mention and enact specific direct, proactive strategies for promoting college pathways (see Table 2). For example, two parents chose classes for their children, another lobbied for an alternate Spanish class placement, and three sought out counselors' advice on college planning. Significantly, these forms of support call for some knowledge of college preparation and/or contact with the school. They also imply a strong social networking orientation—what one parent called "making the right connections"—geared to educational goals (Auerbach, 2002). The Advocates pursued college knowledge, school contacts, and connections diligently, relative to the other parents in the sample, but with difficulty compared with higher SES parents.

35 The Advocates were more aware than other parents in the study of the need for college planning and dealing with gatekeepers along the pathway to college. "I want my son to know that life has a plan," said Alicia, a Chicana hairdresser who had some community college. "I didn't grow up with a plan. I learned later that there's steps in life. You have to take certain steps to be at a certain level." These parents drew on a wider array of more detailed, accurate information sources about college, such as college-educated friends and coworkers, college brochures, and the Internet. They used their social contacts to learn about and negotiate steps along the pathway on behalf of their children, whether getting ideas from fellow parents like Donna or keeping in touch with school security guards to make sure their children were behaving well like Norma, an immigrant mother. They put great faith and energy in the cultivation of social networks, especially with institutional agents at schools who could help their children advance (Stanton-Salazar, 2001). They did this even though parents like Alicia admitted they felt "dumb" and "stuck" in dealing with counselors and administrators.

36 More than other parents in the study, who had little contact with the school, the Advocates reported frequent frustration with being rebuffed by the school bureaucracy. They experienced what Lareau and Horvat (1999) call "moments of social exclusion," due not only to their needs coming into conflict with school practices but due to the school's discounting their limited social and cultural capital. Alicia wondered why "they make it hard" for parents to get everything from scholarship packets to discount lunch tickets:

> A parent like me, who doesn't understand how to get into the university system too well, but is trying, I need the school to help me counsel my son. I told the counselor, "My son's gonna go into university so I want to make sure

The qualitative researcher includes quotes from participants

> his classes are at that level." And he's like, "OK, well, have him come back to my office." It was just like a big runaround. There should be an easier system to guide the kids.

In a sharper social critique, Manuel found fault with a system that claimed to be equal but did not place all students in good classes for college admission (Auerbach, 2002). Likewise, Donna's distrust of the school's treatment of Black, male students prompted her vigilance in monitoring her son's tests and contesting his course grades, which she claimed were often incorrectly calculated.

**37** The Advocates generally persisted in their efforts despite the systemic barriers they faced. They were motivated by strong social mobility aspirations, beliefs in the active parent management of education, and doubts about their children's capacity to negotiate their own access. They portrayed their children as lazy, average, or underachieving students who needed to be pushed if they were to succeed, and as parents, they took responsibility for that pushing. They described their children's education using the pronoun *we* to denote its joint ownership by the parent, the student, and other allies whom parents enlisted in the venture—as in Alicia saying that "we're struggling just to pass" Algebra 2 or in Donna telling her son that "we could have gone to this college" if they had made earlier preparations. These parents' roles in their children's education were central to their identity and to the family's determined agenda for advancement, whether a social climber like Alicia or a protector like Donna. Part of this agenda was the determination to provide the push and help that most Advocates felt had been lacking from their parents in their own schooling.

**38** Despite earlier school success, the children of the Advocates did not do as well as those of the Supporters during high school. They were generally grateful for their parents' help, crediting parents with having kept them on track and seeing parents' push as a sign of caring. As they got older, the students asserted greater independence and the wish to escape parental control, as with Alicia's son opting to transfer schools. As students' grades declined and they resisted parents' push, two of the Advocates pulled back from the hands-on role and underwent a "cooling out" of aspirations—a common response when parents see a drop in student achievement (Hossler et al., 1999). Meanwhile, Donna's son wondered if he could manage at college without his mother's help. Perhaps being raised by Advocates may breed dependence on parents at a juncture when young people need to learn to navigate on their own.

**39** In their propensity to manage their children's student careers, the Advocates resemble more privileged parents with high-status cultural capital

(Baker & Stevenson, 1986; Lareau, 1989, 2003; McDonough, 1997; Useem, 1991). Yet the Advocate parents intervened with less competence, confidence, and effectiveness than did higher SES parents. For example, Donna felt that looking back, "I was storing up information [on college] but not really acting on it the way I should have." Compared to higher status parents, the Advocates not only pursued a different approach but met a less welcome reception by the school (Lareau & Horvat, 1999; Shannon, 1996; Yonezawa, 1997). Moreover, as members of marginalized groups watchful for discrimination and insensitivity, the Advocates had additional work to do as guardians of their children's prospects (Horvat, Weininger, & Lareau, 2003).

**40** The Advocates attempted to use their social networks to leverage access to college-going cultural capital but were at an early stage in the long-term process of capital accumulation, with fewer high-quality resources at their disposal (Gandara & Bial, 1999; Horvat et al., 2003). They focused on the instrumental component of college-going cultural capital or the attempt to work the system to their advantage. This resource, which could be termed "navigational capital," was an outgrowth of the Advocates' social networking orientation and was "under construction" throughout their children's high school years (Auerbach, 2001; Yosso, 2005). Parents' basic understanding of how to navigate institutions—trying to open doors for their children—helped keep students more or less on track for college. This was important for average students who did not seem to have the sense of agency, motivation, or academic skills to persist successfully on their own. Yet because parents' knowledge of the system was only partial, and because their efforts to improve their understanding were rebuffed by the school, the net result also was misunderstandings and detours off the pathway to college.

## Ambivalent Companions: Accompanying the Journey, Holding On to Relationships

**41** A third role orientation, the Ambivalent Companions, lies in a more ambiguous location between the Supporters and the Advocates and is more embedded in family dynamics. This gender-specific category includes four single mothers of daughters: two African Americans, one Chicana, and one Mexican 1.5 generation immigrant who came to the United States as a child. Three of the mothers had some community college, whereas the other was a high school drop-out. They had more familiarity with the American educational system than the Supporters but their college knowledge remained sketchy. These parents supported their children's education through strong emotional support, close communication, and occasional tangible help, such as assisting students with school projects. Although their support was mainly indirect and home-based, like that of the Supporters, the Companions' approach was different in both style and degree because they were more aware of their children's school lives and more assimilated to the dominant culture. Similar to the urban, African American mothers in Meyers et al. (2000), these mothers "actively cheer-lead" to boost their children's self-esteem as a hedge against injury from negative outside influences. Metaphorically, these parents took an occasional hands-off stance, accompanying their children's educational journey and applauding their progress from the sidelines but also anticipating roadblocks. They wanted better opportunities for their daughters but were ambivalent about college as a threat to family ties and obligations, thus conveying mixed messages.

**42** The Companions' complex blend of cheerleading, protectiveness, and ambivalence is evident in this excerpt from a portrait of Joanne, a young Chicana high school drop-out, insurance sales agent, and mother of an average female student:

> I always hated school, ever since I can remember—it didn't really come easy. My daughter is very focused. I wish I was like her when I was her age. She knows what she wants and she's gonna get it, she's got the will. I just try to keep her in the right direction, I don't want her to stray. Everything I missed, I want her to do. For families like ours, where the parents didn't go to college, [the parent's role] is listening to the kids because usually they'll get the information at school. [Parents need to] find a way to get through to them; find out what they want to do and kind of make sure it kind of happens for them. I want her to be able to tell me anything, good or bad, it doesn't matter. She had to educate me about being on the right track [for college]. If she wouldn't have went through all of this [Futures Project], I probably would have been lost on the whole procedure. She just has to realize college is not going to be easy. [A state university campus] is maybe 10 minutes away. She could live at home and she could go to school; she could come home for lunch.

Like the other Companions, Joanne saw her daughter as more academically competent and ambitious than she, Joanne, had been as a student, with more options. On one hand, these mothers lived vicariously through and celebrated their children's relative success; on the other hand, they feared losing their close relationship as students moved away toward unfamiliar worlds.

43 Similar to the Supporters, the Companions valued the parent strategy of giving moral and emotional support for college as central to their approach. They also were more likely than other parents in the study to stress the importance of hard work and of setting limits on their child's behavior as support strategies, perhaps because of the lessons of their own hardships in life. Significantly, although the Companions had somewhat more knowledge of the K-16 system than did the Moral Supporters, they were less likely to prioritize talking with their children about college and career and about as likely to avoid contact with the school (see Table 2).

44 The Companions had a striking psychological bent that led them to put great store in emotional support and communication as the main role for parents. They saw support for education as an extension of their close relationship with their daughters and their wish to maintain that intimacy and ensure their children's happiness and security. In this, they may reflect not only the gendered nature of their role and the mother-daughter bond but a dynamic that is more pronounced in single-parent families. Rather than exhorting students to succeed like the Supporters, or pushing them to advance like the Advocates, the Companions focused on listening to their children to learn their needs and "find a way to get through to them," as Joanne said. According to Estelle, a Mexican-born court clerk, to help children get to college,

> The most important thing [for parents] is to keep an open communication . . . to be able to talk a lot. I find that talking to your children really makes a difference when they grow up because they feel free to say whatever, if it's good or wrong . . . I tried to be close to them, to be very open . . . We'd talk a lot about college and what they [her children] wanted to be. I always paid attention to what they had to say about school, about their teachers.

Estelle believed that if parents and teachers would "pay close attention and make the child feel important" through good communication, students would do better. The focus of communication about school for the Companions was not primarily academic but intrapersonal and social in terms of how the child was feeling about themselves in various classes, activities, and social circles.

45 In their acts of communication, the Companions were mainly concerned with bolstering their daughters' self-esteem and steering them in the right direction, away from the parents' mistakes and struggles. They often drew contrasts between their youth and that of their daughters, as in this portrait of Jolena, an African American medical records clerk:

> My education was hit and miss. My past, it was real bad and real crazy, but thanks be to God, my daughter never missed a beat. She's the only real focused one in the family. I think she's the right type of young lady. I enjoyed watching my baby grow up and feel important and all the things she was doing. I just pointed her in the right direction, that's the only thing I knew.

Jolena involved her child from an early age in almost daily church activities as insurance against risky behavior. As her daughter's confidence faltered during high school, Jolena tried to reassure and protect her. Similarly, Frances, another African American mother, urged her daughter to "keep your head high" and try again whenever she was disappointed in sports or job hunting. As Meyers et al. (2000) observe in a study of low-income African American mothers, the parental habit of "active cheerleading" or applauding one's child's accomplishments can be an antidote to "perceived negative outside influences on self-esteem affecting both academic efforts and social adjustment" (p. 70). This may be one way that Black parents try to inculcate survival skills for living in a racist society (Franklin & Boyd-Franklin, 1985; Ward, 1996).

**46** The Companions took their cue for involvement from their children rather than imposing their own goals. As Joanne said at a parent meeting, "It was important for my daughter for me to be here. It's important for her to go to college, so it's important to me." Likewise, Estelle's aspirations shifted between 2- and 4-year college along with her child's changing goals.

**47** The Companions supported their children's education in several ways, somewhat more directly than the Supporters but less consistently and with less information than the Advocates. For example, all lived outside school boundaries and placed their children at Pacific High for better opportunities and safety through deliberate school choice. Two of the four Companions rarely came to the school but faithfully attended their children's sports events as symbolic of their cheerleading support. These parents often waited until the child expressed a need or the situation was dire before they stepped in with direct help. For example, all of Jolena's contacts with teachers or counselors were initiated by school staff, even after it was clear that her student was failing. An exception was Joanne, who used work-based financial skills to apply for aid online and to protest to a university office when her child did not qualify for a summer program.

**48** The Companions' support was constrained by several factors. First, these mothers were more prone to psychological problems and family crises than others in the study, limiting their attentiveness to school matters. For example, Frances, a hospital clerk with six children, moved several times during the study due to a fire, bad credit, and conflicts with relatives. Each Companion also had an older child who had failed, dropped out, or been incarcerated. Second, they had little information on their students' academic status and little capacity to help them academically. Estelle did not check progress reports and thus did not know when her child began to fail; when Estelle belatedly imposed consequences, her child rebelled and Estelle gave in to preserve the relationship. Third, similar to the Supporters, the Companions relied heavily on the Futures Project as their sole source of college information and expected staff to guide all college planning.

**49** The Companions were more cautious or skeptical about educational opportunities than others in the study due in part to their own disappointing experiences, prompting them to engage in warnings and protective behavior. For example, Joanne advised her child not to take Advanced Placement classes, "If they're an average student, they should just stay where they're at because if the class is too hard for them . . . then they'll be stuck . . . and they'll end up losing." Similarly, she was not sure if her child was mature enough for "the big adventure" of college and often told her, "College is not easy, you know, it's not high school." Having been alienated from school herself, she projected her own experience onto her child. Other parents worried about structural barriers with changes in affirmative action and financial aid policies. "There are so many things that are being taken away now," Frances noted, "they're making it even harder to get in" to college.

**50** The Companions were more likely than others in the study to see college as a threat in addition to an opportunity. They felt threatened by the prospect of students leaving home for college as a disruption of family relationships and routines. This ambivalence led to mixed messages about college. When her child was determined to go to a state college far from home, Estelle said, "I would never tell her no, but I'm dreading it. . . . I would never stop her or disappoint her, but it's hard to accept that she's gonna be gone. Especially being the only girl." Jolena insisted that regarding her daughter's future, "I'm not going to hold her back—I am not," but she added that "if things don't work out the way that she wants them to, my door's always open."

**51** These single mothers, while giving generous emotional support, clearly depended on the mother-daughter bond for their own emotional well-being. Frances and Jolena described sharing fun times with their daughters like they would with a best girlfriend. Frances, with her many troubles, relied on her daughter for daily words of prayer and encouragement as well as babysitting and transporting her younger children: "She's my strength, she keeps me going." She often told relatives and Futures Project staff how "lost" she would be with her daughter gone. The stronger the family bonds and obligations, the more vulnerable these parents were to feeling abandoned for college. All parents struggle to some extent to let go of college-bound children, but this may well play out differently among working-class single mothers and daughters.

**52** The daughters' academic performance ranged from low average to high average, with a marked gap for two students between their capacity for critical thinking and lackluster grades. They generally appreciated their mothers' emotional support but would have liked more tangible support, such as more effort to come to parent meetings related to college. As Estelle's daughter said, her mother was better at childrearing than at helping with school matters. Joanne's daughter complained of academic pressure without help at home, saying, "It's all on me." The turmoil in these relationships increased near graduation, with even the closest mother-daughter pair fighting over college choices and Frances opposing all out-of-town options.

**53** In their cheerleading, protective stance, the Companions resemble many minority parents who deliberately instill self-confidence, pride, and resilience in their children as part of racial socialization to resist the corrosive effects of poverty or racism (Clark, 1983; Fordham, 1996; Franklin & Boyd-Franklin, 1985; Meyers et al., 2000; Ward, 1996; Yosso, 2005). The Companions took pride in their daughters as the hope of an extended family that had generally not succeeded in the system, but the Companions also felt cautious about the future and skeptical about college, extrapolating from their own struggles in school and as single women in the workplace. In their reluctance to deal with school staff, these parents expressed the ambivalence of their student days and their wariness of mainstream institutions (cf. Fordham, 1996; Lareau & Horvat, 1999). In this, they evoke Ogbu's (1987) theory of involuntary minorities, such as African Americans and second-generation Mexican Americans, who tend to be more conflicted than voluntary minorities (first-generation immigrants) about the value of participation in school opportunity structures.

**54** In the end, the Companions supported their children's educational goals by drawing on their reserves of what could be termed "emotional capital," an intuitive, gendered response attuned to their children's feelings and self-esteem. This resource was built on a foundation of years of close mother-daughter communication, but it was complicated by tense parent-teen dynamics and mothers' dependence on their daughters in single-parent households. Child gender, parent gender, and parent marital status shaped the close parent-child bond and parent role construction in these families, with mothers' attempt to hold on to relationships clashing with college goals. The net effect for students was mixed messages and inconsistent support.

Conclusion Section

## From Supporters to Advocates: The Shaping of Parent Roles

Interpreting the research

55 In delineating parent role orientations, this article has stressed the contrasts among them. Yet there were a number of common influences that shaped parent roles across the sample.

56 As anticipated by the conceptual framework, relative differences in social location explain broad within-group contrasts in role construction. All parents pointed to their limited resources for college planning and the struggles that resulted. In Lareau's (1989) terms, the Advocates had a slight "home advantage" of relatively greater educational competence, college knowledge, and school-relevant social networks compared to the Supporters and Companions, who depended exclusively on the Futures Project and their children for college information. In Gandara's (1995) terms, the Advocates also had more access to "middle-class cultural capital" in their understanding of college access and in their view of the role as parents in that process. Parents' contrasting information networks gave rise to different support strategies. Although the Supporters and the Companions identified mainly home-based, indirect forms of help as the most important parent strategies to promote college-going, the Advocates cited more instrumental assistance that required college knowledge or contact with the school (see Table 2).

The qualitative researcher interprets the larger meaning of the findings

57 Parents' educational histories powerfully shaped their aspirations and beliefs about their role. Most spoke bitterly of their lack of educational opportunity, in part due to parents who were obstacles or absent parties in their education (cf. Goldenberg & Gallimore, 1995). Rather than reproduce their own parents' practices, these parents were trying to break with family tradition to forge new roles. As Reay (1998) found in a study of working-class British mothers, such role transformation is a formidable challenge with few guideposts to lead the way. In this study, parents' roles were under construction, with strategies improvised based on sketchy knowledge and changing circumstances (Auerbach, 2001).

The qualitative researcher compares findings to past studies

58 Across the sample, parents took their cue from their children's invitations for involvement, that is, students' academic performance, motivation, responsibility, and requests. The Supporters' view of their children's high academic ability and motivation reinforced their predisposition to be more hands off and to depend on students to navigate their own college pathways. The Advocates saw their academically borderline children as "needing that extra push" and thus took more hands-on, proactive steps. The Companions waited for their daughters to assert aspirations or ask for help rather than impose parental goals or initiate help. In this qualitative study, it was difficult

to separate out the influence of student invitations, as Deslandes and Bertrand (2005) did in their factor analysis, because these psychosocial factors were closely intertwined with other aspects of parent roles. Parent roles were co-constructed with the student, but in the context of families' particular social location, cultural beliefs, and psychodynamics.

**59** Parent roles also were co-constructed with the school, with parents responding to a sense of rebuff or support from staff. Many reported experiencing bureaucratic indifference and alienation at some point in their students' careers. Although this led to disengagement from the high school for the Supporters and Companions, the Advocates persisted in their efforts to gain help or information. Parents' contact with the Futures Project, with its dedicated staff, individual attention, and small parent meetings, mitigated their view of the school as unresponsive to family needs. Yet the project had the unintended consequence of reassuring parents that it was handling all college planning tasks, thus seemingly removing the need for parents' instrumental support.

**60** Although all but one of the parents' students in this study enrolled in a 4-year university after graduation, parent roles had varied impacts on students' experience of "conflict and challenge" (McDonough, 1997) on the pathway to college. The Supporters pointed the way, cleared the path, and did no harm to the college-going efforts of efficacious students. The Advocates, seeing a need and believing in a hands-on role, used social networks to try to make college pathways more manageable for borderline students. The Companions both cheered their daughters' ambitions and discouraged their leaving home, with an ambivalence that may have exacerbated students' doubts and misgivings in preparing for college.

## Reconceptualizing Parent Involvement

**61** Similar to students, parents come to schools with unequal resources for pursuing educational goals and with complex raced/classed/gendered identities, cultural scripts, and family histories or dynamics that shape their relations with institutions. Just as schools need to affirm and accommodate marginalized students, so too, do schools need to transform their understandings of and interactions with working-class parents of color.

**62** The role typology presented here illustrates one set of distinctions among working-class parents of color as they pursue college access for their children. This typology does not presume to be comprehensive but rather to suggest an alternative framework for understanding parent roles beyond mainstream models of involvement. This analysis expands the discourse on parent involvement by focusing in depth on marginalized parents' role constructions—what they think and do—while examining the cultural logics behind their actions. Rather than positing a partnership between home and school and classifying parent involvement in terms of school goals, as in mainstream models, this study recognizes tension between home and school and explores parent support for education in terms of their own values and aspirations for their children. It identifies role orientations that reflect traditional Latino immigrant cultural schemas (Moral Supporters), attempts at social advancement that penetrate privilege (Struggling Advocates), and caution regarding social institutions (Ambivalent Companions) that shape parents' actions in pursuit of educational opportunity. In contrast to the economic, cultural, and social capital activated by higher SES parents, the parents in this study employed the resources of moral, navigational, and emotional capital to attempt to help their children get to college. It is important to enumerate and unpack such family resources to counter the legacy of deficit thinking about families of color and education (Yosso, 2005).

**63** Far from exhaustive or universal, the three role orientations outlined here represent one interpretation of a small group of parents at one school during the crucial high school–college transition. Because the sample was predominantly low SES Latino immigrants, the data is more suggestive for this population than for U.S.-born Chicana and African American parents. This study adds to the literature on the widespread existence of a Moral Supporter orientation among Latino immigrant parents (Auerbach, 2006; Azmitia et al., 1996; Mehan et al., 1996; Valdés, 1996; Villanueva, 1996). Further research is needed to explore other possible role constructions among working-class parents of color who aspire to college for their children. To what extent do the Advocate and Companion categories apply to other groups in other settings, at other points in students' careers, and with other educational goals in mind? Qualitative studies with parents of students of color in other contexts, such as college access programs or Advanced Placement classes, would shed light on this question. So, too, would comparative studies that examine the strategies of families with students in such programs as well as those without the benefit of such programs, with or without parent aspirations for higher education. The Companion orientation is especially intriguing for the dynamics of the intersection of race, class, and gender in both parent-student and home-school relations. How widespread is this stance among single mothers, and to what extent is it tied to student gender? Research on these and other parent role constructions would respond to the call in a recent literature

The qualitative researcher identifies limitations in the study review for more studies of "process-based approaches" to parent involvement among diverse families and of ways families provide support at transition points in student careers (Jordan et al., 2002). In addition, to better understand adolescent student invitations for parent involvement, it would be useful to replicate Deslandes and Bertrand's (2005) French Canadian survey study with racially and economically diverse families in urban high schools in the United States.

**64** This work has several implications for educators and education researchers concerned with families in schools and educational equity. First, we should broaden the value-laden, traditional, middle-class definition of what counts as parent involvement to include more open-ended, emic notions of parent support (*apoyo*) for children's education, advancement, and well-being. Second, we should help educators understand that such support takes multiple forms—some invisible to the school—shaped primarily by parents' social location but also by a web of cultural and psychosocial factors in specific home, school, and community contexts. Third, we must recognize that legitimate goals for parent support extend beyond raising achievement to helping students navigate the system and ensuring their access and opportunity, especially in communities of color with legacies of limited access. Fourth, educators need to engage the broad school community in anticipating, understanding, and reducing sources of conflict in home-school relations, starting with removing barriers to access and communication and responding flexibly to advocacy efforts by/for marginalized families.

The qualitative researcher suggests implications for practice

**65** Finally, schools, parent programs, college access programs, and government initiatives should capitalize on parents' intense concern and need for information to engage more families of color in their children's education, include them in the conversation about students' plans, and launch more students on college pathways (Tierney & Auerbach, 2005). Schools can begin to do this by making information readily available in multiple languages and formats and by creating small-scale, culturally relevant, dialogic parent outreach programs where parents can exchange concerns and information with the help of bicultural educators and parent advocates (Auerbach, 2004).

**66** This study suggests the need for a number of shifts in research on parents and education. In terms of definitions, we must move from seeing parent involvement as a narrow range of traditional practices associated with White, middle-class parents to a wide range of practices by diverse parents at home and at school. Methodologically, we must move beyond surveying discrete behaviors and relying on large national databases to more holistic, in-depth studies of parent roles in particular cultural and

The qualitative researcher suggests implications for future research school contexts, with an emphasis on parents' own perspectives. Conceptually, we must embrace rather than reject the use of race, class, culture, and gender as lenses to examine home-school relations, and we must expand our notion of the goal of parent involvement from merely aiding in the quest for higher test scores to serving diverse families in fulfilling a variety of educational aspirations for their children.

**67** The better educators understand how families support education, the better schools can promote partnerships with informed parent participation and respectful, culturally sensitive, home-school relations. Such collaboration, in turn, will contribute to more equitable outcomes and more manageable "border crossings" between home and school (Phelan, Davidson, & Cao, 1991).

## References


Abrams, L. S., & Gibbs, J. T. (2002). Disrupting the logic of home-school relations: Parent involvement strategies and practices of inclusion and exclusion. *Urban Education, 37*(3), 384-407.

Auerbach, S. (2001). *Under co-construction: Parent roles in promoting college access for students of color.* Unpublished doctoral dissertation, University of California, Los Angeles, Graduate School of Education and Information Studies.

Auerbach, S. (2002). "Why do they give the good classes to some and not to others?" Latino parent narratives of struggle in a college access program. *Teachers College Record, 104*(7), 1369-1392.

Auerbach, S. (2004). Engaging Latino parents in supporting college pathways: Lessons from a college access program. *Journal of Hispanic Higher Education, 3*(2), 125-145.

Auerbach, S. (2006). "If the student is good, let him fly": Moral support for college among Latino immigrant parents. *Journal of Latino Education.*

Azmitia, M., Cooper, C. R., Garcia, E. E., & Dunbar, N. D. (1996). The ecology of family guidance in low-income Mexican American and European American families. *Social Development, 5*(1), 1-23.

Baker, A. J. L., & Soden, L. M. (1998, April). The challenges of parent involvement research. *ERIC Clearinghouse on Urban Education Digest, 134*, 1-4.

Baker, D. P., & Stevenson, D. L. (1986, July). Mothers' strategies for children's school achievement: Managing the transition to high school. *Sociology of Education, 59*, 156-166.

Bourdieu, P. (1973). Cultural reproduction and social reproduction. In J. Karabel & A. H. Halsey (Eds.), *Power and ideology in education* (pp. 487-511). New York: Oxford University Press.

Bourdieu, P. (1987). The forms of capital. In J. G. Richardson (Ed.), *Handbook of theory and research for the sociology of education* (pp. 241-258). New York: Greenwood. (Original work published 1979)

Clark, R. M. (1983). *Family life and school achievement: Why poor Black children succeed or fail.* Chicago: University of Chicago Press.

D'Andrade, R. G. (1992). Schemas and motivation. In R. G. D'Andrade & C. Strauss (Eds.), *Human motives and cultural models* (pp. 23-44). New York: Cambridge University Press.

Delgado-Gaitan, C. (1994a). *Consejos*: The power of cultural narratives. *Anthropology & Education Quarterly, 25*(3), 298-316.

Delgado-Gaitan, C. (1994b). Spanish-speaking families' involvement in schools. In C. L. Fagnano & B. Z. Werber (Eds.), *School, family, and community interaction: A view from the firing lines* (pp. 85-96). Boulder, CO: Westview.

Delgado-Gaitan, C., & Segura, D. A. (1989). The social context of Chicana women's role in their children's schooling. *Educational Foundations, 3*, 71-92.

Deslandes, R., & Bertrand, R. (2005). Motivation of parent involvement in secondary schooling. *Journal of Education Research, 98*(3), 164-176.

Eccles, J. S., & Harold, R. D. (1993). Parent-school involvement during the early adolescent years. *Teachers College Record, 94*(3), 568-587.

Epstein, J. L. (1990). School and family connections: Theory, research and implications for integrating sociologies of education and family. In D. G. Unger & M. B. Sussman (Eds.), *Families in community settings: Interdisciplinary perspectives* (pp. 99-126). New York: Haworth.

Epstein, J. L. (1995, May). School/family/community partnerships: Caring for the children we share. *Phi Delta Kappan*, pp. 701-712.

Fine, M. (1991). *Framing dropouts: Notes on the politics of an urban public high school.* Albany: State University of New York Press.

Fine, M. (1993). [Ap]parent involvement: Reflections on parents, power, and urban public schools. *Teachers College Record, 94*(4), 682-709.

Fordham, S. (1996). *Blacked out: Dilemmas of race, identity, and success at Capital High.* Chicago: The University of Chicago Press.

Franklin, A. J., & Boyd-Franklin, N. (1985). A psychoeducational perspective on Black parenting. In H. P. McAdoo & J. L. McAdoo (Eds.), *Black children: Social, educational and parental environments* (pp. 194-212). Newbury Park, CA: Sage.

Gandara, P. (1995). *Over the ivy wall: The educational mobility of low-income Chicanos.* Albany: State University of New York Press.

Gandara, P., & Bial, D. (1999). *Paving the way to higher education: K-12 intervention programs for underrepresented youth.* Washington, DC: National Center for Education Statistics.

Goldenberg, C., & Gallimore, R. (1995). Immigrant Latino parents' values and beliefs about their children's education: Continuities and discontinuities across cultures and generations. *Advances in Motivation and Achievement, 9*, 183-228.

Henderson, A. T., & Mapp, K. L. (2002). *A new wave of evidence: The impact of school, family, and community connections on student achievement.* Annual synthesis 2002. Austin, TX: Southwest Educational Development Laboratory.

Hoover-Dempsey, K. V., & Sandler, H. M. (1995). Parental involvement in children's education: Why does it make a difference? *Teachers College Record, 97*(2), 310-331.

Hoover-Dempsey, K.V., & Sandler, H. M. (1997). Why do parents become involved in their children's education? *Review of Educational Research, 67*(1), 3-42.

Horvat, E. M., Weininger, E. B., & Lareau, A. (2003). From social ties to social capital: Ciass differences in the relations between schools and parent networks. *American Educational Research Journal, 40*(2), 319-352.

Hossler, D., Schmit, J., & Vesper, N. (1999). *Going to college: How social, economic, and educational factors influence the decisions students make.* Baltimore: Johns Hopkins University Press.

Jordan, C., Orozco, E., & Averett, A. (2002). *Emerging issues in school, family and community connections: Annual synthesis 2001.* Austin, TX: Southwest Educational Development Laboratory.

Lamont, M., & Lareau, A. (1988, fall). Cultural capital: Allusions, gaps and glissandos in recent theoretical developments. *Sociological Theory, 6*, 153-168.

Lareau, A. (1989). *Home advantage: Social class and parental intervention in elementary education*. New York: Falmer.

Lareau, A. (2003). *Unequal childhoods: Class, race, and family life*. Berkeley: University of California Press.

Lareau, A., & Horvat, E. (1999, January). Moments of social inclusion: Race, class and cultural capital in family school relationships. *Sociology of Education, 71, 39-56.*

Lawrence-Lightfoot, S., & Hoffman Davis, J. (1997). *The art and science of portraiture*. San Francisco: Jossey-Bass.

López, G. R. (2001). The value of hard work: Lessons on parent involvement from an (im)migrant household. *Harvard Educational Review, 71*(3), 416-437.

López, G. R., Scribner, J. D., & Mahitivanichcha, K. (2001). Redefining parental involvement: Lessons from high-performing migrant-impacted schools. *American Educational Research Journal, 38*(2), 253-288.

MacLeod, J. (1995). *Ain't no makin' it: Aspirations and attainment in a low-income neighborhood*. Boulder, CO: Westview.

Mattingly, D. J., Prislin, R., McKenzie, T. L., Rodriguez, J. L., & Kayzar, B. (2002). Evaluating evaluations: The case of parent involvement programs. *Review of Educational Research, 72*(4), 549-576.

McDonough, P. (1997). *Choosing colleges: How social class and schools structure opportunity*. Albany: State University of New York Press.

Mehan, H., Villanueva, I., Hubbard, L., & Lintz, A. (1996). *Constructing school success: The consequences of untracking low-achieving students*. New York: Cambridge University Press.

Merriam, S. (2001). *Qualitative research and case study applications in education* (Rev. ed.). San Francisco: Jossey-Bass.

Meyers, B., Dowdy, J., & Paterson, P. (2000). Finding the missing voices: Perspectives of the least visible families and their willingness and capacity for school involvement. *Current Issues in Middle Level Education, 7*(2), 59-79.

Moles, O. C. (1993). Collaboration between schools and disadvantaged parents: Obstacles and openings. In N. F. Chavkin (Ed.), *Families and schools in a pluralistic society* (pp. 21-52). Albany: State University of New York Press.

Oakes, J. (1985). *Keeping track: How schools structure inequality*. New Haven, CT: Yale University Press.

Ogbu, J. U. (1987). Variability in minority school performance: A problem in search of an explanation. In E. Jacob (Eds.), *Minority education: Anthropological perspectives* (pp. 83-111). Norwood, NJ: Ablex.

Olivos, E. M. (2003). *Dialectical tensions, contradictions, and resistance: A study of the relationship between Latino parents and the public school system within a socio-economic structure of dominance*. Unpublished doctoral dissertation, San Diego State University/Claremont Graduate University, San Diego/Claremont, CA.

Peshkin, A. (1988). In search of subjectivity—one's own. *Educational Researcher, 17*(7), 17-21.

Phelan, P., Davidson, A. L., & Cao., H. T. (1991). Students' multiple worlds: Negotiating the boundaries of family, peer, and school cultures. *Anthropology and Education Quarterly, 22*(3), 224-250.

Plank, S. B., & Jordan, W. J. (1997). *Reducing talent loss: The impact of information, guidance, and actions on postsecondary enrollment.* Center for Research on the Education of Students Placed at Risk (CRESPAR) Report #9. Baltimore: Johns Hopkins University Press, CRESPAR.

Reay, D. (1998). *Class work: Mothers' involvement in their children's primary schooling.* London: University College of London Press.

Reese, L., Balzano, S., Gallimore, R., & Goldenberg, C. (1995). The concept of *educación*: Latino family values and American schooling. *International Journal of Educational Research, 23*(1), 57-81.

Reese, L., Gallimore, R., Goldenberg, C., & Balzano, S. (1995). Immigrant Latino parents' future orientations for their children. In R. Macias & R. Garcia Ramos (Eds.), *Changing schools for changing students: An anthology of research on language minorities, schools and society* (pp. 205-230). Santa Barbara: University of California Linguistic Minority Research Institute.

Shannon, S. M. (1996). Minority parental involvement: A Mexican mother's experience and a teacher's interpretation. *Education and Urban Society, 29*(1), 71-84.

Solórzano, D. G. (1992). An exploratory analysis of the effects of race, class, and gender on student and parent mobility aspirations. *Journal of Negro Education, 61*(1), 30-44.

Stanton-Salazar, R. D. (2001). *Manufacturing hope and despair: The school and kin support networks of U.S.-Mexican youth.* New York: Teachers College Press.

Tierney, W., & Auerbach, S. (2005). Toward developing an untapped resource: The role of families in college preparation. In W. Tierney, Z. Corwin, & J. Colyar (Eds.), *Preparing for college: Nine elements of effective outreach* (pp. 29-48). Albany: State University of New York Press.

Tillman, L. C. (2004, spring). African American parental involvement in a post-*Brown* era: Facilitating the academic achievement of African American students. *Journal of School Public Relations, 25,* 161-176.

Treviño, R. E. (2004). *Parent involvement and remarkable student achievement: A study of Mexican-origin families of migrant high-achievers.* Paper presented at the annual meeting of the American Educational Research Association, San Diego, CA.

Useem, E. L. (1991). Student selection into course sequences in mathematics: The impact of parental involvement and school policies. *Journal of Research on Adolescence, 1*(3), 231-250.

Valdés, G. (1996). *Con respeto: Bridging the distances between culturally diverse families and schools. An ethnographic portrait.* New York: Teachers College Press.

Valencia, R. R., & Black, M. S. (2002). "Mexican Americans don't value education!" On the basis of the myth, mythmaking, and debunking. *Journal of Latinos and Education, 1*(2), 81-103.

Villanueva, I. (1996). Change in the educational life of Chicano families across three generations. *Education and Urban Society, 29*(1), 13-34.

Ward, J. V. (1996). Raising resisters: The role of truth telling in the psychological development of African American girls. In B. J. Ross Lendbenter & N. Way (Eds.), *Urban girls: Resisting stereotypes, creating identities* (pp. 85-99). New York: New York University Press.

Wells, A. S., & Serna, I. (1996). The politics of culture: Understanding local political resistance to detracking in racially mixed schools. *Harvard Educational Review, 66*(1), 93-118.

Yin, R. K. (1993). *Applications of case study research.* Thousand Oaks, CA: Sage.

Yonezawa, S. (1997). *Making decisions about students' lives: An interactive study of secondary school students' academic program selection*. Unpublished doctoral dissertation, University of California, Los Angeles, Graduate School of Education and Information Studies.

Yosso, T. J. (2005). Whose culture has capital? A critical race theory discussion of community cultural wealth. *Race, Ethnicity, and Education*, *8*(1), 69-91.

**Susan Auerbach**, PhD, is an assistant professor in the Department of Educational Leadership and Policy Studies at California State University, Northridge. In 2001, she received her doctorate from the University of California, Los Angeles, Urban Schooling Division and the Outstanding Dissertation Award from the Family-School-Community Partnerships Special Interest Group of the American Educational Research Association. Her research interests include parent involvement, college access, leadership for community partnerships and public engagement, and teacher training in the social foundations of education.

*Source:* This article is reprinted from *Urban Education,* Vol. 42, Issue 3, pp. 250–283, 2007. Reprinted with permission of Sage Publications, Inc.

# CHAPTER 2 Quantitative and Qualitative Approaches to Research

*You have learned that research consists of seven steps and that researchers report these steps when they disseminate their research in written reports. Let's add a second idea: Researchers conduct their studies in two ways—using a quantitative approach or a qualitative approach—at each phase in the research process. In this chapter, we explore how researchers conduct the process of research using both quantitative and qualitative approaches.*

## BY THE END OF THIS CHAPTER, YOU SHOULD BE ABLE TO:

- Provide a definition of quantitative and qualitative research to someone who is unfamiliar with the two approaches.
- Explain the differences between the two approaches.
- Identify reasons that researchers use to decide whether to use a quantitative or qualitative approach.
- Assess whether a research study is quantitative or qualitative.
- Consider the quality of quantitative and qualitative research reports.

You have just read two research studies related to parents taking part in their children's education. (If you have not yet read the studies at the end of Chapter 1, go back and read them before continuing with this chapter!) As you read these two studies, you hopefully noticed some similarities between the articles. One similarity is that both articles were about the same general topic: parent involvement in their children's education. The authors also collected and analyzed data in each study. The organization of the two articles was also similar: an introduction to the study's topic, a discussion of the methods, a presentation of results, and a discussion of the conclusions about the study. You may also have noticed differences between these two examples of research. Most notably, the parent involvement study by Deslandes and Bertrand (2005) focused on numbers and reporting statistics about parent involvement. In contrast, the parent role study by Auerbach (2007) focused on words and reporting detailed descriptions of different parent roles.

At a basic level, this difference (numbers vs. words) forms the basis of two different approaches for conducting research: quantitative and qualitative. Today, researchers actively use these two approaches to study most every topic of interest across all disciplines and professional areas. The differences, however, go beyond simply the collection of numbers or words. They permeate throughout the steps of the research process and suggest different criteria for assessing the quality of research studies. Therefore, to be able to understand current research you need to be able to read, understand, and evaluate research using these two different approaches. Let's start by considering a definition for each approach.

*Here's a Tip for Reading Research!*

The rule of thumb to use to determine whether a research study is qualitative or quantitative is to examine how the data were analyzed and the results reported. If the researcher used statistics and reported the results as numbers, then the study is probably quantitative. If the researcher analyzed the meaning of text data and reported the results as themes or categories using only words, then the study is probably qualitative.

For practice identifying the characteristics of quantitative and qualitative research, go to the *Building Research Skills* section under the topic "Introduction to Educational Research" in MyEducationalResearchLab, located at www.myeducationlab.com. Complete the exercise "Recognizing the Characteristics of Quantitative and Qualitative Research" and use the provided feedback to further develop your skills for reading research articles.

## What Is Quantitative and Qualitative Research?

- **Quantitative research** is a type of research in which the researcher studies a problem that calls for an explanation; decides what to study; asks specific, narrow questions; collects quantifiable data from participants; analyzes these numbers using statistics; and conducts the inquiry in an unbiased, objective manner.
- **Qualitative research** is a type of research in which the researcher studies a problem that calls for an exploration; relies on the views of participants; asks broad, general questions; collects data consisting largely of words (or text) from participants; describes and analyzes these words for themes; and conducts the inquiry in a subjective and reflexive manner.

## How Are the Steps of the Research Process Implemented in Quantitative and Qualitative Studies?

Using Figure 2.1 as a guide, we will examine how researchers implement the steps of the research process when conducting quantitative and qualitative studies. This is one of the most important figures in this book because it summarizes the key ideas that you will be learning across the chapters. This figure relates the quantitative and qualitative approaches to the seven steps of the research process. Notice that Figure 2.1 displays a *continuum* for each step. The endpoints for each continuum denote the major characteristics of a quantitative or qualitative study. The characteristics of individual studies fall somewhere along the line between these endpoints. Quantitative studies are usually characterized by the elements on the left and qualitative studies by elements on the right. Let's examine these characteristics in detail for each step.

### Step 1—Identifying a Research Problem

Researchers identify a research problem to limit the subject matter of their study and to suggest the importance of the topic and study for specific audiences. Researchers discuss the research problem in the introduction of their research reports.

**Quantitative research** tends to address research problems requiring:

- a description of trends in a population,
- an explanation of the relationships among variables.

**Qualitative research** tends to address research problems requiring:

- a detailed understanding of a phenomenon,
- an exploration because little is known about the problem.

***Identifying a Research Problem in Quantitative Research.*** In quantitative research, researchers identify research problems that call for an explanation of the trends in a population. For example, a research problem might be that middle school boys have underdeveloped word knowledge because they do not spend enough time reading and teachers do not know what kind of reading materials will appeal to them. This problem calls for describing the trends in middle school boys' reading preferences in order to develop successful reading programs. Quantitative

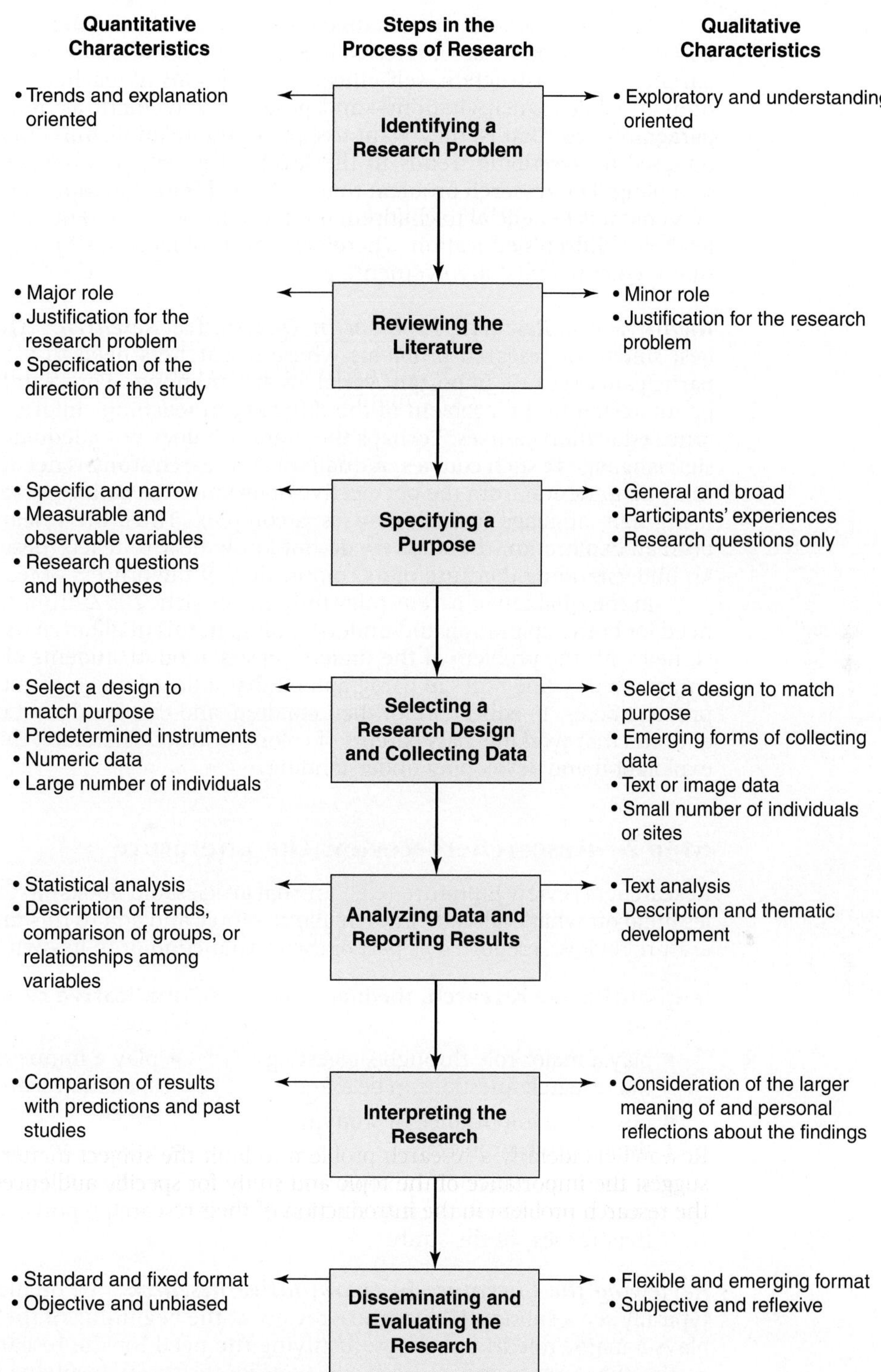


**FIGURE 2.1 Characteristics of Quantitative and Qualitative Research Along Continuua for the Process of Research**

researchers also identify research problems that require the researcher to explain the relationships among variables. A research problem might be that a school district does not understand why certain voters voted against the school bond issue. This problem calls for examining variables such as gender and attitude toward the quality of the schools to identify influences related to how individuals vote on the bond issue.

The authors in the quantitative parent involvement study (Deslandes & Bertrand, 2005) from Chapter 1 are interested in examining the relationship between four factors—parents' role construction, self-efficacy, perceptions of teacher invitations, and perceptions of adolescent invitations—and parent involvement at home and at school (see paragraph 02). That is, they want to explain the relationships among these variables as opposed to describing trends in the levels of parent involvement in secondary-level schooling. The research problem that calls for this explanation arises because parent involvement is beneficial to children, but perhaps not all parents are adequately involved in their children's education. Therefore, this problem calls for explaining the variables that predict parents' involvement.

***Identifying a Research Problem in Qualitative Research.*** Qualitative research is best suited for research problems where researchers need to explore and learn from participants because important variables are unknown. For example, a researcher may be interested in the problem of the difficulty in teaching children who are deaf in distance education courses. Perhaps the literature does not adequately address the use of sign language in such courses. A qualitative research study is needed in order to explore this phenomenon from the perspective of distance education students. Unquestionably, using sign language in such courses is complex. Thus, the research problem requires both an exploration (because we do not know how to teach these children), as well as an understanding (because of its complexity) of the process of teaching and learning.

In the qualitative parent role study (Auerbach, 2007) from Chapter 1 you see the need for both exploration and understanding. In this qualitative study, the author is concerned with the problem of the underrepresentation of students of color in colleges (see paragraph 01). She notes in paragraph 02 that little is known about how parents of color promote access to education for their children, and that we do not understand the different roles that working-class parents of color construct. Therefore, this problem calls for an exploration and developing understanding.

## Step 2—Researchers Review the Literature

Researchers review literature (e.g., journal articles and books) to ensure that their studies build on what is already known about a topic and add to this understanding. The literature review is reported as part of the introduction or in its own introductory section.

In **quantitative research,** the literature tends to:

- play a major role through suggesting the research questions to be asked,
- justify the importance of studying the research problem,
- suggest the direction (purpose statement and research questions or hypotheses) of the study.

In **qualitative research,** the literature tends to:

- play a minor role in suggesting a specific research question to be asked,
- justify the importance of studying the research problem.

***Reviewing the Literature in Quantitative Research.*** In quantitative research, you typically see a substantial literature review at the beginning of the study. This literature plays a major role in two ways: justifying the need for the research problem and suggesting the purpose and research questions for the study. Justifying the research problem means that researchers use the literature to document the importance of the issue examined in the study. The literature also documents a need for the study and directs the purpose statement and research questions or hypotheses. Researchers identify key variables, relationships, and trends from the literature, and use these to provide direction for their studies. A literature review on college students, for example, may show that we know little about the problem of "binge drinking." Existing literature, however, may identify the importance of peer groups and styles of interacting among student peer groups. Thus, important research questions might address how peers and their interaction styles influence binge drinking on college campuses. In this way, the literature in a quantitative study both documents the need to study the problem and provides direction for the research questions.

In the quantitative parent involvement study (Deslandes & Bertrand, 2005), the authors cite extensive literature at the beginning of the article in a section titled "Influences on Parent Involvement." The authors rely on the model of the parent involvement process cited in paragraph 02, and they discuss the literature surrounding the factors that are expected to influence parental involvement (paragraphs 03–10). They begin by reviewing the literature about the demographic or personal factors, such as family size and educational level (see paragraph 03), then they proceed to review the literature about the major factors that they predict will influence parental involvement—parents' role construction (paragraph 05), parents' self-efficacy (paragraph 06), parents' perceptions of teacher invitations (paragraph 07), and parents' perceptions of student invitations (paragraphs 08–10). In this way, the authors establish the research that has been reported in the literature on each of the four factors in the study and foreshadow the research questions that will be addressed.

***Reviewing the Literature in Qualitative Research.*** In qualitative research, the literature review plays a less substantial role at the beginning of the study. Although researchers may review the literature to justify the need to study the research problem, the literature does not direct the research questions. The reason for this is that qualitative research relies on the views of participants in the study and less on the direction identified in the literature by the researcher. Thus, to use the literature to foreshadow or specify the direction for the study is inconsistent with the qualitative approach of learning from participants. For example, one qualitative researcher who studied bullying in schools cited several studies at the beginning of the research to provide evidence for the problem, but did not use the literature to specify the research questions. Instead, this researcher set out to answer the most general, open research question possible, "What is bullying?," to learn how students constructed their view of this experience.

The literature plays more of a minor role in the qualitative parent role study (Auerbach, 2007). The author does include two sections that review literature: "Mainstream and Critical Approaches to Parent Involvement" and "Conceptual Framework." Unlike the quantitative parent involvement study, however, this literature does not foreshadow specific research questions. Instead these sections provide commentary on how parent involvement research has not adequately addressed the needs and experiences of parents of color (see paragraph 06). The author goes on to discuss models available for thinking about parents' roles and argues for the need to understand cultural themes as opposed to specific variables (paragraphs 10–12). Therefore, while this study includes literature, it is used to justify the research problem, but it does not lead to the specific questions asked in the study. The questions are general, allowing the participants to help construct answers. Thus, in a qualitative study, the literature is of secondary importance while the views of the participants are of primary importance.

## Step 3—Researchers Specify a Purpose

Researchers specify a purpose for their research by identifying the major intent of the study and narrowing the intent into specific questions or hypotheses. You can usually find the purpose and questions at the end of the introduction.

In **quantitative research**, the purpose statement, research questions, and hypotheses tend to:

- be specific and narrow,
- seek measurable, observable data on variables.

In **qualitative research**, the purpose statement and research questions tend to:

- be general and broad,
- seek to understand the participants' experiences.

***Specifying a Purpose in Quantitative Research.*** In quantitative research, researchers ask specific, narrow questions to obtain measurable and observable data on variables. The major statements and questions of direction in a study—the purpose statement, research questions, and hypotheses—are specific and narrow because quantitative researchers identify only a few variables to study. Researchers are interested in describing or connecting these variables and therefore need to obtain measures or assessments on an instrument or record scores on a scale from observations. For example, in a study of adolescent career choices, the variable, the role of the school counselor, narrows the study to a specific variable from among many variables that might be studied (e.g., role of parents, personal investment by student). To examine the impact of the school counselor on adolescent career choices, measurable data must be obtained from the students.

In the quantitative parent involvement study (Deslandes & Bertrand, 2005), the authors narrow their focus by selecting a few factors that they predict will explain parental involvement. They state their purpose of the study and the major research questions in paragraph 13. They say that they will examine four factors that might influence parental involvement at home and at school. Thus, their research questions are specific to four factors, and later in the method section, they explain how they will measure these factors (paragraphs 18–23).

***Specifying a Purpose in Qualitative Research.*** In qualitative research, the purpose is much more open ended than in quantitative research. Qualitative researchers state general, broad questions so that they can best learn from participants. They research a single phenomenon of interest (as opposed to several variables in quantitative research) and state this phenomenon in a purpose statement. A qualitative study that examines the "professionalism" of teachers, for example, will seek to learn from high school teachers, "What does it mean to be a professional?" This research question focuses on understanding a single idea—being a professional—and calls for talking to teachers to learn about their experiences, which will yield qualitative data such as quotations.

In the qualitative parent role study (Auerbach, 2007), the author starts her study with broad, open-ended research questions that call for exploring participants' views about their roles as parents in helping their children gain educational access (see paragraph 03). This questioning focuses on understanding what working-class parents of color "think and do" when they want their children to go to college. The researcher's intent is to allow the participants to talk openly about their experiences and perspectives. Later in the method section she describes how she collected data by interviewing and observing parents (paragraph 15).

## Step 4—Researchers Select a Research Design and Collect Data

Once researchers have stated their study's purpose, they select a research design that is suited to address the purpose. The research design provides a blueprint for how researchers will collect, analyze, and report their data. Data collection includes gaining permissions, identifying participants, and collecting information from the participants that will be useful for answering the research questions. These procedures are reported in the methods section of an article.

In **quantitative research**, the data collection tends to consist of:

- selecting a quantitative research design,
- collecting data using instruments with preset questions and responses,
- gathering quantifiable (numeric) data,
- collecting information from a large number of individuals.

In **qualitative research**, the data collection tends to consist of:

- selecting a qualitative research design,
- collecting data using forms with general, emerging questions to permit the participant to generate responses,
- gathering word (text) or image (picture) data,
- collecting information from a small number of individuals or sites.

***Selecting a Research Design and Collecting Data in Quantitative Research.*** Researchers choose to use quantitative research because their problem calls for explanation, the literature provides a specific direction, and the purpose seeks measurable data for several variables. Researchers select a specific strategy for their quantitative research based on the intent of their study. We will learn more about these designs in Chapter 6, but three common quantitative research designs include experimental, correlational, and survey designs. Researchers choose an experimental design if they want to explain whether an intervention (like a new curriculum) causes an outcome (such as better reading performance). Researchers could also choose a correlational design to explain how variables are related to each other or a survey design to describe the trends in attitudes or behaviors of a group.

Across these different quantitative research designs, the collection of data has common characteristics. Researchers use instruments to measure the variables in the study. An instrument is a tool for recording quantitative data. It contains specific questions and response possibilities that the researcher establishes in advance of the study. Examples of instruments are survey questionnaires, checklists that can be used to observe an individual's behaviors, and standardized tests. Researchers administer this instrument to participants, and collect data in the form of numbers. The intent of this process is to apply the results from a small number of people to a large number (called generalizing the results). The more individuals studied, the stronger is the case for applying the results to a large number of people. For example, on a survey sent to 500 parents in a school district, the researcher seeks information about parents' attitudes toward the educational needs of pregnant teenagers in the schools. The researcher selects an instrument called, "Attitudes Toward Education of Pregnant Teenagers" and sends it to 500 parents that represent a cross section of people from all socioeconomic levels in the school district. After collecting and analyzing this data, the investigator will draw conclusions about all parents in this school district based on the representative sample studied.

Data collection is an integral part of the quantitative parent involvement study (Deslandes & Bertrand, 2005). The authors want to test whether the specified factors predict (or are related to) parent involvement at home and at school. Therefore, they designed their study using a correlational design. This quantitative design is so common that the authors did not state the name in the study, but in Chapter 6 we will learn that words such as "predictors" and "regression analyses" (see paragraphs 17, 25) are hallmarks of this quantitative design.

Focusing on data collection, the authors study a large number of parents (i.e., 770) of children in Grades 7, 8, and 9 (American system equivalents to Canadian schools). They survey parents using an adaptation of the instrument, "Sharing the Dream! Parent Questionnaire" as well as items on a questionnaire designed by other researchers to assess parents' perceptions of student invitations (paragraph 16). The survey items are translated into French to fit the Quebec context, and they gather quantifiable data (scores) on the survey (paragraph 18). The authors discuss the scales used to collect the data and how they are scored (i.e., from 1 = disagree very strongly to 6 = agree very strongly).

***Selecting a Research Design and Collecting Data in Qualitative Research.*** As in quantitative research, qualitative researchers generally select a research design to plan how they will conduct their study. We will learn more about these qualitative designs in Chapter 9. An example of a qualitative research design is an ethnographic design, which a researcher chooses to understand the shared culture of a group. Researchers could also choose a grounded theory design if they want to explore individuals' experiences to develop a theory. Although there can be differences in how researchers collect their data depending on the selected research design, all qualitative data collection shares some common characteristics.

In qualitative research, researchers do not begin data collection with a preestablished instrument to measure distinct variables. Instead, researchers seek to learn from the participants in the study. Therefore, they develop forms, called protocols, for recording data as the study proceeds. These forms pose open-ended questions so that the participants can provide their own answers to the questions. Often questions on these forms will change and emerge during data collection. Examples of these forms include an interview protocol, which consists of four or five questions, and an observational protocol, in which the researcher records notes about the behavior of participants. Moreover, qualitative researchers gather text (word) or image (picture) data. Examples of qualitative data might include a typed transcription of the audio recordings from interviews or notes that a researcher recorded while observing participants in their work or family setting. With each form of qualitative data, researchers gather as much information as possible to collect detailed accounts for a final research report.

In the qualitative parent role study (Auerbach, 2007), the author informs us that she has conducted an "ethnographic" study (paragraph 03). This research design is best suited for studies interested in describing the shared culture of groups, such as their beliefs, behaviors, and language. The intent of this study is to understand the cultural roles that parents construct.

In order to understand the different parent roles, the author collects qualitative data from a few parents whose children are participating in a special school-based program (paragraph 14). The researcher does not use instruments constructed by other researchers; instead, she developed her own forms for recording information—an interview protocol—during the project (paragraph 15). This form contains general questions so that the parents can provide their own responses to the questions. She also takes observational notes from meetings attended by the parents.

## Step 5—Researchers Analyze Data and Report Results

In the process of research, researchers analyze their data and report the results of the analysis. These results summarize what the researchers found based on the data collected as part of the study. They are reported within the results section.

In **quantitative research,** data analysis tends to:

- consist of statistical analysis,
- involve describing trends, comparing group differences, or relating variables.

In **qualitative research,** data analysis tends to:

- consists of text analysis,
- involve developing description and themes.

***Analyzing Data and Reporting Results in Quantitative Research.*** In quantitative research, researchers analyze the data using mathematical procedures, called statistics. These analyses consist of breaking down the data into parts to answer the research questions. All quantitative studies describe trends in the data, such as the average response across all participants. In addition, most quantitative studies also include statistical procedures, such as comparing scores between groups or relating scores for individuals that provide information to address the research questions or hypotheses.

In the parent involvement study (Deslandes & Bertrand, 2005), the authors collect responses from the parents of secondary-level students who provide scores on a survey instrument. The survey has questions relating to each of the factors and the parent-involvement outcome measures as shown in Table 2 of the report. The researchers do not use all of the items on the survey because some were found to not be good measures of the factors. As discussed in paragraph 17, they use a statistical procedure (i.e., factor analysis) to help them identify the most important questions for each of the scales (or factors) in the study. With this refined set of questions for each of the factors, they then conduct descriptive analyses (i.e., means and standard deviations as shown in Table 3). They also use the statistical procedure of regression analysis to determine which of the predictors best explain the variation in scores for parent involvement in addition to the personal items (i.e., control variables). From Tables 4 and 5, we see which variables best explain the variation for the measures of parent involvement at home and at school for each grade level (7, 8, and 9). In short, the authors use statistical analysis consisting of three phases—factor analysis, descriptive analysis, and regression analysis. The ultimate goal was to relate variables to see which predictors (the four factors) best explain parental involvement.

***Analyzing Data and Reporting Results in Qualitative Research.*** Qualitative researchers use a different approach for data analysis because the data consist of words or pictures, not numbers. Typically, researchers gather a text database, so the analysis consists of dividing the text into groups of sentences, called text segments, and determining the meaning of each group of sentences. Rather than using statistics, the researcher analyzes words and/or pictures to describe the central phenomenon under study. The result may be a description of individual people or places. In some qualitative studies, the entire report is mostly a long description of several individuals. The result may also include themes or broad categories that represent the findings. In qualitative studies in which researchers both describe individuals and identify themes, a rich, complex picture emerges.

The author of the qualitative parent role study uses text analysis procedures to analyze the collected data (Auerbach, 2007). She reviews the text data consisting of transcripts from interviews, written notes from observations, and documents from the school (see paragraph 15 for data sources). From these data, the author uses a text analysis procedure called coding to identify themes and patterns in the data (see paragraph 16). From her analysis and the emergent themes, the author advances a typology that describes three types of roles constructed by the parents. She describes the moral supporters (paragraphs 23–32), struggling advocates (paragraphs 33–40), and ambivalent companions (paragraphs 41–54). She related these categories to each other in Figure 1, and illustrated their distinguishing characteristics in Table 1. The author also discussed how the different roles were shaped by cultural contexts in paragraphs 55–60 to provide a complex picture of parent roles.

## Step 6—Researchers Interpret the Research

After reporting results, researchers interpret the results and their overall study. The interpretation is discussed within the conclusion section of a report.

In **quantitative research,** the:

- interpretation tends to consist of comparing results with prior predictions and past research.

In **qualitative research,** the:

- interpretation tends to consist of stating the larger meaning of and personal reflections about the findings.

***Interpreting the Research in Quantitative Research.*** In quantitative research, researchers interpret the results of the statistical analyses in light of initial predictions or prior studies. This interpretation is an explanation as to why the results turned out the way they did, and researchers discuss how the results either support or refute the expected predictions. Quantitative researchers also use procedures to ensure that the researchers' personal biases and values do not influence the results. Researchers use instruments that have proven value and that have reliable and valid scores from past uses of the instruments. Researchers also design studies to control for all variables that might introduce bias into a study. They discuss any limitations that occurred in their data collection and analysis procedures.

In the quantitative parent involvement study (Deslandes & Bertrand, 2005), the authors conclude their study with three sections: *Discussion, Implications and Limitations,* and *Conclusion.* They discuss the main results of the study and compare their results with those found in other studies in the literature (paragraphs 32–43). They then proceed to evaluate the study by suggesting the implications and limitations of the results (paragraphs 44–47).

***Interpreting the Research in Qualitative Research.*** After developing a complex picture of the phenomenon under study through a text analysis, qualitative researchers make an interpretation of the meaning of the findings. They may reflect on how the findings relate to existing research or draw out larger, more abstract meanings from the findings. Researchers may also state a personal reflection about the significance of the lessons learned during the study or discuss how their experiences and cultural backgrounds (e.g., Asian American perspectives) affect the interpretations and conclusions drawn. This is an example of qualitative researchers discussing their own role or position in a research study, called being reflexive (reflexivity means that the researchers reflect on their own biases, values, and assumptions and actively write them into their research). This may also involve discussing personal experiences and identifying how researchers collaborated with participants during phases of the project.

In the qualitative parent role study (Auerbach, 2007), the author interprets the three categories of parents that emerged by examining their similarities (paragraphs 55–60) and suggesting the larger meaning of the findings for providing ways to think about parent involvement that provide alternative perspectives to the mainstream approach (see paragraphs 61–62). The author concludes the article by describing the limitations of the study (see paragraph 63) and suggesting implications of the research for practice and future research (paragraphs 64–67). The author also introduces herself into the study by commenting about her role in conducting the study (see paragraph 17). Qualitative researchers typically bring themselves into the written report in some way, such as writing about their experiences when they discuss the procedures or weaving their personal experiences into the report.

## Step 7—Researchers Disseminate and Evaluate the Research

The entire research process culminates in a report that is disseminated to audiences who may benefit from what the researchers learned during the study. Different audiences also evaluate the research process as described within the research report.

In **quantitative research,** the:

- research reports tend to use standard, fixed evaluative criteria and structures,
- researchers tend to take an objective and unbiased approach.

In **qualitative research,** the:

- research reports tend to use flexible, emerging evaluative criteria and structures,
- researchers tend to take a subjective and reflexive approach.

***Disseminating and Evaluating the Research in Quantitative Research.*** Quantitative researchers report research without referring to themselves or their personal reactions. The overall format for a report of a quantitative study follows a predictable pattern: introduction, review of the literature, methods, results, and conclusions. This form creates a standardized structure for quantitative studies. In addition, it also leads to specific criteria that researchers might use to judge the quality of a quantitative research report. For example, researchers examine a quantitative study to see if it has an extensive literature review; tests good research questions and hypotheses; uses rigorous, impartial data collection procedures; applies appropriate statistical procedures; and forms interpretations that logically follow from the data.

Looking at the quantitative parent involvement study (Deslandes & Bertrand, 2005) as a whole, the authors subdivide the report into standard sections typically found in quantitative studies. The study begins with an introduction that includes the literature review and purpose statement and research questions (see paragraphs 01–13), the methods (see paragraphs 14–24), the results (see paragraphs 25–31), and the conclusion (see paragraphs 32–49). The entire study conveys an impersonal, objective tone. The authors do not bring either their biases or their personal opinions into the study. They use proven instruments to measure variables (for example, see paragraphs 18–19), and they employ multiple statistical procedures (see paragraphs 17, 25) to build objectivity into the study.

***Disseminating and Evaluating the Research in Qualitative Research.*** Qualitative researchers employ a wide range of formats to report their qualitative studies. Although the overall general form follows the standard steps in the process of research, the sequence of these "parts" of research tends to vary from one qualitative report to another. A study may begin with a long, personal narrative told in story form or with a more objective, scientific report that resembles quantitative research. With such variability, it is not surprising that the standards for evaluating qualitative research are also flexible. Good qualitative reports, however, need to be realistic and persuasive in order to convince the reader that the study is an accurate and credible account. Qualitative reports typically contain extensive data collection to convey the complexity of the phenomenon or process under study. The data analysis reflects description and themes as well as the interrelation of themes.

Looking at the organization of the qualitative parent role study (Auerbach, 2007) as a whole, it follows a structure similar to that of the quantitative study, although without using traditional headings like "literature review" or "results." In addition, throughout the study the author uses a personal pronoun referring to herself frequently (e.g., "I suggest . . . "). The extensive use of quotes from individuals also accentuates the personal approach in this study.

## What Do You Think?

Consider the following abstract from an article about a study of school counselors. Does this article report a quantitative or qualitative research study?

> The purpose of this article is to investigate correlates and predictors of school counselors' career satisfaction and commitment. Regression analyses of 1,280 Florida counselors' survey responses indicated that positive predictors of career satisfaction included appropriate duties, high self-efficacy, and district and peer supervision, while negative predictors were inappropriate duties and stress. The only positive predictor of career commitment was appropriate counseling duties while the only negative predictor was stress. Results and future directions are discussed. *(Baggerly & Osborn, 2006, p. 197)*

### Check Your Understanding

From this abstract, we can conclude that this article is reporting a quantitative research study. Signals of a quantitative approach include:

- a large number of participants (1280 individuals),
- the researcher wanting to explain predictive relationships,
- an interest in several variables (e.g., career satisfaction, commitment, self-efficacy) instead of a single phenomenon, and
- the use of statistical analysis procedures (regression analyses).

## How Does a Researcher Choose to Use a Quantitative or Qualitative Approach?

For practice understanding how researchers choose a research approach, go to the *Activities and Applications* section under the topic "Introduction to Educational Research" in MyEducational-ResearchLab, located at www.myeducationlab.com. Complete the exercise "Planning Qualitative and Quantitative Studies."

*Here's a Tip for Reading Research!*

Today many researchers are using research designs that combine quantitative and qualitative research. You will find a combination of both approaches in studies using mixed methods designs to best understand a problem. You may also find a researcher combining aspects of both approaches to help solve a practical problem in a local setting in an action research design.

A researcher chooses to use quantitative research when:

- The issue or problem being examined needs to be studied to determine what factors influence an outcome, to explain how variables are related, or to discern broad trends in a population of people.
- A clear direction exists in the literature about the type of questions that need to be examined.
- Ideas can be measured and assessed using instruments.

A researcher chooses to use qualitative research when:

- The topic has been little studied and a need exists to explore the topic with some people.
- The research questions need to evolve from the participants because little is known.
- The setting of the study influences what will be learned.

Other factors also influence this choice, such as the experiences and training of the researcher and their personal preferences. Some researchers are simply more comfortable conducting quantitative research, while others are more comfortable with qualitative research. While these preferences may encourage researchers to be more interested in certain types of research problems, these preferences should be secondary to choosing the approach that is best suited to the research problem being studied.

In the parent involvement study (Deslandes & Bertrand, 2005), the authors' interest grows out of a need to better explain what factors lead parents to decide to become involved in their adolescents' schooling. When prediction is involved, researchers use quantitative research. Alternatively, in the qualitative parent involvement study (Auerbach, 2007), the researcher seeks to understand how parents of students of color construct their roles in assisting their children's access to education, including college. When an exploration is needed, and one in which all of the complexity of a situation must be explored, researchers use qualitative research. To explore is at a different end of the research continuum from explaining the impact of known predictors and measuring their influence (Figure 2.1).

## How Do You Assess the Quality of a Quantitative or Qualitative Study?

Consider the checklists found in Figures 2.2 and 2.3. In it we have listed criteria you might use to assess the quality of a quantitative or qualitative study based on the distinctions we have outlined for the process of research. As implied in the figures, the two

Use the following criteria to evaluate the quality of the research process of a quantitative research report. For each evaluation item, indicate the following ratings:

+ You rate the item as "high quality" for the study.
✓ You rate the item as "ok quality" for the study.
– You rate the item as "low quality" for the study.

In addition to your rating, make notes about each element when you apply these criteria to an actual published study.

| **In a high-quality quantitative research report, the author . . .** | Application to a Published Study | |
|---|---|---|
| | Your Rating | Your Notes |
| 1. States a problem that is best addressed by explaining trends or relationships about specific variables. | | |
| 2. Uses the literature to indicate the questions that need to be answered. | | |
| 3. Presents the purpose and research questions as statements that relate variables and are very specific. | | |
| 4. Gathers numeric data from a large group of participants. | | |
| 5. Reports numbers using statistical information to describe trends, compare groups, or relate variables. | | |
| 6. Makes an interpretation based on the studies of others using an objective approach. | | |

FIGURE 2.2 Criteria for Evaluating the Quality of the Process of Research for a Quantitative Study

approaches to research follow the same steps in the process of research but depart at each phase in the way in which the research is implemented. Therefore, you need to consider different criteria for judging the quality of a study based on whether it is quantitative or qualitative.

In addition to the aspects highlighted in Figures 2.2 and 2.3, all research should meet some basic quality standards. These include:

- The research must be conducted ethically. This means that researchers must treat research participants with respect, such as obtaining their permissions to study them and not deceiving them about the research. It also means that researchers should minimize the risk of harm to participants from the research and to ensure that the benefits and risks of participation are shared with all types of people.
- The steps in the process should fit together. For example, the methods of data collection should relate to the research questions and the type of problem being studied.
- The research should be reported fully and honestly. This means that the research report should include enough detail for the reader to understand what was done to collect and analyze the data and to make his/her own judgment about the quality of the conclusions.

By evaluating the quality and usefulness of published research reports, you are participating in the final step of the overall process of research. Figures 2.2 and 2.3 provide you with general criteria for assessing whether a study is high quality. We will provide more detailed evaluation criteria for each aspect of a research report in the chapters that follow.

Use the following criteria to evaluate the quality of the research process of a qualitative research report. For each evaluation item, indicate the following ratings:

- \+ You rate the item as "high quality" for the study.
- ✓ You rate the item as "ok quality" for the study.
- – You rate the item as "low quality" for the study.

In addition to your rating, make notes about each element when you apply these criteria to an actual published study.

| **In a high-quality qualitative research report, the author . . .** | Application to a Published Study | |
|---|---|---|
| | Your Rating | Your Notes |
| 1. States a problem that is best addressed by exploring participants views because the variables are not known. | | |
| 2. Uses the literature to describe the problem, but not suggest the specific questions that need to be answered. | | |
| 3. Presents the purpose and research questions in an open-ended way so that the researcher is open to participants' views. | | |
| 4. Gathers text or image data from a few individuals. | | |
| 5. Reports words or images and describes the participants' views or identifies themes in their views. | | |
| 6. Makes an interpretation based on his/her own assessment of the results using a subjective and reflexive approach. | | |

**FIGURE 2.3 Criteria for Evaluating the Quality of the Process of Research for a Qualitative Study**

## Reviewing What We've Learned

- There are two main approaches to conducting research: quantitative and qualitative.
- The definition of each approach suggests characteristics that fall at two endpoints of a continuum for describing the procedures for conducting research.
- Look for research problems that call for explanation in quantitative research and for exploration in qualitative research.
- Expect the literature to play a major role in quantitative research and more of a minor role in qualitative research.
- Note that the purpose of quantitative research includes several variables and the purpose of qualitative research focuses on a single phenomenon.
- Recognize that researchers tend to collect data in the form of numbers from a large number of individuals in quantitative research and words and pictures from a small number of individuals in qualitative research.
- Expect the researcher to report the results of statistical analyses in quantitative research and text analyses in qualitative research.
- Expect researchers to compare results with predictions in quantitative research and to discuss the larger meaning of findings in qualitative research.
- Recognize that quantitative research reports will use a standard format and present information objectively while the format of qualitative reports will vary and authors will present information in a more subjective manner.
- When evaluating a study, use criteria that match the overall quantitative or qualitative approach.
- Researchers choose an approach for different reasons, including the type of problem being studied, personal training and experiences, and familiarity with an approach.

## Practicing Your Skills

Reflect back on the quantitative parent involvement and the qualitative parent role studies at the end of Chapter 1. Practice using your skills and knowledge of the content of this chapter by answering the following questions about these articles. Use the answers found in the Appendix to evaluate your progress.

1. List five characteristics of quantitative research that you find in the quantitative parent involvement study.
2. List five characteristics of qualitative research that you find in the qualitative parent role study.
3. Evaluate the quality of the quantitative parent involvement study using the checklist provided in Figure 2.2.
4. Evaluate the quality of the qualitative parent role study using the checklist provided in Figure 2.3.

# PART TWO

# Understanding the Introductions to Research Reports

Recall that we started this text by comparing a researcher who conducts a study to a traveler who takes a journey to a new destination. If you are going to travel to a new place, what do you do before the trip? You probably complete a number of activities, such as deciding where you want to go, packing a suitcase, and planning your itinerary.

Like planning for a trip, researchers also must complete a number of steps at the start of their studies. They decide on a general "destination" by selecting a topic and problem that needs to be studied. Researchers might not pack a suitcase, but they do "pack up" the knowledge that currently exists on the problem by reviewing the literature. With this background information in hand, they specify the specific goal for their research, which sets the agenda for the study they are going to conduct.

Researchers report these preliminary preparations in the *Introductions* of their research reports. You need to read these important sections to understand the context of a study. That is, the introduction in a report should tell you why the study is important, the background that informs the study, and the researcher's goal for conducting the study. In the next chapters, you will learn how to interpret these elements found in the introductions of research reports.

The chapters in Part II are:

- Chapter 3—The Research Problem: Identifying Why a Study Is Important
- Chapter 4—The Literature Review: Examining the Background for a Study
- Chapter 5—The Purpose: Identifying the Goal of a Study

# CHAPTER 3 The Research Problem: Identifying Why a Study Is Important

*A research report starts by introducing the "problem" that the researcher is trying to address. This "statement of the problem" appears in the opening paragraphs of a research article. Authors use this passage to explain the study's importance and to convince you, the reader, to read the rest of the article. You need to know how to read and interpret this important passage to understand the basis for any research study. In this chapter, you will learn how to identify a research problem, what makes a problem important to study, and how to read a "statement of the problem" section that introduces a study.*

**BY THE END OF THIS CHAPTER, YOU SHOULD BE ABLE TO:**

- Define and identify a research problem and explain its importance to a study.
- Describe how a study's research problem differs from its topic and purpose.
- Identify different ways that research studies are important by adding to our knowledge about research problems.
- Describe the types of research problems that fit quantitative studies and qualitative studies.
- Identify and evaluate the five elements that comprise a *statement of the problem* section in a research article.

One of the most challenging aspects of reading research is identifying studies that are important for the topics relevant to you. This is a challenge because when you are just beginning to explore a topic, you may not know a lot about it and that may make it difficult to recognize the value of a study. In addition, you may not know the different ways a topic and study can be important, or what questions to consider about a study's importance. All research reports should answer what we call the "So what?" question; that is, "So what? Why should anyone care about this report?" To be able to answer this question, you need to learn how an author explains:

- the importance of the topic being addressed and
- the importance of the research study for addressing this topic.

Authors write about a study's importance in a *statement of the problem* section of a research article. By learning how to understand this part of a research report, you will be able to identify studies that are important for the topics and problems that interest you.

## What Is a Research Problem?

When reading a research article, start by considering why the study was done in the first place. Researchers should clearly identify the problem that leads to a need for their study and you should look for this information as important background information. **Research problems** are the issues, controversies, or concerns that guide the need for a study. Researchers often represent real problems that need to be solved in our society. You encounter potential research problems every week in the media, problems like:

- the disruptions to people's lives caused by natural disasters,
- the increase in violence on college campuses,
- the controversy about the positive and negative roles of high-stakes testing, and
- the harmful health consequences of adolescent risk-taking behaviors.

## Why Are Research Problems Important?

Problems such as those listed above concern personnel in our schools, classrooms, and communities and affect all kinds of practice. Research generally cannot solve these problems directly, but researchers study these problems in an effort to help policy makers make decisions, to help practitioners solve practical problems, and to provide other researchers with a deeper understanding of the issues. By tying a study to a real-world problem, a researcher shows that the topic that is being studied is important because there is something that needs to be solved. If you understand the research problem an article is trying to address, you can decide whether the study will interest you and whether it pertains to a topic and problem you want to examine.

## How Do You Identify a Study's Research Problem?

You can usually find the research problem in the opening paragraphs of a research article. These paragraphs—which we will call the "statement of the problem"—might be labeled as the *Introduction* or *The Research Problem*, or, as is often the case, they may simply appear as the first few paragraphs of the report without any special heading. Once you locate this opening section, read it to identify what research problem the author discusses.

### Look for a Problem That Needs to Be Solved

Authors usually mention the research problem in the first or second paragraph of the report. As you read the opening paragraphs of a research article, ask yourself:

- Is there a sentence like "A major problem is. . . ."?
- Is there an issue, concern, or controversy that the researcher wants to address?
- What real-world problem needs to be solved?

You are probably aware of many educational and societal problems from your own practice and experiences. Even so, it can be difficult to identify them in research articles. As an example, let's consider an excerpt from the introduction (paragraphs 01–03) of the qualitative parent role study (Auerbach, 2007) from Chapter 1. Ask yourself the questions above as you reread the following passage.

> How do marginalized parents construct their role in promoting their children's access to educational opportunity, specifically college? This question is important in light of persistent patterns of underrepresentation of students of color in 4-year colleges, the well-documented influence of parents on students' aspirations and college pursuit, and calls for greater parent involvement in schooling (Gandara, 1995; Gandara & Bial, 1999; Hossler, Schmit, & Vesper, 1999; McDonough, 1997; Plank & Jordan, 1997). Indeed, parent roles can profoundly affect the extent to which low socioeconomic status (SES) students experience "conflict and challenge" on the pathway to college (Auerbach, 2001; McDonough, 1997).
>
> Traditional parent involvement models of family-school partnerships, and the studies based on them, offer little insight into questions of access. . . . If the norm for students of color is underachievement in K–12 schools and underrepresentation in 4-year colleges, then parents of color with high educational aspirations for their children may need to take deliberate steps to ensure access and counter the tendencies of schools to reproduce inequality (Abrams & Gibbs, 2002; Auerbach, 2001; Delgado-Gaitan & Segura, 1989).
>
> This study draws on 3 years of ethnographic data to illustrate one of many possible alternative typologies of parent roles in the pursuit of educational access. What do parents of color without college experience think and do when they want their high school-age

students to go to college? What shapes their beliefs, goals, and support strategies? . . . With its highlighting of marginalized parents' voices and the cultural logic behind their actions at a critical juncture in student careers, this article suggests directions for reconceptualizing parent roles in education and contributes to a more inclusive discourse on families, schooling, and equity.

We can identify the research problem that this study wants to address in the second sentence of the above excerpt as: "persistent patterns of underrepresentation of students of color in 4-year colleges." That is, the underrepresentation of students of color in college is the issue identified by this study that is of concern to educators and society at large. This is a problem because students' future opportunities are being limited by their lack of representation in college programs. The author is arguing that we need a study that explores parent roles for families of color because we do not know enough about the roles these parents play in helping their children gain access to college.

## Be Careful Not to Confuse the Research Problem with the Study's Topic or Purpose

Did you identify the issue of underrepresentation of students of color in colleges as the research problem from this excerpt, or did you consider another part of passage? A common pitfall for those new to reading research is to confuse a study's research problem with its topic or purpose. For you to better understand research problems, it is helpful to distinguish them from these other two parts of a research report. Let's consider different ways that you might have thought about the research problem in this excerpt.

- ***When looking for the research problem, you might have mistakenly identified the topic.*** Perhaps you thought the research problem was parent involvement. Notice, however, that this is not really a problem that needs to be solved. It is simply the topic of the research report. A research **topic** is the broad subject matter of the study. A study's topic is generally a short phrase that simply summarizes what the study is about, such as "parent involvement." Within the topic, a researcher identifies a problem that is related to the topic, such as "the underrepresentation of students of color in college." A **research problem** is an issue, controversy, or concern that guides the need for a study. See how the research problem falls under the topic in Figure 3.1.
- ***When looking for the research problem, you might have mistakenly identified the study's purpose.*** Perhaps you thought the research problem in the passage was to "illustrate one of many possible alternative typologies of parent roles in the pursuit of educational access." That is a very common answer. However, notice that this is not a problem in society that needs to be solved. Instead this statement describes the study's purpose. From the research problem, the researcher formulates the purpose, as shown in Figure 3.1. This **purpose for research** indicates what the researcher actually intends to do by conducting the study.

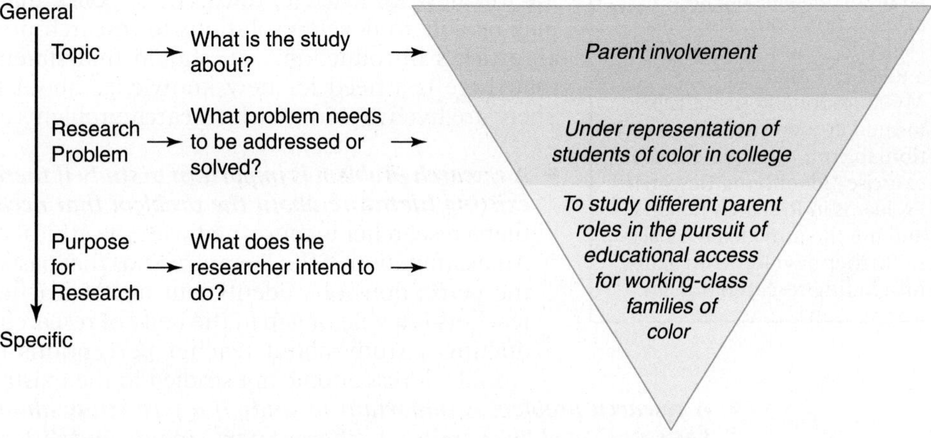


**FIGURE 3.1 Distinguishing Among a Study's Topic, Research Problem, and Purpose**

These three aspects of research—the topic, research problem, and purpose—and their application in the qualitative parent role study are summarized in Figure 3.1. Looking at this figure, you can see that these aspects vary in terms of their breadth from very general (the topic) to more specific (the purpose). As you read research reports, try to distinguish among these parts of research. With this understanding, you can differentiate what the study is about (the topic); the issue, concern, or controversy that is being addressed (the research problem); and what the author intends to do (the purpose).

### What Do You Think?

Consider the following short description of a study. As you read the scenario, ask yourself the following questions: What is the study's research problem? Under what topic does this problem fall? What purpose is formulated from this problem?

> Buck, Leslie-Pelecky, and Kirby (2002) are science educators and researchers interested in the images people hold about scientists. They note that women and minorities are underrepresented in science careers and that some individuals choose not to pursue a career in science due to negative images of scientists. To help address this problem, the purpose of their study was to test the effect of having female scientists visit elementary classrooms on students' perceptions of scientists. They wanted to learn about how children's images of scientists changed after visits from female scientists.

### Check Your Understanding

The research problem behind this study is the underrepresentation of women and minorities in the sciences and the fact that negative images may be contributing to this situation. This is the larger issue or concern that the study wants to address. This problem falls under the broad topic of science education. Narrowing down from the problem, the researchers also stated the purpose of their study (to test the effect of female scientists visiting elementary classrooms).

## What Makes a Research Problem Important to Study?

> For practice identifying important research problems, go to the *Building Research Skills* section under the topic "Selecting and Defining a Research Topic" in MyEducationalResearchLab, located at www.myeducationlab.com. Complete the exercise "Identifying Research Problems in Research Reports" and use the provided feedback to further develop your skills for reading research articles.

Research problems help explain why a study's topic is important, but how do we know if the problem is important to study? Recall from Chapter 1 that research studies contribute to our knowledge about research problems. Therefore, a research problem is important to study when there is a need for new knowledge about the problem. By providing this new knowledge, researchers, policy makers, and practitioners may be able to develop solutions to research problems. When reading an article's introduction, you should find statements that make clear that there is a need for new knowledge about the research problem. There are five ways in which research problems are important to study:

- ***A research problem is important to study if there is a gap or void in the existing literature about the problem that needs to be filled.*** Assume that a researcher is concerned with the ethical climate of high schools. An examination of the literature finds that past research has examined the perceptions of students, but not of teachers. The perspective of teachers is a void or gap in the body of research about this issue. Conducting a study about teacher perceptions of the ethical climate would address a topic not studied in the existing literature.
- ***A research problem is important to study if a past study about the problem has not been replicated by examining different participants and different research sites.*** The value of some research increases when the results can apply broadly to many people and places rather than applying to only one setting where the initial research occurred. The need for results of past studies to be replicated with new participants or

settings is especially important in quantitative experiments. In a quantitative study about a program to promote an ethical climate, for example, past research conducted at a private school in an urban setting can be tested (or replicated) at other sites, such as a rural high school or an all-boys' school. Such sites are new and information from their study will provide new knowledge.

- ***A research problem is important if there is a need to extend past research or examine the topic more thoroughly.*** Some research problems are important because there is a need to extend the research into a new topic or area or to conduct research at a deeper, more thorough level. For example, in our illustration on ethical climate, although research exists on ethical climates, it now needs to be extended to the situation in which students take exams because taking exams poses many ethical dilemmas for students. In this way, the research about the problem is extended to a new topic. This extension is different from the previous example of replication because the investigators extend the research to different topics rather than to different participants and research sites.
- ***A research problem is important to study if there are people whose voices have not been heard, who have been silenced, or who have been rejected in society.*** Research can add knowledge about a problem by presenting the ideas and the words of marginalized individuals and groups (e.g., the homeless, women, racial groups). For example, although past studies on ethical climate have addressed students at predominantly white Midwestern schools, we have not heard the voices of Native Americans on this topic. A study of this topic at a tribal school would therefore report and give voice to Native American students and teachers.
- ***A research problem is important if practice related to the problem needs to be improved.*** Practitioners may need practical knowledge arising from research to inform their practice. By examining the problem, research may lead to the identification of new techniques or technologies, the recognition of the value of historical or current practice, or the necessity to change current practice. For example, a study of ethical issues in a district's schools may lead to a new honor code, new policies about cheating on exams, or new approaches to administering tests.

You now know five different ways that a research problem can be important to study. Let's use this information to consider why the problem of underrepresentation of students of color in college called for the need for new knowledge in the qualitative parent role study. The author implies that there are two reasons why this research problem is important to study. First it is important because there is a need to extend past research about parent involvement by including a new dimension about this topic, namely issues of college access. In addition, this problem is important because there is a need to give voice to working-class families of color that have not previously been heard in the parent involvement literature.

As you begin reading a research article, you should identify the larger research problem being addressed and note how the study will contribute to knowledge about this problem. In addition, from the start you can consider if the identified research problem is more suited to a quantitative or a qualitative study.

## What Types of Research Problems Fit Quantitative and Qualitative Studies?

As discussed in Chapter 2, quantitative and qualitative approaches differ in their essential characteristics. This means that some research problems fit a quantitative approach better and others fit a qualitative approach better. In either case, there should be a match between a study's problem and the approach used. Authors generally provide indications as to whether the study will be quantitative or qualitative from the beginning of the written report, and you should look for this match when reading a study's introduction. What types of research problems are best suited for quantitative and qualitative research? As a general rule of thumb, there are two types of research problems: those that call for *explanation* and those that call for *exploration.*

### Quantitative Research Is Used When the Research Problem Calls for Explanation

Recall the quantitative parent involvement study (Deslandes & Bertrand, 2005) from Chapter 1. The authors made a case that we know little about what factors lead parents to decide to become involved in their adolescents' schooling. That is, we do not know *how to explain* why parents do or do not become involved. Why would a lack of involvement be important? The authors cite literature suggesting that parent involvement results in fewer disciplinary problems and higher grades for students. So, the problem calls for explaining or predicting relationships between parent involvement and other variables. Explaining or predicting relationships among variables is an important characteristic of quantitative research, as we learned in Chapter 2.

### Qualitative Research Is Used When the Research Problem Calls for Exploration

Next consider the qualitative parent role study (Auerbach, 2007) from Chapter 1 and earlier in this chapter. Although it addresses a similar topic to the quantitative parent involvement study, we can see that this study addresses a different type of problem. The research problem called for the author *to explore* the perceptions of parents of color about helping their high school-age children gain access to college without preconceived ideas about what they would find. In Chapter 2, we learned that exploring a problem is a characteristic of qualitative research.

### What Do You Think?

Consider the following passage from a study about practices for hiring new teachers. As you read the paragraph, ask yourself the following questions: Why is the study important? (or how will the study add to knowledge about the problem?) Does the research problem seem to call for a quantitative or a qualitative approach?

> This research also seeks to address a gap in the literature on teacher selection and hiring. During the past two decades, research on teacher recruitment and selection has generated important insights into the decision making of applicants and school administrators who are involved in hiring. . . . To date, however, there has been relatively little research on how schools and districts actually organize and conduct teacher hiring across a broad range of contexts. Moreover, as Young and Delli (2002) have noted, there has been relatively little research in the field of education on the relationship between the hiring process and posthire outcomes. *(Liu & Johnson, 2006, p. 326)*

### Check Your Understanding

From this paragraph, we see that the authors' study is important because it will contribute to knowledge by filling a gap in the literature about teacher selection and hiring. Liu and Johnson (2006) note that we do not know the broad trends that describe hiring decisions across different types of schools and we do not know the relationship between the decisions in the hiring process of new teachers and the outcomes that occur from these decisions. This passage includes indications that the authors are going to conduct a *quantitative* study because they discuss a need for research that measures broad trends and explains the relationship between variables (hiring process decisions and hiring outcomes).

## What Elements Do You Look for When Reading a Statement of the Problem?

You can now identify a research problem, understand why it is important to study, and recognize problems that call for either a quantitative or qualitative approach. It is time to consider the full *statement of the problem* section that introduces a research article and conveys the importance of the topic and study. By carefully reading these passages, you can understand why studies are needed and are valued.

A **statement of the problem** passage conveys the importance of a report by addressing the following five elements:

1. The topic
2. The research problem
3. Evidence for the importance of the problem
4. The knowledge about the problem that is missing
5. The audiences that will benefit from the new knowledge

By recognizing these five elements, you can easily read introductions to research articles and understand the reasons why authors think that their studies are important.

## Find the Topic

When reading a research article, find the topic first. Remember, a research **topic** is the broad subject matter that a researcher addresses in a study. Look for it in the first few sentences of the introduction by asking yourself, "What is this study about?" In many articles, you can find the topic in the article's title or the provided key words, but often these terms are more narrow and specialized than the overall topic. The opening sentences of a statement of the problem passage, however, should start with a broad topic that readers can easily understand. These opening sentences should encourage readers to continue reading, generate interest in the study, and provide an initial frame of reference for understanding the research topic. In this way, the introduction should help you get into a study and encourage you to read beyond the first page.

You can find examples of how researchers state their topics in titles and introduce them in the first sentence of articles in Figure 3.2. Note how these authors ease into their studies' content with general ideas that most readers can understand by introducing their topics of domestic violence, effective teachers, mathematics achievement, and pre-service teachers. The first sentence serves the important function of drawing the reader into a study. Authors frequently write this sentence in a way to cause the reader to pay attention, elicit emotional or attitudinal responses, spark interest, and encourage the reader to continue reading. You will find many articles that start with one of the following types of information: statistical data, a provocative question, a clear need for research, or the intent or purpose of the study. See Figure 3.2 for examples of first sentences that used each of these strategies. When you begin to read a new study, examine the first sentence, assess what topic is being introduced, and consider whether this sentence piques your interest in reading further.

## Identify the Research Problem

After introducing the overall topic, most introductions narrow the topic to a research problem. Recall that a **research problem** is an issue, concern, or controversy that needs to be solved. Researchers conduct studies to help address different problems. Authors may present the research problem as a single sentence or as a couple of short sentences, and it often appears within the first paragraph or two of an article. There are two types of research problems described by authors: practical and literature-based problems.

- ***Practical research problems.*** Sometimes research problems come from issues or concerns found in practice settings, such as schools or clinics. We call these *practical research problems.* For example, can you see the practical issue in the following research problem about the practice of parents delaying their children's entrance to kindergarten?

  Headlines in the Atlanta Journal-Constitution ("Kindergarten," 2003) read, "Kindergarten: Is older wiser?" "Some say 'redshirting' improves readiness." The article featured success stories for children with summer birthdays who delayed entrance to kindergarten. Parents of preschoolers, after reading newspaper articles or talking with other parents, or both, are keenly aware that some parents purposefully delay their child's entrance to kindergarten. A number of parents begin the process even earlier by having their child repeat a 3-year-old preschool program. That phenomenon, especially common in affluent communities and among boys, causes parents with a 5-year-old summer-birthday child to wonder whether they should delay enrollment even when their child seems ready for kindergarten. *(Oshima & Domakeski, 2006, p. 212)*

| **Starting a study about domestic violence with statistical data . . .**<br><br>*Risk of Domestic Violence after Flood Impact: Effects of Social Support, Age, and History of Domestic Violence*<br><br>Petra Clemens, Jennifer R. Hietala, Mamie J. Rytter, Robin A. Schmidt, and Dona J. Reese (1999)<br><br>The Grand Forks flood of 1997 appeared to result in traumatic family-related effects, as reflected in a reported 24% increase in domestic violence between July 1996 and July 1997 (Community Violence Intervention Center, undated). The . . . | **Starting a study about effective teachers with a provocative question . . .**<br><br>*Voices from the Trenches: An Exploration of Teachers' Management Knowledge*<br><br>Deborah A. Garrahy, Donetta J. Cothran, and Pamela H. Kulinna (2005)<br><br>What makes an effective teacher? Early . . . |
|---|---|
| **Starting a study about mathematics achievement with a clear need for research . . .**<br><br>*Effect of Demographic and Personal Variables on Achievement in Eighth-Grade Algebra*<br><br>Leah P. McCoy (2005)<br><br>Mathematics teaching and learning is one of the most serious issues in education. The . . . | **Starting a study about pre-service teachers with the intent or purpose of the study . . .**<br><br>*More than Heroes and Villains: Pre-service Teacher Beliefs about Principals*<br><br>Peter Bodycott, Allan Walker, and John Lee Chi Kin (2001)<br><br>The purpose of this study was to explore how the social context of schools and schooling influence pre-service teachers' personal constructs of the principal. Our interest . . . |

FIGURE 3.2 Examples of Titles and First Sentences Used to Introduce a Study's Topic

The practical problem in this study is that parents are feeling pressured to delay the time when their children start school without understanding the implications of this decision.

- ***Literature-based research problems.*** In other research studies the "problem" is based on a need for further research because there is a gap in our knowledge. The research problem might also be based on conflicting evidence in the literature or theories in the literature that are incomplete. This type of problem is a *literature-based research problem.* For example, see how the authors in the next example discuss a controversy about the impact of student mobility since the literature contains conflicting evidence:

> In the literature on the impact of mobility on children's educational attainment, findings are inconsistent. . . . In sum, the majority of studies that examined achievement at a single point in time found adverse associations of residential and school mobility with subsequent achievement. Findings were reasonably robust, whether or not controls for socioeconomic status were included, and did not depend on the precise measures of either mobility or achievement. However, the two studies, both of European samples, which examined achievement longitudinally, found no association of mobility with subsequent achievement once prior achievement was controlled. *(Heinlein & Shinn, 2000, pp. 349 & 351)*

The problem in this case is based on a need to resolve the existing inconsistencies.

Whether the research problem arises from a practical setting, a need in the research literature, or both, you can identify the issue that leads to a need for the study as you read the introduction and consider whether this problem is important to you.

## Note the Evidence for the Importance of the Problem

Researchers do more than state the problem or issue in their reports. They also provide several reasons for why the problem is important. **Justifying a research problem** means presenting evidence for the importance of the issue or concern. Therefore, as you read an introduction, locate the problem and look for evidence justifying this problem. Providing evidence is an essential aspect of scholarly writing and you need to become comfortable with reading information that helps to justify the importance of the issue. This evidence may appear in a few sentences or in several paragraphs and may include two types.

- ***Evidence from the literature.*** The most scholarly type of evidence for a research problem comes from arguments made in the literature by other researchers that the problem needs to be studied. Researchers provide evidence from experts as previously reported in the literature to justify the importance of the problem. Due to the importance of this practice in research, most quantitative and many qualitative introductions include numerous references to the literature to indicate the existence of the problem, its importance, and why a study is needed. These justifications tell you that not only does the author think the study is needed, but that other authors have also written about the need for studies that address this problem. For example, note how Brotherson, Dollahite, and Hawkins (2005) justify the need for their study about how fathers connect with their children by referencing four other articles that have said that more research on fathering is needed:

  The need for additional research and new perspectives on fathering has been emphasized in recent scholarship (Day & Lamb, 2003; Doherty, 1991; Hawkins & Dollahite, 1997a; Levant, 1992). *(p. 2)*

- ***Evidence from the workplace or personal experience.*** Researchers may also justify their research problem based on evidence from the workplace or their own personal experiences. You can recognize many issues that arise in workplaces, such as issues surrounding treating addiction or approaches to classroom discipline. Therefore, problems related to addiction or discipline may be justified because of their impact on professional settings. Likewise, researchers may describe personal experiences from their lives as evidence for the importance of studying a problem. These personal experiences may arise from intense professional experiences or experiences drawn from childhood or family situations. For example, one researcher justified the need to study students in a multiage middle school by referring to her own experiences in school. The study begins:

  In the spring of 1992, the opportunity to conduct classroom action research was offered to Madison, Wisconsin teachers. Though my daily schedule was already full, I was drawn to this opportunity because of its emphasis on practical, classroom-based research. . . . For me, multicultural curricula, cooperative learning, computer technology, and thematic education were exciting developments in classroom teaching. *(Kester, 1994, p. 63)*

In many qualitative studies, personal experiences are used as evidence for the importance of the problem, especially in those studies with a practical orientation. However, keep in mind that some individuals, such as those trained only in quantitative research, feel that evidence based on experience is not as scholarly as evidence from the literature. Therefore, most articles will not include personal experiences as the only type of justification. Many articles will include evidence from both the literature and from personal and workplace experiences when explaining the importance of the problem.

## Identify the Knowledge About the Problem That Is Missing

Once you have read the problem and the evidence for its importance, look for a sentence (or two) stating that there is something we currently do not know about this research problem. A study is important because the present state of knowledge about the problem is somehow deficient and the study will help to address this deficiency. Authors usually enumerate several deficiencies in the existing literature or practice. A **deficiency in knowledge** means that the past literature or practical experiences of the researchers do not adequately address the research problem. For example, deficiencies in our knowledge may mean that there is a gap in what is known, that past research has not been extended to certain topics, that past studies have not been replicated in specific settings or with different people, or that the voices of marginalized people have not been previously included. A deficiency in practice means that individuals have not identified good and workable solutions for schools or other professional settings.

By stating these deficiencies, the researcher is explicitly explaining that the study is needed because it will address the deficiencies. That is, the research study is needed to fill the gap, extend past research, replicate a study, lift the voices of marginalized people, or add to practice. Here are examples where authors indicate the need for their studies by identifying specific deficiencies in what is known about a problem:

- ***A study is needed to fill a gap in knowledge:*** "Despite the broad scope of this literature, there is little scholarship about how leadership develops or how a leadership identity develops over time." *(Komives, Owen, Longerbeam, Mainella, & Osteen, 2005, p. 593)*
- ***A study is needed to extend past research:*** "While evidence has supported preteaching as an effective supplemental instructional approach, its effectiveness in the area of math has yet to be examined." *(Lalley & Miller, 2006, p. 748)*
- ***A study is needed to replicate previous results:*** "Since parenting processes change in the early adolescent years in the Chinese culture (Shek & Lee, in press), it would be important to replicate the findings of Shek (2006b) in Chinese Secondary 2 students." *(Shek, 2007, p. 569)*
- ***A study is needed to lift the voices of marginalized people:*** "Little research has been conducted describing the perception of friendship and social experiences of adolescents who have Asperger syndrome, and there has been even less qualitative research incorporating children's own words." *(Carrington et al., 2003, p. 211)*
- ***A study is needed to add to practice:*** "Further experimental research is needed to provide educators with information that they can use to make sound decisions about selections and implementation of vocabulary instruction programs and strategies." *(Apthorp, 2006, p. 67)*

Authors often identify two or three reasons why existing research and practice are deficient in addressing the research problem. You can usually find these statements toward the end of the introduction to the study. By looking for these statements, you can clearly understand how a study will add to knowledge about the problem.

## Note the Audiences That Will Benefit from the Knowledge Generated by the Study

The final element of a *statement of the problem* section is the audiences for the study. A study's **audience** consists of individuals and groups who the authors expect will read and potentially benefit from the information provided in the research article. These audiences will vary depending on the nature of the study, but several often considered by researchers include practitioners, policy makers, other researchers, and individuals participating in the studies. For example, note how the authors identified numerous audiences for their study about how rural, low-income families have fun with the following passage:

> The findings from this study can be applied in many different areas. Leisure researchers will gain a better understanding of how rural low-income families have fun and the contexts influencing those choices. In addition, policymakers and rural advocates will gain a better understanding of an important aspect of rural and low-income families' lives. Extension educators and rural community service providers will learn about challenges faced by rural low-income families and strategies used by some families to make fun an important part of their life. Finally, play advocates gain an important understanding about what families with young children see as fun. *(Churchill, Plano Clark, Prochaska-Cue, Creswell, & Ontai-Grzebik, 2007, p. 272)*

*Here's a Tip for Reading Research!*

Note the audiences for a study to see if the study applies to you and your work. This will help you identify research that directly relates to your work as a practitioner. If the author does not identify audiences in the introduction, then look for a discussion of audiences at the end of the study, or ask yourself who could use the information if the deficiency is addressed?

As this example illustrates, authors often name multiple audiences for a study. You will usually find passages such as this at the end of the introduction. These passages explain the importance of addressing the problem for specific audiences. This information personalizes the research so that you can see that the study will potentially provide meaningful information and useful results. By identifying the audience for a study, you can understand who may benefit from the results and consider whether they will be useful for you.

## How Do You Read a Statement of the Problem Passage?

You now are familiar with the five elements that are typically included in a statement of the problem passage that introduces a research study: the topic, the research problem, evidence for the importance of the problem, deficiencies in what is known about the problem, and audiences. Look for these elements when you read an introduction and mark the words *topic, problem, evidence, deficiency,* and *audiences* in the margins next to the sentences where each element is addressed to make it easy for you to follow the flow of ideas. The order in which authors discuss these ideas often matches the flow of ideas as shown in Figure 3.3. This figure shows the five elements as they appear within a generic statement of the problem passage. In addition, this figure highlights how each element was applied within the introduction to the quantitative parent involvement study (paragraphs 01–02) from Chapter 1.

As summarized in Figure 3.3, the authors of the quantitative parent involvement study begin with the *topic* of parent involvement and narrow it to the *problem* of children not receiving the positive benefits if their parents are not involved in their schooling. *Evidence* of the importance of this problem includes prior research about the benefits of parent involvement, such as higher grades and fewer disciplinary problems. Little research, however, has examined the factors that lead parents to be involved in their children's schooling. The evidence, therefore, is *deficient* in explaining parent involvement. A study that addresses this deficiency will be useful for *audiences,* but the authors do not mention any audiences who will benefit from the study in the opening passage. They do, however, mention the benefits of the study for researchers and school personnel in the concluding section of the article. The statement of the problem for this study would have been stronger if these audiences were mentioned in the introduction so we could better understand why the study was important.

> *Here's a Tip for Applying Research!*
>
> Consider addressing each of the five elements in a statement of the problem when describing a problem in your local setting to stakeholders. This will help you explain the importance of the problem and the need for addressing it in a convincing manner.

### What Do You Think?

Read the statement of the problem passage from a new research study in Figure 3.4. As you read the passage, note in the margins as you identify the five elements of the statement of the problem in this introduction.

### Check Your Understanding

In the statement of the problem found in Figure 3.4, the authors introduce the topic (tobacco use) and research problem (number of expected premature deaths due to teenage smoking) in the first paragraph. This illustrates how the topic and the research problem can sometimes blend. They cite evidence for this problem in the second paragraph, such as statistics about the magnitude of the problem and a summary of prior research on the problem. Notice how they included many references to justify the importance of this problem. Following the evidence for the problem, they mention the deficiencies in past studies in the third and fourth paragraphs. For example, little research has examined the social context of high schools or explored students' views. In the final paragraph, they indicate various audiences (e.g., researchers, administrators, and teachers) who may benefit from reading and using this study. Therefore, this passage included all five elements of a statement of the problem.

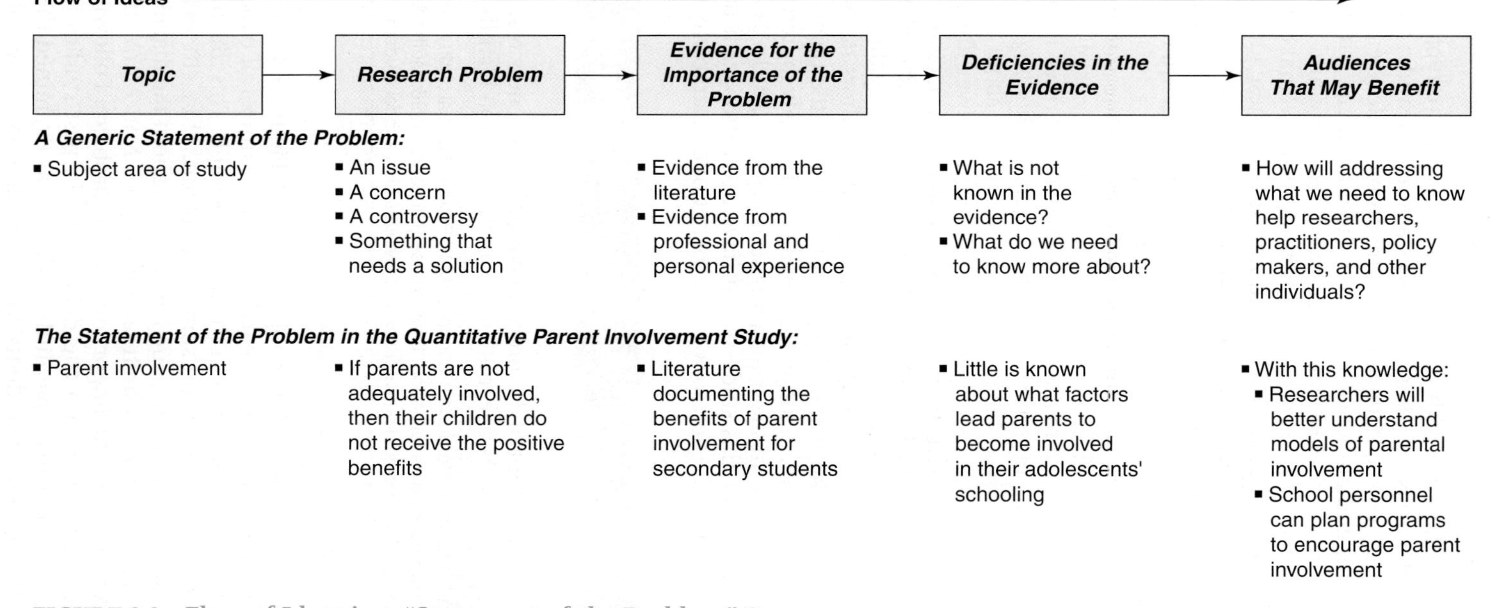

FIGURE 3.3 Flow of Ideas in a "Statement of the Problem" Passage

**In Conversation: High School Students Talk to Students About Tobacco Use and Prevention Strategies**

***Note the Five Elements of the Statement of the Problem***

Tobacco use is a leading cause of cancer in American society (McGinnis & Foege, 1993). Although smoking among adults has declined in recent years, it has increased for adolescents. The Centers for Disease Control (CDC) reported that the incidence of tobacco use among high school students has risen over the past decade from 27.5% in 1991 to 34.5% in 2000 (CDC, 2001). These figures fall well short of the Healthy People 2010 goal of reducing adolescent tobacco use to 16% (U.S. Department of Health and Human Services, 2000). Unless this trend is dramatically reversed, an estimated 5 million American children will ultimately die a premature death due to smoking related diseases (CDC, 1996).

Previous research on adolescent tobacco use in the school context has focused on the following primary topics. Several studies have surveyed public school students, collecting data on initiation of smoking among young people and patterns of escalating tobacco use (CDC, 1998a, 1998b, 1998c; Heishman et al., 1997; Peyton, 2001). Other studies have focused on the prevention of smoking and tobacco use in schools. This research has led to numerous school-based prevention programs and interventions (e.g., Bruvold, 1993; Sussman, Dent, Burton, Stacy, & Flay, 1995). These prevention programs have involved explicit curricular programs (Kolbe et al., 1995; Larsen & Christiansen, 1994; Martin, Levin, & Saunders, 1999) and policy elements, including tobacco bans (Ashley, Northrup, & Ferrence, 1998; Bowen, Kinne, & Orlandi, 1995; Bunch, 1990; CDC, 1994; Northrup, Ashley, & Ferrence, 1998). Fewer studies have examined the schools' role in "quit attempts" or smoking cessation among adolescents. Some investigators have looked at ways to make cessation counseling and support more accessible by offering such services in the school setting (Aveyard et al., 1999; Burton, 1994; Heishman et al., 1997; Pallonen, Prochaska, Velicer, Prokhorov, & Smith, 1998; Pallonen, Velicer, et al., 1998; Sussman, 2001).

Minimal research has focused on high schools as a site where adolescents continue to explore and experiment with tobacco use. During high school, students form peer groups that can contribute to adolescent smoking. Often, peers become a strong social influence that reinforces smoking behavior in general (Engels, Knibbe, Drop, & de Haan, 1997; Ennett & Bauman 1993; Gibbons & Eggleston, 1996; Graham, Marks, & Hansen, 1991; Hansen, Johnson, Flay, Graham, & Sobel, 1988), and belonging to an athletic team, a music group, or the "grunge" crowd can influence thinking about smoking (McVea, Harter, McEntarffer, & Creswell, 1999; Sussman, Dent, Stacy, et al., 1990). Schools are also places where adolescents spend most of their day (Fibkins, 1993) and develop sustained attitudes toward smoking. Schools provide a setting for teachers and administrators to be role models for abstaining from tobacco use and for enforcing policies about tobacco use (Brown, Jr., & Butterfield, 1992; Bunch, 1990; CDC, 1994; Tompkins, Dino, Zedosky, Harman, & Shaler, 1999).

The vast majority of studies looking at smoking within the context of schools have used quantitative research methods; however, schools are also places to explore qualitatively how students view smoking. Rather than using predetermined concepts and theoretical models derived from the adult tobacco literature (Pallonen, 1998; Prochaska et al., 1994), researchers need also to hear how adolescents talk about tobacco use (Ginsburg, 1996; Moffat & Johnson, 2001). Much can be learned from a qualitative study that involves high school students talking with other students about tobacco use. Employing students as co-researchers to gather data not only provides detailed participant views in qualitative research (Creswell, 2002; Ginsburg, 1996) but also offers the opportunity to gather information without biases and perspectives that adults often bring to the study of adolescent smoking.

By examining multiple school contexts, using qualitative approaches, and involving students as co-researchers, we can better understand the complexity of the perceptions held about adolescent tobacco use. This understanding comes from listening to what students have to say about adolescent tobacco use when they talk with other students. With this understanding, researchers can better isolate variables and develop models about smoking behavior. Administrators and teachers can plan interventions to prevent or change attitudes toward smoking, and school officials can assist with smoking cessation or intervention programs.

**FIGURE 3.4 A "Statement of the Problem" Passage in a Study About Adolescent Tobacco Use**

*Source:* This passage is reprinted from Plano Clark, Miller, Creswell, McVea, McEntarffer, Harter, & Mickelson, *Qualitative Health Research,* Vol. 12, Issue 9, pp. 1264–1266, 2002. Reprinted with permission of Sage Publications, Inc.

Use the following criteria to evaluate the quality of a statement of the problem in a research report. For each evaluation item, indicate the following ratings:

+ You rate the item as "high quality" for the study.
✓ You rate the item as "ok quality" for the study.
– You rate the item as "low quality" for the study.

In addition to your rating, make notes about each element when you apply these criteria to an actual published study.

| In a high-quality research report, the author . . . | Application to a Published Study | |
|---|---|---|
| | Your Rating | Your Notes |
| 1. Begins the report by introducing the reader to the general topic in the first sentence. | | |
| 2. Identifies the problem and states it succinctly; may mention several problems. | | |
| 3. Documents the importance of the problem. | | |
| 4. Identifies 2–3 ways that knowledge about the problem is lacking to indicate the need for the study. | | |
| 5. Mentions 2–3 audiences who will benefit from learning the results of the study. | | |
| 6. Provides clues to indicate the need for a quantitative or qualitative approach as found in words such as "explanation" or "exploration." | | |
| 7. Writes the introduction so the reader is encouraged to read on, realizing that an important problem is being studied. | | |

FIGURE 3.5 Criteria for Evaluating a "Statement of the Problem" Passage

## How Do You Evaluate a Statement of the Problem Passage?

By looking for the five elements of topic, problem, evidence, deficiencies, and audiences, you can understand and interpret the statement of the problem in the introduction to a study. Therefore, you now know how to assess your own answer to the "So what?" question when you read a new research article. In addition, Figure 3.5 provides criteria related to the elements of a good *statement of the problem* section. Using this list, you can evaluate the quality of the statement of the problem in any research report.

## Reviewing What We've Learned

- Expect a research article to begin with a statement of the problem passage to convey the importance of the report.
- Look for a research problem—an issue, concern, or controversy—that the investigator presents to convey the importance of the studied topic.
- Be careful not to confuse the research problem with a study's topic or purpose.
- Understand that research is important because it contributes to knowledge of research problems. Problems are important to study when there is a need to fill a gap in the existing literature, replicate a previous study, extend past research, give voice to those unheard, or inform practice.
- Look for indications that the study will use a quantitative or qualitative approach based on whether the problem calls for explanation or exploration.

- Identify the five elements (topic, problem, evidence, deficiencies, and audiences) whenever you read a statement of a problem.
- Start by noting the general topic to learn the general subject matter of a study.
- Identify the research problem and consider whether the problem that needs to be solved is of interest to you.
- Expect the author to provide evidence for the research problem.
- Pay close attention to the deficiencies in our knowledge of the problem that the author describes to learn why the study is important.
- Make note of the audiences that may benefit from the results of the study as indications of the usefulness of the study.

## Practicing Your Skills

At this time, carefully read the "qualitative new teacher study" starting on p. 96 at the end of this chapter. As you read this article, pay close attention to the statement of the problem that appears in the introduction section (paragraphs 01–03).

Once you have read the study, assess your knowledge of the content of this chapter by answering the following questions that relate to the qualitative new teacher study. Use the answers found in the Appendix to evaluate your progress.

1. Examine the first sentence for this study: "Novice teachers in many urban contexts are learning to teach in highly politicized reform environments with heightened emphasis on test scores." Evaluate whether it is an effective first sentence.
2. What research problem(s) does the author mention?
3. How does the author document the importance of the research problem?
4. A research problem is important to study if knowledge about the problem is lacking. What deficiencies in knowledge did the author identify?
5. Did the author mention audiences that will benefit from the new teacher study? If so, who are they? If not, what audiences would you suggest?
6. What indications did you note in this introduction to suggest the need for a qualitative study to address the research problem?

# The Qualitative New Teacher Study

Let's examine another published research study to apply what you have learned about reading research articles and to evaluate how researchers identify a research problem (by completing the *Practicing Your Skills* questions listed on the previous page.) We will refer to this study as the qualitative new teacher study. A formal reference for this study is:

Clayton, C. D. (2007). Curriculum making as novice professional development: Practical risk taking as learning in high-stakes times. *Journal of Teacher Education, 58*(3), 216–230.

As you read this article, note the marginal annotations that signal the major sections of a research report, the steps of the research process, and the major characteristics of qualitative research. In addition, use the following walk-through to help you understand how the steps of the research process are described within the major sections of the report.

### The Introduction Section

- Identifying a research problem (paragraphs 01–03)
- Reviewing the literature (paragraphs 04–06)
- Specifying the purpose (paragraph 03)

The author of the qualitative new teacher study (Clayton, 2007) begins her study by introducing the topic of beginning teachers. She uses the opening passage to indicate the importance of her study by identifying a problem in paragraph 01, providing evidence of the problem and noting a deficiency in the evidence in paragraph 02, and suggesting audiences that may benefit in paragraph 03. Building from the identified deficiency, she states the purpose for this study is to describe how three new teachers learn to teach through a curriculum-making activity (paragraph 03). After the statement of the problem and specifying the purpose, the author provides a brief literature review of what is known and how new teachers learn to teach and develop professionally (paragraphs 04–06).

### The Method Section

- Selecting a design and collecting data (paragraphs 10–14)

The author used a qualitative approach and selected a case study design (paragraph 10). She focused on the stories and experiences of three new teachers participating in a Beginning Teachers' Program (BTP). She collected a variety of sources of qualitative data, including classroom observations, individual and group interviews, and observations and documents from the BTP sessions to address the study's research questions (see paragraph 11 and Table 1). We learn that the questions asked during the interviews changed and emerged during the study (paragraph 12). We also find the author reflecting on her role as researcher and as a staff member of the program in paragraph 14.

### The Results Section

- Analyzing the data and reporting results (paragraphs 12–13 and 07–09, 15–40)

The author describes her data analysis process of reading the data, coding the data, and organizing codes into categories in paragraphs 12–13. She also includes sample codes and categories in Table 2. From this analysis she reports a description of the program (paragraphs 07–09) early in the article. This is indicative of the flexible format used in some qualitative research reports. Then, in the results section, she reports two kinds of findings: description and themes. The results section begins with a general description of the three participants in paragraphs 15–16. Description and themes about how the teachers changed their practices and thinking about teaching are then provided for Alexandra (paragraphs 17–24), Eileen (paragraphs 25–32), and Joanna (33–40).

### The Conclusion Section

- Interpreting the research (paragraphs 41–50)

The author concluded the report with a discussion of her interpretation of the findings of the study. This interpretation includes the author offering the larger meaning of the findings such as how the experiences of the individual teachers tell us about the nature of conceptual change and shifts in practice for new teachers. The author concludes that new teachers may need to first change their practices before they change their thinking about teaching, which is counter to most current teacher development programs. The interpretation suggests implications for practice, such as how individuals who work with new teachers can help them develop professionally (paragraph 47). The author also suggested new questions that future research should examine based on the findings of this study (paragraphs 49–50).

# CURRICULUM MAKING AS NOVICE PROFESSIONAL DEVELOPMENT

## PRACTICAL RISK TAKING AS LEARNING IN HIGH-STAKES TIMES

**Christine D. Clayton**
Pace University

*This qualitative case study presents three novices in urban schools who enacted curricular projects as participants in a university-based professional development program. This experience created an opportunity for practical risk taking, enabling them to consider the consequences of curricular choices in personal terms. Such professional development pivoted on epistemological inquiry grounded in three critical tension areas: management of relationships, curricular ownership, and the sources of classroom knowledge. In these cases, practical risk taking seemed to precede conceptual changes in the teachers' thinking about curriculum itself, raising concerns about how novices learn during an accountability era where such risk taking is often discouraged.*

***Keywords:*** *teacher learning; learning to teach; professional development; beginning teachers; curriculum making; high-stakes times*

Introduction Section

01 Novice teachers in many urban contexts are learning to teach in highly politicized reform environments with heightened emphasis on test scores. Charged with the responsibility of working with increasingly diverse students (Hodgkinson, 2002) to meet ever more prescribed and standardized outcomes, new teachers are caught in the middle—squeezed by the traditional pressures of the new teacher experience (Britzman, 1991; Fuller, 1969; Huling-Austin, 1990; Lortie, 1975; Veenman, 1984) while also facing new pressures born of these high-stakes curricular environments (Clayton, 2007; Kauffman, Moore Johnson, Kardos, Liu, & Peske, 2002). Given these circumstances, concerns about teacher quality are increasingly related to the retention of quality individuals who have the capacity to teach all students well (National Commission on Teaching and America's Future, 2003).

Identifying a research problem

A problem that calls for exploration

02 This article examines an effort to promote curriculum making as professional development among new teachers. Curriculum making, or curricular enactment, considers the central role of the teacher as decision maker in the classroom (Clandinin & Connelly, 1992; Connelly & Clandinin, 1988; Schoonmaker, 2002; Schwab, 1969/1997; Thornton, 1991; Zumwalt, 1989). Rather than viewing curriculum exclusively as a document defined by "experts" external to the classroom, such a perspective is grounded in a notion of enacted curriculum as "the educational experiences jointly created by students and teachers" (Snyder, Bolin, & Zumwalt, 1992, p. 418). In particular, new teachers in the current study engaged in creating and enacting curricular projects with the support of a cohort-based professional development program throughout their 1st year of teaching. In spite of theoretical references in

Qualitative research recognizes the need to listen to participants' "voices"

Journal of Teacher Education, Vol. 58, No. 3, May/June 2007 216-230
DOI: 10.1177/0022487107301377

A deficiency in the knowledge

The qualitative purpose statement and research questions explore a central phenomenon

the literature to curriculum making, little exists that articulates components of curriculum making specifically drawn from empirical data based on novice teachers. Moreover, this gap is exacerbated by a lack of empirical data specifically on the processes of learning to teach through curricular enactment within the context of high-stakes accountability environments (Clayton, 2005).

03 This article presents three portraits of new teachers as they learned to teach through curriculum making. These stories are displayed to make transparent the uneven shifts in thinking and practice that occurred among these teachers. Taken together, they suggest that curriculum making as professional development provided an opportunity for these novices to take practical risks that they otherwise may not have tried given the twin pressures of the 1st-year experience and high-stakes testing. Such professional development pivoted on epistemological inquiries that engaged three tension areas during the 1st year of teaching: managing student relationships, making claims of curricular ownership, and understanding sources of classroom knowledge. Practical risk taking in these instances created opportunities for these novices to consider the consequences of curricular choices in personal terms; these changes in practice, however small, seemed to precede any conceptual changes about curriculum and teaching. And, though many of these tensions were ultimately not resolved for these teachers as they began their 2nd year, the current research shows that engagement of epistemological tensions through such professional development activities led to observable shifts in practical choices made by the three teachers. These findings suggest some important implications about novice teacher learning during an accountability era where such risk taking is often discouraged.

Specifying a purpose for the research

## HIGH-STAKES NEW TEACHER LEARNING

04 In an effort to address the daunting challenges of the 1st year of teaching, a special form of professional development for novices evolved to address concerns regarding attrition and the perceived deficits that new teachers bring to their roles (Gold, 1996). In general, the primary focus of induction programs is the novice teacher's socialization into the system through the development of competence in basic teaching practices. These efforts are typically characterized by a heavy emphasis on technical assistance aimed at classroom and behavior management (Fideler & Haselkorn, 1999), with little attention paid to issues of content and methods (Feiman-Nemser & Parker, 1990). Moreover, they often adopt a transmission model of teacher education, emphasizing discrete skill acquisition, the teacher as technician, and the low, and sometimes only, expectation for new teachers—that they somehow survive the 1st year to return for a second (Wideen, Mayer-Smith, & Moon, 1998).

Reviewing the literature

The literature plays a minor role

05 This limiting perspective of new teachers has contributed, in part, to relegating curriculum issues to an area of peripheral concern among those charged with new teacher learning. When curriculum is addressed in the professional development of new teachers, it is primarily for instrumental purposes such as an orientation to a district's curriculum frameworks or as a training to ensure effective implementation of a prescribed curricular program (Fideler & Haselkorn, 1999; Miller, 1990). Issues of curricular knowledge and knowing are sidelined in traditional programs to promote new teacher learning, despite the fact that novices, particularly in urban environments, face intensifying external curricular mandates to enable all students to achieve at high academic standards. Moreover, a deficit view of the new teacher experience pervades the literature and programs of novice learning where individual deficiencies are highlighted within a static, staged view of learning (Fuller, 1969; Fuller & Brown, 1975). Such a traditional orientation, which often undergirds practices for new teacher learning, narrows the possibilities of scaffolding the new teacher experience as one full of hopeful possibilities for children rather than as a year of desperation and survival for adults.

06 Efforts to challenge and reconceptualize these conventions of new teacher learning, particularly when situated within the technical

rationale (Pinar, 1978; Tickle, 2000) of standards reform and accountability pressures, are important to examine for what they reveal about learning to teach through curriculum making in these high-stakes times. The view of teaching and learning, as codified in the current context of standards reform and federal legislation mandating testing (No Child Left Behind Act, 2002), draws on an epistemology rooted in positivist science where knowledge, which represents truth, can be fragmented, sequenced, transmitted, and measured (McNeil, 2000). Such a view depicts students as consumers of knowledge whose abilities and understandings can be measured on tests with high-stakes consequences for students, teachers, and schools. Such rewards and sanctions for the annual demonstration of received knowledge are presumed necessary to motivate learning, teaching, and the reform of schools (Falk, 2000). Proponents of this view of student learning also invoke these assumptions when linking achievement to teacher learning. In this respect, teachers are viewed in terms of a *conduit* metaphor (Clandinin & Connelly, 1992) where they are to receive and implement the "knowledge-for-practice" as funneled by policy makers and university researchers (Cochran-Smith & Lytle, 1999, p. 250). Within this epistemological framework, it is important to document empirically how new teachers negotiate their own learning through the process of curriculum making that positions knowledge much differently in terms that are personal, relational, and owned by the learners themselves.

Analyzing data and reporting results

## CONTEXT OF THE STUDY

07 This article presents three novices who participated in the Beginning Teachers' Program (BTP) in a large urban district in the Northeast. Founded in 1998, the BTP was an effort to improve the retention of quality teachers through a cohort professional development model that brings teachers from various schools in the same district together for fifteen 2-hr sessions over the course of the year. These ongoing sessions were guided by a job-embedded and constructivist curriculum as well as a BTP facilitator employed by the university where the program originated. The BTP curriculum was anchored on four elements: building community, utilizing professional standards for new teachers, nurturing leadership, and understanding literacy. These four themes spiraled throughout the sessions in the form of activities and discussion topics designed to assist new teachers in constructing new, and increasingly complex, understandings about their professional practice.

Qualitative findings include description

08 Nevertheless, BTP facilitators were prepared to deliver a mindfully designed curriculum built around high-interest topics and through pedagogical methods intended to build learning communities of new teachers around job-embedded discussions of practice as well as to model quality teaching practices (Cuddapah & Clayton, 2007). Such topics included identifying community resources, models of behavior management, self-assessment with Interstate New Teacher Assessment and Support Consortium (INTASC) standards, lesson planning and curriculum design, motivation, alternative assessment, multiple intelligences and literacies, culturally relevant pedagogy, and differentiation. The 2-hr sessions were designed by the facilitators who were provided with BTP "building blocks" as a framework for how to structure each session; these included welcoming and opening, the open forum, a focus on content, active listening, housekeeping, building the portfolio, making connections, and closing with feedback. As the names imply, time for the content of any particular session was built into each 2-hr session but not to the exclusion of creating open space to address new teachers' immediate needs and to encourage highly interactive and fluid discussion among the entire cohort. The sessions documented in the current study were often loosely facilitated to allow for open discussion among the novices, creating an atmosphere of "sustained conversation" over time (Hollingsworth, 1994) among novice peers.

Qualitative researchers use a flexible report format.

09 A culminating experience of the BTP involved the development and enactment of curricular projects initiated by novices. These projects were intended to address an area of challenge identified by the new teachers. With the help of facilitators, new teachers wrote a proposal to enact a curricular project that

**TABLE 1 Relationship of Research Questions and Primary Data Sources**

| | *Primarily addressed by . . .* |
|---|---|
| Research Question 1: How do these new teachers perceive curriculum and their roles as they create and enact new teacher-initiated projects as part of the BTP? | Individual and group interviews, presentations<br>Class and school visits and BTP session notes<br>Archival data |
| Research Question 2: What challenges and opportunities do these new teachers identify as they create and enact new teacher-initiated projects? | Individual and group interviews, presentations<br>Archival data |
| Research Question 3: How do these new teachers feel their participation in the BTP contributes to their conceptualizations about and relationships with curriculum? | Individual and group interviews, presentations<br>BTP session notes<br>Class and school visits<br>Archival data |
| Research Question 4: How do these experiences influence how new teachers position themselves in relation to knowledge and practice? | Individual and group interviews, presentation<br>BTP session notes<br>Classroom and school visits |

NOTE: BTP = Beginning Teachers Program.

The qualitative purpose statement and research questions explore a central phenomenon

The qualitative researcher collects text and image data

would address the area of challenge. They received a US$250 minigrant to enact the project and, at the BTP's year-end celebration, presented their results to fellow new teachers, principals, and district leaders. Through activities grounded in the professional work of teaching, the program aimed to create opportunities for critical reflection that would support the transformative learning (Mezirow & Associates, 1990; Mezirow & Associates, 2000) of 1st-year teachers, enabling shifts in how the teachers viewed students, families, schools, communities, and, ultimately, themselves.

Method Section

## METHOD

10 Drawing from a multiple method qualitative study of six new teachers (Clayton, 2005), I employed case study methods (Merriam, 2001) to develop detailed portraits of new teacher learning while also utilizing aspects of grounded theory (Charmaz, 2000; Glaser & Strauss, 1967; Strauss & Corbin, 1990) to develop theoretical insights about the nature of curriculum making as professional development in the context of high-stakes urban reform. Social constructivist theories (Cochran-Smith & Lytle, 1999; Danielewicz, 2001; Vygotsky, 1978; Wenger, 1998) guided the framing of research questions and the choices of data collection and analysis in ways that focused directly on the individual experiences of novices and their constructed positioning toward knowledge within the socio-historical contexts of accountability reform.

Selecting a research design and collecting data

The literature describes a conceptual framework that informs the qualitative study; it does not direct the study

11 Multiple data collection methods included at least three classroom observations, observation of 15 BTP sessions and the final professional development presentations, three semistructured individual interviews and one group interview, and analysis of all relevant documents and archival materials, including videotape, offered by the teachers and available through the BTP. See Table 1 for explanation of how data collection methods overlapped and reinforced each other to address the study's research questions.

12 Data analysis began during data collection as an integral way of constructing meaning through a review of data and in discussion of those data with participants. Although reflective writing accompanied all data collection procedures and most contacts with the teachers, the research plan built in three checkpoints for systematic analysis; after the first and second individual interviews and after the group interview, these data were analyzed to prepare subsequent interview protocols. After the first interview, transcripts were read to identify possible emergent codes; in addition, passages were identified, usually to clarify teacher meanings to incorporate into the second interview as a focus for discussion. When all second interviews were complete, interview data were analyzed for the first time across all participants, allowing for a comparison of insights between the first and second interviews for each participant and among all participants. Emergent codes from the first review of data were used in conjunction with codes based on

Qualitative researchers use research designs to plan their studies



The qualitative researcher codes the data to develop description and themes

**TABLE 2 List of Categories and Codes Developed Through Data Collection Process and Utilized in Analysis**

| *Categories (and sources of category development)* | *Analysis Codes* |
|---|---|
| Curriculum stance codes (based on emergent codes, Research Questions 1 and 3, and theoretical perspectives) | Curriculum as Big Plan |
| | Curriculum as Guide |
| | Curriculum as Materials |
| | Curriculum as Experience-based |
| | Curriculum as Testing |
| | Curriculum as Standards |
| | Curriculum as Skills |
| | Curriculum as Themes |
| | Curriculum as Real Life |
| | Curriculum as External Mandates |
| | Curriculum as Instruction (what and how you teach in the classroom) |
| | Curriculum as Inquiry (or discovery) |
| Teaching philosophy (based on emergent codes and on Research Questions 1 and 3) | Teacher View (of role of teacher) |
| | Formal Philosophy |
| | Stance toward Students |
| Self-tensions (based on emergent codes, Research Questions 1, 3, and 4, and theoretical perspectives) | "internal war" (in vivo code) |
| | Self-positioning (in relationship to knowledge) |
| | Self-efficacy |
| | Self-becoming (in relation to assuming a professional identity in the classroom) |
| Challenges (based on Research Question 2) | Project Challenges |
| | Teaching Challenges |
| Teaching supports (based emergent codes and on Research Question 2) | Colleagues |
| | Friends |
| | Administration |
| | Staff Development/Staff Developer |
| | Mentor |
| | BTP/cohort |
| | Others |
| | Unexpected |
| | Parents |
| Project Experiences (based on emergent codes, Research Questions 2 and 3, and theoretical perspectives) | Project Motivations |
| | Project Ownership |
| | Project Impact |
| | Critical Classroom Incidents (identified by the teacher and/or myself) |
| Project learnings (based on Research Questions 3 and 4) | About Self |
| | About Students |
| | About Practice |
| | About Planning |
| | About Setting |
| Knowledge stance (based on Research Question 4 and theoretical perspectives) | Knowledge View (what knowledge is of most worth) |
| | Knowledge Source (where knowledge comes from) |
| Researcher Positioning (based on emergent codes and theoretical perspectives) | Tensions |
| | Teacher Response to Researcher |

The qualitative researcher codes the data to develop description and themes

research questions; a list of the curriculum stance codes was discussed with participants during the group interview. Finally, after the group interview, all data were reviewed in relation to an individual participant to construct a vignette that would serve as a text to discuss during the final interview with each participant.

13 After data collection ended, these data were coded and analyzed along two dimensions—across all data types for each participant and across all data types for all participants to develop richly contextualized case portraits and to develop emergent categories that would produce theoretical insights. Utilizing the code list derived through the data collection process, additional codes were constructed in relation to guiding theoretical frameworks to reread the data with these considerations in mind and to help organize the initial open code list into categories for further analysis (see Table 2). The nature of

Qualitative researchers use strategies to validate their findings

The qualitative researcher intentionally selects participants

The qualitative researcher includes a small number of participants

Qualitative researchers take a reflexive and subjective approach

writing about the research process shifted toward more analytical memos that produced the observation of distinct patterns revolving around the three tension areas discussed in this article. Visual charts were utilized to confirm this insight, and the stories of the three individuals highlighted in this article were examined further as most emblematic of these tension areas. QSR NVivo coding software was utilized to track the emerging code list in ways that also enabled multiple layers of analysis.

14 Complicating the methodology of the current study was my position relative to the BTP. During the period of data collection, I was a staff member of the BTP, responsible for several aspects of program development and implementation with a focus on new teacher-initiated projects. This proximity to the program allowed me to gain initial access to the teachers who eventually participated, even though this position may have also compromised how open teachers might have initially felt. To counteract this possibility, I worked to build rapport with teachers through consistent involvement as a participant observer at cohort sessions and in the teachers' classrooms. In addition, past experiences as a teacher enabled me to be sensitive to the experiences of new teachers, though my own novice experiences occurred at different grade levels, and in different state and school contexts prior to the implementation of policies such as high-stakes testing.

Results Section

## THE TEACHERS AND THEIR PROJECTS

15 The three teachers discussed in this article represent the different preparation routes and background experiences characteristic of participants in the larger study and the BTP, in general. Although all considered themselves 1st-year teachers, Joanna and Eileen had taught before—in overseas and private school contexts. During the year of the study, these two English Language Arts teachers held their first full-time positions in two public middle schools housed in the same building; during this period, each pursued master's degrees through different alternative certification programs. Alexandra, a fifth-grade inclusion teacher, came to teaching through a more traditional route, earning a master's degree after beginning a career in business. She had much less experience working directly with students and schools prior to making this career shift, though she came from a family of teachers.

Analyzing data and reporting results

16 Alexandra and Eileen, African Americans, had different background experiences in relation to the African American students they taught. Alexandra was from an upper middle-class suburb in Virginia. Her father, a physicist, and her mother, a teacher and counselor, impressed upon Alexandra a desire to educate "disadvantaged kids" as a "way to give back." Having grown up in public housing in the same city in which she taught, Eileen's motivations to teach were grounded in a desire to "bridge the gap" where she felt she understood the disparities her students faced and she desired to "give back" specifically to African Americans in a "poor neighborhood." Joanna, a White middle-class teacher, proclaimed that teaching was always a "goal." Although she attended a prestigious public university on the West Coast, she began her career teaching in urban schools through an alternative certification route that focused explicitly on addressing the achievement gap. The sections that follow present each teacher's story of curriculum making to describe how this activity unfolded as a form of professional development within high-stakes curricular environments.

### *Altered Visions of Students' Relationship to the Curriculum: Alexandra's Inquiry*

Qualitative findings include description

17 On a sunny day in March of her 1st year, Alexandra stood in the front of a fifth-grade inclusion classroom, asking math questions in a simple call-and-response pattern while a predominantly African American class sat in table groups. Bulletin boards featured student work—visual representations of math problems and typed essays about favorite celebrities. Posted prominently on the door, the class schedule displayed time blocks consumed by literacy and math. On the front chalkboard were two announcements: Reading test 4/15; math test 4/30. After a short and unsuccessful transition to independent reading, Alexandra decided to hand out a cloze passage vocabulary

test. When two boys refused to quiet down, Alexandra approached their desk and ripped up their quizzes in a dramatic manner intended to attract the attention of the class. Across the room, a different female student asked defiantly, "Can I rip up my paper?" as she, then, did so. Alexandra looked on in disgust, and the lesson continued in a haphazard fashion until a visiting guest speaker arrived.

18 This scene was a common one when Alexandra's classroom was observed. Often, Alexandra's stance was adversarial; behavior management was a tactic used to ensure curricular compliance of students whom Alexandra often viewed in deficit terms. Her BTP project—a collection of student narratives based on their interviews of other students in the building—was often used as a lever to impress upon students that engaging curricula was a privilege for those who behaved. Well into her 2nd year, Alexandra's thinking about students seemed firmly fixed, although evidence suggests that subtle changes in practice were supported by curriculum making as professional development in a significant area—the management of relationships with students.

19 *Taking another look.* One key moment came in a BTP cohort session when Alexandra had a pivotal interaction with another novice teacher who challenged her deficit view of students. During a check-in about students' responses to their BTP projects, Alexandra addressed a point that she had mentioned several times previously—her inability to comprehend why her students were not oriented to learning in the same way she was. She expressed disbelief about why qualified students would refuse to go to a more academic middle school, concluding that being smart is some kind of a "put down" in the community.

20 Another teacher, sensing Alexandra's dismay, shared some advice she had received from her father who reminded her that her students were dealing with "deep-rooted social issues." This teacher mentioned incarceration, crack cocaine, and heroin as influences on their students' orientation toward learning. Further dismayed at this seemingly hopeless conclusion, Alexandra talked about a student raised by a parent on crack who was labeled with attention-deficit/hyperactivity disorder (ADHD): "If I remove the child, things improve by 40%."

21 At this point, the other new teacher turned to Alexandra and offered some advice: "You have to find out what they really like and give them special projects."

> Alexandra wondered, "What if they can't handle it?"
> The other teacher then asked, "Did you ask him what he likes to do?"
> Alexandra responded, "No."

22 The teacher, then, shared about how she found out about Elvis's talent in painting and then put that knowledge to use in her curriculum. She shared how Harold wrote two pages on the question of how he had changed from last year to this year, allowing her to learn more about how to motivate him through the leadership curriculum she was developing. Looking Alexandra straight in the eye, she said, "You need to start by asking him." She encouraged Alexandra to begin by having the student write about himself. Alexandra was listening intently, leaning forward and looking intensely interested in an idea that appeared to be a novel one.

23 *Seeing differently: Managing relationships in curriculum making.* During the fall of her 2nd year of teaching, Alexandra independently remembered the interaction with her peer in the cohort the previous year. She recalled that she had her students do an essay on what they liked and what they didn't like about school as a result of that interaction. She admitted that learning about her students through her curriculum was a new practice: "I didn't know to ask any of these questions. . . . I had no idea the response I was going to get." She revealed that it helped her to understand the feelings of her students and to gain insight into their motivations and concerns. This interaction had informed Alexandra's practice; by asking questions and listening to their responses, Alexandra positioned herself to see her students differently—not in terms of what they lacked but in terms of what they might bring to the tasks and processes in the classrooms.

Qualitative findings include themes

24 Still, at this same interview, Alexandra shared that she struggled with similar problems regarding behavior and classroom management. Reading from a short vignette about her that documented the vocabulary quiz incident described above, Alexandra reacted, "I still do that, and they're still unphased. I can't stand it." She continued to talk about "damaged kids," often in stark, deficit terms. She spoke about gunshots, drugs, and "parents that are cracked out" and asked, "So, you know, what do you think is going to be the learning element?" These comments revealed that aspects of Alexandra's thinking about her practice were in some ways locked into her original management perspective even though evidence of subtle, though significant, shifts in practice were noted. Alexandra's story suggests that changes in practice may, indeed, precede shifts in mental models. Such a subtle shift in practice, without evidence of cognitive change, may suggest that the change in Alexandra's practice won't last. Or, perhaps, it may suggest that alterations in practice might, for some teachers, need to precede profound conceptual shifts.

### Shifting Notions of Curricular Ownership: Eileen's Discovery

25 On a visit to Eileen's seventh-grade English and Language Arts classroom on any given day during her 1st year, one might notice a timer attached by magnet to the front of the chalkboard. The kitchen timer gave off a low, unobtrusive beep; however, it was just enough to signal transitions for Eileen's seventh-grade class. There was almost a Pavlovian feel to the order that the timer and Eileen's other management practices created; however, it was also clear that order was not the only objective of Eileen's classroom. On a particular visit in April, just days before the upcoming city-wide English exam, Eileen altered her routine to make space for students who wished to share their journal writing. Students shared poetry and writing about personal matters. After each student shared, the classroom applauded, sometimes raucously, and snapped approval. After all volunteers shared, Eileen passed out test prep books to table groups, and students began their focused practice on comprehension and test-taking strategies.

26 This slice of classroom life illustrated a tension that Eileen experienced daily as a teacher—how to nurture student interest in English and Language Arts. Even in this particular moment where the pressure was on, Eileen responded to "student initiations" (Oyler, 1996, p. 51), making space for student expression and creativity. In this way, she made room for student ownership of the classroom experience. Eileen's BTP project—a school performance celebrating Martin Luther King, Jr.'s legacy and his "I Have a Dream" speech in a predominantly African American school—was actually initiated by her assistant principal. It was written by the assistant principal, assisted by a guidance counselor, and directed by Eileen. Nevertheless, the project provided an opportunity for Eileen to engage the tension of cultivating ownership in the curriculum—first, for herself, and, then, among her students.

27 *Encouraging active participation: The Electric Slide surprise.* Eileen had difficulty committing to an idea for her BTP project so she was relieved when her assistant principal requested that she organize her class to produce a school-wide performance to honor Martin Luther King, Jr. Eileen calculated that she could satisfy the administrator's request, complete BTP requirements, and teach her students needed skills in oral presentation. Unlike other teachers in the study, Eileen had little personal attachment to her BTP project topic; it was simply something to enable her to meet several external demands at once.

Qualitative findings include themes

28 Eileen set up the project to ensure that every student had a role to play as actors, set designers, stagehands, audio-visual (AV) technicians, or directing consultants. Eileen also proposed that a "class-generated rubric" would be used to assess the performance, providing the opportunity for students to assess themselves as a group with the criteria on which they agreed. In spite of these features, students' roles in the project were limited because adults made key choices about the content and process for the performance, narrowing the extent of involvement and the

Qualitative findings include description

personal stake that students might have in the performance.

29 Perhaps because of this fact, Eileen's most surprising moment came when the students claimed a piece of the performance for themselves. During one practice, they decided to create and choreograph their own ending that involved having everyone do the Electric Slide. Well past the end of the project, Eileen remembered this moment vividly: "That was the part of the performance that was probably most memorable. And that was something that was all theirs. All theirs." Lingering on this last phrase as if it were something she was turning over and examining in her mind, Eileen could not quite articulate what she had learned; however, she knew it was a marker moment.

30 When asked indirectly, Eileen shared what she would do differently, offering the Electric Slide surprise as an example of what kinds of curricular possibilities might result if she were to abdicate her role as director and, instead, solicit student participation as directors and writers. Eileen acknowledged the ways the roles that she and the assistant principal assumed, as director and writer, respectively, actually limited possibilities of student ownership. On reflection, she noted that students, in taking the initiative with developing the ending, had taught her a powerful lesson—one that had, indeed, challenged her to assume a new stance for the purpose of nurturing student investment in their curricular experiences.

31 *Seeing new possibilities: Ownership in curriculum making.* Eileen had initially conceptualized the project in terms of ensuring that each student had a particular role to play. By the end of the year, she began to reconceptualize how she could deepen students' ownership of the experience by recognizing the unnecessary limits her own role created for students. By the time she had submitted her project documentation to the BTP, Eileen suggested clearly how she would conceptualize this curriculum differently in the future: "If I were to do this project again, it would be written, directed, produced, and performed by students. They had great ideas that we just did not have time to implement." Eileen's reflection demonstrates a shift in thinking in the direction of constantly expanding the range of opportunities and choices that students would claim—again, to foster a vision of building greater student investment in curricular outcomes. The project, which started out as the inspiration of an assistant principal, became something owned by Eileen first, and then her students. Observing the evolution of ownership in her students probably contributed to her year-end reflections to include students more in the planning "to make it *their* project."

32 During her 2nd year of teaching, evidence existed that these lessons seemed to have some staying power. Eileen was involved in a collaborative project with her colleagues that involved students creating books about their lives. In this project, students acted as authors, layout designers, and publishers. Unlike Alexandra, Eileen's thinking and practice seemed to shift in significant ways through the process of curriculum making as professional development—at least in the area of nurturing student authorship of curricular experiences to build interests and motivation for subject area learning. Like Alexandra, however, the value of curriculum making as professional development appeared to be in how it provided the opportunity for novices to take risks in their practices prior to making particular changes in thinking. In this sense, new teacher learning and, specifically, conceptual shifts about practice were led by actual changes in those practices.

### Changing Conceptions About Knowledge for Teaching and Learning: Joanna's Struggle

33 In handwritten script on a banner of plain white paper, a quote loomed over Joanna's eighth-grade English and Language Arts classroom: "Be the change you want to see in the world. M. Gandhi." Bright posters, many of which were teacher made with explanations of various reading and writing strategies, adorned the wall. Neatly typed poems by students decorated one area of the classroom. Student desks were arranged to support small groupwork. On one side of the room, Joanna had crates for each of her classes filled with a binder for each group

that contained information as the groups prepared poster presentations on various aspects of World War II. The project was designed to provide some historical background for the two novels students were reading in a unit on children and war.

34 This window into Joanna's classroom just before she started her World Cultures BTP project showed Joanna in the midst of the kind of teaching she had wanted to engage in from the beginning of the year. It was a stark contrast to what she reported experiencing earlier as the school geared up for statewide exams in January. In the 6 weeks prior to the exam, Joanna reported that she was told to "abandon all literature" in favor of test prep monitored by a staff developer. When her students took the exam, however, Joanna felt the pressure recede. Not only did the test prep go away but also surveillance of the superintendent's mandated literacy block instruction was also discontinued. Because of these "constraints," she had postponed aspects of the curriculum that she thought extremely valuable such as oral presentation, groupwork, and research in the community. Looking forward to her World Cultures unit, Joanna embraced the freedom to design creative, interdisciplinary units. Excitedly, she exclaimed in anticipation of her project, "I mean, teaching them about culture, art, and literature at the same time—really, what more could you ask for?" Curriculum making as professional development provided Joanna with an opportunity to develop her thinking and practice in the area of what knowledge most counts for teaching and learning.

35 *The value of relational knowledge.* Joanna's BTP project involved students in a group inquiry of one of nine world cultures that Joanna chose. The entire class would learn a bit about all nine cultures; however, each student would be a part of a group team that would conduct a more in-depth inquiry into the culture intended to culminate in a class presentation. Many of these cultures would, indeed, be represented by students' backgrounds, adding a different dimension to the learning experience. Struggling with her vision of project-based inquiry learning and her own beliefs about subject matter expertise for teaching, Joanna sought to provide abundant resources and access to knowledge of these cultures through her own resources and those of other teachers and friends from those particular cultures. Given her aim to make the project "content based," Joanna often cornered herself into the role of disciplinary expert even in spite of her competing desires to act as a facilitator of students' discovery of knowledge.

36 Joanna soon found that the knowledge she engaged her students in would take on a different form. Immersing her students in language, music, food, the arts, and pop culture, she created a curriculum of sensory experiences where students visited museums, sampled the culture's food at ethnic restaurants, and interviewed other teachers and friends from those particular cultures. Such a curriculum required a different kind of engagement with the world. On reflection, Joanna learned that "if they [her students] could develop a relationship with what was being studied . . . then they would *know* it much more." Here, Joanna connected the idea of relationship to knowing and, in so doing, revealed how her notions of what's worth knowing in the classroom had broadened beyond a more one-dimensional notion of knowledge as information to acquire. For Joanna, content knowledge would still be important; the shift was in the scope of what became possible to know in Joanna's classroom.

37 By observing her students as she enacted her project, Joanna came to understand that what's worth knowing in the classroom also had a relational and personal dimension. Such personal knowledge gained through relationships acted not only to "hook" students into learning more traditional forms of knowledge but also had a value in and of itself that may, in fact, surpass the aim to acquire information.

38 In an interview as she was in the middle of enacting her project, Joanna shared that she was coming to understand the value of "human connections" in making "learning come alive." She explained that the "passion" about a subject—in this case, when people shared aspects of their cultures with the students—"really translates to kids" and they

responded "very well." As Joanna came to realize that knowledge was engaging and even inspiring to students when it was acquired as students engaged with others—guest speakers, interviewees, even people in films—her prior notion of knowledge as information held and conveyed by the content expert receded.

39 *Becoming knowledgeable about pedagogy: Sources of classroom knowledge.* This shift in where the sources of classroom knowledge reside did not mean that Joanna relinquished the idea of teachers as knowledgeable experts; to be sure, teachers were to be knowledgeable, this time also in how they pedagogically approached content with students. Joanna discussed her prior conception of teacher as content expert and elaborated on a different view of what content expertise means for teaching and learning:

> Knowing my content extremely well means that when children come across a block in their research I can help them to see what is blocking them, step back and look at the larger picture and suggest names, ideas, books, um, historical facts that then lead them in a direction even though they are blocked.

Joanna's description of how content knowledge aids teaching reveals how she was coming to understand the value of pedagogical content expertise where teachers know how to guide students in navigating difficult aspects of knowledge or how to represent topics to motivate and engage learners (Shulman, 1987). This appeared to be a fundamentally different stance for Joanna, one where it was less important that the teacher know to give information but more important that the teacher know to guide the students in their own discoveries. Here, Joanna recognized that the latter required expertise indeed, but expertise particularly in terms of how to approach the challenges of content as a dilemma of pedagogical practice.

40 Joanna's ideas about classroom knowledge moved on different levels. First, there was a notable change in terms of the value of relational knowledge in making possible powerful learning for her students. Through enacting her BTP project, Joanna learned the central role of such knowledge in facilitating powerful learning to achieve her overall curricular objectives. Then, on the nature of knowledge necessary for classroom teaching, Joanna also came to have a different sense of what mattered most. Through her reflection on the challenges of enacting the BTP project, Joanna came to value expertise in terms of pedagogical content necessary to facilitate discovery learning—not to the exclusion of subject matter knowledge but because, alone, such content expertise was more about her teaching than about the students' learning. In both of these conceptual shifts, Joanna moved in her thinking about the teacher's position toward students and what's worth knowing in the classroom, suggesting important implications for classroom practice. To be sure, Joanna continued to cling to the notion of expertise; however, instead of being a subject expert who provided information and resources to students, Joanna's new positioning required her to become expert in supporting students learning the content that she taught. Like Alexandra and Eileen, Joanna's story of curriculum making suggests that professional development opportunities that facilitate shifts in practice first may, indeed, be necessary to inform conceptual changes in thinking about teaching itself.

Conclusion Section

## DISCUSSION

41 In spite of references to curriculum making in the literature, there exists little that articulates components of curriculum making specifically grounded in empirical data based on novice teachers. This article addresses this gap by beginning to elaborate empirically grounded, theoretical insights about curriculum making as a form of novice professional development that pivot on three critical tension areas: managing student relationships to curriculum, developing claims of curricular ownership, and understanding sources of classroom knowledge. Although novices from any time period may experience these tensions independent of particular professional development activities, the nature of these tensions, and particularly their interaction during the novice experience in an era of high-stakes accountability reforms, were made more visible through curriculum making as professional

The qualitative researcher interprets the larger meanings of the findings

Interpreting the research

Qualitative findings include relating themes

development. These teachers' stories, each of which highlight what is meant by these key areas, offer insight into the nature of conceptual change and shifts in practice with important implications for teacher education and induction programs.

### Conceptual Changes: Shifting the Focus of New Teacher Learning

42 All three teachers showed evidence of shifting views of themselves as teachers as a result of their work on BTP projects. For example, Eileen changed from thinking about being director of the student performance to transferring that authority to students, in effect, with their final scene. Similarly, Joanna's change in knowledge views caused her to replace an image of her expert self with that of a knowledgeable facilitator of students' relational knowing. Although Alexandra's transformation was least dramatic, her struggle to see through her deficit views of students was influenced through an exchange with another teacher, causing Alexandra to turn the gaze inward, even if only slightly, onto her teaching self.

43 These findings suggest that efforts to transform new teachers' thinking from one view of curricular knowledge to another may be misguided. Given the taken-for-granted view of knowledge as information conveyed through the technical rationale of standards reform and accountability, such efforts at conceptual transformation face extraordinary odds. Instead, the epistemological inquiry and self-reflection made possible through curriculum making as a professional development activity created opportunities for these new teachers to consider the consequences of their curricular choices in personal terms that, in turn, may have had more practical benefits for novice teacher development. The distinction here is subtle but important—professional development activities must engage epistemological tensions without expecting epistemological transformations within the limited time frames of current professional development programs for new teachers.

### Practical Shifts: Cultivating Opportunities for Curricular Risk Taking

44 Although conceptual change was less apparent and more subtle, practical shifts that could be attributed to teachers' experience with BTP projects were apparent in observation of all three teachers in their 1st year and in self-reports about teaching during their 2nd years. Alexandra asked students to write an essay that would inform her thinking about curricular connections for her students; in doing so, she shifted their relationship to the curriculum of her classroom. Eileen worked through the problem of cultivating curricular ownership among her students and translated her learning into a project the following year where students had more authority for the products they created. And, finally, Joanna incorporated elements in her World Cultures unit that reflected her evolving conceptions about knowledge. She continued, into her 2nd year, by taking the risk to shift her position in the project from one that provided information to students to that of a facilitator of guided inquiry.

45 These findings suggest that practical shifts were more likely to result from the limited exposure to curriculum making as professional development that these teachers encountered. The experience of BTP projects provided an opportunity for new teachers to take risks that they, otherwise, may not have done given the twin pressures they felt as novices in high-stakes curricular environments. Moreover, the environment of BTP sessions that promoted ongoing and job-embedded conversations among novice peers made it safe for these teachers to act on this opportunity. This professional development activity did not just provide an opportunity to try out an alternative approach; indeed, it required it. Such positive pressure was the support that was necessary to inspire risk taking in an accountability environment that, in many respects, was averse to such risks.

The qualitative researcher identifies limitations in the study

### Tilting Toward Curriculum Making

46 The image of new teacher learning that emerges from this discussion is more appropriately

characterized as tilting toward curriculum making in particular moments of space and time. Rather than making absolute shifts from one view of curriculum and teaching to another, these teachers, on occasion, tilt toward curriculum making and all the epistemological and ontological ideas associated with that view. On other occasions, they tilt in different directions that would, on face value, appear to contradict these views.

47 The representation of change as a tilt in one direction or the other suggests more descriptively the limits and possibilities of new teacher learning through curriculum making as professional development. So much of traditional teacher education and induction focuses on changing teacher thinking, yet these teachers' stories suggest that changes in practice may, indeed, precede conceptual changes. Those who support new teacher learning must think about ways to support teachers like those presented with opportunities to take practical risks for learning in an emotionally safe environment that supports and values those risks.

## CONCLUSIONS

48 In practical terms for programs of new teacher learning, curriculum making can act most effectively as a venue for learning when it engages teachers in considering how to manage the multiple relationships of curriculum making. As Fried (2001) discussed, curriculum involves a "web of relationships" between how teacher and students position themselves toward curricular knowledge in the classroom. Managing these relationships seemed necessary for Alexandra to gain awareness of and then experiment with during her 1st year. Moreover, curricular ownership and epistemological issues are relevant ones to explore with novices; however, for these conversations to be productive, they must be explicitly linked to the consequences for classroom practice. The stories of Eileen and Joanna show that conceptual change is not the short-term goal of new teacher learning; however, explicit engagement of the tensions that emerge naturally in curriculum making are important to have as such opportunities are often disregarded in an accountability era. Given the particular environment in which these teachers were learning to teach, this was a pressure point to encourage possibilities for "tilting" that better characterized the uncertainties of new teacher development in these high-stakes times.

49 Still, many questions remain. Do the shifts in practice demonstrated by these new teachers remain for the long term? Do they lead, over time, to changes in the mental models that undergird those practices? Were some of the "products" or "processes" of curriculum making more important than others in terms of the impact they might have on new teacher retention or student learning? Were the experiences of these teachers, quite possibly, exceptional? If not, how can we use the lessons implied here to think about ways to create the conditions to support teachers, especially those who are new, to take curricular risks in these high-stakes times? Moreover, does practical risk taking in one of the tension areas identified here—managing relationships with students, making claims of curricular ownership, and understanding sources of classroom knowledge—have more staying power in terms of encouraging novices to remain in teaching, to create constructivist, project-based curricula for students, or to promote learning for all students?

50 These questions speak to the kind of research agenda that needs to be pursued in teacher education as revealed in the American Educational Research Association panel report on research and teacher education (Cochran-Smith & Zeichner, 2005; Zeichner, 2005). Longitudinal studies across multiple sites that manage to link program practices, such as curriculum making, with novices' classroom practice and, subsequently, with their students' learning will add insight to these questions. In particular, following candidates from teacher education programs with a curriculum-making perspective and a particular approach to curricular design through the early years of teaching will provide greater insight on epistemological and practical concerns of teaching in these times.

The qualitative researcher suggests implications for practice

The qualitative researcher suggests implications for future research

The qualitative researcher compares findings to past studies

## REFERENCES

Britzman, D. P. (1991). *Practice makes practice: A critical study of learning to teach.* Albany: State University of New York Press.

Charmaz, K. (2000). Grounded theory: Objectivist and constructivist methods. In N. K. Denzin & Y. S. Lincoln (Eds.), *Handbook of qualitative research* (pp. 509-535). Thousand Oaks, CA: Sage.

Clandinin, D. J., & Connelly, F. M. (1992). Teacher as curriculum maker. In P. W. Jackson (Ed.), *Handbook of research on curriculum* (pp. 363-401). New York: Macmillan.

Clayton, C. D. (2005). *Tilting towards curriculum making: Case studies of new teacher-initiated projects as professional development.* Unpublished doctoral dissertation, Teachers College, Columbia University.

Clayton, C. D. (2007). Learning against the grain: New teachers as curriculum makers in high-stakes times. *Excelsior: Leadership in Teaching and Learning, 1*(2).

Cochran-Smith, M., & Lytle, S. L. (1999). Relationships of knowledge and practice: Teacher learning in communities. In A. Iran-Nejad & P. D. Pearson (Eds.), *Review of research in education* (Vol. 24, pp. 249-305). Washington, DC: American Educational Research Association.

Cochran-Smith, M., & Zeichner, K. M. (Eds.). (2005). *Studying teacher education: The report of the AERA panel on research and teacher education.* Washington, DC: American Educational Research Association.

Connelly, F. M., & Clandinin, D. J. (1988). *Teachers as curriculum planners: Narratives of experience.* New York: Teachers College Press.

Cuddapah, J. L., & Clayton, C. D. (2007, February). *Cohort learning among new teachers.* Paper presented at the Annual Meeting of the Association of American Colleges of Teacher Education, New York.

Danielewicz, J. (2001). *Teaching selves: Identity, pedagogy, and teacher education.* Albany: State University of New York Press.

Falk, B. (2000). *The heart of the matter: Using standards and assessments to learn.* Portsmouth, NH: Heinemann.

Feiman-Nemser, S., & Parker, M. B. (1990). Making subject matter part of the conversation in learning to teach. *Journal of Teacher Education, 41*(3), 32-43.

Fideler, E. F., & Haselkorn, D. (1999). *Learning the ropes: Urban teacher induction programs and practices in the United States.* Belmont, MA: Recruiting New Teachers.

Fried, R. L. (2001). *The passionate learner: How teachers and parents can help children reclaim the joy of discovery.* Boston: Beacon.

Fuller, F. F. (1969). Concerns of teachers: A developmental conceptualization. *American Educational Research Journal, 6,* 207-226.

Fuller, F. F., & Brown, O. H. (1975). Becoming a teacher. In K. Ryan (Ed.), *Teacher education* (74th Yearbook of the National Society for the Study of Education) (Vol. Pt. II, pp. 25-52). Chicago: University of Chicago Press.

Glaser, B. G., & Strauss, A. L. (1967). *The discovery of grounded theory: Strategies for qualitative research.* New York: Aldine.

Gold, Y. (1996). Beginning teacher support: Attrition, mentoring, and induction. In J. Sikula, T. Buttery, & E. Guyton (Eds.), *Handbook of research on teacher education* (pp. 548-616). New York: Macmillan.

Hodgkinson, H. (2002). Demographics and teacher education: An overview. *Journal of Teacher Education, 53*(2), 102-105.

Hollingsworth, S. (1994). Sustained conversation: An alternative approach to the study and process of learning to teach. In S. Hollingsworth (Ed.), *Teacher research and urban literacy education: Lessons and conversations in a feminist key* (pp. 3-16). New York: Teachers College Press.

Huling-Austin, L. (1990). Teacher induction programs and internships. In W. R. Houston, M. Haberman, & J. Sikula (Eds.), *Handbook of research on teacher education* (pp. 535-548). New York: Macmillan.

Kauffman, D., Moore Johnson, S., Kardos, S. M., Liu, E., & Peske, H. G. (2002). "Lost at sea": New teachers' experiences with curriculum and assessment. *Teachers College Record, 104*(2), 273-300.

Lortie, D. C. (1975). *Schoolteacher.* Chicago: University of Chicago Press.

McNeil, L. M. (2000). *Contradictions of school reform: Educational costs of standardized testing.* New York: Routledge.

Merriam, S. B. (2001). *Qualitative research and case study applications in education.* San Francisco: Jossey-Bass.

Mezirow, J., & Associates, (Eds.). (1990). *Fostering critical reflection in adulthood. A guide to transformative and emancipatory learning.* San Francisco: Jossey-Bass.

Mezirow, J., & Associates, (Eds.). (2000). *Learning as transformation: Critical perspectives on a theory in progress.* San Francisco: Jossey-Bass.

Miller, J. L. (1990). Teachers as curriculum creators. In J. T. Sears & J. D. Marshall (Eds.), *Teaching and thinking about curriculum* (pp. 85-96). New York: Teachers College Press.

National Commission on Teaching and America's Future. (2003). *No dream denied: A pledge to America's children. A summary report.* Washington, DC: Author.

No Child Left Behind Act, P.L. 107-110 (2002).

Oyler, C. (1996). *Making room for students.* New York: Teachers College Press.

Pinar, W. F. (1978). The reconceptualization of curriculum studies. *Journal of Curriculum Studies, 10,* 205-214.

Schoonmaker, F. (2002). *"Growing up" teaching: From personal knowledge to professional practice.* New York: Teachers College Press.

Schwab, J. J. (1997). The practical: A language for curriculum. In D. J. Flinders & S. J. Thornton (Eds.), *The curriculum studies reader* (pp. 101-115). New York: Routledge. (Original work published 1969)

Shulman, L. S. (1987). Knowledge and teaching: Foundations of the new reform. *Harvard Educational Review, 57*(1), 1-22.

Snyder, J., Bolin, F., & Zumwalt, K. (1992). Curriculum implementation. In P. W. Jackson (Ed.), *Handbook of research on curriculum* (pp. 402-435). New York: Macmillan.

Strauss, A. L., & Corbin, J. (1990). *Basics of qualitative research: Grounded theory procedures and techniques.* Newbury Park, CA: Sage.

Thornton, S. J. (1991). Teacher as curricular-instructional gatekeeper in social studies. In J. P. Shaver (Ed.), *Handbook of research on social studies teaching and learning* (pp. 237-248). New York: Macmillan.

Tickle, L. (2000). *Teacher induction: The way ahead.* Buckingham, UK: Open University Press.

Veenman, S. (1984). Perceived problems of beginning teachers. *Review of Educational Research, 54*(2), 143-178.

Vygotsky, L. S. (1978). *Mind in society. The development of higher psychological processes.* Cambridge, MA: Harvard University Press.

Wenger, E. (1998). *Communities of practice. Learning, meaning, and identity.* Cambridge, UK: Cambridge University Press.

Wideen, M., Mayer-Smith, J., & Moon, B. (1998). A critical analysis of the research on learning to teach: Making the case for an ecological perspective on inquiry. *Review of Educational Research, 68*(2), 130-178.

Zeichner, K. M. (2005). A research agenda for teacher education. In M. Cochran-Smith & K. M. Zeichner (Eds.), *Studying teacher education: The report of the AERA panel on research and teacher education* (pp. 737-760). Washington, DC: American Educational Research Association.

Zumwalt, K. (1989). Beginning professional teachers: The need for a curricular vision of teaching. In M. C. Reynolds (Ed.), *Knowledge base for the beginning teacher* (pp. 173-184). Oxford, UK: Pergamon.

***Christine D. Clayton*** *is an assistant professor in the adolescent education program at Pace University in Pleasantville, New York. She teaches graduate and undergraduate courses in teacher research, content literacy, and curriculum methods. Her research interests include new teachers, learning to teach, curricular thinking, and social justice in teacher education, especially in the context of these high-stakes times. Email: cclayton@pace.edu.*



*Source:* This article is reprinted from the *Journal of Teacher Education,* Vol. 58, Issue 3, pp. 216–230, 2007. Reprinted with permission of Sage Publications, Inc.

CHAPTER

# 4 The Literature Review: Examining the Background for a Study

*Reviewing the literature is an important step in the research process because it provides researchers with information about what is and is not known about the study's topic. Researchers document this information in a "literature review" passage of the report. You can use this passage to understand the context behind a research report. As a practitioner, you also need to develop your own skills for reviewing literature to learn about topics that interest you. In this chapter, you will learn why scholars review the literature, how literature is used in a report, and steps you can use to locate and summarize literature.*

**BY THE END OF THIS CHAPTER, YOU SHOULD BE ABLE TO:**

- Define a literature review and list ways that it is important for researchers and practitioners.
- Describe how authors use literature in their quantitative and qualitative research studies.
- List the different types of literature available.
- Take steps for reviewing the literature about a topic of your choice.
- Prepare a summary of a quantitative and qualitative research report.

As we learned in Chapter 1, an essential step in the process of conducting research is for researchers to review the literature. Researchers need to be aware of the knowledge that exists about the topic and problem they want to study. Knowing how to review the literature, however, is not only important for researchers. Students, practitioners, and policy makers also need to be able to locate, understand, and summarize literature about a topic. You need to understand the role that literature plays in a research report, *and* you need to develop your skills for reviewing literature. In fact, developing these skills is probably the main reason you are taking this class and reading this book! We will consider both types of skills in this chapter, but we will begin by defining what we mean by a literature review.

## What Is a Literature Review?

A **literature review** is a written summary of journal articles, books, and other documents that describes and critiques the past and current state of information about a topic, organizes the literature into sub-topics, and documents a need for a study. In the most rigorous form of research, investigators base this review on research reported in journal articles. A good review, however, might also contain other information drawn from conference papers, books, school reports, and government documents. Regardless of the sources of information, individuals conduct literature reviews to learn about topics, and all researchers review the literature as a step in the research process.

## Why Is Reviewing the Literature Important?

As a student, you have probably been required at some point to go to the library, read some literature, and write a report about what you learned. It is likely that you have a "literature review" project assigned as a requirement for the course you are taking right now. It is true that completing a class assignment is one important reason to review the literature. There are also many additional reasons why researchers and practitioners choose to review the literature.

### Researchers Review the Literature So Their Studies Can Add to the State of Knowledge

At the most basic level, researchers conduct a literature review to document how their study adds to the existing literature. Simply put, researchers cannot know that a study will add to the existing knowledge if they do not know what that knowledge is. This knowledge keeps them from duplicating research that is already available. It also informs them as to how their study can be planned so that it will build on what others have learned. In addition, researchers learn about theories and philosophies that are relevant to their topic areas by reading the literature. They can also see useful models of how others have designed their research studies. Therefore, reviewing the literature provides important background information for researchers about what has been done, what still needs to be done, and how to go about doing it.

### Practitioners Review the Literature to Learn About Topics and Improve Practice

Most of us complete our first literature reviews as class assignments. There are, however, many additional reasons why you should read the research literature. Recall from Chapter 1 that reading research adds to your knowledge, informs your position in policy debates, and suggests improvements for practice. Practitioners of all professions review the literature for these same reasons. By reading a collection of literature, practitioners keep up to date on the latest developments in their field. They also learn about new topics that they have not previously studied. For example, a science teacher may want to look up information to develop effective strategies for a new student who is visually impaired. Practitioners develop new ideas and strategies to try in their practice from reviewing literature.

## How Do You Identify a Report's Literature Review?

Researchers use different strategies for including their literature reviews within research reports. Since the literature review provides the background for a study, you can expect it to appear early in a report. In some reports, you can locate a clearly designated literature review section. In others, you will not find a section that presents the review of the literature. You will find, however, that all researchers weave literature throughout their writings in a research report.

### Look for a Stand-Alone Passage After the Statement of the Problem

When considering the literature review in a research study, look for a stand-alone section where the author presents a literature review. This section may be found immediately after the statement of the problem passage. In some reports the author will use a heading of *Literature Review* for this section. Other commonly used headings include *Background for the Study* or *Conceptual Framework.* Some authors will use a heading that describes the content topic being reviewed, such as "Adolescent Egocentrism and Invulnerability" (Frankenberger, 2004, p. 577). These literature review sections can vary in length from a paragraph or two to multiple pages, depending on the amount of literature that the author chooses to include.

*Here's a Tip for Reading Research!*

Good research will usually include many references within the reports. All these citations can make articles difficult to read. Do not worry about understanding each one individually. Instead, as you read a literature review, focus on the major themes or ideas that the author is describing.

### Note Where Authors Refer to Others' Work

Not all research reports will include a stand-alone literature review section. In many reports the author's review of the literature will be combined with the statement of the problem in one general introduction section. You can identify when authors are referring to "the literature" when they include citations within the text to other published work. These citations often appear in parentheses and include authors' names and the year of the work being cited, such as: (Smith, 2006; Young & Jones, 2004). In some reports, these citations will be indicated with numbers, such as [1, 2] or [3,8]. No matter the format, researchers should clearly indicate where they are using others' ideas by providing citations. These citations indicate the authors' use of the literature and they make it clear that the current study is building on what others have found.

## How Do Researchers Use Literature in Their Reports?

Now you know a short cut for finding literature in a report—look for the citations. Noting citations will tell you *where* a researcher is referring to the literature, but it does not tell you *how* that literature is being used. When you read research reports, you will find five common ways that researchers use literature. These uses include:

- justifying the research problem,
- documenting what is and is not known about the topic,
- identifying the theory or conceptual framework behind a study,
- providing models for the methods and procedures, and
- interpreting results.

Let's examine each of these uses in more detail.

### Literature Provides Evidence for the Research Problem

As we learned in Chapter 3, researchers use references to the literature to provide evidence for the importance of a study's research problem. Literature may be used to document the extent of the problem or the issues and concerns associated with the problem. For example, read how the authors of a study about African American adolescents' career development use literature to provide evidence for a "major concern:"

> In particular, the career development of African American adolescents has been of major concern in light of literature delineating numerous challenges that affect their personal, educational, and career development (Cheatham, 1990; Constantine et al., 1998). (*Constantine, Wallace, & Kindaichi, 2005, p. 307*)

### Literature Documents What Is and Is Not Known About the Topic

Researchers review the literature to document what is known about a topic and to uncover what is not known. Researchers use the literature in their reports to share this knowledge with the readers and to demonstrate that they are sufficiently aware of other research on the topic. Researchers summarize and report this knowledge as part of the statement of the problem or in a stand-alone section. As discussed in Chapter 3, they also clearly state the knowledge that is missing in the available literature to convey the importance of the study with statements such as "little is known about . . ." or "there is a gap. . . ."

### Literature Identifies the Theory or Conceptual Framework Behind a Study

In many studies, researchers identify a perspective from the literature that guides how they approach the topic of their study. These perspectives come from theories and conceptual frameworks discussed in the literature. To understand how a researcher uses the literature this way, we need to consider what theories and conceptual frameworks are.

A **theory** in quantitative research explains and predicts the probable relationship between different variables. Theories develop from research over time. For example, researchers test the relationship that peer groups have an influence on adolescents. This relationship is tested over and over, such as with the Boy Scouts, in church groups, in middle schools, in sports teams, and other settings. Repeatedly the relationship of a positive effect holds true. In light of all this evidence, someone calls this relationship a theory and assigns a name to it. "Smith's theory of peer influence" is born, reported in the literature, and tested further by other researchers. Other examples of theories include a theory about how students learn, a theory about what motivates people, a theory about leadership styles, and a theory about personality.

When researchers plan their studies to test a specific theory, this theory is important background information for the study. Researchers use the literature to document and describe the important elements of the theory. They use this information to select variables and make predictions about expected results. For example, in the study of African American adolescents' career decisions mentioned above, the authors discussed the Social Cognitive Career Theory in their literature review section and used the theory to make predictions for how they expected perceived occupational barriers to be related to career certainty.

In many studies the researchers do not intend to test a specific theory, but they do use a conceptual framework to guide how they think about the study's topic. A **conceptual framework** represents a philosophical perspective or a body of knowledge from the literature that the researcher uses to inform a study. For example, in a study of girls' and women's perceptions of science role models, Buck, Plano Clark, Leslie-Pelecky, Lu, and Cerda-Lizarraga (2008) used a feminist perspective to inform their study and they discussed the use of feminism in the literature review. Similarly, the author of a study about the influence of mandated testing stated that "a particular view of knowledge forms a central underpinning" of the reported study and described a perspective from the literature called "personal practical knowledge" (Craig, 2004, p. 1231). In these examples, the authors used literature to describe a perspective that informs their study, but not something to be tested. That is, they did not set out to test feminism or the idea of personal practical knowledge, but to use these perspectives to think about how to design and interpret their study.

### Literature Provides Models for the Methods and Procedures

In addition to the introduction section of a report, researchers also cite literature when describing their study's methods and procedures. Researchers use the literature to provide models for how to design their studies and to collect and analyze their data. For example, when researchers decide to use a certain instrument for collecting data, they will explain where in the literature they found this instrument. They also use literature to justify the study's research design or decisions about how to select people as participants. This literature may include other published studies that used the same procedures or writing where scholars discuss the procedures that can be used in the research process (like this book). Using procedures that have been discussed in the literature adds rigor to a research report because it shows that the researcher used established procedures and did not just "make things up."

### Literature Helps Authors Interpret Their Results

A final use of literature in research reports is to aid in the authors' interpretation of the results that were found. Researchers cite literature in the final conclusion section of their reports when they compare the new results with past studies in the literature or examine the overall meaning of the results. We will further discuss this use of the literature in Chapter 14.

## What Do You Think?

Look at the following three excerpts taken from a quantitative study (Frankenberger, 2004) that examined the relationship between adolescent smoking behaviors and three characteristics (adolescent egocentrism, risk perceptions, and sensation seeking). For each excerpt, determine how the author appears to be using the literature.

**(a)** "Adolescent invulnerability has roots in Elkind's (1967, 1978) theory of adolescent egocentrism." *(p. 577)*

**(b)** "Extending similar research in the area, this study attempts to capture feelings of invulnerability not just by measuring perceptions of risk (e.g., Arnett, 1990a, 1990b) but also via the widely used Adolescent Egocentrism Scale (AES) (Enright, Lapsley, & Shukla, 1979; Enright, Shukla, & Lapsley, 1980)." *(p. 577)*

**(c)** "Adolescent egocentrism was measured with the AES developed by Enright and colleagues (Enright et al., 1979; Enright et al., 1980)." *(p. 580)*

### Check Your Understanding

All passages make use of the literature as indicated by the references given in parentheses. Excerpt (a) is an example of using the literature to identify the theories and conceptual frameworks behind the study, namely Eklind's theory of adolescent egocentrism. Excerpt (b) is an example of using literature to establish what is and is not known about a topic to justify the importance of the study because the literature needs to be extended. Excerpt (c) is an example of using the literature to provide models for the methods that the researcher actually used in the study. In this case, the author decided to use a measurement instrument that was developed and previously used by others.

## What Role Does Literature Play in Quantitative and Qualitative Studies?

When reviewing the literature, the researcher may select research articles to summarize that use quantitative or qualitative approaches. Both are acceptable. However, as you learned in Chapter 2, the way the researcher uses this literature differs in quantitative and qualitative research. There are three primary differences: the amount of literature cited at the beginning of the study, the use it serves at the beginning, and its use at the end of a study.

### The Literature Plays More of a Major Role in Quantitative Research

In a quantitative study, researchers discuss the literature extensively at the beginning of the study. This serves two major purposes: It justifies the importance of the research problem, and it provides a rationale for the purpose of the study. Investigators locate a theory in the literature, examine the predicted relationship among variables in the theory, and then test the relationships with new participants or at new sites. In many quantitative studies, the authors include the literature in a separate section titled *Review of the Literature* to highlight the important role it plays. This literature directs the study's design by identifying theories to be tested and determining the major variables. Authors also incorporate the literature into the end of the study, comparing the results with prior predictions or expectations made at the beginning.

In the quantitative parent involvement study (Deslandes & Bertrand, 2005) from Chapter 1, the citations to the literature cluster around the beginning and the end of the article. In the opening paragraph, the authors cite studies to document the importance of the problem: the need for parent involvement in their children's educational processes at home and at school. Then, in paragraph 02, the authors explain that a model (or theory) exists in the literature that might explain parent involvement—the Hoover-Dempsey and Sandler model. They also present research questions consistent with factors in this model that are expected to influence parent involvement: parents' role construction, parents' self-efficacy, perceptions of teacher invitations and perceptions of adolescent invitations. The paragraphs that follow (paragraphs 03–09) represent the literature review about these four factors, and paragraph 10 introduces the idea that grade level will also influence parent involvement. In Paragraph 11 the authors identify the deficiencies in what is known in this literature. Then, when you see paragraph 13, which presents the intent or purpose of the study, it makes sense because we now know that four factors and grade level will be of primary importance in this study. The authors also use literature when they discuss the measures that they use to collect data (e.g., see paragraph 16). Finally, the authors return to the literature in paragraphs 34–43 by comparing their results to other studies in the literature, as well as to the theory mentioned at the beginning of the article.

### The Literature Plays More of a Minor Role in Qualitative Research

Similar to quantitative research, qualitative researchers mention the literature at the beginning of the study to document the importance of the research problem. Unlike quantitative studies, qualitative authors often do not discuss the literature extensively at the beginning of a study. This allows the views of the participants to emerge without being constrained by the views of others from the literature. In some qualitative studies, researchers describe a conceptual framework that informs the research. This framework does not set the direction of the study or introduce predictions like a theory in a quantitative study. Qualitative researchers also cite literature to compare and contrast past studies with the major findings in the study. This contrast and comparison is not the same as prediction in quantitative research. In qualitative inquiry, researchers do not make predictions about findings. They are more interested in whether the findings of a study support or modify existing ideas and practices advanced in the literature.

In the qualitative parent role study (Auerbach, 2007) from Chapter 1, the author begins her article by citing literature to document the research problem of underrepresentation of students of color in colleges (see paragraphs 01–02). The purpose and research questions (paragraph 03) did not follow from the literature. Rather, the questions are general and open ended so the researcher will learn from the participants. After stating the study's purpose, the author does present literature about two perspectives that guide this study. First, she discusses a "critical approach" in paragraphs 04–09, which is described as "examining parent involvement as socially constructed and politically contested through the lenses of race, class, culture, and gender" (paragraph 07). Second, she describes that her study is informed by Hoover-Dempsey and Sandler's model (paragraphs 10–12). Interestingly, this is the same theory used in the quantitative parent involvement study. Those authors used this theory to direct their quantitative questions, which is a different use than in the qualitative parent role study. The author also cites literature in the method section (paragraphs 15–17) to justify her procedures. Finally, she uses literature to help interpret the larger meaning of the results of the study. In the conclusion section (see paragraphs 55–67) the author discusses how the three parent types both reinforce and depart from findings in past research and suggests ways that the literature needs to be adapted.

## What Do You Need to Conduct Your Own Literature Review?

So far in this chapter, we have focused on how to recognize and interpret researchers' use of literature within their research reports. It is not enough for you to understand how others use literature. You also have to develop your skills for locating and summarizing literature and writing a literature review. These skills include being familiar with the kinds of literature that are available. You also need to learn the steps that go into reviewing the literature and writing a literature review. We address each of these issues in turn. It is our intention that you develop the skills necessary to conduct your own literature reviews. Therefore, the provided steps will be described in terms that you can directly apply. Keep in mind as you read, however, that these steps are the same ones that researchers take when they review the literature.

## What Types of Literature Are Available to Review?

There are many different kinds of literature available for review. Figure 4.1 provides a useful classification system of the literature. Modified from a classification originally developed by Libutti and Blandy (1995), the figure is a guide to three types of literature available, including summaries and books, journal articles, and early stage materials. These types of literature vary in terms of the standards for the quality of information and the timeliness of the ideas presented.

### Summaries and Books

**Summaries** are major publications that provide overviews of the literature and research on topics of current interest. For example, encyclopedias such as the *Encyclopedia of Educational Research* (Alkin, 1992) are useful. Another type of summary is the handbook. Handbooks provide a comprehensive overview of research in a specific topic area. Examples of handbooks include the *Handbook of Research and Policy in Art Education* (Eisner & Day, 2004) and the *Handbook of Research on Mathematics Teaching and Learning* (Grouws, 1992). Summaries are usually written by a group of leading specialists in the field. They are a good place to turn to first learn about a topic. They can introduce you to a new problem area and help you identify important issues. Since they represent major publications, they take time to be produced and usually will not reflect the most recent research findings. Also, they tend to be expensive and therefore can be difficult to obtain unless available in a local library.

Academic libraries have extensive collections of books that authors have written on a broad range of topics. The books most useful in reviewing the literature are those that summarize research studies or report conceptual discussions. Textbooks used in classes are less useful because they typically do not contain reports of single research studies. You can identify books through online catalogs for libraries or booksellers. Books that report research studies give you an in-depth picture of the research because they are longer than other publications, such as journal articles. Although books can provide a thorough picture of one study, reviewing books limits your overall view of research because few studies are published in book form.

**FIGURE 4.1 A Classification of Types of Literature**
*Source:* Adapted from Libutti & Blandy (1995) and Creswell (2008).

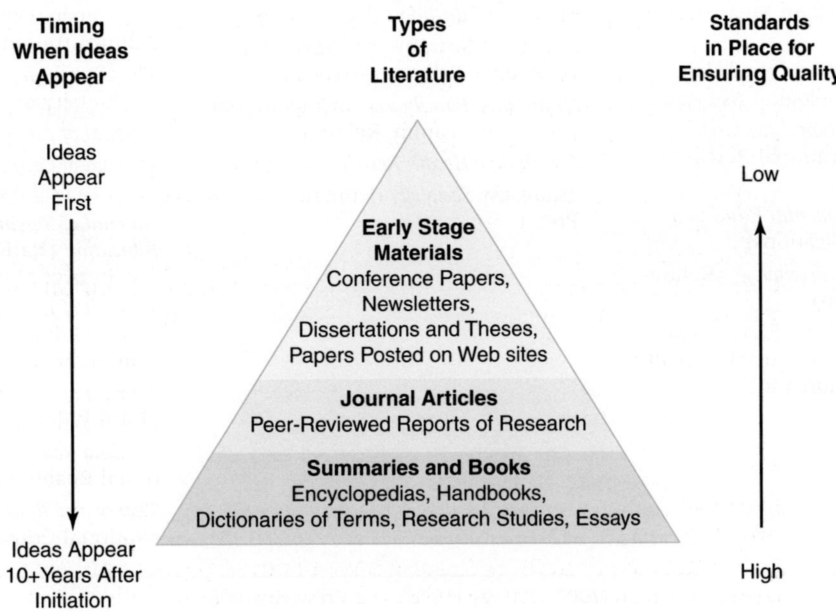

## Journal Articles

**Journal articles** that report research are the prime source for a literature review. Scholarly research journals are published at regular intervals (e.g., quarterly or monthly). The best research journals are **peer-reviewed journals**. For these journals, potential authors submit their research reports to a journal's editor in hopes that it will be acceptable for publication. Each submitted manuscript undergoes a rigorous peer-review process. This means that the editor sends copies of the manuscript to other experts in the field who critique it for the quality of the methods and its contribution to the existing knowledge. The editor uses this information to decide what is published in each issue of the journal. Therefore, articles published in scholarly research journals are generally high quality reports of recent research studies. They present the literature in the original state and present the viewpoint of the original author. Research articles also provide the details of original research better than summary and book sources.

> *Here's a Tip for Applying Research!*
>
> Look to the literature to learn about topics that interest you in your practice. Be open to reading different types of literature. Keep in mind, however, that journal articles are the best sources to use for a literature review because they are current and of high quality.

There are many scholarly journals available across all the disciplines and fields you can imagine. For example, Table 4.1 lists a sample of journals that publish research in education and the social sciences. The journals in Table 4.1 are listed based on their emphasis on the quantitative approach, the qualitative approach, or both. This classification is a rough guide because journal preferences shift over time and with appointments of new editors and editorial boards. However, a classification such as this highlights the numerous publications where you can find both quantitative and qualitative research.

**TABLE 4.1 Select Journals that Emphasize Quantitative and Qualitative Research or Both**

| Journals Emphasizing Quantitative Research | Journals Emphasizing Qualitative Research | Journals Emphasizing Both Quantitative and Qualitative Research |
|---|---|---|
| *Applied Measurement in Education* (National Council for Measurement in Education) | *Anthropology and Education Quarterly* (Council on Anthropology and Education) | *American Educational Research Journal* (American Educational Research Association) |
| *Journal of Educational Measurement* (National Council on Measurement in Education) | *International Journal of Qualitative Studies in Education* (Falmer Press) | *Educational Administration Quarterly* (University Council Educational Administration) |
| *Journal of Educational Psychology* (American Psychological Association) | *Journal of Narrative and Life History* (Lawrence Erlbaum Associates) | *The Elementary School Journal* (University of Chicago Press) |
| *Journal of Educational Research* (American Educational Research Association) | *Qualitative Family Research* (National Council on Family Relations) | *Journal of Adolescent Research* (Sage) |
| *Journal of Experimental Education* (HELDREF Publications) | *Qualitative Health Research* (Sage) | *Journal of Counseling and Development* (Counseling Association) |
| *Journal of School Psychology* (Behavioral Publications) | *Qualitative Sociology* (Human Sciences Press) | *Journal of Research in Mathematics Education* (National Council of Teachers of Mathematics) |
| *Research Quarterly for Exercise and Sport* (American Alliance for Health, Physical Education and Recreation) | | *Journal of Research in Music Education* (Music Educators National Conference) |
| | | *Journal of Research in Science Teaching* (John Wiley and Sons) |
| | | *Reading Research Quarterly* (International Reading Association) |
| | | *Theory and Research in Social Education* (National Council Social Studies) |

*Sources:* Adapted from Frankel and Wallen (2000), Preissle (1996), and Creswell (2008).

### Early Stage Materials

The final major category of literature (Figure 4.1) comprises materials at an early stage of development. Such **early stage literature** consists of studies posted to Web sites, papers presented at conferences, professional-association newsletters, drafts of studies available from authors, and student theses and dissertations. For example, electronic journals and research studies posted to Web sites and available online represent a growing source of research. This type of literature can be interesting because it is where new ideas and results may first appear. Unfortunately, because this work is typically early in its development, it also means that reviewers (e.g., journal editors or book publishers) have probably not screened the work for quality. That is, materials found on Web sites are often not monitored to ensure their quality. Therefore, although this type of literature is easily accessible, you must be cautious of the conclusions until the results appear in more rigorous outlets, such as scholarly journals.

### What Do You Think?

Suppose you want to learn about recent research on a topic of interest, such as bullying. What kind of literature might be most useful?

Now suppose you also want to get an overview of a topic that is new to you, such as the use of music therapy for young children with developmental disabilities. What kind of literature might be most useful?

### Check Your Understanding

Journal articles are the best type of literature to learn about current research on a topic. They are reviewed, represent quality publications, and report recent information.

Using a summary such as an encyclopedia or handbook is a good way to get an overview for a topic that is new to you. Summaries are written by leading specialists so they are generally high quality, but they probably will not include the most recent findings about a topic.

## What Are the Steps for Reviewing the Literature?

For practice locating and selecting literature about a topic, go to the *Activities and Applications* section under the topic "Reviewing the Literature" in MyEducationalResearchLab, located at www.myeducationlab.com. Complete the exercise "Conduct a Database Search."

Regardless of whether you are a researcher planning a study, a practitioner interested in learning about a topic, or a student working on a class assignment, there is a set of common steps that are used to search for and locate literature for a literature review. Although conducting a literature review follows no prescribed path, individuals typically go through four interrelated steps. Knowing these steps helps you read and understand the literature discussed in a research study. In addition, these steps provide you with a framework for looking for literature on a topic for your own personal use or practice. These steps are:

- Identify key terms.
- Use search strategies to locate literature.
- Select relevant documents that are of good quality.
- Take notes on the key aspects of each selected document.

We will discuss specific strategies to use for each of these steps. In addition, for each step we will briefly consider how it could be applied in a literature review conducted to learn about weapon possession and violence in middle schools.

### Step 1—Identify Key Terms Related to the Topic of the Literature Review

Today you can easily search for literature (or most anything else) from the comfort of your school, home, or work computer. Searching by computer is a fantastic tool, but it only works well if you are able to tell the search programs what it is you want it to find. Therefore, the first step to searching for literature is identifying your topic and narrowing it to a few key terms. These key terms should be one or two words or short phrases. Choose these terms carefully because they are important for initially locating literature in a library or through an online search. To identify these terms, you can use several strategies, such as:

- Pose a short, general question that you would like answered by reviewing the literature. Select the two or three words in this question that best summarize the primary topics.
- Write a preliminary "working title" for a project and select two to three keywords in the title that capture the central idea.
- Use words that authors report in the literature. You might be interested in how different students learn and read a journal article that refers to these differences as "learning styles." You can use these words as key words for this topic.

Let's suppose you are interested in learning about student violence in general and weapon possession by middle school students in particular. You might start by writing a working title for your project, "Student Violence and Weapon Use by Middle School Students." Therefore, you might consider the words *violence, weapon,* and *middle school* as key terms for this topic.

### Step 2—Use Search Strategies to Locate Literature

Having identified key terms, you can begin the search for literature. There is so much literature available that you need to develop efficient strategies for searching. Fortunately, you probably have experience searching for information on friends or finding favorite music using Google™ or other Internet search engines. You might be tempted to search for literature the same way by accessing Web sites and exploring the information available on a topic. Although this process may be convenient, recall that not all literature posted online is dependable or of high quality. Instead, you should search places that are set up specifically to help individuals identify scholarly literature on topics. These places include academic libraries and electronic databases.

***Using academic libraries for literature reviews.*** A sound approach is to begin your search in an academic library housed at a college or university. By physically searching an academic library's catalogs and stacks, you will save time because you will find comprehensive holdings not available through other sources. Although a town or city library may yield some useful literature, an academic library typically offers the largest collection of materials, especially research studies. Academic libraries typically have online catalogs of their holdings so that you can search the library materials easily to find summaries and books on your topic.

***Searching electronic databases to find research articles.*** The best sources for literature reviews consist of journal articles reported by the individuals who actually conducted the research or originated the ideas. You can find journals in the stacks at your academic library, but it would take too much time to review them all by hand. Therefore, to locate journal articles on your topic, you should search the electronic databases available. Five useful databases that offer easy retrieval of journal articles and other documents related to educational, social, and health topics are listed in Table 4.2. If you access these databases through your library, they may also indicate which documents

> *Here's a Tip for Applying Research!*
>
> If you are having trouble locating research on your topic, go to an academic library and ask for help from the Reference Librarian. They are experts at locating information and all the ones that we have met have been delighted to help students and professionals locate literature.

> *Here's a Tip for Applying Research!*
>
> When possible, access an electronic database through an academic library. This will provide you with free access to more journal articles than are available directly through the Web sites available to the general public.

TABLE 4.2 Useful Electronic Databases for Searching for Research Journal Articles

1. ***Educational Resources Information Center*** (ERIC, 1991):
   - The ERIC database consists of two parts: (1) major educational and education-related journals and (2) documents including conference papers, project and technical reports, speeches, unpublished manuscripts, and books.
   - You can search ***ERIC*** on the Internet (www.eric.ed.gov) or online through academic libraries that have purchased access.
2. ***Psychological Abstracts*** (APA, 1927–):
   - This database provides a comprehensive source of psychological literature.
   - You can search the database through ***PsycINFO*** on the Internet (www.apa.org) or online through academic libraries that have purchased access.
3. ***Sociological Abstracts*** (Sociological Abstracts, Inc., 1953–):
   - This database provides access to the world's literature in sociology and related disciplines.
   - The database is available from Cambridge Scientific Abstracts or online through academic libraries that have purchased access.
4. ***EBSCO Information Services:***
   - This service provides online access to more than 150 databases and thousands of e-journals.
   - Academic libraries purchase the services of EBSCO or individuals can purchase articles of interest through the pay-per-view feature (www.ebsco.com).
5. ***PubMed:***
   - The PubMed database is a service of the U.S. National Library of Medicine and provides access to biomedical and life science publications, including free access to research funded by the National Institutes of Health through ***PubMed Central.***
   - You can search the full ***PubMed*** database (www.pubmed.gov) and the ***PubMed Central*** database (www.pubmedcentral.nih.gov) on the Internet.

are available directly in the library. Usually you will want to search more than one database to find all relevant literature on your topic.

When you use one of the databases listed in Table 4.2, you can simply enter your key terms into the main search box. A better strategy is to use the "Advanced Search" feature to help you search for documents that meet specific criteria. Here are a few tips that we use when searching a database. You can refer to the example "Advanced Search" screenshot in Figure 4.2 to see how each of the tips was applied in a search for articles about violence and weapon possession in middle schools through the ERIC Web site (www.eric.ed.gov).

- ***Use multiple key terms, but not too many.*** Two or three broad key terms (as shown in Figure 4.2) can help you identify literature clearly related to your topic. One key word that is too general (such as "violence") can get you thousands of hits! Using too many key terms or terms that are very specific (such as "bring a knife to school") may cause you to get too few hits and miss many good documents.
- ***Use "logic" terms to combine multiple key words.*** Most database searches will let you use logic terms to combine key words in different ways. Consider the following:
  - The word "AND" means that two (or more) words must appear within a document to meet the search criteria. For example, the search in Figure 4.2 will only identify literature that includes the terms *violence* AND *middle school.*
  - The word "OR" means that at least one of the terms must appear in a document. For example, a document will satisfy the search criteria shown in Figure 4.2 if it has either the term *weapon* or *gun,* but it does not have to have both words.
  - Use quote marks to search for an exact phrase. By putting the words "middle school" in quotes, as in Figure 4.2, it requires a match to that exact phrase. This can reduce the number of extra hits that could occur for other uses of the word middle (such as an article about children in the middle of their siblings).
- ***Focus on recent literature.*** The purpose of a literature review is to document the current state of knowledge about a topic. Therefore, consider limiting your search to

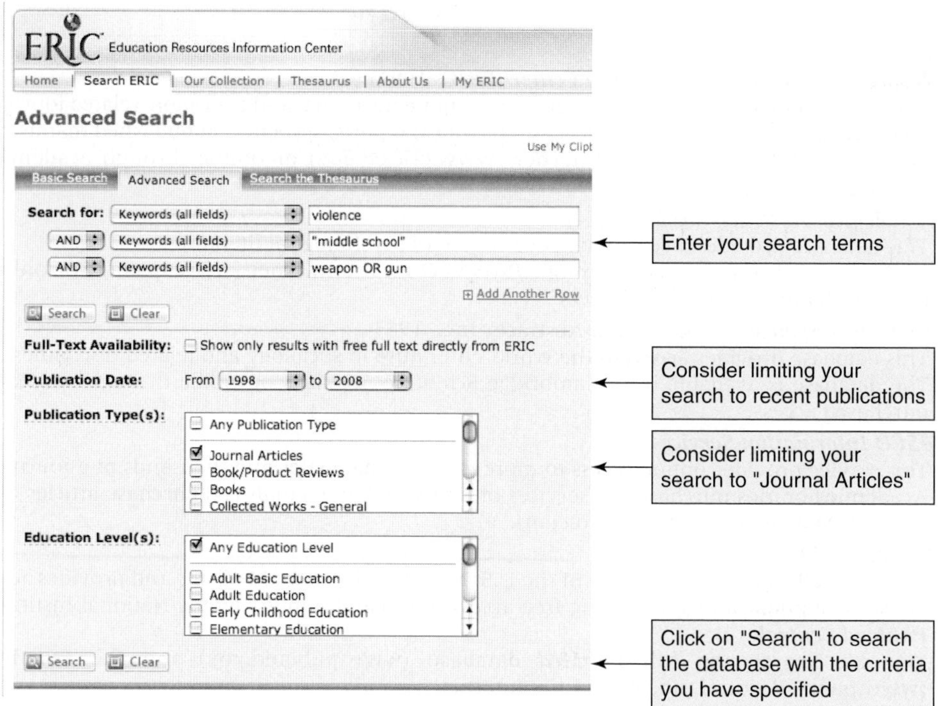


**FIGURE 4.2 Conducting an Advanced Search Using the ERIC Database**

*Source:* From Education Resources Information Center (ERIC) Web site, 2008, http://www.eric.ed.gov. Reprinted with permission from the U.S. Department of Education.

research that has been published in the past 10–15 years. If you are interested in recent research, you can limit your search to certain publication dates. The search shown in Figure 4.2 was limited to 1998—the present (2008 at the time the screen shot was made).

- ***Begin your search by looking for journal articles.*** As we stated before, journal articles represent the best sources for finding ideas that are current and of good quality. Therefore, when first starting to look for literature on a topic, consider limiting your search to journal articles (see check box under "Publication Type(s)" in Figure 4.2). Once you have examined that literature, you might return and search more broadly to include documents like conference papers and dissertations.

Once you conduct a search, the database will display a list of all documents that met your search criteria. For example, when we ran the search shown in Figure 4.2, we found six articles that satisfied the criteria. When you obtain a list of hits from a search, you can click on the name of each document to view more detailed information. An example of a detailed record for a journal article is displayed in Figure 4.3. Notice that this record includes information about the article, whether the publication was peer-reviewed by other scholars to ensure quality, and a summary abstract about the article's content, including who wrote the abstract (in this case it was provided by the author). You can review these details about each document to decide whether it is a good source for you to use in your literature review.

## What Do You Think?

Suppose you want to review the literature to learn about research related to teaching science for students with visual impairments. What key words might you use? In what database would you start searching for literature?

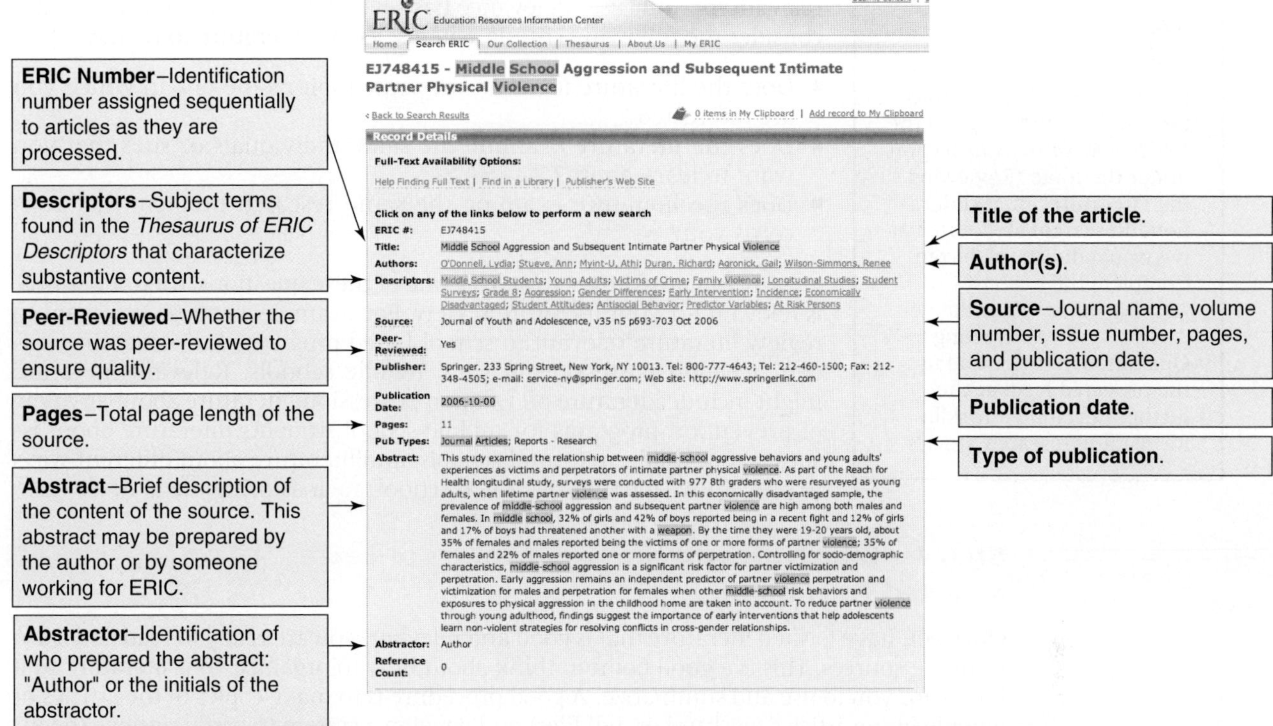


**FIGURE 4.3 Example of an ERIC Journal Article Record Detail**

*Note:* The highlighted words are the words that were used in the ERIC search. In this example, the search terms include: violence, weapon, and middle school. The search also used the criteria of journal articles and a publication date between 1998–2008.
*Note:* The format of an ERIC Journal Article Record Detail will vary according to the source from which the database is accessed. The above format is from the www.eric.ed.gov Web page.
*Source:* From Education Resources Information Center (ERIC) Web site, 2008, http://www.eric.ed.gov. Reprinted with permission from the U.S. Department of Education.

### Check Your Understanding

A good place to start thinking about a search is to write down a project title or question that you want answered. An example is: What strategies are available to teach science to students who are visually impaired? To find literature related to this question, key terms might include: *visual impairment, teaching,* and *science.* Since this is an educational topic, ERIC would be a good database to search. Another potentially good database would be PsycINFO.

## Step 3—Select Literature That Is of Good Quality and Relevant

Let's return to the major steps in conducting a literature review. The process begins with identifying keywords and locating resources. Good sources are those that follow the definition of research consisting of posing questions, collecting data, and forming results or conclusions from the data. You should include both quantitative and qualitative research studies in your review. Each form of research has advantages and provides insight for our knowledge base about any educational or social science topic. Depending on your topic, you may also find documents like school reports (such as about new programs) of interest, but you have to keep in mind that report documents are often not reviewed for quality and they may not include any research component.

You also want to select literature that is relevant for your review. You might quickly scan each source identified from your search, noting the title, the contents of the abstract, and major headings in the study. This examination helps determine if the source is

For practice writing abstracts for research studies, go to the *Building Research Skills* section under the topic "Reviewing the Literature" in MyEducationalResearchLab, located at www.myeducationlab.com. Complete the exercises "Abstracting a Quantitative Article" and "Abstracting a Qualitative Article" and use the provided feedback to further develop your skills for reading research articles.

relevant for your use. Relevance has several dimensions, and you might consider the following criteria when selecting literature to review:

- Does the literature focus on the same topic as the one in which you are interested?
- Does the literature examine the same individuals or sites that you want to learn about?
- Does the literature examine the same research problem that concerns you?

If you answer yes to at least one of these questions, then the source is relevant for your literature review. For example, suppose you want to review literature relevant to school-based programs for preventing student weapon possession in rural middle schools. Relevant literature might include literature on weapon possession, literature about any type of prevention programs for middle school students, literature about issues facing children in rural schools, and literature about different ways to prevent weapon possession at school, such as using metal detectors.

### Step 4—Take Notes on the Key Aspects of Each Selected Document

Once you have located literature that is good and relevant, you are ready to read and learn from the sources. This is a good point to think about how to organize your literature so it is easy for you to use and summarize. A good procedure is to make copies of the articles or download the articles (as .html or .pdf files) and develop a system to easily retrieve the information. Copyright laws permit the duplication of only one complete article without the permission of the publisher. Organize the literature in a way that makes sense to you, such as by author, by topic (e.g., possession of weapons, prevention programs, and effects of weapons), or by participant (e.g., middle school, high school, and college).

In addition to organizing the literature, you also have to read it! It is a good idea to record your own set of notes about each source as you read. This process yields a useful record so that you can remember the details of the studies. A systematic approach for summarizing literature is to develop an abstract for each source. An abstract is a summary of the major aspects of a study or article, conveyed in a concise way (about 350 words for this purpose). Be careful **not** to use the abstract provided at the beginning of a journal article. It is usually too brief to be useful for this purpose because of word limitations imposed by journal editors. Also, if you use it as it is written, you need to directly reference it so that you do not plagiarize the authors. You should write your own summary abstracts of articles and materials to avoid plagiarizing someone else's words and to prepare an abstract that is useful for your purposes.

Here is a good strategy for taking notes that abstract a quantitative or qualitative research study. For each source, you might identify the:

- reference to the source,
- research problem,
- purpose, research questions or hypotheses,
- data collection procedures, and
- results or findings of the study.

A complete abstract reporting these five elements for the quantitative parent involvement study from Chapter 1 is shown in Figure 4.4. Notice in this abstract that the summaries of each element are short. A complete reference to the work is listed at the top so that the abstract is fully documented. (The format for writing these references will be addressed later in this chapter.) These elements were also used to write a summary abstract for the qualitative parent role study from Chapter 1. As shown in Figure 4.5, the abstract starts with a complete reference to the article and includes a brief summary of each element.

The elements abstracted in the quantitative and qualitative examples illustrate typical information extracted from research studies. When abstracting other forms of writing (such as theoretical papers or school reports), you may include additional information in which you critique or assess the strengths and weaknesses of the document. In addition, you might also indicate the implications of each source for practice.

**FIGURE 4.4 Sample Abstract for a Quantitative Research Study**

**Reference:**

Deslandes, R., & Bertrand, R. (2005). Motivation of parent involvement in secondary-level schooling. *The Journal of Educational Research, 98*(3), 164–175.

**Research Problem:**

Parent involvement has been shown to be beneficial for high school students; it is associated with higher grades, higher aspirations, and fewer disciplinary problems. Despite its benefits, little is known about the factors that influence high school students' parents to become involved. The Hoover-Dempsey and Sandler model predicts that four psychological constructs are related to parent involvement: parents' role construction, self-efficacy, perceptions of teacher invitations to become involved, and perceptions of student invitations. No one has tested the constructs in this model for predicting parent involvement across different secondary grade levels.

**Purpose, Research Questions, or Hypotheses:**

The purpose of this quantitative correlational study was to examine whether the four psychological constructs are related to parent involvement for three secondary grade levels. The specific research question was: "What are the relative contributions of parents' role construction, self-efficacy, perceptions of teacher invitations, and perceptions of adolescent invitations to predict parent involvement at home and at school in Grades 7, 8, and 9?" (p. 166).

**Data Collection Procedure:**

The researchers distributed survey packets to parents via 45 classroom teachers at five selected public high schools in the areas around Quebec, Canada. The resulting sample included 770 parents. The parents completed questionnaires developed to measure the constructs of interest.

**Results:**

The results supported two separate models to explain parents' involvement at home and at school. In terms of parent involvement at home, the results for parents with students in Grade 7 largely supported the model, with 3 of the 4 constructs being significant predictors (perceived teacher invitations were missing). Parents' role construction was significantly related to involvement at home for Grades 7 and 9. Parents' perceptions of student invitations was a significant predictor for all grades. In terms of parent involvement at school, the authors found a greater influence of parents' role construction and that teacher invitations was a significant predictor for all grades. Implications of these results suggest the importance of working with adolescents to develop strategies to invite their parents to become involved at home and the importance of developing teacher invitations for parent involvement at school.

**FIGURE 4.5 Sample Abstract for a Qualitative Research Study**

**Reference:**

Auerbach, S. (2007). From moral supporters to struggling advocates: Reconceptualizing parent roles in education through experience of working-class families of color. *Urban Education, 42*(3), 250–283.

**Research Problem:**

The author states that students of color are underrepresented in colleges. Parents play an important role, but the current models of parent involvement do not address issues of access. Lower-SES and minority families experience constraints that influence their access to college. The voices of parents of color have not been sufficiently heard.

**Purpose and Research Questions:**

The purpose of this qualitative ethnographic study was to explore how parents of color construct their roles in pursuit of educational access for their children. The study is informed by critical approaches and existing models of parent involvement. The research questions are: "What do parents of color without college experience think and do when they want their high school-age students to go to college? What shapes their beliefs, goals, and support strategies?" (p. 251).

**Data Collection Procedure:**

Sixteen parents were purposefully selected from a program to promote college access for high school students in Los Angeles. The primary source of data was in-depth semi-structured parent interviews. Other sources included observations of program meetings, interviews with school staff and students, and school documents. The author collected data over three years.

**Findings:**

A typology of three roles constructed by the parents emerged from the qualitative data: moral supporters, ambivalent companions, and struggling advocates. These constructed roles differed along dimensions such as mode of support to children, goal of support, and the frame of reference for the support. The author concludes that current models of parent involvement need to be modified to recognize the tensions that exist between schools and some parents. She suggests that schools need a better understanding of working-class parents of color and need to broaden their ideas of what counts as parent involvement.

## How Do You Write a Literature Review?

In many cases individuals read literature simply to learn about a topic for themselves. Reading literature and taking notes is sufficient for this purpose. In other cases, however, individuals want to summarize the information to share it with others. If you plan to share the information, then you will probably want to write a literature review that summarizes what you have learned. The nature of this review will differ depending on its purpose. A student preparing a literature review for her class may write it differently from a teacher preparing a literature review report for his principal, who will write it differently from a researcher writing the literature review section of her research article. Each of these individuals, however, will organize the literature into themes, summarize the major themes, include citations, and conclude the review by relating what they learned to the purpose for conducting the review.

### Organize the Literature Into Themes

As you organize and take notes on the articles, you will begin to understand the content of your literature review. In other words, a conceptual picture will begin to emerge. This conceptual picture usually involves organizing the studies in themes, or groupings of studies, that discuss similar sub-topics within your larger topic. One good way to develop this conceptual picture is to create a visual diagram that allows you to organize the literature in your mind. This visual picture results in a map of the reviewed literature. A **literature map** is a figure or drawing that displays the research literature (e.g., research studies) on a topic. This visual picture helps you make sense of your literature. It is also useful for conveying the current picture of the literature on a topic to others, such as to colleagues at work or to an audience at a conference.

Figure 4.6 gives an example of a literature map created by a student who examined literature about the consequences of different educational accountability policies (Zhvania, 2007). At the top of the figure she lists the topic: educational accountability policies. Below the top level, she identifies two sub-topics: the elements of accountability policies and the consequences of accountability policies. Within each of these areas, she identifies themes in the literature that she read, such as effective approaches to accountability, issues of high-stakes teaching, and consequences to school, teacher, and student behavior. Under each theme, she lists the research studies that she reviewed. In the center of the map, Zhvania advances her proposed study to extend the literature by addressing the question, "What are the effects of policies that promote rewards on student performance?"

Zhvania's literature map includes several useful design features that you can include in a literature map. Here are some guidelines to follow when constructing your own literature map:

- Identify the key term for your general topic and place it at the top of the map.
- Take your reviewed sources and sort them into groups of related topical areas or "families of studies." These families represent the themes you find in the literature. Think in terms of three to five broad groupings to focus on the big ideas of the literature.
- Provide a name for each theme based on the articles in the group. Use this theme name as a label for each box. In each box, list the key sources you found in your literature search that fit that theme.
- Indicate your own work on the map. For example, if you review the literature to identify a strategy to use to promote parent involvement at your school, then indicate where your preferred strategy comes out of the literature. Draw a box near the bottom of the figure that says "our proposed program." In this box you could describe the program that you think your school should consider adopting based on your literature review. This helps others understand how the proposed program comes out of the literature.

> *Here's a Tip for Reading Research!*
>
> Literature maps can also help you understand someone else's literature review. Consider drawing your own map of the literature described within a study's literature review. This visual picture may help you see the big picture of what the author is presenting.

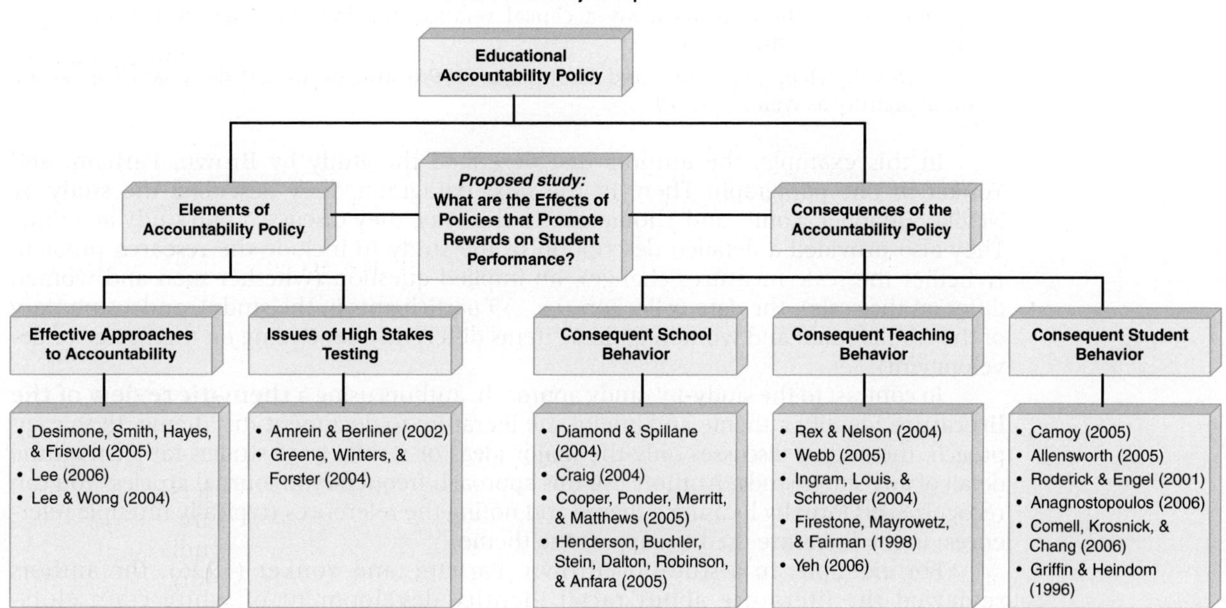


**FIGURE 4.6 A Sample Literature Map**
*Source:* Used by permission of Nino Zhvania, 2007.

## Write a Summary of the Major Themes

Once the literature is organized, then the writing process begins. But how do you report what you learned from the literature? Using your literature map as a guide, you write a summary of what you learned from the literature for each of the major themes that you identified. There are two common styles for writing this summary:

- a study-by-study literature review or
- a thematic literature review.

One approach to summarizing literature is to describe each reviewed study one at a time. In this way, a **study-by-study review of the literature** provides a detailed summary of each study grouped under a broad theme. This detailed summary of each study is usually one paragraph in length and includes the elements of an abstract shown in Figures 4.4 and 4.5. This form of literature review typically appears in journal articles that summarize the literature and in student work, such as class papers, theses, or dissertations. When presenting a study-by-study review, authors link the summaries of the studies using transitional sentences. They also organize the summaries under subheadings that reflect the major themes in the reviewed literature (i.e., the topics identified in boxes of the literature map).

The following review of the literature about cross-cultural competency and multicultural education in the journal *Review of Educational Research* by McAllister and Irvine (2000) illustrates a study-by-study review. Here, the authors discuss the research that addresses Helms's racial identity model one study at a time.

> Brown, Parham, and Yonker (1996) employed the White Racial Identity Scale to measure change in the white racial identity of thirty-five white graduate students who participated in a sixteen-week multicultural course. Eighty percent of the participants had had previous multicultural training and most of them had had experiences with people from at least two different racial backgrounds, though the nature of these experiences is not defined. The authors designed the course based on three areas—acquisition of self knowledge, cultural knowledge, and cross-cultural skills—and they used a variety of teaching methods such as lectures, talks by guest speakers, and simulations. Results indicated that at the end of the course women endorsed more items than men did in the pseudo-independence stage on

> the White Racial Identity Scale, and men endorsed more items than women did in the autonomy stage. The authors draw a causal relationship between the course and those changes found in the group.
>
> Neville, Heppner, Louie, and Thompson (1996) also examined the change in White racial identity as well . . . *(p. 8)*

In this example, the authors first described the study by Brown, Parham, and Yonker in one paragraph. Then, in the next paragraph, they described the study by Neville, Heppner, Louie, and Thompson. In this way, they discussed one study at a time. They also provided a detailed description of the study to include the research problem (whether the scale measures change), an implied question (whether men and women differ on the scale), the data collection (i.e., 35 participants in the study), and a summary of the results (men and women endorse items differently depending on their stage of development).

In contrast to the study-by-study approach, authors using a **thematic review of the literature** identify a theme and briefly cite literature to document this theme. In this approach, the author discusses only the major ideas or results from studies rather than the detail of any single study. Authors use this approach frequently in journal articles. You can recognize this form by locating a theme and noting the references (typically multiple references) to the literature used to support the theme.

For example, in a study by Brown, Parham, and Yonker (1996), the authors reviewed the literature about racial identity development of white counselors-in-training in a course on racial identity attitudes of white women and men. This passage, appearing in an early section in the study, illustrates a thematic literature review approach:

> Among other things, racial identity is a sense of group belonging based on the perception of a shared racial heritage with a specific group and, as such, it has an impact on personal feelings and attitudes concerning distinguishable racial groups (Helms, 1990; 1994; Mitchell & Dell, 1992). Researchers agree that White Americans generally are not challenged to ask themselves, "What does it mean to be White?" (Pope-Davis & Ottavi, 1994) . . . *(p. 511)*

In this case, the authors review the literature about the theme "racial identity" and briefly mention multiple references to support the theme. The authors do not discuss the details of each reference separately.

## Include Citations to the Literature

> *Here's a Tip for Applying Research!*
>
> If you read a study that has implications for your practice, be sure to record the full citation of this source. You will be able to present a more convincing argument to others if you can tell them the source from which you found evidence for an idea.

Regardless of how you write about the literature you read, you must include citations (or references) to the sources that are reviewed. You must give credit to these sources, so as to not plagiarize others' work. To **plagiarize** means to represent someone else's ideas and writings as if they were your own. It is not only rude to plagiarize someone else's work, but it is wrong to do. In many cases it can result in serious consequences such as failing a class or losing a job. Therefore, the best policy is to *always* give credit to proper sources.

We have already seen how abstracts can include a complete reference (or citation) to the information in the literature (see Figures 4.4 and 4.5). Although there are many ways that this information could be recorded, you should adopt a common style for reporting this information. **Style manuals** are available that provide a structure for citing references, as well as other aspects of writing, including labeling headings and constructing tables. Numerous style guides are available that discuss formats for writing a research report. The choice of a style guide is usually determined by some one else, such as by your teacher, your advisor, or the editor of a journal. The *Publication Manual of the American Psychological Association,* 5th edition (APA, 2001), style manual is the most popular style guide in educational and social research. We will focus on the format it recommends for reporting citations.

**FIGURE 4.7 Examples of Within-Text References in APA Style**

| Type of Reference | Within-Text Examples |
|---|---|
| Single author | Rogers (2004) compared reaction times for athletes and nonathletes in middle schools.<br>Research has examined differences between athletes and nonathletes (Rogers, 2004). |
| Two authors | Bacyn and Alon (2008) tested the effectiveness of group learning on reaction times.<br>Studies have also tested the effectiveness of group learning (Bacyn & Alon, 2008). |
| Three or more authors, first mention in a paper | The difficulty of test taking and reaction times has been examined by Smith, Paralli, John, and Langor (1994).<br>Reaction times are important considerations for test design (Clark, Peabody, & Johnson, 2002). |
| Three or more authors, subsequent mention in a paper | The study of test taking and reaction times (Clark et al., 2002) . . . |
| Multiple references (listed in alphabetical order) | Past studies of reaction times (Clark et al., 2002; Gogel, 1992; Lucky & Jones, 1994; Rogers, 2004; Smith et al., 1994) showed. . . . |
| Direct quote | Reaction times are defined as "the time to react to an unexpected stimulus" (Milz & Hass, 1999, p. 42). |

There are two approaches related to writing citations found in the APA style:

- within-text references and
- end-of-text references.

**Within-text references** are references cited in a brief format within the body of the text to provide credit to authors. APA style lists several conventions for citing these in-text references. You can find examples of with-in text references using the APA style in Figure 4.7. Key features of this style include the following elements:

- Use only the last names of authors, listed in the order they appear in the article.
- Include the year of the publication.
- If there is more than one author, write out the word "and" if the names are used as part a sentence text or use "&" if the names are referenced within parentheses.
- If a reference has three or more authors, write the names the first time and then only list the first name followed by "et al." (meaning "and others") subsequently.
- If you use a direct quote from the source, include the page number of the quote.

**End-of-text references** are the references listed at the end of a research report. Common forms are listed in Figure 4.8. In the APA style, these forms include the following features:

- They are double spaced and listed alphabetically by the last name of the first author.
- The end-of-text reference list must include **all** the references mentioned in the body of the paper and **only** the references mentioned in the body of the paper.
- The first line is left adjusted and the subsequent lines are indented. This is called a *hanging indent.*
- Only the first word in the title of a book or journal article is capitalized. You also capitalize proper nouns and the first word after a colon, if present.
- All words in the name of a journal are capitalized and italicized.

| Type of Reference | End-of-Text Examples |
|---|---|
| Journal article | Carrington, S., Templeton, E., & Papinczak, T. (2003). Adolescents with Asperger syndrome and perceptions of friendship. *Focus on Autism and Other Developmental Disabilities, 18*(4), 211–218. |
| Book | Meyer, R. C. (1996). *Stories from the heart.* Mahwah, NJ: Lawrence Erlbaum and Associates. |
| Chapter from a book | Skinner, D., Matthews, S., & Burton, L. (2005). Combining ethnography and GIS technology to examine constructions of developmental opportunities in contexts of poverty and disability. In T. S. Weisner (Ed.), *Discovering successful pathways in children's development: Mixed methods in the study of childhood and family life* (pp. 223–239). Chicago: University of Chicago Press. |
| Conference paper | Zedexk, S., & Baker, H. T. (1971, May). *Evaluation of behavioral expectation scales.* Paper presented at the meeting of the Midwestern Psychological Association, Detroit, MI. |

**FIGURE 4.8 Examples of End-of-Text References in APA Style**

## What Do You Think?

Note the following information about an article published in a journal. Using this information, write a sentence that includes a within-text reference to this article using the APA style. Next, write an end-of-text reference for this article using the APA style.

*Article Title:* Use of Songs to Promote Independence in Morning Greeting Routines for Young Children with Autism

*Author Names:* Petra Kern, Mark Wolery, and David Aldridge

*Name of Journal:* Journal of Autism and Developmental Disorders

*Volume Number:* 37

*Issue Number:* 7

*Year of Publication:* 2007

*Pages of the Article:* 1264–1271

### Check Your Understanding

One example sentence with a within-text reference is:

One study examined the use of songs to promote the independence of children with autism (Kern, Wolery, & Aldridge, 2007).

Another example sentence with a within-text reference is:

Kern, Wolery, and Aldridge (2007) examined the use of songs to promote the independence of children with autism.

Be careful to use the ampersand ("&") when a reference with multiple authors appears in parentheses, but write out the word "and" when the in-text reference is part of the sentence text.

An end-of-text reference to this study is:

Kern, P., Wolery, M., & Aldridge, D. (2007). Use of songs to promote independence in morning greeting routines for young children with autism. *Journal of Autism and Developmental Disorders, 37*(7), 1261–1271.

### Provide Your Conclusions About the Literature

Once you have summarized the literature, you have to decide how to end your literature review. First, restate the major themes. Ask yourself, "What are the major results and findings from all of the studies I have reviewed?" Your answer to this question will result in the identification of three or four themes that summarize the literature. Then, briefly summarize what you learned about each theme. The summaries should emphasize the big ideas under each major heading in the literature review and highlight what the reader needs to remember from the summary of the review.

Besides stating the major themes in a review, you should also suggest how the literature informs your work. For example, if you are a practitioner reviewing the literature to learn what is known about different available programs, then you should conclude the literature review with a statement giving your recommendation for which program should be adopted by your organization based on what you learned from the literature. If you are reviewing literature for a research study, then you might advance reasons why the current literature is deficient and why we need additional research on the topic. These reasons address ways the proposed study will add to knowledge and they justify the importance of the research problem.

## How Do You Evaluate a Literature Review?

Now that you know how individuals conduct and write literature reviews, you can more easily interpret and evaluate the literature review sections included as part of the introductions of research reports. Recall that the purpose of including a literature review is for the author to inform readers about the background for the study. Good, rigorous research is grounded in the knowledge that exists in the literature. Figure 4.9 provides criteria for assessing the quality of the *Literature Review* section based on these elements. Using this list, you can evaluate the quality of the literature review discussions in any research report.

Use the following criteria to evaluate the quality of a literature review in a research report. For each evaluation item, indicate the following ratings:

- \+ You rate the item as "high quality" for the study.
- ✓ You rate the item as "ok quality" for the study.
- − You rate the item as "low quality" for the study.

In addition to your rating, make notes about each element when you apply these criteria to an actual published study.

| **In a high-quality research report, the author . . .** | Application to a Published Study | |
|---|---|---|
| | Your Rating | Your Notes |
| 1. Reviews literature on the study's topic. | | |
| 2. Covers recent literature (last 10–15 years). | | |
| 3. Includes high quality publications, focusing primarily on journal articles (research and otherwise). | | |
| 4. May also include books and conference papers to develop an up-to-date description of the literature. | | |
| 5. Includes numerous citations that are accurately cited according to an appropriate style manual. | | |
| 6. Comprehensively shows the literature on a topic and positions the study within this literature (such as with a literature map). | | |

**FIGURE 4.9 Criteria for Evaluating a Study's Literature Review**

## Reviewing What We've Learned

- Recognize that reviewing the literature is useful for researchers conducting research and practitioners wanting to learn about topics and improve their practice.
- Look for a literature review passage and the author's use of citations to other published work when you read research reports.
- Expect to find references to the literature in the introduction of a report, but also in the method and conclusion sections.
- Assess the ways that an author uses the literature.
- Recognize that quantitative researchers use literature to direct their study's purpose and questions and qualitative researchers do not.
- Focus on research studies published in journal articles when you review literature on a topic.
- Use strategies to search for literature, including identifying key terms, searching academic libraries and electronic databases, selecting relevant literature, and making notes on the studies you select.
- Write a literature review by organizing the literature into themes, summarizing each theme, including citations for each source, and stating your conclusions about how the literature informs your situation.

## Practicing Your Skills

Practice using your skills and knowledge of the content of this chapter by answering the following questions. Use the answers found in the Appendix to evaluate your progress.

**1.** Assume that you wish to conduct a literature review on the topic of the increasing incident of teenage pregnancies in high schools today. What two or three words would you use to search for research on this topic using the ERIC database?

**2.** Consider the following excerpts from the qualitative new teacher study (Clayton, 2007) at the end of Chapter 3. Determine how the author is using the literature.

   **a.** Social constructivist theories (Cochran-Smith & Lytle, 1999; Danielewicz, 2001; Vygotsky, 1978; Wenger, 1998) guided the framing of research questions and the choices of data collection and analysis in ways that focused directly on the individual experiences of novices and their constructed positioning toward knowledge within the sociohistorical contexts of accountability reform. *(paragraph 10)*

   **b.** In spite of theoretical references in the literature to curriculum making, little exists that articulates components of curriculum making specifically drawn from empirical data based on novice teachers. Moreover, this gap is exacerbated by a lack of empirical data specifically on the processes of learning to teach through curricular enactment within the context of high-stakes accountability environments (Clayton, 2005). *(paragraph 02)*

   **c.** I employed case study methods (Merriam, 2001) to develop detailed portraits of new teacher learning while also utilizing aspects of grounded theory (Charmaz, 2000; Glaser & Strauss, 1967; Strauss & Corbin, 1990) to develop theoretical insights about the nature of curriculum making as professional development in the context of high-stakes urban reform. *(paragraph 10)*

**3.** Using Figure 4.5 as a guide, develop an abstract for the qualitative new teacher study found at the end of Chapter 3.

# CHAPTER 5 The Purpose: Identifying the Intent of a Study

*Authors start their research studies by providing information about the research problem and literature, but this information does not tell you what they intend to do. Researchers indicate their intent by writing one or more sentences that state their specific aims for conducting a study. These sentences are only a small part of a report, but they represent the most important statements for understanding any research study. In this chapter, you will learn how to identify a study's purpose, as well as the key elements that are included for specifying the purposes of quantitative and qualitative studies.*

**BY THE END OF THIS CHAPTER, YOU SHOULD BE ABLE TO:**

- Identify how authors express the intent of their studies as purpose statements, research questions, and hypotheses.
- List the elements that comprise quantitative purpose statements.
- Identify the different types of variables in a quantitative research study.
- List the elements that comprise quantitative research questions and hypotheses.
- List the elements that comprise a qualitative purpose statement.
- Identify the central phenomenon in a qualitative research study.
- List the elements that comprise qualitative research questions.

For a given research problem and literature review, there are several different studies that a researcher could do to address deficiencies in the literature. When you read a report, you do not want to know what *could* be done; you want to know what the researcher actually intended to do. Conducting research consists of the researcher asking a question, collecting information, and analyzing the information to answer the question. Researchers indicate the question they are asking by specifying the purpose for their research study. You need to locate the statements that convey a study's purpose to learn what a researcher is trying to accomplish. By learning how to interpret a study's purpose, you will be well on your way to understanding any research study.

## What Is a Study's Purpose?

Recall from Chapter 1 that researchers specify a purpose for their research as one of the essential steps of the process of research. A **purpose for research** indicates the researcher's major intent or aim for conducting the research study. Researchers often provide one purpose statement that conveys the major focus of the study, the participants in the study, and the location of the study. The purpose statement is then narrowed to research questions or predictions that the researcher plans to address. This step sets the direction and goals for a research study.

Specifying the purpose may be the most important step in the process of research. As shown in Figure 5.1, a researcher builds the purpose for a study from the identification of a research problem and the literature. By setting the aim for the

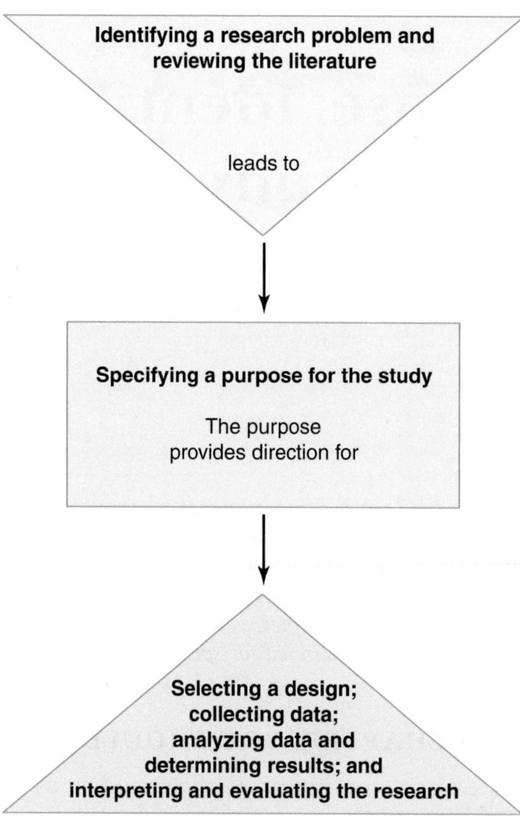


**FIGURE 5.1 The Central Role of Specifying a Purpose in the Process of Research**

study, the researcher determines the direction for all the steps that follow. Researchers select their approach or design and decide how to collect, analyze, and report their data in response to their study's purpose. Therefore, this is a very important aspect of all research studies.

## How Do You Identify a Study's Purpose?

Research reports include one or more sentences that convey the researcher's intent for conducting the study. The statements that a researcher writes to specify the purpose of a study serve as signposts in a written report similar to a thesis statement or objectives in term papers you may have written. Researchers often place this information at the end of the introduction section, either immediately following the statement of the problem or the literature review. In some reports you will find the study's purpose stated in both of these locations. In addition to placing the purpose in different locations within a report, researchers also use different styles for writing these sentences in a study: purpose statements, research questions, and hypotheses.

### Look for the Study's Purpose Statement

The **purpose statement** is a statement that advances the overall direction or focus for the study. Researchers describe the purpose of a study in one or more succinctly formed sentences. It is used both in quantitative and qualitative research and is typically found as the last sentence of the "statement of the problem" passage (discussed in Chapter 3). You can recognize purpose statements because researchers typically use a phrase such as "The purpose of this study is . . ."

A quantitative version of a purpose statement for a study addressing teacher–parent communications and student achievement follows:

> The purpose of this study is to examine the relationship between the use of Internet communication between teachers and parents and student achievement on tests in high school social studies in a Midwestern school district.

A qualitative version might be:

> The purpose of this study is to explore parent stories regarding Internet communications with teachers concerning their students in one Midwestern school district.

## Look for Research Questions

**Research questions** are questions in quantitative or qualitative research that narrow the purpose statement to specific questions that researchers seek to answer. Unlike the single statement found in a purpose statement, researchers typically state multiple research questions so that they can fully examine a topic. In some studies, the researcher provides both a purpose statement and research questions. This is a good presentation style that clarifies both the general and specific directions of a study. The research questions are typically at the end of the statement of the problem passage or immediately following the review of the literature. To locate research questions, look for passages in which authors identify the questions they are addressing. For example, a quantitative research question would be:

> Do parent–teacher Internet communications affect student performance in the classroom?

A qualitative research question is:

> What types of Internet experiences do parents have with teachers concerning the performance of their children?

## Look for Hypotheses

*Here's a Tip for Reading Research!*

The purpose statement, research questions, and hypotheses are the most important sentences in any research report. When you find these major signposts in a report, mark them with a highlighting pen or by drawing a box around them. This will help you to quickly refer back to these statements as you read the rest of the report.

**Hypotheses** are statements used only in quantitative research in which the investigator makes a prediction or a conjecture about the outcome of a relationship among attributes or characteristics. They serve to narrow the purpose statement to specific predictions. These predictions are not simply an educated guess. Researchers base their hypotheses on results from past research. If the literature includes studies where investigators have found certain results, then researchers can offer predictions as to what other investigators will find when they repeat the study with new people or at new sites based on the earlier results. You will typically find these hypotheses stated at the end of the introduction. Investigators also place them immediately after the review of the literature or in a separate section titled "Hypotheses." Usually researchers advance several hypotheses. An example of a hypothesis is:

> Students in high schools in the school district in which parents and teachers communicate through the Internet will have higher test scores than students whose parents and teachers do not communicate through the Internet.

# How Does the Purpose Differ in Quantitative and Qualitative Studies?

All research reports include statements or questions to convey a researcher's intent for conducting the study. The components of good purpose statements and research questions, however, differ for quantitative and qualitative research. Therefore it is helpful for us to consider how the purpose in quantitative research is similar to and different from qualitative research before we learn about the details that go into composing purpose statements, research questions, and hypotheses. Let's review the ideas that we introduced in Chapter 2 about specifying a purpose for quantitative and qualitative research.

### Quantitative Researchers Specify Purposes That Are Narrow and Specific

In quantitative research, the investigator writes a purpose statement, research questions, and hypotheses that tend to be specific and narrow. The investigator seeks to measure differences among two or more groups, changes over time in individuals, or how well factors are able to predict individuals' attitudes or behaviors. The purpose statement, research questions, and hypotheses are considered to be specific and narrow because the investigator identifies only a few variables to study. Quantitative researchers often test theories that predict how variables are related. They state hypotheses that convey these predictions and then test the hypotheses using statistics during data analysis. They employ a closed stance by identifying variables and selecting instruments to collect data before the study begins. Quantitative research questions and hypotheses are set at the start and do not change during the study.

### Qualitative Researchers Specify Purposes That Are Broad and General

Qualitative researchers develop purpose statements and research questions that tend to be broad and general. Qualitative researchers do not test predictions and therefore hypotheses are not appropriate in qualitative research. Instead of testing theories, the qualitative researcher seeks a deep understanding of the views of individuals or a group. The purpose statement and research questions focus on a single broad concept—a central phenomenon—instead of a set of specific variables. In qualitative research, the inquirer uses more of an open stance and often changes the phenomenon being studied, or at least allows it to emerge during the study. The research questions, therefore, may change based on what is learned from the participants.

With these general differences in mind, you are ready to learn the elements that go into developing and interpreting the purpose of quantitative and qualitative studies. Because of their differences, we will examine each approach separately, starting with quantitative research.

## How Do Researchers Specify a Quantitative Purpose?

Researchers consider five elements as they specify the purpose for a quantitative research study. These elements include:

1. ***The participants***—who will be studied (e.g., teacher aides or parents of infants).
2. ***The research site***—the location of the study (e.g., Midwestern elementary schools or the southern United States).
3. ***A theory*** (if appropriate)—the literature that directs the study (e.g., Smith's theory of career development or a theory of gender roles).
4. ***The major variables***—the specific topics or characteristics that will be measured and about which the researcher wants to learn (e.g., job satisfaction and number of years at school or gender, child age, and caregiving attitudes).
5. ***The overall intent***—what it is that the researcher wants to learn. Three common quantitative research intents include wanting to describe trends for a variable, compare groups in terms of a variable, or relate variables to other variables.

Recognizing these five elements will assist you with identifying the purpose specified for any quantitative research study. The key to understanding quantitative purpose statements, research questions, and hypotheses, however, is developing an understanding of variables. Therefore, we next consider the types of variables that are used in quantitative research.

## What Are Quantitative Variables?

A **variable** is a characteristic or attribute of an individual or an organization that researchers can measure or observe and varies among the individuals or organizations studied. Variables are the key ideas or concepts about which researchers collect information to address the purpose of their quantitative study. Some examples of variables studied in research are leadership style of administrators, achievement in science by students, and interpersonal communication skills of counselors.

***Variables are characteristics and attributes.*** Characteristics of individuals refer to personal aspects about them, such as their grade level, age, or income level. An attribute represents how an individual or individuals in an organization feel, behave, or think. For example, individuals have self-esteem, engage in smoking, or display the leadership behavior of being well organized. Researchers define their variables in a specific way so they can be measured. For example, a researcher may be interested in student achievement and defines a variable of grade point average that can be measured.

***Variables can be measured.*** Measurement means that the researcher records information from individuals to measure attributes or characteristics. Examples of measurement include having individuals answer questions on a questionnaire (e.g., a student completes questions on a survey asking about self-esteem) or observing an individual and recording scores on a checklist (e.g., a researcher watches a student playing basketball and records scores on dribbling techniques). By measuring a variable, the researcher assigns a number or score for the attribute or characteristic of interest for each individual. For example:

- Gender varies by two possible scores: female = 1 and male = 2.
- Grade point average varies along a range of scores: scores vary from 0.00 to 4.00.

***The scores for a variable are measured in categories or as continuous.*** When researchers measure variables, they expect the scores to vary (hence the name variable). When variables vary it means that different individuals may be assigned different scores. Researchers score variables in two ways. First, they might group the scores into a limited number of categories. A variable measured *in categories* is a variable that changes among a small number of groups (or categories). Here are examples of variables that vary by categories:

- Variable: smoking status. Categories: smoker = 1 and nonsmoker = 2.
- Variable: type of instruction. Categories: groups of students who experience lectures = 1, groups of students who experience discussion = 2, and groups of students who experience classroom activities = 3.

A second type of variable is based on measuring scores along a continuum. A variable measured as *continuous* is a variable measured by the researcher on a point along a continuum of scores, from low to high scores. The most straightforward example of a continuous score would be age (e.g., from 25 years old to 65 years old). Often continuous scores indicate the extent to which individuals agree or disagree with an idea or rate the level of importance of an issue. We also find continuous scores used for performance measures like test scores (0% to 100%).

## What Types of Variables Are Specified in a Quantitative Purpose?

Quantitative researchers use different types of variables in their purpose statements, research questions, and hypotheses. We can think of the different types as a "family" of variables because the types tell us how the variables are related to each other. Understanding the family of variables requires learning the definition of each type of variable and understanding its role in providing direction for a study.

This family is shown in Figure 5.2. A useful way to think about organizing these types of variables is to consider them in a cause-and-effect relationship where the variables on the left side tend to influence (or cause or predict) those on the right side (the

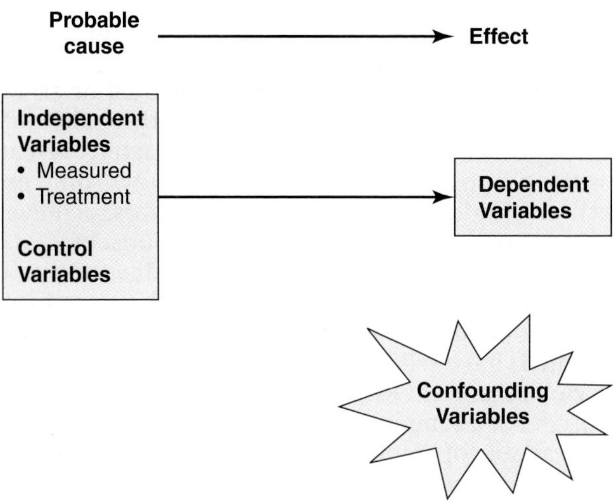


**FIGURE 5.2 The Family of Variables in Quantitative Studies**

outcomes). To identify the different roles that variables play in the family, ask yourself the following:

1. What outcomes is the study trying to explain or measure? (the dependent variables)
2. What factors are expected to influence the outcomes? (the independent variables)
3. What other variables are important to measure (or control) that might influence the outcomes? (the control variables)
4. What variables might influence the outcomes, but cannot or will not be measured in the study? (the confounding variables)

Let's consider how these different types of variables can be applied to an everyday situation. Consider a fender-bender car accident as an example. The outcome (dependent variable) was that you hit another car at a stop sign—rammed right into the back of it. You caused this fender-bender because you were talking on your cell phone (independent variable). It might have been caused by the slick pavement (control variable), but the skies were sunny and it had not rained for days. The fact that you were daydreaming might have contributed to the accident (confounding variable), but this fact would be difficult to measure after the accident. See how this works? Now take another situation in your life this last week, and list the dependent, independent, control, and confounding variables in your own cause-and-effect situation.

Now let's consider these four types of variables in a little more depth.

## Dependent Variables

Look at Figure 5.2. On the right-hand side are the dependent variables. A **dependent variable** is an attribute or characteristic that is dependent on, or influenced by, the independent variables. This is generally the variable that the researcher wants to measure or predict—the one of most interest. Examples of dependent variables from education are achievement scores on a test, the organizational climate of a junior high school, the leadership skills of principals, or the cost effectiveness of student affairs programs in colleges. Researchers often study multiple dependent variables in a study. You may find dependent variables labeled as the outcome, effect, or criterion variables. To locate dependent variables in a study, examine purpose statements, research questions, and hypotheses for outcomes that the researcher wishes to predict or explain. Ask yourself, "What is the outcome in this study?"

## Independent Variables

On the left side of Figure 5.2 are the independent variables. An **independent variable** is an attribute or characteristic that influences or affects an outcome or dependent variable. In Figure 5.2, the arrow shows how the independent variables influence the dependent variables. In research studies, you will find the independent variables called factors, treatments, predictors, or manipulated variables. Researchers measure this type of variable distinctly (or independently) from the dependent variable. They select these variables as worthy of study because they expect them to influence the outcomes. Researchers study independent variables to see what effect or influence they have on the outcome. For instance, consider this research question:

> Do students who spend more instructional time in class on math have higher math scores than students who spend less time?

From this question we find that the researcher is interested in an outcome of math scores and expects that time on math instruction will influence the scores. Therefore, we find that time on math instruction is the independent variable and math scores is the dependent variable.

There are two main types of independent variables: measured variables and treatment variables. Each serves a slightly different purpose in quantitative research.

- ***Measured Variables.*** Most independent variables represent existing characteristics or attributes of individuals that a researcher decides to measure for a study. These variables are *measured variables* because they are measured by the researcher, but he/she does not manipulate these variables. Measured variables can be scored in categories (e.g., gender) or on a range of continuous scores (e.g., attitude about distance learning).
- ***Treatment Variables.*** Another important type of independent variable is used when a researcher actually applies some kind of treatments to the participants. This variable is used in experiments. In an experiment, a researcher treats one group of participants to specific activities and withholds them from another group. (We will learn more about this approach to research in Chapter 6.) The question is whether the group that receives the activities scores differently on the dependent variable than the group without the activities. Because researchers give or withhold activities to individuals in the groups, the groups are treated or manipulated by the researcher. A treatment variable is measured in categories (received or denied activities) representing each group. Experimental researchers refer to these groups as levels (i.e., level 1, level 2).

In the following example, the treatment variable is the type of instruction used by the teacher in a middle school math classroom:

> In a study of student achievement outcomes in a math classroom, the researcher gives one group of students small-group discussions (level 1) and the other group receives traditional lecture (level 2).

In this example, the independent variable "type of instruction" is considered a treatment variable because the researcher manipulates the conditions received by the groups.

### Control Variables

A **control variable** is a type of independent variable that is not of central interest to the researcher, but that the researcher measures because it may also influence the dependent variable. A control variable is a variable that must be considered (or controlled) because the researcher cannot change it or cannot remove it from the participants. Typically control variables are personal attributes or characteristics, such as gender, ethnicity, socioeconomic status, or prior knowledge. These variables are controlled through statistical procedures (you will learn more about statistical procedures in Chapter 8). Using special statistical procedures, the researcher is able to statistically account for their effects during the data analysis.

### Confounding Variables

The final variable included in Figure 5.2 is the confounding variable. In this illustration, confounding variables are not directly in the probable cause-and-effect sequence, but are extraneous or uncontrolled variables. **Confounding variables** are attributes or characteristics that the researcher does not directly measure, but that may influence the relationship between the independent and dependent variables. These variables get in the way of research because researchers may not know that they should be measured. They may also be too difficult to measure because their effects cannot be easily separated from those of other variables. For example, for a high school student it may be impossible to separate an individual's race and prior discriminatory experiences as predictors of attitudes toward school. Thus, researchers measure the variables they can identify (e.g., race) and then explain a limitation of their results (e.g., race was so interconnected with discriminatory experiences that it could not be easily separated as an independent measure). All quantitative studies have the potential for confounding variables because it may not be possible to measure all variables that influence an outcome. Good quantitative studies reduce the threats from confounding variables by carefully selecting the independent variables that are measured and controlling the conditions of the study.

### Researchers Use Theories to Connect the Different Types of Variables

You might be wondering how researchers decide which variables will be the independent and which will be the dependent. Recall the discussion of theories from Chapter 4. Theories explain and predict the probable relationship among different variables. In other words, theories provide the reason for the arrows that connect the independent variables to the dependent variables in Figure 5.2. Therefore, in many quantitative studies, researchers use a theory from the literature that predicts the likely impact of the independent variables on the dependent variables. Because this theory deals with humans whose behavior cannot be perfectly predicted, we say that the independent variable *probably* causes the dependent variable. The idea of probable causation is that researchers attempt to establish a likely cause-and-effect relationship between variables, rather than prove the relationship.

## What Do You Think?

Consider the quantitative parent involvement study (Deslandes & Bertrand, 2005) that you read at the end of Chapter 1. Recall the following passage from this study:

> We explored how the psychological constructs, as defined in Hoover-Dempsey and Sandler's model (1995, 1997), influence the parent involvement process . . . We addressed the following research question: What are the relative contributions of parents' (a) role construction, (b) self-efficacy, (c) perception of teacher invitations, and (d) perception of adolescent invitations to predict parent involvement at home and at school? (paragraph 02)

Using this passage, can you identify the independent and dependent variables for this study? What theory guided the authors' use of these variables?

### Check Your Understanding

The outcome that these authors wanted to explain was parent involvement. Specifically, this study used two dependent variables: parent involvement at home and parent involvement at school. They measured different variables that they expected to influence this outcome. That is, the independent variables were parents' role construction, self-efficacy, perception of teacher invitations, and perception of adolescent invitations. They selected these variables based on a theory in the literature developed by Hoover-Dempsey and Sandler.

## How Do Researchers Write Quantitative Purpose Statements?

Recall that researchers write purpose statements to convey the overall intent of their study. These statements:

- usually begin with words such as "The purpose of this study . . ." or "The aim of this study. . . ." and
- include the five elements for specifying a quantitative purpose: the participants, research site, theory (if applicable), major variables, and overall intent.

Here are examples of purpose statements written for three different types of intents.

***Example 1—A Quantitative Purpose Statement to Describe Variables***
If the intent is to describe variables, the researcher writes a purpose statement such as:

> The purpose of this study is to describe (the variable) for (participants) at (the research site).

The following purpose statement is an example of this form:

> The purpose of this study is to describe attitudes about high-stakes testing for special education teachers at U.S. elementary schools.

In this example, the variable is *attitudes about high-stakes testing,* the participants are *special education teachers,* and the research site is *U.S. elementary schools.* We do not have independent and dependent variables in this example because the researcher is *not* relating or comparing two or more variables.

***Example 2—A Quantitative Purpose Statement to Relate Variables***
If the intent is to relate two or more variables, the researcher might write a purpose statement such as:

> The purpose of this study is to test (the theory) by relating (the independent variable) to (the dependent variable) for (participants) at (the research site), controlling for (the control variables).

The following purpose statement is an example of this form:

> The purpose of this study is to relate leadership style to autonomy for teachers in high schools in the northwest, controlling for gender and school size.

In this example, the independent variable is *leadership style,* the dependent variable is *autonomy,* and the control variables are *gender* and *school size.* In addition, we learn that the participants are *teachers* and the research site is *northwest high schools.* There was no theory stated.

*Here's a Tip for Applying Research!*

Good research studies *should* include clear purpose statements. Unfortunately, authors do not always make them clear. Use the models in this chapter to write a good purpose statement for any study you read. This sentence will help you clarify the intent of any study. In addition, since it will be stated in your own words, you can use it if you are writing a summary of the study for a literature review.

***Example 3—A Quantitative Purpose Statement to Compare Groups***
If the intent is to compare two or more groups in terms of an outcome variable, the researcher might write a purpose statement such as:

> The purpose of this study is to test (the theory) by comparing (group 1 of the independent variable) with (group 2 of the independent variable) in terms of (the dependent variable) for (participants) at (the research site).

The following purpose statement is an example of this form:

> The purpose of this study is to test Smarts' (1999) theory of leadership by comparing autocratic leaders with consensus-building leaders in terms of the satisfaction of teachers in New York high schools.

In this example, the researcher identifies a theory (*Smarts' theory of leadership*), one independent variable with two levels (*leadership style as autocratic or consensus-building*), one dependent variable (*satisfaction*), the participants (*teachers*), and the research site (*New York high schools*). No control variables are stated in this example.

## What Do You Think?

Using the models of good quantitative purpose statements, see if you can identify the main features of the following purpose statement.

> "The purpose of the current study was to use SAT scores and Tracey and Sedlacek's psychosocial variables to predict Asian American students' GPA and retention in the first year of college." (Ting, 2000, p. 444)

### Check Your Understanding

Let's first consider the features that are present in this purpose statement. It included the following elements:

*Theory:* A theory developed by Tracey and Sedlacek.

*Independent variables:* SAT scores and psychosocial variables.

*Dependent variables:* GPA (grade point average) and retention in the first year of college.

*Words that indicate the intent to relate variables:* The purpose of the study was to use independent variables "to predict" the dependent variables.

*Participants:* Asian American college students.

This purpose statement is missing the research site. If you read the full study, you can learn that the study took place at one Southeastern public land-grant research university. It would have been helpful if the author had specified that information in the purpose statement.

## How Do Researchers Write Quantitative Research Questions?

Researchers use the following strategies to write quantitative research questions:

- Identify the key elements of participants, research site, theory (if applicable), major variables, and question intent.
- Phrase them as questions, beginning with the words "how," "what," or "why" and ending with a question mark.
- List the variables in the order as shown in Figure 5.2: independent variables first, dependent variables second, and control variables third.

Let's examine examples of three common forms of research questions available in quantitative research: descriptive questions, relationship questions, and comparison questions.

***Example 1—Quantitative Descriptive Research Questions***

Researchers use a descriptive question when they want to describe participants' responses to a single variable or question. This single variable may be an independent, a dependent, or a control variable. A researcher might write:

> How frequently do (participants) (variable) at (the research site)?

An example of a descriptive research question might be:

> How frequently do African Americans feel isolated on college campuses?

This example identifies one variable, *feelings of isolation.* It also identifies the participants and sites (*African Americans* on *college campuses*).

***Example 2—Quantitative Relationship Research Questions***

Researchers may want to examine the relationship between two or more variables. Relationship questions seek to answer questions about the magnitude and direction of the relationship between two or more variables. These questions often relate different types of variables in a study, such as independent variables to dependent variables, or dependent variables to control variables. The most common case occurs when researchers relate the independent variable to the dependent variable. A researcher might write:

> How does (the independent variable) relate to (the dependent variable) for (participants) at (the research site)?

As applied to the relationship between isolation and ethnic identity, an example relationship research question could be:

> How do feelings of isolation relate to (or influence) the ethnic identity of African Americans in the United States?

In this example we find the researcher is relating an independent variable (*feelings of isolation*) to the dependent variable (*ethnic identity*).

***Example 3—Quantitative Comparison Research Questions***

Researchers might ask a comparison question to find out how two or more groups on an independent variable differ in terms of one or more outcome variables. In experimental studies, the researcher provides some intervention to one group and withholds it from the second group. Other studies may compare individuals based on existing groups, such as by gender. A researcher might write:

> How does (group 1 of the independent variable) compare to (group 2 of the independent variable) in terms of (the dependent variable) for (participants) at (the research site)?

An example of a research question comparing African Americans and Euro Americans is:

> How do African Americans and Euro Americans compare (or differ) in their perceptions of ethnic identity?

In this example, the researcher is comparing two racial groups so *race* is the independent variable. The dependent variable is *perceptions of ethnic identity.*

## What Do You Think?

Read the following examples of research questions taken from research studies. For each, identify the type of research question (descriptive, relationship, or comparison).

**(a)** "Do appropriate duties, inappropriate duties, self-efficacy, frequency of district and peer supervision, and perceived stress correlate with school counselors' career satisfaction?" (Baggerly & Osborn, 2006, p. 199)

**(b)** "Does technology access differ for children attending high-poverty and low-poverty schools?" (Judge, Puckett, & Bell, 2006, p. 53)

**(c)** "What are elementary school principals' perceptions of music learning outcomes as they are currently being met?" (Abril & Gault, 2006, p. 10)

### Check Your Understanding

Research question (a) is an example of a relationship research question. The words "correlate with" are equivalent to "relate to." The researchers are interested in whether numerous independent variables (appropriate duties, inappropriate duties, self-efficacy, frequency of district and peer supervision, and perceived stress) relate to one dependent variable (career satisfaction) for school counselors.

Research question (b) is an example of a comparison research question. The word "differ" provides an indication of the comparison. The researchers are interested in comparing two groups of schools (high-poverty and low-poverty) in terms of a dependent variable (technology access).

Research question (c) is an example of a descriptive research question. The researchers are interested in describing a single variable (perceptions of music learning outcomes) for elementary school principals.

## How Do Researchers Write Quantitative Hypotheses?

For practice writing hypothesis statements, go to the *Activities and Applications* section under the topic "Selecting and Defining a Research Topic" in MyEducationalResearchLab, located at www.myeducationlab.com. Complete the exercise "Writing Research Hypotheses."

Hypotheses are an alternative form for writing quantitative researcher questions that researchers use to narrow the purpose in quantitative research. Hypotheses advance a prediction about what the researcher expects to find in the study. They are used to predict how two or more variables are related. That is, a hypothesis may predict the expected changes for the groups, such as less or more favorable or no changes (e.g., no difference), or the expected relationships among variables, such as a positive relationship or no relationship. Since hypotheses are predictions involving multiple variables, researchers do not use hypotheses to describe a single variable.

There are two types of hypotheses: null hypotheses and alternative hypotheses. Researchers actually need both types in a research study, but they generally only write one or the other into their reports. Here is an example of each type.

***Example 1—Quantitative Null Hypotheses***

The null hypothesis (often indicated as $H_0$) is the most traditional form of writing a hypothesis. Null hypotheses make predictions about all possible people that researchers might study (i.e., called the general population). Null hypotheses predict that there is *no relationship* between independent and dependent variables or *no difference* between groups of an independent variable on a dependent variable. A null hypothesis might begin with the phrase "There is no difference" among groups, or "There is no relationship" between variables. The following statement illustrates how a null hypothesis can use the language "no difference."

> There is no difference between (independent variable, group 1) and (independent variable, group 2) in terms of (dependent variable) for (participants) at (the research site).

An example of a null hypothesis might be:

> There is no difference between students placed at-risk and those not-at-risk in terms of student achievement on math test scores for third-grade students.

Notice that this is a null hypothesis because it predicts "no difference." This example has one independent variable (*at-risk status*) with two levels (*placed at risk* or *not at risk*). It also identifies one dependent variable (*achievement on math test scores*).

***Example 2—Quantitative Alternative Hypotheses***

In contrast to the null hypothesis, researchers may choose to write an alternative hypothesis into their reports. Researchers use an alternative hypothesis (often indicated as $H_A$ or $H_1$) when they expect there will be a difference based on a theory or results from past research reported in the literature. They usually write an alternative hypothesis so that it predicts the direction of a change, difference, or relationship for variables in the population of people. A researcher selects a sample of people from a population and predicts that the scores will be higher, better, or changed in some way. This form for writing hypotheses is encountered in the literature more than null hypotheses.

A researcher might write an alternative hypothesis that predicts the direction when relating two variables such as:

> (the independent variable) will be (positively, negatively) related to (the dependent variable) for (participants) at (the research site).

An example of this alternative hypothesis is:

> Time spent studying will be positively related to reading test scores for athletes in rural high schools.

Note how this example predicts that the two variables (*time spent studying* and *reading test scores*) will be related and that they will be related in a certain way, namely "positively." Therefore, this is an example of an alternative hypothesis because it predicts a specific direction to the relationship for the population (*athletes in rural high schools*).

## What Do You Think?

Read the following examples of hypotheses taken from research studies. For each, identify the type of hypothesis (null or alternative) and the independent and dependent variables.

**(a)** "We hypothesized that perceived occupational barriers would be negatively predictive of career certainty . . . in a sample of African American adolescents." (Constantine et al., 2005, p. 311)

**(b)** "We hypothesized that women when compared with men would score lower in ethnocentrism, intercultural communication apprehension, prejudice, and ambiguity intolerance." (Kim & Goldstein, 2005, p. 269)

### Check Your Understanding

Hypothesis (a) is an example of an alternative hypothesis. The authors identify an independent variable (perceived occupational barriers) and dependent variable (career certainty). They predict that these two variables will be "negatively" related, thereby predicting the direction of the relationship. If the authors had written a null hypothesis, it might have been: "We hypothesized that perceived occupational barriers would not be related to career certainty."

Hypothesis (b) is also an example of an alternative hypothesis. The authors are interested in gender (women and men) as an independent variable and in several dependent variables (e.g., ethnocentrism, intercultural communication apprehension, prejudice, and ambiguity intolerance). They use an alternative hypothesis because they predict that women will score lower than men on these dependent variables. If the authors had written a null hypothesis, it might have been: "We hypothesized that there would be no difference between women and men in terms of ethnocentrism, intercultural communication apprehension, prejudice, and ambiguity intolerance."

You now have a basic understanding of the forms that researchers use to convey the purpose of their quantitative studies. The provided examples of quantitative purpose statements, research questions, and hypotheses fit the narrow and specific intents of most quantitative research. In contrast, recall that *qualitative* studies are generally conducted with a different intent in mind. Researchers conduct qualitative research to address purposes that are general and broad. Therefore, qualitative researchers write purpose statements and research questions that reflect the focus of their qualitative studies.

## How Do Researchers Specify a Qualitative Purpose?

Researchers consider four elements as they specify the purpose for a qualitative research study. These elements include:

1. ***The participants***—who will be studied (e.g., new teachers or homeless adolescents).
2. ***The research site***—the location of the study (e.g., rural schools in Nebraska or an urban Asian city).
3. ***The central phenomenon***—the one concept that will be studied and about which the researcher wants to learn (e.g., the process of adjusting to rural settings or cultural norms on the street).
4. ***The overall intent***—what it is that the researcher wants to learn. Common qualitative research intents include wanting to explore, describe, or understand.

Recognizing these four elements will assist you with identifying the purpose specified within any qualitative research study. You also need to develop an understanding of what is meant by a central phenomenon in qualitative research.

## What Is a Qualitative Central Phenomenon?

Researchers conducting qualitative research do not specify a set of variables. Instead, qualitative researchers focus their attention on a single phenomenon that is central to their inquiry. A **central phenomenon** is the concept or process explored in a qualitative research study. For example, as a concept, it could be:

- the ethnic identity of Chinese American immigrants.

As a process it might be:

- the process of negotiation by a female superintendent with her principals.

These examples illustrate the expression of the central phenomenon in a few words. They also show a focus on a single concept or a single process. This single focus is different from quantitative research that emphasizes relating two or more variables (e.g., "How do alienation and isolation relate for the female superintendent?") or comparing groups (e.g., "How do female principals and superintendents compare in their alienation?"). This comment is not to suggest that researchers may not explore comparisons or relationships in qualitative inquiry. Comparisons and relationships may emerge as the qualitative data analysis proceeds (we will discuss qualitative data analysis further in Chapter 11). The qualitative inquirer, however, begins by identifying a single idea, focus, or concept to explore before gathering data.

> For practice interpreting the purpose statement in a qualitative research report, go to the *Building Research Skills* section under the topic "Selecting and Defining a Research Topic" in MyEducationalResearchLab, located at www.myeducationlab.com. Complete the exercise "Identifying a Qualitative Purpose" and use the provided feedback to further develop your skills for reading research articles.

A picture might best express the differences between explaining variables in quantitative research and exploring a central phenomenon in qualitative research. As shown in Figure 5.3, one way to visualize this difference is by contrasting the explanation of an outcome (or dependent variable) by an independent variable (on the left of the figure) with the different image for a central phenomenon (on the right side of the figure). Rather than using cause-and-effect logic as in quantitative research, the qualitative researcher seeks to explore and understand one single phenomenon. To understand a single phenomenon requires the researcher to consider the multiple external forces that shape this phenomenon. At the beginning of a study, the qualitative researcher cannot predict the nature of external forces (i.e., Which ones will be important? How will they exercise influence?). The arrows about forces shaping the central phenomenon are multidirectional. The qualitative researcher wants to understand this phenomenon in all its complexity instead of limiting the view to a set of predetermined variables.

**FIGURE 5.3 Comparing How Researchers Explain or Predict Variables Versus How They Explore or Understand a Central Phenomenon**

**Quantitative Research**

Explaining or Predicting Variables:

$X \longrightarrow Y$

The independent variable ($X$) influences the dependent variable ($Y$).

**Qualitative Research**

Exploring or Understanding a Central Phenomenon:

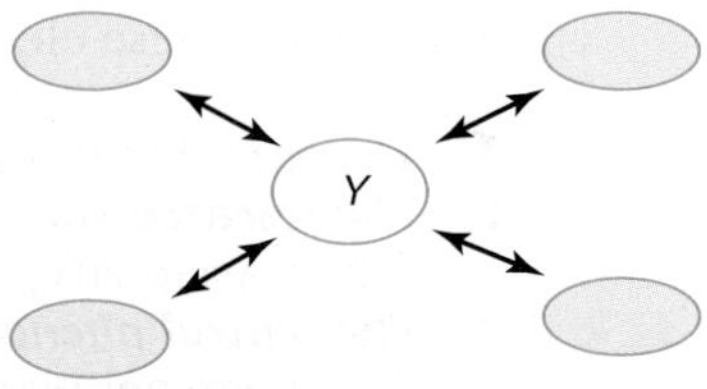


In-depth understanding of the central phenomenon $Y$; external forces shape and are shaped by $Y$.

## How Do Researchers Write Qualitative Purpose Statements?

Recall that researchers write purpose statements to convey the overall intent of their study. These statements:

- usually begin with words such as "The purpose of this study . . . " or "The aim of this study . . . ." and
- should include the four elements for specifying a qualitative purpose: the participants, research site, central phenomenon, and overall intent.

Here is an example of a purpose statement written for a qualitative study.

***Example 1—A Qualitative Purpose Statement***
Researchers indicate the intent of their qualitative studies with purpose statements such as:

> The purpose of this qualitative study is to (explore/discover/understand/describe) (the central phenomenon) for (the participants) at (the research site).

An example for a study about Internet classroom learning is:

> The purpose of this qualitative study is to describe classroom learning using the Internet for five high-school students participating in a sign language class.

Notice that this statement identifies the study as a "qualitative" study. It also identifies one central phenomenon that the researcher wants to describe: classroom learning using the Internet. This statement also indicates that the participants are five high-school students and that the research takes place in a sign language class in a high school.

### What Do You Think?

Using the characteristics of good qualitative purpose statements, see if you can identify the main features of the following purpose statement.

> "The purpose of this study was to understand the processes a person experiences in creating a leadership identity." *(Komives et al., 2005, p. 594)*

### Check Your Understanding

Let's first consider the features that are present in this purpose statement. It included the following elements:

> *Central phenomenon:* Creating a leadership identity (a process).
> *Words that indicate the intent to explore:* The purpose of the study was to "understand" this process.

This purpose statement is missing a clear identification of the participants and the research site. If you read the full study, you can learn that the study took place at one large mid-Atlantic research university. The participants included undergraduate students from this university. The purpose statement also did not identify that the study is qualitative. Putting these elements together, the authors could have written their purpose statement as:

> The purpose of this qualitative study was to understand the processes a person experiences in creating a leadership identity for undergraduate students at a large mid-Atlantic research university.

## How Do Researchers Write Qualitative Research Questions?

Research questions in qualitative research focus the purpose of a study into questions. Qualitative research questions are open-ended, general questions that the researcher would like answered by conducting the study. When writing good qualitative research questions, researchers:

- Pose only a few, general questions. Using only a few questions places emphasis on learning from participants, rather than learning what the researcher seeks to know.
- Identify the key elements of participants, research site, central phenomenon, and question intent.
- Phrase them as questions, beginning with the words "how" or "what."
- Use neutral, exploratory language and refrain from conveying an expected direction.
- Are open to questions emerging or changing to reflect the participants' views of the central phenomenon and the researcher's growing understanding of it.

Let's examine two types of research questions used in qualitative research: the central research question and subquestions.

*Example 1—A Central Research Question in Qualitative Research*
The **central research question** is the overarching question that the researcher explores in a qualitative research study. The central research question is the most general question that the researcher can ask. The intent of this approach is to open up the research for participants to provide their perspectives and not to narrow the study to the researcher's perspective. The researcher states this question at the end of the introduction using neutral and nondirectional language. The central research question is usually a brief and very general question that specifies the central phenomenon, such as:

> What is (the central phenomenon) for (the participants) at (the research site)?

The following example illustrates a central research question for a study of creativity:

> What is creativity for five students at Roosevelt High School?

Note how this question begins with the word "what" to signal the need for an exploration. This question also identifies the central phenomenon of creativity. The study participants are five students and the study takes place at a school that is referred to as Roosevelt High School.

A good qualitative central research question should be written so that it provides some direction for the study but does not leave the direction wide open. When you read a central question that is too open, you do not have enough information to understand the project. Alternatively, when the central question is too specific or too laden with assumptions, it does not offer enough latitude for the researcher to understand participants' views. Narrow research questions may indicate that the researcher was not sufficiently open to learning about the central phenomenon from participants. In this case, the researcher may have unintentionally shaped the views of participants in one direction or another.

In Table 5.1, several specific examples illustrate central research questions stated in terms that are too general, too focused, or too laden with assumptions. First a poor exaple is given, followed by a better, improved version. In the first example, the author states a central question so broadly that readers and audiences do not understand the central phenomenon under study. This situation often occurs when qualitative researchers take too literally the concept of open-ended questions to mean anything goes.

In the second example of Table 5.1, the author focuses the question too much. By asking about specific activities on a committee, the researcher may miss the larger process at work in the committee and lose important information for the research report. In the final example, the researcher starts with the assumption that the committee is "alienated" from the school board. Although this may be the case, the specification of a direction may severely limit what the inquirer can learn from a situation. To open the situation by asking about the "role of the school board" includes the possibility that the role may be alienating, supportive, or may serve some combination of roles. Note, however, that some qualitative researchers choose to use an advocacy approach for their studies and bring to the research assumptions about power imbalances and alienation of groups in society based on issues such as gender, race, disability, sexual orientation, or class.

**TABLE 5.1 Problems Typically Found in Central Research Questions in Qualitative Research**

| Problem | Poor Example of a Central Research Question | Better Example of a Central Research Question |
|---|---|---|
| Question is too general | What is going on here? | What is the process being used by the curriculum committee at the elementary school? |
| Question is too focused | How did the committee make a decision about the curriculum for a new foreign language program? | What is the process of the curriculum committee in making decisions about the curriculum? |
| Question is too laden with assumptions | How did the curriculum committee address its alienation from the school board? | What was the role of the school board in the curriculum committee's deliberations? |

***Example 2—Subquestions in Qualitative Research***

In addition to a central question, qualitative researchers pose subquestions. These subquestions refine the central question into subquestions to be addressed in the research. These subquestions contain many of the same elements as central questions (i.e., open ended, emerging, neutral in language, and few in number), but they provide greater specificity about the study's direction. Researchers often write subquestions such as:

> What is (the subquestion issue) for (participants—optional information) at (the research site—optional information).

If the researcher states the participants and research site in the central question or purpose statement, then they will not repeat this information in the subquestions. The issue subquestions follow immediately after the central question as follows:

> What is self-esteem for high school students? (central question)
> What is self-esteem as seen through friends? (subquestion)
> What is self-esteem for the student's family? (subquestion)
> What is self-esteem as experienced in extracurricular activities in school? (subquestion)

As these examples illustrate, the central phenomenon, self-esteem, is divided into three topical areas (or issues) that the researcher explores.

## What Do You Think?

Read the following passage from the qualitative parent role study (Auerbach, 2007) from Chapter 1. What is the study's central phenomenon? What types of research questions did the author pose?

> "This study draws on 3 years of ethnographic data to illustrate one of many possible alternative typologies of parent roles in the pursuit of educational access. What do parents of color without college experience think and do when they want their high school-age students to go to college? What shapes their beliefs, goals, and support strategies?" (paragraph 03)

### Check Your Understanding

The first sentence in this passage is a purpose statement that provides the general intent of the study. The purpose statement clearly identifies the central phenomenon (parent roles in the pursuit of educational access) and the use of a qualitative ethnographic approach. This statement, however, did not clearly identify the participants or research site. The participants—parents of color—are identified in the first research question. The two research questions are subquestions that serve to focus the purpose to specific issues that will be addressed in the study (what parents think and do and what shapes these beliefs and strategies). They are open-ended, exploratory questions that indicate that the author is open to learning from participants.

## How Do You Evaluate a Study's Purpose?

You have now learned the important elements that go into specifying a purpose for quantitative and qualitative research studies. When you examine a research study, you want to first identify each of these elements to understand what the study is about. If a study's purpose is not clear, then you can only guess what the researcher was trying to do. Figure 5.4 also provides a series of criteria you can use to evaluate the purpose in a quantitative and qualitative study. As you apply these criteria to research studies, they will assist you in considering whether the purpose is specified in a rigorous way that is consistent with the quantitative or qualitative approach. For a given study, you can rate the elements of the study's purpose based on how well the author described and justified the information. Few studies will satisfy every criterion. For example, a quantitative study may include research questions or hypotheses, but usually not both.

FIGURE 5.4 Criteria for Evaluating the Quality of a Study's Purpose

Use the following criteria to evaluate the quality of the purpose in a research report. For each evaluation item, indicate the following ratings:

+ You rate the item as "high quality" for the study.
✓ You rate the item as "ok quality" for the study.
– You rate the item as "low quality" for the study.

In addition to your rating, make notes about each element when you apply these criteria to an actual published study.

| In a high-quality research report, the author writes a purpose statement that . . . | Application to a Published Study | |
|---|---|---|
| | Your Rating | Your Notes |
| 1. Uses words such as "purpose" or "aim" to signal the reader. | | |
| 2. Is concise and clearly states the intent of the study. | | |
| 3. Consists of relationships among variables (quantitative study) or specifies a central phenomenon (qualitative study). | | |
| 4. Identifies the participants and sites in a general way. | | |
| 5. May mention a theory if one is being used to direct or inform the study. | | |
| **In a high-quality research report, the author writes research questions that . . .** | | |
| 6. Use words such as "What," "How," or "Why" (quantitative study) and "What" and "How" (qualitative study). | | |
| 7. Consist of relationships among variables (quantitative study) or specify a central phenomenon or subquestions (qualitative study). | | |
| 8. Indicate a relationship among variables (quantitative study) or use neutral, exploratory language (qualitative study). | | |
| 9. Are set at the start of the study by the researcher (quantitative study) or allowed to emerge and change during the study (qualitative study). | | |
| **In a high-quality research report, the author writes hypotheses that . . .** | | |
| 10. Predict how two or more variables are related (quantitative study only). | | |
| 11. Make predictions based on past results reported in the literature (quantitative study only). | | |

## Reviewing What We've Learned

- Identify purpose statements, research questions, and hypotheses as signals of the major direction or intent of a study.
- Look to the purpose statement to learn the author's overall direction or objective of the study.
- Expect the author to narrow or focus the purpose of the study with research questions or hypotheses.
- When reading a quantitative purpose, identify the dependent, independent, and control variables.
- Look for research questions or predictions in the form of hypotheses in addition to the quantitative purpose statement.
- When reading a qualitative purpose, identify the central phenomenon of the study.
- Look for the central research question as the most general question that the researcher can ask in a qualitative study.
- Note if the central question has been divided into subquestions.
- Assess whether the researchers provided clear statements of their purpose.

## Practicing Your Skills

At this time, read carefully the "quantitative goal orientation study" starting on p. 154 at the end of this chapter. As you read this article, pay close attention to how the researchers specify the purpose for the study (paragraphs 09-10).

Once you have finished reading this study, assess your knowledge of the content of this chapter by answering the following questions about the practice studies. Use the answers found in the Appendix to evaluate your progress.

First consider the quantitative goal orientation study (at the end of this chapter).

1. Identify the main variables used in this study. That is, what are the (a) independent and (b) dependent variables? (c) Is the independent variable a measured variable or a treatment variable? (d) What might be an example of a confounding variable?
2. Using the examples provided in this chapter, write a good purpose statement for this study. How does your purpose statement compare to the statements that the authors provided in paragraphs 09 and 16? Did the authors include the elements of a good purpose statement?
3. Using the examples provided in this chapter, write (a) a comparison research question, (b) a null hypothesis, and (c) an alternative hypothesis that fits this study.

Now consider the qualitative new teacher study (at the end of Chapter 3).

4. Identify the central phenomenon explored in this study.
5. Using the examples provided in this chapter, write a good purpose statement for this study. How does your purpose statement compare to the one that the author wrote into the study (see paragraph 03)? Did the author include the elements of a good purpose statement?
6. Using the examples provided in this chapter, write (a) a central research question and (b) a subquestion that fit this study.

# The Quantitative Goal Orientation Study

Let's examine another published research study to apply what you have learned about reading research articles and to evaluate how researchers specify the purpose for their research (by completing the *Practicing Your Skills* questions listed on the previous page). We will refer to it as the quantitative goal orientation study. It is:

> Self-Brown, S. R., & Mathews, S., II. (2003). Effects of classroom structure on student achievement goal orientation. *Journal of Education Research, 97*(2), 106–111.

As you read this article, note the marginal annotations that signal the major sections of a research report, the steps of the research process, and the major characteristics of quantitative research. In addition, use the following walk-through to help you understand how the steps of the research process are described within the major sections of the report.

## The Introduction Section

- Identifying a research problem (paragraphs 01–09)
- Reviewing the literature (paragraphs 02–09)
- Specifying the purpose (paragraphs 09–10)

The authors of the quantitative goal orientation study (Self-Brown & Mathews, 2003) introduce their topic of student goal orientation. They then immediately identify a research-based problem (paragraph 01). They note that there has been a "paucity of research" about the effect of classroom structure on students' goal orientation. As they review the relevant literature and past research related to this problem in paragraphs 02–09, they also note a practical problem that students who adopt a performance goal orientation tend to develop maladaptive strategies, such as avoiding difficult tasks and having little interest in academic activities. Therefore, the authors suggest that there is an important problem that calls for explaining the effect of variables like classroom structure on students learning and performance goal orientations. The authors conclude their introduction by stating their general purpose (paragraph 09) and three specific hypotheses for how they expect different classroom structures to affect students' goal orientations (paragraph 10). These statements are narrow in focus and identify the key variables of interest in the study (e.g., classroom structure, learning goals, and performance goals).

## The Method Section

- Selecting a design and collecting data (paragraphs 11–24)

The authors describe their overall design and methods for collecting data to address their stated purpose. They first describe their participants (71 students in two fifth-grade classes and one fourth-grade class) in paragraph 11. They also restated their study's purpose and identified their major independent and dependent variables in paragraph 16. This study uses a quasi-experiment design (we will learn more about these in Chapter 6) to test whether different classroom structures affect students' goal setting. Each class was randomly assigned to a different classroom structure by the researchers: token economy, contingency contract, or control. The researchers manipulated the materials that the children received in the different classes. The authors describe in detail the materials and procedures that students experienced in each classroom and how the researchers collected their data (see paragraphs 12–15 and 17–24). They collected a set of quantitative data based on counting the number of performance and learning goals set by each child.

## The Results Section

- Analyzing the data and determining results (paragraphs 16 and 25–27)

The authors mention their data analysis procedures in paragraph 16. They present their results in paragraphs 25–27 and in two tables. They provide descriptive information about two variables: learning goals and performance goals. This information includes the average value (called the mean, *M*) for each variable for each group in Table 1. The rest of the results used statistical procedures to determine whether significant differences existed among the three groups in terms of the dependent variables. The researchers found that there was a difference among the three groups in terms of the learning and performance goals set. Specifically, the token economy group set significantly more performance goals than learning goals and the contingency contract group set significantly more learning goals than performance goals. They also found that there was no significant difference in the goals set by the control group.

## The Conclusion Section

- Interpreting the research (paragraphs 28–33)

The authors concluded their report with a discussion of what they learned. They first summarized the major results in paragraph 28. They next compared the results to their predictions and to past research (paragraphs 28–31). They also described some important limitations of the study, such as not being able to control for differences among the classroom teachers (paragraph 32). This means that the results must be interpreted with caution as there may be confounding variables related to the classrooms that account for the differences among the groups. The authors also suggested future research based on the results (paragraph 32). Finally, they discussed possible implications of their results for encouraging positive effects for elementary students' learning (paragraph 33).

# Effects of Classroom Structure on Student Achievement Goal Orientation

**SHANNON R. SELF-BROWN**
**SAMUEL MATHEWS, II**
**University of West Florida**

ABSTRACT **The authors assessed how classroom structure influenced student achievement goal orientation for mathematics. Three elementary school classes were assigned randomly to 1 classroom structure condition: token economy, contingency contract, or control. Students in each condition were required to set individual achievement goals on a weekly basis. The authors assessed differences in goal orientation by comparing the number of learning vs. performance goals that students set within and across classroom structure conditions. Results indicated that students in the contingency-contract condition set significantly more learning goals than did students in other classroom structure conditions. No significant differences were found for performance goals across classroom structure conditions. Within classroom structure conditions, students in the contingency-contract group set significantly more learning goals than performance goals, whereas students in the token-economy condition set significantly more performance goals than learning goals.**

**Key words: classroom structure, goal orientation, mathematics**

Introduction Section | Identifying a research problem

01 Over the last 35 years, considerable research and writings have addressed the relationship between the classroom learning environment and student goal orientation. However, only a paucity of research has focused on establishing a link between the classroom evaluation structure, differences in students' goal orientation, and classroom strategies for the creation of specific goal orientations within the classroom (Ames, 1992c). In this study, we addressed those issues.

02 Students' goal orientation has been linked to contrasting patterns that students exhibit when they attend to, interpret, and respond to academic tasks (Dweck & Leggett, 1988). One leading model of goal orientation focuses on two goal orientations—performance goals and learning goals. According to the model, students who set performance goals are focused on demonstrating their abilities to outside observers such as teachers, whereas students who set learning goals seek to increase their competence regardless of the presence of outside observers (Kaplan & Migdley, 1997). Researchers have found consistent patterns of behavior that are related directly to the types of goals that students establish (Dweck, 1986; Nichols, 1984; Schunk, 1990).

Reviewing the literature

A deficiency in the knowledge

03 Generally, researchers have concluded that a negative relationship exists between performance goals and productive achievement behaviors (Greene & Miller, 1996; Zimmerman & Martinez-Pons, 1990). Adoption of a performance goal orientation means that ability is evidenced when students do better than others, surpass normative-based standards, or achieve success with little effort (Ames, 1984; Covington, 1984). Consequently, those students often avoid more difficult tasks and exhibit little intrinsic interest in academic activities (Ames, 1992c; Dweck, 1986; Nicholls, 1984). Students with a performance goal orientation can become vulnerable to helplessness, especially when they perform poorly on academic tasks. That result occurs because failure implies that students have low ability and that the amount and quality of effort expended on tasks is irrelevant to the outcome (Ames, 1992c).

A problem that calls for explanation

04 In contrast, researchers have consistently found evidence for a positive relationship between learning goals and productive achievement behaviors (Ames & Archer, 1988; Greene & Miller; 1996; Meece, Blumenfeld, & Hoyle, 1988). Students who are focused on learning goals typically prefer challenging activities (Ames & Archer, 1988; Elliot & Dweck, 1988), persist at difficult tasks (Elliot & Dweck; Schunk, 1996), and report high levels of interest and task involvement (Harackiewicz, Barron, & Elliot, 1998; Harackiewicz, Barron, Tauer, Carter, & Elliot, 2000). Those students engage in a mastery-oriented belief system for which effort and outcome covary (Ames, 1992a). For students who are focused on learning goals, failure does not represent a personal deficiency but implies that greater effort or new strategies are required. Such persons will increase their efforts in the face of difficult challenges and seek opportunities that promote learning (Heyman & Dweck, 1992). Overall, researchers have concluded that a learning-goal orientation is associated with more adaptive patterns of behavior, cognition, and affect than is a performance-goal orientation

*Address correspondence to Shannon R. Self-Brown, 1714 College Drive, Baton Rouge, LA 70808. (E-mail: sselfb1@lsu.edu)*

The literature plays a major role

(Ames & Archer, 1988; Dweck & Leggett, 1988; Nicholls, Patashnick, & Nolen, 1985).

05 In several empirical studies, researchers have established a relationship between the salience of certain goal orientations and changes in individual behavior (Ames, 1984; Elliot & Dweck, 1988; Heyman & Dweck, 1992; Schunk, 1996). Previous laboratory studies have created learning and performance goal conditions by manipulating the instructions provided to children regarding the tasks at hand (Ames, 1984; Elliot & Dweck, 1988). Results from those studies indicate that children who participated in performance goal conditions, in which instructions made salient the external evaluation of skills and/or competitive goals, most often attributed their performance on tasks to ability. Those children also exhibited reactions that were characteristic of a helpless orientation, giving up easily and avoiding challenging tasks. In contrast, children exposed to learning-goal conditions, for which instructions focused on improving individual performance and further developing skills, typically attributed their performance to effort. Those children demonstrated mastery-oriented responses toward tasks by interpreting failures as opportunities to acquire information about how to alter their responses in order to increase their competence.

06 Schunk (1996) conducted a study in a classroom setting to investigate the influence of achievement goal orientation on the acquisition of fractions (Schunk, 1996). Similar to the laboratory studies, learning and performance goal conditions were established through a distinction in teacher instructions. Results indicated that students in the learning-goal condition had higher motivation and achievement outcomes than did students in the performance-goal condition. The results of that study suggested that varying goal instruction within the classroom can influence students' goal perceptions and achievement-related behavior on academic tasks.

07 Given that achievement goal orientation is an important predictor of student outcomes in educational settings, researchers must attend to the classroom environment variables that are necessary so that children orient toward a learning-goal orientation versus a performance-goal orientation (Church, Elliot, & Gable, 2001). Researchers have suggested that such variables as the instructional and management practices that teachers use can influence the type of achievement goals that students set (Ames & Ames, 1981; Kaplan & Maehr, 1999; Meece, 1991). One major element of instructional and management practices within a classroom is the structure of classroom evaluation that teachers use in their daily practices. A focus on the type of evaluation, that is, striving for personal improvement or performing to attain a teacher's goal for external reward may be related to students' goal orientation (Ames, 1992c).

08 Typical evaluation in elementary classrooms compares students against a normative standard, such as that required to pass a course or to receive a reward within a token economy system (Brophy, 1983). Token economy systems provide students with tangible reinforcers and external incentives for meeting normative standards. Although token economy programs have received empirical support for improving student behavior and academic responding in a variety of school subjects, this classroom structure can have paradoxical and detrimental effects when applied with no regard for the varying degrees of students' capabilities (Lepper & Hodell, 1989). For instance, a student who has a learning disability in mathematics will not be motivated by the same amount of tokens to complete mathematics assignments as other students in the same classroom who have average abilities in this subject. In addition, the type of evaluative structure that stems from a token economy tends to increase the perceived importance of ability and public performance in the classroom, which makes performance-goal orientation salient to students (Ames, 1992c).

The literature specifies the direction of the qunatitative study

09 To promote a learning-goal orientation, Ames (1992c) suggested a type of classroom structure in which student evaluation is based on personal improvement and progress toward individual goals. The use of contingency contracts as an evaluative tool likely would place emphasis on these variables. Contingency contracting creates an agreement for learning and performing between a student and teacher. Success is based solely on each student's individual performance, according to the goal that he or she sets (Piggott & Heggie, 1986). Contracting allows each student to consider his or her unique needs and competencies when setting goals and places responsibility for learning and performing on the student (Kurvnick, 1993). The use of contingency contracting has been an effective intervention for improving students' academic behavior in a variety of academic subjects (Murphy, 1988). It encourages students to become active participants in their learning with a focus on effortful strategies and a pattern of motivational processes that are associated with adaptive and desirable achievement behaviors (Ames, 1992c). One question that remains, however, is whether an intervention such as contingency contracting will lead to an increase in learning goals relative to performance goals. In this study, we addressed that question.

10 We manipulated classroom structures to assess the effects on student goal orientation. Each intact classroom was assigned randomly to either a token-economy classroom structure, contingency-contract classroom structure, or a control classroom structure. We assessed student goal orientation by comparing the number of learning and performance goals that students set according to the classroom-structure condition. On the basis of previous research, we hypothesized that the type of classroom structure would be linked directly to the achievement goals that students set. Our prediction was as follows: (a) The token-economy classroom structure would be related positively to student performance-goal orientation, (b) the contingency contract classroom structure would be related positively to student learning-goal orientation, and (c) the control classroom structure would be unrelated to student goal orientation.

Specifying a purpose for the research

The quantitative purpose statement and research questions are narrow and specific.

The quantitative purpose statement and research questions call for observable and measurable data.

## Method

Method Section

Quantitative researchers include a large number of participants

*Participants*

11 Students from three classrooms at a local elementary school participated in this study. Participants included 2 fifth-grade classes and 1 fourth-grade class. Each of the three intact classrooms was randomly assigned to one of the three classroom evaluation structure conditions. Twenty-five 5th-grade students were assigned to the token economy condition, 18 fourth-grade students to the contingency contract condition, and 28 fifth-grade students to the control condition.

Selecting a research design and collecting data

*Materials*

12 Materials varied according to the classroom evaluation structure condition. The conditions are described in the following paragraphs.

13 *Token economy.* Students in this condition were given a contract that (a) described explicitly how tokens were earned and distributed and (b) listed the back-up reinforcers for which tokens could be exchanged. Students received a contract folder so that the contract could be kept at their desk at all times. Students also received a goals chart that was divided into two sections: token economy goals and individual goals. The token economy goals section listed the student behaviors that could earn tokens and the amount of tokens that each behavior was worth. The individual goals section allowed students to list weekly goals and long-term goals for mathematics. Other materials used for this condition included tokens, which were in the form of play dollars, and back-up reinforcers such as candy, pens, keychains, and computer time cards.

14 *Contingency contract.* Students in this condition were given a contingency contract that described the weekly process of meeting with the researcher to set and discuss mathematics goals. Students received a contract folder so that the contract could be kept at their desk at all times. Participants also received a goals chart in which they listed weekly and long-term goals for mathematics. Gold star stickers on the goals chart signified when a goal was met.

15 *Control.* Students in this condition received a goals chart identical to the one described in the contingency contract condition. No other materials were used in this condition.

*Design*

16 In the analysis in this study, we examined the effect of classroom evaluation structure on students' achievement goals. The independent variable in the analysis was classroom structure, which consisted of three levels: token economy, contingency contract, and control. The dependent variable was goal type (performance or learning goals) that students set for mathematics. We used a two-way analysis of variance (ANOVA) to analyze the data.

Quantitative researchers use research designs to plan their studies

*Procedure*

17 Each of three intact classrooms was assigned randomly to one of three classroom evaluation structure conditions: token economy, contingency contract, or control. We applied those classroom evaluation structure conditions to mathematics. The mathematics instruction in each classroom was on grade level. Throughout the study, teachers in the participating classrooms continued to evaluate their students with a traditional grading system that included graded evaluation of mathematics classwork, homework, and weekly tests.

Quantitative researchers manipulate the conditions experienced by participants

18 Student participants in each classroom structure condition completed a mathematics goal chart each week during a one-on-one meeting with the first author. The author assessed goals by defining them as performance goals or learning goals, according to Dweck's (1986) definitions. Further procedures were specific to the classroom structure condition. The treatments are described in the following paragraphs.

19 *Token economy.* The first author gave a contract to the students, which she discussed individually with each of them. When the student demonstrated an understanding of the terms of the contract, the student and author signed the contract. Reinforcement procedures were written in the contract and explained verbally by the author, as follows:

> For the next six weeks you can earn school dollars for completing your math assignments and/or for making A's or B's on math assignments. For each assignment you complete, you will earn two school dollars. For every A or B you make on a math assignment, your will earn four school dollars. At the end of the five weeks, if you have an A or B average in math and/or have turned in all your math assignments, you will earn ten school dollars. These are the only behaviors for which you can earn school dollars. Your teacher will pay you the dollars you earn on a daily basis following math class.

20 Tokens were exchanged on a weekly basis when students met with the author. The process was explained to students as follows: "Once a week you can exchange your school dollars for computer time, pens, markers, keychains, notepads, or candy. You must earn at least ten school dollars in order to purchase an item."

21 A goals chart also was provided for the students in the token economy condition. At the top of the goals chart, target behaviors that could earn tokens were identified. Beneath the token economy goals, a section was provided in which students could write their own mathematics goals. During the weekly meeting time that students met with the author, they (a) traded tokens for back-up reinforcers, (b) received reminders of the target behaviors that could earn tokens, and (c) wrote individual mathematics goals on the goals chart.

Quantitative researchers use strategies to ensure the reliability and validity of instruments

22 *Contingency contract.* Students who participated in this condition received a folder with a contract provided by the author. The terms of the contract were presented verbally by the author, as follows:

**TABLE 1. Means and Standard Deviations for Learning Goals and Performance Goals, by Classroom Structure**

| Classroom structure | Learning goals *M* | Learning goals *SD* | Performance goals *M* | Performance goals *SD* |
|---|---|---|---|---|
| Token economy | .75 | 1.59 | 4.95 | 2.15 |
| Contingency contract | 14.27 | 3.98 | 5.55 | 3.95 |
| Control | 5.36 | 5.39 | 5.61 | 1.96 |

Quantitative findings include descriptive statistics

The quantitative researcher represents results in figures and tables

**TABLE 2. Summary of Tukey Post Hoc Test for Classroom Structure-by-Goals Interaction**

| | *Classroom structure results* |
|---|---|
| Token economy | Performance goals > learning goals |
| Contingency contract | Learning goals > performance goals |
| Control | Performance goals = learning goals |
| | *Goals results* |
| Learning goals | Token economy < control < contingency contract |
| Performance goals | Token economy = control = contingency contract |

Quantitative researchers collect information in the form of numbers

> Each week we will meet so that you can set goals for math. You will be allowed to set weekly goals and long-term goals. When we meet we will look over the goals you set for the previous week. We will identify the goals you have met and place a gold star beside them on your goals chart form. We will discuss the goals you did not meet and you can decide whether to set those goals again or set new ones.

23 Contracts were discussed individually with each student, and once the student demonstrated an understanding for the terms of the contract, the student and the author signed the contract.

Students in the contingency contract condition received a goals chart, which was divided into sections according to the week of the study. Below the weekly sections, a long-term goals section was provided. During the weekly meeting time, the previous week's goals were reviewed. Students received gold stars and positive verbal feedback, contingent on effort when they met a particular goal. Students then set weekly and long-term mathematics goals for the upcoming week.

24 *Control.* Students in this condition received an individual goals chart identical to the one used in the contingency contract condition. The author met one-on-one with students on a weekly basis so they could write short-term and long-term goals for mathematics on their goals chart. The students did not discuss their goals with the author. Furthermore, the students did not receive verbal feedback or external rewards for achieving their goals from the teacher or author. Thus, this condition simply served as a control for goal setting and time spent with the author.

Results Section

## Results

25 We computed an ANOVA by using a two-factor mixed design (classroom structure by goal type) to determine the frequency of learning and performance goals set according to classroom structure condition. Table 1 shows the cell means for learning and performance goals that students set as a function of classroom structure. Results indicated a significant main effect for classroom structure, $F(2, 67) = 36.70, p < .0001$, as well as a significant classroom structure-by-goals interaction, $F(2, 67) = 31.35, p < .0001$.

Quantitative findings include inferential statistics

26 We computed a Tukey post hoc test to determine the significant differences between classroom structure-by-goals on the ANOVA. A summary of post hoc results are shown in Table 2. In our post hoc analysis, we concluded that students in the contingency contract condition set significantly more learning goals than did students in the other conditions. Students in the control condition set significantly more learning goals than did students in the token-economy group. There were no significant differences between the numbers of performance goals that students set according to classroom structure conditions.

27 Within the contingency contract group, students set significantly more learning goals than performance goals. In the control group, there were no significant differences between the number of learning and performance goals that students set. In the token-economy group, students set significantly more performance goals than learning goals.

## Discussion

Conclusion Section

28 Results from the goal analyses indicated significant differences within and across classroom structure conditions. Those results were consistent with the theoretical relationship predicted by Ames (1992c) and the hypothesis in this study that the type of classroom evaluation structure would

Analyzing data and reporting results

Quantitative researchers use statistical analyses to describe trends, relate variables, and compare groups

Quantitative researchers use research designs to plan their studies

Quantitative researchers compare results to predictions

Interpreting the research

influence student goal orientation. Students who were in the contingency-contract condition set significantly more learning goals than performance goals and significantly more learning goals than did students in the other classroom structure conditions. Students in the token-economy condition set significantly more performance goals than learning goals. There were no significant differences within the control classroom for the number of learning versus performance goals that students set. However, students in that classroom did set significantly more learning goals than did students in the token-economy condition. There were no significant differences for the amount of performance goals that students set across classroom-structure conditions.

29 Our results support the idea that a contingency contract classroom structure, in which students were evaluated individually and allowed to determine their own achievement goals, led students to adopt a learning-goal orientation versus a performance-goal orientation. In this classroom structure, student evaluation was focused on individual gains, improvement, and progress. Success was measured by whether students met their individual goals, which creates an environment in which failure is not a threat. If goals were met, then students could derive personal pride and satisfaction from the efforts that they placed toward the goals. If goals were not met, then students could reassess the goal, make the changes needed, or eliminate the goal. A classroom structure that promotes a learning-goal orientation for students has the potential to enhance the quality of students' involvement in learning, increase the likelihood that students will opt for and persevere in learning and challenging activities, and increase the confidence they have in themselves as learners (Ames, 1992b).

30 In contrast, students in the token-economy classroom structure were rewarded for meeting normative standards and tended to adopt a performance-goal orientation. That is an important finding because token economies have been successful in changing student behavior in classrooms, so teachers may implement this intervention without concern for the special needs of students (McLaughlin, 1981). Students are not motivated by the same amount of tokens for given assignments because of individual differences. Students with lower abilities will likely become frustrated and helpless. According to Boggiano & Katz (1991), children in that type of learning environment typically prefer less challenging activities, work to please the teacher and earn good grades, and depend on others to evaluate their work. As a result, the token-economy classroom evaluation structure makes ability a highly salient dimension of the learning environment and discourages students from setting goals that involve learning and effort.

31 The number of performance goals that students set did not differ across classroom structure conditions. Students in the contingency-contract and control conditions set similar numbers of performance goals as compared with those in the token-economy condition. That result likely occurred because throughout the study teachers continued to evaluate all students on their schoolwork with a traditional grading system. It would have been ideal if a nontraditional, individually based evaluative system could have been implemented in the contingency-contract condition to assess whether this would have altered the results.

Quantitative researchers take an objective approach

32 There were limitations to this study. One limitation was that it did not control for teacher expectancies and how these may have influenced students' goal setting. Another potential limitation was that mathematics was the only subject area used for this study. Further studies should include additional academic areas, such as social studies, humanities, and science to investigate whether similar results will ensue.

Quantitative researchers identify limitations in the study

Quantitative researchers suggest future research

33 This study provides strong evidence that the classroom evaluation structure can influence student achievement goal orientation. Specifically, we demonstrated that in a classroom structure that emphasizes the importance of individual goals and effort, learning goals become more salient to students. That result can lead to many positive effects on elementary student's learning strategies, self-conceptions of ability and competence, and task motivation (Smiley & Dweck, 1994). Students' achievement goal orientation obviously is not contingent on any one variable, but it is comprised of the comprehensive relationship between classroom processes and student experiences. Understanding the influence of classroom evaluation structure on student goal orientation provides a foundation for further research of other potentially related variables.

Quantitative researchers suggest implications for practice

## NOTES

Shannon Self-Brown is now in the Department of Psychology at Louisiana State University.

We would like to thank Lucas Ledbetter for assisting in data collection. We would also like to thank the teachers and students at Jim Allen Elementary for participating in the project.

## REFERENCES

Ames, C. (1984). Achievement attribution and self-instructions under competitive and individualistic goal structures. *Journal of Educational Psychology, 76,* 478–487.

Ames, C. (1992a). Achievement goals and the classroom motivational environment. In D. L. Schunk & J. L. Meece (Eds.), *Student perceptions in the classroom* (pp. 327–343). Hillsdale, NJ: Erlbaum.

Ames, C. (1992b). Achievement goals, motivational climate, and motivational processes. In G. C. Roberts (Ed.), *Motivation in sport and exercise.* Champaign, IL: Human Kinetics Books.

Ames, C. (1992c). Classroom: Goals, structures, and student motivation. *Journal of Educational Psychology, 84,* 261–271.

Ames, C., & Ames, R. (1981). Competitive versus individualistic goal structures: The salience of past performance information for causal attributions and affect. *Journal of Educational Psychology, 73,* 411–418.

Ames, C., & Archer, J. (1988). Achievement goals in the classroom: Student learning strategies and motivation processes. *Journal of Educational Psychology, 80,* 260–267.

Boggiano, A. K., & Katz, P. (1991). Maladaptive achievement patterns in students: The role of teachers' controlling strategies. *Journal of Social Issues, 47,* 35–51.

Brophy, J. E. (1983). Conceptualizing student motivation. *Educational Psychologist, 18,* 200–215.

Church, M. A., Elliot, A. J., & Gable, S. L. (2001). Perceptions of classroom environment, achievement goals, and achievement outcomes. *Journal of Educational Psychology, 93,* 43–54.

Covington, M. C. (1984). The motive for self worth. In R. Ames & C.

Ames (Eds.). *Research on motivation in education: Student motivation* (Vol. 1, pp. 77–113). San Diego, CA: Academic Press.

Dweck, C. (1986). Motivational processes affecting learning. *American Psychologist, 41*, 1040–1048.

Dweck, C., & Leggett, E. L. (1988). A social-cognitive approach to motivation and personality. *Psychological Review, 95*, 256–273.

Elliot, E. S. & Dweck, C. S. (1988). Goals: An approach to motivation and achievement. *Journal of Personality & Social Psychology, 54*, 5–12.

Greene, B., & Miller, R. (1996). Influences on achievement: Goals, perceived ability, and cognitive engagement. *Contemporary Educational Psychology, 21*, 181–192.

Harackiewicz, J. M., Barron, K. E., & Elliot, A. (1998). Rethinking achievement goals: When are they adaptive for college students and why? *Educational Psychologist, 33*, 1–21.

Harackiewicz, J. M., Barron, K. E., Tauer, J. M., Carter, S. M., & Elliot, A. J. (2000). Short-term and long-term consequences of achievement goals: Predicting interest and performance over time. *Journal of Educational Psychology, 92*, 316–330.

Heyman, G. D., & Dweck, C. S. (1992). Achievement goals and intrinsic motivation: Their relation and their role in adaptive motivation. *Motivation and Emotion, 16*, 231–247.

Kaplan, A., & Midgley, C. (1997). The effect of achievement goals: Does level of perceived academic competence make a difference? *Contemporary Educational Psychology, 22*, 415–435.

Kaplan, A., & Maehr, M. L. (1999). Achievement goals and student well-being. *Contemporary Educational Psychology, 24*, 330–358.

Kurvnick, K. (1993). Contracting as a motivational teaching tool: An agreement for learning offering simplicity, flexibility, and opportunity. *Journal of College Science Teaching, 22*, 310–311.

Lepper, M. R., & Hodell, M. (1989). Intrinsic motivation in the classroom. In C. Ames & R. Ames (Eds.), *Research on motivation in education* (Vol. 3, pp. 73–105). San Diego, CA: Academic Press.

McLaughlin, T. F. (1981). An analysis of token reinforcement: A control group comparison with special education youth employing measures of clinical significance. *Child Behavior Therapy, 3*, 43–50.

Meece, J. L. (1991). The classroom context and children's motivational goals. In M. Maehr & P. Pintrich (Eds.), *Advances in achievement motivation research* (pp. 261–286). Greenwich, CT: JAI.

Meece, J. L., Blumenfeld, P. C., & Hoyle, R. H. (1988). Students' goal orientation and cognitive engagement in classroom activities. *Journal of Educational Psychology, 80*, 514–523.

Murphy, J. J. (1988). Contingency contracting in schools: A review. *Education and Treatment of Children, 11*, 257–269.

Nicholls, J. (1984). Achievement motivation: Conceptions of ability, subjective experience, task choice, and performance. *Psychological Review, 91*, 328–334.

Nicholls, J. G., Patashnick, M., & Nolen, S. (1985). Adolescents' theories of education. *Journal of Educational Psychology, 77*, 683–692.

Piggott, H. E, & Heggie, D. L. (1986). Interpreting the conflicting results of individual versus group contingencies in classrooms: The targeted behavior as a mediating variable. *Child & Family Behavior Therapy, 7*, 1–15.

Schunk, D. H. (1990). Goal setting and self-efficacy during self-regulated learning. *Educational Psychologist, 25*, 71–86.

Schunk, D. H. (1996). Goals and self-evaluative influences during children's cognitive skill learning. *American Educational Research Journal, 33*, 359–382.

Smiley, P. A., & Dweck, C. S. (1994). Individual differences in achievement goals among young children. *Child Development, 65*, 1723–1743.

Zimmerman, B. J., & Martinez-Pons, M. (1990). Student differences in self-regulated learning: Relating grade, sex, and giftedness to self-efficacy and strategy use. *Journal of Educational Psychology, 82*, 51–59.

# PART THREE

# Understanding the Methods and Results of Quantitative Research Reports

Recall the idea that conducting research is like taking a journey. We learned that researchers report their preliminary considerations for their journeys in introduction sections. These include: why they want to go (the research problem), what they know about the destination (the literature review), and their goals for the trip (the purpose). With these decisions in place, researchers are ready to take their journeys.

When the preliminary considerations call for explanation and measurement of specific variables, researchers choose to take a quantitative research "journey." Researchers using this approach plan the details of their "itineraries" from the start. Before collecting any information, quantitative researchers set the plan for the study, such as who will be involved, where they will go, and what they will do and see along the way. For a quantitative study, you can say that all the decisions are made before the researcher "leaves home." This type of trip may not permit much flexibility, but quantitative researchers ensure that they gather consistent information about the specific variables to answer their research questions.

Once the study is complete, quantitative researchers report the details of their itineraries in the method section of a research report. Their research itineraries include the specific plan for the study, called a research design, and the procedures used to collect and analyze data. They report the results of their journey in a separate section, the results section. The results are like the pictures that a traveler takes and shares to document a trip. You will now examine the different ways that quantitative researchers design, conduct, and report results so you can better understand the method and results sections of quantitative research reports.

The chapters in Part III are:

- Chapter 6—Quantitative Research Designs: Recognizing the Overall Plan for a Study
- Chapter 7—Quantitative Data Collection: Identifying How Information Is Gathered
- Chapter 8—Quantitative Data Analysis and Results: Examining What Was Found in a Study

CHAPTER

# 6 Quantitative Research Designs: Recognizing the Overall Plan for a Study

*You have learned to identify studies that used quantitative research to explain trends and relationships among variables. Identifying the overall approach of a study is a good start to understanding any quantitative report. You will have a more advanced understanding, however, if you also recognize the types of quantitative research designs that researchers use when conducting their studies. Quantitative research designs provide overall plans for conducting studies to address different purposes. This chapter introduces five common types of quantitative designs, reviews their key characteristics, and suggests strategies for identifying and evaluating the quantitative research designs reported in published studies.*

## BY THE END OF THIS CHAPTER, YOU SHOULD BE ABLE TO:

- Explain why research designs are important in quantitative research.
- Name five different quantitative research designs.
- List key characteristics for each of the quantitative research designs.
- Identify the quantitative design used in a reported study.
- Evaluate the quantitative research design as reported in a research article.

We now focus our attention on studies that use a quantitative approach to the process of research. Recall from Chapter 5 that researchers use quantitative research for different purposes. For example, consider the following brief descriptions of three quantitative studies.

- A researcher wanted to determine whether voters that receive negative political advertisements are more likely to vote in a local election than voters that do not receive negative ads (Niven, 2006). He mailed negative ads to one group of voters and no negative ads to another group. He then compared the percentage of voters from each group that voted in the election.
- A team of researchers wanted to examine the extent to which the variables of perceived barriers and parental support predict levels of career certainty and career indecision for African American high schools students (Constantine et al., 2005). They administered questionnaires to a group of students to measure the four variables and then analyzed the data to look for the extent that the variables were related.
- Researchers wanted to describe the beliefs that the general public holds about father involvement with their children (Andrews, Luckey, Bolden, Whiting-Fickling, & Lind, 2004). They carefully selected individuals that were thought to be representative of the public and surveyed them about their beliefs.

As these examples illustrate, researchers have different types of purposes for their quantitative research studies. You may also notice some differences in the procedures. For example, in one study the researcher manipulated the conditions that the participants experienced (receiving or not receiving negative ads). Another study emphasized the selection of participants so that they were representative of a larger group (the general public). You can see that there are also some common procedures in the above examples, such as measuring variables like parental support, voter turnout, or beliefs about father involvement.

Researchers design their studies using a range of procedural options. They select an overall plan, called a research design, to guide their choices among all possible procedures that they could use. By learning to identify these plans, you will have a better understanding of how the methods and results follow from a study's purpose. The different designs also suggest standards you can use to evaluate studies that interest you.

## What Are Quantitative Research Designs?

Recall that quantitative research is research in which the researcher decides what to study about a research problem; asks specific, narrow questions; collects numeric data from participants; analyzes these numbers using statistics; and provides objective explanations about trends and relationships among variables. Within the process of conducting research, a **research design** is a set of procedures that researchers use to collect, analyze, and report their data in a research study. From these two concepts, we can advance the following definition: **Quantitative research designs** are sets of procedures for collecting, analyzing, and reporting numeric data to assess specified variables to answer research questions that call for explanation.

Figure 6.1 summarizes the general characteristics of quantitative research (as we introduced in Chapter 2) and indicates how quantitative research designs fit within the process of research. Researchers select a research design based on their purpose for conducting research. Quantitative research designs, such as true experiments or survey research, provide researchers with a guiding blueprint for how they collect, analyze, and report data in their studies.

FIGURE 6.1 Quantitative Research Designs in the Process of Research

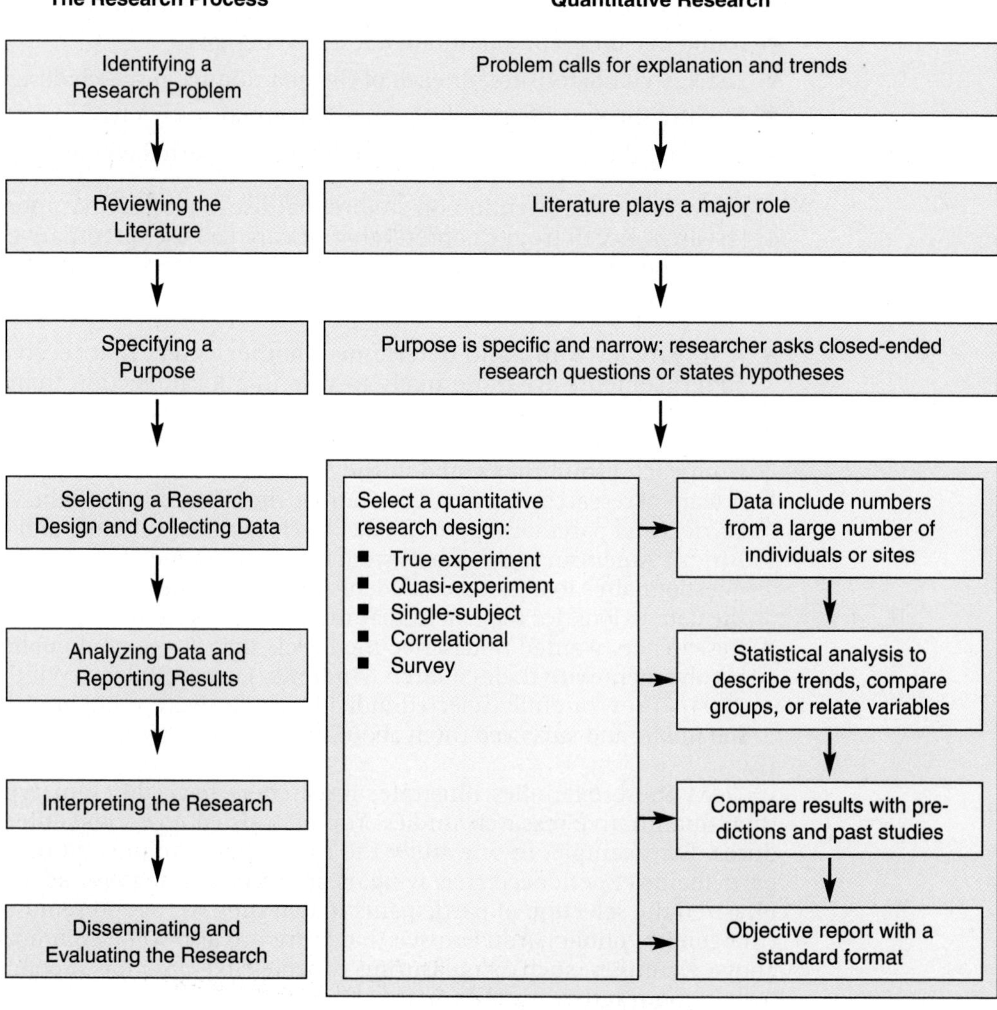

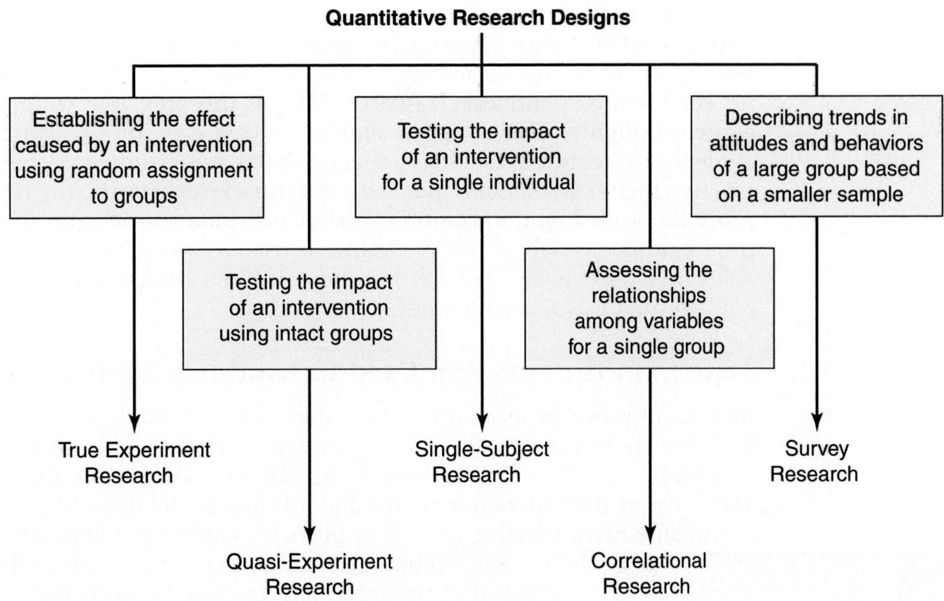


FIGURE 6.2 Types of Quantitative Research Designs and Their Use

## How Did Different Types of Quantitative Research Develop?

The development of quantitative research designs has grown alongside the developments in statistical and measurement procedures. Surveys of educational issues in the community began in the late nineteenth century. The idea of comparing the attitudes or performance of two groups, the basic concept behind experimental research, also took hold in the early twentieth century, drawing on the lessons learned from psychology. Researchers further developed these early models of design into more complicated designs involving multiple groups and multiple tests. Today, researchers have identified the types of experiments, their strengths and weaknesses, and expanded quantitative approaches to include correlational studies and survey research (Campbell & Stanley, 1963; Kerlinger, 1964; Shadish, Cook, & Campbell, 2002).

While new designs continue to be advanced and refined, there is a basic set of research designs used in most quantitative research. For this text, we will focus on five common quantitative designs that we find frequently reported in the literature. As summarized in Figure 6.2, the five quantitative designs that we consider are:

- true experiments,
- quasi-experiments,
- single-subject research,
- correlational research,
- survey research.

## What Is the True Experiment Research Design?

You are probably familiar with the idea of conducting experiments from your daily life and perhaps from experiences in science classes. In general, **experiments** are quantitative procedures that researchers use to test an idea (or practice or procedure) to determine whether it influences an outcome or dependent variable. The researcher first decides on an idea with which to experiment, assigns individuals to experience it (and have other individuals experience something different), and then determines whether those who experienced the idea (or practice or procedure) performed better on some outcome than those who did not experience it. For example, a researcher might want to test whether a special health curriculum can change student's attitudes toward weapons in schools.

We are going to learn about three kinds of experiments in this chapter, the first of which is called a true experiment. True experiments (also called *randomized experiments, intervention trials,* and *randomized control trials*) are often referred to as the "gold standard" for conducting quantitative research. Why is this approach to quantitative research regarded so highly? This design is simply the best way for a researcher to be able to conclude that a treatment (such as a special after-school study hall) causes a certain outcome (such as higher grade point average). In **true experiments,** the researcher uses a special procedure called randomization to assign individual participants to different conditions of the treatment variable. This procedure is used as a way to control for confounding variables (like parents that ensure that their children complete their homework) that might explain the measured outcomes.

## True Experiments Are Used to Establish Probable Cause and Effect

Researchers use experiments when they want to establish probable cause and effect between their independent and dependent variables. This means that they attempt to control all variables that influence the outcome except for the independent variable. Then, when the independent variable influences the dependent variable, they can say the independent variable caused or probably caused the dependent variable.

Researchers use a true experiment when they want to be highly certain that the treatment caused the outcome. True experiments provide researchers with the best procedures for controlling all the variables that might influence the outcome because the researcher controls many aspects of the study, including the assignment of each individual to a treatment or control condition. Researchers choose this design when they have the ability to assign each individual to a group instead of using preexisting groups of people, such as classrooms in a school. True experiments are frequently used in medical research where researchers need to be highly certain that a treatment is effective (e.g., does a vaccine really prevent a disease?) and have sufficient funding to implement the procedures of a true experiment. Other examples of studies using true experiments include testing whether an eating disorder prevention program reduced the incidence of eating disorders in adolescent girls (Favaro, Zanetti, Huon, & Santonastaso, 2005) or testing whether a reading summer camp intervention improved reading achievement of first-grade children (Schacter & Jo, 2005).

For practice understanding the report of a true experiment, go to the *Building Research Skills* section under the topic "Experimental Research" in MyEducationalResearchLab, located at www.myeducationlab.com. Complete the exercise "Identifying Steps in the Research Process for an Experimental Study" and use the provided feedback to further develop your skills for reading research articles.

## Key Characteristics of True Experiments

You can identify a research study using a true experimental design by looking for the following key characteristics:

- ***The researcher randomly assigns individual participants to groups to control for confounding variables.*** Experimenters identify participants and assign each individual to a group (e.g., treatment or control) so that each person has an equal chance of being assigned to any group. This random assignment of individuals is essential. If a researcher does not randomly assign the individual participants, then the design is not a true experiment.
- ***The researcher manipulates the conditions experienced by participants in different groups.*** The researcher actually does something to the participants as part of the study, with different participants receiving different experiences. For example, a researcher may provide special nutritional information to new mothers in the treatment group and the usual information about care of newborns to new mothers in a control group. A control group in an experiment is the group that receives the usual experience instead of the special treatment.
- ***The researcher statistically compares groups on an outcome measure.*** The researcher measures the outcome of interest (e.g., health of infants at six months) and statistically compares the scores among the groups to test for differences.
- ***The researcher draws conclusions consistent with a true experiment.*** True experiments are set up so that the only difference between the groups is the treatment and everything else is equal. Therefore, the researcher can make strong claims that the

treatment caused the measured effect since they controlled for confounding variables with procedures such as random assignment.

### An Example of a True Experiment Study

Unger, Faure, and Frieg (2006) used a true experiment to study the effect of an eight-week training program on gait and perceptions of body image. Their participants included 31 adolescents with spastic cerebral palsy from one school. The researchers randomly assigned the participants to one of two groups: treatment or control. For the 21 individuals assigned to the treatment group, the researchers provided an eight-week program that included specially designed physical exercises. No special training was provided to the individuals in the control group during the study. The researchers measured the participants' gait and perceptions of body image at the beginning of the study and after the eight-week program was complete. They statistically compared the scores for the two groups and found that the treatment group's scores for gait and perceptions of body image improved more than those from the control group. Therefore, the authors concluded that the school-based strength-training program caused improvements in participants' gait and perceptions of body image.

This true experiment illustrates a study seeking to establish that a school based strength-training program (the cause) improves gait and perceptions of body image (the effects) for adolescents with spastic cerebral palsy from one school. The authors randomly assigned participants to groups and manipulated the conditions experienced by the groups (some received the program, some did not). They measured the dependent variables before and after the treatment was complete and used statistical procedures to compare groups based on their scores. They used the results to draw conclusions about the treatment causing specific outcomes.

### What Do You Think?

Suppose you are reading a collection of research articles related to the problem of childhood obesity. How might a true experiment be used to study this topic? What characteristics would you expect to find in this study?

#### Check Your Understanding

A researcher might use a true experiment design to test whether setting a daily goal of 10,000 steps and carrying a pedometer results in healthier weights for middle school girls. In this study, we would expect the researcher to identify a large number of participants, such as girls from across an urban area. She could then randomly assign each participating girl to one of three groups. The researcher manipulates the experiences of the groups by: (a) giving a pedometer to the girls in one group and asking them to watch how far they walk each day, (b) giving a pedometer to the girls in the second group and asking them to try to reach a goal of 10,000 steps each day, and (c) not providing a pedometer to the girls in the control group. The researcher measures each girl's weight at the start of the study and at the end and compares the changes in weight across the three groups. From this study we might learn that having a specific goal along with a pedometer causes adolescent girls to obtain healthier weights compared to the control group and to girls who carried a pedometer without a goal.

How might a true experiment study be used to study a topic of interest to you?

## What Is the Quasi-Experiment Research Design?

There are many experimental situations in which researchers need to use groups that exist naturally or are already formed (such as students grouped into classrooms). **Quasi-experiments** are a type of experiment that uses intact groups. The researcher assigns groups to the different conditions, but does *not* randomly assign individual participants. This occurs because the experimenter cannot artificially create groups for the experiment. For example, studying a new math program may require using existing fourth-grade classes and designating one as the experimental group and one as the control group. Randomly assigning students to the two groups is not possible because it would disrupt classroom learning. Instead the researcher randomizes at the classroom level. Quasi-experiments have the advantage of being easier to conduct than true experiments because existing groups are used. The use of intact groups, however, introduces the possibility of other influences that might explain the outcomes. For example, suppose the children in one class had a special math curriculum the year before. If they performed better than the control group, we cannot know if it was because of the new math program or because of their prior experiences. Therefore, one cannot draw strong conclusions about cause-and-effect from a quasi-experiment.

*Here's a Tip for Reading Research!*

It can be a challenge to distinguish between true and quasi-experiments because authors may use the term "random assignment" in both. Look to see what is being assigned randomly. If each individual is randomly assigned to a condition, then it is a true experiment. If the random assignment is made to existing groups, then it is a quasi-experiment.

## Quasi-Experiments Are Used to Determine the Effect of a Treatment for Intact Groups

Like true experiments, researchers choose to use quasi-experiments for the design of their studies when they want to determine whether a treatment causes the desired effect. Researchers also choose this design when they plan to compare groups, but have to administer the treatment to existing groups such as students in specific classes, teachers at different schools, or counselors working in specific clinics. Because many situations call for using intact groups (schools, colleges, or school districts), quasi-experimental designs are frequently used.

### Key Characteristics of Quasi-Experiments

Authors often refer to their quasi-experiment research design as an *experiment* in their research reports. Therefore, you can recognize the use of a quasi-experiment by looking for the following key characteristics:

- ***The researcher uses intact groups of participants.*** The researcher uses participants who are already within existing groups because it is not practical or possible to assign individuals randomly.
- ***The researcher manipulates the conditions experienced by participants in different groups.*** Although existing groups are used, the researcher still manipulates the conditions that are experienced by the groups. For example, a researcher may manipulate conditions by having students in one first-grade class receive healthy snacks at break time and those in another class receive the traditional cookie.
- ***The researcher statistically compares groups on an outcome measure.*** Like in true experiments, the reseracher measures the outcome of interest (e.g., children's attitudes about fruits and vegetables) and statistically compares the scores between the different groups. Quasi-experiments often measure additional variables as control variables (such as parents' attitudes about serving fruits and vegetable at home) that will influence the outcome in addition to the treatment.
- ***The researcher draws conclusions consistent with a quasi-experiment.*** The researcher can make moderate claims that the treatment caused the measured effect if they accounted for other variables that may influence the outcome. The researcher may also make modest claims about the practicality of the treatment since it was administered in a regular setting, such as a classroom.

## An Example of a Quasi-Experiment Research Study

Vooijs and van der Voort (1993) used a quasi-experiment design to study the impact of a curriculum designed to encourage critical viewing of violence on television by children. The researchers identified six elementary schools to test this curriculum. They randomly assigned three schools to use the curriculum and three schools to not use it. Students in Grades 4 through 6 at the assigned schools completed the curriculum. The researchers measured a range of dependent variables (e.g., readiness to see violence and approval of violent actions) and control variables (e.g., gender and grade level) from the participants at all six schools. The variables were assessed before the treatment was administered (a pre-test), after the treatment (a post-test), and then again two years later (a follow-up test). Using a range of statistical analyses, they found that the curriculum had positive effects, such as increasing students' readiness to see violence and decreasing their approval of violent actions of the "good guys."

This study illustrates an example of a quasi-experiment study. The researchers manipulated the conditions of participants, but used intact groups (six schools). The researchers compared the groups in terms of the dependent variables, while statistically controlling for numerous other variables that may have also influenced the outcomes. They conducted the research to test whether the curriculum impacted students as expected.

### What Do You Think?

Suppose you are reading a collection of research articles related to the problem of childhood obesity. How might a quasi-experiment design be used to study this topic? What characteristics would you expect to find in this study?

### Check Your Understanding

A researcher might use a quasi-experiment to study the effect of daily recess time for third-graders. In this study, we would expect to find that the purpose of the study is to test the effect of daily recess time on dependent variables, such as student attentiveness. The study would use intact groups (such as existing third-grade classrooms), and the researcher would manipulate the conditions by having the treatment groups receive daily recess time while the control groups receive breaks within the regular classroom. After the treatment conditions had been applied for a number of weeks, the researcher measures the outcome variables and compares the groups.

How do you think a quasi-experiment could be used to study a topic of interest to you?

## What Is the Single-Subject Research Design?

Suppose that an investigator wants to experimentally study the behavior of a single individual instead of groups of individuals. **Single-subject research** is a set of procedures that involves the study of single individuals, their observation over a baseline period, and the administration of an intervention. This is followed by further observation during and after the intervention to determine if the treatment affects the outcome. For example, researchers tested whether students with intellectual disabilities in a community vocational setting are able to independently transition between tasks when they are prompted with a handheld prompting system (Cihak, Kessler, & Alberto, 2008). This design does not include random assignment. In addition, it includes the study of single individuals rather than a group of subjects. Therefore, while true and quasi-experiments often use a control group for comparison with a treatment group, the individual subject becomes his/her own control in a single subject experiment. Single-subject research is also referred to as *N of 1 research, behavior analysis,* or *multiple baseline design*. Authors also use letters to indicate variants of this design such as *AB design* or *ABAB design,* where *A* stands for measurements made without the treatment and *B* stands for measurements made during the treatment.

### Single-Subject Designs Are Used to Test Interventions for Individuals

Researchers use single-subject designs when they seek to determine whether an intervention impacts the behavior of a single participant. They also use this design for situations

For practice understanding the report of a single-subject research study, go to the *Building Research Skills* section under the topic "Single-Subject Experimental Research" in MyEducationalResearchLab, located at www.myeducationlab.com. Complete the exercise "Identifying Steps in the Research Process for a Single-Subject Study" and use the provided feedback to further develop your skills for reading research articles.

where they have the opportunity to observe the person's behavior over time. By observing the individual over a prolonged period of time and recording the behavior before, during, and after the intervention, the researcher assesses whether there is a relationship between the treatment and the target behavior or outcome. Researchers may use this design to target multiple behaviors of one individual, such as the verbal responses of a student who is selectively mute in three different school settings (Beare, Torgerson, & Creviston, 2008). They may also test the impact of an intervention on several individuals by staggering when the intervention is applied to each. This approach was used in the study of the handheld prompting system where four individuals received the handheld system intervention over time to show that changes in transition behavior were clearly associated with the start of the intervention for each individual (Cihak et al., 2008).

## Key Characteristics of Single-Subject Research

Single-subject research designs have the following key characteristics:

- ***The researcher examines the effect of a treatment on a single individual.*** The investigator studies a small number of single individuals.
- ***The researcher establishes a baseline of behavior and then manipulates the conditions experienced by the individual.*** Prior to administering the intervention, the researcher establishes a stable baseline of information about the individual's behavior. A stable baseline means that behavior for an individual varies little over several sessions or days. The researcher then applies an intervention and continues to repeatedly measure behavior (i.e., the outcome) throughout the experiment based on making observations and recording scores for each individual. In some studies the researcher will remove and reapply the intervention to verify that it is the cause of the measured effects.
- ***The researcher plots the individual's behavior over many points of time on a graph and visually inspects the data for change.*** After administering the intervention, the researcher notes the patterns of behavior and plots them on a graph. This pattern may be ascending, descending, flat, or variable. Data are typically analyzed by visually inspecting the data rather than by using statistical analysis. In particular, the researcher notes how the behavior of the individual has changed during the intervention, after withdrawing the intervention, or during multiple interventions.
- ***The researcher draws conclusions about whether the individual's behavior meaningfully changed.*** The single-subject researcher can make strong claims as to whether the participant's behavior has meaningfully changed and that this change was caused by the intervention.

## An Example of a Single-Subject Research Study

Kern et al. (2007) used a single-subject design to study the impact of the use of songs in assisting two young children with autism in transitioning into their inclusive child care classrooms each morning. The treatment was the use of a morning greeting song composed by a music therapist for each child. The outcomes included five specific behaviors, such as greeting the teacher or indicating goodbye to the caregiver. The researchers established a baseline for each child by observing the number of successful behaviors completed over six days. They continued to record the behaviors when the intervention was enacted, removed, and then reinstated. The resulting graphs of behavior clearly demonstrate that the two children improved their greeting routine behaviors at times when the music therapy intervention was in place.

This study illustrates an example of a single-subject research. The researchers wanted to affect the behavior of individual students and applied a treatment (the morning song) to each on an individual basis. Numerous observations were recorded before, during, and without the intervention to establish its effect on a child's behavior. The researchers graphed the resulting data by individual and analyzed it visually, without the use of statistics.

## What Do You Think?

Suppose you are reading a collection of research articles related to the problem of childhood obesity. How might a single-subject design be used to study this topic? What characteristics would you expect to find in this study?

### Check Your Understanding

A researcher might use a single-subject design to study the impact of a system that requires a child to peddle a bicycle-like machine while playing video games for a child who is severely overweight. In this study, the researcher is interested in increasing the amount of physical activity in which the child engages on a daily basis. Baseline activity data could be collected while the child has access to his usual video game. Then the game could be replaced with the version that requires that the child peddle for the game to function. The researcher would continue to observe the amount of activity on a daily basis to see if the intervention successfully changed the child's behavior.

How might a single-subject design be used to study a topic of interest to you?

# What Is the Correlational Research Design?

There are many situations in which researchers are unable or uninterested in providing an intervention. Instead they want to examine the association or relation between two or more variables without manipulating what individuals are experiencing. **Correlational research designs** are procedures in quantitative research in which investigators measure the degree of association (or relationship) between two or more variables using the statistical procedure of correlational analysis. This degree of association, expressed as a number, indicates the extent to which the two variables are or are not related or whether one can predict another. To accomplish this, a researcher studies a single group of individuals, rather than two or more groups as in most experiments. In this design, researchers do not attempt to control or manipulate the variables as in an experiment; instead they relate, using the correlation statistic, two or more scores for each individual (e.g., a student motivation and a student achievement score for each individual). You can often identify studies using this design by terms such as *correlation, multiple regression* (a statistical technique), or *prediction.*

## Correlational Research Is Used to Assess the Relationships Among Variables

Researchers choose to use a correlational research design when they seek to relate two or more variables to see if they influence each other, such as the relationship between teachers who endorse developmentally appropriate practices, and their use of the whole-language approach to reading instruction (Ketner, Smith, & Parnell, 1997). This design allows a researcher to predict a dependent variable, such as the prediction that ability, quality of schooling, student motivation, and academic coursework influence student achievement (Anderson & Keith, 1997). Researchers also use this design when they know and can apply statistical knowledge based on calculating the correlation statistical test.

## Key Characteristics of Correlational Research

Correlation designs are very common and share these key characteristics:

- ***The researcher studies a single group of participants.*** The researcher selects a single group of individuals, such as children in one school, teachers who teach science, or adults that serve as mentors. The researcher does not assign individuals to groups.

- ***The researcher collects information for each major variable.*** The researcher collects the same information in the same manner from all individuals. There is no intervention and the researcher does not manipulate the experiences of different participants.
- ***The researcher statistically relates variables.*** Researchers use a wide range of statistical procedures (e.g., correlation or multiple regression) to test for relationships among variables. Researchers are interested in determining the tendency or pattern for two (or more) variables or two sets of data to vary consistently. In the case of only two variables, this means that two variables co-vary together. For example, when time spent studying goes up, scores on the final exam also go up; therefore these variables have a positive relationship. It might also be true that as students' anxiety about a test increases, their final exam scores go down. These two variables have a negative relationship.
- ***The researcher concludes the extent to which variables are related to each other.*** Researchers using this design cannot conclude that some variables *cause* an effect in other variables because the researcher did not use random assignment or manipulate the conditions (like in an experimental design). For example, a researcher may find that an increase in attendance at swimming pools is related to an increase in domestic violence incidences. It is not the case that swimming causes domestic violence, but these variables are related because both increase when the temperature goes up.

## An Example of a Correlational Research Study

Malecki and Demaray's (2003) study of predictors of carrying a weapon to school is an example of correlational research. The study sought to identify whether variables (such as gender, grade level, or perceptions of social support) predict whether students have carried a weapon to school. The researchers studied one group of 461 students from one urban middle school. All participants completed a questionnaire that assessed the variables of interest to the researchers. Once the data were gathered, the researchers used correlation and regression statistical procedures to determine that prior risk behaviors (like being arrested), gender, grade level, and support together were significant predictors of carrying a weapon to school.

This correlational research illustrates a study of the relationships among variables for a single group. The researchers did not attempt to change students' weapon carrying behaviors and instead wanted to understand the relationship among various demographic and social variables to weapon possession. The researchers used analysis procedures to statistically test for relationships among the variables.

### What Do You Think?

Suppose you are reading a collection of research articles related to the problem of childhood obesity. How might a correlational research design be used to study this topic? What characteristics would you expect to find in this study?

### Check Your Understanding

A researcher might use a correlational research design to examine which variables are related to a child having an unhealthy weight. We would expect the researchers to study a single group (such as tenth-graders). The researchers would identify variables they expect to be related to a child's weight, such as the child's family income, parent's education status, self esteem, age, and height. The researcher would gather information about each variable from every child and analyze the data looking to see which variables are best at predicting a child's weight. This study would not determine which factors cause obesity, but it could identify variables useful for identifying children who may be at a greater risk for developing obesity.

How might correlational research be used to study a topic of interest to you?

## What Is the Survey Research Design?

*Here's a Tip for Reading Research!*

The word "survey" is used extensively in research reports. Sometimes it refers to a type of questionnaire used to gather information from individuals. For example, you have probably responded to a survey over the telephone. Any quantitative study can use a survey for gathering information. In contrast, a *survey research design* is a set of procedures that includes decisions about who to study, how to collect data, and how to report results.

For practice understanding the report of a survey research design, go to the *Building Research Skills* section under the topic "Survey Research" in MyEducationalResearchLab, located at www.myeducationlab.com. Complete the exercise "Identifying Steps in the Research Process for a Survey Study" and use the provided feedback to further develop your skills for reading research articles.

In some quantitative research, a researcher may seek to describe trends in a large population of individuals. In this case, a survey is a good design to use. **Survey research designs** are procedures in quantitative research for administering a survey or questionnaire to a small group of people (called the *sample*) in order to identify trends in attitudes, opinions, behaviors, or characteristics of a large group of people (called the *population*). A hallmark of this design is that the researcher carefully selects a group of people to study to ensure that they are representative of a larger population about which they want to make conclusions. For example, if researchers want to describe the risky behaviors of high school students in a school district (the population), then they might select a sample of boys and girls that represent all high school grades and each school in the district.

### Survey Research Is Used to Describe Trends in a Population

Researchers use a survey to describe trends, such as community interests in school bond issues or state or national trends about mandatory student uniform policies. Researchers also use a survey to determine individual opinions about policy issues, such as whether students need a choice of schools to attend. Surveys help identify important beliefs and attitudes of individuals at one point in time, such as college students' beliefs about what constitutes abusive behaviors in dating relationships. They are also used to follow attitudes over time, such as with graduates 5, 10, and 15 years after college to learn about their present careers. Researchers describe trends by identifying the average opinion or the range of attitudes held by individuals.

### Key Characteristics of Survey Research

Because the term survey is used extensively in quantitative research, it does not always tell you that a study used a survey research design. To identify this design, look for the following key characteristics in the report:

- ***The researcher studies the attitudes, opinions, or behaviors of a large group.*** The researcher is primarily interested in *describing* how a group of people in society (a population) thinks or acts. This is different from wanting to change or predict how people think and act.
- ***The researcher chooses a large number of participants using random selection.*** The researcher wants to select participants to study that are representative of all members of the larger group because the goal is to generalize the results from the participants to the whole population. Selecting them at random from a list of all members of the group is the best way to accomplish this. Survey researchers also select a large number of participants so that the results are more likely to resemble those of the population.
- ***The researcher gathers information and describes trends in the data.*** Researchers gather information with survey questionnaires that ask about individuals' attitudes, opionions, or behaviors. The data is primarily analyzed to describe the average and range of responses.
- ***The researcher makes conclusions about the larger population.*** Researchers using a survey design are most interested in drawing conclusions from the study to the larger population.

### An Example of a Survey Research Study

An example of survey research can be found in Abril and Gault's (2006) study of elementary principals. These authors wanted to describe principals' perspectives about elementary music education. They obtained a list of all elementary principals that belong to a major national organization and randomly selected 350 individuals' names. They mailed a survey questionnaire to each selected person and 61 percent of them returned a completed form. The researchers analyzed the data to describe what principals think elementary children should do in music class, what the curricular goals should be, and what barriers they perceive to elementary music education.

This study illustrates a survey research study. The researchers aimed to provide a general picture of how elementary principals currently think about music education. They carefully selected a sample using procedures to ensure that participants would likely represent the opinions of all principals. The researchers gathered information about principals' opinions and reported a description of their responses.

### What Do You Think?

Suppose you are reading a collection of research articles related to the problem of childhood obesity. How might a survey research design be used to study this topic? What characteristics would you expect to find in this study?

### Check Your Understanding

A researcher might use a survey research design to study attitudes about children's weight of school nurses in the state. The researcher may begin by acquiring a list of all school nurses in the state and randomly selecting a group to participate in the study. The researcher would design a survey that asks questions about the nurses' attitudes such as, "To what extent do you think obesity is a problem for children?" After the data are gathered, the researcher describes the trends in the responses and makes conclusions about how all school nurses in the state think about children's weight.

Now, how might a survey research design be used to study a topic of interest to you?

## How Do You Identify the Research Design in a Research Article?

We have now reviewed five quantitative research designs, including reasons researchers use them and their key characteristics. With this information, you can figure out what research design was used when reading a published quantitative research article. We suggest taking three steps to identify a study's quantitative research design.

1. ***Look to see if the author names the design in the title of the article.*** For example, note how the following titles indicate the research design that was used:
   - "What Do You Want to Tell Us about Reading? A Survey of the Habits and Attitudes of Urban Middle School Students" (*Hughes-Hassell & Lutz, 2006*)
   - "School Counselors' Career Satisfaction and Commitment: Correlates and Predictors" (*Baggerly & Osborn, 2006*)
2. ***Examine the purpose statement to see if it suggests the study's research design.*** Researchers select their research designs to match their studies' purposes. Sometimes authors include the name of the research design in their purpose

statement. If not, you can find clues about the design when you read the purpose. For example, if the purpose is to test the impact of an intervention, then the researcher will use an experiment. If the purpose is to identify variables that predict certain behaviors or attitudes, then the researcher will use a correlational design. If the purpose is to describe trends in a large group, then the researcher will use a survey design.

3. ***Examine the procedures described within the method section of the report.*** Quantitative researchers often will not name their designs in their reports. This is because they can be recognized by the specific procedures that a researcher uses. As you read the method section, look for procedures that suggest the research design. You can use the following questions to recognize these procedures. The design that usually calls for each procedure is indicated within parentheses.
   - Did the author study two or more groups (true or quasi-experiment), one group (correlational or survey), or one individual (single subject)?
   - Did the author randomly assign individuals to groups (true experiment) or use intact groups (quasi-experiment)?
   - Did the author randomly select individuals to participate (survey study) or use individuals that were conveniently available (experiments or correlational)?
   - Did the author provide a treatment to some individuals (true, quasi-, or single-subject experiment) or collect data without manipulating the conditions experienced by participants (correlational or survey)?
   - Did the analysis focus on describing trends (survey), relating variables (correlational), comparing groups (true or quasi-experiment), or inspecting graphs of an individual's data (single subject)?

## What Do You Think?

Consider the following abstract from a published study about African American adolescents' career issues. Which design do you think the authors used and what is your evidence?

> This study examined the extent to which perceived occupational barriers and perceived parental support predicted career certainty and career indecision in a sample of African American adolescents. Perceived occupational barriers were positively predictive of career indecision, and perceived parental support was positively associated with career certainty. The results provided support for the importance of considering contextual variables, such as perceived occupational barriers and perceived parental support, in the career decision-making processes of African American adolescents. The results also highlighted the salience of social cognitive career theory in conceptualizing career-related issues in African American high school students. Future research directions are discussed. (*Constantine et al., 2005, p. 307*)

### Check Your Understanding

This study is an example of a quantitative study using a correlational research design. Evidence for this design includes: (a) the study of a single group, (b) no mention of a treatment or intervention, (c) an interest in identifying variables that predict other variables, and (d) a discussion of results in terms of positive associations between variables.

Use the following criteria to evaluate the quality of the research design in a quantitative research report. For each evaluation item, indicate the following ratings:

+ You rate the item as "high quality" for the study.
✓ You rate the item as "ok quality" for the study.
– You rate the item as "low quality" for the study.

In addition to your rating, make notes about each element when you apply these criteria to an actual published study.

| In a high-quality quantitative research report, the author . . . | Application to a Published Study | |
|---|---|---|
| | Your Rating | Your Notes |
| 1. Identifies the type of research design used so you know their plan for conducting the study. | | |
| 2. Discusses the key characteristics of the design so you know they used rigorous procedures of data collection, analysis, and interpretation within the selected design. | | |
| 3. Explains the reason for choosing the design. | | |
| 4. Matches the selected research design to the study's stated purpose, research questions, and hypotheses. | | |
| 5. Cites up-to-date references about the research design within the method section to indicate the author's knowledge about the design. | | |

FIGURE 6.3 Criteria for Evaluating the Quality of a Study's Quantitative Research Design

## How Do You Evaluate a Study's Quantitative Research Design?

Recognizing the design used in a quantitative study is an important step to understanding and evaluating its report. Figure 6.3 provides a checklist you can use to assess an author's implementation of a quantitative research design. Keep in mind that in a good, rigorous quantitative study, the design matches the purpose and the methods of collecting, analyzing and reporting data match the design.

Researchers conduct quantitative research to explain trends and relationships about variables for a large group of people. Therefore, the quality of a quantitative research study also depends on (a) how well the researcher can make claims about the resulting trends and relationships and (b) how well the findings can be applied to a larger group. Researchers can make stronger claims about the variables they study when they use sound procedures for measuring the variables, manipulate the conditions and control for other important factors that may influence the outcomes, and use appropriate statistical procedures to draw their conclusions. Researchers can make stronger claims that their results generalize to the larger group if they studied a large number of participants that were selected to be similar to the overall group of interest.

## Reviewing What We've Learned

- Quantitative research designs are sets of procedures for collecting, analyzing, and reporting quantitative data to address different types of research purposes.
- Quantitative research designs have developed along with more advanced statistical and measurement procedures.
- Determine the type of quantitative research design when reading a study, such as experimental, quasi-experimental, single-subject, correlational, and survey research.

- Assess whether the selected research design is best suited to develop explanations about the variables of interest.
- Expect the procedures for selecting and/or assigning participants to be consistent with the research design.
- Consider whether the researcher is manipulating the experiences of participants.
- Look for the use of statistical procedures associated with the selected design.
- Ask yourself whether the author can conclude that the independent variable(s) caused an effect in the dependent variable(s) based on the design used in the study.
- Ask yourself whether the author can conclude that results readily apply to a larger population based on the design used in the study.
- Assess the choice of a quantitative research design by considering whether the key characteristics of the design match the study's purpose.

## Practicing Your Skills

Practice using your skills and knowledge of the content of this chapter by answering the following questions about the practice research studies. Use the answers found in the Appendix to evaluate your progress.

Consider the quantitative parent involvement study at the end of Chapter 1.

1. Identify the research design used in this study. List three pieces of evidence for your answer.
2. Does the research design match the study's purpose?
3. What types of claims can the author make based on the design used?

Consider the quantitative goal orientation study at the end of Chapter 5.

4. Identify the research design used in this study. List three pieces of evidence for your answer.
5. Does the research design match the study's purpose?
6. What types of claims can the author make based on the design used?

# CHAPTER 7 Quantitative Data Collection: Identifying How Information Is Gathered

*Once researchers have selected an overall research design for addressing the purpose of their quantitative study, they next consider the details of implementing this plan. In particular, researchers share information about how they collected their quantitative data in the method section of quantitative research reports. It provides you with details that are essential for understanding how a study was conducted. These details include how the researchers selected participants, the instruments used to record quantitative data, and the procedures employed for gathering the information in a rigorous and ethical manner. In this chapter, you will learn how to understand the procedures researchers report using to collect quantitative data.*

## BY THE END OF THIS CHAPTER, YOU SHOULD BE ABLE TO:

- Define quantitative data collection and list the major elements that researchers report.
- Describe a study's sample and identify the strategy the researcher used to select sites and participants.
- Identify the instruments that a researcher used and look for evidence that the instruments will provide good data.
- Understand the procedures a researcher used to collect quantitative data.
- Evaluate the collection of quantitative data as reported in a research article.

Think back to the definition of research you learned in Chapter 1. Recall that at the general level, research consists of posing a question, collecting data about the question, and presenting an answer to the question. Therefore, collecting data is at the heart of the research process. Researchers dedicate much attention and effort to planning, implementing, and reporting their quantitative data collection.

You need to carefully examine the details of data collection when you read any quantitative research report. This tells you whether the report meets the definition of research. More importantly, the details of how the researcher collected the data will help you understand the context of the study's results because it tells you what data were collected and from whom. This information will help you assess whether the research procedures were conducted in a rigorous and ethical manner that is consistent with a quantitative approach. When a researcher reports good procedures for collecting quantitative data, you can feel more confident in the results based on that data. Therefore, you need to be familiar with the important aspects of quantitative data collection to judge the quality of any quantitative study. Let's begin by reviewing data collection in the process of conducting quantitative research.

## What Is the Process of Collecting Quantitative Data?

Recall the general characteristics of quantitative data collection that you learned in Chapter 2. Quantitative data collection consists of:

- selecting participants that are representative of a larger group;
- gathering information from a large number of participants; and
- collecting numeric data using instruments with predetermined questions and responses.

These elements point to the major characteristics of collecting quantitative data in response to research purposes that call for quantitative information. While they suggest important attributes of quantitative data collection, they do not tell you how to interpret information about data collection included in a quantitative research report. Therefore, let's begin to examine these issues by considering how you locate and read information about quantitative data collection.

## How Do You Identify a Study's Quantitative Data Collection?

You can find an author's discussion of quantitative data collection in the method section of a quantitative research report. This section usually has the heading *Method* in quantitative studies, and it follows directly after the introduction and literature review. The method section is where researchers describe their procedures (i.e., their method) for conducting the study.

As we introduced in the previous chapter, the method section may include a description of the study's research design. Most of the method section, however, will focus on how the researcher actually gathered information from people or organizations. Because this data collection is central to conducting research, researchers generally describe the same categories of information when discussing their data collection methods. Let's think about these categories by reading the following excerpt from a quantitative research report. This correlational study investigated whether smoking status and gender are related to specific variables, such as egocentrism, for adolescents (Frankenberger, 2004). As you read this passage, think about the kind of information the author is telling you about how she collected her data.

> *Here's a Tip for Reading Research!*
>
> Authors include subheadings to organize the presented information. Therefore, use the subheadings to help make sense of the information that you read.

***Method***

*Participants*

Participants were 215 male (52%) and female (48%) high school students ranging in age from 14 to 18 ($M$ = 15.91, $SD$ = 1.14). Because prior research on adolescent egocentrism has historically used White, middle-class samples, data were collected at a high school in the predominantly middle-class neighborhood of a medium-sized city in the Pacific Northwest. Students were predominantly White (77%). Of the original 223 surveys administered, 8 were excluded from the analysis because of missing data.

*Procedure*

Students completed a self-administered questionnaire during one of their health classes. The questionnaire was titled "You and Your Opinions About Cigarette Smoking" and included measures of adolescent egocentrism, sensation seeking, risk perceptions, and questions regarding smoking behavior. Participants were informed that the results of the survey were anonymous and confidential. Participation was voluntary.

*Instruments*

*Adolescent egocentrism.* Adolescent egocentrism was measured with the AES [Adolescent Egocentrism Scale] developed by Enright and colleagues (Enright et al., 1979; Enright et al., 1980). The scale consists of three five-item subscales for the imaginary audience, personal fable, and self-focus. For each item, participants are asked to rate the importance of a statement on a scale ranging from 1 = not important to 5 = very important. The AES has demonstrated acceptable to good levels of internal consistency ranging from Cronbach's alpha = .78 (Enright et al., 1979) to Cronbach's alpha = .83 (Enright et al., 1980). Scores were calculated by summing across the five items for each subscale. . . . *(Frankenberger, 2004, pp. 580–581)*

### Look for Information About the Sites and Participants

We learned several details about how the researcher collected data by reading this passage. The author begins by informing us where she collected the data (the site) and from whom (the participants). We learn that she collected data from 215 students at one high school in the Pacific Northwest. We also learn the reason that she selected this school when she noted that this school had characteristics similar to those used in past research on this topic.

### Note the Procedures for Collecting Data

After telling us about the sites and participants, the author next described the general procedures for how she collected her data. The procedures included having students complete a questionnaire during health class. In addition, we find that the author is concerned with the treatment of her participants. She notes that she informed the students that their information would be kept confidential and that their participation was voluntary.

### Identify the Instruments Used to Gather Quantitative Data

After providing general information about collecting data, the author discussed the instruments used to collect data in detail. For the instrument described in this excerpt, she noted its name (Adolescent Egocentrism Scale), who developed it, the types of responses collected with this instrument, and information about the scores from this instrument.

From this one example, we find there are three categories that provide essential information about how a quantitative researcher collected data during a study:

- the participants and sites,
- the general procedures, and
- the specific data collection instruments.

These categories also provide you with a framework for reading and evaluating a quantitative research report. Let's examine each of these categories in more detail.

## How Do Quantitative Researchers Select Sites and Participants?

When starting the process of collecting quantitative data, researchers must make decisions regarding who will participate in the research. These decisions include identifying the general group to which their research questions apply, selecting the people from the group who will provide information in the study, and including enough participants to be able to make conclusions about the general group.

For practice understanding the sample in a research study, go to the *Building Research Skills* section under the topic "Selecting a Sample" in MyEducationalResearchLab, located at www.myeducationlab.com. Complete the exercise "Sampling in a Quantitative Study" and use the provided feedback to further develop your skills for reading research articles.

### The Group of Interest Is Identified

Quantitative research is about describing trends, relationships, or differences for a group of people or organizations. Quantitative researchers need to clearly identify the general group in which they are interested. This general group is referred to as a population. A **population** is a group of individuals who have the same characteristic. Populations can be small, such as all administrators in one school district. Usually populations are large, such as all elementary principals in a state, all eighth-grade science students in the country, or all girls participating in high school sports in a city. The population is important in quantitative research because it is the group about which the researcher wants to learn.

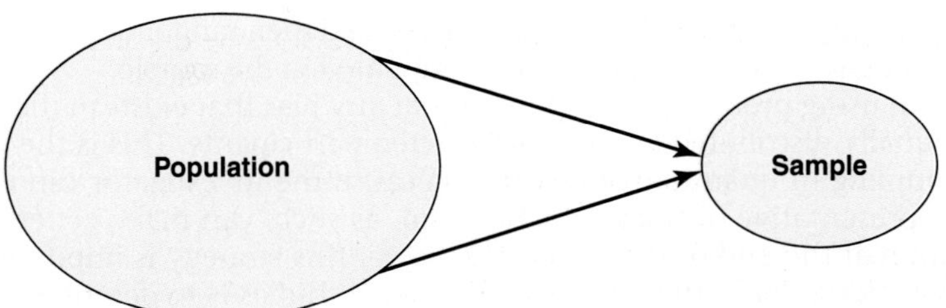


**Population**
- All elementary principals in the state
- All community college students
- Female high school student athletes
- Departments of education

**Sample**
- A collection of principals from one state
- Students attending one community college
- Girls on the basketball and tennis teams at three high schools
- Departments of education from 10 states

FIGURE 7.1 Populations and Samples

## Participants Are Selected That Are Representative of the Population

Researchers generally conduct quantitative research because they want to learn about a population. If the population is large (as is often the case), then the researcher probably will not collect data from every person or organization in the group. It simply would take too long, cost too much, or be too difficult to locate everyone in a group. What do quantitative researchers do in this situation to learn about the population?

Researchers need to select individuals who are part of the population for their studies. That is, from all possible people or organizations in the population, they select a sample for study from the population. A **sample** is a subgroup of the population that the researcher plans to study for generalizing about the population. As illustrated in Figure 7.1, researchers can select different possible samples from populations of interest. For example, a researcher may be interested in elementary principals (the population) and selects a collection of principals from around the state as the sample for a research study.

In order to be able to learn about a population, the researcher selects individuals or schools that are representative of the entire group of individuals or organizations. Representative refers to the selection of individuals from a sample of the population, such that the individuals selected are typical of the population under study. A **representative sample** means that the individuals selected for the sample from the wider population are typical of the wider population. For example, if the population of elementary school principals is 75 percent female, 70 percent middle class, and 30 percent from rural settings, a representative sample of the population of elementary school principals would be made up of about 75 percent females, about 70 percent of the individuals would be middle class, and about 30 percent of the sample would be assigned to rural schools. When the individuals included in the sample are representative, the researcher is able to draw conclusions from the sample about the population as a whole. Therefore, we need to consider the different strategies that researchers use to select their samples.

## Sampling Strategies Are Used

Researchers employ different approaches for selecting individuals or organizations for the samples in their studies. These selection approaches are called **sampling strategies**. There are two types of sampling strategies that researchers use in quantitative studies: probability and nonprobability sampling.

***Probability Sampling.*** The most rigorous sampling strategy for quantitative research is probability sampling. In **probability sampling** the researcher selects individuals (or units, such as schools) from the population through a random process so that each individual has a known chance (or probability) of being selected. You can think of probability sampling as the researcher putting everyone's name from the population into a hat and drawing out names at random to participate in the study. The most common example of this sampling strategy is *random sampling* where the researcher selects participants at random from the larger group. Another example is *stratified random sampling* where the researcher first stratifies the population into groups (such as boys and girls) and then randomly selects participants from each group to ensure the groups are represented in the sample.

The advantage of using probability sampling is that any bias that exists in the population should be equally distributed among the selected participants. This is the most rigorous form of sampling in quantitative research because the investigator can claim that the sample is representative of the population and, as such, can make generalizations to the population at the end of the study. The use of this strategy is important in studies using a survey design because the purpose of these studies is to describe trends in a population (as discussed in Chapter 6).

It is not always possible to use probability sampling. Probability sampling requires that the researcher obtain a list of *every* person in the population. In many studies it is too expensive to obtain such a list because the population is so large, such as a list of all third-graders in the state. In other cases, it may be impossible to obtain a list because no relevant records exist, such as a list of all children who are homeless. Probability sampling is also difficult in experimental studies where a researcher wants to manipulate the conditions experienced by participants. In these studies it may be ethically or practically not feasible to select participants at random.

***Nonprobability Sampling.*** In cases where probability sampling is not feasible, a researcher uses nonprobability sampling. In **nonprobability sampling**, the researcher selects individuals because they are available, convenient, and represent some characteristic the investigator seeks to study. For example, in the excerpt we reviewed at the start of this chapter, the author selected convenient participants from one school.

While this strategy is easier to use than probability sampling, its use limits the conclusions that researchers can make about the results. For example, a researcher who studies teachers at one inner city middle school cannot draw conclusions about middle school teachers in general because these teachers may be different from the typical middle school teacher in some important ways (such as if all teachers had more than 20 years teaching experience). In many studies, however, the researcher is not interested in generalizing findings to a population, but only in describing differences in, or relationships between, variables for a small group of participants. In such studies a sampling strategy based on convenience is sufficient.

Whichever strategy is used, quantitative researchers should explain the specific type of sampling strategy used in their report. Sometimes authors identify these strategies by name, but often they simply describe what they did and you have to deduce the strategy type from this information. You read about the sampling, sites, and participants in an article to understand who participated in a study and why the author selected those individuals. As you read a method section of a quantitative report, identify whether a probability or nonprobability sampling strategy was used. Use this information to determine whether the results are representative of a larger population or they are limited to the individuals that participated in the study.

## What Do You Think?

Consider the quantitative goal orientation study (Self-Brown & Mathews, 2003) found at the end of Chapter 5. Read the following passage from this study. What type of sampling strategy did the author use? Is the sample representative?

> Students from three classrooms at a local elementary school participated in this study. Participants included 2 fifth-grade classes and 1 fourth-grade class.

### Check Your Understanding

From this passage, we can conclude that the authors used a *nonprobability sampling strategy* to select students that were convenient at one elementary school. The school and sampled students are not representative of all elementary students. Therefore, the results may not generalize beyond the students that were studied.

## The Sample Includes a Large Number of Participants

It is important to consider the size of a study's sample in addition to how it was selected. The **sample size** is the number of participants (or organizations) that actually participated in the study. Researchers report the sample size by stating it in the text or using a shorthand such as "$N = 52$," where $N$ stands for the "number of participants" and = stands for "equals."

A general rule of thumb for quantitative research is that the larger the size of the sample, the better. This is because a larger sample means that there is less of a chance that the sample will be different from the population. The difference between the sample estimate and the true population score is called sampling error. In other words, **sampling error** is the difference between the data collected from the sample (sample estimate) and what the researcher would get if data were collected from the whole population (true population score). Unfortunately, unless a researcher collects data from everyone in the population, the true population score cannot be known and the researcher does not know for sure whether she has a large or small sampling error. For example, suppose a researcher wants to know how elementary school principals feel about differentiated instruction and, by random chance, happens to select a small sample that hates differentiated instruction. In this case the study may have a large sampling error, especially if the general population feels positively about differentiated instruction. Researchers do their best to reduce the chance of sampling error by selecting as large a sample as possible.

Many considerations influence the sample size that a researcher uses in a quantitative study. In some studies, the sample size may be limited to the number of participants who are willing to participate in the study. In other cases, factors such as access, funding, the overall size of the population, and the number of variables will also influence the size of the samples. The best way for researchers to pick their sample size is to use precise estimates of the number of participants needed as derived from sample size tables or special formulas that have been developed. You can feel more confident that the sample is large enough when a researcher reports using procedures like a sample size formula to determine the size of their sample.

In addition to looking for information explaining the sample size when you read a report, use the following guidelines as estimates of the sample sizes needed for the different research designs discussed in Chapter 6. These estimates are based on the size needed for typical statistical procedures so that the sample is likely to be a good estimate of the characteristics of the population (we will learn more about this in Chapter 8). These recommended samples sizes are:

- approximately 15 participants (or more) in each group in a true or quasi-experiment,
- one participant (or more) in a single-subject study (with data collected over many points in time),
- approximately 30 participants (or more) for a correlational study that relates variables, and
- approximately 350 individuals (or more) for a survey study, but this size will vary depending on several factors, including the size of the overall population.

## What Do You Think?

Consider the following passage from a quantitative survey study. What is the sample size? What sampling strategy appeared to be used to select the participants? What population does the sample represent?

> A random sample of 350 was drawn from a list of 8,506 active elementary public school principals enrolled as members of the National Association of Elementary School Principals . . . Surveys were returned from principals representing various regions of the United States: Midwest (32%), Northeast (27%), South (26%), and West (15%). These proportions closely reflected the membership of the population from which the sample was drawn . . . Respondents ($N = 214$) reported the length of their service as elementary school administrators to be as follows: under 1 to under 5 years (28.5%), 5 to under 10 years (30.8%), and 10 or more years (40.7%). *(Abril & Gault, 2006, p. 11)*

### Check Your Understanding

From this passage we learn that the author contacted 350 individuals, but the actual sample size of individuals that participated was 214. That is, $N = 214$. The authors used probability sampling to identify their participants by randomly selecting them from a list of principals who belong to a national organization. The population of this study is all principals who belong to National Association of Elementary School Principals in the United States. Due to the extensive membership of this organization and its representation of all areas of the United States, this sample is likely representative of all U.S. elementary principals. We should, however, be a little cautious about generalizing the results since so many contacted principals did not respond. This could be a problem if the ones who did not respond tend to think differently from those who did respond.

## How Do Quantitative Researchers Collect Information?

Once you have determined a study's population and who participated, you are ready to consider the type of information that the researcher gathered from these participants. Researchers gather information in order to be able to answer their research questions. In quantitative research, researchers need to obtain information about each of their variables from their participants. This means that researchers specify their variables, determine the type of instrument needed to collect the information for each variable, and select instruments that are good quality. This process is summarized in Figure 7.2 for a variable called "test anxiety."

### Specifying the Variables

To determine what data need to be collected, the researcher first identifies the variables in the study from the research questions and hypotheses. We learned in Chapter 5 that these variables include independent, dependent, and control variables. Variables represent characteristics or attributes that vary among participants. Researchers must specify their variables in a way that they can be measured (i.e., assigned a numeric score). For example, a researcher interested in math performance for high school students could

FIGURE 7.2 The Flow of Activities for Collecting Quantitative Data

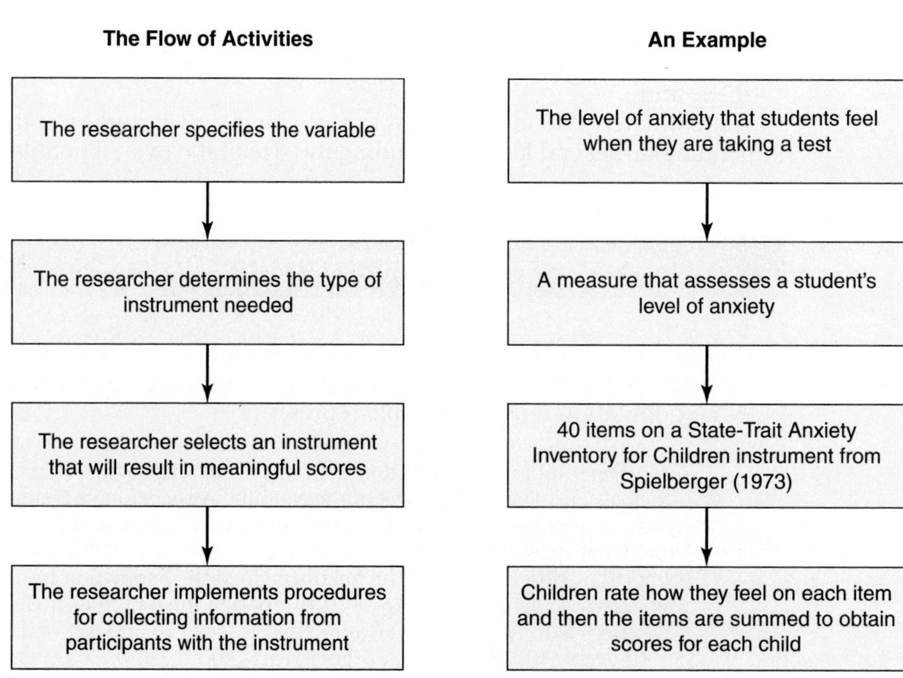

define this variable as a grade point average for algebra class. This grade point average can be measured and will vary among the students (from a low of 0.0 to a high of 4.0).

## Determining the Type of Instrument Needed to Gather Information

Once researchers specify their variables, they next identify the types of data that will measure the variables. Researchers collect quantitative data on instruments. An **instrument** is a tool for measuring, observing, or documenting quantitative data. Determined before the researchers collect data, the instrument may be a test, questionnaire, tally sheet, log, observational checklist, inventory, survey, or assessment instrument. Researchers use instruments to measure achievement, assess individual ability, observe behavior, develop a psychological profile of an individual, or interview a person. There are five general types of quantitative instruments used in research. A summary of each type with examples of items that might be included on such an instrument is illustrated in Figure 7.3. You can consider these different types to understand what information a researcher gathered in a study.

- ***Demographic Forms.*** Researchers collect demographic forms to gather basic facts about and characteristics of their participants. Common types of demographic information collected by researchers include gender, age, race, and annual income.

<table>
<tr><th>Type of Instrument</th><th>Definition</th><th>Examples of Items That Might Appear on This Type of Instrument</th></tr>
<tr><td>Demographic Form</td><td>Instruments used to gather facts about or characteristics of participants</td><td>1. Gender<br>_____ Male (0)<br>_____ Female (1)<br><br>2. Age in years<br>_____ 19 or younger (1)<br>_____ 20–29 (2)<br>_____ 30–39 (3)<br>_____ 40–49 (4)<br>_____ 50 or older (5)</td></tr>
<tr><td>Performance Measure</td><td>Instruments used to assess individuals abilities and achievement</td><td>3. A sample item from a math achievement test:<br>If $x$ is 25% of 40 and $y$ is 50% of $x$, then what is $y$?<br>A. $y = 2$<br>B. $y = 4$<br>C. $y = 5$<br>D. $y = 8$<br>E. $y = 10$</td></tr>
<tr><td>Attitudinal Measure</td><td>Instruments used to measure individuals' attitudes</td><td>4. Bullying is a big problem at my middle school.<br>1. Strongly disagree<br>2. Disagree<br>3. Neither agree nor disagree<br>4. Agree<br>5. Strongly agree</td></tr>
<tr><td>Behavioral Observation</td><td>Instruments used to record individuals' behaviors</td><td>5. Time teacher spends speaking in Spanish during 10 minutes of Spanish II class:<br><table><tr><td>Minute of lesson</td><td>1</td><td>2</td><td>3</td><td>4</td><td>5</td><td>6</td><td>7</td><td>8</td><td>9</td><td>10</td></tr><tr><td>Teacher activity</td><td></td><td></td><td></td><td></td><td></td><td></td><td></td><td></td><td></td><td></td></tr></table>Teacher activity = S = Speaking in Spanish<br>Teacher activity = E = Speaking in English<br>Teacher activity = B = Speaking in both English and Spanish<br>Teacher activity = N = Not speaking</td></tr>
<tr><td>Factual Information</td><td>Information gathered from public records</td><td>6. Number of days recorded as absent: ________<br>7. Number of days suspended from school: ________</td></tr>
</table>

FIGURE 7.3 Types of Instruments, Their Definitions, and Examples of Items

- ***Performance Measures.*** Researchers collect performance measures to assess an individual's ability to perform on an achievement test, intelligence test, aptitude test, interest inventory, or personality assessment inventory. Participants take tests that measure their achievement (e.g., the Iowa Test of Basic Skills), their intelligence (e.g., Wechsler), or their aptitude (e.g., Stanford-Binet). In addition, researchers gather data with instruments that measure an individual's career interests or assess personality traits.
- ***Attitudinal Measures.*** Researchers also measure attitudes of individuals. Researchers use attitudinal measures when they measure participants' feelings toward topics (e.g., assessing positive or negative attitudes toward giving students a choice of school to attend). These measures often ask participants to rate their level of agreement for multiple statements on a scale from strongly agree to strongly disagree. The researcher then adds up the scores on these multiple statements for each individual. This type of attitudinal measure is very common and is often referred to as a "Likert scale" after the person (Rensis Likert) who wrote about its use.
- ***Behavioral Observations.*** Some variables require researchers to collect data on specific behaviors. Researchers observe behavior and record scores on a checklist or scoring sheet. Behavioral observations are made by selecting an instrument (or using a behavioral protocol) on which to record a behavior, observing individuals for that behavior, and checking points on a scale that reflect the behavior (behavioral checklists). The advantage of this form of data is that researchers can measure an individual's actual behavior, rather than simply record their views or perceptions. However, behaviors may be difficult to score, and gathering them is a time-consuming form of data collection.
- ***Factual Information.*** Factual information or personal documents consist of numeric, individual data available in public records. Examples of these types of data include grade reports, school attendance records, student demographic data, and census information. As long as these documents are available in the public domain, researchers can access and use them. Some documents, such as grade or health information, cannot be easily accessed by investigators because federal regulations protect the privacy of individuals.

Researchers select from these types of quantitative instruments to determine how they will measure their variables. The type is often determined by what the researcher wants to measure (e.g., attitudes or behaviors). It also depends on what is feasible. For example, researchers may want to observe how frequently students are bullied on the playground, but observing all students all day is not feasible. Instead they have students report their attitudes about how often they feel that they are bullied on the playground on an instrument. When you read a report, you should note what type of measure was used for each variable and whether that type seemed appropriate considering what the researcher wanted to learn. More importantly than the type, you also want to consider whether the instruments are of good quality and likely to result in meaningful data. Let's now consider the idea of an instrument's quality.

## Understanding What Makes a Good Instrument

Researchers often use instruments that have been developed by other researchers. In some studies, however, no instrument may exist for measuring the variable of interest so the researchers need to develop their own instruments. In either case, researchers should provide evidence that they are using a good instrument. Instruments are good if they result in the collection of data that provides a good measure of the variable of interest. What makes an instrument good or bad? Let's start to answer this question by considering a measurement instrument with which you are probably already familiar.

Suppose you want to study an obesity prevention program by measuring the weight of each participating child at the beginning and end of the school year. You do not have much money, so you buy two old bathroom scales at a garage sale. These bathroom scales are now your instruments to measure the variable weight. You decide to try out these bathroom scales with your daughter who weighs 85 pounds (according to her recent visit to the doctor, who you know has a good scale). That afternoon you ask her to stand on scale #1 three times and you record the following scores: 36 pounds, 36 pounds, and 35 pounds. You ask her to do the same with scale #2 and obtain the following scores: 82 pounds, 91 pounds, and 86 pounds. Knowing that your daughter weighs 85 pounds, are either of these two bathroom scales good measures?

As the bathroom scale example illustrates, it can be easy for researchers to obtain numbers, but it is important that they obtain *good* numbers from their instruments. If numbers are not accurate or if they fluctuate without reason like the two bathroom scales in the example, then the numbers are not useful. There are two criteria useful for assessing whether scores from an instrument are good quality:

- the scores need to be reliable and
- the scores need to valid.

***The Scores from Instruments Should Be Reliable.*** **Reliable** means that scores from an instrument are stable and consistent. Scores should be nearly the same when researchers administer the instrument multiple times. If you stand on a bathroom scale once and then again five minutes later, you expect to record nearly the same weight since it is unlikely your weight changed in five minutes. In our example, scale #1 was reliable (scores were consistently at about 36 pounds), but scale #2 was not reliable (scores varied over 10 pounds even though the girl's weight did not change). Another aspect of reliability is that scores from the items on an instrument need to be consistent. When an individual answers certain questions one way, the individual should consistently answer closely related questions in the same way.

A goal of good research is to have measures or observations that are reliable. Scores from a bathroom scale may be unreliable simply because the spring inside is broken. Scores from a research instrument, however, may not be reliable for several reasons. Different factors can result in unreliable data, such as the questions on the instrument are ambiguous and unclear, or the procedures for completing the instrument vary such as some students get 30 minutes to answer the questions and others are only permitted 10 minutes.

***The Scores from Instruments Should Be Valid.*** **Valid** means that the scores from an instrument make sense, are meaningful, and enable the researcher to draw good conclusions from the sample to the population. If we consider a bathroom scale, then we expect the weight value to accurately measure a person's weight. That is, if the person weighs 85 pounds then we expect the scale to record a value around 85 pounds. Likewise, a quantitative instrument should assign scores to individuals that are meaningful. For example, if a student excels at reading, then you expect him to obtain a high score on an instrument aimed at measuring reading performance.

*Here's a Tip for Applying Research!*

If your school wants to use a test for important decisions, be sure to ask if there is evidence that the test will give scores that are reliable and valid with individuals in your setting.

For practice assessing the instruments described in a quantitative research report, go to the *Building Research Skills* section under the topic "Selecting Measuring Instruments" in MyEducationalResearchLab, located at www.myeducationlab.com. Complete the exercise "Evaluating the Measuring Instruments Used in a Quantitative Study" and use the provided feedback to further develop your skills for reading research articles.

In addition to reliable scores, good research must have measures or observations that are also valid. Scores from a bathroom scale may not be valid because the needle indicating a weight is no longer calibrated (such as if it reports 36 pounds instead of 85 pounds). There are many reasons why scores from a research instrument may not be valid. Consider an instrument that intends to measure overall achievement in a foreign language class. The scores would not be valid if the questions only asked about vocabulary even though the class emphasized grammar, speaking, and culture in addition to vocabulary. Therefore, the questions have to be appropriate to the topic and they have to cover the full range of content that is relevant to the variable being measured. Likewise an instrument has to be written at an appropriate level to be valid. The SAT test may be valid for high school students wanting to go to college, but it would not be a valid test to give to third-graders.

Reliability and validity are bound together in complex ways. These two terms sometimes overlap and at other times are mutually exclusive. Validity can be thought of as the larger, more encompassing term when you assess the choice of an instrument. Reliability is generally easier to understand as it is a measure of consistency. In order to comprehend these concepts more fully, it may be necessary to untangle their relationship. If scores are not reliable, they are not valid; scores need to be stable and consistent first before they can be meaningful. Additionally, the more reliable the scores from an instrument, the more valid the scores may be (however, scores may still not measure the particular construct and may remain invalid). The ideal situation exists when scores are both reliable and valid.

## How Do You Assess the Instruments Used in a Report?

You have now learned many concepts that are important for quantitative data collection: variables, instruments, reliability, and validity. You should look for information about each of these aspects when reading about the instruments used to gather quantitative data. Here are some strategies you can use to identify this information within a quantitative research report:

- ***Identify the major variables.*** Examine the purpose statement, research questions, and hypotheses. In addition, note that authors often discuss the instruments they used in a study by the variables they represent. Therefore, many studies include subheadings that identify the variables. Consider underlining each of these major variables as you read a report so you are clear as to what the researcher is measuring.
- ***Note the type of instrument used to measure each variable.*** Ask yourself whether it is a demographic, performance, attitudinal, observational, or factual measure.
- ***Look for evidence that the scores from the instrument are reliable.*** Evidence of reliable scores may include the following:
  - The scores from the instrument are consistent over time when the instrument is administered more than once to the same individuals. Researchers collect scores at two times and check that they relate (or correlate) at a positive, reasonably high level ($r = .6 - 1.0$). Authors may refer to this as test-retest reliability.
  - The scores from multiple questions are consistent with each other (called internal consistency or Cronbach's alpha, $\alpha$). The scores for all questions should relate to each other at a positive, high level (Cronbach's alpha = $.7 - 1.0$).
  - If multiple raters are used (such as with an observational checklist), the different raters scored items in a consistent way (called inter-rater reliability). Raters in quantitative research should agree 90–100 percent of the time.
- ***Look for evidence that the scores from the instrument are valid.*** Evidence of valid scores may include the following:
  - The authors include a citation to the literature indicating that the instrument was previously developed and used for research purposes.
  - If the authors developed their own instrument, they include the items asked so the reader can judge whether they address the concept being measured in a clear and unambiguous way.
  - Experts assessed that the items on the instrument cover the appropriate content. Authors may refer to this as content validity.
  - The scores from the instrument are a meaningful indicator of the general concept or variable of interest. There are two types of evidence that scores are meaningful. The researcher may expect that the scores are related in certain ways (positive or negative) to other variables and checks to see that the scores match these expectations (called construct validity). The researcher may also expect that scores will not be related to other variables and checks to see that the scores are unrelated as expected (called discriminant validity).

Let's apply this set of strategies to the study excerpt that you read at the start of this chapter. Here is the paragraph about one of the instruments in that study. As you read it again, consider whether you think this study used a good instrument.

> *Adolescent egocentrism.* Adolescent egocentrism was measured with the AES [Adolescent Egocentrism Scale] developed by Enright and colleagues (Enright et al., 1979; Enright et al., 1980). The scale consists of three five-item subscales for the imaginary audience, personal fable, and self-focus. For each item, participants are asked to rate the importance of a statement on a scale ranging from 1 = not important to 5 = very important. The AES has demonstrated acceptable to good levels of internal consistency ranging from Cronbach's alpha = .78 (Enright et al., 1979) to Cronbach's alpha = .83 (Enright et al., 1980). Scores were calculated by summing across the five items for each subscale. *(Frankenberger, 2004, pp. 580–581)*

In the paragraph, the author clearly identified the major variable that is being measured, namely adolescent egocentrism. As we read on, we learn that the author actually has three variables related to this concept: imaginary audience, personal fable, and self-focus. The author provides evidence that the scores from this instrument are reliable (i.e., consistent) to an "acceptable to good" level since Chronbach's alpha is greater than .7. The author also provides limited evidence for the validity of the scores by using an instrument that has been previously reported in the literature (see references to the work of Enright and colleagues).

### What Do You Think?

Read the following passage about quantitative data collection. (a) What variable is discussed? (b) What type of measure is used? (c) What evidence do you note that the researcher selected a good instrument?

> *Intercultural communication apprehension.* Neuliep and McCroskey's (1997a) Personal Report of Intercultural Communication Apprehension (PRICA) was used to assess anxiety associated with real or anticipated intercultural interaction. The higher the score on this 14-item scale, the greater apprehension indicated. In two studies using this scale with U.S. samples, good internal consistency was obtained, with Cronbach's alpha equal to .92 (Lin & Rancer, 2003; Neuliep & Ryan, 1998). Neuliep and McCroskey (1997a) reported support for the construct and discriminant validity of the PRICA. Lin and Rancer (2003) found significant correlations between the PRICA and a measure of intercultural willingness to communicate. *(Kim & Goldstein, 2005, p. 270)*

### Check Your Understanding

From this passage we learned the following: (a) The authors discuss how they plan to measure a variable called *intercultural communication apprehension.* (b) This instrument sounds like it is an attitudinal measure because it measures participants' attitudes about interacting with other cultures. (c) The authors provide extensive evidence that this is a good instrument. We learn that the scores from this instrument tend to be reliable. They note that "good internal consistency" was obtained in previous studies (Chronbach's alpha = .92). In terms of the instrument's validity, we learn that this instrument has been previously used, and that its validity has been supported by two studies that examined how its scores relate to other measures.

## What Procedures Do Researchers Use When Collecting Quantitative Data?

In addition to information about participants and instruments, quantitative research reports should also include a description of the procedures used to collect data. The actual process of collecting quantitative data differs depending on the research design, participants, and instruments used. There are, however, three important procedures for every quantitative data collection process. These are ethical practices, the use of standardized procedures, and anticipating "threats" to a study's conclusions.

### The Procedures Should Be Ethical

Above all else, the collection of quantitative data should be ethical and respect individuals and sites. Federal legislation requires that researchers guarantee participants certain rights and request their permission to be involved in a research study. No matter how interesting a study's topic, researchers should only collect data using ethical procedures. If the data collection procedures are not ethical, then the study should not get published, and it certainly should not receive your attention. Here are some indications that the researcher used ethical procedures during data collection.

- ***The researcher obtained permission to conduct their study from their local campus.*** Most researchers work for universities that are required to have institutional review boards (IRBs). The IRBs are charged with reviewing research procedures before studies start to ensure they represent ethical practices for conducting research on human subjects. When a researcher reports that they have received such approval, then you know that an ethics committee has reviewed their procedures.
- ***The researcher obtained permission to collect data within an organization.*** By noting that access to an institution (such as a school or clinic) was permitted, the researcher is informing readers about their ethical practices.
- ***Researchers must obtain permission from individuals who participate in their studies.*** This involves informing them about the purpose of the research, without deception. It also includes taking steps to protect the privacy and confidentiality of individuals who participate in the study. Investigators should be sensitive to the potential harm that participants may experience because of research and ensure that the potential benefits outweigh any risk for harm. Participation should be voluntary and individuals should give their informed consent before participating. If the participants include minors, then in most instances the researcher must also take steps to secure parental informed consent in addition to having the children agree to participate.

## The Data Should Be Collected in a Standardized Way

Researchers must also take care to conduct their studies so that they collect good quantitative data. It is important that quantitative researchers use standard procedures for collecting all of their data. This means that they try to collect their questionnaire, observation, or interview data in a similar way from all participants. When procedures vary, researchers may introduce bias into the study and the data for individuals may not be comparable for analysis. There are different ways that data collection procedures may be standardized.

> *Here's a Tip for Applying Research!*
>
> The contexts in which individuals provide data can influence their responses. If you want to collect good information (say on an end-of-chapter test), you want to use uniform procedures, such as giving everyone the same amount of time. In addition, make sure that your questions are clear and cover the content so that the test will be more likely to produce meaningful scores.

- Researchers use instruments with **close-ended questions** that include preset options from which the participant can respond.
- Researchers give all participants the same directions for completing the instruments and have them complete the measures under similar conditions (such as having the same amount of time to take a test or making sure students do not talk to each other while filling out a questionnaire about attitudes).
- When collecting observational data, the observers must be adequately trained so that they can recognize the target behaviors and make records that are in a usable form.

Consider the following passage as an example of using standardized procedures: "Between mid–October and mid–November 2000, 1st-year seminar students completed an extensive survey packet during a class period. Volunteer participants were read instructions for completing the questionnaire and then did so at their own pace during the survey administration session" (Kim & Goldstein, 2005, p. 272). This passage indicates that the researchers collected their data in a standard way (i.e., all participants were provided one class period to complete the surveys, data were collected during one month in the semester, and the researchers read the instructions out loud to ensure that participants received the same directions).

## Threats to Studies' Conclusions Should Be Anticipated

In addition to having good instruments and standardized and ethical procedures, quantitative researchers also need to implement procedures that will allow them to make meaningful conclusions about their research questions and hypotheses from the data. There are two special types of conclusions that are desired in quantitative research. These are:

- the researcher wants to claim that the independent variables really caused changes in the dependent variables and

- the researcher wants to claim that the findings can be generalized from the sample to a larger population.

Good quantitative studies include procedures that anticipate the threats to these types of claims. In fact, being able to make these claims in a valid way is so important that they have been given their own special names in quantitative research: internal validity and external validity. Just as researchers want the scores from their instrument to be valid, they also want to design their data collection procedures in a way so that their conclusions are valid.

***Using Procedures to Increase a Study's Internal Validity.*** **Internal validity** in quantitative research is the extent to which a researcher can claim that the independent variable caused an effect in the dependent variable. Recall from Chapter 6, researchers conduct different types of experiments (true experiments, quasi-experiments, and single subject experiments) for the purpose of establishing that a treatment causes an effect. Therefore, one way that researchers increase a study's internal validity is by choosing an experimental design instead of a survey or correlational design.

To show that the independent variable caused an outcome, the researcher tries to control for spurious variables that may also influence the outcome. Good experimental procedures include:

- randomly assigning individuals to treatment groups so that differences among individuals are spread across the groups;
- measuring other variables that need to be controlled, such as giving a pretest or assessing individuals for attitudes that may be relevant to how they respond to a treatment; and
- manipulating the activities that participants receive so that they are similar across groups except for the treatment related to the independent variable.

***Using Procedures to Increase a Study's External Validity.*** **External validity** in quantitative research is the extent to which a researcher can generalize the results from the study sample to a population. As a general rule, studies using a survey design are more generalizable (i.e., have higher external validity) than experimental or correlational studies. This is because survey studies are designed for the purpose of describing trends in a larger population.

In order to conclude that the results can generalize from the study's sample to a larger population, the researcher needs to provide evidence that their sample is representative. Good survey procedures include:

- randomly selecting individuals from the population to participate in the study;
- examining demographic information of participants to see that they are similar to the larger group; and
- using procedures to encourage as many people as possible to respond to the study's measurement instruments. This results in a larger sample size and reduces the number of nonrespondents. If many people do not respond, then the results may not generalize because the people who chose to respond may be different from those who do not.

Both internal and external validity are important in quantitative research. It is difficult, however, to achieve high levels of both because they are related to each other in complex ways. Researchers achieve a high level of internal validity by controlling all extra variables. The more variables are controlled, however, the less generalizable the results become. Let's consider an example to see the relationship between these two ideas.

Suppose researchers want to test whether a new reading curriculum causes better reading achievement. They might set up an experiment that compares students randomly assigned to receive the new curriculum to those assigned to receive standard instruction. There are many possible influences on reading achievement—such as the effectiveness of the teacher, available reading materials, and time spent practicing. To control for these effects, the researchers have the children from a local magnet school come to a special program in their laboratory for six weeks during the summer. At the laboratory, the researcher provides instruction to both groups and mandates that all children put in a set amount of time practicing each day with research assistants. Therefore, if the results show better achievement for the students in the experimental group, we can feel fairly certain that the new curriculum caused this achievement. That is, this study has a high level of internal validity. These results, however, will not generalize to real schools and classrooms that have a range of teachers and children who may or may not complete their homework each day. Therefore, this study also has relatively low external validity.

### What Do You Think?

Recall the quantitative parent involvement study (Deslandes & Bertrand, 2005) from Chapter 1. Read the following passage from this study. What procedural issues do the authors discuss?

> We collected all the data from survey respondents by means of questionnaires in late spring 2001. Following the school principals' acceptance to participate in the study, we mailed nearly 2,560 parent questionnaires to the schools. Forty-five classroom teachers from five schools volunteered to send the questionnaires to 1,500 parents via the students. The package included a letter that explained the purpose of the study and requested voluntary participation. The participation rate was approximately 51% (770 parents accepted from the 1,500 questionnaires that were sent home).

### Check Your Understanding

The authors touch on a number of procedural issues related to their study in these few sentences. First, we find evidence that they employed ethical practices because they describe getting the permission of principals, and including information to inform parents about the study's purpose. Second, we learn important procedural details, such as when the researchers collected the data and under what conditions parents received the questionnaires. Third, we learn that the researchers tried to obtain a large and representative sample of parents across numerous schools. We also learn that many parents did not return the questionnaires, so we have to question whether the study's results will apply to all parents, or if the parents who respond may be somehow different from those parents who did not respond. Therefore, the results may be somewhat representative of all parents, but the claims for external validity would be stronger if a true probability sample had been obtained and if more parents had responded.

## How Do You Evaluate a Study's Quantitative Data Collection?

It is essential to understand the basics of quantitative data collection to understand any quantitative research report. As you identify the elements of the quantitative data collection in a report, you can also assess how well the researcher implemented them in the study. Use the criteria for a high-quality report provided in Figure 7.4 to assess an author's implementation of quantitative data collection. These items evaluate whether the author provides sufficient information about the sample, instruments, and procedures in the report. In addition, they examine the extent to which the researchers collected the data in a manner consistent with a good quantitative research approach. The authors should provide enough information for you to understand what was done and why it was done that way. Good quantitative research studies will incorporate most of the criteria listed in Figure 7.4.

## Reviewing What We've Learned

- Look under the heading of *Method* in a research study for the data collection procedures.

Use the following criteria to evaluate the quality of a quantitative study's data collection as specified within a research report. For each evaluation item, indicate the following ratings:

+ You rate the item as "high quality" for the study.
✓ You rate the item as "ok quality" for the study.
– You rate the item as "low quality" for the study.

In addition to your rating, make notes about each element when you apply these criteria to an actual published study.

| **In a high-quality quantitative research report, the author . . .** | Application to a Published Study | |
|---|---|---|
| | Your Rating | Your Notes |
| 1. Clearly identifies the population so you know the group about which the authors are trying to learn. | | |
| 2. Explains the sampling strategy used so you know how individuals were selected. | | |
| 3. Uses probability sampling, if possible, to ensure that the participants are likely to be representative of the population. | | |
| 4. States the sample size so you know how many people provided data for the study. | | |
| 5. Uses a large sample size and explains why the sample size is sufficiently large. | | |
| 6. Identifies the instruments used to measure each variable. | | |
| 7. Provides evidence that the scores from each instrument are reliable and valid. | | |
| 8. Includes information about the procedures that indicate that the research was conducted ethically, used standardized procedures, and anticipated threats to the conclusions. | | |

FIGURE 7.4 Criteria for Evaluating the Quality of a Study's Quantitative Data Collection

- Recognize that this *Method* section contains information about who participated in the study and where it was conducted, the types of data collected, and the quality of the instruments and the data collection procedures.
- Identify the group or population that is being studied.
- Search for the individuals or sample who actually provided data for the study.
- Determine whether the sample was selected using a rigorous method (e.g., probability sampling).
- See whether a large sample size is used.
- Determine the types of data collection, such as demographics, performance or attitudinal measures, behavioral observations, and factual information.

- Assess whether good instruments were used in terms of reliability and validity.
- Ask yourself whether the researchers used good ethical practices, collected their data in a standard way, and anticipated possible threats to their conclusions.

## Practicing Your Skills

At this time, read carefully the "quantitative youth literacy study" article starting on p. 197 at the end of this chapter. As you read this article, pay close attention to the discussion of data collection that appears in the method section (paragraphs 12–16).

Once you have read the study, assess your knowledge of the content of this chapter by answering the following questions that relate to the quantitative youth literacy study. Use the answers found in the Appendix to evaluate your progress.

1. From what sites and participants did the authors collect their quantitative data? How were they selected? What was the size of the sample?
2. What instrument did the authors use to learn about youth leisure activities? Do you think the scores from this instrument are good? Explain your thoughts.
3. What procedures did the authors describe related to their quantitative data collection?
4. The authors state a limitation of their study is that the results may not be representative of all students (paragraph 28). What could the researchers have done differently during data collection to make their results more generalizable?
5. The authors found a significant difference between grades in the use of e-mail. Can they claim that grade level caused this difference based on how they collected the data? Why or why not?

# The Quantitative Youth Literacy Study

Let's examine another published research study to apply what you have learned about reading research articles and to evaluate how researchers collect quantitative data (by completing the *Practicing Your Skills* questions listed on the previous page.) A formal reference for this study is:

Nippold, M. A., Duthie, J. K., & Larsen, J. (2005). Literacy as a leisure activity: Free-time preferences of older children and young adolescents. *Language, Speech, and Hearing Services in Schools, 36,* 93–102.

As you read this article, note the marginal annotations that signal the major sections of a research report, the steps of the research process, and the major characteristics of quantitative research. In addition, use the following walk-through to help you understand how the steps of the research process are described within the four major sections of the report.

## The Introduction Section

- Identifying a research problem (paragraphs 01–11)
- Reviewing the literature (paragraphs 04–08)
- Specifying the purpose (paragraph 09)

The authors of the quantitative youth literacy study (Nippold et al., 2005) describe the importance of reading for helping youth develop knowledge about words and language throughout the introduction. They discuss the benefits of reading for language development, thereby implying that a problem exists if youth do not read because they will not have these benefits. They conclude their introduction with a strong statement that children with language disorders will face additional problems with their language development if they do not enjoy or participate in reading (paragraph 10). The authors use literature to justify the importance of reading (paragraphs 01–03) and include a study-by-study literature review of studies that have examined the relationship between reading and word knowledge in paragraphs 04–08.

In paragraph 09 the authors state that there is a deficiency in the literature because little is known about current youth reading habits. The authors show that they will address this deficiency by stating the purpose of their study in the form of three goals in paragraph 09. This overall purpose is to describe current trends in preferences and habits for free time and reading for youth ages 11–15 years in Oregon. The researchers suggest that this knowledge will benefit speech-language pathologists who work with children that have language disorders so that they can suggest appropriate reading materials for these children (paragraph 10).

## The Method Section

- Selecting a design and collecting data (paragraphs 12–16)

The authors describe their methods for collecting data to address their stated purpose. Although the research design is not identified by name, this study uses a survey research design to describe trends in youth reading. The authors describe the participants of their study (paragraphs 12–14). They selected a total of 200 children (half girls, half boys) from Grades 6 and 9 from a middle and high school in one middle-income neighborhood in western Oregon.

The researchers used a survey questionnaire to collect data from the participants. They chose to develop this questionnaire themselves and therefore there is no information about its use from prior research. The researchers did include a copy of the questions in the article's appendix. From these questions we can see that the survey included three questions with many close-ended response options. The researchers describe a number of procedures that they used to gather information with this survey. We learn in paragraph 13 the procedures that they used to collect this information in an ethical manner, including notifying parents about the study and assuring individuals that their participation is voluntary. In addition, the researchers took steps to make sure that the survey was administered in a standard way by reading the questions out loud and giving students time to indicate their responses (see paragraph 15).

## The Results Section

- Analyzing the data and reporting results (paragraphs 17–23)

The authors present their results in paragraphs 17–23 and in three tables (one per item on the questionnaire). The tables provide descriptive information about the percentage of participants that indicated each of the provided response options. The authors also highlight the most popular activities in paragraphs 17 and 21. In addition, the researchers analyzed the data to compare responses by grade (sixth vs. ninth) and gender (boys vs. girls). They found a number of significant differences in the preferred ways to spend free time, but few significant differences related to time spent reading and preferred reading materials.

## The Conclusion Section

- Interpreting the research (paragraphs 24–32)

The authors concluded their report with a discussion of what they learned. They first summarized the major results in paragraph 24. They next compared the results to past research (paragraphs 25–27). They also evaluated their research study in this section. They described some important limitations of the study such as not being able to generalize to all students (paragraph 28). They also suggested future research based on the results (paragraph 28). Finally, they provided an extensive discussion of the implications of their results for encouraging youth reading habits (paragraphs 29–31).

LSHSS

# Literacy as a Leisure Activity: Free-Time Preferences of Older Children and Young Adolescents

Marilyn A. Nippold
Jill K. Duthie
Jennifer Larsen
University of Oregon, Eugene

Introduction Section

Identifying a research problem

01 Literacy plays an important role in the development of language during the school-age and adolescent years. Typically developing youth acquire new vocabulary at an impressive rate of 2,000 to 3,000 words per year (Nagy & Scott, 2000; White, Power, & White, 1989), resulting in a working knowledge of at least 40,000 different words by the senior year of high school (Nagy & Herman, 1987). One factor promoting this

ABSTRACT: **Purpose:** Literacy plays an important role in the development of language in school-age children and adolescents. For example, by reading a variety of books, magazines, and newspapers, students gain exposure to complex vocabulary, and reading becomes a prime opportunity for learning new words. Despite the importance of reading for lexical development, little is known about the pleasure reading habits of today's youth. The first goal of this investigation was to examine the preferences of older children and young adolescents with respect to reading as a leisure-time activity and its relationship to other free-time options that are likely to compete for their attention. The second goal was to examine the amount of time that young people spend reading for pleasure each day and the types of materials they most enjoy reading. The third goal was to determine if preferences for free-time activities and reading materials would evince age- and gender-related differences during the period of development from late childhood through early adolescence (ages 11–15 years). The findings could serve as a reference point for understanding what is reasonable to expect of students during this age range.
**Method:** The participants were 100 sixth graders (mean age = 11;7 [years;months]) and 100 ninth graders (mean age = 14;8) attending public schools in western Oregon. Each group contained an equal number of boys and girls, all of whom spoke English as their primary language and were considered to be typical achievers. All participants completed a survey concerning their preferred free-time activities and reading materials. They also reported the average amount of time they spent reading for pleasure each day.
**Results:** The most popular free-time activities were listening to music/going to concerts, watching television or videos, playing sports, and playing computer or video games. Least preferred activities were cooking, running or walking, writing, and arts and crafts. Reading was moderately popular. The most popular reading materials were magazines, novels, and comics; least popular were plays, technical books, and newspapers. Interest in pleasure reading declined during this age range (11–15 years), and boys were more likely than girls to report that they spent no time reading for pleasure.
**Clinical Implications:** Given the importance of reading to lexical development in school-age children and adolescents, reading should be promoted as a leisure activity during these years. School-based speech-language pathologists (SLPs), in their role as language consultants, can benefit from understanding the pleasure-reading patterns of today's youth. It is especially important for SLPs to monitor these patterns in students who have language disorders, as it is common for these young people to experience deficits in reading and in lexical development. Fortunately, much can be done in school settings to encourage strong literacy habits in all students if SLPs work collaboratively with teachers, principals, psychologists, librarians, parents, and students. Suggestions are offered for ways to encourage young people to spend more time reading for pleasure.

KEY WORDS: lexical development, literacy, pleasure reading, school-age children, adolescents enormous growth in lexical development is the increased exposure to written language that occurs as children become proficient readers (Miller & Gildea, 1987). Compared to spoken language (e.g., conversations, television shows), written language (e.g., newspapers, novels) contains a greater variety of complex and low-frequency words, and becomes a prime opportunity for learning the meanings of words, particularly after the fifth grade (Cunningham & Stanovich, 1998; Stanovich & Cunningham, 1992). By this time, decoding and fluency skills have improved in most students to the point where reading has become a tool for gaining new knowledge, which includes the learning of words that occur in textbooks for older children and adolescents (Chall, 1983). Increased word knowledge leads to stronger reading comprehension, which, in turn, leads to further lexical expansion (Sternberg & Powell, 1983). Thus, there is an ongoing reciprocal relationship between language and literacy development in youth.

02 Learning the meanings of unfamiliar words is a gradual process (Beck & McKeown, 1991) that requires an understanding of subtle nuances and the ability to use those words in different contexts (Nagy & Scott, 2000). A single exposure to an unfamiliar word is unlikely to result in this degree of knowledge, and studies have shown that many new words are learned as a result of having repeated exposure to them while reading (Jenkins, Stein, & Wysocki, 1984; Nagy, Herman, & Anderson, 1985; Schwanenflugel, Stahl, & McFalls, 1997). The mechanisms by which this occurs have been studied in detail. Research has shown that upon exposure to an unfamiliar word, the learner begins to determine its meaning through the use of key metalinguistic strategies—morphological analysis (Anglin, 1993; Nagy, Diakidoy, & Anderson, 1993; White et al., 1989; Wysocki & Jenkins, 1987) and contextual abstraction (Miller & Gildea, 1987; Sternberg, 1987; Sternberg & Powell, 1983). Either or both of these strategies may be used depending on the analyzability of the target word and the quality of context clues surrounding it (Nippold, 2002). For example, consider a child who encounters the word *mineralogy* in a newspaper article about volcanoes. Knowledge of the lexical morpheme *mineral* and the derivational morpheme *-ology* can help the learner determine that the word refers to the science of chemicals found in the ground, a conjecture supported by sentences contained in the article, such as, "And when they [the scientists] thought to compare the *mineralogy* of their samples with known Missoula sediments, they were surprised to find that no one had ever examined the clay in detail.... Their idea was confirmed when they compared the minerals of the clay and material known to have been ejected by Mount Mazama" (Bolt, p. A9). These strategies offer a viable alternative to less efficient methods of word learning such as the use of a dictionary (Nippold, 1998).

03 Nagy and Herman (1987) estimated that children encounter 15,000 to 30,000 unfamiliar words a year from reading only 25 min per day, and argued that up to one half of student vocabulary growth may result from reading. Additionally, Miller and Gildea (1987) reported that students who are avid readers acquire larger vocabularies than those who read less frequently. Indeed, studies have found a consistent link between the amount of time spent reading and word knowledge in both children and adults.

04 Cunningham and Stanovich (1991) conducted a study to determine if there was a relationship between print exposure, vocabulary, and other skills in fourth- through sixth-grade children ($N$ = 134). Print exposure was measured by a title recognition task (TRT) consisting of a checklist of children's book titles and a series of foils. Additional measures were obtained for vocabulary, verbal fluency, nonverbal problem-solving ability, and general knowledge. Oral vocabulary was measured by a group-administered selection from the Peabody Picture Vocabulary Test—Revised (PPVT–R; Dunn & Dunn, 1981); reading vocabulary was measured by a checklist composed of real words and nonword foils; and verbal fluency was measured by a task in which the children wrote down as many words as they could from four different categories, each in 45 s. Using hierarchical regression analyses to control for age and nonverbal ability, the investigators found that print exposure as measured by the TRT uniquely predicted oral vocabulary, reading vocabulary, verbal fluency, and general knowledge.

Reviewing the literature

The literaure plays a major role

05 Similarly, Stanovich and Cunningham (1992) conducted a study to determine if differences in print exposure were associated with word knowledge in young adults who were college students ($N$ = 300). Participants were administered formal tests of reading vocabulary, oral vocabulary, verbal fluency, reading comprehension, and cognitive ability (nonverbal analogical reasoning). They also were asked to fill out questionnaires that assessed their exposure to print, including their familiarity with authors (Author Recognition Test) and magazines (Magazine Recognition Test). Controlling for reading comprehension and cognitive ability in the participants, hierarchical regression analyses revealed that the level of print exposure uniquely predicted each measure of word knowledge: reading vocabulary, oral vocabulary, and verbal fluency.

06 West, Stanovich, and Mitchell (1993) also demonstrated a strong relationship between print exposure and word knowledge. Adult participants ($N$ = 217) were selected from an airport lounge on the basis of their observed reading behavior, and were classified as either "readers" or "nonreaders" according to how they spent their waiting time. Each participant was then administered a vocabulary checklist and a series of tasks to measure print exposure (i.e., recognition of authors, magazines, and newspapers) and nonprint exposure (i.e., recognition of television shows, films, and actors). Readers received higher scores on print exposure than nonreaders, but the groups did not differ on nonprint exposure. It was also determined that higher scores on print exposure were significantly related to vocabulary scores, whereas higher scores on nonprint exposure were not. Hierarchical regression analyses indicated that all three measures of print exposure—recognition of authors, magazines, and newspapers—accounted for unique variance in vocabulary while controlling for participant age and amount of education.

07 This is not to argue that reading is the only source of word learning. Clearly, people can learn new words from other sources such as listening to lectures and news reports,

talking with informed individuals, and watching educational television shows (Rice, 1983). Nevertheless, reading is a prime source of word exposure, particularly for complex and low-frequency words, and there is evidence from research that the amount of time spent reading is closely associated with word learning—a relationship that holds during childhood and adulthood (e.g., Cunningham & Stanovich, 1991; Stanovich & Cunningham, 1992; West et al., 1993). This suggests that reading should be promoted, not only as a school-based activity, but as a leisure-time activity as well.

**08** Beyond exposure to new words, reading for pleasure offers additional benefits. Summarizing past research, Worthy, Moorman, and Turner (1999) reported that when children and adolescents engage in voluntary reading about topics that truly interest them, their effort, motivation, and attitudes about reading improve. They also reported that allowing students to read simpler materials such as comics and magazines can improve their basic reading skills (e.g., fluency), leading to increased confidence. This, they suggested, could encourage students to tackle more technical reading materials in school.

A deficiency in the knowledge

Specifying a purpose for the research

The quantitative purpose statement and research questions call for observable and measurable data

**09** Although most speech-language pathologists (SLPs) probably would agree that reading is an important activity that should be promoted in young people, little is known about today's youth and their views concerning the value of reading for pleasure in relation to the multitude of options that exist for spending one's leisure time. Hence, the first goal of the present study was to investigate the preferences of older children and young adolescents with respect to reading as a leisure-time activity and its relationship to other free-time options that are likely to compete for their attention. The second goal was to examine the amount of time that young people spend reading for pleasure each day and the types of materials they most enjoy reading. The third goal was to determine if preferences for free-time activities and reading materials would evince age- and gender-related differences during the period of development from late childhood through early adolescence (ages 11–15 years). The findings could serve as a reference point for understanding what is reasonable to expect of students during this age range.

**10** This developmental period was of interest because students are beyond the fifth grade, a time when reading has become a primary tool for learning the meanings of new words (Stanovich & Cunningham, 1992). This is also a time when socializing with peers takes on greater importance. In a cross-sectional study, Raffaelli and Duckett (1989) examined the socialization patterns of boys and girls ($N$ = 401) during the ages of 10 to 15. They found that, as age increased, students spent greater amounts of time socializing with friends (e.g., talking on the phone and talking in person), a pattern that characterized girls more so than boys. They also found that as age increased, peer interactions made greater contributions to students' personal well-being. At the same time, however, parents remained an important source of information and advice, a finding confirmed by other investigators (e.g., Rawlins, 1992). Given these findings, it is important to examine the literacy habits of children and adolescents during this age range when socialization might be expected to displace solitary activities such as reading, and when differences in the behavior patterns of boys and girls sometimes emerge.

Selecting a research design and collecting data

The quantitative purpose statement and research questions are narrow and specific

A problem that calls for explanation

**11** In public schools today, SLPs frequently work with school-age children and adolescents having language disorders. In an effort to conduct intervention that is relevant and ecologically valid, SLPs increasingly serve as consultants to other school professionals who work with those same students (Whitmire, 2000), such as teachers, psychologists, and librarians. Many students with language disorders experience difficulties in learning to read (Bashir, Wiig, & Abrams, 1987; Catts, Fey, Zhang, & Tomblin, 2001; Catts & Kamhi, 1999; Nippold & Schwarz, 2002; Stothard, Snowling, Bishop, Chipchase, & Kaplan, 1998) and have long-standing deficits in lexical development (Kail, Hale, Leonard, & Nippold, 1984; Kail & Leonard, 1986; McGregor, Newman, Reilly, & Capone, 2002). Students with language disorders who do not enjoy reading are likely to receive less exposure to new vocabulary through text—a situation that can exacerbate their limitations in word knowledge. Given the contribution that reading makes to lexical development, SLPs need to understand the literacy habits of today's youth in order to provide appropriate recommendations in their role as language consultants in public school settings.

Method Section

Quantitative researchers select participants that are representative of a population

Quantitative researchers include a large number of participants

## METHOD

### Participants

**12** The participants were 100 sixth-grade children (50 boys, 50 girls) with a mean age of 11;7 (years;months; range = 11;1–12;1) and 100 ninth-grade adolescents (50 boys, 50 girls) with a mean age of 14;8 (range = 14;1–15;7). All participants were enrolled in a public middle school (sixth graders) or high school (ninth graders) located in a lower middle-income neighborhood in western Oregon. According to teacher report, the students represented a range of ability levels and were considered to be typical achievers. None had a known history of language, learning, or cognitive deficits, and none was receiving special education services. More than 90% of the participants were of European American descent, and all reported that English was their primary language spoken at home.

**13** Teachers at each school were asked to volunteer their classes. This request resulted in the recruitment of five sixth-grade English classes and five ninth-grade English classes. A passive consent procedure was employed. The parents of all students enrolled in those 10 classes were provided with a letter informing them of the nature of the study and indicating that it was an optional activity to be carried out during regular school hours. If any parents objected to their son or daughter participating in the study, they were able to communicate that by returning a form letter to the school. No students were pressured to participate, and all were assured that it was a voluntary activity. Students were told that their individual performance would remain confidential. In addition, they were able to indicate their own willingness to participate by signing an assent form on the day of testing. Students who were not participating in the study were allowed to work quietly at their desks or go to the school library during the testing.

14 The Oregon Department of Education Web site (http://www.ode.state.or.us) reported that 13.8% of the students in this school district live in poverty, as compared to 14.3% for the state as a whole. The Web site also reported the percentage of students who met or exceeded the state benchmarks in reading, based on their performance on the Oregon Statewide Assessment (OSA). In Oregon, this test is administered every year to all students in grades three, five, eight, and ten. The participants in this investigation would have taken the test during their fifth- or eighth-grade year. Although individual student scores were not available, it was reported that, for this district, 75% of the fifth graders met or exceeded the performance standards that year as compared to 79% for the state, and 54% of the eighth graders met or exceeded the standards as compared to 64% for the state. These results suggest that the participants in this investigation were fairly representative of students in Oregon. However, the results also suggest that some of the participants, particularly those in ninth grade, may not have met the performance standards in reading despite the fact that none had been identified as having special needs.

## Procedures

15 All participants were tested in large-group fashion in their classrooms at school by one of the investigators. They were asked to complete a two-page survey, the "Student Questionnaire" (see Appendix), designed especially for the present study. To ensure that all participants were listening to the directions and performing the task, the examiner read each question aloud, paused, and allowed time for them to mark their own answers.

16 The survey required approximately 10 min to complete and consisted of three main questions. Question 1, which asked how students spent their free time, provided a list of activities that were thought to be of interest to middle-school and high-school students. As a result of investigator observations of young people and discussions with their parents, it was believed that these activities might be good candidates to compete for students' time and attention. In addition to activities that are primarily solitary (e.g., reading, writing), the list contained activities that could be carried out either alone or with others (e.g., shopping, media events, sports, games). The category of "other" was also provided to allow students to write in any favorite activities that were not included in the list. Question 2 asked the students to estimate how much time they typically spent each day reading for pleasure outside of the school day, followed by a set of options (e.g., none, 5–10 min, 10–20 min). Question 3 provided a list of common reading materials (e.g., poems, novels, newspapers) and asked the students to indicate which types they enjoyed reading for pleasure. The opportunity to indicate "none of the above" and "other" (write in) was provided to compensate for anything that had been omitted from the list. Upon completion of the testing, all students were rewarded with a ballpoint pen.

Quantitative researchers collect information in the form of numbers

## RESULTS

Results Section

17 Table 1 reports the results of Question 1, free-time activities, showing the percentage of students who selected each item as something they liked to do. For all students combined ($N$ = 200), the most popular activities were listening to music/going to concerts (78%), watching television or videos (77%), playing sports (68%), and playing computer or video games (63%). Least popular activities were cooking (32%), running or walking (33%), writing (34%), and arts and crafts (38%). Reading (51%) was a moderately popular activity. For the category of "other," the most popular write-in activity was spending time with friends (e.g., sleepovers, playing with friends, visiting friends' homes, having friends come to visit), especially for girls. Fourteen sixth graders (4 boys, 10 girls) and 11 ninth graders (2 boys, 9 girls) wrote in this activity.

Analyzing data and reporting results

Quantitative findings include descriptive statistics

18 For each activity listed on the questionnaire, the data were analyzed using a 2 × 2 (grade × gender) analysis of variance (ANOVA) with Bonferroni corrections for multiple comparisons (adjusted alpha = .003). Effect sizes were computed using the eta coefficient (Meline & Schmitt, 1997) and were interpreted as follows: small = .10–.23; medium = .24–.36; large = .37–.71 (Cohen, 1969, p. 276). For grade, statistically significant main effects were obtained for swimming, $F(1, 196) = 13.25$, $p = .0003$, $\eta = .25$; riding a bicycle or scooter, $F(1, 196) = 20.86$, $p < .0001$, $\eta = .31$; using e-mail $F(1, 196) = 9.90$, $p = .0019$, $\eta = .22$; and reading, $F(1, 196) = 15.70$, $p = .0001$, $\eta = .27$. Effect sizes were small for using e-mail and medium for swimming, riding a bicycle or scooter, and reading. Tukey's studentized range (honestly significant difference [HSD]) test ($p = .05$) indicated that ninth graders showed a stronger preference than sixth graders for e-mail, whereas sixth graders showed a stronger preference than ninth graders for swimming, riding a bicycle or scooter, and reading.

Quantitative researchers use statistical analyses to describe trends, relate variables, and compare groups

19 For gender, statistically significant main effects were obtained for playing computer or video games, $F(1, 196) = 23.14$, $p < .0001$, $\eta = .32$; playing sports, $F(1, 196) = 15.05$, $p = .0001$, $\eta = .27$; talking on the phone, $F(1, 196) = 20.74$, $p < .0001$, $\eta = .31$; using e-mail, $F(1, 196) = 14.03$, $p = .0002$, $\eta = .26$; shopping, $F(1, 196) = 83.36$, $p < .0001$, $\eta = .55$; writing, $F(1, 196) = 73.30$, $p < .0001$, $\eta = .52$; and cooking, $F(1, 196) = 9.52$, $p = .0023$, $\eta = .22$. Effect sizes were small for cooking; medium for playing computer or video games, playing sports, talking on the phone, and using e-mail; and large for shopping and writing. Tukey's (HSD) test ($p = .05$) showed that boys preferred playing computer or video games and playing sports, whereas girls preferred talking on the phone, using e-mail, shopping, writing, and cooking. No interactions between grade and gender were statistically significant.

Quantitative findings include inferential statistics

20 Table 2 reports the results of Question 2, the amount of time spent reading for pleasure. For each time block, the data were analyzed using a 2 × 2 (grade × gender) ANOVA



Quantitative researchers ask participants close-ended questions

Quantitative researchers use strategies to ensure the reliability and validity of instruments

**Table 1.** Percentage of students who responded positively to each item listed under the question, "How do you like to spend your free time?" (standard deviations are reported).

| | *Grade 6* | | | *Grade 9* | | | *Grades 6 & 9* | | |
|---|---|---|---|---|---|---|---|---|---|
| | *Boys* | *Girls* | *Combined* | *Boys* | *Girls* | *Combined* | *Boys* | *Girls* | *Combined* |
| A. watching TV or videos | 88 | 74 | 81 | 74 | 70 | 72 | 81 | 72 | 77 |
| | (33) | (44) | (39) | (44) | (46) | (45) | (39) | (45) | (43) |
| B. playing computer or video games | 82 | 58 | 70 | 74 | 36 | 55 | 78 | 47 | 63 |
| | (39) | (50) | (46) | (44) | (48) | (50) | (42) | (50) | (49) |
| C. playing sports | 82 | 56 | 69 | 78 | 54 | 66 | 80 | 55 | 68 |
| | (39) | (50) | (46) | (42) | (50) | (48) | (40) | (50) | (47) |
| D. running or walking | 32 | 26 | 29 | 30 | 42 | 36 | 31 | 34 | 33 |
| | (47) | (44) | (46) | (46) | (50) | (48) | (46) | (48) | (47) |
| E. swimming | 54 | 64 | 59 | 38 | 30 | 34 | 46 | 47 | 47 |
| | (50) | (48) | (49) | (49) | (46) | (48) | (50) | (50) | (50) |
| F. skating | 46 | 42 | 44 | 54 | 22 | 38 | 50 | 32 | 41 |
| | (50) | (50) | (50) | (50) | (42) | (49) | (50) | (47) | (49) |
| G. riding a bicycle or scooter | 78 | 70 | 74 | 56 | 32 | 44 | 67 | 51 | 59 |
| | (42) | (46) | (44) | (50) | (47) | (50) | (47) | (50) | (49) |
| H. playing cards or board games | 64 | 40 | 52 | 36 | 32 | 34 | 50 | 36 | 43 |
| | (48) | (49) | (50) | (48) | (47) | (48) | (50) | (48) | (50) |
| I. talking on the phone | 38 | 64 | 51 | 50 | 84 | 67 | 44 | 74 | 59 |
| | (49) | (48) | (50) | (51) | (37) | (47) | (50) | (44) | (49) |
| J. using e-mail | 28 | 42 | 35 | 38 | 74 | 56 | 33 | 58 | 46 |
| | (45) | (50) | (48) | (49) | (44) | (50) | (47) | (50) | (50) |
| K. listening to music/going to concerts | 68 | 80 | 74 | 74 | 90 | 82 | 71 | 85 | 78 |
| | (47) | (40) | (44) | (44) | (30) | (39) | (46) | (36) | (42) |
| L. shopping/going to the mall | 28 | 72 | 50 | 26 | 90 | 58 | 27 | 81 | 54 |
| | (45) | (45) | (50) | (44) | (30) | (50) | (45) | (39) | (50) |
| M. reading | 58 | 70 | 64 | 30 | 44 | 37 | 44 | 57 | 51 |
| | (50) | (46) | (48) | (46) | (50) | (49) | (50) | (50) | (50) |
| N. writing | 12 | 52 | 32 | 06 | 64 | 35 | 09 | 58 | 34 |
| | (33) | (50) | (47) | (24) | (48) | (48) | (29) | (50) | (47) |
| O. cooking | 22 | 48 | 35 | 22 | 36 | 29 | 22 | 42 | 32 |
| | (42) | (50) | (48) | (42) | (48) | (46) | (42) | (50) | (47) |
| P. arts & crafts | 34 | 54 | 44 | 28 | 36 | 32 | 31 | 45 | 38 |
| | (48) | (50) | (50) | (45) | (48) | (47) | (46) | (50) | (49) |
| Q. other (write in)___________ | 46 | 40 | 43 | 44 | 44 | 44 | 45 | 42 | 44 |
| | (50) | (49) | (50) | (50) | (50) | (50) | (50) | (50) | (50) |

The quantitative researcher represents results in figures and tables

(with Bonferroni corrections; adjusted alpha = .006). Effect sizes were computed using the eta coefficient (Cohen, 1969; Meline & Schmitt, 1997). For grade, no statistically significant main effects were obtained. For gender, the only statistically significant main effect was obtained for "none," $F(1, 196) = 9.29$, $p = .0026$, $\eta = .21$, where boys selected this option more frequently than did girls. The effect size was small. No interactions between grade and gender were statistically significant.

21 Table 3 reports the results of Question 3, preferred reading materials, showing the percentage of students who said they liked each type of material. For all students combined ($N = 200$), the most popular reading materials were magazines (63%), novels (52%), and comics (41%); least popular were plays (12%), technical books (15%), and newspapers (16%). The category of "other" (27%) was moderately popular. For other, some students wrote in the names of specific books (e.g., *Harry Potter*) or themes (e.g., pets, adventure, science fiction, sports, biographies, mystery, horror) they enjoyed.

22 For each type of material, the data were analyzed using a 2 × 2 (grade × gender) ANOVA (with Bonferroni corrections; adjusted alpha = .005). Effect sizes were computed using the eta coefficient (Cohen, 1969; Meline & Schmitt, 1997). For grade, a statistically significant main effect was obtained only for magazines, $F(1, 196) = 9.95$, $p = .0019$, $\eta = .22$. The effect size was small. Tukey's (HSD) test ($p = .05$) indicated that ninth graders showed a stronger preference than sixth graders for magazines.

23 For gender, a statistically significant main effect was obtained only for poems, $F(1, 196) = 19.57$, $p < .0001$, $\eta = .30$. The effect size was medium. Tukey's (HSD) test ($p = .05$) indicated that girls showed a stronger preference than boys for poems. No interactions between grade and gender were statistically significant.

Conclusion Section

## DISCUSSION

24 Given the importance of reading to lexical development in school-age children and adolescents, this study was conducted to investigate the views of young people with respect to reading as a leisure activity in relation to other free-time options that are likely to compete for their attention. Fortunately, the results indicate that reading is at

Interpreting the research

**Table 2.** Percentage of students who selected each option in response to the request, "Please estimate how much time you spend each day, on average, reading for pleasure outside of the school day" (standard deviations are reported).

| | *Grade 6* | | | *Grade 9* | | | *Grades 6 & 9* | | |
|---|---|---|---|---|---|---|---|---|---|
| | *Boys* | *Girls* | *Combined* | *Boys* | *Girls* | *Combined* | *Boys* | *Girls* | *Combined* |
| A. none | 14 | 02 | 08 | 20 | 06 | 13 | 17 | 04 | 11 |
| | (35) | (14) | (27) | (40) | (24) | (34) | (38) | (20) | (31) |
| B. 5–10 minutes | 16 | 10 | 13 | 28 | 22 | 25 | 22 | 16 | 19 |
| | (37) | (30) | (34) | (45) | (42) | (44) | (42) | (37) | (39) |
| C. 10–20 minutes | 12 | 14 | 13 | 10 | 14 | 12 | 11 | 14 | 13 |
| | (33) | (35) | (34) | (30) | (35) | (33) | (31) | (35) | (33) |
| D. 20–30 minutes | 22 | 28 | 25 | 12 | 22 | 17 | 17 | 25 | 21 |
| | (42) | (45) | (44) | (33) | (42) | (38) | (38) | (44) | (41) |
| E. 30–60 minutes | 22 | 28 | 25 | 18 | 18 | 18 | 20 | 23 | 22 |
| | (42) | (45) | (44) | (39) | (39) | (39) | (40) | (42) | (41) |
| F. 1–2 hours | 12 | 18 | 15 | 06 | 12 | 09 | 09 | 15 | 12 |
| | (33) | (39) | (36) | (24) | (33) | (29) | (29) | (36) | (33) |
| G. 2–3 hours | 0 | 0 | 0 | 04 | 0 | 02 | 02 | 0 | 01 |
| | (0) | (0) | (0) | (20) | (0) | (14) | (14) | (0) | (10) |
| H. more than 3 hours | 02 | 0 | 01 | 02 | 06 | 04 | 02 | 03 | 03 |
| | (14) | (0) | (10) | (14) | (24) | (20) | (14) | (17) | (16) |

Quantitative findings include descriptive statistics

**Table 3.** Percentage of students who responded positively to each item listed under the question, "What kinds of materials do you like to read for pleasure?" (standard deviations are reported).

| | *Grade 6* | | | *Grade 9* | | | *Grades 6 & 9* | | |
|---|---|---|---|---|---|---|---|---|---|
| | *Boys* | *Girls* | *Combined* | *Boys* | *Girls* | *Combined* | *Boys* | *Girls* | *Combined* |
| A. poems | 14 | 24 | 19 | 08 | 48 | 28 | 11 | 36 | 24 |
| | (35) | (43) | (39) | (27) | (50) | (45) | (31) | (48) | (43) |
| B. short stories | 38 | 40 | 39 | 18 | 44 | 31 | 28 | 42 | 35 |
| | (49) | (49) | (49) | (39) | (50) | (46) | (45) | (50) | (48) |
| C. plays | 10 | 16 | 13 | 04 | 16 | 10 | 07 | 16 | 12 |
| | (30) | (37) | (34) | (20) | (37) | (30) | (26) | (37) | (32) |
| D. novels | 44 | 64 | 54 | 42 | 56 | 49 | 43 | 60 | 52 |
| | (50) | (48) | (50) | (50) | (50) | (50) | (50) | (49) | (50) |
| E. comics | 58 | 38 | 48 | 36 | 32 | 34 | 47 | 35 | 41 |
| | (50) | (49) | (50) | (48) | (47) | (48) | (50) | (48) | (49) |
| F. technical books | 28 | 12 | 20 | 10 | 08 | 09 | 19 | 10 | 15 |
| | (45) | (33) | (40) | (30) | (27) | (29) | (39) | (30) | (35) |
| G. newspapers | 18 | 06 | 12 | 22 | 16 | 19 | 20 | 11 | 16 |
| | (39) | (24) | (33) | (42) | (37) | (39) | (40) | (31) | (36) |
| H. magazines | 50 | 54 | 52 | 62 | 84 | 73 | 56 | 69 | 63 |
| | (51) | (50) | (50) | (49) | (37) | (45) | (50) | (46) | (49) |
| I. none of the above | 04 | 04 | 04 | 06 | 02 | 04 | 05 | 03 | 04 |
| | (20) | (20) | (20) | (24) | (14) | (20) | (22) | (17) | (20) |
| J. other (write in)_________ | 36 | 30 | 33 | 14 | 26 | 20 | 25 | 28 | 27 |
| | (48) | (46) | (47) | (35) | (44) | (40) | (44) | (45) | (44) |

least a moderately popular free-time activity for students in the 11- to 15-year age range. Yet at the same time, the study indicates that many other activities are preferred over reading, such as listening to music/going to concerts, watching television or videos, playing sports, and playing computer or video games. The study also indicates that interest in reading as a free-time activity declines during these years, whereas interest in using e-mail increases, consistent with the trend for young people to spend more time socializing with peers as they transition into adolescence (Raffaelli & Duckett, 1989).

25 Differences between boys and girls also emerged. Boys preferred playing computer or video games and playing sports; girls preferred talking on the phone, using e-mail, shopping, writing, and cooking. Boys were more likely than girls to report that they spent no time reading for pleasure. For all students combined, the most popular reading materials were magazines, novels, and comics; least popular were plays, technical books, and newspapers. Older students showed a stronger preference than younger ones for magazines, and girls showed a stronger preference than boys for poems.

26 Reports have indicated that the amount of time that is spent reading predicts word knowledge (e.g., Cunningham & Stanovich, 1991; Stanovich & Cunningham, 1992; West et al., 1993). This is thought to occur because written



Quantitative researchers compare results to prior research

Quantitative researchers take an objective approach

language exposes learners to large numbers of unfamiliar words, leading them to infer the meanings of those words through metalinguistic strategies—morphological analysis and contextual abstraction (Nippold, 1998). Because word knowledge plays a critical role in academic success and in other intellectual pursuits (Sternberg & Powell, 1983), it is important that school-age children and adolescents spend time reading a variety of materials and that their interest in reading continues into adulthood. Pleasure reading can expose students to new words and allow them to cultivate a positive attitude toward reading as they refine their basic reading skills (e.g., fluency), building confidence in themselves as readers (Worthy et al., 1999).

**27** This is not to say that other free-time activities are unimportant. For example, in the present study, many participants indicated that they enjoyed socializing with friends through phone calls, e-mail, and personal visits. Because socializing is an activity that offers emotional support and contributes to personal well-being through the lifespan (Raffaelli & Duckett, 1989; Rawlins, 1992), it should be encouraged. In addition, many participants reported that they enjoyed physical activities such as playing sports, swimming, and riding a bicycle or scooter—all of which can benefit one's health. Nonetheless, it is helpful to know where reading fits into the larger picture of free-time options for today's youth, some of whom spend little or no time reading for pleasure.

Quantitative researchers suggest implications for practice

## STUDY LIMITATIONS

**28** One limitation of the present study is that it focused only on students who were attending public schools located in lower middle-income neighborhoods in western Oregon. It is possible that different results might have been obtained in schools representing additional socioeconomic levels located in diverse regions of the United States. Another caveat is that the present study focused exclusively on leisure-time reading and did not investigate the amount of time that students spent on other types of reading, such as that required for school assignments. It seems possible that some of the students who reported spending little time reading for pleasure (e.g., ninth graders) may have been spending more time reading for school assignments, particularly if they were college bound. These possibilities should be investigated in future research. In addition, the literacy habits of various subgroups should be examined. This could include, for example, students who have been identified as having language and/or reading disorders, and those who show different levels of reading proficiency (e.g., strong, average, weak).

Quantitative researchers identify limitations in the study

Quantitative researchers suggest future research

## IMPLICATIONS

**29** In any case, if students are successfully engaging in large amounts of academic reading, there is no reason to be concerned about their exposure to new vocabulary words. However, for those who spend little time reading for pleasure or for school assignments, steps should be taken to promote their interest in reading. School-based SLPs should take note of these patterns, particularly as they occur in children and adolescents with language disorders, as it is common for these young people to experience deficits in reading and in word learning (e.g., Catts & Kamhi, 1999; Kail et al., 1984; Kail & Leonard, 1986; McGregor et al., 2002; Nippold & Schwarz, 2002). In addition, SLPs should note the pleasure-reading habits of struggling readers, as these students also could benefit from increased opportunities to read. As indicated earlier, a certain portion of students in this district (and in many districts in Oregon) failed to meet the state standards in reading as tested by the OSA, data that were obtained from the Oregon Department of Education Web site. Information concerning the literacy habits of students who are struggling to meet state standards can be helpful as SLPs consult with other professionals who may be less familiar with the reciprocal relationship between language and literacy development.

**30** Fortunately, much can be done in school settings to encourage strong literacy habits in all students as SLPs work collaboratively with teachers, principals, psychologists, librarians, parents, and the students themselves. For example, the activities described below could be spearheaded by the school-based SLP:

- *Organize book clubs at school.* High schools and middle schools may offer clubs similar to the successful "Oprah book clubs" that were broadcast on national television. For this activity, books were selected by the television talk show host Oprah Winfrey and read by the general public, followed by interactive discussions on television. Similarly, a ninth-grade book club might vote on a selection of student-recommended books to be read by the club and discussed during their weekly meetings, facilitated by student leaders. For a sixth-grade club, options might include the *Harry Potter* books, which are frequently enjoyed by older children and young adolescents. In addition to their intriguing story lines, these books contain a wealth of low-frequency words used in colorful and imaginative ways, as evidenced in the following passage from *Harry Potter and the Goblet of Fire* (Rowling, 2000):

  > Slowly, magnificently, the ship rose out of the water, gleaming in the moonlight. It had a strangely skeletal look about it, as though it were a resurrected wreck, and the dim, misty lights shimmering at its portholes looked like ghostly eyes. Finally, with a great sloshing noise, the ship emerged entirely, bobbing on the turbulent water, and began to glide toward the bank. (p. 245)

  Book clubs with different themes (e.g., mystery, adventure, animals) and reading levels (e.g., strong, average, weak) could be organized, and reluctant readers could receive academic credit for participating. In organizing these clubs, students should be grouped so that weaker readers are not competing with stronger ones and being subjected to peer ridicule. As appropriate, weaker readers might be asked to lead book clubs for younger students in order to build their own confidence as readers. Alternatively, they might be assigned to book clubs led by mature and supportive adults. For example, a successful book club in an Oregon high school, started by a school librarian, includes senior citizens (e.g., retired teachers) who volunteer their time, helping to engage the students in lively discussions about the books and sharing their unique generational perspectives (Williams, 2003). In working with weaker readers, volunteers will need to understand the students' difficulties and know how to manage them positively. Thus, the SLP may need to train and supervise these volunteers carefully.

- *Provide incentives and reward students for reading books and other materials (e.g., magazines, newspapers, plays) at school and at home.* For example, on completing a book, article, or play, a student could earn a ticket to deposit in a special box in the principal's office. At regular intervals, a ticket could be drawn and a desirable prize could be awarded to the lucky ticket holder.
- *Provide blocks of class time each day (e.g., 25 min) for "sustained silent reading" (SSR), where all students are required to read a book, magazine, or newspaper of their choice.* Given that many children, as they transition into adolescence, show less interest in reading as a leisure activity, it is beneficial to provide this type of structured opportunity for them to read during the school day. Immediately following each SSR block, students can be requested to spend the next 5 min discussing what they read with a classmate, thereby appealing to the adolescent need for socialization and peer interaction.
- *Encourage students to visit the school library and to take books home.* Ensure that the library contains an adequate supply of books for students of differing backgrounds, interests, and levels of reading proficiency. This should include multiple copies of books that have been adapted for weaker readers such as classic novels (e.g., *The Red Badge of Courage*, *David Copperfield*, *Treasure Island*) and short biographies of sports heroes and movie stars (PCI Educational Publishing, 2003). Given the findings of the present study, simplified books on sports (e.g., baseball, football, hockey) might be of interest to ninth-grade boys, many of whom indicated enjoyment of sports-related leisure activities but little interest in reading for pleasure. A selection of high-interest books on tape also should be available for students who require additional support when reading.
- *Take note of students' preferred reading materials and encourage their use.* Based on the results of the present study, SLPs can expect to find differences in reading preferences based on a student's age or gender. For example, as shown in Table 3, poems were of less interest to ninth-grade boys than to ninth-grade girls, but both boys and girls enjoyed magazines. Given that research has shown that popular magazines can provide exposure to low-frequency words (Cunningham & Stanovich, 1998), magazines should be acceptable for free-time reading.
- *Conduct informal surveys of students in the district to determine the names of specific magazines, comics, and books that are currently popular with boys and girls at different grade levels, information that may change rather quickly.* Stocking school libraries and classrooms with these particular materials can help to motivate reluctant readers and generate interest in pleasure reading.
- *Explore with students their reasons for rejecting certain types of reading materials.* For example, a ninth-grade boy's dislike for poems may stem from having been forced to read adult-selected works depicting themes that were irrelevant to him (e.g., Emily Dickinson's poems on love). Providing students with a wide range of options depicting themes that interest them, such as horror (e.g., "The Raven" by Edgar Allan Poe, 1884) or adventure (e.g., "Paul Revere's Ride" by Henry Wadsworth Longfellow, 1963), may encourage them to explore this genre.
- *Encourage parents to support these efforts by making them aware of the importance of reading and requesting their assistance through parent–teacher organizations designed to secure materials and personnel for the school library.* Additionally, parents can be asked to hold daily sessions at home where they read and discuss with their child or adolescent favorite books, magazines, comic strips, or sections of the newspaper (e.g., sports, movies, television, advice). Contrary to popular myth, as children become adolescents, they continue to enjoy spending time with their parents and other family members (Raffaelli & Duckett, 1989).

**31** For additional information on ways to promote strong literacy habits in school-age children and adolescents, SLPs may wish to consult various Web sites. For example, the International Reading Association (IRA; http://www.reading.org) is an excellent resource for lists of books that are of high interest to adolescents, as judged by students in Grades 7 through 12 attending schools in the United States. This Web site also provides research-based information on how to assist struggling readers, which often includes children and adolescents with language disorders.

**32** It is difficult to overestimate the importance of reading during childhood and adolescence. Yet the present study indicates that as children become adolescents, their interest in reading as a leisure activity may decline as other free-time options compete for their attention. A decline in reading is problematic for students who avoid all other kinds of reading and for those whose language and literacy skills are weak. Fortunately, suggestions such as those offered above can be implemented quite easily, and it is clear that much can be done within school settings to maintain and even expand students' enthusiasm for reading when their individual needs and preferences are considered. Given the intellectual rewards that can accrue from a lifetime of reading, a modest investment in adolescent literacy programs can bring monumental rewards to society.

## ACKNOWLEDGMENTS

We express sincere gratitude to the children and adolescents who participated in this research project and to the teachers and administrators who granted permission for the project to take place at their schools and who helped to schedule the testing sessions.

## REFERENCES

**Anglin, J. M.** (1993). Vocabulary development: A morphological analysis. *Monographs of the Society for Research in Child Development, 58*(10), Serial No. 238.

**Bashir, A. S., Wiig, E. H., & Abrams, J. C.** (1987). Language disorders in childhood and adolescence: Implications for learning and socialization. *Pediatric Annals, 16,* 145–156.

**Beck, I., & McKeown, M.** (1991). Conditions of vocabulary acquisition. In R. Barr, M. L. Kamil, & P. B. Mosenthal (Eds.), *Handbook of reading research* (Vol. 2, pp. 789–814). White Plains, NY: Longman.

**Bolt, G.** (2004, March 26). Scientists link valley's clay soil to Mount Mazama ash spew. *The Register-Guard,* pp. A1, A9.

**Catts, H. W., Fey, M. E., Zhang, X., & Tomblin, J. B.** (2001). Estimating the risk of future reading difficulties in kindergarten children: A research-based model and its clinical implementation. *Language, Speech, and Hearing Services in Schools, 32,* 38–50.

**Catts, H. W., & Kamhi, A. G.** (1999). *Language and reading disabilities.* Boston: Allyn & Bacon.

**Chall, J. S.** (1983). *Stages of reading development.* New York: McGraw-Hill.

**Cohen, J.** (1969). *Statistical power analysis for the behavioral sciences.* New York: Academic Press.

**Cunningham, A. E., & Stanovich, K. E.** (1991). Tracking the unique effects of print exposure in children: Associations with vocabulary, general knowledge, and spelling. *Journal of Educational Psychology, 83,* 264–274.

**Cunningham, A. E., & Stanovich, K. E.** (1998, Spring/Summer). What reading does for the mind. *American Educator,* 8–15.

**Dunn, L. M., & Dunn, L. M.** (1981). *Peabody Picture Vocabulary Test–Revised.* Circle Pines, MN: American Guidance Service.

**Jenkins, J. R., Stein, M. L., & Wysocki, K.** (1984). Learning vocabulary through reading. *American Educational Research Journal, 21,* 767–787.

**Kail, R., Hale, C. A., Leonard, L. B., & Nippold, M. A.** (1984). Lexical storage and retrieval in language-impaired children. *Applied Psycholinguistics, 5,* 37–49.

**Kail, R., & Leonard, L.** (1986). *Word-finding abilities in language-impaired children (ASHA Monograph 25).* Rockville, MD: American Speech-Language-Hearing Association.

**Longfellow, H. W.** (1963). *Paul Revere's ride.* New York: Crowell.

**McGregor, K. K., Newman, R. M., Reilly, R. M., & Capone, N. C.** (2002). Semantic representation and naming in children with specific language impairment. *Journal of Speech, Language, and Hearing Research, 45,* 998–1014.

**Meline, T., & Schmitt, J. F.** (1997). Case studies for evaluating statistical significance in group designs. *American Journal of Speech-Language Pathology, 6*(1), 33–41.

**Miller, G. A., & Gildea, P. M.** (1987). How children learn words. *Scientific American, 257*(3), 94–99.

**Nagy, W., Diakidoy, I., & Anderson, R.** (1993). The acquisition of morphology: Learning the contribution of suffixes to the meanings of derivatives. *Journal of Reading Behavior, 25*(2), 155–171.

**Nagy, W. E., & Herman, P. A.** (1987). Breadth and depth of vocabulary knowledge: Implications for acquisition and instruction. In M. McKeown & M. E. Curtis (Eds.), *The nature of vocabulary acquisition* (pp. 19–36). Hillsdale, NJ: Erlbaum.

**Nagy, W. E., Herman, P. A., & Anderson, R.** (1985). Learning words from context. *Reading Research Quarterly, 20,* 233–253.

**Nagy, W. E., & Scott, J. A.** (2000). Vocabulary processes. In M. L. Kamil, P. B. Mosenthal, & R. Barr (Eds.), *Handbook of reading research* (Vol. 3, pp. 269–284). Mahwah, NJ: Erlbaum.

**Nippold, M. A.** (1998). *Later language development: The school-age and adolescent years* (2nd ed.). Austin, TX: Pro-Ed.

**Nippold, M. A.** (2002). Lexical learning in school-age children, adolescents, and adults: A process where language and literacy converge. *Journal of Child Language, 29,* 474–478.

**Nippold, M. A., & Schwarz, I. E.** (2002). Do children recover from specific language impairment? *Advances in Speech-Language Pathology, 4*(1), 41–49.

**PCI Educational Publishing.** (2003). *Special education & learning differences catalogue: Middle school, high school & adult.* San Antonio, TX.

**Poe, E. A.** (1884). *The raven.* New York: Harper & Brothers.

**Raffaelli, M., & Duckett, E.** (1989). "We were just talking...": Conversations in early adolescence. *Journal of Youth and Adolescence, 18,* 567–582.

**Rawlins, W. K.** (1992). *Friendship matters: Communication, dialectics, and the life course.* New York: DeGruyter.

**Rice, M.** (1983). The role of television in language acquisition. *Developmental Review, 3,* 211–224.

**Rowling, J. K.** (2000). *Harry Potter and the goblet of fire.* New York: Scholastic.

**Schwanenflugel, P., Stahl, S., & McFalls, E.** (1997). Partial word knowledge and vocabulary growth during reading comprehension. *Journal of Literary Research, 29,* 531–553.

**Stanovich, K. E., & Cunningham, A. E.** (1992). Studying the consequences of literacy within a literate society: The cognitive correlates of print exposure. *Memory & Cognition, 20*(1), 51–68.

**Sternberg, R. J.** (1987). Most vocabulary is learned from context. In M. G. McKeown & M. E. Curtis (Eds.), *The nature of vocabulary acquisition* (pp. 89–105). Hillsdale, NJ: Erlbaum.

**Sternberg, R. J., & Powell, J. S.** (1983). Comprehending verbal comprehension. *American Psychologist, 38,* 878–893.

**Stothard, S. E., Snowling, M. J., Bishop, D. V. M., Chipchase, B. B., & Kaplan, C. A.** (1998). Language-impaired preschoolers: A follow-up into adolescence. *Journal of Speech, Language, and Hearing Research, 41,* 407–418.

**West, R. F., Stanovich, K. E., & Mitchell, H. R.** (1993). Reading in the real world and its correlates. *Reading Research Quarterly, 28,* 35–50.

**White, T. G., Power, M. A., & White, S.** (1989). Morphological analysis: Implications for teaching and understanding vocabulary growth. *Reading Research Quarterly, 24,* 283–304.

**Whitmire, K.** (2000). Action: School services. *Language, Speech, and Hearing Services in Schools, 31,* 194–199.

**Williams, A.** (2003, December 15). Young, old find common ground in the pages of some good books. *The Register-Guard*, pp. B1, B4.

**Worthy, J., Moorman, M., & Turner, M.** (1999). What Johnny likes to read is hard to find in school. *Reading Research Quarterly, 34*(1), 12–27.

**Wysocki, K., & Jenkins, J. R.** (1987). Deriving word meanings through morphological generalization. *Reading Research Quarterly, 22,* 66–81.

Received April 5, 2004
Accepted May 12, 2004
DOI: 10.1044/0161-1461(2005/009)

Contact author: Marilyn A. Nippold, PhD, Professor, Communication Disorders and Sciences, College of Education, University of Oregon, Eugene, OR 97403. E-mail: nippold@uoregon.edu

Appendices

## APPENDIX. STUDENT QUESTIONNAIRE

Please tell us a little about yourself by answering the following questions. There are no "right or wrong" answers. We just want to know more about you and your interests.

1. How do you like to spend your free time?
   Circle all that apply:

   A. watching TV or videos
   B. playing computer or video games
   C. playing sports (e.g., basketball, baseball, football, soccer, etc.)
   D. running or walking
   E. swimming
   F. skating (skate board or roller blades)
   G. riding a bicycle or scooter
   H. playing cards or board games (e.g., Monopoly, chess, checkers, etc.)
   I. talking on the phone with friends or relatives
   J. using e-mail with friends or relatives
   K. listening to music/going to concerts
   L. shopping/going to the mall
   M. reading (e.g., books, magazines, newspapers, etc.)
   N. writing (e.g., diary, poetry, notes to friends, etc.)
   O. cooking
   P. arts & crafts
   Q. other (write in)________________________________

2. Please estimate how much time you spend each day, on average, reading for pleasure outside of the school day. This includes reading that you **choose** to do. Circle the **one** best answer:

   A. none
   B. 5–10 minutes
   C. 10–20 minutes
   D. 20–30 minutes
   E. 30–60 minutes
   F. 1–2 hours
   G. 2–3 hours
   H. more than 3 hours

Quantitative researchers ask participants close-ended questions

3. What kinds of materials do you like to read for pleasure? Circle all that apply:

   A. poems
   B. short stories
   C. plays
   D. novels
   E. comics
   F. technical books (e.g., auto repair, science, history, computers, etc.)
   G. newspapers
   H. magazines
   I. none of the above
   J. other (write in)________________________________

CHAPTER

# 8 Quantitative Data Analysis and Results: Examining What Was Found in a Study

*Quantitative research is about more than collecting data. Researchers analyze their data with statistics to answer their research questions and test their hypotheses. This data analysis process produces the results that researchers report in their studies. Learning about the results of a study is probably why you choose to read a research report. You need to know how to read and interpret different types of statistical results to understand what researchers found in a quantitative study. In this chapter, you will learn about the process that researchers use to analyze quantitative data and how the results of this process are reported.*

**BY THE END OF THIS CHAPTER, YOU SHOULD BE ABLE TO:**

- Describe the process for analyzing quantitative data in a research study.
- Locate where researchers describe how they analyzed their quantitative data and where they report their results in research articles.
- List the steps that researchers use to analyze quantitative data.
- Know how to recognize descriptive results that answer descriptive research questions.
- Know how to recognize inferential results that answer comparison and relationship research questions.
- Evaluate the analysis of quantitative data and results as reported in a research article.

Many students dread reading this chapter as soon as they see the word statistics. The use of statistics has a bit of a bad reputation. You might think that statistical procedures are hard to learn. You might also be concerned that people can use statistics to come up with whatever answer they want. In reality, however, statistics is simply a set of useful mathematical tools for summarizing large amounts of data and uncovering evidence for relationships that exist within numeric data. Learning to use tools effectively takes time, and learning to use statistics is no different. Once learned, however, you will be able to tell which statistics are best for certain tasks and to evaluate statistical results in other's work.

This book will not teach you how to calculate different statistics. You can take a stats course from a friendly statistician to learn to do that. Instead, this book focuses on the thinking and logic behind using statistics in the process of analyzing quantitative data. By understanding why researchers use statistics and the different kinds of statistical results that researchers report, you can make sense of the results reported in quantitative research studies. We will first consider the general quantitative data analysis process before we jump into the detail of each step of this process.

## What Is the Process of Analyzing Quantitative Data?

Researchers who collect data in the form of numbers need to use quantitative analysis procedures to make sense of this data. During quantitative data analysis, researchers analyze the data using mathematical procedures, called *statistics,* and represent the results in tables, figures, and explanations. These analyses consist of breaking down the

FIGURE 8.1 The Process of Quantitative Data Analysis

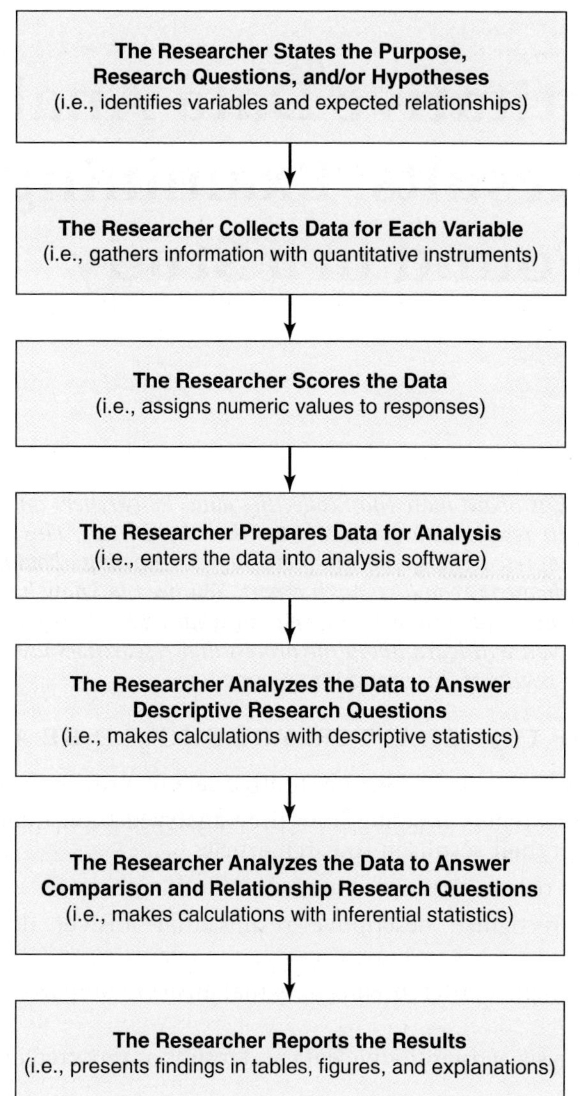


data into parts to answer the research questions. Statistical procedures, such as comparing groups or relating scores for individuals, provide information to address a study's research questions and hypotheses.

The quantitative data analysis process unfolds in a very linear fashion. This means that the researcher generally finishes one step before moving to the next. You can visualize the major steps in this process by examining the "top-down" approach to quantitative analysis in Figure 8.1. As shown in the figure, data analysis begins when quantitative researchers state their purpose, research questions, and hypotheses. These statements specify the direction of the study, including the specific variables and expected relationships among variables. Recall from Chapter 5 that quantitative researchers are interested in three main types of questions: descriptive, relationship, and comparison.

Once the study's direction is specified, researchers collect data for each variable, such as using a questionnaire with items that ask about students' motivation and class grade. After data collection is complete, researchers assign numbers by scoring the responses and prepare the data for analysis. For example, if a student reported his grade as a B, the researcher scores it as 3.0. Researchers then analyze the data to answer their descriptive research questions using procedures called descriptive statistics. These analyses find the average level of motivation in the sample and the high and low motivation scores. From descriptive analyses, quantitative researchers move to analyses that use inferential statistics to address their relationship and comparison questions.

For example, they use the collected data to test whether motivation and grade point average are related. Finally, researchers represent and report the results of these different analysis procedures.

## How Do You Identify a Study's Quantitative Data Analysis and Results?

There are two types of information about quantitative data analysis that you can find within a quantitative research report. First, researchers report details specific to their procedures for implementing the process outlined in Figure 8.1. Second, researchers also report the specific results that resulted from this analysis process.

### Look to the Method Section for a Description of the Analysis Process

The first place you may find information about quantitative data analysis is within the method section. As we learned in Chapter 7, the focus of this section is on reporting the procedures for data collection. Many quantitative research reports, however, will also include an overview of the data analysis procedures in the method section. You may find this discussion presented under a subheading such as *Data Analysis* or *Statistical Analyses*. In general, authors provide only a brief overview of the specific statistical choices they made to analyze the study's quantitative data. For example, read the following excerpt about data analysis that the authors provided in the method section of an experimental study testing the effectiveness of a strength training program provided as a treatment to adolescents with cerebral palsy:

> Data were analyzed using Statistica (version 6) . . . To determine differences between the control and experimental groups from pre to post measurement, repeated measures ANOVA was used, and in all cases violations of assumptions were checked. A 5% significance level was used. *(Unger et al., 2006, p. 473)*

Note that this excerpt does not provide a description of the full analytic process. It does, however, tell us information such as the software used for the analysis (i.e., Statistica), the focus on comparing groups (i.e., "determine differences between the control and experimental groups"), the name of the test that was used (i.e., "repeated measures ANOVA"), and information about criteria for judging the results of the test (i.e., "a 5% significance level").

As this passage illustrates, the method section may contain detailed information without much explanation as to what it means. Surprisingly, many quantitative research articles do not explicitly discuss information about data analysis. This is because all quantitative researchers follow basically the same analysis process (see Figure 8.1), with the differences emerging in the choice of statistical procedures. Therefore, many researchers go right from describing their procedures for data collection to presenting their statistical results.

### See How the Research Questions and Hypotheses Are Answered in the Results Section

Quantitative researchers report the results of their data analysis in major sections of their articles. Almost without exception, this section is called *Results*. In this section, researchers report the results obtained for the statistical procedures used to address the study's research questions and hypotheses. Therefore, when you read the results of a quantitative study, you learn the results of the study. In addition, the results section will include information so you can identify the details of the analysis process used to obtain the results.

## How Do Researchers Analyze Quantitative Data?

You probably know that analyzing quantitative data involves statistics in some way, but you may not know what this means or how a researcher actually uses statistics. It is helpful to know about these procedures to follow the process in a quantitative report.

As Figure 8.1 introduced, this process involves a number of distinct steps after data collection:

- scoring the data;
- preparing the data for analysis;
- analyzing the data to answer descriptive research questions;
- analyzing the data to test comparison and relationship hypotheses; and
- reporting the results of data analysis.

## Step 1—Researchers Score the Data

Researchers cannot analyze their data with statistics unless the data have been recorded in a numeric form. The first step of analyzing quantitative data therefore is for the researcher to assign scores. **Scoring data** means that the researcher assigns a numeric score (or value) to each response category for each question on the instruments used to collect data. In some cases the score is obvious. If you ask a child to indicate her age and she responds 10 years, then the response could be scored as 10. For many quantitative variables, the researcher needs to develop a plan for how to score different responses. The key is that all individuals who respond the same way should end up with the same score. For instance, suppose that parents respond to a survey asking them to indicate their attitudes about choice of a school for children in the school district. One question might be:

> Please indicate the extent to which you agree with this statement:
> "Students should be given an opportunity to select a school of their choice."
>
> ___________ Strongly agree
> ___________ Agree
> ___________ Undecided
> ___________ Disagree
> ___________ Strongly disagree

Assume that a parent checks "Agree." How does the researcher score this response? To analyze the data, the researcher will assign scores to responses, such as strongly agree = 5, agree = 4, undecided = 3, disagree = 2, and strongly disagree = 1. Based on these assigned numbers, all parents who checks "Agree" would receive a score of 4 for this item. Researchers score their data in consistent ways so that they are reliable and valid, as we discussed in Chapter 7.

## Step 2—Researchers Prepare the Quantitative Data for Analysis

Once researchers have scored the data, the next procedure is to prepare the data for analysis. This procedure includes selecting a computer program, entering the data into the program, and determining the types of scores to analyze.

One of the first data analysis decisions a researcher makes is to select a computer program to analyze their quantitative data. Statistical software programs are available that can store the data collected in a study and calculate different statistical quantities from these data. Researchers often name the program they used in their reports. This informs the reader that the researcher used a sophisticated program. In addition, not all programs calculate some advanced statistics in the same way, so by informing readers as to what program was used, other researchers learn the context of how calculations were made. Two frequently used programs are SPSS (Statistical Package for the Social Sciences, http://www.spss.com) and SAS/STAT (http://www.sas.com).

After a researcher has carefully entered all the data into a computer program, the next step is to determine the types of scores to analyze. You will find two types of scores commonly mentioned in research reports. Figure 8.2 presents examples of two types of scores collected for three students: single-item scores and summed scores on a scale.

- ***Single-Item Scores.*** Researchers often examine single-item scores. A **single-item score** is an individual score assigned to each question for each participant in a study. These scores provide a detailed analysis of each person's response to each item on an

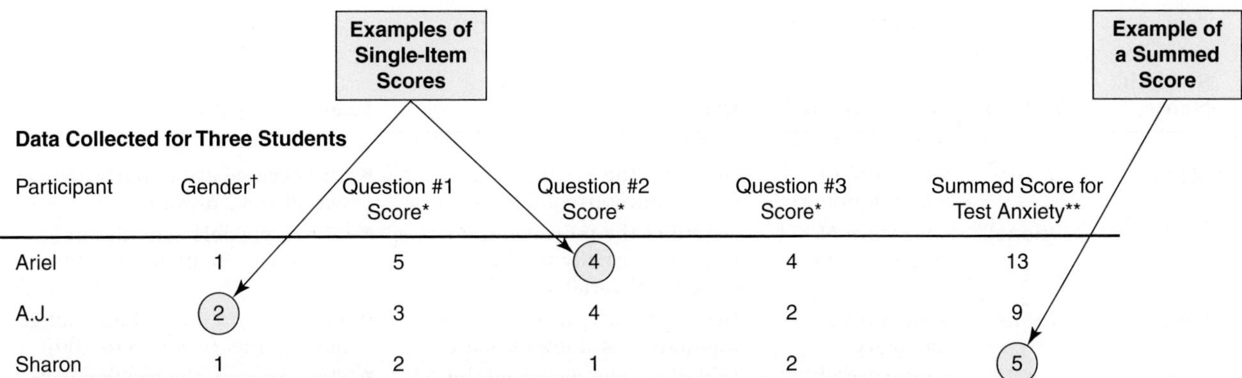


**Data Collected for Three Students**

| Participant | Gender† | Question #1 Score* | Question #2 Score* | Question #3 Score* | Summed Score for Test Anxiety** |
|---|---|---|---|---|---|
| Ariel | 1 | 5 | 4 | 4 | 13 |
| A.J. | 2 | 3 | 4 | 2 | 9 |
| Sharon | 1 | 2 | 1 | 2 | 5 |

†Gender responses scored: 1 = female; 2 = male.
*Question responses scored: 5 = strongly agree; 4 = agree; 3 = undecided; 2 = disagree; and 1 = strongly disagree.
**Test Anxiety: Calculated by summing scores from Questions #1, 2, and 3.

**FIGURE 8.2** Two Types of Scores Used in Quantitative Data Analysis

instrument. In Figure 8.2, all three participants have single-item scores indicating their level of agreement for questions 1, 2, and 3. Single-item scores are also frequently used for demographic information, such as the variable "gender" in Figure 8.2.

- ***Summed Scores.*** Single items often do not completely capture a participant's perspective and are not adequately reliable or valid if the question is poorly worded (as discussed in Chapter 7). One solution to these problems is for the researcher to form scales based on responses to multiple questions. **Summed scores** are the scores of an individual added over several items that measure the same variable. Researchers add the scores from single items to compute an overall score for a variable. As shown in Figure 8.2, the three participants—Ariel, A. J., and Sharon—have provided responses to three questions. The researcher sums the three scores for each individual to provide a summed score for the variable "test anxiety" that represents all three questions. Summed scores are very common from performance and attitudinal measures.

## Step 3—Researchers Use Descriptive Statistics to Answer Their Descriptive Questions

Once the data are prepared, researchers are ready to begin their statistical analyses. Researchers analyze their data to address each of their research questions or hypotheses. Think back to the types of research questions presented in Chapter 5. One type of question that researchers ask is descriptive questions to describe trends in the data for single variables. Examples of such descriptive questions are:

- What is the self-esteem of middle school students?
- How varied are teachers' level of satisfaction?
- How was a student's performance relative to other students?

For practice interpreting descriptive statistics results, go to the *Building Research Skills* section under the topic "Descriptive Statistics" in MyEducationalResearchLab, located at www.myeducationlab.com. Complete the exercise "Understanding Descriptive Statistics" and use the provided feedback to further develop your skills for reading research articles.

Researchers use descriptive statistics to answer questions like these for independent, dependent, or control variables. **Descriptive statistics** are statistical tools that help researchers summarize the overall tendencies in the data, provide an assessment of how varied the scores are, and provide insight into where one score stands in comparison with others. These three ideas are called the central tendency, variability, and relative standing.

You will find results from descriptive statistics reported in almost all quantitative research studies. Table 8.1 provides a key for recognizing the most common descriptive statistics that you will read. This table lists the name, symbol, and use of each statistics along with a concrete example of how it might be applied in a study. Because these statistics

TABLE 8.1 A Key for Recognizing Common Descriptive Statistics

| Statistic Name | Symbol | Type of Statistic | Use | Example Applications |
|---|---|---|---|---|
| Mean | *M* or $\bar{X}$ | A measure of central tendency | Describes the average value of a continuous variable | ■ The average age of participants was *M* = 12.6 years. |
| Mode | (none) | A measure of central tendency | Describes the most common response, usually used for categorical variables | ■ Of five possible activities in gym class, the mode was "line dancing." |
| Range | (none) | A measure of variability | Describes the spread between the highest and lowest score | ■ The class test scores had a range of 65 points (from 35 to 100). |
| Standard deviation | *SD* | A measure of variability | Describes how dispersed the data points are about the mean | ■ The scores on the spelling test (*M* = 85.5, *SD* = 12.3) were more spread out than those on the math test (*M* = 85.5, *SD* = 5.5). |
| Percentile rank | % | A measure of relative standing | Describes the percentage of participants with scores at or below a particular score | ■ The student scored 81 on the test, which is at the 73rd percentile. He scored higher than 73% of the students. |
| Z score | *z* | A measure of relative standing | Converts an original score into a relative score measured in units of standard deviations | ■ Jennifer is very tall for this sample. Her height has a *z* score of +3. Mark is short compared to others in the sample. His height has a z score of −2.1. |

are so common, researchers will often use the symbol (e.g., *M* or *SD*) in a report instead of giving the name of the statistic.

Let's examine what researchers learn by using each type of descriptive procedure.

***Describing Central Tendency.*** Researchers describe the central tendency of their data for each variable. Descriptions of **central tendency** are single numbers that summarize a collection of scores. Researchers choose a statistic to describe central tendency based on whether the variable is measured as continuous or in categories. Recall from Chapter 5 that continuous scores fall along a range (such as test scores measured from 0 to 100) and categorical scores fall in distinct categories (such as single, married, or divorced). Two common statistics for central tendency are the mean and the mode.

- The mean is the most common statistic used to describe the responses of all participants to items on an instrument. The **mean** is the total of the scores divided by the number of scores. That is, the mean is the average score for the variable across all the participants. Researchers often use the symbol *M* or $\bar{X}$ when they report mean values. For example, a researcher reports the average score on a spelling test as *M* = 85.5. The mean is used for variables that are measured as continuous, such as age, self-esteem, or test scores.
- The **mode** is the score that appears most frequently in a list of scores. It is used when researchers want to know the most common response for a variable. Researchers use the mode for reporting about variables with categorical values. For example, suppose a researcher provided seventh-grade girls with a list of three possible activities for gym class and asked them to indicate their preferred choice. If 15 girls chose volleyball, 22 girls chose swimming, and 38 girls chose line dancing, then we can see that "line dancing" was the most popular choice. That is, the "line dancing" response is the mode.

***Describing Variability.*** When summarizing a set of scores for a continuous variable, it is not enough for a researcher to report the mean. Let's examine a practical example to understand this statement. Suppose two classes of third-grade students took a spelling test, and both classes had the same mean score: *M* = 85.0. It sounds like the classes scored the same, but suppose all students' scores fell between 80 and 90 for one class, but for the other class scores fell between 35 and 100. Even though both classes had the same average, we see that their scores differed in another way. In one class the scores varied only a little (indicating that all students performed similarly), but they varied a lot in the other class (indicating that performance was not very uniform).

Researchers use descriptions of **variability** to indicate the spread of scores collected for a variable. This information helps us see how dispersed the responses are to items on an instrument. The variability of a variable also plays an important role in many advanced statistical calculations. As shown in Table 8.1, range and standard deviation are commonly reported to indicate the amount of variability in a distribution of scores.

- The most straightforward indication of the variability of scores is when researchers look at the range of scores. The **range of scores** is the difference between the highest and the lowest scores for a variable. In the example of the spelling test just described, one class had a range of 10 points (between a low of 80 and a high of 90) and the other had a range of 65 points (between 35 and 100).
- The most commonly used measure of variability in research is called the standard deviation. The **standard deviation** is a measure of how dispersed the data are about the mean value for a variable. As such, it provides useful information about the dispersion or spread of scores in a dataset. This measure of variability is reported almost any time a researcher gives a mean value for a variable. Authors often use the abbreviation ***SD*** to indicate a standard deviation, and it usually is reported right after a mean value. For example, a researcher notes the scores on a spelling test as $M = 85.5$, $SD = 5.5$.

  The meaning of the standard deviation can be illustrated when we graph a theoretical distribution of scores, as shown in Figure 8.3. If we collected sample after sample of scores for a variable, and plotted them on a graph, they would look like a bell-shaped curve as shown in Figure 8.3. This graph is called a *normal distribution* or *normal probability curve*. Looking at the figure, the shaded areas indicate the percentage of scores likely to fall within each standard deviation about the mean. Therefore, the standard deviation is a helpful indicator describing the spread of the scores. For example, 68 percent (34% + 34%) of the scores are expected to fall between +1 and −1 standard deviations from the mean. That is, if a researcher reported the scores on a spelling test as $M = 85.5$, $SD = 5.5$, we can expect that about 68 percent of the scores on this test should fall between 80.0 and 91.0.

***Describing Relative Standing.*** There is one more type of descriptive statistic that researchers include in their quantitative data analysis: descriptions of relative standing. Descriptions of **relative standing** are statistics that describe one score relative to a group of scores.

- A measure of relative standing is the percentile rank. A **percentile rank** of a particular score is the percentage of participants in the distribution with scores at or below a particular score. Researchers use a percentile rank to determine where in a distribution of scores an individual's score lies in comparison with other scores. For example, if a student completed a math test and scored at the 73rd percentile, this means that the

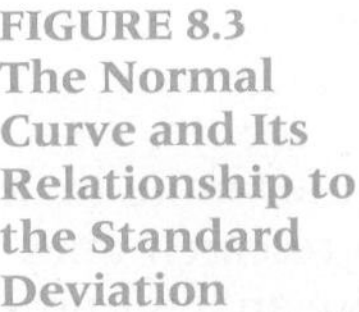
FIGURE 8.3 The Normal Curve and Its Relationship to the Standard Deviation

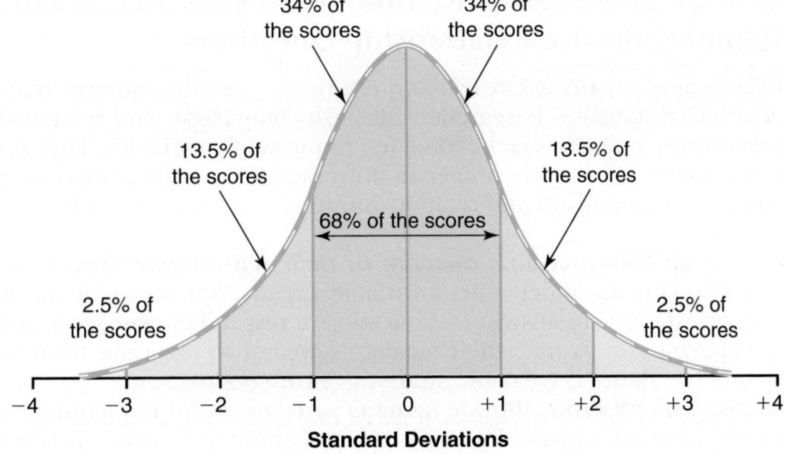

student scored better than 73 percent of the students who took the test. It also means that 27 percent of the students scored higher.

- Another measure of relative standing is the standard **z score**. Researchers calculate z scores by converting an original score (such as height measured in inches) into a relative score measured in units of standard deviations. The standard z score has the advantage that researchers convert a set of data so that it has a mean of 0 and a standard deviation of 1. The z score is helpful because it conveys how an individual's score compares to the group at large. For example, if you read that a first-grader has a height of 54 inches, you may not know what to make of it. Is this average? Is this tall or short? Suppose instead you read that a first-grader's height had a z score value of +3 standard deviations. If you look back at Figure 8.3, you can find that the expectation is that 97.5 percent of the scores for a variable should be less than +3 standard deviations. Therefore, we can conclude that a student whose height has a z score of +3 is very tall relative to other first-graders!

## What Do You Think?

Consider the following results reported in Table 1 of the quantitative goal orientation study (Self-Brown & Mathews, 2003) found at the end of Chapter 5. What variables are being described? What descriptive statistic(s) did the authors use? What do these statistics tell you about the contingency contract group in the study's sample?

| | Learning goals | | Performance goals | |
|---|---|---|---|---|
| | *M* | *SD* | *M* | *SD* |
| Contingency contract group | 14.27 | 3.98 | 5.55 | 3.95 |

### Check Your Understanding

In this excerpt, the authors are providing descriptive information about two variables: learning goals and performance goals. For each variable, the authors reported the values for mean (*M*) and standard deviation (*SD*). The values of the mean tell us the average number of learning goals and performance goals written by the participants within the contingency contract group. We see that, on average, this group wrote 14.27 learning goals and 5.55 performance goals. The values of the standard deviation indicate the spread of the scores about the mean. We see that each set of scores had approximately the same amount of variability because the standard deviations are practically equal (3.98 and 3.95).

## Step 4—Researchers Use Inferential Statistics to Answer Comparison and Relationship Questions

Researchers usually ask research questions or state hypotheses that call for more than descriptive statistics. Researchers also ask comparison and relationship research questions. These questions go beyond describing single variables. They require analysis procedures that allow a researcher to draw conclusions about two or more variables. Examples of comparison and relationship research questions include:

- ***How do boys and girls compare in their self-esteem?*** This question compares two groups on the independent variable (gender) in terms of the dependent variable (self-esteem). To answer this question, a researcher assesses whether the differences between groups (i.e., their means) is greater or less than what we would expect to find by chance if we could study the entire population.
- ***Does an optimistic attitude relate to satisfaction for elementary teachers?*** To answer this question, a researcher assesses whether the relationship between the two variables

(optimistic attitude and satisfaction) is more than what we would expect to find by chance if the researcher could study the entire population.

When researchers are interested in how groups compare or how variables are related, they need analytic procedures that consider two (or more) variables at a time. In addition, they want to infer results from a sample to a population. Researchers use **inferential statistics** to address these two aspects. The basic idea of these statistical procedures is to look at scores from a sample, and use the results to draw inferences or make predictions about the population. Recall from Chapter 7 that researchers usually cannot study the entire population because of size and cost, so instead they examine a sample that has been carefully chosen from the population. At the heart of using inferential statistics to make conclusions about a population is the concept of hypothesis testing. You need to learn about this concept to understand quantitative results.

**Hypothesis testing** is a procedure that researchers use to obtain their results by comparing an observed value from a sample with a population value to determine whether a difference or relationship exists in the population. Researchers start by stating a hypothesis about the population, which is not known. They then collect data from a sample of the population and use the information to make a judgment about the hypothesis. Note that researchers use evidence from a sample to make a conclusion about the larger population.

For practice identifying the process that researchers use to test hypotheses, go to the *Building Research Skills* section under the topic "Inferential Statistics" in MyEducationalResearchLab, located at www.myeducationlab.com. Complete the exercise "Understanding the Use of Hypothesis Testing" and use the provided feedback to further develop your skills for reading research articles.

A researcher's use of hypothesis testing is like having a crime scene investigator (a CSI) gather evidence about a crime and go to court to testify. Sometimes the evidence can be overwhelming, and it is easy for the court to conclude that a person is guilty or not guilty. In other cases, the evidence can be unclear and then the court must deliberate and people may not feel very confident in their decision. In either case, it is always possible that the evidence was misleading, although the CSI's job is to try to prevent that from happening. Similarly, in the process of hypothesis testing, the researcher gathers information and determines whether there is sufficient evidence to find the data "guilty," that is, to find that a difference or relationship exists.

There are guidelines about the standards used in court cases to judge whether a person is found guilty or not guilty. Likewise hypothesis testing provides researchers with objective procedures for judging whether there is sufficient evidence for or against a given hypothesis. These guidelines include five steps that researchers take in hypothesis testing. Researchers:

1. identify a null and alternative hypothesis;
2. set the criterion for making a decision, called the alpha value;
3. collect data from a sample;
4. compute the sample statistic; and
5. make a decision about rejecting or failing to reject the null hypothesis.

Figure 8.4 illustrates these steps along with an example application. Knowing about these steps informs you how researchers report their research results.

**1.** ***The researcher identifies a null and alternative hypothesis.*** As discussed in Chapter 5, a null hypothesis is a prediction about the population and is typically stated using the language of "no difference" (or "no relationship"). An alternative hypothesis, however, indicates a difference (or relationship), and the direction of this difference may be positive or negative. Researchers specify *both* a null and an alternative hypothesis for each hypothesis test. Example hypotheses from a study about adolescent smoking and depression are shown in Figure 8.4.

**2.** ***The researcher sets the criterion for rejecting the null hypothesis, called the alpha level.*** Unless a researcher collects data from every person in a population, the true value of the population remains unknown. Statistics are mathematical tools for estimating the probability that certain results could occur simply based on chance, instead of based on real differences or relationships in the population. Therefore, statistics do not *prove* a hypothesis. Researchers do, however, use statistics to say whether there is a reasonably good chance that a relationship or difference exists. To make certain that a researcher's biases or hopes do not affect the results, researchers set an objective standard

FIGURE 8.4
The Steps of Hypothesis Testing

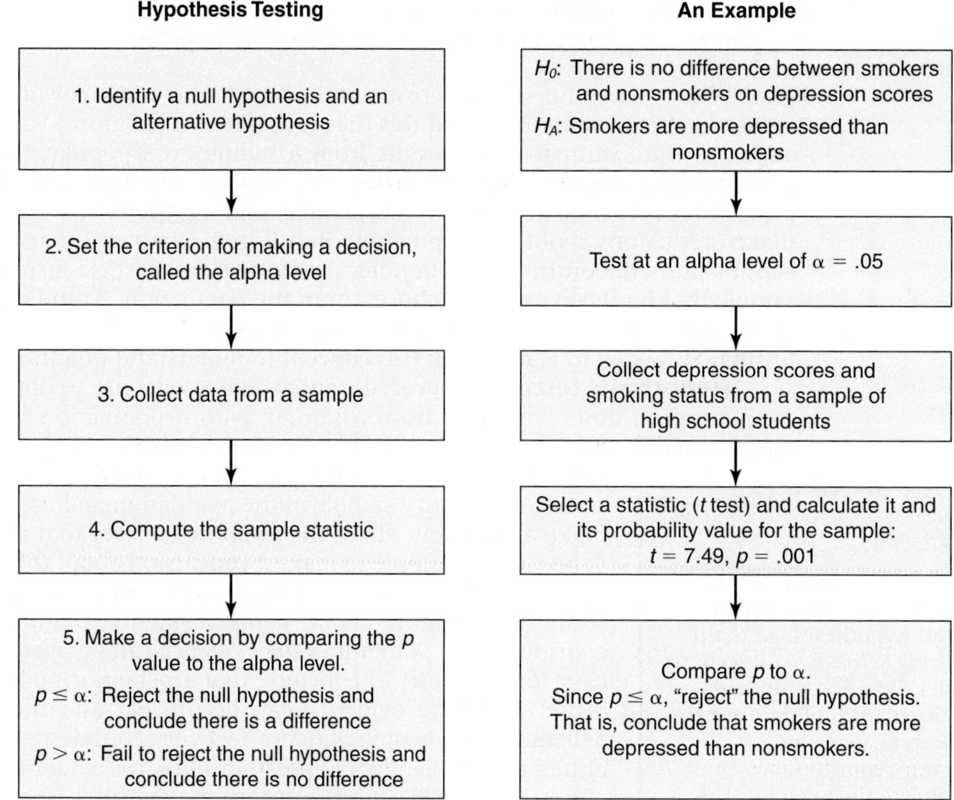


for how certain they need to be about the results before they are willing to reject the idea that no relationship or difference exists. This is called "setting the alpha value" or "setting the level of significance."

The **alpha level** ($\alpha$) is the maximum risk that researchers are willing to take that they make a mistake when they conclude that they have sufficient evidence that there is a difference or a relationship. As the example in Figure 8.4 illustrates, researchers in education and social sciences traditionally set their alpha at a level of .05. What does this mean? This simply means that researchers are willing to take up to a 5 percent chance that they will be wrong when they conclude that there is a difference or there is a relationship. Another way to say this is that for as much as 5 percent of all the research that finds there is a difference or there is a relationship, the truth is that no such difference or relationship exists in the population. The problem is that no one knows which studies are the ones that get it wrong. Therefore, the scientific community has decided that, in general, it is acceptable to get it wrong at most 5 percent of the time. Some researchers will reduce their risk for a study and pick a smaller alpha value such as .01 (risk getting it wrong at most 1 percent of the time). Some researchers will also report that they corrected their alpha level (made it lower than .05) because they are running multiple tests with the same data set and want their total risk across all tests to remain no greater than 5 percent.

*Here's a Tip for Reading Research!*

Note that the alpha level (e.g., $\alpha = .05$) is different from Cronbach's alpha introduced in Chapter 7. The *alpha level* represents the maximum risk that a researcher is willing to take for rejecting a null hypothesis by mistake. *Cronbach's alpha* is a measure of how consistent items are on an instrument. Both types of alpha may appear in a method section, but they represent different concepts.

**3.** ***Collect data from a sample.*** Researchers collect data by administering an instrument or recording behaviors on a check sheet for participants as discussed in Chapter 7. They also score this data and prepare it for analysis, as discussed earlier in this chapter.

**4.** ***Compute the sample statistic to compare groups or relate variables.*** Once researchers have their data entered into a statistical analysis program, they are ready to compute a statistic for the sample. Researchers must select the statistical test that is appropriate for their hypotheses. There are *many* inferential statistics available to researchers. You can think of these statistics as falling into two types: those used to

TABLE 8.2 A Key for Recognizing Common Statistics for Comparing Groups

| Statistic Name | Symbol | Use | How to Interpret* | Example Applications |
|---|---|---|---|---|
| *t*-test | $t$ | To test for a difference between 2 groups in terms of 1 dependent variable | ■ There is a significant difference between the groups if $p \leq \alpha$ | ■ Compare boys and girls on time spent reading |
| Analysis of variance (ANOVA) | $F$ | To test for a difference among 2 or more groups in terms of 1 dependent variable | ■ There is a significant difference among the groups if $p \leq \alpha$ | ■ Compare four groups (freshmen, sophomores, juniors, and seniors) on time spent studying |
| Analysis of covariance (ANCOVA) | $F$ | To test for a difference among 2 or more groups in terms of 1 dependent variable, controlling for at least one control variable | ■ There is a significant difference among the groups if $p \leq \alpha$ | ■ Compare three groups (treatment 1, treatment 2, and treatment 3) in terms of their final test score, controlling for scores on a pre-test |
| Multiple analysis of variance (MANOVA) | $F$ | To test for a difference among 2 or more groups in terms of 2 or more dependent variables | ■ There is a significant difference among the groups if $p \leq \alpha$ | ■ Compare men and women who are married, single, or divorced in terms of their life satisfaction scores and depression scores |
| Chi square | $\chi^2$ | To test for a difference among groups in terms of a categorical dependent variable | ■ There is a significant difference among the groups if $p \leq \alpha$ | ■ Compare men and women in terms of their political party affiliation (democratic, republican, or independent) |
| **Measures of Effect Size:** | | | | |
| Effect size | *ES* or $d$ | To assess the effect size for a significant *t* test | ■ Consider whether the author describes the effect as small, medium, or large | ■ To judge whether a statistically significant difference between two groups also has practical significance |
| Eta squared | $\eta^2$ | To assess the effect size for a significant ANOVA test | ■ Consider whether the author describes the effect as small, medium, or large | ■ To judge whether a statistically significant difference among groups also has practical significance |

*$\alpha$ refers to the "alpha level." It is set by the researcher, usually at a level of $\alpha = .05$.

*compare groups* and those used to *relate variables*. The most commonly used statistics for comparing groups are listed in Table 8.2 and those used for relating variables are listed in Table 8.3. Use these tables to assist with interpreting the statistics you find when you read research reports.

Researchers use several considerations when selecting an appropriate statistical test. These considerations include the type of question being addressed (comparison or relationship). Researchers also must consider factors such as the number of independent and dependent variables in their hypotheses, whether control variables are included in the analysis, and whether the data for each variable are measured as continuous or categorical. Once researchers select a statistical test, they use the computer to calculate the statistic that corresponds to that test. Here is a brief overview of the three most common statistical tests you will find in your reading:

- ***The* t *test.*** Researchers use a *t* test and report the *t* statistic when they want to compare two groups (representing the independent variable) in terms of one continuous dependent variable. For example, a *t* test would be appropriate if a researcher wanted to compare boys and girls in terms of the time spent reading.
- ***The ANOVA test.*** Researchers use an ANOVA test and report an *F* statistic when they want to compare more than two groups in terms of one continuous dependent variable. For example, an ANOVA test would be appropriate if a researcher wanted to compare freshmen, sophomores, juniors, and seniors in terms of the time spent reading.

TABLE 8.3 A Key for Recognizing Common Statistics for Relating Variables

| Statistic Name | Symbol | Use | How to Interpret* | Example Applications |
|---|---|---|---|---|
| Pearson correlation | $r$ | To test for a relationship between two variables | ■ There is a significant relationship if $p \leq \alpha$; the sign of $r$ indicates whether the relationship is positive (+) or negative (−) and the value of $r$ (0–1.00) indicates the strength of the relationship | ■ Determine whether time spent studying is related to grade point average |
| Multiple regression | $R$ | To determine the degree to which 2 or more independent variables are related to (or predict) 1 dependent variable | ■ The value of $R$ indicates the association of the combination of the independent variables with the dependent variable | ■ Determine whether grade point average, SAT score, and depression combined predict retention in the first year of college |
| Beta | $\beta$ | To provide a standardized measure of each independent variable's individual contribution to the dependent variable in a multiple regression analysis | ■ Compare the beta values for each independent variable in a multiple regression equation to see which ones are most important | ■ Determine the individual contribution of grade point average, SAT score, and depression for predicting retention in the first year of college |
| **Measures of the Strength of Relationships:** | | | | |
| Coefficient of determination | $r^2$ | To assess the proportion of variability in one variable accounted for by a second variable | ■ Consider this value as the percentage of variance in one variable that is explained by a second variable | ■ Time spent studying explained 49% of the variability in the final test score ($r^2 = .49$) |
| $R$ squared | $R^2$ | To assess the proportion of variability in the dependent variable accounted for by the combination of independent variables in the regression equation | ■ Consider this value as the percentage of variance in the dependent variable accounted for by the combination of predictor variables | ■ Time-on-task, motivation, and prior achievement together predict 34% of the variability in student learning ($R^2 = .34$) |

*$\alpha$ refers to the "alpha level." It is set by the researcher, usually at a level of $\alpha = .05$.

- ***The Pearson correlation coefficient.*** Researchers use the Pearson correlation coefficient and report an $r$ statistic when they want to test for a relationship between two continuous variables. For example, a correlation coefficient would be appropriate if a researcher wanted to relate time spent studying and grade point average.

  When researchers compute a statistic for a sample, they actually obtain two important values. One is the value of the statistic (e.g., $t$, $F$, or $r$) for the sample's data. The other is the $p$ value. A ***p* value** is the probability ($p$) that a result (e.g., the value of $t$, $F$, or $r$ calculated for the collected data) could have been produced by chance if the null hypothesis were true for the population. It is actually this $p$ value that researchers use to make a decision as to whether the data provide sufficient evidence for the alternative hypothesis. Looking back at Figure 8.4, the researcher in the example conducted a $t$ test and found $t = 7.49$ and that $p = .001$ for this value of $t$ for the sample of students.

5. ***Make a decision about "rejecting" or "failing to reject" the null hypothesis.*** Now the researcher has all the information needed to make a decision. There are two possible decisions for any hypothesis test:

- ***The researcher rejects the null hypothesis and concludes there is a difference or relationship***—that is, the two groups are sufficiently different (or the relationship is sufficiently large) that we conclude that it is very unlikely that the null hypothesis is true. In other words, the data support the conclusion that there is a difference (or a relationship). For example, if the data show that girls spend significantly more time reading than boys, then we reject the null hypothesis and conclude that there is a difference and that girls spend more time reading than boys.

- ***The researcher fails to reject the null hypothesis and concludes there is no difference or relationship***—that is, the two groups are not very different (or the relationship is not very large), so we conclude that there is not sufficient evidence to reject the null hypothesis. In other words, the data support the conclusion that there is no difference (or no relationship). For example, if the data show that girls spend about the same amount of time reading as boys, then we fail to reject the null hypothesis and conclude that there is not a difference between boys and girls.

Now all that remains is deciding what criterion to use to decide whether there is sufficient evidence. It turns out that researchers set this criterion level early in the process by setting their alpha level! Therefore, in the end the researcher makes a decision simply by comparing the $p$ value from their sample statistic to the specified alpha level. If you examine the information from the example study in Figure 8.4, we see that the researcher set $\alpha = .05$ and found $p = .001$. These values tell us that the researcher is willing to take up to a 5 percent risk that the results occurred by chance, but found that there is only a 0.1 percent chance that the observed result from the sample could have occurred by chance. Therefore, since the $p$ value is less than or equal to the alpha value, the researcher concludes that the null hypothesis can be rejected. This means, there is a statistically significant difference between the groups. A *statistically significant* result is found when the observed $p$ value is equal to or less than the predetermined alpha level set by the researcher. If the $p$ value is greater than alpha, then the researcher concludes that the study did not find evidence of a relationship or difference. This is a *non-significant* result (sometimes abbreviated as "ns" in reports). When this happens, the study does not prove that the null hypothesis is true, but it does not provide enough evidence to reject it either.

> *Here's a Tip for Reading Research!*
>
> Hypothesis testing sets a strict, objective standard for judging whether a result is statistically significant. Close is not good enough. If a $p$ value is even a tiny bit higher than the alpha level, you still conclude that there is no difference or no relationship.

Statistical significance tells us whether there is evidence of a relationship among variables or a difference between groups, no matter how small the relationship or difference may be. If the sample size is very large, even a very small difference will be statistically significant because it is unlikely that the difference occurred only by chance. However, this result does not tell us whether the result has any practical significance. Researchers today are often concerned with practical significance in addition to statistical significance. They use a separate indicator called an effect size to indicate the practical significance of any statistically significant result.

**Effect size** is a means for identifying the practical strength of the conclusions about group differences or about the relationship among variables in a quantitative study. Effect sizes tell us how different the sample values are and allow us to make a judgment as to whether this is significant based on our knowledge of practical issues, such as the measures, the participants, and the data collection effort. There are many different ways to calculate effect sizes depending on the type of inferential statistic that was used. Tables 8.2 and 8.3 list a few common forms that researchers use when comparing groups or relating variables. For each kind of effect size, researchers adopt a standard for judging whether a measured effect is small, medium/moderate, or large. Researchers usually state how they interpret the size of the effect that they report (e.g., small, medium, or large), so you can determine whether the result has practical significance.

> *Here's a Tip for Applying Research!*
>
> Statistically significant results are important for adding to knowledge. Results that also have practical significance, however, show promise for being useful for practical applications. If you are looking for research results that can apply to your practice, pay particular attention to results about which the authors describe having large effect sizes.

As an illustration, let's consider the example of a statistical difference between smokers and nonsmokers in terms of depression from Figure 8.4. When examining the difference in the mean scores for two groups, the researcher reports that, "there is a large effect ($ES = 1.6$)." This tells you that the difference has practical significance because the effect is large. Therefore, practitioners concerned with smokers will also want to consider providing treatment for depression in addition to helping them quit smoking.

## What Do You Think?

Consider the following three results. Assume that alpha = .05 for each study. Based on the ideas of hypothesis testing and Tables 8.2 and 8.3, what do you conclude about each reported result? Consider what type of hypothesis is being tested, what statistic is reported, the *p* value of the statistic for the sample, and whether there is sufficient evidence to reject the null hypothesis in each case.

**(a)** Girls reported receiving more rewards overall (from both parents and teachers) than did boys: $F(1, 132) = 22.93, p < .001$. *(Davis, Winsler, & Middleton, 2006)*
**(b)** Career satisfaction is correlated with appropriate duties ($r = .14, p < .01$) for career counselors. *(Baggerly & Osborn, 2006)*
**(c)** There was no association between state-anxiety scores and number of test problems answered correctly for the students ($\beta = .11$, ns). *(Weber & Bizer, 2006)*

### Check Your Understanding

Passage (a) is a hypothesis test comparing girls and boys in terms of the number of rewards received. The researchers reported an *F* statistic for their data with $p < .001$. Since *p* is less than .05, there is sufficient evidence to reject the null hypothesis (that there is no difference). We conclude that the researchers found a statistically significant difference.

Passage (b) is a hypothesis test relating two variables (career satisfaction and appropriate duties). The researchers reported an *r* statistic for their data with $p < .01$. Since *p* is less than .05, there is sufficient evidence to reject the null hypothesis (that there is no relationship). We conclude that the researchers found a statistically significant relationship.

Passage (c) is also a hypothesis test relating multiple variables (e.g., state-anxiety scores) to the number of test problems answered correctly. The researchers reported a $\beta$ statistic (a type of multiple regression statistic). They did not state the *p* value, but they did state "ns." NS stands for "nonsignificant." This means that *p* is more than .05. There is not sufficient evidence to reject the null hypothesis and we conclude that the two variables are not related.

## How Do Quantitative Researchers Report Their Results?

When researchers conclude the statistical testing, they next turn to representing the results in tables and figures and stating results in a discussion. Researchers prepare this information to include in the results section of their reports. Several points might help you understand the contents of a published results section.

First, keep in mind that authors write their results sections to addresses the research questions and hypotheses. A typical approach is for the researcher to respond to each question or hypothesis one by one in the order in which they were introduced earlier in the study. In reporting the results, the researcher also stays close to the statistical findings without drawing broader implications or meaning from them. A results section includes:

- tables that summarize statistical information,
- figures (charts, pictures, drawings) that portray variables and their relationships, and
- detailed explanations about the statistical results.

## Researchers Summarize Their Results in Tables

Researchers display information in tables that summarize statistical results to research questions or hypotheses. A **table** is a summary of quantitative information organized into rows and columns. (See examples in Figures 8.2, 8.5 and 8.6.) Typically, tables for reporting results contain quantitative information, but they might contain text information as well (such as variable names or descriptions of groups). Tables are very useful for reporting quantitative results because they can summarize a large amount of data in a small amount of space. You will find that tables contain important information about a study's results. Here are some guidelines for reading tables.

- Researchers generally present one type of inferential test per table. Sometimes, however, they combine data from different analyses into a single table. For example, descriptive results (mean, standard deviation, and range) are often combined within one table.
- Researchers give each table a title that describes its contents. Use the title to understand the type of information being presented.
- In addition to the title, look at the labels for each column and row to grasp the meaning of a table. These labels will often represent specific variables and computed statistics.
- Authors typically include notes that provide additional information about the tables. These notes usually appear in a small font at the bottom of the table. Often these notes include information about the size of the sample reported in the study, the alpha level used in hypothesis testing, and the actual *p* values.

The tables in Figures 8.5 and 8.6 illustrate these guidelines for two common types of tables that report statistical results.

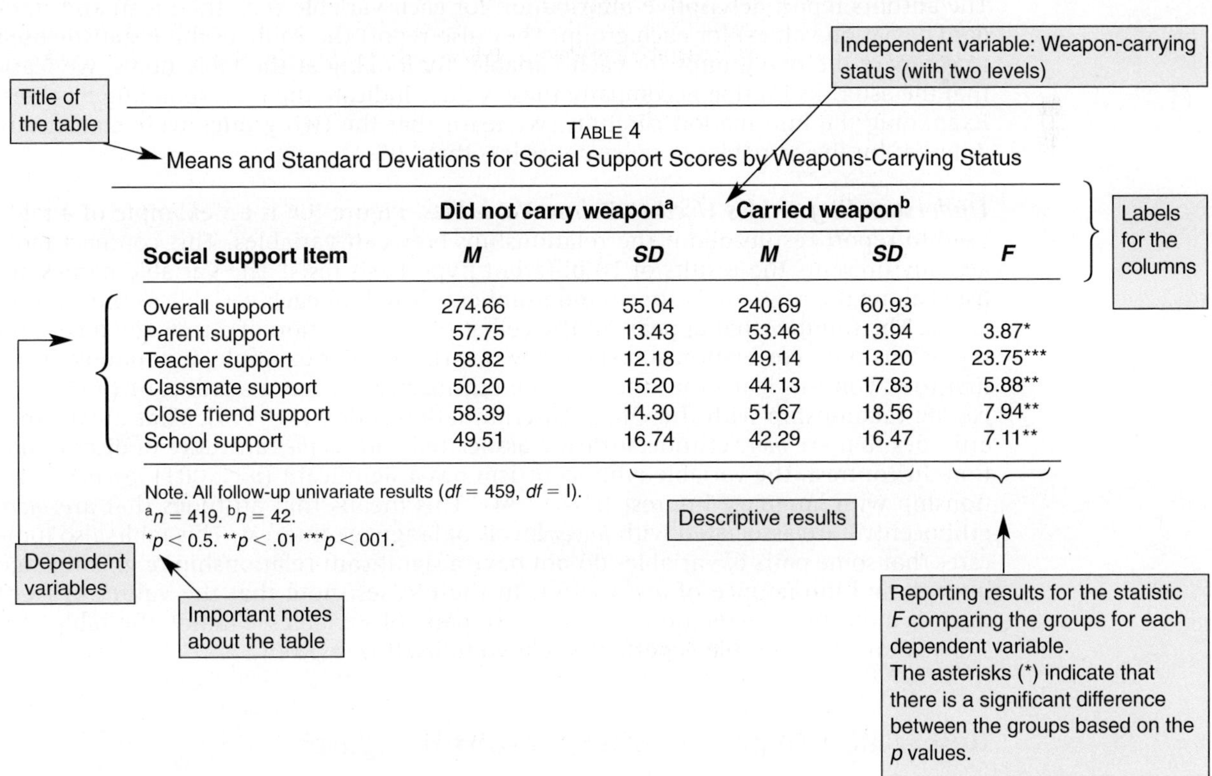


TABLE 4
Means and Standard Deviations for Social Support Scores by Weapons-Carrying Status

| | Did not carry weapon[a] | | Carried weapon[b] | | |
|---|---|---|---|---|---|
| **Social support Item** | *M* | *SD* | *M* | *SD* | *F* |
| Overall support | 274.66 | 55.04 | 240.69 | 60.93 | |
| Parent support | 57.75 | 13.43 | 53.46 | 13.94 | 3.87* |
| Teacher support | 58.82 | 12.18 | 49.14 | 13.20 | 23.75*** |
| Classmate support | 50.20 | 15.20 | 44.13 | 17.83 | 5.88** |
| Close friend support | 58.39 | 14.30 | 51.67 | 18.56 | 7.94** |
| School support | 49.51 | 16.74 | 42.29 | 16.47 | 7.11** |

Note. All follow-up univariate results ($df = 459$, $df = l$).
[a]$n = 419$. [b]$n = 42$.
*$p < 0.5$. **$p < .01$ ***$p < 001$.

**FIGURE 8.5 A Table Summarizing the Results Comparing Two Groups**

*Source:* This table is reprinted from Malecki and Demaray, *Journal of Emotional and Behavioral Disorders,* Vol. 11, Issue 3, p. 175, 2003. Reprinted with permission of Sage Publications, Inc.

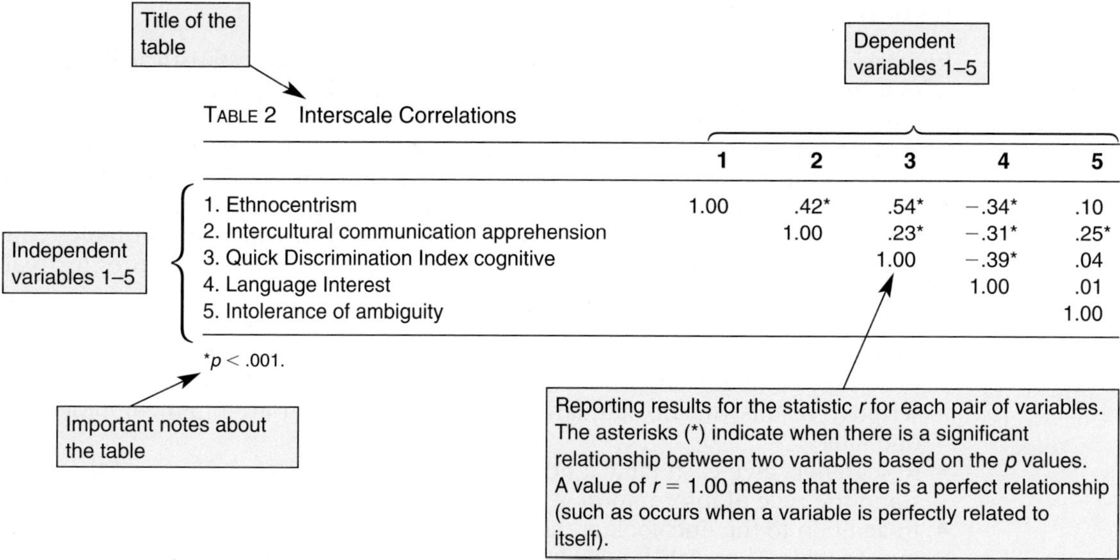


TABLE 2 Interscale Correlations

| | 1 | 2 | 3 | 4 | 5 |
|---|---|---|---|---|---|
| 1. Ethnocentrism | 1.00 | .42* | .54* | −.34* | .10 |
| 2. Intercultural communication apprehension | | 1.00 | .23* | −.31* | .25* |
| 3. Quick Discrimination Index cognitive | | | 1.00 | −.39* | .04 |
| 4. Language Interest | | | | 1.00 | .01 |
| 5. Intolerance of ambiguity | | | | | 1.00 |

*$p < .001$.

**FIGURE 8.6 A Table Summarizing the Results Relating Variables**

*Source:* This table is reprinted from Kim and Goldstein, *Journal of Studies in International Education,* Vol. 9, Issue 3, p. 273, 2005. Reprinted with permission of Sage Publications, Inc.

***Understanding Tables Used to Compare Groups.*** Figure 8.5 is an example of a table used to compare groups. Specifically, this table provides information on six dependent variables for two groups: students who have carried a weapon and those who have not. The authors report descriptive information for each variable (i.e., the mean and standard deviation values) for each group. They also report the value of the *F* statistic used to compare the two groups for each variable. By looking at the table notes, we learn that the asterisks (*) that accompany these values indicate the corresponding *p* values. Examining the information carefully, we learn that the two groups were statistically different for five variables because *p* was less than .05.

***Understanding Tables Used to Relate Variables.*** Figure 8.6 is an example of a table used to report results about the relationships between variables. This compact table actually presents the results of 10 different hypothesis tests! The variable names are listed along the rows and a shorthand number is listed for each variable as the column labels. The number that appears in the cell at the intersection of a row and a column represents the *r* correlation statistic for two variables. For example, if you look at the first row, you can learn that the variable ethnocentrism has a significant ($p < .001$) *positive* relationship with the Quick Discrimination Index ($r = .54$). That means that attitudes that are *more* ethnocentric are associated with *higher* attitudes of discrimination. In contrast, the variable ethnocentrism has a significant ($p < .001$) *negative* relationship with language interest ($r = -.34$). This means that attitudes that are *more* ethnocentric are associated with *lower* levels of language interest. This table also indicates that some pairs of variables do not have a significant relationship (e.g., language interest and intolerance of ambiguity). In these cases, note that the values of *r* are near 0, indicating no relationship for those pairs of variables. Finally, the table also shows that each variable is perfectly related to itself ($r = 1.00$).

## Researchers Represent Their Results in Figures

Tables are very common in quantitative research, but authors also choose to include figures in many studies. A **figure** is a summary of quantitative information presented as a chart, graph, or picture that shows relations among scores or variables. Figures can be helpful when a picture can better convey information than a table. Figures are

**FIGURE 8.7 A Figure Summarizing the Results from a Study Using a Single Subject Design**

*Source:* This figure is reprinted from Cihak, Kessler, and Alberto, *Education and Training in Developmental Disabilities,* Vol. 43, Issue 1, p. 107, 2008. Reprinted with permission of the Division on Developmental Disabilities of the Council for Exceptional Children.

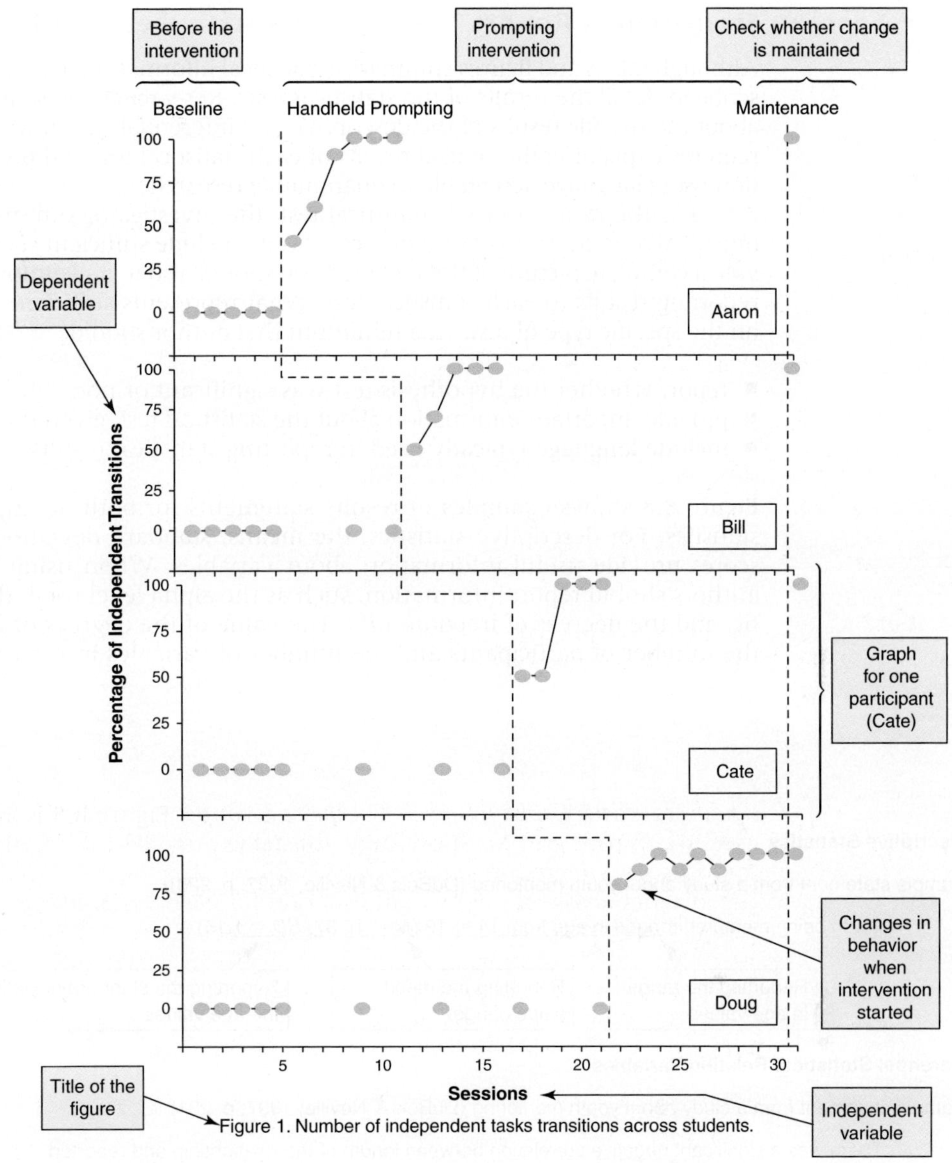


suitable for visually presenting information in graphs and pictures in results sections of studies.

***Understanding Figures Used to Visually Display Results.*** There are many types of figures used to report quantitative results. While their form may vary, they generally present a visual picture of how one variable is related to or affected by another variable. In figures, the figure title is placed at the bottom of the figure. This is different from table titles, which are placed at the top of the table (see the tables in Figures 8.5 and 8.6). Figure 8.7 presents an example of a figure used to display a graph from a single-subject study that tested a prompting system to help students with intellectual disabilities transition through specific tasks. This figure is actually a composition of four graphs combined into one figure. Each graph shows the percentage of successful transitions achieved in a given session plotted as a function of time (or sessions) for four students. The dashed line that cuts across the middle of the four graphs shows the point in time when the intervention was started for each student. By visually displaying the students' scores over time, we are able to easily see how the percentages increased with the start of the intervention treatment for each student. This type of visual display helps to provide a convincing picture of cause and effect when the study includes too few participants to use inferential statistics.

## Researchers Report Their Results with Detailed Explanations

Although tables and figures summarize statistical information, researchers also need to describe in detail the results of the statistical tests. Researchers present detailed information about the specific results of the descriptive and inferential statistical analyses. This process requires explaining the central results of each statistical test and presenting this information using language acceptable to quantitative researchers.

For the results to each statistical test, the investigator summarizes the findings in one or two sentences. These sentences should include sufficient statistics in order to provide a complete picture of the results. They should also include information necessary for reporting results to each statistical test. What represents sufficient information depends on the specific type of test. At a minimum that author should:

- report whether the hypothesis test was significant or not;
- provide important information about the statistical test, given the statistics; and
- include language typically used in reporting statistical results.

Figure 8.8 shows examples of results statements for both descriptive and inferential statistics. For descriptive statistics, the means, standard deviations, and the range of scores provide useful information about variables. When using inferential statistics, authors should report information, such as the alpha level used, the chosen test statistic, and the degrees of freedom (*df*). The value of the degrees of freedom is related to the number of participants and the number of variables in the calculation. It is listed

**Descriptive Statistics**

Example statement from a study about youth mentoring (DuBois & Neville, 1997, p. 228):

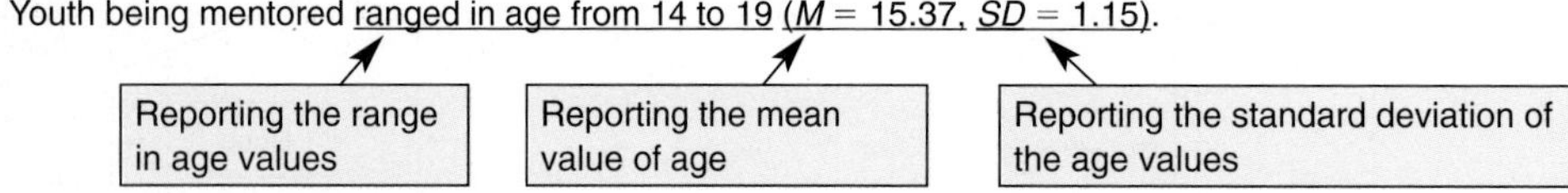


**Inferential Statistics: Relating Variables**

Example statement from a study about youth mentoring (DuBois & Neville, 1997, p. 231):

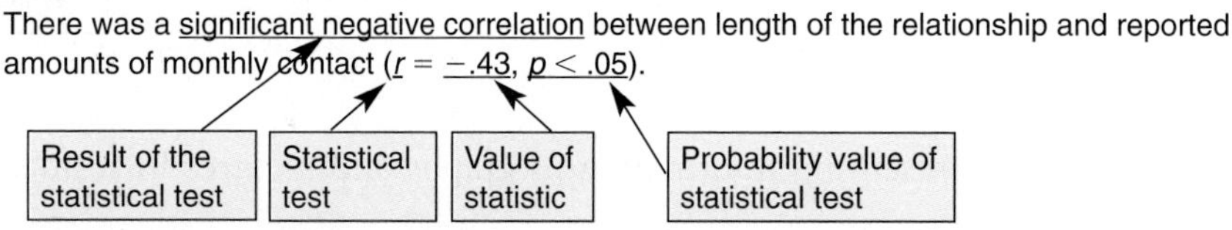


**Inferential Statistics: Comparing Groups**

Example statement from a study comparing two note-taking interventions: partial graphic organizer (GO) and complete GO (Robinson et al., 2006, p. 105):

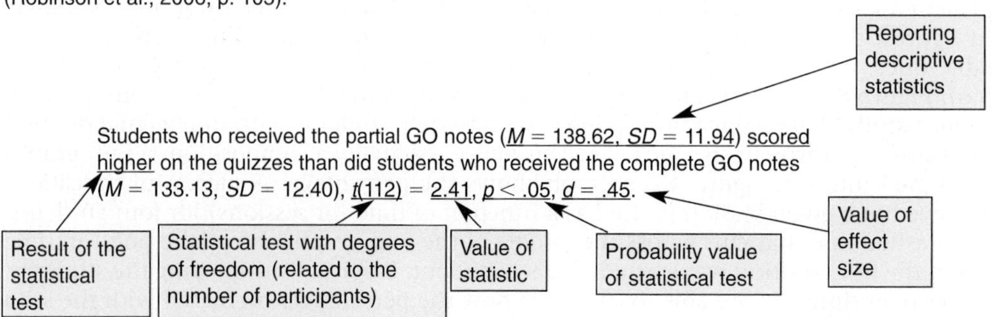


**FIGURE 8.8 Examples of Descriptive and Inferential Results Statements**

in parentheses with the statistic, such as: $F(1, 84)$. Researchers report these numbers because they are important parameters that the computer programs consider when they estimate the $p$ value for the statistic. In addition, authors also report the value of the test statistic and the actual $p$ value. They often also report the effect size. When reading quantitative results, look for this information to interpret the results of the study.

## What Do You Think?

Consider the following excerpt from the results reported in a quantitative study about graduate student attitudes about cheating (McCabe, Butterfield, & Treviño, 2006). How did the authors report these results? How do you know which results were significant?

> "Table 1 shows the bivariate correlation analyses for the total graduate student sample . . . Correlational analysis supports Hypotheses 2, 4, and 5, suggesting that cheating behavior is inversely related to the perceived certainty of being reported by a peer and understanding and acceptance of academic integrity policies and positively related to perceptions of peer cheating behavior. Hypothesis 3, which predicted an inverse relation between academic dishonesty and the perceived severity of penalties, was not supported in any of the samples." *(p. 298)*

**TABLE 1 Intercorrelations of Study Variables**

| **Measures** | *N* | 1 | 2 | 3 | 4 | 5 |
|---|---|---|---|---|---|---|
| 1. Peer behavior | 4457 | — | | | | |
| 2. Acceptance of policy | 4525 | −.29* | — | | | |
| 3. Severity of penalties | 4699 | −.28* | .59* | — | | |
| 4. Certainty of reporting | 5105 | −.24* | .31* | .21* | — | |
| 5. Academic dishonesty | 3455 | .28* | −.11* | −.03 | −.13* | — |

$^*p < .05$. $^{**}p < .01$. $^{***}p < .001$.

## Check Your Understanding

The authors presented their results in two ways: in a summary table and in a detailed discussion. From this part of the detailed discussion, we learn that they are presenting the results to address each of the study's hypotheses. Looking at the table, we see that the authors report how many participants completed each variable (the values of $N$). We also learn that the reported results are addressing hypotheses about the relationships between variables. Noting that an asterisk (*) indicates a significant relationship, we see that all of the presented relationships were significant except one. No relationship was found between academic dishonesty and severity of penalties (indicated by the absence of an asterisk). Looking at the other values we find that some relationships are positive (such as certainty of reporting and acceptance of policy, $r = .31$) and others are negative (such as peer behavior and severity of penalties, $r = -.28$).

## How Do Researchers Analyze Data and Report Results When Using the Different Research Designs?

Recall from Chapter 6 that authors present results that match the study's research design. Each of the major design types typically calls for the researcher to analyze the data and report results in certain ways, such as the following:

- If an investigator used a *true experiment* or a *quasi-experiment*, then you can expect that the results will emphasize inferential statistics that compare groups. The presentation of the results usually includes tables (similar to Figure 8.5) and description, and possibly graphs.
- If an investigator used a *single-subject experiment*, then you can expect that the results will emphasize graphical displays in figures that show data over time for single individuals (e.g., Figure 8.7). Researchers do not use inferential statistics in these designs because they are not attempting to make inferences about a population.
- If an investigator used a *correlational design*, then you can expect that the results will emphasize inferential statistics that relate variables. Results usually include tables (like Figure 8.6) and description.
- If an investigator used a *survey design*, then you can expect that the results will emphasize descriptive statistics that describe single variables. Results usually include description, tables, and graphs. Some relationship and comparison results may be examined as well.

## How Do You Evaluate a Study's Quantitative Data Analysis and Results?

As you read and identify the components of a study's quantitative data analysis and results, you can also assess how well the researcher implemented these aspects within the study. Use the criteria provided in Figure 8.9 to assess an author's implementation of quantitative data analysis and the way the author reported the findings. These items evaluate whether the author provides sufficient information about the analysis process and reports the results in a manner consistent with quantitative hypothesis testing. For each statistical test, authors should provide enough information for you to understand the data analysis and whether the results provide sufficient evidence for or against the stated hypotheses.

## Reviewing What We've Learned

- Look to the *Method* section for the data analysis procedures and the *Results* section for the results of these procedures.
- Recognize that researchers use a linear process for analyzing quantitative data.
- Expect the data analysis process to consist of assigning numeric scores to each response, preparing the data for analysis, analyzing the data to address the research questions or hypotheses, and reporting results.
- Look to see that the researcher scored the data in a consistent way.
- Look for summed scores for the major variables.
- Search the results for measures of central tendency, variability, and relative standing for each major variable.
- Determine the inferential statistics used to address comparison and relationship research questions.
- Search for the alpha level used for any hypothesis tests.
- For each reported result, identify the statistic, its $p$ value, and whether the finding is statistically significant.

Use the following criteria to evaluate the quality of a quantitative study's data analysis and results as specified within a research report. For each evaluation item, indicate the following ratings:

+ You rate the item as "high quality" for the study.
✓ You rate the item as "ok quality" for the study.
– You rate the item as "low quality" for the study.

In addition to your rating, make notes about each element when you apply these criteria to an actual published study.

| **In a high-quality quantitative research report, the author . . .** | Application to a Published Study | |
|---|---|---|
| | Your Rating | Your Notes |
| 1. States the statistical analyses used to answer the research questions. | | |
| 2. Indicates how the data collected from the instruments were scored. | | |
| 3. Indicates the computer program used so you know how the statistics were calculated. | | |
| 4. Reports descriptive analyses so you know a summary of the sample's responses to each major variable. | | |
| 5. Reports inferential statistics to address the comparison and relationship hypotheses. | | |
| 6. Uses an alpha level of .05 or less. If not, the author explains why not so you understand why they are willing to take a greater risk of incorrectly finding a significant result. | | |
| 7. Reports the value of the statistic, the associated *p* value, and the effect size (if a statistically significant result is found) so you can make your own conclusions about a research question. | | |
| 8. Provides clearly formed tables and figures so you can interpret the information provided. | | |
| 9. Provides results that answer the research questions and address the hypotheses. | | |

FIGURE 8.9 Criteria for Evaluating the Quality of a Study's Quantitative Data Analysis and Report of Results

- Assess whether a statistically significant result also has practical significance.
- Determine the results reported for each research question, looking at tables, figures, and discussion.
- Ask yourself whether the researchers analyzed the data and reported the results in an objective way that matches the study's design.

## Practicing Your Skills

Return to the quantitative youth literacy study found at the end of Chapter 7, starting on p. 199. Pay close attention to the discussion of the results that appear in paragraphs 17–23 and Tables 1–3.

Practice using your skills and knowledge of the content of this chapter by answering the following questions about this study. Use the answers found in the Appendix to evaluate your progress.

1. What kinds of analyses (descriptive or inferential) are reported in Tables 1, 2, and 3?
2. What kinds of analyses (descriptive or inferential) are reported in paragraph 19?
3. The authors report the following result about reading poems in paragraph 23: "for gender, a statistically significant main effect was obtained only for poems, $F(1, 196) = 19.57$, $p < .0001$, $\eta = .30$. The effect size was medium." How does this result represent the five steps of hypothesis testing?
4. In paragraph 20 the authors state that they set alpha = .006 for a set of statistical tests. What does this mean?

# PART FOUR

# Understanding the Methods and Results of Qualitative Research Reports

Let's return to the idea that conducting research is like taking a journey. Researchers take qualitative research journeys in order to explore a topic area and learn from participants' views. As with quantitative research, qualitative researchers start with a reason for taking the trip (the problem), a general idea of what is known (the literature review), and an overall goal of where they are headed (the purpose). Unlike quantitative research, however, qualitative researchers do not preplan all of the details of their studies from the start. They learn as they go and adjust their path based on what they learn. Two benefits of exploring new territory this way when you travel are that you can follow up on unexpected and interesting findings and develop an in-depth understanding of the area. This flexible and emerging approach is useful in many qualitative research studies.

Although qualitative research journeys are more flexible than those taken in a typical quantitative research study, they still represent research studies that use rigorous and systematic procedures to implement the steps of the research process. Authors describe their qualitative procedures—their overall design and how they collected and analyzed data—in the method sections of their reports. They share what they found from these procedures in results sections. You will now examine the different ways that researchers design, conduct, and report results from their qualitative research studies so you can better understand the methods and results sections of qualitative research reports.

The chapters in Part IV are:

- Chapter 9—Qualitative Research Designs: Recognizing the Overall Plan for a Study
- Chapter 10—Qualitative Data Collection: Identifying How Information Is Gathered
- Chapter 11—Qualitative Data Analysis and Results: Examining What Was Found in a Study

CHAPTER

# 9 Qualitative Research Designs: Recognizing the Overall Plan for a Study

*You are familiar with identifying studies that used qualitative research to explore a research problem from Chapter 2. Identifying the overall approach of a study is a good start to understanding any qualitative report. A better understanding will arise if you also recognize and evaluate the types of qualitative research designs that researchers use when conducting their studies. Qualitative research designs provide overall plans for conducting studies to address different purposes. This chapter introduces five common types of qualitative designs, reviews their key characteristics, and suggests strategies for identifying and evaluating the qualitative research designs reported in published studies.*

### BY THE END OF THIS CHAPTER, YOU SHOULD BE ABLE TO:

- Explain why research designs are important in qualitative research.
- Describe how qualitative research developed from alternative perspectives to quantitative research.
- Name five different qualitative research designs.
- List key characteristics for each of the qualitative research designs.
- Identify the qualitative design used in a reported study.
- Evaluate the qualitative research design as reported in a research article.

We now focus our attention on studies that use a qualitative approach to the process of research. Recall from Chapter 5 that researchers conduct qualitative studies for the purposes of exploring, describing, or understanding a central phenomenon. As we found when discussing quantitative research in Part III, there are several different ways that a researcher can conduct a qualitative study depending on exactly what he/she wants to explore, describe, or understand. In many qualitative studies, researchers use a basic **thematic approach to qualitative research** to describe the multiple perspectives held about a topic. In this generic approach, researchers collect qualitative data, develop themes as results, and discuss general conclusions from the themes. We will learn more about these general procedures in Chapters 10 and 11.

Today, however, more and more researchers are using formal research designs to guide their procedures for collecting, analyzing, and reporting data in their qualitative studies. Authors using a design-based approach write clues into their reports that identify the design they are using. For example, examine the following statements (with italics added for emphasis) that appear as the first sentences in the method sections of several research reports:

- "This research study incorporated a blending of symbolic interactionalism and *narrative inquiry* in order to better understand Julie's journey as she completed her fifth year of teacher's college." (Rushton, 2004, pp. 64–65)
- "The research design for this study was informed by the *phenomenological* tradition of inquiry." (Landreman, Rasmussen, King, & Jiang, 2007, p. 277)
- "Because the purpose of the study was to understand how a leadership identity develops, a *grounded theory* methodology was chosen." (Komives et al., 2005, p. 594)

- "A *collective case study* of one high school's music department in the Midwestern United States, consisting of four music teachers, served as the focus." (Scheib, 2003, p. 126)
- "To more fully understand the perspective of the adolescent female, I undertook a year-long *ethnographic* study at one midwestern junior high school . . . "(Finders, 1996, p. 72)

As these examples illustrate, authors embed special terminology such as *narrative inquiry, phenomenological, grounded theory, case study,* and *ethnographic* to identify the research designs that they used in their studies. If you know the meaning of these words and the designs they represent, then these single sentences tell you a lot about the procedures the researcher used to conduct their study and the type of results you can expect them to report.

As a reader of research reports, you need to be familiar with the different types of qualitative research design. By recognizing the design used, you will have a more sophisticated understanding of what a study tried to accomplish and how the study's methods and results followed from the stated purpose. You will also have an expanded vocabulary for talking about different types of qualitative research. This vocabulary should be helpful for your class assignments and tests, but will also help you make sense of and evaluate studies that interest you.

## What Are Qualitative Research Designs?

You learned earlier in this book that *qualitative research* is research conducted to explore research problems by collecting text and image data to understand participants' views about a research problem. You also learned that a *research design* is a set of procedures that researchers use to collect, analyze, and report their data in a research study. Putting these two ideas together provides us with the following definition: **Qualitative research designs** are sets of procedures for collecting, analyzing, and reporting text and image data to answer research questions by exploring participants' views.

Figure 9.1 summarizes the general characteristics of qualitative research (as we introduced in Chapter 2) and indicates how qualitative research designs fit within the

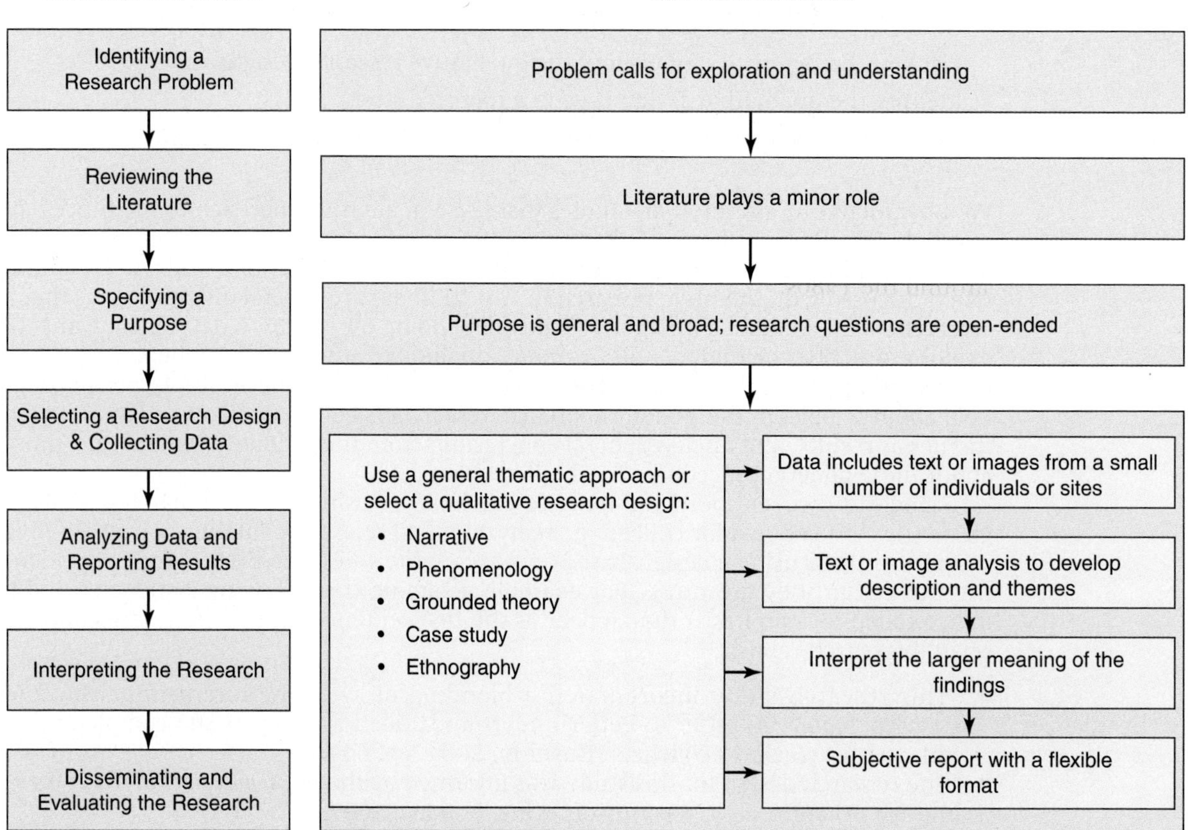


FIGURE 9.1 Qualitative Research Designs in the Process of Research

process of research. Researchers select a research design that fits their purpose for conducting research. Qualitative research designs, such as grounded theory or case study, provide researchers with a blueprint to guide how they conduct and report their studies. These designs, therefore, also provide you with a blueprint for understanding different types of qualitative studies reported in the literature.

## Why Are Qualitative Research Designs Useful?

At this point you might be asking yourself, "Why is research so complicated? Isn't it enough to just recognize that a study used a qualitative approach?" In addition to providing a more complex picture of research, considering research designs also provides a far more interesting and useful picture than just considering the overall approach. Think about the value of understanding different styles of music. If you are familiar with different styles of music, you can conclude that a song is an example of jazz, country, rock and roll, or classical. Each of these categories represents a different genre of music and each genre has its own history, identifying characteristics, and standards to determine if it is a good example. Knowing about different types of music helps musicians decide what music is appropriate to play in different situations. As a listener, you also have a better understanding of and appreciation for the music you hear if you are able to recognize different styles.

Like knowing about different styles of music, learning about different styles of qualitative research design is an important part of understanding research. With this knowledge, you can assess whether a design was best suited to study a given research purpose. Knowing the definitions of different qualitative research designs and being familiar with their characteristics, you can also understand and appreciate the different ways that researchers collect, analyze, and report their qualitative studies.

## How Did Different Types of Qualitative Research Develop?

Although the basis for traditional quantitative research grew out of the physical sciences, the ideas for qualitative research started in the late 1800s and early 1900s in fields such as anthropology and sociology. For example, qualitative studies of the poor in Europe, anthropological reports about indigenous cultures, and the fieldwork of sociologists with immigrants in inner-city Chicago all appear in social science research before the 1940s (Bogdan & Biklen, 1998). Although a few researchers were using these ideas, the actual use of qualitative research did not become prevalent in fields such as education until around the 1980s.

By the late 1960s, philosophers of education called for an alternative to the traditional quantitative approach. The traditional approach, they felt, relied too much on the researcher's view of education and lacked information on the research participant's view. They felt that traditional investigations created a contrived situation in which the research participant was taken out of context and placed within an experimental situation far removed from his or her personal experiences. To counter these traditional approaches, philosophers of education suggested an alternative way to think about research, called *naturalistic inquiry* or *constructivism,* to remedy these deficiencies (Lincoln & Guba, 1985). The central perspective of these new approaches emphasized the importance of the participant's view, stressed the setting and context (e.g., a classroom) in which the participants expressed their views, and highlighted the meaning people personally held about educational issues.

From these new perspectives for thinking about research, several writers began to focus on the procedures for conducting research based on the naturalistic or constructivist perspectives, namely qualitative research. Writers developed procedures such as writing general qualitative research questions, conducting on-site interviews and observations, and analyzing data for themes (e.g., Glesne & Peshkin, 1992; Miles & Huberman, 1994; Tesch, 1990). Along with these efforts arose a discussion about breaking qualitative research approaches into different types, such as case study and grounded theory research (e.g., Creswell, 2007; Stake, 1995; Strauss & Corbin, 1990). Different types of

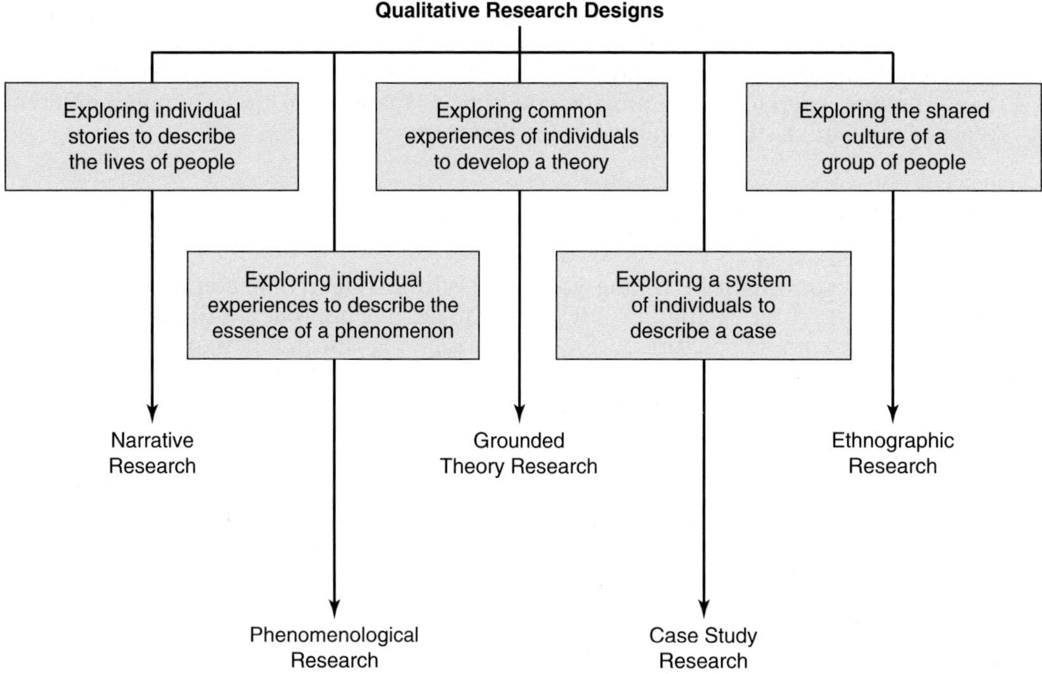


FIGURE 9.2 Types of Qualitative Research Designs and Their Use

qualitative research designs emerged from different disciplines to address different research purposes. They also encourage researchers to use procedures that go beyond analyzing data only for themes.

Today researchers have a wide range of possible research designs for conducting qualitative research. In fact, because of the flexible nature of qualitative research, even saying how many designs exist is a challenge! We have found qualitative textbooks that discuss 3 designs (Richards & Morse, 2007), 5 designs (Creswell, 2007), and even 17 (wow!) qualitative designs (Hatch, 2002). In addition, some researchers use a general thematic approach without a specific design and others choose to combine aspects of two or more designs. The trend today, however, is for researchers to use a design-based approach to their qualitative studies. For this text, we will focus on five common designs that we find frequently reported in the literature. The five designs that we will examine are summarized in Figure 9.2. These designs are:

- narrative research,
- phenomenological research,
- grounded theory research,
- case study research, and
- ethnographic research.

## What Is the Narrative Research Design?

In some qualitative research, a researcher wishes to tell the stories of one or two individuals. **Narrative research designs** are qualitative procedures in which researchers describe the lives of individuals, collect and tell stories about these individuals' lives, write narratives about their experiences, and discuss the meaning of those experiences for the individual. *Stories* are descriptions of individuals' lives and experiences as they unfold over time. Narrative researchers study stories such as the life of the first Native American to serve as a principal in a state, the experiences of a few first-year teachers in rural communities, or the story of a student who commits a violent act at school.

### Narrative Research Has Developed Through Literary Approaches

Despite substantial interest in narrative research, its methods are still in development. Consequently, there is little agreement about its form at this time. Writers in literature, history, anthropology, sociology, sociolinguistics, and education all have developed procedures for conducting narrative research. For example, these discussions have included procedures for conducting biographies, autobiographies, personal experience stories, and teachers' stories. An overview of the use of this research design for education emerged in the work of educator D. Jean Clandinin (2000, 2007) and her work with Michael Connelly. Three trends in the field of education support the use of narrative research (Cortazzi, 1993). First, there is an emphasis on teacher reflection. Second, more emphasis is being placed on teachers' knowledge—what they know, how they think, how they develop professionally, and how they make decisions in the classroom. Third, educators seek to bring teachers' voices to the forefront by empowering teachers to talk about their experiences. Narrative research is currently a popular design in education because it provides researchers with a set of procedures that suits these emphases.

## Narrative Research Is Used to Describe Individuals' Lives Over Time

For practice understanding the report of a narrative research study, go to the *Building Research Skills* section under the topic "Narrative Research" in MyEducationalResearchLab, located at www.myeducationlab.com. Complete the exercise "Identifying Steps in the Research Process for a Narrative Study" and use the provided feedback to further develop your skills for reading research articles.

Narrative research captures stories—an everyday form of data that is familiar to most people. Researchers select the narrative research design when they have individuals willing to tell their stories to help explore a research problem. Narrative research is well suited for focusing on studying individuals rather than groups or abstract patterns across many individuals. This design focuses on events experienced by an individual over time and the settings, actions, contexts, and people involved in these events. It is used when a researcher wants to uncover practical, specific insights that emerge from an individual's personal experiences. Therefore, narrative research is a good design for an investigator who wants to produce results that are useful for practitioners, such as educators or health-care providers. For example, researchers use narrative designs to learn how women respond to being informed that they are HIV-infected (Stevens & Doerr, 1997), follow one preservice teacher's placement in an inner-city school (Rushton, 2004), or describe the life history of a man with a mental disability (Angrosino, 1994).

## Key Characteristics of Narrative Research

You can identify a research study using a narrative research design by looking for terms such as *narrative research, narrative inquiry,* and *stories*. When reading a narrative study, examine the text for the following key characteristics:

- ***The researcher's purpose is to explore individual experiences as told through stories.*** The narrative researcher focuses on telling and understanding the stories of individual lives as told in a chronology of events that occurred over time.
- ***The researcher collects field texts that document the individual's story in his or her own words.*** The researcher collects data, called field texts, that provide the story of the individual. The story may be told in personal conversations or interviews, journal entries, letters, or other documents.
- ***The researcher analyzes the data to retell the individual's story.*** The researcher "restories" the data by identifying story elements and organizing them in a logical sequence.
- ***The researcher reports a chronological retelling of the story, the context for the story, and themes from the story.*** After completing the analysis, the narrative researcher presents the story in chronological order, including the contexts that provide the setting of the story, and identifies themes that emerged from the story.

## An Example of a Narrative Research Study

Huber and Whelan (1999) used a narrative design to study the story of Naomi's (a teacher) experience of miseducation occurring within our schools. Naomi experienced contradictions, gaps, and silences in her work at school; particularly centered around the placement of a special needs student in her classroom and the interactions that followed between her and other professionals at the school. The researchers collected Naomi's story through conversations among a group of five teachers during an 18-month period. They analyzed the conversations and stories of Naomi by retelling her story, presenting the themes that emerged from this story (including classroom- and borders-related themes), and interpreting the meaning of her story in terms of her power of resistance.

This narrative study illustrates a study of one individual—Naomi—and the story of her experience as a teacher. The authors focused on telling her story as it unfolded in time by using the data collected in Naomi's own words through interview conversations. The analysis in this study included retelling her story, developing themes from the story, and providing an interpretation of the meaning of the story for Naomi and other educators.

### What Do You Think?

Suppose you are reading a collection of research articles related to the problem of bullying at schools. How might a narrative study be used to study this topic? What characteristics would you expect to find in this study?

### Check Your Understanding

A researcher might use a narrative design to tell and analyze the story of one high school student's experiences of being the victim of bullying from a group of classmates. In this study, we would expect to find a focus on the individual and his story. The researcher would collect data from the student that tells the story through conversations and documents, such as his personal diary or artwork. The analysis of the story would be reported in the article by retelling the story in a logical order (what happens first and then what happens next), identifying themes of information that emerged from the story (such as helplessness or isolation), and interpreting the meaning of the story for the individual.

How might a narrative study be used to study a topic of interest to you?

## What Is the Phenomenological Research Design?

In some studies researchers want to identify what is common about how several individuals experience a phenomenon instead of describing an individual's story. A **phenomenological research design** is a set of qualitative procedures that a researcher uses to understand a single phenomenon by collecting information about and describing essential aspects of the experiences (events, interactions, meanings, etc.) of several individuals who have experienced the phenomenon. Examples of experiences include failing a test for middle school students, teaching advanced placement courses for high school teachers, or having your first child start kindergarten. This approach assumes that all individuals have unique experiences of a phenomenon. Phenomenology seeks to uncover the meaning of the phenomenon and its underlying essence by interviewing several individuals who have experienced it.

### Phenomenological Research Has Developed Through Philosophical Ideas

Phenomenology began as a philosophical movement early in the twentieth century with the writings of a mathematician named Edmund Husserl. This philosophical perspective advances the idea that the reality of a phenomenon can only be perceived within one's experience with it, and therefore it cannot be separated from that experience. Building from this philosophy, the phenomenological research design emerged as an approach to research in psychology, sociology, and education for describing phenomena of interest to research problems. Writers, such as Clark Moustakas (1994), Max van Manen (1997), and Renata Tesch (1990), offer specific approaches and methods for conducting studies based on a phenomenological approach.

*Here's a Tip for Reading Research!*

You might be confused with the different uses of the word "phenomenon" in qualitative research. You will often find this term used in a general way when authors refer to the "central phenomenon" that is being explored in the study. This use of phenomenon occurs in all types of qualitative research. In contrast researchers report using a "phenomenological design" when they want to describe *the meaning of how people experience a phenomenon.*

## Phenomenological Research Is Used to Understand the Essence of an Experience

Researchers choose to use phenomenology for the design of their studies when they need to understand the essence of a phenomenon as it is experienced by individuals. This design is especially useful when little is known about the meaning of the phenomenon of interest. Researchers who are interested in the philosophical roots of phenomenology often make use of this design. To use this approach, the researcher must be interested in learning about a single phenomenon as it is actually experienced. Therefore, the researcher must also have access to individuals who have had the experience and are able to describe it. For example, a researcher could use phenomenology to study reinvestment for individuals who participated in a youth mentoring program (Moerer-Urdahl & Creswell, 2004), the acquisition of a vision of social justice for expert multicultural educators (Landreman et al., 2007), and parents' experiences of raising a gifted African American child (Huff, Houskamp, Watkins, Stanton, & Tavegia, 2005).

## Key Characteristics of Phenomenological Research

You can identify a study using a phenomenological research design by looking for terms such as *phenomenology* or *phenomenological.* When reading a phenomenology, examine the text for the following key characteristics:

- ***The researcher's purpose is to determine the essence of a single phenomenon.*** The phenomenological researcher wants to understand the experiences that individuals have related to a single phenomenon.
- ***The researcher sets aside his or her own experiences about the phenomenon and collects data from people who have experienced it.*** In a step called bracketing, the researcher reflects on his/her own prior knowledge about the phenomenon and sets this knowledge aside to focus on learning from particiapnts. The researcher generally collects data by interviewing people who have experienced the phenomenon, but documents, art, or observations may also be used.
- ***The researcher analyzes the data for significant statements and meaning about the the phenomenon.*** A phenomenological researcher identifies all significant statements about the phenomenon. The researcher then analyzes the underlying meaning of the statements to develop themes about and descriptions of the phenomenon.
- ***The researcher reports themes, description, and the essence of the phenomenon.*** At the end of a phenomenology, the researcher reports themes about the phenomenon, descriptions of what is experienced and how it is experienced, and a statement of the essential essence of the experience.

## An Example of a Phenomenological Research Study

McVea, Harter, McEntarrffer, and Creswell (1999) used a phenomenological design to study the meaning of student tobacco use at one high school. The researchers trained high school students to conduct group interviews with classmates and school personnel, and 72 individuals participated in the interviews. The researchers reported analyzing the data by identifying significant statements (provided in the appendix of the article) and core themes such as social benefits, rebellion, and dialogue between smokers and nonsmokers. They concluded with a description of the meaning of student tobacco use as experienced by four groups (the hall, the "hill," the debate team, and the cross-country team) as well as a statement of the overall essence of student tobacco use at City High School. From these findings, the authors suggest possible interventions for the school.

This phenomenological study illustrates a study of a single phenomenon—student tobacco use at City High School. The researchers focused on understanding this phenomenon from the perspective of those who experience it, including students, teachers, and administrators at the school. The researchers analyzed the interview data to identify themes, to describe the contexts in which the phenomenon is experienced, and to provide the essence of the experience.

### What Do You Think?

Suppose you are reading a collection of research articles related to the problem of bullying at schools. How might a phenomenological design be used to study this topic? What characteristics would you expect to find in this study?

### Check Your Understanding

A researcher might use a phenomenology to study the meaning of being a bully. In this study, we would expect to find that the purpose of the study is to describe the lived experiences of this phenomenon (being a bully). The researcher would collect interview data from individuals known to engage in bullying behaviors toward others. The researcher would also bracket her own expectations about bullies so she could focus on learning from her participants' experiences. The report would describe themes related to being a bully, describe what it means to be a bully and how being a bully is experienced, and offer a statement describing the essence of what it means to be a bully.

Now, how might a phenomenology be used to study a topic of interest to you?

## What Is the Grounded Theory Research Design?

For some research problems, researchers need to do more than develop description. **Grounded theory research designs** are systematic, qualitative procedures that researchers use to generate a general explanation (called a *grounded theory*) that explains a process, action, or interaction among people. For example, grounded theorists might study the process principals use to mentor new elementary teachers, the action of coping with stress for undergraduate freshmen at large universities, or the interactions between school counselors and parents with a child with persistent behavior problems in middle school. The procedures for developing this theory include collecting primarily interview data, developing and relating categories (or themes) of information, and composing a figure or visual model that portrays the general explanation. In this way, the explanation is grounded in the data from participants.

### Grounded Theory Research Developed in Sociology

The procedures for conducting a systematic grounded theory design were first developed in the 1960s by two sociologists studying the terminally ill (Glaser & Strauss, 1967). Corbin and Strauss (2008) formally described the procedures to conduct a systematic grounded theory design. Other researchers such as Glaser (1992) and Charmaz (2006) working with Bryant (2007) have advanced more flexible strategies for developing theories using grounded theory designs. The systematic and flexible designs for grounded theory are widely used in research today to develop theories related to important issues and problems.

### Grounded Theory Research Is Used to Develop a Theory

Researchers use grounded theory when they need a broad theory or explanation of a process, action, or interaction. A researcher chooses this design to generate a theory when the current existing theories do not address the problem or participants of interest. Because a theory produced from a grounded theory study is "grounded" in the data, it actually works in practice, is sensitive to individuals in a setting, and represents the complexities actually found in the process, action, or interaction. Thus, it provides a better explanation than a theory borrowed off-the-shelf. For instance, in the study of certain populations (e.g., children with attention disorders), existing theories may have little applicability to special populations (e.g., child immigrants from Latin America) and therefore a new or modified theory needs to be developed. Grounded theory is also used when the purpose of the study is to examine a process, such as how students develop as writers (Neff, 1998), or how high-achieving African American and Caucasian women's careers develop (Richie, Fassinger, Linn, & Johnson, 1997). It also is used to explain an action of people, such as participation in an adult education class (Courtney, Jha, & Babchuk, 1994), or an interaction among people, such as the support department chairs provide for faculty researchers (Creswell & Brown, 1992).

## Key Characteristics of Grounded Theory Research

Grounded theory studies can usually be identified by the use of the term *grounded theory*. When reading a grounded theory study, watch for the following key characteristics:

- ***The researcher's purpose is to develop a theory that explains a process.*** The grounded theory researcher should identify a process, action, or interaction that is the focus of the study. The study examines this process in order to generate a theory about it.
- ***The researcher collects data in the form of interviews.*** The grounded theory researcher most often uses interviews with people who have experienced the process, action, or interaction of interest to provide the data necessary to develop a theory.
- ***The researcher systematically analyzes the data using multiple stages of coding.*** Systematic grounded theory designs can be recognized by the researcher's use of three stages of data analysis. In open coding, the researcher develops categories from the collected data. In axial coding, the researcher identifies one category that is at the heart of the process and then relates it to the other categories. Finally, the researcher conducts selective coding to produce propositions or hypotheses grounded in the data.
- ***The researcher reports a model and propositions to describe the theory.*** A grounded theory report presents the theory that has been developed in the article text, in a visual model that depicts the theory, and in proposition or hypothesis statements.

## An Example of a Grounded Theory Research Study

Komives et al. (2005) used a grounded theory design in their study of how college students develop a leadership identity. They stated the purpose of their study as "to understand the processes a person experiences in creating a leadership identity" (p. 594). To develop a theory of this process, the researchers conducted three interviews with each of 13 diverse college students who had been identified as demonstrating leadership qualities. They reported using a systematic process of open coding, axial coding, and selective coding to analyze the data. From their analysis, the researchers found a six-stage process for developing a leadership identity. This process was connected to the categories of developmental influences, developing self, group influences, changing view of self with others, and broadening view of leadership. Komives et al. presented a visual model of how the categories related to the six stages of the developmental process and discussed the implications of the theory in their discussion.

This grounded theory study illustrates the study of a process—development of a leadership identity—as experienced by a number of individuals. The researchers collected their data through interviews and used a systematic approach to analyzing their data to identify the process and the themes that relate to this process. They brought their findings together into a visual diagram that depicts the process and illustrates the developed theory.

### What Do You Think?

Suppose you are reading a collection of research articles related to the problem of bullying at schools. How might a grounded theory design be used to study this topic? What characteristics would you expect to find in this study?

### Check Your Understanding

A researcher might use a grounded theory design to study the process by which middle school students cope with being bullied. In this study, we would expect the author to discuss the need to develop a theory explaining the coping process and to collect data by interviewing victims of bullying at different middle schools. He would analyze the data in stages to develop themes about the process, produce a diagram showing how the themes are interrelated, and suggest hypotheses that result from this new theory.

How might a grounded theory design be used to study a topic of interest to you?

## What Is the Case Study Design?

The designs described so far have emphasized exploring individuals' perspectives and experiences. Sometimes researchers want to examine the complexities of a system instead of individuals and then they choose to use a case study design. A **case study research design** is a set of qualitative procedures to explore a bounded system in depth. The bounded system of interest represents the *case* being studied. A *system* of interest can be a program, event, or activity involving individuals. *Bounded* means that the case is separated out for research in terms of time, place, or some physical boundaries. Examples of cases that could be studied include a third-grade class using a new vocabulary curriculum for a school year, a theater group preparing a theatrical production during the fall semester, or a school board establishing budget priorities over three years. The case study researcher collects multiple types of data to develop an in-depth picture, describes the case within its setting, and explores themes about the case.

### Case Study Research Developed Across Disciplines

Early examples of case studies are found starting in the 1920s when sociologists conducted studies to depict and describe ordinary life in U.S. cities. These case studies described topics such as the life of Polish immigrants, the Jewish ghetto, the taxi-dance hall, and the professional thief. Today, many scholars write about case study designs such as Robert Stake (1995), Sharan Merriam (1998), and Robert Yin (2003). Case studies are common in educational research where researchers seek to describe educational systems, such as a classroom, a school, or a college campus.

For practice understanding the report of a case study, go to the *Building Research Skills* section under the topic "Case Study Research" in MyEducationalResearchLab, located at www.myeducationlab.com. Complete the exercise "Identifying Steps in the Research Process for a Case Study" and use the provided feedback to further develop your skills for reading research articles.

### Case Study Research Is Used to Describe a Case

Researchers choose to use a case study design if they want to provide an in-depth exploration of a case in order to better understand a research problem. Case study researchers often focus their studies on a program, event, or activity involving individuals. Therefore, the case may be a single individual (e.g., a teacher), several individuals separately or in a group (e.g., several teachers), or a program, events, or activities (e.g., the implementation of a new math program). A case may be selected for study because it is unusual and has merit in and of itself, such as a bilingual elementary school. Alternatively, the focus of a qualitative study may be a specific issue, with a case (or cases) used to illustrate the issue. For example, a researcher wants to study the issue of campus violence and selects a campus to study as a case because it had experienced a violent event (Asmussen & Creswell, 1995). Case studies may also include multiple cases, called a *collective case study* (Stake, 1995), in which multiple cases are described and compared to provide insight into an issue. A case study researcher might examine several agencies to illustrate alternative approaches to managing foster care cases.

## Key Characteristics of Case Study Research

Depending on the number of cases, you can identify this design by finding the terms *case study, collective case study,* or *multiple case study.* When reading a case study, look for the following key characteristics of a case study design:

- ***The researcher's purpose is to study a case.*** The case study researcher should identify a single case or multiple cases as the object of study. Each case should be a system of individuals bounded by time, place, and/or physical boundaries.
- ***The researcher collects multiple forms of data.*** The researcher seeks to develop an in-depth understanding of the case or cases by collecting multiple forms of data (e.g., interviews, observations, pictures, scrapbooks, videotapes, and e-mails). Providing this in-depth understanding requires that only a few cases be studied, because for each additional case examined, the researcher has less time to devote to exploring the depths of any one case.
- ***The researcher analyzes the data for description and themes.*** A case study researcher analyzes the data to provide a rich description of the case and to develop themes or patterns of information that emerge about the case.
- ***The researcher reports description, themes, and lessons learned.*** A case study report includes a description of the case, a presentation of the thematic results, and an interpretation of the lessons learned from the case.

## An Example of a Case Study Research Study

Scheib's (2003) study of four high school music teachers is an example of a case study. The study sought to describe the complicated lives of four music teachers and to examine the stressors that the music teachers face as they balance their different roles. The author spent one semester at the school observing the teachers at school, conducting interviews with the teachers, and collecting documents, such as teacher handbooks and concert programs. After describing a profile of each teacher in the report, the author identified six themes that emerged about the role stress perceived by each teacher: role ambiguity, role conflict, role overload, underutilization of skills, resource inadequacy, and nonparticipation. From the individual case analyses, the author compared the four individuals and found that the teachers experience stress that arose from conflict and tension between their expectations based on prior experiences with music programs and the resources available at their current school.

This case study illustrates a study of four bounded systems—specific individuals—and a description of patterns of stress for all four teachers. The researcher focused on the issue of role stress and conducted an in-depth examination of four cases to illustrate this issue. Multiple forms of data were collected, and the analysis results consisted of both description and themes.

### What Do You Think?

Suppose you are reading a collection of research articles related to the problem of bullying at schools. How might a case study design be used to study this topic? What characteristics would you expect to find in this study?

### Check Your Understanding

A researcher might use a case study design to study bullying events that occur among the children in one sixth-grade classroom during a school year. In this study, we would expect to find the identification of a case (bounded by one class at one school during one school year), the collection of multiple types of data (such as observations in the class and during recess; interviews with the teacher, students, and parents; and documents stating the school's policy about bullying), and data analysis focused on description and theme development. The study's results would include a description of the case, themes that emerged about bullying events, and suggestions of lessons learned from the study.

How might a case study be used to study a topic of interest to you?

## What Is the Ethnographic Research Design?

When studying a group of individuals, researchers may want to do more than describe what is happening in a case. **Ethnographic research designs** are qualitative research procedures for describing, analyzing, and interpreting a culture-sharing group's shared patterns of behavior, beliefs, and language that develop over time. Central to this definition is culture. *Culture* is "everything having to do with human behavior and belief" (LeCompte, Preissle, & Tesch, 1993, p. 5). It can include language, rituals, communication styles, and economic and political structures. To understand the patterns of a culture-sharing group, the ethnographer spends considerable time in the field interviewing, observing, and gathering documents about the group in order to understand their culture-sharing behaviors, beliefs, and language.

### Ethnographic Research Developed from Cultural Anthropology

The roots of educational ethnography lie in cultural anthropology. In the late nineteenth and early twentieth centuries, anthropologists explored "primitive" cultures by visiting other countries and becoming immersed in their societies for extensive periods. Educational ethnographers began to apply these strategies to study the culture of educational groups starting in the 1950s. For example, Jules Henry depicted elementary school classrooms and high schools as tribes with rituals, culture, and social structure (LeCompte et al., 1993). Contemporary educational ethnographers like David Fetterman (1998) and Harry Wolcott (1999) have written about techniques for using ethnography to study educational issues.

For practice understanding the report of an ethnographic research study, go to the *Building Research Skills* section under the topic "Ethnographic Research" in MyEducationalResearchLab, located at www.myeducationlab.com. Complete the exercise "Identifying Steps in the Research Process for an Ethnographic Study" and use the provided feedback to further develop your skills for reading research articles.

### Ethnographic Research Is Used to Explore a Group's Culture

Researchers conduct ethnographies when the study of a group provides understanding of a larger cultural issue. This means that the researcher has access to a culture-sharing group to study—one that has been together for some time and has developed shared values, beliefs, and language. The researcher seeks to capture the "rules" of behavior, such as the informal relationships among teachers who congregate at favorite places to socialize (Pajak & Blasé, 1984) or the tacit rules for reading teen magazines by a group of best friends at one junior high school (Finders, 1996). The culture-sharing group may be narrowly framed (e.g., teachers, students, or staff members) or broadly framed (e.g., studying entire schools and their success, innovation, or violence). The culture-sharing group may be a family as in the ethnographic study of a 12-year-old child with Down syndrome and his family (Harry, Day, & Quist, 1998). Ethnography is the best design when researchers want to examine a group in the setting where they live and work and provide a detailed day-to-day picture of events, such as the thoughts and behaviors of a search committee hiring a new principal (Wolcott, 1974, 1994).

## Key Characteristics of Ethnographic Research

You can identify a study using an ethnographic research design by looking for terms such as *ethnography* or *ethnographic.* When reading a study reporting an ethnography, look for the following key characteristics in the report:

- ***The researcher studies a culture-sharing group.*** The ethnographer identifies an intact culture-sharing group of individuals to study. Generally members of this group have interacted with each other for sufficient time for the group to develop its own culture.
- ***The researcher conducts extensive fieldwork.*** The ethnographer develops an understanding of the cultural patterns of the group through extensive time spent conducting fieldwork with members of the group. This fieldwork emphasizes observing the group, but may also include collecting interviews, documents, and other artifacts.
- ***The researcher analyzes the data for shared patterns of behaviors, beliefs, and language.*** Ethnographic researchers analyze their data to identify shared patterns of behavior, beliefs, and language that the culture-sharing group adopts over time. A shared pattern in ethnography is a common social interaction that stabilizes as a tacit rule or expectation of the group (Spindler & Spindler, 1992).
- ***The researcher reports a cultural portrait and personal reflections.*** When writing up the report, the ethnographer presents a cultural portrait of the group—a detailed, rich rendering of individuals and scenes that depict what is going on in the culture-sharing group and the setting, situation, or environment that surrounds the cultural group being studied. In addition, the ethnographic researcher also discusses his or her role in the study in a way that honors and respects the site and participants.

## An Example of an Ethnographic Research Study

An example of an ethnography can be found in Swidler's (2000) study of a one-teacher country school. This author considers schools to be cultural settings and designed this study to examine the shared practices of one specific country school made up of one teacher and 12 students spanning kindergarten through eighth grades. He collected data over six months, including extensive observations, interviews, and artifacts and documents. The results paint a descriptive portrait of life at the school, including its setting in the community, the teacher and individual students, and their shared practices during a typical school day. The author interprets his views of the teacher's use of a conservative recitation-driven pedagogy within the cultural contexts in which the school exists. These important community values include the socialization of the community's children, the desire for children's success in high school, a distrust of youth culture, and defending the community's way of life.

This study illustrates an ethnographic study of a culture sharing group—a one-teacher school within a small rural community—to learn about the shared patterns of beliefs, behaviors, and language. The researcher conducted extensive fieldwork. He developed a rich, detailed portrait of daily life at this school and interpreted it within the cultural contexts of the group.

## What Do You Think?

Suppose you are reading a collection of research articles related to the problem of bullying at schools. How might an ethnographic design be used to study this topic? What characteristics would you expect to find in this study?

### Check Your Understanding

A researcher might use an ethnographic design to study a group of children and parents that frequent one popular park in an inner city neighborhood where bullying occurs to understand the cultural patterns that emerge from this group. In this study, we would expect to find an emphasis on the cultural aspects of the group, the collection of extensive fieldwork (with an emphasis on conducting observations at the park), and data analysis focused on identifying shared behaviors, attitudes, and language related to the issue of bullying within the group (such as how parents react to bullying or the language kids use to talk about bullies and victims). The report would end with a rich, detailed description of the park's setting and typical life at the park and a discussion of the cultural themes that emerged.

Now, how might an ethnographic design be used to study a topic of interest to you?

## How Do You Identify the Research Design Reported in a Qualitative Research Article?

We have now reviewed five qualitative research designs, including their history, reasons that researchers use them, and their key characteristics. With this information in hand, the challenge now becomes figuring out what research design was used when reading a published qualitative research article. We suggest trying four steps to identify a qualitative research design.

*Here's a Tip for Applying Research!*

Some qualitative research designs are more likely to produce results that suggest direct implications for practice. Look to narrative studies and case studies to find results that might easily fit your setting. In contrast, phenomenology, grounded theory, and ethnography studies are best suited for developing broad patterns across several individuals or larger groups. Look to studies using these designs to find results that provide a more abstract explanation or description of the topic, which may be more useful for researchers than for practitioners.

1. ***Look to see if the author named one of the five designs in the title of the article.*** For example, note how the following titles clearly state the research design that was used:
   - "The Experiences of Parents of Gifted African American Children: A Phenomenological Study" (*Huff et al., 2005*)
   - "Using Narrative Inquiry to Understand a Student-Teacher's Practical Knowledge while Teaching in an Inner-City School" (*Rushton, 2004*).
2. ***Examine the purpose statement to see if it suggests the study's research design.*** Many qualitative purpose statements will name the design used, such as saying "The purpose of this ethnographic study is. . . ." Some studies, however, will not state the design in the purpose statement. They will, however, state a purpose that suggests the appropriate design by what type of central phenomenon the researcher wants to study (e.g., an individual's story, an experience, a process, a system, or a culture-sharing group). For example, in the grounded theory study by Komives et al. (2005), the purpose statement read: "The purpose of this study was to understand the processes a person experiences in creating a leadership identity" (p. 594). Although this statement did not identify the study as using grounded theory, we expect it is a grounded theory study since it is the study of a process.
3. ***Read the beginning paragraphs of the method section and look for a statement that identifies the design.*** Authors will often describe the design that was used as one of the first topics addressed in the method section of a qualitative report. For example, Komives et al. (2005) followed up their purpose statement (in the previous paragraph) with the following sentence at the start of the method section: "Because the purpose of the study was to understand how a leadership identity develops, a grounded theory methodology was chosen" (p. 594).
4. ***Examine the methods and results section to identify how the author collected, analyzed, and reported the data.*** The surest way to recognize the research design used in a study is to assess the procedures that the author used for collecting, analyzing, and reporting the data and decide whether they match one of the major design types. In fact, this is always an important step in identifying a design. Some authors mistakenly claim to use a type of design (such as ethnography) when they really

mean that they are using a general qualitative thematic approach. In addition, we have seen a few studies that claim to use case study, grounded theory, narrative, and ethnography—all in one article! When in doubt, you should consider the procedures the author actually *used* and not rely on the word(s) they happen to state.

### What Do You Think?

Consider the following information from a published study (Asmussen & Creswell, 1995). Which design do you think the authors used and what is your evidence?

*Title*: Campus Response to a Student Gunman

*Purpose Statement*: The study presented in this article is a qualitative case analysis that describes and interprets a campus response to a gun incident. (p. 576)

*Excerpt from the First Paragraph in the Method Section*: . . . We also limited our study to the reactions of groups on campus rather than expand it to include off-campus groups (for example, television and newspaper coverage). This bounding of the study was consistent with an exploratory qualitative [research design]. . . . We identified campus informants, using a semistructured protocol that consisted of five questions. . . . We also gathered observational data, documents, and visual materials. . . . (p. 578)

### Check Your Understanding

This study is an example of a qualitative study using a case study research design. The authors do not inform us of the type of design in the title. When we turn to the purpose statement, we find the use of the phrase "case analysis," which suggests the study may be a case study. More importantly, as we continue reading we can find several key characteristics of the case study research design in the excerpts. For example, the authors report wanting to "describe and interpret" the case in their purpose statement. A review of the full study will show that the authors report a detailed description of the event as well as themes that emerged about the event (such as "fear" and "safety"). The authors also note that their study was "bounded," another common feature of case study designs. Finally, we note that they collected multiple types of data in order to build an in-depth description.

## How Do You Evaluate a Study's Qualitative Design?

Recognizing the design used in a qualitative study is a great step to understanding its report, but you do not want to stop there. Understanding research designs means that you can also use a design's characteristics to help evaluate a study. We will discuss the details of qualitative data collection and analysis procedures in upcoming chapters, but for now, you can focus on the overall plan described for a study and whether the key characteristics of that plan were implemented. Figure 9.3 provides criteria you can use to assess an author's discussion of a qualitative research design. In a high-quality qualitative study, the researcher implements a formal research design that matches the purpose, and the methods of collecting, analyzing and reporting the data match this design.

## Reviewing What We've Learned

- Assess whether a qualitative study used a general thematic approach or a more formal research design.
- Note that qualitative research designs are sets of procedures for collecting, analyzing, and reporting data to address different types of research purposes.
- Realize that qualitative research and the different designs emerged as an alternative to more traditional quantitative perspectives about research.

Use the following criteria to evaluate the quality of the research design in a qualitative research report. For each evaluation item, indicate the following ratings:

+ You rate the item as "high quality" for the study.
✓ You rate the item as "ok quality" for the study.
– You rate the item as "low quality" for the study.

In addition to your rating, make notes about each element when you apply these criteria to an actual published study.

| **In a high-quality qualitative research report, the author . . .** | Application to a Published Study | |
|---|---|---|
| | Your Rating | Your Notes |
| 1. Uses a specific qualitative design rather than a "generic" general thematic approach. | | |
| 2. Identifies the type of research design used so you know the plan for conducting the study. | | |
| 3. Includes up-to-date references about the design within the method section to indicate the author's knowledge about the design. | | |
| 4. Matches the selected research design to the study's purpose and research questions. | | |
| 5. Uses rigorous procedures of data collection, analysis, and interpretation within the selected design. | | |

**FIGURE 9.3 Criteria for Evaluating the Quality of a Study's Qualitative Research Design**

- Determine the type of qualitative research design, such as narrative research, phenomenology, grounded theory, case study, and ethnography.
- Assess whether the selected research design is best suited to explore the specified central phenomenon.
- Expect the data collection procedures to be consistent with the research design.
- Look for the data analysis to utilize procedures associated with the selected design.
- Anticipate the kinds of results that will be reported based on a study's research design.
- Assess qualitative research designs by considering whether the key characteristics of the design were implemented to address the study's stated purpose.

## Practicing Your Skills

Practice using your skills and knowledge of the content of this chapter by answering the following questions. Use the answers found in the Appendix to evaluate your progress.

1. In your own words describe why it can be helpful to recognize the research design used when reading a qualitative research report.
2. Read the following statements and identify the design you think the researcher used to conduct the study. Explain your choice and why this design matches the study.
   - "In this article, I detail findings from a qualitative case study that examined African American elementary and secondary students' descriptions of teaching practices and learning environments within urban contexts." (*Howard, 2002, p. 425*)

- "Our goals were to develop theoretical concepts about processes of adolescent emotional development and how settings can facilitate these processes." (*Larson & Brown, 2007, p. 1084*)
- "The narrative structures and meanings of the preservice teachers' stories, written while the preservice teachers were enrolled in a secondary methods course, were examined with the goal of gaining insight into the preservice teachers' emerging identities as mathematics teachers." (*Lloyd, 2006, p. 57*)

3. Return to the qualitative parent role study at the end of Chapter 1. Identify the research design used in this study. List three pieces of evidence for your answer and discuss whether this design matches the study's purpose.
4. Return to the qualitative new teacher study at the end of Chapter 3. Identify the research design used in this study. List three pieces of evidence for your answer and discuss whether this design matches the study's purpose.

# CHAPTER 10 Qualitative Data Collection: Identifying How Information Is Gathered

*You can understand the general plan for a qualitative study by recognizing the research design that was used, but that does not inform you as to what the researcher actually did to collect data during the study. Authors report the details of how they collected their qualitative data in the method section of their research articles. These details include the selection of sites and participants, the identification of the types of data, and the procedures used to gather the desired information in an ethical manner. In this chapter, you will learn how to understand the procedures qualitative researchers report using to implement qualitative data collection.*

**BY THE END OF THIS CHAPTER, YOU SHOULD BE ABLE TO:**

- Define qualitative data collection and list the major elements that researchers report.
- Describe a study's sample and identify the strategy the researchers use to select sites and participants.
- Name the types of qualitative data researchers collect during a study.
- Understand the issues researchers confront while collecting qualitative data.
- Evaluate the collection of qualitative data as reported in a research article.

As we learned in Chapter 1, an essential element that separates research from other types of scholarly work is the collection (and subsequent analysis) of data. This step in the research process is so important that it merits its own section in any research report. It is important for you to examine a study's data collection process because the results that a researcher produces can only be as good as the collected data. Like with quantitative data collection, qualitative researchers address a similar set of issues related to their data collection. These include:

- selecting participants and sites,
- choosing a data collection method, and
- implementing data collection procedures.

While the issues are similar to quantitative research, qualitative researchers have special considerations in mind as they implement the qualitative data collection step of their studies. These considerations speak to questions such as: How should a qualitative researcher select participants? How many participants should be included in a qualitative study? What types of data are appropriate? What issues are confronted during data collection?

The answers to these questions relate to the overall purpose of exploring a topic and, more specifically, to the particular research design being used. When reading qualitative research, you need to be able to understand how a researcher collected qualitative data. Let's begin by reviewing data collection in the process of conducting qualitative research.

## What Is the Process of Collecting Qualitative Data?

You were introduced to the process that researchers use to collect qualitative data in Chapter 2. Building on this earlier discussion, we can identify four elements specific to qualitative data collection. Qualitative data collection consists of:

- intentionally selecting sites and participants based on the places and people that can best help provide understanding of the central phenomenon;
- gathering information from a small number of sites and participants to develop rich detail and understandings;
- collecting word (text) or image (picture) data using forms with open-ended, emerging questions to permit participants to generate their own responses; and
- being sensitive to the challenges and ethical issues of gathering information face to face and often in people's homes or workplaces.

These four elements provide you with an overview of what to expect when reading about data collection in a qualitative report. They also point to criteria you can use to evaluate a study's data collection that are specific to a qualitative approach. You have probably already noticed some differences between quantitative and qualitative data collection. For example, in quantitative research we look to see that a study collected data from a large number of people, but we have a different standard to use for qualitative research. To evaluate qualitative research, you need to be able to apply criteria that are appropriate for qualitative data collection.

## How Do You Identify a Study's Qualitative Data Collection?

*Here's a Tip for Reading Research!*

When available, use subheadings to identify the information presented in a method section. Many qualitative reports will include subheadings such as *Sample*, *Site* or *Setting*, *Participants*, and *Data Collection*. These labels will help you grasp how the author organized the information.

You can find an author's discussion of data collection in the method section of a qualitative research article or report. This section generally has a heading such as *Method*, *Methodology*, or *Procedures* in qualitative studies. As we discussed in the previous chapter, the method section often begins with a brief statement introducing the qualitative research design, but the bulk of the text in this section describes how the author implemented data collection during the study. While every method section reflects the unique circumstances and procedures used in a study, they all tend to address a common set of important elements.

To consider the elements discussed for qualitative data collection, let's examine the following excerpt from Howard's (2002) qualitative case study about African American students' descriptions of teaching practices and learning environments. As you read this passage, think about the kind of information the author is telling you.

> ***Method***
>
> The students who participated in the [qualitative case] study were chosen from five urban elementary and secondary schools located in the northwestern and midwestern areas of the United States. The students ranged from second to eighth grades. A purposeful sample of 30 students was used for the study, 17 girls and 13 boys. A cross-selection of students, based on academic achievement and classroom behavior per their teachers' classifications, were identified to serve as participants for the study. Thus, the students fell into low-, medium-, or high-achievement and behavioral categories. This choice of selection was also made to reduce the likelihood that students would give glowing testimonials of their teachers that may not have been indicative of their true perceptions of their learning environments.
>
> Data collection occurred during the 1998–1999 school year. Semi-structured interviews were done with the students to gain insight into their perceptions of school in general, and of their teachers' pedagogy as it related to degrees of effectiveness or ineffectiveness. Each student was interviewed once individually and once in a group setting of two to three with selected classmates who were also participants in the study. The interviews, which occurred on the students' school premises, lasted approximately 30 to 60 min each, and were tape-recorded and transcribed. Data-collection methods also included classroom observations that occurred two to three times a week, and lasted from 30 to 90 min per visit . . . (*Howard, 2002, pp. 429–430*)

### Look for Information About the Sites and Participants in the Method Section

We learned several details about how the researcher collected data in this qualitative study by reading this passage. The author begins by informing us about where he collected the data (the sites) and from whom (the participants). He collected data at five elementary and secondary schools in the northwestern and midwestern regions of the United States. In addition, we learn that the participants included 30 children at these schools. He selected them so that they ranged in age from second to eighth-grade and had different levels (low, medium, or high) of academic achievement and behaviors.

### Identify the Types of Qualitative Data Gathered

After telling us about the sites and participants, the author next identified the types of data that he gathered. Specifically we learned that he collected individual and group interviews with the children. The author also reports gathering classroom observations.

### Note the Procedures and Issues Related to Collecting Data

The researcher provided information beyond the type of data collected. These details include information about how he collected the data (types of interviews and for how long), where data collection occurred (at the schools), and how the information was recorded (tape-recording). While not included in this passage, the author could also have provided information about issues that arose during data collection (such as how he gained access to the schools) and any ethical considerations that played a role in the research (such as how he received permission to interview the children).

These categories—the sites and participants; types of data; and procedures and issues—provide essential information about what a qualitative researcher actually did while collecting data during a study. They also provide you with a framework for reading and evaluating a research report. Let's examine each of these categories in more detail.

## How Do Researchers Select the Sites and Participants for Their Qualitative Studies?

In order to understand how qualitative researchers select participants and sites, it is helpful to consider how this selection process differs from what we previously learned about quantitative research. Once we understand this difference, then we can focus on the specific selection strategies used by qualitative researchers.

### The Qualitative Approach Is Different from Quantitative Research

Recall that the intent of qualitative inquiry is not to generalize to a population like quantitative research. Instead, qualitative research seeks to develop an in-depth exploration of a central phenomenon, such as creating community in a classroom or the experience of being a bully. To best understand this central phenomenon, the qualitative researcher intentionally selects individuals and sites instead of selecting them randomly.

The distinction between quantitative probability sampling and qualitative purposeful sampling is portrayed in Figure 10.1. In quantitative research, the focus is on using probability sampling, selecting representative individuals for the sample, and generalizing from these individuals to a population. Often this process results in testing theories that explain the population. In contrast, the qualitative researcher selects sites and people that can best help develop an understanding about a central phenomenon. This understanding emerges through a detailed exploration of the people or sites. It provides information that is useful, that helps us learn about the phenomenon, or that gives voice to individuals who have not been heard.

> For practice understanding the sample in a research study, go to the *Building Research Skills* section under the topic "Selecting a Sample" in MyEducationalResearchLab, located at www.myeducationlab.com. Complete the exercise "Sampling in a Qualitative Study" and use the provided feedback to further develop your skills for reading research articles.

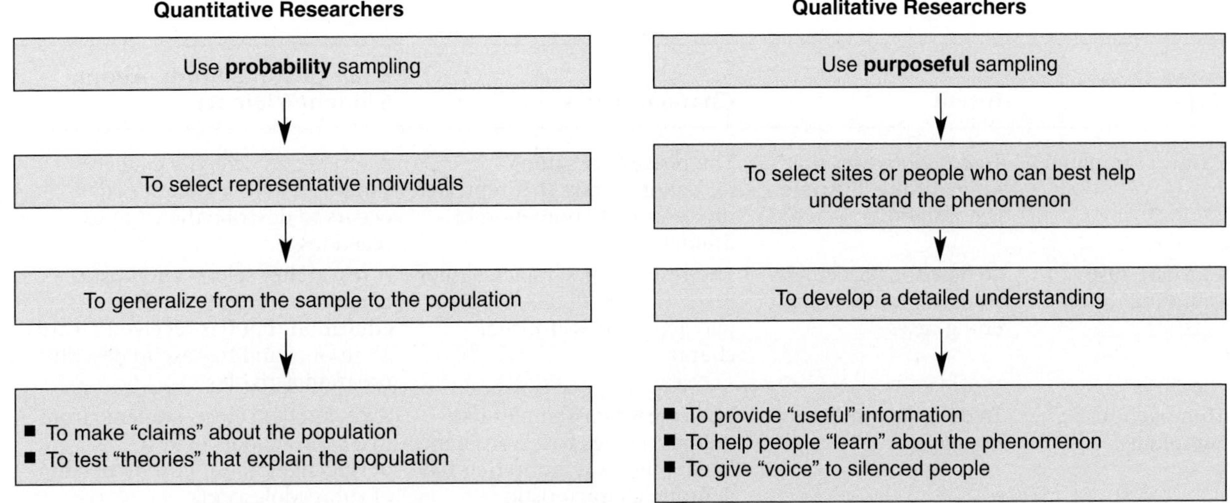


**FIGURE 10.1 Differences Between Sampling in Quantitative and Qualitative Research**

## Participants Are Intentionally Selected

The research term used for qualitative sampling is purposeful sampling. **Purposeful sampling** means that researchers intentionally select sites and individuals to learn about or understand the central phenomenon. The standard used in choosing sites and participants is whether they are "information rich" (Patton, 2002, p. 230). For example, a qualitative researcher may decide to study a site (e.g., one college campus), several sites (three small liberal arts campuses), individuals or groups (freshman students), or some combination (purposefully sample two liberal arts campuses and several freshman students on those campuses). Purposeful sampling thus applies to both sites and individuals. Purposeful sampling is important for good qualitative research because it demonstrates that the researcher tried to identify the best sites and participants to learn about the central phenomenon.

## Purposeful Sampling Strategies Guide the Selections

Qualitative researchers use several different strategies to implement purposeful sampling in their studies. Table 10.1 summarizes nine different purposeful sampling strategies found in the literature (Patton, 2002). Each of these strategies has a different intent and different characteristics. Researchers choose the strategy that best matches their studies' purposes, such as the examples included in Table 10.1. All strategies apply to sampling a single time or multiple times during a study. They can be used to sample individuals, groups, or entire organizations and sites. The following samples illustrate three of the most frequently used strategies.

- ***Maximal variation sampling:*** "We used purposive sampling to ensure that a range of experiences was obtained (Lincoln & Guba, 1985). We selected for interviews (from the 59 students who identified themselves as bullied during the current school term) five children who had a high or low score on the physical, relational, and racial items." (*Mishna, 2004, p. 236*) This research team used the maximal variation sampling strategy to select participants who varied across three characteristics in order to best describe the different perspectives about bullying.
- ***Homogenous sampling:*** "Students were recommended for participation by their language arts teachers at the end of the previous school year. I asked the teachers to recommend girls who met the definition of a struggling reader and who did not have a history of being absent." (*Hall, 2007, p. 134*) This researcher used the homogenous sampling strategy to select individuals who are similar (girls who struggle to read and attend school regularly) in order to describe a subgroup.
- ***Snowball sampling:*** "More than half of the respondents were found through a snowball sample technique. A work colleague in Boulder, a native of Grand Forks, provided two names of women as my initial contacts. At the end of each interview I asked my respondents to recommend someone 'different from themselves' for my

**TABLE 10.1 Types of Purposeful Sampling Strategies**

| Type | Intent | Characteristics | Example for a Study About Student Violence |
|---|---|---|---|
| Critical sampling | To describe cases that dramatically illustrate the situation | The researcher samples exceptional cases that represent the central phenomenon in dramatic terms | A researcher selects a college campus where a violent event occurs to describe the campus reactions |
| Extreme case sampling | To describe particularly troublesome or enlightening cases | The researcher samples outlier cases or individuals that display extreme or unusual characteristics | A researcher selects an autistic education program in elementary education that has received awards as an outstanding case to describe program activities |
| Homogenous sampling | To describe a subgroup in depth | The researcher samples individuals or sites based on membership in a subgroup that has defining characteristics | A researcher selects students from five rural schools to describe perspectives about gun ownership of rural adolescents |
| Maximal variation sampling | To describe diverse perspectives | The researcher samples cases or individuals that differ on some characteristic or trait (e.g., different age groups) | A researcher selects students based on school type (rural, suburban, and urban) and gender (male and female) to explore diverse experiences about student violence |
| Theory or concept sampling | To generate a theory or explore a concept | The researcher samples individuals or sites because they can help the researcher generate or discover a theory or specific concepts within the theory | A researcher is developing a theory about coping strategies of adolescents incarcerated for weapons charges and identifies students who have experiences that can inform this theory |
| Typical sampling | To describe cases that are typical | The researcher samples persons or sites that are typical or average | A researcher selects principals that represent schools in a state that report an average number of violent events per school year |
| Confirming/ disconfirming sampling | To explore cases that confirm or disconfirm emergent findings | The researcher samples individuals to test or confirm preliminary findings | During a study, a researcher finds that Hispanic girls report different experiences with violence than African American girls. The researcher selects additional girls from these two groups to confirm these preliminary findings. |
| Opportunistic sampling | To take advantage of emerging insights | The researcher samples individuals or sites to take advantage of unfolding opportunities that will help answer research questions | While conducting a study of school anti-violence programs, the researcher learns about a special program at another school and decides to select individuals from that school |
| Snowball sampling | To locate people or sites to study | The researcher samples individuals or sites based on the recommendations of others | A researcher studying the perceptions of gang members about violence asks interviewees to invite other individuals to participate |

next interview, in order to increase diversity of the sample, a strategy that worked well." (*Fothergill, 1999, pp. 128–129*) This researcher used the snowball sampling strategy to select individuals after the study begins based on the recommendations of participants to identify participants unknown to the researcher.

Qualitative researchers should describe and defend the specific type of sampling strategy used in their report. Sometimes authors identify these strategies by name, but often they only describe what they did and you have to deduce the strategy type from this information. As you read a method section, identify the sampling strategy that was used and how the strategy was implemented to understand who participated in the study and why the author selected those individuals and sites.

## What Do You Think?

Recall the excerpt at the start of this chapter. Reread the following passage. Using the types listed in Table 10.1, determine the purposeful sampling strategy the author used.

> The students ranged from second to eighth grades. A purposeful sample of 30 students was used for the study, 17 girls and 13 boys. A cross-selection of students, based on academic achievement and classroom behavior per their teachers' classifications, were identified to serve as participants for the study. Thus, the students fell into low-, medium-, or high-achievement and behavioral categories. *(Howard, 2002, p. 429)*

### Check Your Understanding

From this passage, we can conclude that the author used a maximal variation sampling strategy to select diverse individuals to participate in the study. The sampled students were purposefully selected to vary on the characteristics of gender, academic achievement, and classroom behavior.

## A Small Number of Participants Are Selected

Authors report the *number* of selected people and sites in addition to the strategy used to select the sample. This number is a study's sample size. You will find the sample size stated in a study's method section. Here are some general guidelines to consider when reading about the sample size reported for qualitative research studies:

- It is typical in qualitative research to study a few individuals or a few cases. This is because the overall ability of a researcher to provide an in-depth picture diminishes with the addition of each new individual or site. One objective of qualitative research is to present the complexity of a site or of the information provided by individuals.
- In some studies, a researcher might study a single individual or a single site. In other studies, the number may be several, ranging from 2 or 3 to 30 or 40. Because of the need to report details about each individual or site, too many cases can become unwieldy and result in superficial perspectives.
- Researchers consider the specific design (i.e., ethnography, case study, grounded theory, phenomenology, and narrative research) for conducting their qualitative study when deciding on the size of their sample. The design suggests the numbers of individuals needed to study. Sample sizes range from studying one or two individuals in a narrative study, to studying 20 to 30 individuals in a grounded theory study, to studying an entire group of people in an ethnographic study.

Let's consider some specific examples to see how many individuals and sites were used. Qualitative researchers may collect data from single individuals. For example, in the qualitative case study of Basil McGee, a second-year middle school science teacher, Brickhouse and Bodner (1992) explored his beliefs about science and science teaching and how his beliefs shaped classroom instruction. Elsewhere, several individuals participated in a qualitative grounded theory study. The researchers examined 25 nonsmoking parents of adolescent children who smoke (Small, Brennan-Hunter, Best, & Solberg, 2002). More extensive data collection was used in a qualitative ethnographic study of the culture of fraternity life and the exploitation and victimization of women. Rhoads (1995) conducted 12 formal interviews and 18 informal interviews, made observations, and collected numerous documents from the fraternity members.

### What Do You Think?

Consider the following passage from the qualitative parent role study (Auerbach, 2007) from Chapter 1. What is the sample size? What sampling strategy was used?

> A small, purposeful sample of parents of Futures students was selected to explore the role constructions of working-class parents of color who lack a college education but aspire to college for their children. Although not representative of Latino or African American parents at the school or generally, the sample reflects the preponderance of immigrant families in the project and variation on characteristics that could affect parent roles. The sample consisted of 16 working-class parents from 11 families. *(paragraph 14)*

### Check Your Understanding

From this passage we learn that the author studied a sample of 16 parents in the study. These parents appeared to be selected using a homogenous sampling strategy. All of the participants shared the characteristics of being from a working-class background, being a parent of color (African American or Latino), not possessing a college education, and having a child in the Futures program.

## What Types of Information Do Qualitative Researchers Collect?

For practice understanding procedures used to collect qualitative data, go to the *Building Research Skills* section under the topic "Qualitative Data Collection" in MyEducationalResearchLab, located at www.myeducationlab.com. Complete the exercise "Collecting Data for a Qualitative Study" and use the provided feedback to further develop your skills for reading research articles.

Researchers identify the types of data that they collected to address their research questions in the method section. In qualitative research, these types of data share several characteristics. The qualitative researcher poses general, broad questions to participants, and allows them to share their views relatively unconstrained by the researcher's perspective. The researcher often collects multiple types of information and adds new forms of data during the study. Further, the researcher engages in extensive data collection, spending a great deal of time at the site where people engage in the phenomenon under study. At the site, the qualitative researcher gathers detailed information to establish the complexity of the central phenomenon.

We can see the varied nature of types of qualitative data when they are placed into the following four categories:

- interviews and questionnaires,
- observations,
- documents, and
- audiovisual materials.

Table 10.2 shows each category of data collection listed, the type of data it yields, and a definition for that type of data. Variations on data collection in all four areas are emerging continuously, and you can notice a wide variety when reading several qualitative research reports. Most recently, videotapes, student portfolios,

TABLE 10.2 Types of Qualitative Data Collection

| Data Type | Format of Data | Definition of Type of Data | When It Is Typical Used |
|---|---|---|---|
| Interviews | Transcriptions | Unstructured text data obtained from transcribing audiotapes of interviews or by transcribing open-ended responses to questions on questionnaires | ■ Useful for recording information that cannot be observed or providing detailed personal information<br>■ Primary form of data collection in grounded theory studies and phenomenologies<br>■ Also frequently used in narrative research, case studies, and ethnographies |
| Observations | Fieldnotes and drawings | Unstructured text data and pictures recorded during observations by the researcher | ■ Useful for recording information as it naturally occurs<br>■ Also helpful when participants have difficulty verbalizing their ideas<br>■ Often used in ethnographies and case studies |
| Documents | Hand-recorded notes about documents or optically scanned documents | Public (e.g., notes from meetings) and private (e.g., journals) records available to the researcher | ■ Useful for providing information from public and private records<br>■ Frequently used in narrative studies, ethnographies, and case studies |
| Audiovisual materials | Pictures, photographs, videotapes, objects, or sounds | Audiovisual materials consisting of images or sounds from people or places recorded by the researcher or someone else | ■ Supplements text data with visual and sound information<br>■ Use is growing in all types of qualitative research |

and the use of e-mails are attracting increasing attention as forms of data found useful by qualitative researchers. Researchers choose one or more types of data based on the research design they are using and the type of information that will best answer their research questions. Some general guidelines of when researchers use each type of data are also provided in Table 10.2. Now let's take a detailed look at each of the categories to understand the different ways that researchers gather qualitative data.

## How Do Researchers Interview Individuals?

Gathering data through interviews is probably the most common approach to qualitative data collection that you will find in published reports. A qualitative **interview** occurs when a researcher asks one or more participants general, open-ended questions and records their answers. Qualitative researchers ask open-ended questions so that the participants can best voice their experiences unconstrained by any perspectives of the researcher or past research findings. An **open-ended question** allows the participant to create his/her own options for responding. For example, in a qualitative interview of athletes in high schools, the interviewer might ask "How do you balance participation in athletics with your schoolwork?" The athlete then creates a response to this question without being forced into response possibilities.

There are five aspects you should consider when researchers use interviews as part of their qualitative studies: the reason for using interviews, the type of interviews, the questions asked during the interview, the record made during the interview, and the information about the interview process included in the report.

### Examine Why the Researcher Chose to Collect Interviews

Researchers choose to collect data through interviews because they provide useful information when participants cannot be directly observed. This type of data also permits participants to describe detailed personal information. The interviewer has control over the types of information received since he/she can ask specific questions to elicit this information. Qualitative interviews can be appropriate in studies using any of the available qualitative research designs. They are the primary type of data collected in most grounded theory and phenomenological studies, but are useful for learning from participants in case studies, ethnographies, and narrative studies as well.

## Identify the Type of Interview

There are a number of approaches to interviewing, and they each appear frequently in reported studies. Researchers choose the one—a focus group interview, a one-on-one interview, a telephone interview, an e-mail interview, a questionnaire, or some combination—that will allow them to best learn the participants' views and answer their research questions.

- ***Focus group interviews:*** Researchers choose focus group interviews to collect shared understanding from several individuals as well as to get views from specific people. A **focus group interview** is the process of collecting data through interviews with a group of people, typically four to six individuals. The researcher asks a small number of general questions and elicits responses from all individuals in the group. Focus groups are implemented when the interaction among interviewees will likely yield the best information and when interviewees are similar to and cooperative with each other. Due to the group format, they are not appropriate if the researcher wants to learn about sensitive topics or learn the details about an individual's experiences. An example of the use of focus groups is a study where high school students, with the sponsorship of a team of researchers, conducted focus group interviews with other students to learn their perceptions about the use of tobacco (Plano Clark et al., 2002).
- ***One-on-one interviews:*** A popular, but time-consuming and costly approach is for the researcher to conduct individual interviews. The **one-on-one interview** is a data collection process in which the researcher asks questions to and records answers from only one participant at a time. The researcher may conduct several one-on-one interviews, such as asking teachers and counselors to provide their impressions of a violent event at a school. One-on-one interviews are ideal for interviewing participants who are articulate, who can share ideas comfortably, and who are not hesitant to speak.
- ***Telephone interviews:*** It may not be possible for a researcher to gather groups of individuals for an interview or to visit one on one with single individuals. The participants in a study may be geographically dispersed and unable to come to a central location for an interview. In this situation, a qualitative researcher may choose to conduct telephone interviews. Conducting a qualitative **telephone interview** is the process of gathering data from individuals by asking a small number of general questions over the telephone. These forms of interviews are convenient, but the researcher is unable to observe the participant's behaviors and facial expressions during the interview.
- ***E-mail interviews:*** **E-mail interviews** consist of collecting open-ended data through interviews with individuals using computers and the Internet. They are also useful for researchers collecting qualitative data from a geographically dispersed group of people. This form of interviewing provides rapid access to large numbers of people and a detailed, rich text database for qualitative analysis. It can limit the amount of probing or follow-up questions that are easy to ask during a conversation. Although a fairly new type of qualitative data, its use in research studies is undoubtedly increasing with the increased availability and use of computers in the population.
- ***Open-ended questions as part of a questionnaire:*** A final type of qualitative interview occurs when a researcher asks some open-ended questions as part of a questionnaire that also includes closed-ended items. This type of data collection allows a researcher to net two types of information. The researcher gains quantitative information to support theories and concepts in the literature from the predetermined, closed-ended items. At the same time, the researcher can use the open-ended responses to explore reasons for the close-ended responses and identify comments

people might have that are beyond the responses to the close-ended questions. For example, a researcher might ask:

> Indicate the extent of your agreement or disagreement with this statement:
> "Student policies governing binge drinking on campus should be more strict."
> ☐Strongly agree ☐Agree ☐Undecided ☐Disagree ☐Strongly disagree
> Please explain your response in more detail.

In this example, the researcher started with a closed-ended question and five predetermined response categories. This question is followed with an open-ended question in which the participants indicate reasons for their responses.

## Note the Way the Researcher Organizes the Interview Questions

It is important for the researcher to have some means for structuring the interview and taking careful notes. An **interview protocol** is a form designed by the researcher that contains instructions for the process of the interview, the questions to be asked, and space to take notes of responses from the interviewee. This form serves the purpose of reminding the interviewer of the questions and providing a means for recording notes. Researchers will often include their interview protocol as an appendix to the report or list the main questions in the method section.

Examine Figure 10.2 to see an interview protocol that was included as an appendix for a research article (Plano Clark et al., 2002). This study included focus group interviews to learn about high school students' perceptions of tobacco use. You can find many features that are typical of interview protocols by reviewing this figure. The protocol begins with a general question to help the participants become at ease (often called an "icebreaker" question). It also includes only a few questions, which are stated in a broad, open-ended fashion to let the respondents determine their own options for answering the questions. In addition to the main numbered questions, this protocol also indicates probing questions with the bulleted items. **Probes** are sub-questions under each main question that the researcher asks to elicit more information. Researchers use probes to encourage participants to clarify what they are saying and to urge them to elaborate on their ideas.

FIGURE 10.2 A Sample Interview Protocol Published as the Appendix of a Research Article

**APPENDIX Focus Group Interview Protocol**

1. First, I'd like to go around the room and have each person say their first name and one thing they would like us to know about themselves. (This is an icebreaker and can be modified.)
2. Think back over the course of the past month. Describe for me times when you have or you have seen people using tobacco.
   - Where were you?
   - What was going on?
   - Who was using it?
   - How did you react?
   - Can you give me some examples? (May have to specifically ask: What about chewing tobacco?)
3. Tell me what students at this school think about tobacco.
   - Can you give me an example?
   - Could you tell me more?
   - What do you mean by that?
4. How would you describe the rules for tobacco use at this school?
   - What do students think about the rules?
   - How are they enforced?
5. We've mostly been talking about tobacco use at school. Now I would like for you to tell me what happens outside of school.
   - Other experiences the past month with tobacco?
   - What about the role of advertising, films, television?
   - What about experiences at home, with friends, at work?
6. Could you tell me what you think quitting is like for smokers?
   - How do you think it is different for people who are younger compared to people who are older?

*Source:* This appendix is reprinted from Plano Clark et al., *Qualitative Health Research*, Vol. 12, Issue 9, p. 1280, 2002. Reprinted with permission of Sage Publications, Inc.

## Note How the Researcher Recorded the Data During the Interview

As with all types of data collection, the researcher needs to make a record of the collected data during interviews. The researcher will typically record field notes on the interview protocol during the interview. It is difficult, however, to write down all aspects of the conversation as it is happening. Most often, the interviewer also audiotapes the questions and responses during the interview. Qualitative interviewers use recording procedures, such as having high quality microphones and good recording equipment, as part of their data collection process. Audiorecording of interviews provides a detailed record of the interview and good qualitative studies should record interview conversations whenever possible.

## Look for Details About the Interviews in the Report

As you can see, there are many procedures involved with collecting qualitative interviews as part of a research study. Researchers describe these procedures when they report their studies so that readers like you can understand how they collected their data. This information is reported in the method section and usually includes the following details:

- the type of interviews,
- who the interviewer and interviewees were,
- where the interviews occurred and for how long,
- what questions were asked and whether probes were used, and
- how the interviewer recorded the conversation.

## What Do You Think?

Read the following excerpt from a study about how at-risk students persist in school (Knesting & Waldron, 2006). Identify (a) the type of interviews, (b) who the interviewer and interviewees were, (c) where the interviews occurred and for how long, (d) what questions were asked and whether probes were used, and (e) how the interviewer recorded the conversation.

> Individual interviews were conducted with all 17 students recommended for participation. Interviews took place in either a back corner of the school library or an empty classroom . . . Students were asked four open-ended questions: (a) If I were a new student here, what would you tell me about this school? What would you show me? (b) Tell me some things I might like about this school; (c) Tell me some things I might not like; and (d) If I were a student at this school who was thinking about dropping out, what advice would you give me? Is there anybody here at school that you would suggest that I talk with about my decision? . . . Interviews took place in classrooms or offices and lasted between 45 to 60 min . . . All interviews were conducted by the first author. They were audiotaped, transcribed, and then returned to participants for feedback and clarification. To help ensure understanding of interviewee responses, during the interviews answers were reflected back and probing questions used to seek clarification. *(p. 601)*

### Check Your Understanding

From this passage we learned the following: (a) The study included one-on-one interviews. (b) The first author (Knesting) conducted the interviews with students. (c) The interviews took place at the students' schools and each interview lasted between 45 and 60 minutes. (d) The interviewer asked four main questions and used probes for clarification. (e) The interviewer audiotaped the interview conversations.

## How Do Researchers Observe Individuals?

Next to interviews, observations represent a frequently used form of qualitative data collection. If you are an educator, then you probably have in mind the process of collecting observational data in a specific school setting when you think of observations. Observations can actually occur in many settings beyond schools, such as museums, school board meetings, doctors' offices, homes, or sporting events. Qualitative **observation** is the process of gathering open-ended, firsthand information by observing people and places at a research site. This information might include descriptions of the participants, the physical setting, events, and activities. In observing a classroom, for example, a researcher may observe and record the layout of the room, activities by the teacher and students, the interactions between the students and teacher, and the student-to-student conversations.

Researchers make several decisions related to observing individuals. First, researchers explain why observations are appropriate for the study. In addition, researchers note the observer's role during the observations, how many times they observed, how they recorded data during the observation, and details of the observation process.

### Examine Why the Researcher Chose to Collect Observations

*Here's a Tip for Applying Research!*

Look to studies where the researcher collected interviews to learn individuals' perspectives and to studies where the researcher collected observations to learn what individuals actually do.

Researchers choose to collect qualitative observations when observational data address their research questions. This type of qualitative data gives a researcher the opportunity to record information as it naturally occurs in a setting, to study actual behavior, and to study individuals who have difficulty verbalizing their ideas (e.g., preschool children). Ethnographers often include observations so that they can actually observe the shared language, behaviors, and beliefs of the culture-sharing group of interest. Observations are a common type of data collected by case study researchers when they study classrooms or other settings. Observations are also useful in grounded theory studies that are examining an action or interaction.

### Look for the Researcher's Role as an Observer

Using observations requires that the researcher adopt a particular role as an observer. Many possible roles exist (see Spradley, 1980) and no one role is suited for all situations. These observational roles fall along a continuum from the researcher not participating in the setting to being an active participant. It is useful to think of observers using one of three roles:

- ***Nonparticipant observational role:*** A **nonparticipant observer** is an observer who visits a site and records notes without becoming involved in the participants' activities. The nonparticipant observer is an outsider who sits on the periphery or some advantageous place to watch and record the phenomenon under study (i.e., the back of the auditorium during play practice). This role works well if the researcher does not want to disrupt the activities or is not familiar enough with the site and people to participate.
- ***Participant observational role:*** A **participant observer** is an observational role adopted by researchers when they take part in activities in the setting they observe. As a participant, the researcher assumes the role of an inside observer who engages in activities at the study site and records information at the same time as participating in activities. This role offers opportunities to see experiences from the views of participants to truly learn about a situation.
- ***Changing observational role:*** In many observational situations, it is advantageous for the researcher to shift or change roles. A changing observational role is one where researchers adapt their role to the situation. For example, the researcher might enter a site and observe as a nonparticipant, simply needing to look around during the early phases of research. Then he/she slowly becomes involved as a participant. Sometimes the reverse happens, and a participant becomes a nonparticipant. Engaging in both

roles permits the researcher to be subjectively involved in the setting, as well as to see the setting more objectively.

### Expect Researchers to Conduct Multiple Observations Over Time

Using observations requires that the researcher observe multiple times. Researchers generally start with broad observations, noting the general landscape or activities (such as sketching the layout of a classroom and the general activities that unfold during the day). As they become familiar with the setting, they narrow their observations to specific aspects (e.g., a small group of children interacting during reading time). A broad-to-narrow perspective is helpful because of the extensive amount of information available in an observation. To truly gain an understanding of a setting and individuals, researchers make observations over an extended period of time, such as six months to multiple years.

### Note How Researchers Record Observational Fieldnotes

The data recorded during an observation are called *fieldnotes*. **Fieldnotes** are text (words) recorded by the researcher during an observation in a qualitative study. Researchers record two types of fieldnotes: descriptive and reflective. Descriptive fieldnotes record a description of the observed events, activities, and people (e.g., what happened). Reflective fieldnotes record personal thoughts that researchers have that relate to their insights, hunches, or broad ideas or themes that emerge during the observation (e.g., what sense they make of the site, people, and situation). The fieldnotes become the data that the researcher analyzes in the study.

### Look for Details About the Observations in the Report

Researchers report details about their observations such as where they occurred and who was observed. In addition, researchers report who conducted the observations, the observer's role, the number of observations, the length of time of the observations, and how the observer recorded the data. For example, the following passage describes the observations conducted in an ethnographic study of a one-room country school: "My data collection has included participant-observation and narrative fieldnotes from Bighand School for the first 6 months of the 1998–1999 academic year (August–February), at least 2 days/week and in several return visits" (Swidler, 2000, p. 9). Note how from this one sentence we have learned that the author conducted observations at the school, he used a participant-observation role, and he recorded fieldnotes during his multiple observations during a six-month period of time.

## How Do Researchers Collect Documents?

A third valuable source of information that researchers collect in qualitative research is documents. **Documents** consist of public and private records that qualitative researchers obtain about a site or participants in a study. Examples of public documents are minutes from meetings, official memos, and records in the public domain. Private documents consist of personal journals and diaries, letters, personal notes, and jottings individuals write to themselves. Other materials such as e-mail comments or Web site data illustrate both public and private documents, and they represent a growing data source for qualitative researchers. These sources can provide valuable information in helping researchers understand central phenomena in qualitative studies and are often used in ethnographies, case studies, and narrative studies. For example, in a case study of a high school music department, the researcher noted his collection of documents by writing: "School policy publications (e.g., student handbooks, teacher handbooks, job descriptions, mission statements), documents sent to students and parents, and concert programs were also collected for analysis" (Scheib, 2003, p. 126).

> *Here's a Tip for Reading Research!*
>
> In studies using a grounded theory and phenomenological design, researchers often collect only one type of data. In many case studies and ethnographies, however, the researchers collect multiple types of data. You can understand studies that report multiple types of data by considering which of the four types (observations, interviews, documents, or audiovisual materials) each data source represents.

## How Do Researchers Collect Audiovisual Materials?

> *Here's a Tip for Applying Research!*
>
> When gathering information about a topic in your own practice (such as evidence about a student's progress), consider gathering multiple types of qualitative information to develop a richer picture. This could include talking with individuals (e.g., the student, his parents, his teachers), observing behaviors (e.g., what the student does in the classroom and on the playground), collecting documents (e.g., examples of writing, attendance records), and examining audiovisual materials that may be available (e.g., artwork that the student produced).

The final form of qualitative data is audiovisual material. **Audiovisual materials** consist of images or sounds that researchers collect to help them understand the central phenomenon under study. Used with increasing frequency in qualitative research, images or visual materials include photographs, videotapes, digital images, paintings, and unobtrusive measures (e.g., evidence deduced from a setting, such as physical traces such as footsteps in the snow). One growing approach in using photography is the technique of photo elicitation. In this approach, participants are shown pictures (their own or those taken by the researcher) and asked to discuss the contents. These pictures might be personal photographs or albums of historical photographs. Here is an example of a description of the use of photographs with interviews in a qualitative study of parents raising a child with a disability:

> During the first home visit, lasting approximately an hour, researchers explained the study, obtained informed consent, and gave the parents disposable cameras with 24 to 27 color exposures. Researchers asked parents to photograph images of life that were important to them over a 2-week period . . . At the end of 2 weeks, researchers retrieved the camera and scheduled a second home visit. During the second home visit, lasting approximately 1½ to 2 hours, participants described the significance of each image. Grand tour questions included (a) "Tell me about photograph #1" and (b) "Why did you take this photograph?" Follow-up probes occurred spontaneously. *(Lassetter, Mandleco, & Roper, 2007, p. 459).*

### What Do You Think?

Consider the following passage from paragraph 11 of the qualitative new teacher study (Clayton, 2007) from Chapter 3. What types of data did the author collect?

> Multiple data collection methods included at least three classroom observations, observation of 15 BTP sessions and the final professional development presentations, three semistructured individual interviews and one group interview, and analysis of all relevant documents and archival materials, including videotape, offered by the teachers and available through the BTP.

### Check Your Understanding

From this passage we learn that the author collected observations (in classrooms and in the program sessions), interviews (one-on-one interviews and a focus group interview), documents from the program, and audiovisual materials (videotaped materials). The use of multiple types of data is an indicator of a good case study approach.

## What Issues Occur During Qualitative Data Collection?

You can now recognize the basics of any study's qualitative data collection by identifying the sites, participants, and type(s) of collected data. In addition, researchers report important procedural issues related to their qualitative data collection. Researchers who engage in qualitative studies typically face field issues when collecting data that they need to resolve. Also, because qualitative research typically involves going to the research sites of the participants, staying a considerable time, and asking detailed questions, ethical issues are likely to arise that need to be anticipated.

## Challenges in Gaining Access and Gathering Data

Qualitative researchers negotiate a wide range of issues in the field. One such issue is gaining access to the research site. In qualitative research, the researcher often needs to seek and obtain permissions from individuals and sites at many levels. Because of the in-depth nature of extensive and multiple interviews with or observations of participants, it is helpful for the researcher to make use of a gatekeeper. A **gatekeeper** is an individual who assists in the identification of places to study, has an official or unofficial role at the site, provides entrance to a site, and helps researchers locate people. For example, a gatekeeeper may be a teacher, a principal, or the informal leader of a special program who has insider status at the site the researcher plans to study. Another issue that arises is successfully recruiting participants. Researchers may discuss how they contacted participants, what information was shared with them, and whether a financial incentive was provided to participating individuals.

Researchers may also describe special circumstances that arose during data collection as a third issue. For example, consider the following statement about issues faced by an ethnographer during her study of junior high girls' literacy practices:

> Early, there were moments in which I was tested by focal students. On several occasions, a girl would not allow me to see a note that she deemed "too obscene." I did not report such incidents as writing on a restroom wall or faking illness to avoid an exam. I avoided conveying any negative judgment, and as the study progressed, I slowly gained their trust and was permitted to receive literacies still deemed "too gross" for parents or teachers. *(Finders, 1996, p. 74).*

This researcher is sharing information about how she gained access to her participants and the challenges she faced in collecting her data.

## Ethical Issues

In gathering data for a qualitative project, a researcher seeks an in-depth description of a central phenomenon. Participants may be asked to discuss private details of their life experiences over a period of time. This process requires a sufficient level of trust based on a high level of participant disclosure. Because of the intimate nature of this research, numerous ethical issues must be anticipated and handled appropriately.

- ***Participants have certain rights that must be respected.*** In all steps of the research process, researchers need to engage in ethical practices, particularly during data collection. Individuals who participate in a study have certain rights. Before participating in research, individuals need to know the purpose and aims of the study, how the results will be used, and the likely social consequences the study will have on their lives. They also have the right to refuse to participate in a study and to withdraw at any time. When they participate and provide information, their anonymity is protected and guaranteed by the researcher. Individuals are not to be offered excessive financial inducements to participate in a project. Participants also have the right to gain something from a study. Researchers need to actively look for ways to give back (or reciprocate) to participants in a study because the participants have freely provided their time. For example, in one study involving individuals with HIV, the author shared book royalties with the participants in the study. In another study, a researcher volunteered to help supervise lunchroom activities in exchange for information from students in the school.
- ***Reports should protect participants' anonymity.*** Researchers need to protect the anonymity of the participants. In some qualitative studies, researchers assign pseudonyms to participants or develop a composite picture of the group rather than focus on any single individual to protect the anonymity of participants. Authors may also choose not to identify the specific research site, such as referring to a school simply as a "Midwestern elementary school," as an additional way to protect participants' identities.
- ***Ethical guidelines exist to guide researchers efforts.*** Researchers can locate ethical standards to use in research from several professional associations. Examples of professional associations that offer helpful guidelines include those from the American Educational Research Association (AERA) (*Ethical Standards of the American Educational Research Association,* Strike et al., 2002), the American Psychological Association (APA) (*Ethical*

*Principles of Psychologists and Code of Conduct*, 2003), and the Joint Committee on Standards for Educational Evaluation (*Program Evaluation Standards*, adopted November 21, 1980; amended through September 20, 1995). Practicing ethics, however, is a complex matter that involves much more than merely following a set of static guidelines such as those from these professional associations. Conducting research ethically requires researchers to actively interpret these principles for their individual projects, tailoring these ethical guidelines to suit the unique contexts of their research and participants.

Researchers demonstrate that they consider ethical issues by discussing specific steps that they have taken when they report their studies. These details include information about securing approval for the research from their university's institutional review board (often referred to as the "IRB"), as well as from the site and obtaining individuals' permission to participate in the study. For example, Plano Clark et al. (2002) noted in their study of adolescents' perceptions of tobacco use, "We began by obtaining permissions for the study from the human subjects review board and the district office and principals of the four high schools" (p. 1266).

## How Do You Evaluate a Study's Qualitative Data Collection?

Qualitative researchers use different standards than quantitative researchers to judge the quality of their data collection. Recall from Chapter 7 that quantitative researchers are concerned with drawing valid conclusions about how independent and dependent variables are related and generalizing their results to a larger population. In contrast, qualitative researchers are concerned with drawing conclusions that provide in-depth descriptions and that are credible.

Use the criteria provided in Figure 10.3 to assess an author's implementation of qualitative data collection. The qualitative data collection should be sufficiently rich

Use the following criteria to evaluate the quality of a qualitative study's data collection as specified within a research report. For each evaluation item, indicate the following ratings:

- \+ You rate the item as "high quality" for the study.
- ✓ You rate the item as "ok quality" for the study.
- – You rate the item as "low quality" for the study.

In addition to your rating, make notes about each element when you apply these criteria to an actual published study.

| | Application to a Published Study | |
|---|---|---|
| **In a high-quality qualitative research report, the author . . .** | Your Rating | Your Notes |
| 1. Purposefully samples a small number of sites/participants so that rich detail can be provided. | | |
| 2. Recruits individuals who can help answer the study's research questions. | | |
| 3. Collects extensive data to provide a credible and rich description of the central phenomenon. | | |
| 4. Identifies specific types of qualitative data collection. | | |
| 5. Has an organized means for recording the data (e.g., an interview protocol and audiorecording). | | |
| 6. Uses open-ended questions to learn the participants' perspectives. | | |
| 7. Discusses field issues and ethical issues that occurred during data collection. | | |

FIGURE 10.3 Criteria for Evaluating a Study's Qualitative Data Collection

and rigorous to provide an in-depth description and credible understanding of the study's central phenomenon. Researchers ensure the quality of their descriptions by limiting the number of participants to a small number. They also collect extensive data sets that include rich details that convey the inherent complexity. The description is enhanced when the researcher spends a longer time in the field learning about the phenomenon. Researchers can make claims that are more credible when they provide information about how the data represent participants' perspectives (as opposed to those of the researcher). The credibility of a study is also enhanced when the data represent different perspectives and sources and accurate records of the data are made during data collection.

## Reviewing What We've Learned

- Look under the heading of *Method* or *Procedures* in a qualitative research report for the data collection procedures.
- Recognize that the method section contains information about who participated in the study, where it was conducted, the types of data, and the data collection procedures.
- Search for the individuals or sample that actually provided data for the study.
- Determine whether the sample was selected using a rigorous method (e.g., purposeful sampling) that will provide rich data for the study's purpose.
- See if a small sample size is used.
- Determine the types of data collection, such as interviews, observations, documents, and audiovisual materials.
- Assess whether the researcher made detailed records of the data, such as audio-recordings and fieldnotes.
- Ask yourself whether the researchers used good ethical practices and described the field issues faced during the data collection.

## Practicing Your Skills

At this time, read carefully "the qualitative classroom management study" article starting on p. 267 at the end of this chapter. As you read this article, pay close attention to the discussion of data collection that appears in the method section (paragraphs 08–13).

Once you have read the study, assess your knowledge of the content of this chapter by answering the following questions that relate to the qualitative classroom management study. Use the answers found in the Appendix to evaluate your progress.

1. From what sites and participants did the authors collect their qualitative data? Did the authors purposefully sample a small number of participants and sites?
2. What type(s) of data did the authors collect to learn about the teachers' perceptions of classroom management? Why did this type(s) of data fit (or not fit) the study's purpose?
3. What procedures did the authors describe related to their qualitative data collection?
4. What are some examples of field and ethical issues that confronted the researchers in this study?

# The Qualitative Classroom Management Study

Let's examine another published research study to apply what you have learned about reading research articles and to evaluate how researchers collect qualitative data (by completing the *Practicing Your Skills* questions listed on the previous page.) A formal reference for this study is:

> Garrahy, D. A., Cothran, D. J., & Kulinna, P. H. (2005). Voices from the trenches: An exploration of teachers' management knowledge. *Journal of Educational Research, 99*(1), 56–63.

As you read this article, note the marginal annotations that signal the major sections of a research report, the steps of the research process, and the major characteristics of qualitative research. In addition, use the following walk-through to help you understand how the steps of the research process are described within the four major sections of the report.

## The Introduction Section

- Identifying a research problem (paragraphs 01–06)
- Reviewing the literature (paragraphs 01–04)
- Specifying the purpose (paragraph 07)

The authors of the qualitative classroom management study (Garrahy et al., 2005) begin by reviewing literature related to effective teachers and the knowledge that teachers need to possess to be effective (paragraphs 01–04). From this literature, they note that little research has examined one particular type of teacher knowledge: class management (paragraph 04). They justify the importance of this topic for their study because of its impact on student learning and job satisfaction (paragraph 06). They conclude their introduction in paragraph 07 by stating their central research question (What do elementary physical education teachers know about management?) and two sub-questions (How that knowledge is gained, and how it changes over time). They also note different audiences that can benefit from the research, including teacher educators and administrators.

## The Method Section

- Selecting a design and collecting data (paragraphs 08–13)

The authors describe their methods for collecting data to understand the central phenomenon of teacher's knowledge of class management in the *Method* section. The researchers did not name a research design. This study includes many procedures typical of grounded theory research including: examining a process (how knowledge was gained), using an iterative data analysis process, identifying categories from the data and examining the causal conditions (teacher history), strategies, and contextual factors around the central phenomenon. The authors, however, did not advance a theory or propositions at the end of the study. Therefore, this study could be described as using a general thematic approach with many procedures typical of grounded theory research.

The authors purposefully selected 20 elementary physical education teachers for their sample because they were known through their professional affiliations and they represented a diverse range of experiences and contexts (paragraph 08). The primary data source included one-on-one interviews and telephone interviews (paragraph 09). In addition, the researcher conducted limited observations at the schools of 12 of the participants. During the interviews, the researchers asked 10 broad questions (see Appendix A) and audiotaped the conversation to obtain a complete record (paragraph 09).

## The Results Section

- Analyzing the data and reporting results (paragraphs 10–13 and 14–28)

The authors described their process of analyzing the data in paragraphs 10–13 in the method section. This iterative process involved reading the transcribed interviews, coding the transcripts, and refining the codes into three major themes. The authors used numerous strategies to ensure the credibility of their findings such as asking participants to review their transcripts (paragraph 09) and basing the findings on multiple teachers and multiple researchers' perspectives (paragraph 13).

The final results include three major themes that describe teacher's perceptions of classroom knowledge and how that knowledge is gained and changes over time. The authors describe each theme in detail, providing participant quotes to add richness to the descriptions. The themes are: knowledge origin and influences (paragraphs 15–20), knowledge evolution (paragraphs 21–25), and knowledge content (paragraphs 26–28).

## The Conclusion Section

- Interpreting the research (paragraphs 29–37)

The authors concluded their report with a discussion of what they learned. They first summarized the major results in paragraph 29. They also compared the results to past research (e.g., paragraph 30) and discussed the larger meaning of the results. From these results, the authors also suggested implications for practice, such as how teacher education programs might change to provide preservice teachers with an expanded view of classroom management. The researchers also noted limitations of their study (such as the results did not identify best practices) and suggested research needed in the future (paragraph 37).

# Voices From the Trenches: An Exploration of Teachers' Management Knowledge

Qualitative research recognizes the need to listen to participants' "voices"

A deficiency in the knowledge

The literature plays a minor role

DEBORAH A. GARRAHY
Illinois State University
DONETTA J. COTHRAN
Indiana University

PAMELA H. KULINNA
Arizona State University

ABSTRACT Classroom management is a critical component of effective teaching. Despite its importance, little information is available about how teachers gain and use knowledge about management in their classrooms. The authors examined elementary physical education teachers' development and use of pedagogical knowledge related to class management. The authors interviewed 20 elementary teachers (14 women and 6 men). A constant comparison process guided data analysis. Trustworthiness measures included triangulation of data sources, member checks, and a search for negative cases. Results reveal insights into teachers' knowledge origins and influences, evolution, and content regarding class management.

Introduction Section

Key words: classroom management, effective teaching, elementary physical education teachers

Identifying a research problem

01 What makes an effective teacher? Early attempts to answer that question focused on teacher characteristics and processes (Connelly, Clandinin, & He, 1997). A more recent and promising approach to answering the question focuses more on what teachers know and how this knowledge leads to the decisions they make in their classes. Schempp (1993) suggested that understanding teaching requires an understanding of teachers' knowledge bases.

02 Calderhead (1996) summarized research on teacher knowledge and proposed a three-stage evolution of focus. The first stage occurred in the 1970s and focused on teacher decision making. The second stage included "teachers' perceptions, attributions, thinking, judgments, reflections, evaluations, and routines" (Calderhead, p. 710). The third stage consisted of an emphasis on teachers' knowledge and beliefs. That focus drives much of the current educational research on teacher knowledge.

Reviewing the literature

03 Researchers have proposed a number of frameworks for categorizing teacher knowledge (e.g., Carter & Doyle, 1987; Shulman, 1987). Although each framework is unique, nearly all of them include some version of the following knowledge domains: (a) pedagogical knowledge, (b) subject-matter knowledge, and (c) pedagogical content knowledge. *General pedagogical knowledge* is not subject-matter specific and includes generic teaching knowledge (e.g., management, instructional strategies) about effective teaching that might be applicable in a wide variety of educational settings. *Subject-matter knowledge* is a teacher's knowledge of, and about, the content that he or she will teach. *Pedagogical content knowledge* is an integration of general pedagogical and specific subject-matter knowledge. Although Marks (1990) suggested that a precise distinction between types of knowledge is somewhat arbitrary, the distinctions have served, and continue to serve, as useful research heuristics.

04 Pedagogical knowledge, particularly as it is related to management, has not been a common focus of current research in education. Borko and Putnam (1996) noted that "General pedagogical knowledge of classroom management has sometimes received short shrift" (p. 675). The absence of investigations into teachers' pedagogical knowledge, which is related to management, is problematic because class management is an aspect of teaching that consistently challenges teachers of all experiential levels and content areas, and, as Graber (2001) suggested, "is central to the development of expertise and matures with experience" (p. 495). Even rarer than research on teachers' pedagogical knowledge of management, however, is research that incorporates the voices of teachers and their perspectives on learning about class management, particularly in special subject-matter areas outside the traditional classroom.

05 What is class management and why is it important? Rink (2002, p. 136) defined *class management* as the "arranging of the environment for learning and maintaining and developing student-appropriate behavior and engagement in the content." Educators and, presumably, parents see management as the primary factor by which quality instruction and student learning occur (Lewis, 1999). Discussions of management frequently focus on student behavior and control; that is a critical component of class management. That focus is not, however, the only component, and for the pur-

*Address correspondence to Deborah A. Garrahy, Campus Box 5121, Illinois State University, Normal, IL 61790–5121. (E-mail: dagarra@ilstu.edu)*

A problem that calls for exploration

poses of this study, we viewed management as a broad range of actions that teachers take to ensure a quality learning environment.

06 For example, within physical education, primary factors in classroom management would include, but not be limited to (a) establishing routines (attendance, distribution and return of equipment, lesson closure); (b) developing class expectations and consequences with students; (c) teacher consistency; and (d) maintaining student cooperation throughout the lesson for maximum time on task (Rink, 2002). Effective management is the foundation from which learning can occur. In addition to its impact on student learning, the ability to manage effectively is an important factor in teacher job satisfaction. Management struggles have been linked to teacher stress and burnout (Schottle & Peltier, 1991) and to an inability to care about students (Chemlynski, 1996).

07 We attempted to address the lack of available research on pedagogical knowledge from teachers' perspectives. The specific research questions that guided this study were,

1. What do elementary physical education teachers know about management?

2. How was that knowledge gained, and did the knowledge of elementary physical education teachers change over time? Understanding what teachers know and how they know it should provide insights into preservice education and inservice education. With better insights into teacher knowledge bases, teacher educators, researchers, and administrators can improve professional development plans to better meet teachers' needs. Improved teacher management would then likely lead to increased learning opportunities for students.

The qualitative purpose statement and research questions explore a central phenomenon

Specifying a purpose for the research

Method Section

## Method

Selecting a research design and collecting data

### *Participants and Setting*

08 Twenty Caucasian elementary physical education teachers (14 women and 6 men) volunteered to share their personal knowledge base about class management. We knew the participants from their professional affiliations as university practicum supervisors, as committee members, or as conference attendees. Professional teaching experiences ranged from 1 to 28 years; average experience was 15 years. Participants represented urban, suburban, and rural public school settings. School demographics varied widely—some schools reported a majority Caucasian student body, whereas other schools served primarily African American and Hispanic students.

### *Data Collection and Analysis*

Analyzing data and reporting results

09 Participant interviews were the primary source of data collection for this study. We interviewed 12 teachers individually at their school, which allowed for limited researcher observation and interactions with students. Those interactions allowed us to observe classroom management. To maximize the variety of teachers involved in the study, we conducted telephone interviews with 8 teachers, but only when we had prior knowledge of the teacher and of the quality of the physical education program, and when on-site interviews could not be arranged. The interviews lasted from 45–90 min. An interview guide (Patton, 2002) structured the conversations; topics included personal teaching history, perceived effectiveness of various management strategies, and contextual factors. Sample interview questions and probes are included in Appendix A. We audiotaped, transcribed, and returned the interviews to the teachers for a member check of the data. A few teachers elaborated on answers or made grammatical corrections to their responses, but they did not suggest any substantive changes.

The qualitative researcher asks participants open-ended questions

10 We analyzed the data by using the constant comparison and analytic induction methods to identify emerging common themes across the respondents (LeCompte & Preissle, 1993). We began the data analysis by reading through each transcription numerous times to become intimately familiar with the data. We individually established a personal coding system with initial emergent themes. We compared coding systems by seeking common themes among all of us. During discussions, we collapsed, merged, or rejected themes. We followed the same pattern throughout the analysis, which produced four iterations.

The qualitative researcher codes the data to develop description and themes

11 The following example describes the iterative process. During the initial coding review, we established eight themes, each with its own subcategories. Fifteen subcategories emerged during the first iteration. One theme, Trial and Error, included the following subcategories: University and College Learning, Professional Development, and Experience. Trial and Error, along with its subcategories, were collapsed during the second iteration to Learning Management. Continued analysis produced a third iteration titled Changes in Teachers; Knowledge Evolution emerged as the final theme.

12 Through the iterative analysis of the data, we agreed on final dominant themes. To be considered a final theme, we had to agree on the significance of the theme, and at least one third of the participants had to have addressed the issue in their interview. The themes were Knowledge Origin and Influences, Knowledge Evolution, and Knowledge Content. Appendix B provides examples of transcript excerpts under the dominant themes.

13 We took a number of steps to ensure trustworthiness. First, we asked participants to elaborate on and clarify information during a member check of their interviews. Second, data triangulation occurred via comparisons of different teachers in varied schools and settings. Similarly, the use of multiple researchers served as another type of triangulation. Finally, we conducted a search for and analysis of negative cases to seek alternative explanations for emergent themes. Only one negative case emerged, and it related to respondents' views on the importance of teacher education programs. Both per-

The qualitative researcher collects text and image data

The qualitative researcher includes a small number of participants

The qualitative researcher intentionally selects participants

Qualitative researchers use strategies to validate their findings

Qualitative findings include themes

Results Section

spectives are provided in the results section. All other themes were affirmed by the absence of negative cases.

## Results

14 Teachers provided key insights into their management pedagogical knowledge base growth and development. In the following sections, we discussed the themes of teachers' knowledge origin and influences, evolution, and content. In sections of the results in which a specific teacher is quoted, we used parentheses to identify the teacher's years of experience and whether he or she taught in a suburban, urban, or rural school.

### *Knowledge Origin and Influences*

Analyzing data and reporting results

15 The teachers (pseudonyms are used throughout) in this study attributed their pedagogical knowledge development about management to a variety of sources, including children, colleagues, and professional development. Few teachers, however, gave credit to their teacher education programs.

16 The two most commonly cited and related sources of knowledge were trial and error and children. Jamie (7 years, urban) said, "It's trial and error. You just learn by experience and every child is different and every experience is different and I think you learn better tools to make the flow a little easier for both of you." Anna (6 years, suburban) agreed: "It's trial and error method the first couple of years. I had some problems and I would try and fail and if it didn't work out, you tried something else." Willingness to learn, or the necessity of learning, from failure was a key management knowledge growth. As John (20 years, suburban) described,

> I had all the activities lined up. I was going to overwhelm them with things. But what I neglected to do was to have an opening [set induction]. They came in the door and they saw all this stuff laid out [equipment] and they just ignored me. That taught me right away that I needed to meet them at the door and have established what they are to do when they enter my classroom. That's what really started my awareness that management is important.

17 Classroom teachers generally work with a specific grade level, whereas elementary physical educators work with all the children at the school (e.g., K–6). Such diversity requires that physical educators use multiple strategies that are developmentally appropriate for children. Teachers acknowledged that the management strategy that worked for one class did not necessarily work in the next class. Therefore, many physical educators sought help from their colleagues, which revealed that much of the educators' knowledge base was gained from other teachers and from professional endeavors. Donna (7 years, suburban) attributed most of her knowledge base about management to her supervising teacher. Donna said, "My student teaching had a huge impact. His name was John and he taught me so much, taught me how to deal with kids. It was great. He still calls me and I call him."

18 Other teachers admitted that they taught, at least initially, as they were taught as public school students. Holly (9 years, urban) acknowledged, "I stepped into my first teaching experience teaching like my high school PE teachers taught me. It's probably like parenting in that you remember how maybe teachers that you had handled things." Being able to interact with other teachers, not just physical educators, continued to assist in their development. Linda (12 years, urban) remarked,

> If I have trouble with something, I'll go ask our assistant principal, the home-school advisor and the classroom teacher. She knows the kids better than anyone else and might have a little tip that I can tell the child. You really have to work together with your staff.

19 Teachers also addressed the need for, and importance of, continued professional development. For some teachers, continued professional development meant attending conferences and workshops, whereas other teachers focused on reading professional journals and books. Speaking of how her teaching had changed, Catherine (21 years, suburban) reported the following about the modifications to her teaching and management styles:

> . . . [Change] came from watching other teachers teach and going to workshops. Professional development is critical. Every teacher that goes into a new situation is going to teach the way they've been taught and then is going to say "Hey, you know, I really don't need to do this" or "I need to do a little bit more of this."

Another teacher spoke of how professional development changed the way in which she taught. Lucy (12 years, urban) recognized that

> What helped me more than anything was the year I went to the first PACE conference. All of a sudden there was so much stuff to teach. Before I didn't feel like there was a lot of help out there for elementary education. It changed the way I felt about physical education. . . . The key is keeping the kids interested in what you're doing. And I think through continuing education and networking with other teachers . . . if they [students] are interested, there's going to be less discipline problems.

Teachers recognized the value in visiting other schools, the role of professional conferences, workshops, courses, and staying current in the professional literature as tactics for continually refining their management skills.

20 Most participants agreed that their college programs provided minimal assistance in developing their management knowledge base. Only 1 physical educator (Elizabeth, 11 years, suburban) claimed that she learned a great deal about how to manage children from her college program. Teachers believed that either their undergraduate experiences did not address management or they experienced a conflict between the material that was taught at the university and the material that was applied in the school setting. Several teachers described their first years of teaching and perceived lack of adequate preparation as being "eaten alive," "thrown to the wolves," and "sinking or swimming." Dustin

The qualitative researcher includes quotes from participants

(12 years, suburban) recalled, "They didn't teach much of it when I was in college. In fact they didn't teach any of it." Anna (6 years, suburban) and others recalled their classes in management theory but found that their college experiences did not match their school setting.

> Somebody should have been more realistic about management, specifically about elementary physical education and the number of children you have in class. How do you adapt your classroom atmosphere to account for 50, 56, 58 kids at a time? You [the researcher] come in tomorrow and you'll see four double classes. It's all management.

Others, although critical of their undergraduate experience, acknowledged the role of the practicum experiences that they received. Brian (10 years, suburban) observed, "You don't learn that [management] until you start doing your student teaching and your practical work so that's why I believe practical work is an essential part of undergraduate starting right at the beginning with pre-student teaching."

*Knowledge Evolution*

21 Teachers discussed the evolutionary process of their pedagogical knowledge related to management. One 20-year veteran found that learning to manage his class was "a gradual thing. You learn a lot. The people that do their best learn from others or borrow from others, if you are willing to keep changing, learning and evolving." Often, such evolutionary knowledge resulted in very different practices from their entry-level management skills. In addition to new techniques, teachers reported philosophic changes in their management approach. Janice (28 years, urban) stated that,

> I think when I first started I jumped on kids a little too quick so I was very authoritative when I first started. Now it seems the more I teach the more I'm trying to understand kids and really I guess I take my time with them. I've learned the last few years to take a whole different look at what is really going on in their lives and why they're actually acting the way they are.

Dustin (12 years, suburban) concurred: "I've begun to try to understand the kids a little bit more. I try to get to know the kids better from a personal standpoint. I'm less autocratic and I'm a little more democratic." In general, teachers revealed changing to a more humanistic approach by focusing on the students' feelings and self-esteem as a factor in their behavior (Williams, 1999). When asked what prompted such changes, some teachers said that they gained confidence in their teaching abilities, which allowed them to look outward and focus on students' needs, problems, and behaviors.

22 Teachers also cited changing contextual influences as the prompt for their evolution. When asked about his management evolution, Brian (10 years, suburban) noted that "I had to change because kids have changed." Teachers cited out-of-school changes as well as in-school changes. Out-of-school changes included single-parent homes, lack of parental behavioral expectations, and dysfunctional families. Teachers spoke of the need to know their students, which included information regarding students' lives at home. Janet (16 years, suburban) advised,

> Be aware of the total picture and not just the kid's misbehavior. What things are they bringing into the classroom from home? I don't think that you learn any of that really until you are in the situation. Poverty, abuse—physical and sexual. I was never taught about how to deal with any of that.

23 Teachers believed that family issues led to changes in student behavior and reported more frequent aggressive behaviors by more students over the years. Janet continued describing her classes: "I'm seeing a lot of aggression. I see more and more every year that just get very upset when things do not go their way. They're screaming and yelling at me or other kids." In addition to more aggression, teachers noted an increase in disrespectful behavior. Anna (6 years, suburban) remarked, "I just think that things have changed so much as far as parents and adults being figures of respect. Generally speaking, so many children that I have nowadays will question your authority more and will talk back." Also, teachers like Brian (10 years, suburban) observed a lack of parent involvement in many aspects of the students' lives but specifically in parents' dealing with behavioral situations at school:

> Ninety-nine percent of the time, I do not hear from parents once they get the behavioral report sent home. They sign it and return it, but they don't say, "Hey what was he doing?". . . . It's a pity and that's surprising. If my kid got in trouble I would say "What happened? Why'd you do this?" As a parent I would want the whole story.

In several cases, teachers observed that parents were accomplices in their child's poor behavior.

24 In-school changes also influenced teachers' management evolution. Several teachers noted that corporal punishment was a common practice when they began their careers and that as corporal punishment was removed or severely limited in their school districts, teachers found new techniques to handle student misbehavior. Some elementary physical educators spoke of how they had used exercise as punishment and yelled at students, acknowledging that they were teaching the same way that they had been taught. However, most of the teachers perceived themselves differently, and were working toward "becoming a more peaceful teacher." Elizabeth (11 years, suburban) addressed the exercise-as-punishment shift:

> No, I don't believe in that, I mean, then I feel like you're punishing them by having them do something that I actually want them to do for life, and I am trying to encourage. I want them to run. I want them to go out and do stuff. I want them to do push-ups if they want everyday. So, no I do not discipline that way.

25 The current litigious environment had teachers reconsidering even "positive" touches. Jane (16 years, suburban) described her apprehension about any physical contact with children:

Conclusion Section

> You are thinking about that more. I give hugs and high fives, and [pats] on the head. But even with one of my favorite kids I just don't do things that I probably used to do. One day I put my hand on his shoulder and he was joking. He said "I'm going to sue you. You can't touch me." I think he was joking, but I took a step back.

*Knowledge Content*

26 Even though teachers claimed a personal and eclectic pedagogical knowledge gained from numerous experiential resources, their verbalized knowledge bases were similar. First, teachers in all settings described the need for consistency in their interactions with students and in establishing routines. Teachers found that consistency provided children with a safe environment. Dustin (12 years, suburban) remarked that "Kids have to know exactly where you are coming from and after that I need to be fair, firm, and consistent. Kids feel comfortable in your class when they know what to expect." Consistency not only related to what teachers expected from children but also to the teachers' ability to follow through on their own policies. Brian (10 years, suburban) recalled that when he first started teaching, he overlooked some behaviors and attributed them to the notion that "they're just being kids." He then realized that "they'll catch onto that and try to take advantage."

27 Second, teachers' pedagogical knowledge involved a humanistic approach, which included teachers speaking with children individually, developing mutual respect, modeling desired behaviors, and knowing their students. Peggy (6 years, suburban) believed that "Good behavior should be expected. However, when a child is misbehaving I try to talk to them one on one. I try to remove them from their audience. I don't like to embarrass them so that everyone can hear." Other teachers shared Patricia's (28 years, urban) sentiment regarding respect:

> Respect has to start with the teacher. Teachers have to render respect to children. You have to model it. If I start yelling and screaming, they are going to do the same thing. Children do not know what respect is until they see it.

Respondents also addressed the need to not only model the behaviors they desired but also to acknowledge behaviors when demonstrated by students. Lucy (12 years, urban) learned that "You don't have to point out the negative behaviors, they already know what they are. Try to point out what's positive." Knowing students also was important because such knowledge related to students' experiences at home and at school-related events. Catherine (21 years, suburban) made sure that she had "contact with every child in your room, every lesson. It does not have to be skill related. Maybe you noticed their name on the wall for something special, like reading. It makes them feel special."

28 Finally, the elementary physical education teachers had a plethora of strategies for teaching and reinforcing their expectations. Most of the teachers used multiple rewards and consequences (e.g., verbal praise, letters to parents, time out, written assignments, and grade reductions) as ways to improve student behavior. Teachers also spoke of the need for students to acknowledge responsibility for their behaviors. Having students help to establish the desired classroom behaviors aided them in assuming responsibility for their learning experiences. For instance, Bill (28 years, suburban) found that,

> At the beginning of the year I ask them to tell me what things we should do or not do as a class [rules and expectations]. They give me feedback. I put them on a piece of paper. When it comes to about the same ideas that I have, what a classroom should/not do, not destroying equipment or not touching the equipment until we are ready . . . [when it comes to arguments] sometimes I have the students talk it out. I say "It seems like you two are having a little disagreement. Instead of a time out, they will sit down and talk about it. Then you come back and 95–99% of the time they come back and say they have settled it. It is another alternative to me to trying to help them. . . . they are helping each other.

In addition, several teachers incorporated written documentation of student misbehavior, which is sometimes referred to as a Physical Education Resolution Sheet. When students were removed from an activity, they had to explain the incident in writing. Upon completion of the assignment, teacher and student reviewed the incident together. Tasks such as those assisted teachers in helping students reflect and become accountable for their behaviors.

Interpreting the research

### Discussion and Implications

29 Our intention was to examine elementary physical education teachers' perspectives on their pedagogical knowledge of classroom management. Regardless of whether one is a novice or a veteran teacher, classroom management continues to be a primary concern of educators (Goyette, Dore, & Dion, 2000). Our results provide insights as to how teachers acquired and implemented their knowledge about class management over time. The findings also suggest that learning to manage one's classroom is an ongoing, developmental process influenced by personal and contextual forces.

30 Similar to Schempp's (1993) case study of a high school physical education teacher, the elementary teachers in this study most valued knowledge that came from personal practice. Shulman (1987) called that process of learning from doing "wisdom of practice." Teachers believed strongly in their wisdom of practice and the wisdom of their colleagues' practice.

31 Teachers did not, however, give much credence to knowledge from their teacher education programs. It is not clear whether the teachers' undergraduate programs did not address management techniques or whether the teachers were unable to interpret such information prior to their professional immersion. Borko and Putnam (1996) stated that "Prospective teachers may not see the relevance of their pedagogy courses to the process of learning to teach

Qualitative researchers take a reflexive and subjective approach

The qualitative researcher interprets the larger meaning of the findings

The qualitative researcher compares findings to past studies

The qualitative researcher suggests implications for practice

and they may not attend closely to the information or the experiences offered by the courses" (p. 681). It is also possible that teachers learned valuable information in their teacher education programs but had since forgotten the source of that knowledge over time. The data from this sample, however, are not strongly supportive of that possibility because novice to veteran teachers consistently gave little credit to their college preparation programs, with the exception of practicum experiences.

32 The elementary physical educators in this study valued the role of hands-on experiences and were quick to suggest the addition of more practicum opportunities into undergraduate programs. Teacher education programs might provide progressive, well-defined observations and opportunities so that students could interact with numerous educators in various environments (e.g., K–12; urban, rural, and suburban schools). Such exchanges would provide multiple-management frameworks for new knowledge and reflection. By combining those observations and early teaching experiences with college coursework, teacher educators can help preservice teachers interpret their new knowledge in relation to the programmatic message of the teacher education program—a message that can otherwise be missed (O'Sullivan, 1996; Pagano & Langley, 2001).

33 Fernandez-Balboa, Barrett, Solmon, and Silverman (1996) suggested that prospective teachers use cognitive maps to help them define and reflect on their current knowledge base and on how new material fits within their current knowledge network. Similarly, Clandinin (2000) claimed that teacher education programs must recognize the knowledge that teachers have gained from practice and then begin with "what preservice teachers already know rather than what should be taught to them" (p. 29). Similar strategies are clearly needed with in-service education programs because teachers' most valued knowledge comes from self and other practicing teachers, rather than from theory decontextualized from personal school settings.

34 The teachers in this study used multiple classroom management strategies, which varied from the limited resources that high school physical educators believed they could use in their classes (Cothran & Ennis, 1997). On average, the teachers in this study had taught for 15 years, yet they spoke consistently of their willingness to change and seek information to improve their classroom management skills. Although comparisons based on such small samples must be used cautiously, it is intriguing for one to think about what might cause the difference between elementary and high school physical education teachers' management knowledge and use.

35 Unlike high schools, most elementary schools have only one physical education teacher in the building; thus, the elementary teachers are isolated from other physical education colleagues. The same also is true for elementary art and music teachers. Might that isolation work to the advantage of the elementary teachers? Perhaps elementary physical educators may feel more flexible in their managerial endeavors because the pressure to conform to the practices of their peers is absent.

The qualitative researcher identifies limitations in the study

36 The findings provide intriguing initial insights into teachers' pedagogical knowledge origins, development, and content. However, consumers of educational research might want to identify "best practices" in classroom management as a result of this study. We did not attempt to label any of our findings as best practices because we believe that such identification is up to the reader. We imagine that there are numerous definitions of best practice, as well as definitions for the highly individualistic manner in which it is interpreted. The teachers in this study did not mention best practices as technically described by researchers and teacher educators. The teachers judged their practices by those that worked for them in their daily settings.

37 Research is needed to continue to clarify the exact content of teachers' knowledge and to learn how "lessons learned" can be disseminated to other teachers. Additional information also is needed in relation to teachers' knowledge bases at different grade levels and in differing contexts. Schempp, Manross, Tan, and Fincher (1998) claimed that "To teach one must know" (p. 342). The key to future research seems to be an exploration of the question, What must teachers know? We provide some insight into possible answers to that question, and with additional work in the field, educators can be better prepared with the knowledge needed to maximize the effectiveness of the teaching–learning process.

The qualitative researcher suggests future research

## REFERENCES

Borko, H., & Putnam, R. T. (1996). Learning to teach. In D. C. Berliner & R. C. Calfee (Eds.), *Handbook of educational psychology* (pp. 673–708). New York: Macmillan.

Calderhead, J. (1996). Teachers: Beliefs and knowledge. In D. C. Berliner & R. C. Calfee (Eds.), *Handbook of educational psychology* (pp. 709–725). New York: Macmillan.

Carter, K., & Doyle, W. (1987). Teachers' knowledge structures and comprehension processes. In J. Calderhead (Ed.), *Exploring teachers' thinking* (pp. 147–160). London: Cassell.

Chemlynski, C. (1996). Discipline as teaching. *Education Digest, 61*, 42–44.

Clandinin, J. (2000). Learning to teach: A question of knowledge. *Education Canada, 40*, 28–30.

Connelly, F. M., Clandinin, D. J., & He, M. F. (1997). Teachers' personal practical knowledge on the professional knowledge landscape. *Teaching and Teacher Education, 13*, 665–674.

Cothran, D. J., & Ennis, C. D. (1997). Students' and teachers' perception of conflict and power. *Teaching and Teacher Education, 13*, 541–553.

Fernandez-Balboa, J. M., Barrett, K., Solmon, M., & Silverman, S. (1996). Perspectives on content knowledge in physical education. *Journal of Physical Education, Recreation, and Dance, 67*, 54–67.

Goyette, R., Dore, R., & Dion, E. (2000). Pupils' misbehaviors and the reactions and causal attribution of physical education student teachers: A sequential analysis. *Journal of Teaching in Physical Education, 20*, 3–14.

Graber, K. C. (2001). Research on teaching in physical education. In V. Richardson (Ed.), *Handbook of research on teaching* (pp. 491–519). Washington, DC: American Educational Research Association.

LeCompte, M. D., & Preissle, J. (1993). *Ethnography and qualitative design in educational research.* San Diego, CA: Academic Press.

Lewis, R. (1999). Teachers coping with the stress of classroom discipline. *Social Psychology of Education, 3*, 155–171.

Marks, R. (1990). Pedagogical content knowledge from a mathematical case to a modified conception. *Journal of Teacher Education, 41*, 3–11.

O'Sullivan, M. (1996). What do we know about the professional preparation of teachers? In S. Silverman & C. Ennis (Eds.), *Student learning in*

*physical education: Applying research to enhance instruction* (pp. 315–337). Champaign, IL: Human Kinetics.
Pagano, K., & Langley, D. J. (2001). Teacher perspectives on the role of exercise as a management tool in physical education. *Journal of Teaching in Physical Education, 21*, 57–74.
Patton, M. Q. (2002). *Qualitative research and evaluation methods* (3rd ed.). Thousand Oaks, CA: Sage.
Rink, J. E. (2002). *Teaching physical education for learning*. Boston: McGraw-Hill.
Schempp, P. G. (1993). Constructing professional knowledge: A case study of an experienced high school teacher. *Journal of Teaching in Physical Education, 13*, 2–23.
Schempp, P. G., Manross, D., Tan, S. K., & Fincher, M. D. (1998). Subject expertise and teachers' knowledge. *Journal of Teaching in Physical Education, 17*, 342–356.
Schottle, D. A., & Peltier, G. L. (1991). Should schools employ behavior management consultants? *Journal of Instructional Psychology, 23*, 128–130.
Shulman, L. S. (1987). Knowledge and teaching: Foundations of the new reform. *Harvard Educational Review, 57*, 1–22.
Williams, R. L. (1999). The behavioral perspective in contemporary education. *The Teacher Educator, 35*, 44–60.

## APPENDIX A
## Sample Interview Questions and Possible Follow-Up Probes

1. Where did you learn to manage your classes?

   *Can you discuss how your management philosophy has changed over the years? Was there a particularly influential individual?*

2. If I were a new teacher, what advice would you give me?
3. How do you teach students about your rules and management?

   *What strategies do you use for children who follow your directions and expectations?*

4. What kinds of things do you do when a student's behavior is inappropriate?
5. How much of your time and energy is spent on management?
6. When a student misbehaves, what is the effect on you? Your students?
7. Integration and mainstreaming are common in physical education. How does it affect your classes?
8. Does student behavior impact grades?
9. Why do you think students misbehave?
10. The most frequent behaviors are those minor ones like talking and not following directions. What works for those behaviors?

    *You mentioned a few key ideas. Where do you come up with these new ideas?*

*Note*. Interview questions are numbered; follow-up probes are italicized.

The qualitative researcher asks participants open-ended questions

**APPENDIX B**
**Transcript Excerpts**

| Knowledge Origin and Influence | Knowledge Evolution | Knowledge Content |
|---|---|---|
| "The first day I was in charge of a class, I had 10 activities all lined up. . . . I was not going to not have enough for them to do. . . . I neglected to have an opening and they just ignored me. That taught me right away to meet them at the door or establish what they have to do when they enter my classroom." | "I have a little different student clientele . . . but I have probably changed more than some of the students. I am less autocratic, more democratic. I try to give choices. I keep myself calm better and make better decisions. I don't get upset. I got upset easier in my first few years as a starting teacher." | "I use the infamous time-out. I usually give them a few chances. . . . I go back and talk to them and ask do you know what you did wrong? How are you going to make it better? . . . Our first few classes, I let the students brainstorm and come up with what will make our class run smoothly." |
| "My first few teaching experiences really gave me some real insight to what I had to do. . . . " | "I'd say that I probably had to lighten up a little bit. The first morning that I started is etched in my skull. And now we're at a point now . . . back when I was in school, you know . . . it was nothing to get paddled. I mean I had a hat trick on me in sixth grade about three times. But now you don't do those things to kids." | "Something I learned is that you've gotta talk to the kids individually and as a group . . . call them aside and talk to them." |
| "It was trial and error. They didn't teach me much in college. In fact they didn't teach any of it." | "I think that they don't have the consistency at home. They don't have discipline at home. And they don't have it at school. I think that kids were taught more to respect the adult or the teacher. And that's just really lessened over the years. I don't feel that's what is being taught at home." | "Proximity, staying close to the kids helps nip it in the bud. . . . I will sit them down and talk to them. . . . I like to teach by example." |
| "I would say that most of it was trial and error. . . . And sometimes by other teachers, their suggestions and so on. But I think the majority of it came from trial and error . . . just seeing what worked." | ". . . kids have changed. You know you have to find that line every year of how much can I joke with these kids . . . and that's true with every class. And some years, you just can't let your hair down at all." | "You need to know what kind of control and discipline you are comfortable with and can teach. You need to make sure it is practical and fair to the kids. To me that is #1." |

The qualitative researcher includes quotes from participants

*Source: Journal of Educational Research,* Vol. 99, Issue 1, pp. 56–63, 2005. Reprinted with permission of the Helen Dwight Reid Educational Foundation. Published by Heldref Publications, 1319 Eighteenth St., NW, Washington, DC 20036-1802. 

CHAPTER

# 11 Qualitative Data Analysis and Results: Examining What Was Found in a Study

*If you are similar to most students, then the main reason you want to read research is to find out what researchers have learned about topics that are important to you. Therefore, when you read a qualitative research report, you are probably most interested in reading the insights that resulted when the researcher analyzed the collected data. For qualitative research studies, this means that you need to be able to understand the general qualitative analysis process and the format by which researchers report their qualitative findings. In this chapter, you will learn the steps researchers use to analyze and present their findings in a qualitative research study.*

**BY THE END OF THIS CHAPTER, YOU SHOULD BE ABLE TO:**

- Describe how researchers analyze qualitative data and list the major elements of this process.
- Locate where researchers describe how they analyzed their qualitative data and where they report their results in research articles.
- List the steps that researchers report using to analyze qualitative data.
- Know how to identify results in the form of description and themes when reading a qualitative research article.
- Evaluate the analysis of qualitative data and findings as reported in a research article.

Research would not be research without the analysis of collected data. It is an essential step and, in qualitative research in particular, it can be the step in the research process that requires the most time and effort from the researcher. Despite all the work that goes into qualitative data analysis, researchers often only report a paragraph or two about *how* they analyzed the data and instead focus much attention on the actual *findings* that emerged from the analysis. As a reader of research, however, you need to understand both the process of analyzing qualitative data and how the results of this process are reported to fully appreciate and interpret the findings presented in a qualitative research report. Let's first consider data analysis in the process of conducting qualitative research.

## What Is the Process of Analyzing Qualitative Data?

Researchers who collect qualitative text or image data need to use qualitative analysis procedures to make sense of this data. Qualitative data analysis consists of a researcher using systematic procedures to develop description and themes from text and image data about a central phenomenon. You can visualize the major steps in this process by examining the bottom-up approach to qualitative analysis in Figure 11.1. As shown in the figure, qualitative researchers collect data and prepare the data for analysis. This analysis consists of the researcher developing a general sense of the data, coding for description and themes about the central phenomenon, and writing up the findings. Here are some features of this process.

FIGURE 11.1 The Process of Qualitative Data Analysis

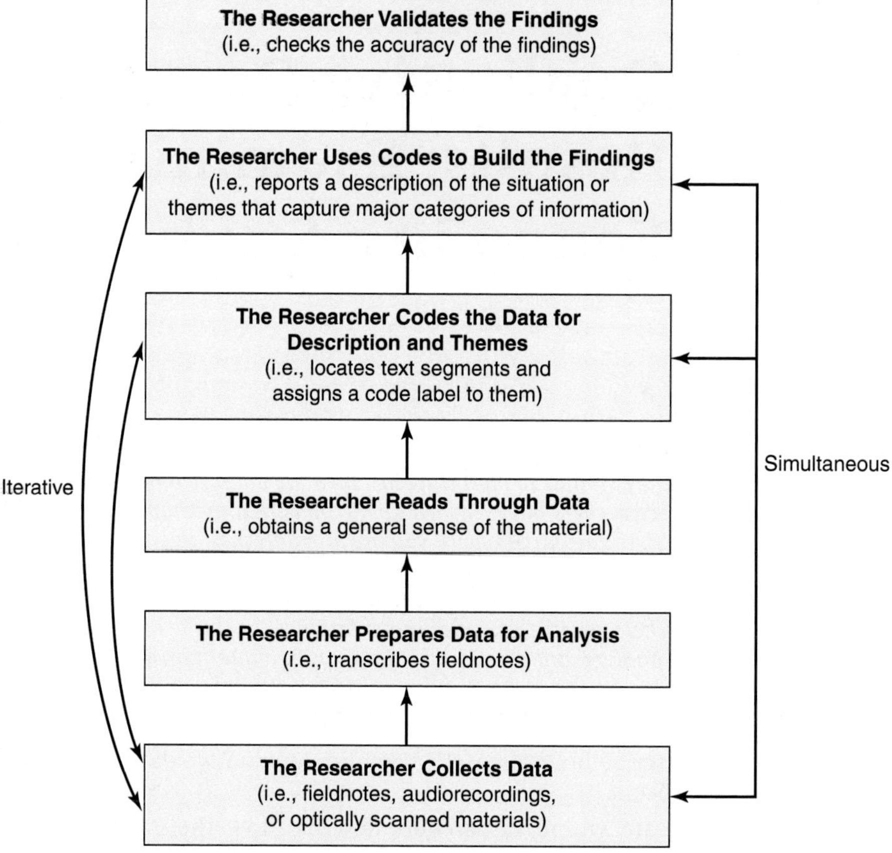


- It is *inductive* in form, going from the detailed data (e.g., transcriptions or typed observational fieldnotes) to the general (e.g., codes and themes). Keeping this in mind helps you understand how qualitative researchers produce broad themes or categories from diverse databases. Although the initial analysis consists of subdividing the data (later we will discuss *coding* the data), the final goal is to generate a larger picture.
- It involves a *simultaneous* process of analyzing while the researcher is also collecting data. In qualitative research, the data collection and analysis (and perhaps the report writing) are simultaneous activities. That is, the researcher may analyze collected information at the same time as collecting additional data.
- The phases are also *iterative*, in which the researcher cycles back and forth between data collection and analysis. In qualitative research, researchers might collect stories from individuals, and, as their analysis of the stories proceeds, they may return to the participants for more information to fill in gaps in their stories.
- Qualitative researchers analyze their database by reading it several times and conducting an analysis each time. Each time a researcher reads the database, he/she develops a deeper understanding about the information supplied by the participants.
- Qualitative research is *interpretive* research in which the researcher makes a personal assessment as to a description that fits the situation or themes that capture the major categories of information. The interpretation that one researcher makes of a transcript, for example, may differ from the interpretation that someone else makes. This does not mean that one interpretation is better or more accurate; it simply means that each researcher brings his/her own perspective to the interpretation.

From this beginning description, you can already identify some differences between how researchers analyze qualitative data compared to quantitative data. For example, in quantitative research the investigator first completes data collection and then moves to data analysis. The traditional quantitative process is much more linear than the simultaneous and iterative process used in most qualitative studies.

## How Do You Identify a Study's Qualitative Data Analysis and Results?

When qualitative researchers write up reports of their studies, they include two elements related to data analysis. They report the actual process they used to analyze the data and they report the results that emerged from this process.

### Look to the Method Section for a Description of the Analysis Process

You can find an author's discussion of data analysis in the method section of a qualitative research article, usually immediately following the discussion of data collection. In many studies the author will use a subheading of *Data Analysis* to let you know where the discussion of the analysis process occurs. Generally authors provide only an overview of the steps they took to analyze the data. Read the following information that the author provided in the methods section of the qualitative parent role study (Auerbach, 2007) at the end of Chapter 1 for a description of a study's data analysis process:

> All interviews were taped and transcribed verbatim in English or Spanish, with Spanish translated by a native speaker assistant. Interview data were triangulated with field notes from 3 years of participant observation of Futures & Families parent meetings and other family-school interactions as well as student interviews from the Futures Project database, school staff interviews, academic transcripts, and school documents.
>
> Topical, theoretical, and en vivo codes were used to identify emerging themes and patterns, with particular attention to how parents made meaning of their roles. Case summaries, data displays, and narrative analysis revealed further patterns and irregularities in the data and created an audit trail for findings. The extended period of fieldwork, use of thick description, and multiple methods helped strengthen validity and reliability according to current standards for qualitative research (Merriam, 2001). Validity also was enhanced by colleague checks, member checks, and analytical memos to monitor researcher subjectivity (Peshkin, 1988). *(paragraphs 15–16)*

This passage conveys details about the general steps used by researchers to analyze qualitative data. These details included:

- ***Preparing the data.*** The author transcribed the interview audiotapes and the data were translated as necessary.
- ***Exploring and coding the data.*** The author read through the data (e.g., interview transcripts, observation fieldnotes) and began to assign "codes" to the data.
- ***Developing description and themes.*** The author identified "themes and patterns" that emerged from the analyzed data. These themes and patterns form the three parent roles found in the study.
- ***Validating the findings.*** The author provided information about how she ensured the credibility of the findings, such as by checking findings with colleagues, spending an extended amount of time in the field, and using multiple data collection methods.

> *Here's a Tip for Reading Research!*
>
> Pay special attention to the opening paragraph of the results section to obtain an overview of the findings. This paragraph will help you understand the information that the author will be presenting, such as how many themes or what kinds of descriptions.

### Look to the Results Section for the Findings Produced by the Analysis Process

Authors typically devote a great deal of attention to describing and explaining what was found as a result of the data analysis process. Due to the importance of the results in a qualitative research article, they are reported in their own section. This section may be called *Results* like in quantitative studies, but qualitative investigators often prefer to use the word *Findings* as the heading because it sounds more open to having learned from participants. In some qualitative studies, the authors may choose to use a heading that describes what was found, such as in the qualitative parent role study, where the author used the major heading "An Alternative Role Typology: From Moral

Supporters to Struggling Advocates" (paragraph 18) to signal the start of the findings section. In order to understand the types of results that authors report in the results section of qualitative studies, you need to know about the qualitative analysis process.

## How Do Researchers Analyze Qualitative Data?

For practice identifying the steps of qualitative data analysis, go to the *Building Research Skills* section under the topic "Qualitative Research: Data Analysis and Interpretation" in MyEducationalResearchLab, located at www.myeducationlab.com. Complete the exercise "Analyzing Data for a Qualitative Study" and use the provided feedback to further develop your skills for reading research articles.

If you are unfamiliar with qualitative data analysis procedures, you may be thinking that it must be very simple: The researcher talks to a few individuals and then writes up a summary of what was said. Good qualitative data analysis, however, is *not* simply summarizing what people had to say. Qualitative data analysis is a systematic, rigorous, and thoughtful process that researchers use to uncover larger patterns about the central phenomenon from the collected data. Even if you do not plan to conduct such analyses yourself, you need to develop an appreciation of this process to be able to effectively read and assess qualitative research reports.

The qualitative data analysis process includes four major steps:

- preparing the data;
- exploring and coding the data;
- developing description and themes from the codes; and
- validating the findings.

### Step 1—Researchers Prepare Their Data

Due to the vast amount of information collected in most qualitative studies, researchers must take steps to prepare their data for analysis. You might remember from Chapter 10 that qualitative researchers obtain words through interviewing participants or by writing fieldnotes during observations or obtain sounds and images from documents or audiovisual materials. Researchers prepare the image, audiovisual, or document data that they collected by creating a digital copy (such as by scanning an image or document) that can be used for analysis purposes.

Researchers also convert the collected words into computer files for analysis. **Transcription** is the process of converting audiotape recordings or fieldnotes into typed text. The most complete procedure is for the researcher to transcribe all interviews and observational notes. As a general rule of thumb, it takes approximately four hours to transcribe one hour of audiotape. Hence, the process of transcription is labor-intensive. It also yields extensive data. For example, a 30-minute interview will often result in about 15 pages of single-spaced transcribed text! Researchers may transcribe the information themselves or they may use a transcriptionist to type the text files. The best procedure is for the researcher to type the transcription verbatim. This means that *all* spoken words are typed as well as unspoken events such as [*pause*] to indicate when interviewees take a lengthy break in their comments or [*laughter*] when the interviewee laughs. Although preparing transcriptions represents a great deal of the researcher's effort, good transcriptions are essential for the qualitative researcher to be able to conduct a thorough analysis of the collected data.

*Here's a Tip for Applying Research!*

Just as it takes longer to grade an essay exam than a multiple-choice text, it can be very labor intensive to make sense of a collection of text information. If you want to gather text information for a topic related to your practice, consider how you will organize and analyze this information to keep from being overwhelmed.

In addition to preparing the data, researchers need to decide whether to analyze the data by hand or to use a computer. Here is an overview of these two options:

- ***Analyzing qualitative data by hand*** means that researchers read the data, mark them by hand, and divide them into parts by hand. Traditionally, analyzing text data by hand involves using colored highlighting markers to mark parts of the text or cutting and pasting (with scissors and tape!) text sentences onto cards. For example, note how the following researcher described analyzing his data by hand: "I began

**TABLE 11.1 Qualitative Data Analysis Software Commonly Mentioned in Research Reports**

- *Atlas.ti* (Scientific Software Development, http://www.atlasti.com)
- *Ethnograph* (Qualis Research, http://www.qualisresearch.com)
- *HyperRESEARCH* (Research Ware, http://www.scolari.com)
- *MAXqda* (Verbi Software, http://www.maxqda.com)
- *NUD*IST* (QSR International, http://www.qsrinternational.com)
- *NVivo* (QSR International, http://www.qsrinternational.com)

to index themes with various highlighted colors and with notes in the margins" (Rushton, 2004, p. 65). Some qualitative researchers prefer to hand-analyze their data. A hand-analysis can be used in projects with relatively small databases (e.g., less than 500 pages of text).

- ***Analyzing qualitative data with a computer*** means that researchers use a computer program to facilitate the process of analyzing the qualitative data. Unlike the computer programs used to analyze quantitative data, qualitative computer programs *do not* analyze the data for researchers. They do, however, provide several features that help a researcher analyze a qualitative database. These features include storing data, organizing data, enabling the researcher to assign labels or codes to the data, and facilitating searching through the data and locating specific text. Computer-assisted analysis is ideal for researchers who have large databases and/or an interest in technology.

Many qualitative data analysis software programs are commercially available to researchers today, and you may see them referred to by name in many qualitative research reports. The most common programs are listed in Table 11.1 so you can recognize their names. Authors name the specific software package that they used because it informs readers about an important detail of the data analysis process. For example, the author of a study on bullying identified the particular software package used for data analysis by writing: "The interviews were analyzed using grounded theory (Creswell, 1998), with NVivo qualitative software to organize the data (Richards, 1999)" (*Mishna, 2004, p. 237*).

## Step 2—Researchers Explore and Code Their Data

Once the qualitative data are prepared, researchers begin their formal analysis. They start by exploring the data. A **preliminary exploratory analysis** in qualitative research consists of the researcher exploring the data to obtain a general sense of the data, memoing ideas, thinking about the organization of the data, and considering whether more data are needed. The researcher may write memos in the margins of fieldnotes, transcripts, or under photographs to help in this initial process of exploring the data. These memos are short phrases, ideas, concepts, or hunches that occur to the researcher. Look for evidence of this exploratory step in research reports. For example, the authors of a study about multicultural educators noted their exploratory analysis step when they wrote: "Each team member read every transcript to gain a sense of the whole experience communicated by participants" (*Landreman et al., 2007, p. 279*).

Once inquirers have explored the data, they begin to code the text and image data. Coding is the process of segmenting and labeling text (or images) to form descriptions and broad themes in the data. No two researchers code in exactly the same way, but most follow the same general procedure. Considering a visual model like the one in Figure 11.2 will help you understand this procedure. The objective of the **coding process** is for the inquirer to make sense of the database by dividing it into text or image segments, labeling the segments with codes, examining codes for overlap and redundancy, and collapsing these codes into broad themes. Thus, this is an inductive process of starting with lots of data segments and building up from the data to several codes and then to a few themes. You will find researchers using terms for variations of this process, such as analytic induction, constant comparison, or thematic development.

**FIGURE 11.2 A Visual Model of the Coding Process in Qualitative Research**

*Source:* Adapted from Creswell (2008).

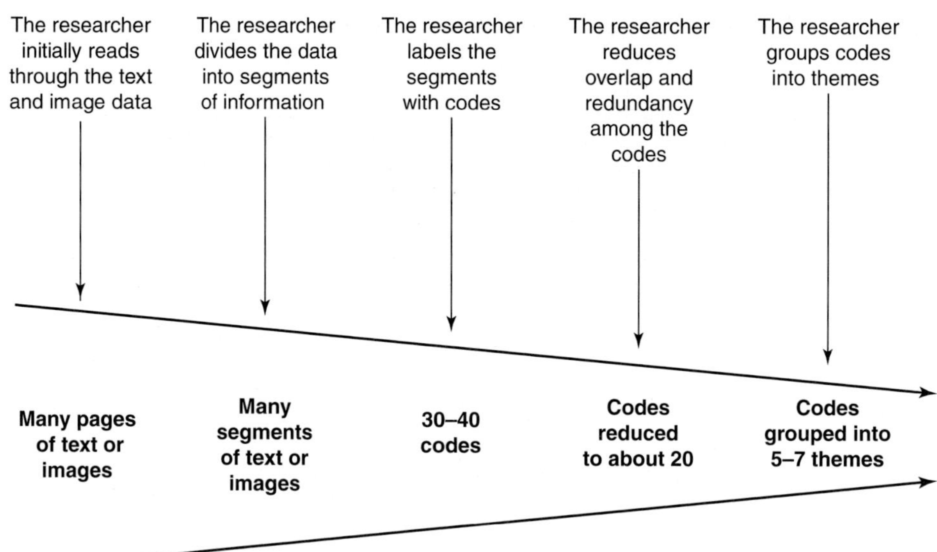


The coding process is at the heart of all qualitative data analysis. It is what makes qualitative data analysis rigorous. Specifically, the researcher identifies segments of text (or images), places a bracket around them, and assigns a code that describes the meaning of the text segment. **Codes** are labels that the inquirer uses to describe the meaning of a segment of text or an image. Codes can address many different topics, such as those listed here:

- setting and context (e.g., classroom),
- perspectives held by participants (e.g., poor learners),
- participants' ways of thinking about people and objects (e.g., problem children),
- processes (e.g., disruptions during the class),
- activities (e.g., student sitting quietly),
- strategies (e.g., teacher giving time-out), and
- relationship and social structure (e.g., students talking to each other).

Researchers determine their codes in different ways. In a few qualitative projects, researchers start with specific topics of interest and they use these topics as codes to identify the data that relates to those topics. In most qualitative analyses, however, the researcher does not start with predetermined codes. These researchers read the data and create codes based on the meaning of the data. These codes can be phrased in standard educational terms (a researcher referring to "a classroom") or expressed in the researcher's own language (a statement about "students talking to each other"). Researchers may also state codes in the participant's actual words (i.e., a student's perspective about other students, such as "poor learners"), which are called *in vivo* codes.

Figure 11.3 shows a sample transcript from an interview that has been coded by a researcher. This transcript resulted from an interview for a project exploring changes in the curriculum in a rural high school (Jones, 1999). Overall, the interviewee talks about changes in the high school from a traditional curriculum to a school based on service-learning in the community. Jones asks questions during the interview and "LU," the interviewee, provides responses. Notice the following features of the coding process illustrated in this figure.

- The researcher located sentences that seem to "fit together" to describe one idea and drew a bracket around them. These represent text segments.
- The researcher assigned a code label to each text segment and recorded the codes on the left side. The researcher used only two or three words for each code label. In some cases these were the actual words used by the participant, "LU."

**The Process of Reconstructing Curriculum in a Rural High School Setting**

| Codes Here | | Themes (and Other Ideas) Here |
|---|---|---|
| | JJ: One thing, Lucy, that I've heard talked about was the fact that schools reflect the strengths of communities. What do you perceive as strengths of Greenfield as a community and how that relates to schools? | |
| *Close-knit community* | LU: Well, I think Greenfield is a fairly close-knit community. I think people are interested in what goes on. And because of that, they have a sense of ownership in the schools. We like to keep track of what our kids are doing and feel a connection to them because of that. The downside of that perhaps is that kids can feel that we are looking TOO close. But most of the time, that is the nurturing environment that we do provide an atmosphere of concern and care. | *Potential theme: The community* |
| *Health of community or community values* | To back up, you said the health of the community itself is reflected in schools. A lot of times communities look at schools and say they are not doing this or they aren't doing that, or we're missing something in our schools. I think perhaps we look at the school and see, this is probably a pretty conservative community overall, and look to make sure that what is being talked about in the schools really carries out the community's values. | *Idea: Getting a good sense here for the community and its values* |
| *Change is threatening* | There is a little bit of an idealization I think, perhaps in terms of what we thought of "basic education." And I think there might be a tendency to hold back a little bit too much because of that idealization of "you know, we learned the basics, the reading, the writing and the arithmetic." So you know, any change is threatening. And I think that goes for the community as well as what we see reflected at the school. Sometimes that can get in the way of trying to do different things. I think, again, idealization, older members of the community forget some of the immaturity that they experienced when they were in school and forgetting that kids are kids. So there is a little bit too much of that mental attitude. But for the most part, I think there is a sense of we're all in this together, and concern for the kids. | *A good quote* |
| | JJ: In terms of looking at leadership strengths in the community, where does Greenfield set in a continuum there with planning process, understanding the need to plan, forward-thinking, visionary people. You talked about that a little bit before. | *Potential theme: Leaders* |
| *Visionary skills of talented people* | LU: I think there are people that have wonderful visionary skills. I would say that the community as a whole would be . . . would not reflect that. I think there are people who are driving the process, but the rest of the community may be lagging behind a little bit. I think we have some incredibly talented people who become frustrated when they try to implement what they see as their . . . | *Idea: Returns to description of community again* |

**FIGURE 11.3 Coding a Page from a Sample Interview Transcript**

*Source:* Reprinted with permission of Jean E. Jones, Ph.D.

> ***Here's a Tip for Reading Research!***
>
> Recognize that qualitative data analysis is very labor intensive. A well-done coding process may take many months to complete, as the researcher understands the meaning of an extensive dataset.

- The researcher also recorded reflections (e.g., "getting a good sense here for the community and its values") and potential themes (e.g., "community") on the right side.
- The researcher placed boxes around keywords that could be used as codes or broad ideas or themes.

As the project progresses, the researcher applies this coding process to all the data, which often includes many hundreds of pages of text (wow!). Researchers continually evaluate the list of codes they have generated. As they code more of the data, they work to group similar codes together and to combine redundant codes. As they make sense of the data, they try to reduce the total number of codes to a manageable number, such as 25 or 30, that represent the most important ideas about the central phenomenon. As the list of codes is refined, the researcher uses them to build five to seven themes and descriptions of the setting or participants. **Themes** (also called *categories*) are similar codes aggregated together to form a major idea in the database. The reason for the small number of themes is that it is best to write a qualitative report providing detailed information about a few themes rather than general information about many themes. A **description** is a detailed rendering of people, places, or events in a setting in qualitative research. The researcher might use codes, such as "seating arrangements," "teaching approach," or "physical layout of the room," to build description of a classroom where instruction takes place.

## Step 3—Researchers Use Codes to Build Their Results

In a qualitative research study, the researcher analyzes the data to form answers to the research questions. **Describing and developing themes from the data** consists of answering the major research questions and forming an in-depth understanding of the central phenomenon through description and thematic development.

***Building Description.*** When researchers build description into their qualitative findings, they include a detailed rendering of people, places, or events in a setting. In providing this detailed information, the researcher aims to transport the reader to a research site or help the reader visualize a person. In some forms of qualitative research design, such as in ethnography or in case studies, the researcher provides a considerable description of the setting. Developing detail is important, and the researcher analyzes data from all sources (e.g., interviews, observations, documents) to build a portrait of individuals or events.

Let's examine part of a descriptive passage from the qualitative new teacher study (Clayton, 2007) you read in Chapter 3 as an illustration of an author providing description. Figure 11.4 describes one of the teachers in the study as taken from the author's report. The discussion of this teacher and events in her classroom illustrates several features of description used in many qualitative research reports. The labels indicate that:

- The passage starts broadly with the day and teacher's context and then focuses down into the classroom's details and finally the events in the classroom on this one day. This broad-to-narrow description helps the reader understand the context or place of the teacher and provides a sense of a real place where this teacher is teaching.
- The author uses vivid details to create the description. We know, for example, what is posted on the bulletin boards and what announcements are written on the chalkboard.
- The action comes alive with the use of action verbs and movement-oriented modifiers and adjectives. The teacher did not simply take the papers; she "ripped up" the papers.
- The author does not make an interpretation or evaluate the situation—she simply reports the facts as recorded in the data sources.

**FIGURE 11.4 Elements of Description in a Narrative Passage**

*Source:* Clayton (2007, paragraph 17).

| | |
|---|---|
| The description builds from broad to narrow to situate the reader in the place or context | On a sunny day in March of her 1st year, Alexandra stood in the front of a fifth-grade inclusion classroom, asking math questions in a simple call-and-response pattern while a predominantly African |
| Details are provided | American class sat in table groups. Bulletin boards featured student work—visual representations of math problems and typed essays about favorite celebrities. Posted prominently on the door, the class schedule displayed time blocks consumed by literacy and math. On the front chalkboard were two announcements: Reading test |
| Just the "facts" are described without interpreting the situation | 4/15; math test 4/30. After a short and unsuccessful transition to independent reading, Alexandra decided to hand out a cloze passage vocabulary test. When two boys refused to quiet down, Alexandra |
| Action verbs and vivid modifiers and adjectives are used → | approached their desk and ripped up their quizzes in a dramatic manner intended to attract the attention of the class. Across the room, a different female student asked defiantly, "Can I rip up my |
| Quotes are used to emphasize ideas and add realism → | paper?" as she, then, did so. Alexandra looked on in disgust, and the lesson continued in a haphazard fashion until a visiting guest speaker arrived. |

- The passage includes quotes to provide emphasis and realism in the account. These quotes are usually short. In a brief journal article, writers need to be concerned about space available for the narrative and generally keep the quotes as short as possible.

***Building Themes.*** In addition to description, the development of themes is another way that researchers analyze qualitative data. Because themes are similar codes aggregated together to form a major idea in the database, they form a core element in qualitative data analysis. Like codes, themes have labels that typically consist of only a few words (e.g., "self-tensions," "teaching supports"). In order to convey rich detail about the emergent themes, authors generally report only five to seven themes in the results of their qualitative research studies. There are several types of themes that you might find discussed in reports, such as expected themes (e.g., consequences of tobacco use) or surprising themes (unenforced school tobacco-use policies).

Researchers report rich details about the themes that emerged from their codes. Figure 11.5 is a portion of the discussion of the "students' experiences" theme found in a study about adolescent perceptions of tobacco use (Plano Clark et al., 2002). You might consider "students' experiences in high schools" to be an expected theme because we might expect tobacco use to be present during the high school years. The marginal annotations mark important elements that the authors used in developing this theme. These elements include:

- ***Use of quotes.*** The authors include short quotes (exact words from participants) from their focus group interviews to add realism to the passage. You can identify these quotes

**FIGURE 11.5 Elements of Theme Development in a Narrative Passage**

*Source:* Plano Clark et al. (2002, pp. 1270–1271). Reprinted with permission of Sage Publications, Inc.

**What Are the Students' Experiences with Tobacco in High Schools?**

Turning directly to the high school years, the students view tobacco as a common, pervasive phenomenon in their lives. For most, their frame of reference is the use of cigarettes and, to a lesser extent, smokeless (or chewing) tobacco. They reflect on the presence of tobacco among high school students, family members, parents, teachers, and personnel in jobs where they work when not in school. They find themselves surrounded by tobacco users to the point where they feel that "everybody" uses tobacco. It is interesting how they estimate how many students at their schools are at least occasional smokers, from "more than half" to "everyone." Although the rate of use of chewing tobacco is considered lower than that of cigarettes, many students indicate that chewing tobacco is popular with certain groups, such as athletes, because smokeless tobacco is "easy to hide."

A related issue is the location where tobacco is used. Several students mention that it is "everywhere," such as in public places (e.g., restaurants and punk music shows) and personal locations (such as "work," "the ride to school," and "at home"). "Everywhere" also pertains to on or near school grounds, even though the high schools have explicit policies against the use of tobacco products by students. Smokers, they say, including underage smokers, are able to get around these rules. In fact, all four high schools have a recognized location either on or adjacent to school property where students go to smoke with little fear of retribution. Although these unofficially designated smoking areas, such as "smoker's corner" or "the park," are the primary locations for students to smoke, other locations are also mentioned. These areas include restrooms, the parking lot, a back staircase, and the locker room. Smokers can be seen throughout the school day, including before and after school and during all breaks between classes. Chewers are seen during school and even in class. The invisible nature of chewing tobacco seems to lead to more blatant in-school and in-class use of this form of tobacco as opposed to cigarettes.

The picture of a world where tobacco use is perceived as common results in high school students' being desensitized to tobacco use. Due to its high visibility, students appear to feel surrounded by the use of tobacco products at school and outside of school, resulting in their acceptance of tobacco use. As an MHS student explains, high school students "become numb to it just 'cause so many people [their] age do it." A UHS student echoes a similar sentiment by saying, "[Smoking] seems normal 'cause everybody does it."

Evidence for theme based on short quotes

Evidence for theme based on multiple perspectives

Within the theme there are multiple subthemes (prevalence, where tobacco is used, desensitized)

Subthemes add complexity to the passage

Quotes used to provide voice of participants

*Here's a Tip for Reading Research!*

Good qualitative findings include multiple perspectives and points of view. This means that the researcher has learned about the complex perspectives that people hold about the topic. This is different from quantitative research that emphasizes determining average trends.

when the authors use quotation marks (e.g., " "). In many studies the authors will also use the exact wording of participants for the theme name.

- ***Use of subthemes under a major theme.*** It is useful to see that the authors have major themes and several subthemes subsumed under each major theme. The major theme is "What Are the Students' Experiences with Tobacco in High Schools?" Under this major theme, the authors discuss the following minor themes: prevalence of tobacco use, where tobacco is used, and students feeling desensitized.
- ***Use of multiple perspectives.*** The authors analyzed the data for multiple perspectives on this theme. The term **multiple perspectives** means that the researcher provides several viewpoints from different individuals and sources of data as evidence for a theme. Multiple perspectives are important when conveying the complexity of the central phenomenon in qualitative research. In this passage, for example, the authors report the perspectives of many students, including those from different school settings.

This passage does not include one further element of theme development. A realistic presentation of information does not present only one side or the other. In an attempt to capture the complexity of situations, qualitative researchers analyze their data for contrary evidence. **Contrary evidence** is information that does not support or confirm the themes and provides contradictory (but realistic) information about a theme. What might this contrary evidence be for this theme? Had the authors searched for this evidence they might have found that some students do not perceive that many people use tobacco at their school.

***Relating Multiple Themes.*** You will find many qualitative studies in the literature that stop with only reporting description and themes. In more sophisticated studies, however, the author will report the individual themes and then will relate the themes to each other. Two examples of relating themes are layering the themes and interconnecting the themes.

- ***Layering the themes*** means that the researcher represents the data using embedded levels of themes. This occurs when the researcher subsumes minor themes within major themes and then includes major themes within broader themes. The entire analysis becomes more and more complex as the researcher works *upward* toward broader levels of abstraction. Asmussen and Creswell (1995) layered their themes about a campus reaction to a gunman incident by subsuming their five major themes (denial, fear, safety, retriggering, and campus planning) within two broader themes (social-psychological and psychological).
- ***Interconnecting the themes*** means that the researcher connects the themes to display a chronology or sequence of events, such as when qualitative researchers generate a theoretical and conceptual model or connect the themes to tell a larger story found in the data. The authors of the theme illustrated in Figure 11.5 interconnected the five major themes in a larger story. Note how the following statement explains these connections:

> As we report these themes in the next section, we organize them into a story line about adolescent use of tobacco. This story line reports how individuals begin smoking; how smoking becomes a pervasive influence in school lives; how attitudes are formed about smoking at school and in personal lives; how these attitudes, in turn, shape what it means to be a smoker; and, ultimately, how these experiences influence student suggestions for tobacco use prevention. (*Plano Clark et al., 2002, p. 1269*)

## Step 4—Researchers Validate Their Results

Throughout the process of data collection and analysis, researchers need to make sure that their findings and interpretations are accurate so the findings will be credible. **Validating findings** means that the researcher determines the accuracy and credibility of the findings through strategies, such as member checking or triangulation. Unlike quantitative researchers, qualitative researchers are not typically concerned with being objective. Qualitative researchers note that all research is interpretive (or subjective). Therefore qualitative researchers believe that all researchers should be self-reflective about their role in the research, how they are interpreting the findings, and their personal and political history that shapes their interpretation. Thus, reflecting on the analysis process and establishing the accuracy and credibility of the findings is of upmost importance. Although you may find authors describing many different strategies for validating their qualitative findings, our attention here will be on four forms frequently used by qualitative researchers: bracketing, triangulation, member checking, and auditing.

- Because qualitative data analysis is a subjective process, researchers reflect on their personal viewpoints and how they shape their interpretations of the data. One way that researchers address this issue is through bracketing. **Bracketing** is a process by which a researcher reflects on his or her own views and experiences related to the study's central phenomenon, describes these perspectives in writing, and then works to set them aside (or "bracket" them) during the analysis process. Although personal bias can never be totally eliminated, bracketing helps to ensure that the researcher's perspectives do not overwhelm the perspectives of the participants.
- Qualitative inquirers triangulate different data sources to enhance the accuracy of a study. **Triangulation** is the process of corroborating evidence about a finding from different individuals (e.g., a principal and a student) or types of data (e.g., observational fieldnotes and interviews). The inquirer examines each information source and finds evidence to support a theme. This helps to ensure that the study will be accurate because the information draws on multiple sources of information or individuals.
- Researchers check their findings with participants in the study to determine whether their findings are accurate. **Member checking** is a process in which the researcher asks one or more participants to check the accuracy of the findings. This process involves taking the findings back to participants and asking them (in writing or in an interview) about the accuracy of the report. Researchers ask participants about many aspects of the study, such as whether the description is complete and realistic, the themes are accurate, and the interpretations are fair and representative.
- Researchers may also ask a person *outside* the project to conduct a thorough review of the study and report back, in writing, the strengths and weaknesses of the project. This is the process of conducting an **external audit**, in which a researcher hires or obtains the services of an individual outside the study to review different aspects of the research. The auditor reviews the project and writes or communicates an evaluation of the study. Some researchers may conduct a less formal review of their study's process, often called a *peer review.* A researcher using peer review discusses his/her research process with a knowledgeable colleague to review the procedures as they unfold during the study.

## What Do You Think?

Consider the description of data analysis provided in paragraphs 12–14 of the qualitative new teacher study (Clayton, 2007). You can find these paragraphs starting on page 101 the end of Chapter 3. What qualitative data analysis procedures do you identify in these paragraphs?

### Check Your Understanding

The author reports on the process of analyzing the data in paragraphs 12–13. Consistent with qualitative research, the author reports analyzing data simultaneously with collecting data. She prepared the data by creating transcripts and choosing to use a computer software program (namely NVivo). She reported reading the transcripts and undergoing a coding process (paragraph 12). The groups of codes formed larger themes, as described in paragraph 13 and nicely illustrated in Table 2. While the author did not explicitly mention validation strategies, we do learn that she discussed initial findings with participants (paragraph 12), which is an example of member checking. Finally, the researcher also discussed her role and perspectives in paragraph 14, which helps us understand how her experience with the program may have influenced her findings.

# How Do Qualitative Researchers Report Their Findings?

After researchers have analyzed their qualitative data—coded the data, analyzed it for description and themes, layered and interconnected the themes, and validated the results—they report findings to their research questions. Researchers report their findings by constructing a narrative to explain what they have found in response to their research questions, by displaying findings in tables and figures, and by matching their findings to their research design.

## Researchers Report Their Findings in Narrative Discussions

The primary form for representing and reporting findings in qualitative research is a narrative discussion. A **narrative discussion** is a written passage presented in the results section of a qualitative report in which authors summarize, in detail, the findings from their data analysis. There is no set form for this narrative, which can vary widely from one study to another. Examples of different forms include a discussion that presents a chronology (or story) of events, a discussion that describes events and setting, or a discussion that describes a model of a process. The researcher's decision about how to report the findings depends on the purpose of the research, the research design, and the type of data analyzed. However, it is helpful to identify some narrative elements that are frequently used. Here are some common narrative elements that researchers use when reporting their qualitative findings:

- ***Writing in vivid detail.*** Researchers report descriptions of an individual, event, or activity and include details so that readers feel like they are taken to the site or have met the individual. Note the detail found in a few sentences of a descriptive passage about a gunman incident on a college campus:

  > The gunman pointed the rifle at the students, swept it across the room, and pulled the trigger. The gun jammed. Trying to unlock the rifle, he hit the butt of it on the instructor's desk and quickly tried firing it again. Again it did not fire. By this time, most students realized what was happening and dropped to the floor, overturned their desks, and tried to hide behind them. After about twenty seconds, one of the students shoved a desk into the gunman, and students ran past him out into the hall and out of the building. (*Asmussen & Creswell, 1995, pp. 576–577*)

- ***Reporting quotes from interview data or from observations of individuals.*** These quotes represent the exact words of participants. Researchers select quotes that capture feelings, emotions, and ways people talk about their experiences.
- ***Organizing ideas by presenting major themes and sub-themes.*** To convey the complexity of the findings, researchers include several sub-themes within each major theme. For example, in a study about how nonsmoking parents struggle when their children start to smoke (Small et al., 2002), the authors reported subthemes for each major theme using subheadings. Under the theme "discovering the smoking," the sub-themes included seeing the evidence, putting the pieces together, confirming the behavior, reacting to the discovery, and secrecy.
- ***Reporting multiple perspectives and contrary evidence.*** Researchers include multiple perspectives about a theme based on different individuals, sources of information, or multiple views held by one person. Contrary evidence also helps to convey the complexity of a phenomenon and the differences in individuals' experiences.
- ***Including dialogue.*** Researchers may include actual dialogue from participants to provide support for themes. For example, in a study about students' perceptions of effective teachers, Howard (2002) provides this dialogue between a teacher (Hazel) and one of her students to support the theme "making school seem like home."

  > **HAZEL [SPEAKING TO STUDENT]:** Where's your book report?
  >
  > **STUDENT:** I don't have it. (long pause) I didn't finish it.
  >
  > **HAZEL:** You didn't finish it? (with emphasis) What are you waiting for to get it done? Christmas?
  >
  > **STUDENT:** No.
  >
  > **HAZEL:** Alright then, get it done! (p. 433)

- ***Stating dialogue in the participants' native language or dialect.*** A study that examines the life histories of African American women by Nelson (1990) includes examples of *code-switching* of African American dialect to convey the casual kitchen-table discourse:

  > I'm trying to communicate a shoe box full when you only give them (the words) a matchbox. I'm trying to relate the spiritual meaning. (p. 151)

- ***Using metaphors and analogies.*** Literary devices are useful for conveying the richness of the findings. In reporting on the competition and concerns surfacing during the implementation of distance education in the state of Maine, Epper (1997) writes metaphorically about how student and citizen support is a "political football" game:

  > As the bickering went on, many students stood by watching their education dreams tossed around like a political football. Some were not content to sit on the sidelines. From the islands, valleys, backwoods, and far reaches of the state came letters to the faculty senates, legislators, and newspapers. (p. 566)

- ***Specifying tensions and contradictions in individual experiences.*** Researchers include tensions and contradictions to convey the complexity of the central phenomenon. For example, Huber and Whelan (1999) discuss the tension a teacher feels between being in control in her classroom and the out-of-class pressure that she experiences from her school coordinator.
- ***Including personal interpretations.*** Researchers reflect on how personal experiences shape the interpretation of the data, recognizing that all data analysis is based on multiple sources of interpretation (the participant, the researcher, and the readers of the research)

## Researchers Represent Their Findings with Visual Displays

In addition to narratively describing the findings, qualitative researchers often display their findings visually by using figures or pictures that augment the discussion (Miles & Huberman, 1994). Examples of different ways that researchers display qualitative findings are:

- ***Comparison tables.*** In some studies, researchers create visual images of the information in the form of a comparison table or a matrix, a table that compares groups on one of the themes (e.g., freshmen and seniors in terms of "students' experience with tobacco"). In a qualitative study of the meaning of "professionalism," a researcher collected statements from both women and men teachers in a school. Statements from these teachers, shown in Table 11.2, are included in a comparison table to show that females and males can differ in their approaches to professionalism.
- ***Hierarchical tree diagrams.*** Researchers use this type of diagram to visually represent themes and the layers among themes. The hierarchical tree diagram in Figure 11.6 illustrates the major themes (layer 3) and broader categories (layer 4) that emerged from a case study about a campus reaction to a gunman incident (Asmussen & Creswell, 1995).
- ***Figures.*** In some qualitative studies, researchers present a figure that illustrates how themes and categories relate to each other. Figures with boxes to show the connections among themes are common in studies using a grounded theory design. For example, Figure 11.7 depicts the findings from a grounded theory study by Creswell

**TABLE 11.2 A Sample Comparison Table Used to Represent Information in a Qualitative Report**

| Statements About "Professionalism" from Female Participants | Statements About "Professionalism" from Male Participants |
|---|---|
| ■ Helping fellow teachers is part of my day.<br>■ When another teacher asks for advice, I am generally a good listener.<br>■ It is important, once I achieve a certain level of experience, that I become a mentor to other teachers, especially new ones.<br>■ Caring about how other teachers employ high standards in their classroom is a sign of my own professionalism. | ■ Being concerned about following the coordinator's advice about curriculum shows a high level of professionalism.<br>■ It is important to be in charge in the classroom and to be aware of student off-task behavior.<br>■ I set standards for myself, and try to achieve these goals each year.<br>■ It is necessary that each teacher "pull" his or her weight in this school—a sure sign of professionalism. |

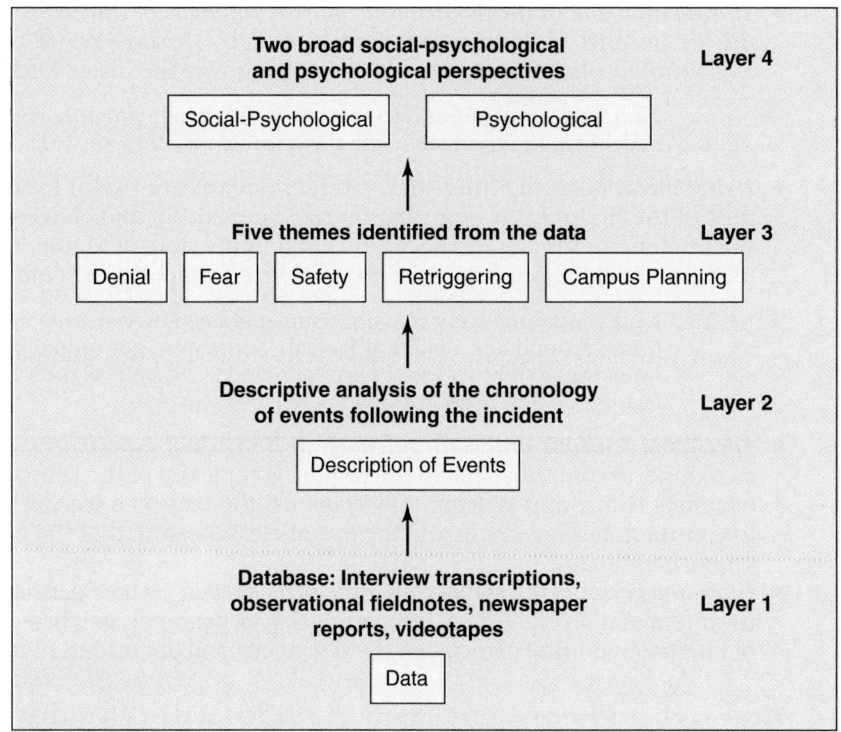


FIGURE 11.6 A Hierarchical Tree Diagram to Portray Theme Layers in a Qualitative Report

*Source:* Adapted from Asmussen & Creswell (1995).

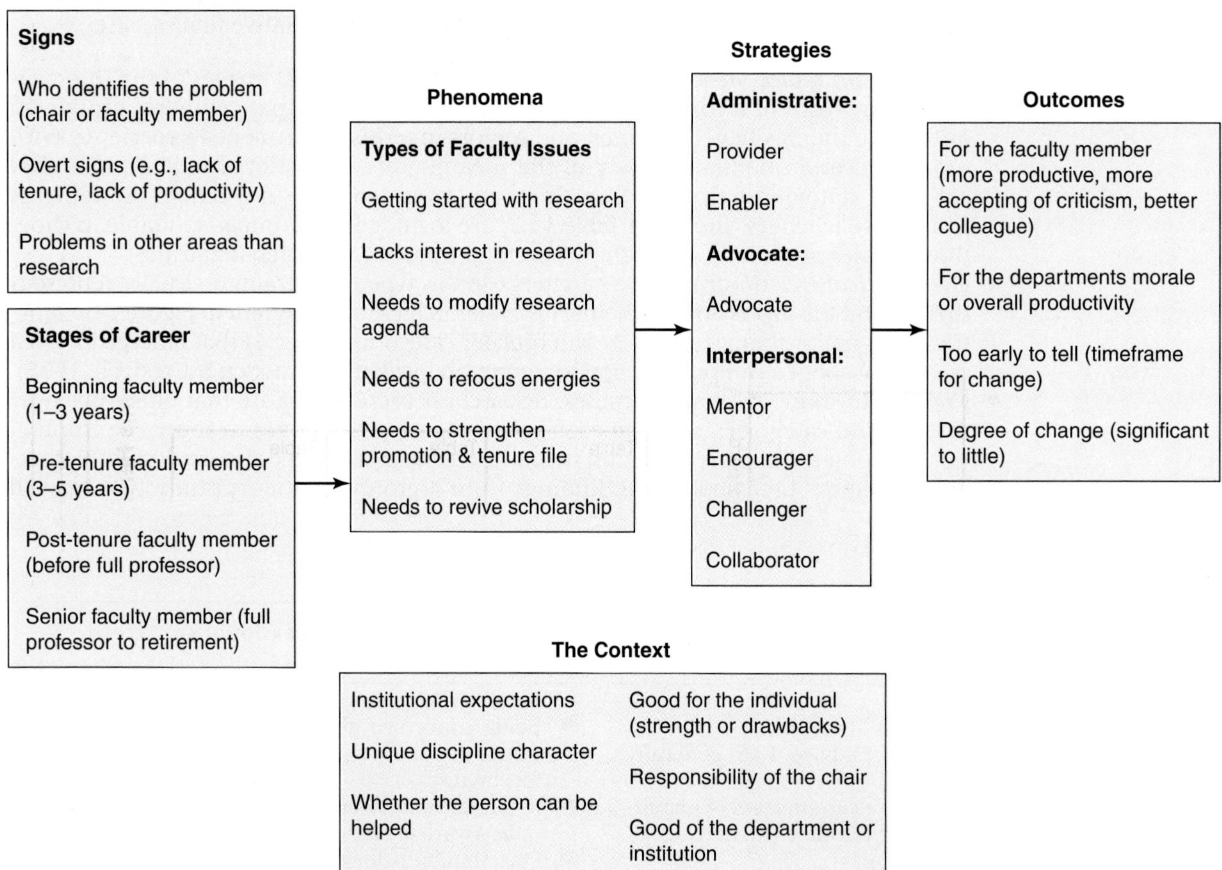


FIGURE 11.7 Interconnecting Themes or Categories in a Figure in a Qualitative Report

*Source:* Creswell, J. W. & M. L. Brown. *How Chairpersons Enhance Faculty Research: A Grounded Theory Study*. *16*:1 (1992), 57, Fig. 1. 

and Brown (1992) that examined the practices used by 33 academic department chairs to enhance the research of faculty in their college or university units. The authors identified numerous themes within each box and used arrows to show the connections among the boxes.

- ***Maps.*** Researchers may use maps to depict the physical layout of the study's setting. As shown in Figure 11.8, Miller, Creswell, and Olander (1998) display the physical setting of a soup kitchen in their study. The authors provided this diagram so that readers could visualize where different activities happened.
- ***Demographic tables.*** Researchers use demographic tables to describe personal or demographic information for each person or site in the research. In a study of the types of technology used by instructors in college classrooms, the researcher described each instructor and his or her primary delivery style in a demographic table, shown in Table 11.3. The six individuals studied in this qualitative study displayed

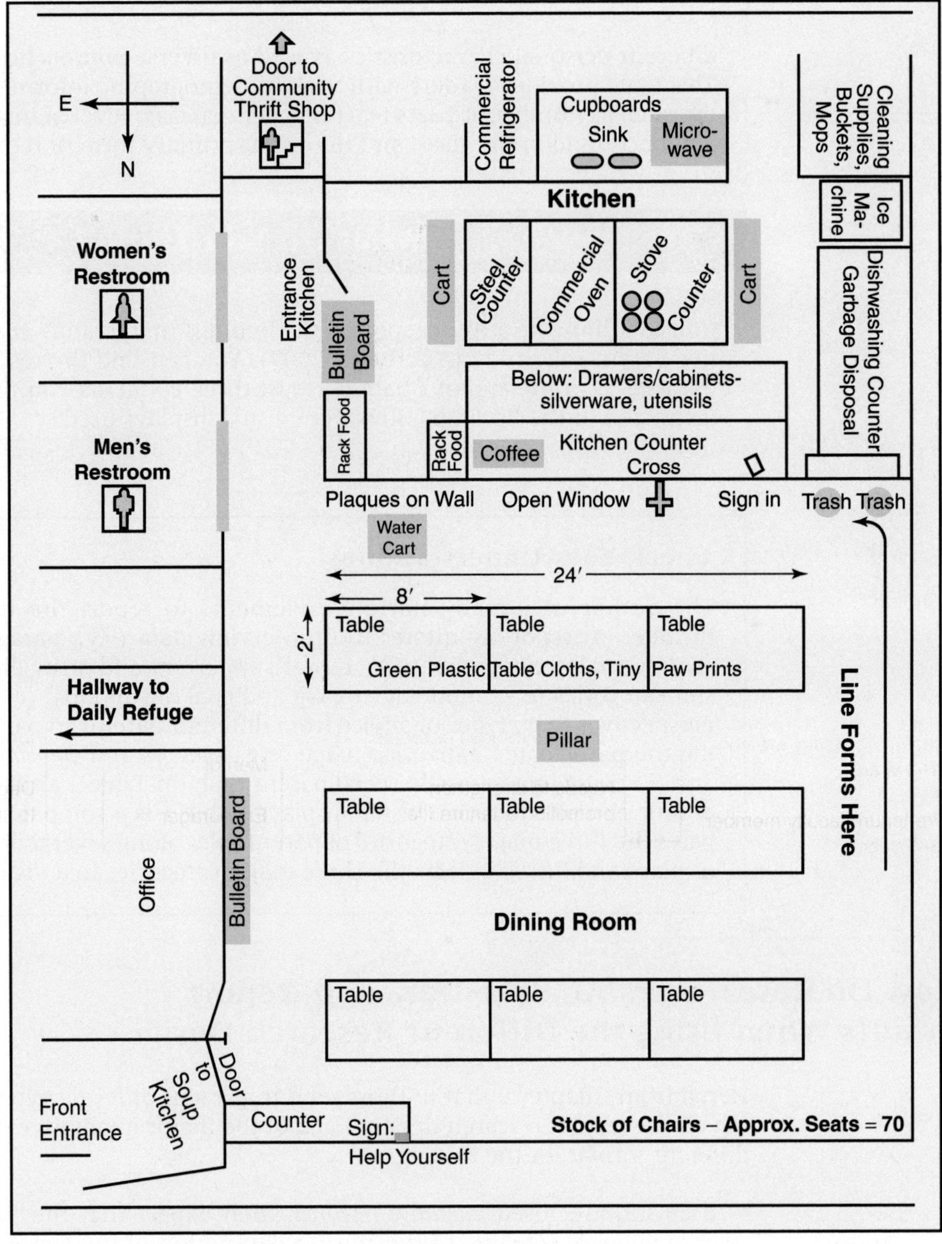


**FIGURE 11.8** Sample Map of the Physical Layout of a Setting in a Qualitative Report

*Source:* Miller, D. M., Creswell, J. W., & Olander, L. S. (1998). Writing and retelling multiple ethnographic tales of a soup kitchen for the homeless. *Qualitative Inquiry, 4*(4), 475. Copyright © 1998 by Sage Publications. Reprinted by permission of Sage Publications, Inc.

**TABLE 11.3 A Sample Demographic Table Used to Represent Information in a Qualitative Report**

| Name | Years Teaching | Gender | Class Level of Instruction | Instructional Approach in the Classroom | Primary Form of Technology in the Classroom |
|---|---|---|---|---|---|
| Rosa | 25 | Female | 12 | Discussion | Internet |
| Harry | 20 | Male | 11 | Critique | Not used |
| Joan | 18 | Female | 11 | Discussion | Web site and Internet |
| Ray | 20 | Male | 12 | Interactive | Web site, Internet, wireless laptops |
| Jamal | 15 | Male | 11 | Discussion | Not used |
| Yun | 36 | Male | 10 | Lecture | Internet |

different personal characteristics as well as diverse approaches to using technology. This table provides readers with various demographic information for each instructor, such as number of years teaching, gender, class level of instruction, instructional approach used in the class, and his or her primary form of technology use.

### What Do You Think?

Consider how the author reported the findings (paragraphs 18–54) in the qualitative parent role study (Auerbach, 2007). You can find the results section starting on page 39 at the end of Chapter 1. List three elements you find in the narrative discussion of the findings. How were visual displays used?

### Check Your Understanding

The author uses many narrative elements to report the findings. Examples include: (a) reporting quotes from interview data (e.g., paragraph 24); (b) presenting major categories (e.g., moral supporters and struggling advocates) and sub-categories (e.g., mode of support and goal of support); (c) reporting multiple perspectives (e.g., types of advice from different parents in paragraph 27); (d) using the participants native language (e.g., *consejos* and *empeño* in paragraph 27); and (e) using metaphors for each parent type (in Table 1 and paragraph 21). The author also provides two visual displays. Table 1 is a comparison table that compares the three major categories of parent roles along several dimensions. Figure 1 displays and interconnects the three major categories in a visual picture.

## How Do Researchers Analyze Data and Report Results When Using the Different Research Designs?

Recall from Chapter 9 that authors tend to present different types of findings depending on the study's research design. Each of the major qualitative design types calls for a different format for the findings:

- If an inquirer used *narrative research*, then expect that the findings will include a chronological retelling of the story, a description of the context for the story, and a description of themes that emerged from the story.
- If an inquirer used *phenomenological research*, then expect that the findings will include major themes about the central phenomenon along with presenting descriptions of

what and how the phenomenon is experienced and a statement of the essence of the experience.

- If an inquirer used *grounded theory research*, then expect that the findings will present a visual model of the interconnections among themes and a discussion of the theory described by and hypotheses suggested by these connections.
- If an inquirer used *case study research*, then expect that the findings will report a description of the case and the themes that emerged about the case.
- If an inquirer used *ethnographic research*, then expect that the findings will present a detailed description of how a group behaves, thinks, or believes as well as the context, or setting, of the group.

## How Do You Evaluate a Study's Qualitative Data Analysis and Findings?

As you read a qualitative research report, you can evaluate the researcher's process for analyzing the qualitative data in the study. Use the criteria provided in Figure 11.9 to assess an author's implementation of qualitative data analysis and the reported the findings. These items evaluate whether the author provides sufficient information about the analysis process, including preparing the data, coding the data, developing findings from the data, and validating the findings. In addition, they will help you evaluate whether the author reported rich, detailed findings that match the qualitative approach in general and a specific research design in particular. Overall authors should provide

Use the following criteria to evaluate the quality of a qualitative study's data analysis and findings as specified within a research report. For each evaluation item, indicate the following ratings:

+ You rate the item as "high quality" for the study.
✓ You rate the item as "ok quality" for the study.
– You rate the item as "low quality" for the study.

In addition to your rating, make notes about each element when you apply these criteria to an actual published study.

| **In a high-quality qualitative research report, the author . . .** | Application to a Published Study | |
|---|---|---|
| | Your Rating | Your Notes |
| 1. Analyzes the data to respond to each research question. | | |
| 2. Discusses preparing the data, including transcribing the data verbatim so an accurate record is available for analysis. | | |
| 3. Uses a software program to facilitate the analysis of all the collected data. | | |
| 4. Uses multiple stages of analysis (reading, memoing, coding, theme and description development, and relating themes). | | |
| 5. Uses at least three strategies to validate his/her findings. | | |
| 6. Discusses how his/her role influenced the interpretation of the findings. | | |
| 7. Reports 5-7 themes and builds multiple perspectives, subthemes, and quotes into the theme descriptions. | | |
| 8. Includes a rich description of people, places, or events in a setting so you feel like you have met the people or are in the setting. | | |

FIGURE 11.9 Criteria for Evaluating a Study's Qualitative Data Analysis and Findings

enough information for you to understand the data analysis and to assess whether the findings provide a rich description, are credible, and provide sufficient information to address a study's research questions.

## Reviewing What We've Learned

- Look to the method section (often called *Procedures*) for the qualitative data analysis procedures and the results section (often called *Findings*) for the findings from these procedures.
- Recognize that researchers use a process for analyzing qualitative data that is simultaneous and iterative with data collection.
- Expect the data analysis process to consist of preparing the data for analysis, exploring and coding the data, developing description and themes, and validating the findings.
- Look to see that the researcher transcribed the interview recordings and observation fieldnotes.
- Look for evidence of a process of assigning codes to the text and grouping codes to build description and themes.
- Assess the strategies used to help validate the credibility of the findings.
- Search the results for description of people, places, or activities.
- Identify the major themes that emerged from the data analysis and consider how they address the study's research questions.
- Search for a layering or interconnecting of the themes.
- For the reported findings, expect elements such as quotes, vivid detail, and multiple perspectives.
- Determine how the findings are reported, looking at narrative discussion, tables, and figures.
- Ask yourself whether the researchers analyzed the data and reported the findings in a descriptive and credible way.

## Practicing Your Skills

Return to the qualitative classroom management study (Garrahy et al., 2005) found at the end of Chapter 10, starting on page 269. Practice using your skills and knowledge of the content of this chapter by answering the following questions about this article. Use the answers found in the Appendix to evaluate your progress.

1. Review the *Method* section of this study (paragraphs 08–13). What evidence can you find that the authors implemented the following major steps of qualitative data analysis: preparing the data, exploring and coding the data, and developing description and themes from the codes?
2. How did the authors validate their findings?
3. What type of results did the authors report? If the results included themes, what major themes were found?
4. Consider the following three excerpts from the findings reported in this study. What narrative elements did the authors use in each of the excerpts?
   a. Most participants agreed that their college programs provided minimal assistance in developing their management knowledge base. Only 1 physical educator (Elizabeth, 11 years, suburban) claimed that she learned a great deal about how to manage children from her college program. *(paragraph 20)*
   b. Knowledge Evolution
      Teachers discussed the evolutionary process of their pedagogical knowledge related to management . . . Teachers cited out-of-school changes as well as in-school changes . . . *(paragraph 21)*
   c. Finally, the elementary physical education teachers had a plethora of strategies for teaching and reinforcing their expectations. Most of the teachers used multiple rewards and consequences (e.g., verbal praise, letters to parents, time out, written assignments, and grade reductions) as ways to improve student behavior. Teachers also spoke of the need for students to acknowledge responsibility for their behaviors. *(paragraph 28)*

# PART FIVE

# Understanding Reports That Combine Quantitative and Qualitative Research

Throughout this book we have used the analogy of "taking a journey" to think about how researchers conduct their research. Recall that some journeys are highly structured with set agendas, like many quantitative research studies that focus on explanation. Other journeys are like qualitative research, focusing on exploration. They are flexible and emerging, where people's decisions about where to go next are based on what they have learned along the way.

It will probably come as no surprise to you to learn that some people like taking trips that include both set agendas as well as time to explore to more fully get to know new territory. Likewise, many of today's interesting research problems call for explanation *and* exploration. Whether focusing on contributing to knowledge or solving local problems, researchers studying these problems may choose to combine *both* quantitative and qualitative research to best understand their research problems and questions. You will now learn about two different research approaches that scholars, including many practitioners, use to combine quantitative and qualitative information. This knowledge will help you understand research reports using some of the most up-to-date approaches to research.

The chapters in Part V are:

- Chapter 12—Mixed Methods Research: Research That Mixes Quantitative and Qualitative Approaches
- Chapter 13—Action Research Designs: Research for Solving Practical Problems

CHAPTER

# 12 Mixed Methods Research: Research That Mixes Quantitative and Qualitative Approaches

*Researchers today can choose between two accepted approaches—quantitative and qualitative research—when conducting their studies. With both types of data available, some researchers combine quantitative data and qualitative data to understand their research problems. The use of these mixed approaches is one of the newest developments in research methods. When researchers use a mixed methods approach, they often use a specific research design to guide their studies' procedures. You need to recognize these different mixed methods designs to better understand studies that include quantitative and qualitative data. This chapter introduces four types of mixed methods designs, identifies their key characteristics, and suggests strategies for you to use to identify and evaluate mixed methods reports.*

## BY THE END OF THIS CHAPTER, YOU SHOULD BE ABLE TO:

- Explain why researchers choose to use mixed methods research.
- State key events in the development of mixed methods research.
- Name four different mixed methods research designs.
- List key characteristics for each of the mixed methods designs.
- Identify the mixed methods design used in a reported study.
- Evaluate the mixed methods design as reported in a research article.

As we write this book, researchers' interest in combining quantitative and qualitative research within single studies is growing across all disciplines. Studies that "mix" these two approaches are called "mixed methods research." There are many mixed methods studies published in the literature. As a reader of research you may find that mixed methods studies are particularly complex to understand. By definition, mixed methods studies include two datasets (one quantitative and one qualitative) and two types of analyses (statistical and thematic). For example, here is how one author described his mixed methods study about the career development of college students:

> The current investigation sought, first, to establish quantitative gender differences in college students' career maturity. Next, interviews were conducted with approximately one third of the participants to provide information about qualitative career development differences. Qualitative analyses allowed for an exploration of the role conflicts and perceived barrier differences between women and men and the impact of such differences in the career development process. (*Luzzo, 1995, p. 320*)

Notice how this example refers to quantitative research (quantitative gender differences in career maturity) *and* qualitative research (qualitative analyses of interviews that explored students' perceptions). The author combined these two datasets to develop a more complete understanding of the gender differences in college students' career maturity. Using more than one data collection and analysis procedure in a study means that the author has a lot of information to explain in a mixed methods report. Learning about mixed methods research designs will give you a framework for understanding published reports that make use of this increasingly popular approach to research.

## What Are the Characteristics of Mixed Methods Research?

As an approach to conducting research, mixed methods research has the following characteristics:

- It is considered a distinctive approach to research that spans the entire process of research, as illustrated in Figure 12.1.
- Researchers use this approach when the combination of both quantitative and qualitative methods provides a better understanding of the research problem and questions than either method by itself.
- It is an approach that has different types of research designs that researchers can use.
- Mixed methods research designs incorporate the collection and analysis of the two types of data at the same time, in a sequence, or some combination.
- The designs also involve mixing—connecting or integrating—both forms of data at some stage in the research.

## Why Do Researchers Choose to Conduct Mixed Methods Studies?

Researchers collecting both quantitative and qualitative data probably sounds like a good idea to you. It just makes sense to include both types of data to have the best of both worlds, so to speak. Collecting both types of data, however, requires special considerations by the researcher compared to conducting a study that is quantitative *or*

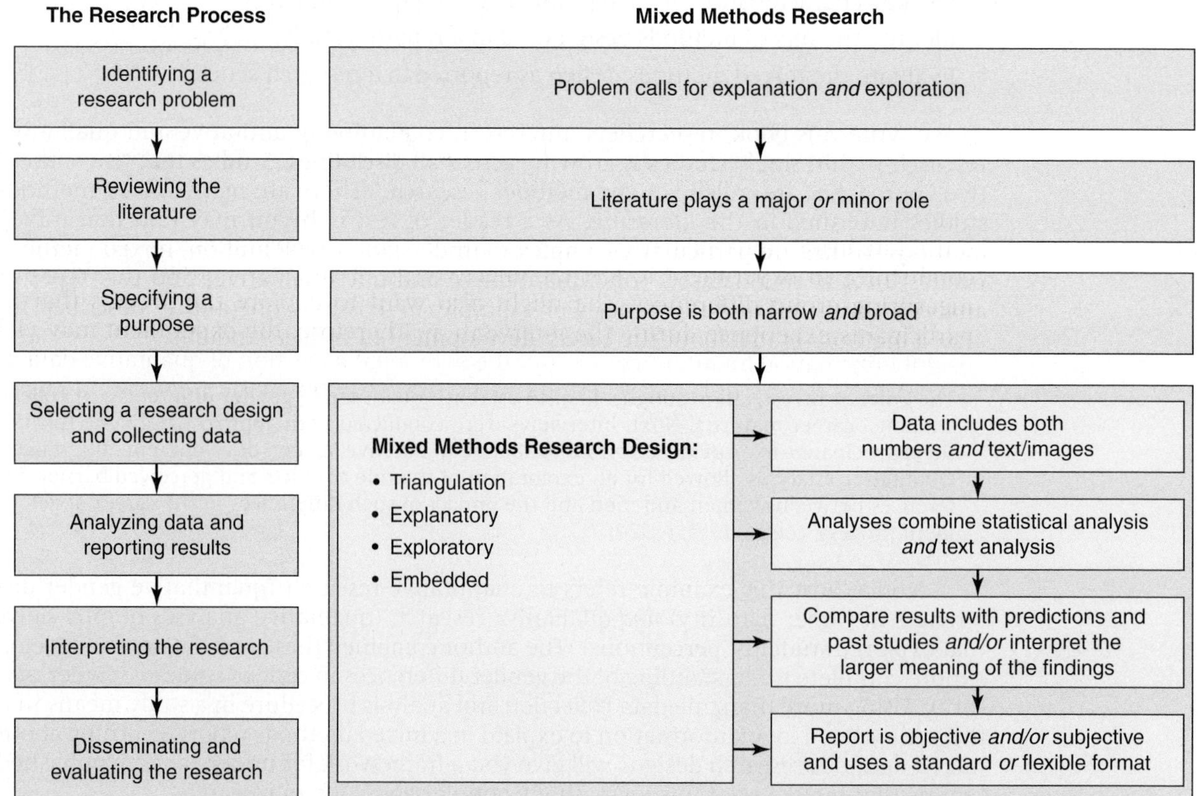


FIGURE 12.1 Mixed Methods Research Designs in the Process of Research

qualitative. In addition, for many research purposes a quantitative *or* qualitative approach works best. Researchers that use mixed methods, therefore, have important reasons for choosing to combine the two approaches. Look for the researcher's reason for mixing methods when you read any mixed methods report.

### Mixed Methods Can Combine the Strengths of Quantitative and Qualitative Data

*Here's a Tip for Applying Research!*

When you want to gather information related to your practice (such as a student's performance), consider whether you can obtain a more complete picture by including both quantitative (e.g., test scores) and qualitative (e.g., documents such as portfolio evidence) information.

There are several reasons that call for a researcher to use a mixed methods design. In general, researchers conduct mixed methods studies when both quantitative and qualitative data, together, provide a better understanding of the research problem than either type by itself. Mixed methods research allows a researcher to build on the separate strengths of both quantitative and qualitative data. Quantitative data, such as scores on instruments, yield specific numbers that can be statistically analyzed, can produce results to assess the frequency and magnitude of trends, and can provide useful information to describe trends about a large number of people. In contrast, qualitative data, such as open-ended interviews that provide actual words of people in the study, offer many different perspectives on the study topic and provide a complex picture of the situation. By combining quantitative and qualitative data, the researcher can develop a more complete picture of social phenomena.

### Mixed Methods Can Build from One Type of Data to the Other

Investigators also conduct mixed methods studies when one type of research (qualitative or quantitative) is not enough on its own to address the research problem. In such cases, the researcher needs to collect a second database to extend, elaborate on, or explain an initial database. For example, a researcher may first explore a topic qualitatively to build themes and then use those themes to develop an instrument. He can then collect quantitative data with that instrument to extend the initial qualitative findings. Another researcher might engage in a mixed methods study when she wants to follow quantitative results with a qualitative exploration to obtain more detailed, specific information that can help explain the results of statistical tests.

### Mixed Methods Can Answer Two Questions

Sometimes researchers use a mixed methods approach when they have two different, but related questions that they want to answer. For example, a researcher might be conducting an experiment to test the effectiveness of an intervention. In addition to measuring group differences, she might also want to explore the process that the participants experience during the intervention. Therefore, the experiment may yield useful information about outcomes, but the additional collection of qualitative data develops a more in-depth understanding of how the experimental intervention actually worked.

## How Do Researchers Choose a Mixed Methods Design?

Once researchers have decided to conduct a mixed methods study, they choose a mixed methods research design to guide how to implement the quantitative and qualitative procedures. A **mixed methods research design** is a set of procedures for collecting, analyzing, and mixing both quantitative and qualitative methods in a study to understand a research problem (Creswell & Plano Clark, 2007). From Figure 12.1, you might imagine that there are numerous ways that researchers can combine quantitative and qualitative procedures in their studies. For example they might collect one type of data (e.g., qualitative) before the other type (e.g., quantitative) or they might collect them both at the same time. Researchers choose a mixed methods research design to give them a plan for how to combine these two approaches in one study. These designs are distinguished by three decisions that the researcher makes about combining the quantitative and qualitative aspects of the study.

- ***The researcher considers the timing for the quantitative and qualitative data collection.*** Timing means that the researcher either collects the two datasets at the same time (concurrent timing) or collects one dataset after the other (sequential timing).
- ***The researcher considers the relative priority of the quantitative and qualitative components for addressing the research questions.*** A mixed methods researcher may place a greater emphasis on one method compared to the other. Therefore, mixed methods studies may have a quantitative priority or a qualitative priority. Some studies use an equal priority where both methods are emphasized equally.
- ***The researcher considers when in the study to mix the two datasets.*** The researcher chooses to compare, relate, link, or synthesize the two datasets. This mixing occurs during data collection, between data collection and data analysis, during data analysis, or in the interpretation of the results of the study. This combination is what makes a mixed methods study *mixed*.

These three considerations are at the heart of the different mixed methods designs. They also provide you with a framework for recognizing the most common ways that researchers combine quantitative and qualitative research within published reports. Before we examine the different designs in details, let's first review how mixed methods research developed as a new way of conducting research.

## How Did Mixed Methods Research Develop?

Mixed methods research did not start becoming widely recognized and accepted until the end of the twentieth century. Since mixed methods research is fairly new, not everyone is familiar with it as a legitimate approach to research. Therefore, it is helpful to know a little about its historical development. From this development, you can also learn important concepts that are central to researcher's reporting of mixed methods studies today.

Early examples of researchers combining quantitative and qualitative data in their studies go back to the 1930s. From the early days, Jick's (1979) study of anxiety and job insecurity during organizational mergers is a classic example of combining quantitative and qualitative data. He collected surveys, semistructured interviews, observations, and archival materials to provide a "rich and comprehensive picture" (p. 606). His work encouraged scholars to think about combining quantitative and qualitative data in rigorous ways because he illustrated the procedure of triangulating quantitative and qualitative data. *Triangulation*, a term drawn from naval military science, is the process where sailors use multiple reference points to locate an object's exact position at sea. Applied to research, it meant that investigators could improve their inquiries by collecting different kinds of data bearing on the same phenomenon. The three points to the triangle are the two sources of the data (quantitative and qualitative in mixed methods research) and the phenomenon under study. This process could improve inquiries by using the strengths of one type of method to offset the weaknesses of the other, resulting in a better understanding. For example, in a study of middle school principal leadership, qualitative observations can provide the context in which this leadership is enacted and help clarify quantitative statistical relationships and numeric findings. To triangulate or converge quantitative and qualitative data in a single study continues to be an attractive approach to mixed methods research today.

As more researchers began combining the two approaches, others expressed concern with this new approach. Recall that different philosophies serve as the foundations for quantitative and qualitative research (as we introduced in Chapter 9). Quantitative research is based on objective stances to knowledge where researchers can measure variables and establish cause and effect. In contrast, qualitative research is based on

**FIGURE 12.2 A Notation System for Mixed Methods Studies**

*Source:* Adapted from Morse (1991).

**Sample Notations:**

| | |
|---|---|
| Study #1: | QUAL + QUAN |
| Study #2: | QUAN → qual |

**Notation Used:**

- + indicates the simultaneous or concurrent collection of quantitative and qualitative data.
- → indicates the sequential collection of quantitative and qualitative data.
- Uppercase letters indicate a priority or increased weight for the quantitative (QUAN) and/or qualitative (QUAL) data.
- Lowercase letters indicate a lower priority or weight for either the quantitative (quan) or qualitative (qual) data.

subjective stances to knowledge where each participant experiences his/her own reality and researchers seek to describe these multiple perspectives. Many individuals felt that quantitative and qualitative research cannot be mixed because it is not possible to mix the philosophies behind them. In the 1980s and 1990s, great debates ensued at academic conferences and in professional writings about the legitimacy of conducting mixed methods research.

Despite the debates, mixed methods research continued to evolve. Researchers adopted other perspectives that are compatible with mixing methods, such as using two philosophies in one study (Greene & Caracelli, 1997) or using a philosophy of pragmatism that emphasizes developing knowledge that works for the situation at hand (Tashakkori & Teddlie, 1998). In addition, scholars devoted increased attention to describing the reasons that researchers should use mixed methods and the procedures useful in mixed methods designs. For example, in addition to triangulation, researchers could collect quantitative and qualitative data separately in two phases so that data from one source could enhance, elaborate, or complement data from the other source (Greene, Caracelli, & Graham, 1989).

One important advance was the development of a notation system to help people write about and think about mixed methods designs. A notation system designed by Morse (1991) became central to scholars thinking about different procedures for mixing methods. This system, shown in Figure 12.2, is a way for researchers to portray the procedures in mixed methods designs. This useful system appears in many reports of mixed methods studies even today. Note that a researcher can use shorthand labels for quantitative (quan) and qualitative (qual) to simplify the terms. Figure 12.2 also portrays two different example procedures. As shown in Study #1, a researcher emphasizes both quantitative and qualitative data and integrates the two datasets in the study. In Study #2, the investigator emphasizes quantitative data in the first phase of a study, followed by a lesser emphasis on qualitative data in the second phase of the study. Later in this chapter we consider names for these designs.

Today the discussion has turned to viewing mixed methods research as a separate approach to research. For many scholars, mixed methods research now stands along side quantitative and qualitative as a third approach to conducting research. Advocates for mixed methods research have written entire chapters and books on its use in the social and health sciences (Creswell, 2003; Creswell & Plano Clark, 2007; Greene, 2007; Tashakkori & Teddlie, 2003). In addition, refinements continue in understanding important issues, such as the process of integrating quantitative and qualitative data analysis. Several authors have developed classifications of the common types of mixed methods designs. From this current picture, we focus our attention on four designs that researchers commonly use when they collect both quantitative and qualitative data. These designs are summarized in Figure 12.3 and discussed in the following sections. They include:

- triangulation mixed methods,
- explanatory mixed methods,
- exploratory mixed methods, and
- embedded mixed methods.

*Here's a Tip for Applying Research!*

Note that we cited recent writers when discussing the history of mixed methods research. Turn to these specialized resources if you want to learn more about this design.

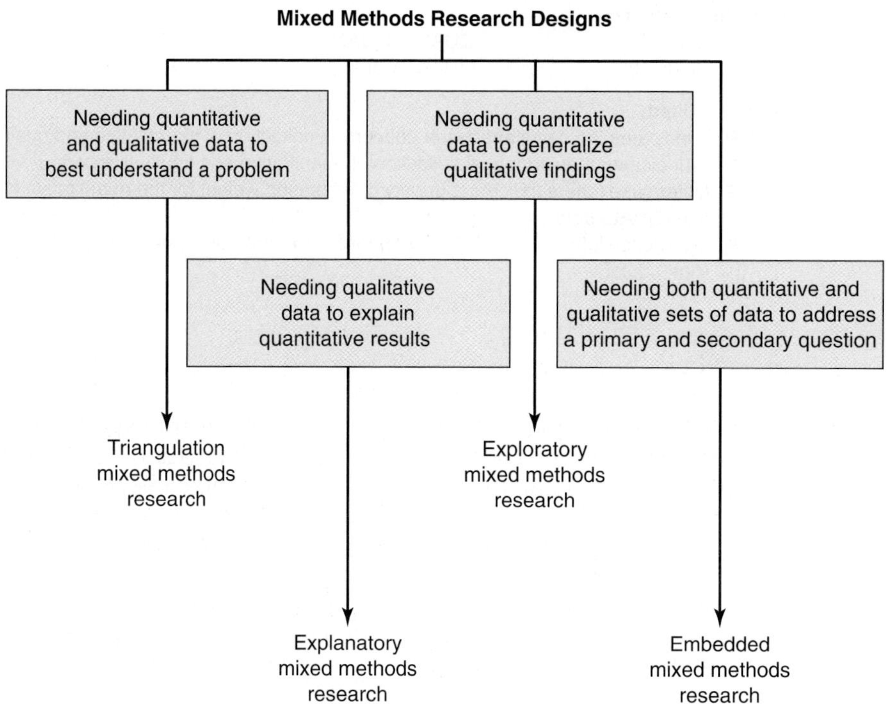


FIGURE 12.3 Types of Mixed Methods Research Designs and Their Use

## What Is the Triangulation Mixed Methods Design?

From the historical sketch, you have already gained a familiarity with the triangulation design. The **triangulation mixed methods design** is a set of procedures that researchers use to simultaneously collect both quantitative and qualitative data, analyze both datasets separately, compare the results from the analysis of both datasets, and make an interpretation as to whether the results support or contradict each other. You can see the analogy of the triangle in Figure 12.4 where the two different types of research "point to" a better understanding of the phenomenon (the interpretation). A basic rationale for this design is that each data-collection form supplies strengths to offset the weaknesses of the other form. For example, quantitative scores on an instrument from many individuals provide strengths to offset the weaknesses of qualitative documents from a few people. Alternatively, qualitative, in-depth observations of a few people offer strengths to quantitative data that does not adequately provide detailed information about the context in which individuals provide information (e.g., the setting).

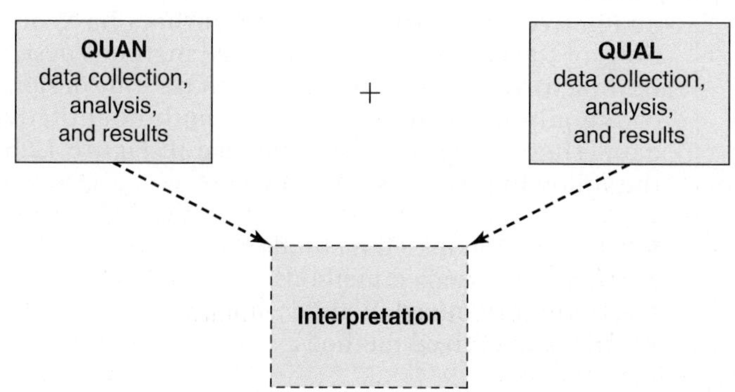


FIGURE 12.4 The Triangulation Mixed Methods Design

## The Triangulation Design Is Used to Compare Quantitative and Qualitative Results

The triangulation design enables a researcher to gather information that uses the best features of both quantitative and qualitative data collection. Researchers choose this design to combine the advantages of each form of data; that is, quantitative data provide for generalizability, whereas qualitative data offer information about the context or setting. It is useful when a researcher wants to have qualitative results that illustrate the meaning or context of quantitative statistical results. This design is also a good choice for researchers who want to establish results that have been corroborated with both quantitative and qualitative information. By comparing quantitative and qualitative results, this design is useful for discovering inconsistencies in the results when the quantitative and qualitative information do not agree. For example, results from a quantitative survey may indicate low community support for a new school program for teenage mothers, but qualitative focus group interviews might show that individuals are highly supportive of the new program. Some researchers view such a disagreement as troubling. Others, however, see it as an ideal opportunity to learn even more about the phenomenon by examining why the inconsistent results emerged. For example, further examination would show that the desperate attitudes about the program for teenage mothers result from the community knowing little about the program specifics.

## Key Characteristics of the Triangulation Design

Researchers use different terms to signal the use of a triangulation mixed methods design. In addition to *triangulation*, look for *concurrent* or *parallel*. These terms indicate that the researcher collected the quantitative and qualitative data at the same time, or with procedures that are parallel to each other. In addition to these terms, you can recognize a triangulation mixed methods design by identifying the following characteristics in a written report:

- ***The researcher needs both quantitative and qualitative approaches to understand the problem.*** The researcher wants to provide a complete picture of the phenomenon being studied. Both methods are needed in order to describe generalizations and trends along with participant perspectives.
- ***The researcher collects the quantitative and qualitative data concurrently during the study.*** The researcher collects both types of data during the same phase of the research process, often at the same time. For example, qualitative documents about what students learn in preschool are reviewed at the same time that the researcher collects quantitative observations on student behavior using a checklist. This concurrent timing is indicated with a "+" in Figure 12.4.
- ***The researcher gives equal priority to both quantitative and qualitative data.*** The researcher values both quantitative and qualitative data and sees them as approximately equal sources of information in the study. For example, interview data are as important as the scores gathered on an instrument. This equal priority is indicated by the uppercase "QUAN" and "QUAL" designations in Figure 12.4.
- ***The researcher compares the results from the quantitative and qualitative analyses to determine whether the two databases yield similar results.*** The researcher analyzes the two data sets separately (i.e., in parallel) and then directly compares the results. For instance, qualitative themes identified during interviews are compared to the statistical results obtained from responses to a survey about the same ideas as the themes.

## An Example of the Triangulation Design

In a triangulation mixed methods study, Russek and Weinberg (1993) collected quantitative and qualitative data at the same time to understand the implementation of technology in an elementary school. They examined how 16 elementary school teachers implemented two sets of supplementary mathematics lessons, one utilizing the calculator and one utilizing the computer. To study this process, they conducted qualitative interviews with teachers and administrators, made informal classroom observations, examined school documents, and obtained teacher responses to open-ended questions on questionnaires. Quantitatively, they gathered classroom observation checklists and lesson and workshop evaluation forms, and collected two self-reported measures of teacher feelings, attitudes, and concerns (i.e., the self-evaluation questionnaire and the stages of concern questionnaire). They compared results from teacher questionnaires with interview themes about using both the calculator and computers in the classroom. Finding inconsistencies in the results, they attributed this difference to the teachers' reluctance to put on paper what they revealed freely in their oral remarks. They also felt that the questionnaire was less valid because the teachers might have felt that the questionnaires would become part of their permanent personnel record.

### What Do You Think?

Suppose you are reading a collection of research articles related to the problem of alcohol abuse by adolescents. How might a triangulation mixed methods design be used to study this topic? What characteristics would you expect to find in this study?

### Check Your Understanding

A researcher might use a triangulation design to provide a complete picture of adolescents' reasons for using alcohol. She might ask high school students to complete a survey indicating whether they have used alcohol and if so, the reasons for the use. During the same semester, the researcher could also conduct focus group interviews with small groups of high school students to learn about their perceptions of adolescents' alcohol use. As the researcher analyzes the results, she will consider both sets of data as equally important for helping her understand adolescents' reasons. She will also compare the trends obtained through the surveys with the themes that emerged from the interviews to see whether they confirm each other.

How might a mixed methods triangulation design be used for a topic of interest to you?

## What Is the Explanatory Mixed Methods Design?

*Here's a Tip for Reading Research!*

When reading a mixed methods report, look for a diagram of the procedures to help you understand the flow of activities in the mixed methods study. If such a visual is not present, you may want to sketch out the sequence of activities using the figures in this chapter as models.

Instead of collecting data at the same time, a mixed methods researcher might collect some quantitative information first and then collect qualitative information in a second phase. This design, shown in Figure 12.5, is an explanatory mixed methods design. An **explanatory mixed methods design** consists of first collecting and analyzing quantitative data and then collecting qualitative data to help explain or elaborate on the quantitative results. The rationale for this approach is that the quantitative data and results provide a general picture of the research problem, but further information, specifically through qualitative data collection, is needed to refine, extend, or explain the general picture. For example, quantitative survey results may describe trends in parental involvement in school athletics, but not explain why certain parents are not involved. Qualitative interviews collected with non-involved parents can then help the researcher explain the quantitative trends.

FIGURE 12.5 The Explanatory Mixed Methods Design

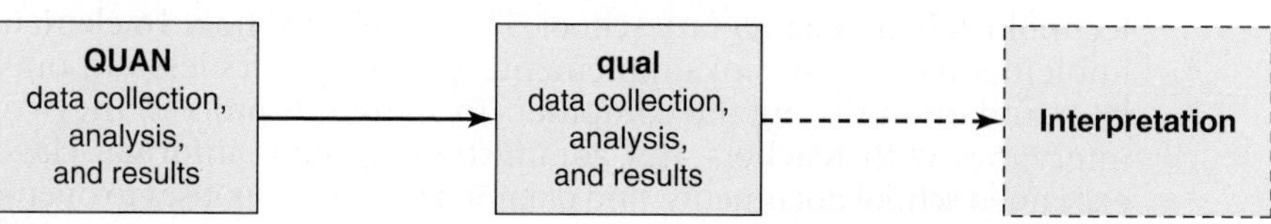

## The Explanatory Design Is Used to Explain Quantitative Results with Qualitative Data

The explanatory design captures the best of both quantitative and qualitative data—to obtain quantitative results from a population in the first phase, and then refine or elaborate these findings through an in-depth qualitative exploration in the second phase. Researchers choose to use this design when they have a research problem that calls for explanation, but the quantitative dataset by itself is not adequate. This design is particularly useful when researchers obtain unexpected quantitative results because they can collect a second set of qualitative data to help explain why the results occurred. This design also works well when the researcher needs to collect quantitative information first to identify the best participants to include for the qualitative data collection. For example, a researcher could use the quantitative data to identify individuals who have high achievement to participate in qualitative interviews about the perceptions of high achievers. An advantage of this design is that it has two clearly identified quantitative and qualitative phases (see Figure 12.5). Researchers often present these studies in two sections, with each phase clearly identified with headings in the report. This also makes it easier for you to understand the reports using this design!

## Key Characteristics of the Explanatory Design

You can identify studies that report an explanatory design with the terms *explanatory*, *sequential*, or *two-phase* and checking to see if the researcher collected the quantitative data first. As you read an explanatory mixed methods study, expect the following characteristics:

- ***The researcher needs a second qualitative phase to explain the initial quantitative results.*** The researcher wants to provide a complete explanation of the research problem and questions, but the quantitative results are not enough. A second, qualitative phase is needed so that the researcher can explain or elaborate on the initial quantitative results.
- ***The researcher collects the two datasets in a sequence, with the quantitative data collected first.*** The researcher begins the report by describing the quantitative data collection, analysis, and results. Generally the secondary qualitative data collection follows after the researcher has analyzed the quantitative data and found the quantitative results. This sequential timing is indicated with an "→" in Figure 12.5.
- ***The researcher usually places a priority on the quantitative data.*** In many explanatory mixed methods studies, the author uses a quantitative emphasis. The author indicates this emphasis by discussing the quantitative phase first, having it represent a major aspect of the data collection, and having an overall goal of explanation. The second phase of the research study is then a small qualitative component. The "QUAN" and "qual" shorthand in Figure 12.5 indicates this unequal priority.
- ***The researcher uses the qualitative data to refine the results from the quantitative data.*** The researcher connects the qualitative data collection to the initial quantitative results. The qualitative data helps the researcher refine the quantitative results by exploring a few typical cases, probing a key result in more detail, or following up with outlier or extreme cases. In this way the two phases are connected to each other because the researcher collects the qualitative data to follow up on the quantitative results.

## An Example of the Explanatory Design

A two-phase project by Ivankova and Stick (2007) is a good example of an explanatory design. Their research examined the persistence of students enrolled in an educational leadership doctoral program that was delivered using online technology. They described their purpose as:

> . . . to identify factors contributing to students' persistence in the [program] by obtaining quantitative results from a survey of 278 current and former students and then following up with four purposefully selected individuals to explore those results in more depth through a qualitative case analysis. (p. 3)

The authors began their study with a quantitative phase. They collected and analyzed survey data to determine the factors (e.g., self-motivation and faculty) that predicted students' persistence in the program. Once these results were obtained, they used the quantitative data to select one typical individual (in terms of the quantitative data) from each of four groups (students beginning, matriculated, graduated, or withdrawn from the program). The authors felt that these individuals could best provide detailed information about different perspectives of each group in a secondary qualitative phase. They then collected qualitative information about each individual, including interview data, program records, and documents such as coursework. The qualitative descriptions resulting from the four cases helped to explain the quantitative survey results. For example, the quantitative results pointed to student attitudes about the high quality of the program and the qualitative results helped to explain how this quality was experienced.

### What Do You Think?

Suppose you are reading a collection of research articles related to the problem of alcohol abuse by adolescents. How might an explanatory mixed methods design be used to study this topic? What characteristics would you expect to find in this study?

### Check Your Understanding

A researcher might use an explanatory mixed methods design to provide a better explanation of why adolescents first start to drink alcohol. The researcher asks high school students to complete an instrument indicating at what age and in what circumstances they had their first alcoholic drink. He could then analyze the quantitative data to test a hypothesis that boys and girls who start drinking at a young age are more likely to do so at home. The quantitative results may include a surprising finding, such as there is a difference in the circumstances of first drinks for boys compared to girls. The researcher then decides to collect a qualitative data set to learn girls' stories of having their first alcoholic drinks. The researcher uses this qualitative data to help explain the quantitative results.

How could a mixed methods explanatory design be used to study a topic of interest to you?

## What Is the Exploratory Mixed Methods Design?

Rather than first collecting or analyzing quantitative data as is done in the explanatory design, the mixed methods researcher can begin a two-phase study with qualitative data. As illustrated in Figure 12.6, an **exploratory mixed methods design** consists of first collecting and analyzing qualitative data to explore a topic and then collecting quantitative data to help extend or generalize the qualitative results. The rationale for this design is that the qualitative data and results provide an exploration and description of the research problem, but then a quantitative data collection is needed to expand on, generalize, or test this description with a larger sample. A common application of this design is to explore a phenomenon, identify themes, develop an instrument based on the thematic findings, and subsequently administer the instrument to many people to see if the themes generalize to the larger group.

**FIGURE 12.6 The Exploratory Mixed Methods Design**

## The Exploratory Design Is Used to Generalize Qualitative Results with Quantitative Data

The exploratory design is appropriate when a researcher has a research problem that requires an exploration, but also calls for quantitative results that can go beyond or expand on the initial qualitative findings. One advantage of this approach is that it allows the researcher to identify measures actually grounded in the data obtained from study participants. Therefore, this design is particularly useful when existing instruments, variables, and measures may not be known or available for the population under study. The researcher can initially explore views by listening to participants rather than approach a topic with a predetermined set of variables. The researcher may also develop a model by collecting and analyzing qualitative data from a few individuals. This model can then be quantitatively tested in a secondary quantitative phase. Like the explanatory mixed methods design, researchers also choose the exploratory mixed methods design because the two phases makes this design simpler to implement and report than the triangulation design.

## Key Characteristics of the Exploratory Design

You can identify studies that report an exploratory mixed methods design with the terms *exploratory, instrument development model, sequential,* or *two-phase,* and checking to see if the researcher first implemented a qualitative phase. As you read an exploratory mixed methods study, identify the following characteristics:

- ***The researcher needs a second quantitative phase to build on the initial qualitative results.*** The researcher wants to provide a detailed exploration of the research problem and questions, but qualitative results are not enough. A second, quantitative phase is needed so that the researcher can expand on or generalize the initial qualitative results.
- ***The researcher collects the two datasets in a sequence, with the qualitative data collection first.*** The researcher presents the study in two phases. The first phase involves qualitative data collection (e.g., interviews, observations) with a small number of individuals. This phase is followed by quantitative data collection (e.g., a survey) with a large, randomly selected number of participants in a second phase. The arrow (→) in Figure 12.6 indicates this sequential timing.
- ***The researcher usually emphasizes the qualitative data more than the quantitative data.*** In many exploratory mixed methods studies, the author uses a qualitative priority. This emphasis occurs through presenting the overarching research question as an open-ended question or discussing the qualitative results in more detail than the quantitative results. This unequal priority is indicated by the "QUAL" and "quan" designations in Figure 12.6.
- ***The researcher plans on the quantitative data to build on or expand the initial qualitative findings.*** The intent of the researcher is to use quantitative results to extend the qualitative findings. The initial qualitative exploration leads to generalizable trends through the second quantitative phase. In this way the quantitative data build on and connect to the qualitative results.

## An Example of the Exploratory Design

In an exploratory mixed methods study, Milton, Watkins, Studdard, and Burch (2003) used qualitative data to develop an instrument, which they used to gather quantitative data. They wanted to understand changes in the size of adult education graduate programs. Little previous work had examined this problem, so they needed to begin their study by exploring the topic before they could attempt to measure it. The authors wrote:

> First, qualitative analysis of interview data was used to identify and define factors related to recent changes in programs and to generate survey items. Survey methodology was then used to measure faculty and administrators' perceptions of these factors' influence on changes in the size of graduate programs. (*p. 27*)

The qualitative first phase of the study consisted of interviews with 11 faculty and administrators representing a variety of adult education programs. From this data, the researchers identified three broad categories (e.g., program integration, responsiveness to change, and leadership) that relate to changes in program size. The researchers developed the qualitative categories into a questionnaire and pilot-tested the new instrument. In the second phase of the study, they then selected a representative sample and gathered self-reported survey data from faculty. They analyzed the data statistically to determine which factors predicted changes in the size of programs. They concluded by discussing what they learned from the results and offering suggestions of how program faculty might work to help their own programs thrive.

### What Do You Think?

Suppose you are reading a collection of research articles related to the problem of alcohol abuse by adolescents. How might an exploratory mixed methods design be used to study this topic? What characteristics would you expect to find in this study?

### Check Your Understanding

A researcher might use an exploratory mixed methods design to develop and test a model of how parents come to seek help for their adolescent children's drinking problems. The researcher starts by interviewing a few parents across the county who have enrolled their children in a local treatment program. He analyzes the qualitative data to develop a model of the process parents undergo to seek help for their child. He next wants to expand these results by seeing if the model generalizes to many parents' experiences. He develops a questionnaire that includes items about each step identified in the model and administers it to a large number of parents in the region who have enrolled their children in similar programs. From the two sets of results, he can describe the steps and also discuss the trends for how often each step occurs across a large number of parents.

In what way could a mixed methods exploratory design be used to study a topic of interest to you?

## What Is the Embedded Mixed Methods Design?

A fourth form of mixed methods design is similar to the previous designs, with some important exceptions. The **embedded mixed methods design** is a set of procedures for collecting one type of data (quantitative or qualitative) within a larger study that is guided by the other method (qualitative or quantitative), having the secondary dataset address a different question than the primary dataset, and using the secondary dataset to augment the implementation and/or interpretation of the primary method. The basic rationale for this design is that a researcher needs to enhance a traditional quantitative or

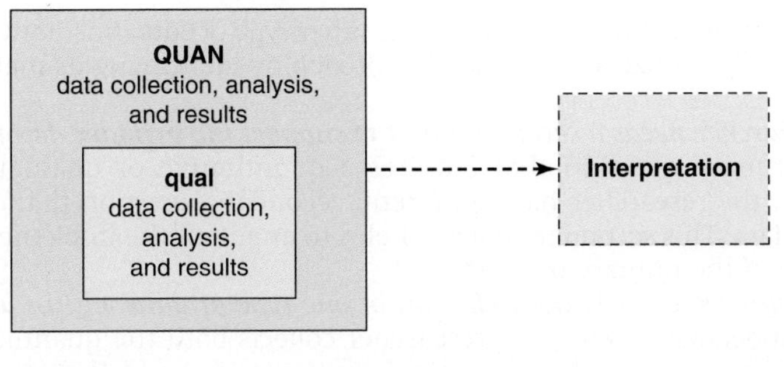


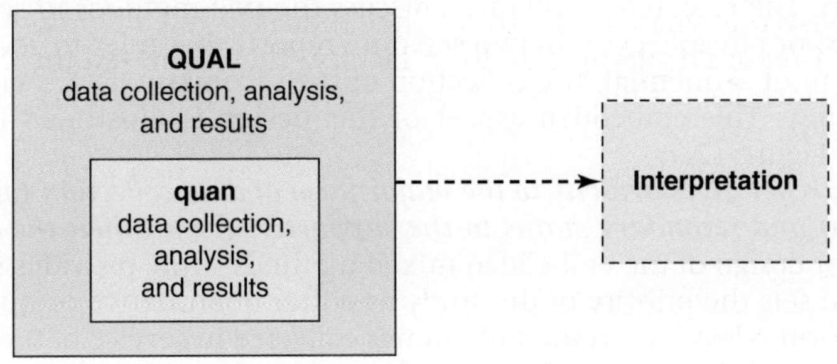


FIGURE 12.7 Two Examples of the Embedded Mixed Methods Design

qualitative design (such as those we learned in Chapters 6 and 9) by asking a secondary question that calls for a different type of data embedded within the other design. You can see the embedded nature of this design in Figure 12.7. For example, during a quantitative experiment, the investigator decides to collect qualitative data at the same time as the intervention to examine how participants in the treatment condition are experiencing the intervention. The primary aim of the study, in this case, is to examine the impact of the experimental treatment on the outcome. The addition of qualitative data enables the researcher to *also* explore how participants are experiencing the process of the experiment. As another approach a researcher could embed quantitative data into a qualitative design. For example, a researcher conducting a qualitative case study gathers secondary quantitative data to help explain attitudes in a community that inform the context of the case.

## The Embedded Design Is Used to Enhance a Larger Study with a Secondary Dataset

This design enables a researcher to use different methods to address different, but related, questions. For example, quantitative data are more effective for recording outcomes of an experiment and qualitative data are more effective for exploring how individuals are experiencing the process of the intervention. This design also works well for researchers who are more experienced and comfortable with specific quantitative or qualitative designs (e.g., quantitative experimental or correlational designs or qualitative case study or narrative research designs). These researchers can place their focus on the primary method, but still enhance their understanding of the overall research problem by examining a secondary question within the larger study.

## Key Characteristics of the Embedded Design

You can identify studies that report an embedded mixed methods design with the terms *embedded* or *nested*. Other key terminology that you may notice includes the terms *primary* and *secondary* to indicate the relative status of the two datasets. Authors name a specific quantitative or qualitative design (e.g., an experiment or ethnography) while also mentioning the collection of the other type of data (qualitative or quantitative). You will also recognize an embedded approach by identifying its main characteristics:

- ***The researcher needs a second dataset to support the primary design.*** The researcher has a primary question that requires a quantitative or qualitative approach. In addition, the researcher has a different, secondary question that calls for the other type of data. This secondary dataset helps to augment the implementation or understanding of the primary method.
- ***The researcher embeds the collection of one type of data within a larger design.*** In many embedded designs, the researcher collects both the quantitative and qualitative data at roughly the same time. In some embedded designs, however, the researcher may collect the secondary form of data before or after the primary data collection. The researcher will often discuss the two methods in separate sections of the report or possibly even in two separate reports that refer to each other. Whether concurrent or sequential, the collection of the secondary data is embedded within a larger study. This embedded aspect of this design is illustrated by the concentric boxes in Figure 12.7.
- ***The researcher gives priority to the major form of data collection (often the quantitative data) and secondary status to the supportive form (often the qualitative data).*** The larger design of the embedded mixed methods study provides the overall framework and sets the priority of the study as either quantitative or qualitative. The secondary form is less important and often is collected in service of the primary method. The priority of the primary form is indicated by the "QUAN" and "QUAL" designations in Figure 12.7.
- ***The researcher uses the secondary form of data to augment or provide additional sources of information not provided by the primary source of data.*** The augmentation that arises from the second data set occurs by addressing a different question than asked for the primary form of data. For example, the collection of qualitative data during an experiment may be to understand the *process* the participants are going through, whereas the quantitative data assesses the *impact* of the treatment on the outcomes.

## An Example of the Embedded Design

Harrison's (2007) study of an undergraduate mentoring program in teacher education illustrates the embedded mixed methods design. Using quantitative correlational analysis, she followed 18 undergraduates in a leadership program over two years as they learned how to forge mentor-mentee relationships in an undergraduate teacher education program. Harrison collected quantitative data on an instrument, the Working Alliance Inventory (WAI), during six administrations over a 2-year period. This quantitative information represented the major source of information during her study, and her correlation model suggested that a number of factors (e.g., number of times the mentors–mentees met) influence the building of positive relationships. She also collected limited qualitative data in the form of three focus group interviews with the students. She plotted the longitudinal trends in relationship building using the WAI scores over time, and then used the secondary data, the focus group information, to help her understand why some mentor–mentees forged closer relationships, plateaued, or formed more distant relationships over time. Her study is a good example of an embedded design with a major quantitative correlational component and a smaller, supportive qualitative focus group component.

### What Do You Think?

Suppose you are reading a collection of research articles related to the problem of alcohol abuse by adolescents. How might an embedded mixed methods design be used to study this topic? What characteristics would you expect to find in this study?

### Check Your Understanding

A researcher might use an embedded mixed methods design to test the effectiveness of a new alcohol treatment program aimed at teaching adolescents alternative strategies for dealing with stress. The researcher designs a true experiment where adolescents who have been cited for alcohol possession are randomly assigned to either the new program or to the usual punishment of community service. She has participants in both groups complete a quantitative measure about their attitudes about and recent experiences with alcohol consumption before the treatment and then six months later to look for differences between the groups. At the same time of this quantitative experiment, the researcher also gathers qualitative interview data with individuals completing the new program to understand how they are experiencing the program materials. Therefore, the quantitative dataset is of primary importance to test the effectiveness of the program, and the qualitative dataset is secondary information about the program's process.

How might an embedded design be used to study a topic of interest to you?

## How Do You Determine if a Study Is Mixed Methods?

You are now familiar with four mixed methods designs that researchers use to combine quantitative and qualitative data within one study. At this point it is helpful to reflect on useful strategies for identifying mixed methods designs reported in the published literature. This means first determining that a report is a mixed methods study. Since this approach to research is relatively new, it is not always easy to determine if a study used mixed methods. One strategy you can use is to ask the following questions to help identify a study as mixed methods research:

1. ***Is there evidence in the title?*** Read the report's title to determine if it includes words such as *quantitative and qualitative, mixed methods,* or other related terms to signify the collection of both quantitative and qualitative data. Related terms might be *integrated, combined, triangulation, multimethod, mixed model,* or *mixed methodology.*

2. ***Is there evidence in the data collection procedures?*** Examine the method section and determine if the authors discuss collecting two types of data. Mixed methods studies will include forms of quantitative data (i.e., numbers) and qualitative data (i.e., words or images) as part of the data collection. Strong mixed methods studies will also explicitly discuss how the two datasets are mixed.

3. ***Is there evidence in the purpose statement or the research questions?*** Examine the abstract or the introduction of the study to identify the purpose or research questions. Mixed methods studies should include statements that indicate that the researcher intends to collect both quantitative and qualitative data during the study.

For practice identifying a mixed methods study in the literature, go to the *Activities and Applications* section under the topic "Mixed Methods Research" in MyEducationalResearchLab, located at www.myeducationlab.com. Complete the exercise "Identifying Mixed Methods Research."

## How Do You Identify a Mixed Methods Design in a Study?

If the answers to the above questions are yes, then you have identified the study as mixed methods. To help understand the information that is presented in the report, determine the type of mixed methods design the author is using. Using the following four questions, you can identify most mixed methods designs commonly used in research reports.

For practice identifying the type of mixed methods design used in a study, go to the *Building Research Skills* section under the topic "Mixed Methods Research" in MyEducationalResearchLab, located at www.myeducationlab.com. Complete the exercise "Evaluating a Mixed Methods Study" and use the provided feedback to further develop your skills for reading research articles.

**1.** ***What is the timing of collecting the quantitative and qualitative data?*** Determine whether the qualitative data is collected before or after the quantitative data or if they are collected concurrently.

**2.** ***What priority or weight does the researcher give to the quantitative and qualitative data collection?*** Determine if the quantitative and qualitative data appear to be treated equally in the report or if the authors give more emphasis to one form of data.

**3.** ***Why does the researcher combine the two types of data?*** The researcher may need both forms of data to best understand a complex problem, to use one type of data to expand on the other, or to augment a design based on the other type. To understand a mixed methods study, you need to identify why the author needed both types of data.

**4.** ***How does the researcher mix the data?*** The two forms of data might be analyzed separately and then combined or contrasted, connected from one set of results to a second type of data collection, or embedded one within the other. A mixed methods study is not mixed unless the author combines the two datasets in some meaningful way.

## What Do You Think?

Consider the following excerpts from three published studies. What design do you think each of the authors used? What evidence do you have from the passages? How can you represent it using the mixed methods notation system in Figure 12.2?

**(a)** "The study included two stages: first a quantitative stage, consisting or self-administered questionnaires addressing each of the hypotheses; and second, a qualitative stage, including interviews focused on a more limited set of issues." (*Vittersø, Akselsen, Evjemo, Julsrud, Yttri, & Bergvik, 2003, p. 207*)

**(b)** "Locating our project within the mixed methods framework provided by Hanson et al., our longitudinal data were collected concurrently throughout the project; equal weight was given to the quantitative and qualitative data; and data were analyzed separately, compared, and contrasted." (*Bikos et al., 2007, p. 30*)

**(c)** "Findings from a qualitative analysis provided complex and rich information about young adults' perceptions of mattering to their current romantic partners. Responses were used to develop a scale that was administered in Study 2 to a sample ($N = 99$) of young adults in romantic relationships." (*Mak & Marshall, 2004, p. 469*)

### Check Your Understanding

Each of the study excerpts mentions the collection of quantitative and qualitative data. Therefore, we can conclude that all three represent mixed methods studies. Excerpt (a) is from a study that used an explanatory mixed methods design. We know this because the authors discuss using two stages, with the quantitative stage first followed by a qualitative stage. This study can be represented as: QUAN → qual. Excerpt (b) comes from a study that used a triangulation mixed methods design. We know this because the authors collected the two datasets concurrently, gave them equal priority, and analyzed them separately before comparing them. This study can be represented as: QUAN + QUAL. Excerpt (c) comes from a study that used an exploratory mixed methods design. We know this because the authors first collected and analyzed a set of qualitative data. They then used the qualitative results to develop a scale, which was subsequently used to collect quantitative data in a second phase. This study can be represented as: QUAL → quan.

## How Do You Evaluate a Study's Mixed Methods Design?

Like other research approaches, mixed methods studies are based on specific designs that address certain types of research problems and have key characteristics that differentiate them from other designs. With the information you have learned in this chapter, you now have the skills needed to identify the design used in a mixed methods study and evaluate the author's use of that design. Evaluating a mixed methods study requires you to assess a study in different ways. First, since the study includes both quantitative and qualitative data, you should assess the quantitative procedures using criteria presented in Chapters 6–8 and the qualitative procedures using criteria presented in Chapters 9–11. In addition to evaluating the two parts, you also need to consider how well the author implemented and reported the major mixed methods design characteristics. The criteria provided in Figure 12.8 are useful for evaluating a mixed methods design as you read a study's report. These criteria focus on the procedures needed to successfully mix the quantitative and qualitative components within a study.

Use the following criteria to evaluate the quality of a mixed methods study as specified within a research report. For each evaluation item, indicate the following ratings:

- \+ You rate the item as "high quality" for the study.
- ✓ You rate the item as "ok quality" for the study.
- – You rate the item as "low quality" for the study.

In addition to your rating, make notes about each element when you apply these criteria to an actual published study.

| **In a high-quality mixed methods research report, the author . . .** | Application to a Published Study | |
|---|---|---|
| | Your Rating | Your Notes |
| 1. Describes that mixed methods is the best approach to answer the study's research questions because either quantitative or qualitative is inadequate by itself. | | |
| 2. Incorporates both quantitative and qualitative data collection and analysis. | | |
| 3. Explicitly combines or mixes the two datasets. | | |
| 4. Uses rigorous quantitative and qualitative procedures of data collection and analysis. | | |
| 5. Frames the study within one of the mixed methods research designs. | | |
| 6. Provides a visual diagram of the procedures to clarify the timing, priority, and mixing within the study. | | |
| 7. Signals to the reader that the study is using mixed methods (e.g., in the title, purpose statement, and methods section) to indicate their awareness of this research design. | | |

FIGURE 12.8 Criteria for Evaluating a Mixed Methods Study

## Reviewing What We've Learned

- Recognize that reports of research studies that combine quantitative and qualitative research are becoming more common.
- Identify studies using a mixed methods approach by the collection, analysis, and mixing of both quantitative and qualitative data to best understand a research problem.
- Identify the reason that a researcher uses mixed methods, such as needing to develop a complete picture, needing to build from one method to another, or having two different but related questions.
- Look for the timing of the quantitative and qualitative methods to be either sequential (two phases) or concurrent (one phase).
- Assess whether the study prioritizes the quantitative or the qualitative approach, or if both methods are equally important for addressing the study's purpose.
- Identify how the author mixed the quantitative and qualitative components, such as comparing results, connecting from one set of results to another data collection, or embedding one within a design associated with the other.
- Use a notation system to describe the flow of activities in the mixed methods study.
- Determine the type of mixed methods research design when reading a study, such as triangulation, explanatory, exploratory, or embedded.

## Practicing Your Skills

At this time, read carefully the "mixed methods learning environment study" article starting on page 315 at the end of this chapter. As you read this article, pay close attention to the use of the quantitative and qualitative components throughout the study.

Once you have read the study, assess your knowledge of the content of this chapter by answering the following questions that relate to the mixed methods learning environment study. Use the answers found in the Appendix to evaluate your progress.

1. Give three pieces of evidence that this study is a good example of mixed methods research.
2. Why did the researchers choose to conduct a mixed methods study instead of a quantitative or qualitative study?
3. Identify this study's mixed methods design and indicate this design using the mixed methods notation system.
4. In what way(s) did the authors combine or mix the two datasets?

# The Mixed Methods Learning Environment Study

"Let's examine another published research study to apply what you have learned about reading research articles and to evaluate how researchers use a mixed methods design (by completing the *Practicing Your Skills* questions listed on the previous page.)" A formal reference for this study is:

> Aldridge, J. M., Fraser, B. J., & Huang, T. I. (1999). Investigating classroom environments in Taiwan and Australia with multiple research methods. *Journal of Educational Research, 93*(1), 48–62.

As you read this article, note the marginal annotations that signal the major sections of a research report, the steps of the research process, and the major characteristics of mixed methods research. In addition, use the following walk-through to help you understand how the steps of the research process are described within the four major sections of the report.

## The Introduction Section

- Identifying a research problem (paragraphs 01–03)
- Reviewing the literature (paragraphs 04–09)
- Specifying the purpose (paragraphs 02, 09)

The authors (Aldridge, Fraser, & Huang, 1999) introduce the broad research problem early in the opening paragraphs (01–03). They state that they need to understand cross-national differences in classroom learning environments and the factors that influence a country's learning environment. This understanding is needed to better inform researchers about important variables and about the assumed attitudes within one's cultural setting. The authors note a deficiency in that no studies have compared learning environments between Australia and other Southeast Asia countries. They might have made a stronger argument for the importance of their study by drawing additional evidence from practice (such as the need for national educational policies to be based on an understanding of a culture's learning environment) and stating specific audiences who could benefit from this knowledge (such as principals and policy makers).

This research problem passage indicates a strong quantitative focus on the need to compare countries. The authors mention quantitative topics such as the importance of variables (paragraph 01), an investigation of factors (paragraph 02), and the desire to validate a questionnaire (paragraph 03) as part of their study. Because the problem is stated as an examination of variables and the differences between two countries, the authors are foreshadowing a quantitative emphasis (QUAN) for this study. The substantial use of references to the literature in the *Background* section (paragraphs 04–09) is consistent with a strong quantitative orientation to the study.

The purpose statement in paragraph 02 ("The research involved . . . ") continues to emphasize a strong quantitative component to this study: the "comparison" of classroom learning environments. This statement also introduces the concept that both quantitative and qualitative methods will be used, indicating a mixed methods study. In paragraph 09, the authors introduce their reason for mixing methods. We learn that the quantitative data are needed to "replicate previous research" and the qualitative data are needed to "explore" students' perceptions. Therefore, quantitative methods alone are inadequate for this study.

## The Method Section

- Selecting a design and collecting data (paragraphs 10–22)

We learn that the initial quantitative results led to more questions and served as a "springboard for further data collection" involving qualitative methods in paragraph 12.

Consequently, although not identified by name, the authors framed their study by using an explanatory design with an initial quantitative phase followed by a second qualitative phase to explore the results about learning environments in more detail.

The initial quantitative data collection is introduced first in this explanatory design (paragraphs 13–16). It consists of a large sample ($n$ = 1,081 in Australia and $n$ = 1,879 in Taiwan), collection of numeric data, and a focus on instruments (i.e., What is Happening in this Class? and Test of Science Related Attitudes). An anomalous result emerged from the quantitative phase. The Australian students had more positive perceptions of their classroom environments, but the Taiwanese students had more positive attitudes toward their science classes (see paragraph 27). Therefore, the authors conducted a second qualitative phase to explain this anomaly. The authors collected data from students and teachers in four classes in Australia and Taiwan (see paragraphs 18–21). They conducted extensive in-class observations and interviews with students and teachers, yielding text data for analysis.

## The Results Section

- Analyzing the data and reporting results (paragraphs 23–99)

The authors report quantitative results using statistical analyses (paragraphs 17, 23–27). The analysis included descriptive statistics about the two countries (e.g., factor loadings, means, and standard deviations) and inferential statistics that tested for differences between the students in Australia and Taiwan. This section displayed an increasingly detailed analysis from general examination of the instrument (paragraphs 23–25) to trends and specific comparisons.

The qualitative results were reported (paragraphs 20, 28–99) to help explain the performance of the instrument as well as perceptions of learning environments within each country. The authors' main qualitative findings began with in-depth descriptions of a science class in each of the two countries. They then reported five themes identified across the two sets of findings: "Nature of the curriculum," "Pressures experienced by teachers," " Respect for the teacher," "Questioning techniques," and "Educational aims." The authors included multiple perspectives throughout, including both students and teachers from the two countries and the frequent use of quotes to capture the voice of the participants.

## The Conclusion Section

- Interpreting the research (paragraphs 100–107)

The authors interpret the results in the *Discussion* section. Here we find a summary and interpretation of the quantitative results (paragraphs 101–103). Then the interpretation turns to the qualitative results, focusing on the larger meaning of the findings within the overall context of the study (paragraphs 104–107). The authors end by noting the significance of their study and the need for further research on this topic using a mixed methods approach.

# Investigating Classroom Environments in Taiwan and Australia With Multiple Research Methods

**JILL M. ALDRIDGE**
**BARRY J. FRASER**
**Curtin University of Technology, Australia**

**TAI-CHU IRIS HUANG**
**National Kaohsiung Normal University, Taiwan**

ABSTRACT **Multiple research methods from different paradigms were used in this interpretive study to explore the nature of classroom environments in a cross-national study involving Taiwan and Australia. When English and Mandarin versions of a questionnaire assessing student perceptions of 7 dimensions of the classroom learning environment were administered to 50 classes in each country, data analysis supported the reliability and factorial validity of the questionnaire and revealed differences between Taiwanese and Australian classroom environments. The data provided a starting point from which other methods (such as observations, interviews, and narrative stories) were used to gain a more in-depth understanding of the classroom environments in each country. Findings are represented in the form of stories and interpretive commentaries.**

troduction ection

01 Educational research that crosses national boundaries offers much promise for generating new insights for at least two reasons (Fraser, 1996). First, there usually is greater variation in variables of interest (e.g., teaching methods, student attitudes) in a sample drawn from multiple countries than a sample drawn from one country. Second, the taken-for-granted familiar educational practices, beliefs, and attitudes in one country can be exposed and questioned when researchers from two countries collaborate on studies involving teaching and learning in two countries.

dentifying a research roblem

02 Comparative studies of classroom learning environments in Australia and other countries have been limited. To date, there are no studies that compare the classroom learning environments found in Australia with those found in neighboring countries of Southeast Asia. The present research involves six Australian and seven Taiwanese researchers who worked together on a cross-national study of learning environments in Taiwan and Australia. The research involved a comparison of classroom learning environments in Taiwan and Australia, as well as an investigation of socio-cultural factors that influence the learning environment in each country.

Specifying a purpose for the research

03 This study is distinctive because it combined multiple research methods as recommended by Denzin and Lincoln (1994) and Tobin and Fraser (1998). We tried to validate a learning environment questionnaire for use in two countries, to identify differences between Taiwanese and Australian classroom environments, and to identify factors that influence learning environments in different cultures.

Reviewing the literature

## Background

04 The importance of the classroom learning environment has been increasingly recognized over the past 20 years. Considerable progress has been made in the conceptualization, assessment, and investigation of the important but subtle concept of learning environment (Fraser, 1986, 1994, 1998; Fraser & Walberg, 1991; Wubbels & Levy, 1993). In the past, the most common means of measuring the learning environment has been through the use of perceptions; that has led to insights into the learning environment through the eyes of the participants, rather than through the eyes of an external observer. The use of qualitative methods in learning environment research (Tobin, Kahle, & Fraser, 1990) also has provided a more in-depth understanding of learning environments. The combining of quantitative and qualitative methods has been a feature of recent research (Tobin & Fraser, 1998).

05 Most classroom environment research has involved students in Western countries. The field originated in the United States with pioneering work using the Learning Environment Inventory (LEI; Walberg, 1979) and the Classroom Environment Scale (CES; Moos, 1979); that was followed by work in the Netherlands with the Questionnaire on Teacher Interaction (QTI; Wubbels & Levy, 1993) and in Australia with the Individualized Classroom Environment

*Address correspondence to Barry J. Fraser, Science and Mathematics Education Centre, Curtin University of Technology, GPO Box U1987, Perth, 6845, Western Australia.*

Questionnaire (ICEQ; Fraser, 1990). Although those instruments have been used and validated in a number of countries, many of the questionnaires overlap in what they measure; some contain items that might not be pertinent in current classroom settings. In the present study, we used the What is Happening in this Class? (WIHIC) questionnaire to collect data. The questionnaire was developed by Fraser, McRobbie, and Fisher (1996) and combines scales from past questionnaires with contemporary dimensions to bring parsimony to the field of learning environments.

06 Although a recent literature review (Fraser, 1998) shows that the majority of the classroom environment studies involve Western students, a number of important studies have been carried out in non-Western countries. Early studies established the validity of classroom environment instruments that had been translated into the Indian (Walberg, Singh, & Rasher, 1977) and Indonesian (Schibeci, Rideng, & Fraser, 1987) languages, and they replicated associations between student outcomes and classroom environment perceptions. Recently, Asian researchers working in Singapore (Chionh & Fraser, 1998; Goh, Young, & Fraser, 1995; Teh & Fraser, 1994; Wong & Fraser, 1996) and Brunei (Riah & Fraser, 1998) have made important contributions to the field of learning environments.

07 In Singapore, the growing pool of literature that is related to classroom learning environments across different subjects includes computing (Khoo & Fraser, 1998; Teh & Fraser, 1994), geography (Chionh & Fraser, 1998), mathematics (Goh, Young, & Fraser, 1995), and science (Wong & Fraser, 1996; Wong, Young, & Fraser, 1997). Also, a study from Brunei reported how the introduction of new curricula has influenced learning environments in high school chemistry classes (Riah & Fraser, 1998). The questionnaires used in those studies were written in English and validated for use in Singapore. Studies in Singapore (Chionh & Fraser, 1998), Brunei (Riah & Fraser, 1998), and Korea (Kim, Fisher & Fraser, in press) were conducted simultaneously with the present study and, like the present study, used the WIHIC questionnaire to collect data pertaining to the classroom learning environment. The studies in Singapore and Brunei validated an English version of the WIHIC questionnaire, whereas the study in Korea validated a Korean version of the questionnaire. The findings in each study replicate those of past studies, reporting strong associations between the learning environment and student outcomes for almost all scales. Although the studies provide useful information to educators regarding classroom environment dimensions that could be manipulated to improve student outcomes, they do not identify causal factors associated with the classroom environments.

08 In Hong Kong, qualitative methods, in the form of open-ended questions, were used to explore students' perceptions of the learning environment in ninth-grade mathematics classrooms (Wong, 1993, 1996). That study reported that many students identified the teacher as the most crucial element in a positive classroom learning environment. Those teachers kept order and discipline while creating an atmosphere that was not boring or solemn. They interacted with students in ways that could be considered friendly and showed concern for the students. Also in Hong Kong, Cheung (1993) used a multilevel approach to determine the effects of the learning environment on students' learning. The findings of that study provide insights that could help explain why Hong Kong was ranked among the leading countries in physics, chemistry, and biology in the IEA Third International Science Study (Keeves, 1992).

09 The present interpretive study went beyond past research in non-Western countries to involve a multimethod approach that emerged in light of new findings. This study was used not only to replicate previous research but also to explore causal factors associated with students' perceptions of their learning environment. Furthermore, by drawing on a range of paradigms, we extended past research in the field of learning environments by piecing together a more in-depth understanding of socio-cultural influences on the classroom environments created in each country.

Method Section

## Research Method

10 It has been widely accepted that the paradigm used will shape the way in which the researcher perceives the world (Feyerbend, 1978; Kuhn, 1962; Lakatos, 1970). In cross-cultural studies, cultural representations are constructed in terms of the researcher's own culture, thus making method and methodology inseparable (van Maanen, 1988).

11 Comparative studies in education have the luxury of being able to draw their methodology from a range of disciplines including psychology, sociology, philosophy, and anthropology. There is no single scientific method that applies to comparative studies; the choice will invariably depend on the research questions posed (Denzin & Lincoln, 1994). The issue of which paradigm is most appropriate depends largely on the situation and the appropriateness of the measure, although it is widely agreed that multiple methods in comparative research are useful to achieve greater understanding (Keeves & Adams, 1994; Tobin & Fraser, 1998).

12 In the present interpretive study, we drew on multiple research methods that were combined to help examine and compare science classroom learning environments in Taiwan and Australia from different perspectives. Triangulation was used to secure an in-depth understanding of the learning environment and to provide richness to the whole. The idea of *grain sizes* (the use of different-sized samples for different research questions varying in extensiveness and intensiveness) in learning environment research (Fraser, 1999) has been used effectively in studies that combine different research methods (Fraser & Tobin, 1991; Tobin & Fraser, 1998), and it was used to guide the collection of data for this study. Initially, a large-scale quantitative probe (involving the collection of data from 1,081 students in Australia and 1,879 students in Taiwan using the WIHIC ques-

Mixed methods researchers provide reasons for using mixed methods

Selecting a research design and collecting data

Mixed methods researchers consider the timing of the quantitative and qualitative methods

tionnaire and an attitude scale) provided an overview of the learning environments in each country. In the spirit of this interpretive inquiry, the data posed more questions than it answered. A sense of the problem was developed during observations that reshaped the inquiry toward an examination of socio-cultural influences that might affect what was considered to be a desirable learning environment in each country. The data collected using the questionnaires were then used as a springboard for further data collection involving different research methods including interviews with participants, observations, and narrative stories.

Mixed methods researchers use research designs to plan their studies

*Initial Data Collection and Analysis*

13 We used the recently developed WIHIC questionnaire to measure students' perceptions of their classroom environment. The data provided an overview of the learning environment in each country and a starting point from which comparisons could be made. The WIHIC was developed by Fraser, McRobbie, and Fisher (1996) to bring parsimony to the field of learning environments by combining the most salient scales from existing questionnaires with new dimensions of contemporary relevance to assess the following seven dimensions of the classroom environment:

Mixed methods researchers collect quantitative data

1. *Student cohesiveness* (extent to which students know, help, and are supportive of one another)
2. *Teacher support* (extent to which the teacher helps, befriends, trusts, and shows interest in students)
3. *Involvement* (extent to which students have attentive interest, participate in discussions, perform additional work, and enjoy the class)
4. *Investigation* (emphasis on the skills and processes of inquiry and their use in problem solving and investigation)
5. *Task orientation* (extent to which it is important to complete activities planned and to stay on the subject matter)
6. *Cooperation* (extent to which students cooperate rather than compete with one another on learning tasks)
7. *Equity* (extent to which students are treated equally by the teacher)

The Appendix contains the items from the WIHIC that survived the factor and item analysis described later in this article.

14 In addition, we used an eight-item scale to assess students' satisfaction in terms of enjoyment, interest, and how much they anticipated science classes according to a scale from the Test of Science Related Attitudes (TOSRA; Fraser, 1981).

15 The instruments were translated into Chinese by team members based in Taiwan. The next step involved an independent back translation of the Chinese version into English by team members who were not involved in the original translation (Brislin, 1970). Then the Australian researchers checked the back translations and, for some items, that necessitated the modification of the original English version, the Chinese translation, or both.

16 The final 70-item version of the questionnaire, along with the attitude survey, were administered to a sample of 1,081 Grade 8 and 9 general science students from 50 classes in 25 schools in Western Australia and 1,879 Grade 7–9 students from 50 classes in 25 schools in Taiwan. Of the classes sampled in Western Australia, 38 were from within the metropolitan area of the capital city, Perth, and the remaining 12 classes were from rural schools. The sample in Taiwan was selected from three areas—northern Taiwan (Taipei), central Taiwan (Changhua), and southern Taiwan (Kaohsiung). In Taiwan, 25 classes were biology classes and 25 were physics classes; in Australia, all 50 classes were general science classes. The samples from both countries were drawn from coeducational government schools that could be considered typical and representative of science classes in each country.

17 The data collected using the questionnaires were analyzed to provide information regarding the reliability and validity of the questionnaires in each country and to inform researchers of the differences and similarities between students' perceptions in each country.

Mixed methods researchers analyze quantitative data and report results

*Qualitative Data Generation and Analysis*

18 The data from the questionnaires were used not only to provide a parsimonious and economical view of learning environments in each country, but also as a starting point from which qualitative data were collected using classroom observations, interviews with teachers and students, and narrative stories written by the researchers.

19 Observations were carried out in the classes of four teachers in Australia and Taiwan. Teacher selection was based on their willingness to be involved in the study. Narrative stories, in keeping with Denzin and Lincoln's (1994) fifth moment, were used to portray archetypes of science classrooms in each country. Stories were used to represent a way of knowing and thinking (Carter, 1993; Casey, 1995) with the use of the researcher's images, understandings, and interpretations of the learning environments in each country. The stories were used with their interpretations and subsequent commentaries to provide a second layer of representation (Geelan, 1997).

20 At least 3 students from each of the eight classes were interviewed initially on the basis of student responses to selected questionnaire items. Analysis of the interviews raised more in-depth questions related to the learning environment and cultural aspects. Observations were also the source of many student interview questions about various actions that had taken place and student views about the classroom environment. The analysis of each interview raised more questions that were asked in proceeding interviews.

21 The teachers of the eight classes also were interviewed to determine their reasons for various actions and to learn whether the classroom environments created by different teachers were influenced by socio-cultural factors. As with the students, we asked more questions in our attempt to

Mixed methods researchers collect qualitative data

piece together our understanding of the learning environments in each country.

22 The cross-cultural nature of the present study led to a multimethod approach to allow triangulation of the methods and cross-validation of the data. The data collected using the different research methods was complementary and formed a more complete and coherent picture of the learning environments in each country (Denzin & Lincoln, 1994).

Results Section

Mixed methods researchers analyze quantitative data and report results

## Results

### *Quantitative Data*

23 *Validation of the WIHIC Questionnaire.* Data collected from the 50 classes in Taiwan and the 50 classes in Australia were analyzed in various ways to investigate the reliability and validity of the 70-item version of the WIHIC questionnaire in both countries. Principal components factor analysis followed by varimax rotation resulted in the acceptance of a revised version of the instrument, which comprised 56 items (8 items in each of the seven scales; see Appendix). The a priori factor structure of the final version of the questionnaire was replicated in both countries; nearly all items had a factor loading of at least .40 on their a priori scale but on no other scale (see Table 1).

24 Table 1 also reports the internal consistency reliability (Cronbach alpha coefficient) of each of the seven 8-item scales for two units of analysis (individual and class mean). Using the class mean as the unit of analysis, we found that scale reliability estimates ranged from .87 to .97 in Australia and from .90 to .96 in Taiwan.

25 We used an analysis of variance (ANOVA) to determine the ability of each WIHIC scale to differentiate between the perceptions of students in different classes. The $\eta^2$ statistic was calculated to provide an estimate of the strength of association between class membership and the dependent variable (WIHIC scale). The ANOVA results for Taiwan and Australia are reported in Table 2. Each scale differentiated significantly between classes ($p < .01$) in both Taiwan and Australia. The amount of variance in scores accounted for by class membership (i.e., $\eta^2$) ranged from .07 to .15 in Australia and from .07 to .36 in Taiwan.

26 *Differences between Australia and Taiwan in learning environment and student attitudes.* Table 2 shows the differences in mean environment and attitude scores for Taiwan and Australia. Although the differences were small, Australian students consistently perceived their learning environments more favorably than did Taiwanese students (see Table 2). *T* tests for paired samples, using the class as the unit of analysis, were used to investigate whether differences in scale scores between Australia and Taiwan were statistically significant. Students in Australia consistently viewed their classroom environment (in terms of WIHIC scales) more favorably than did students in Taiwan. There was a statistically significant difference ($p < .05$) for the Involvement, Investigation, Task Orientation, Cooperation and Equity scales.

27 An interesting anomaly arose in the finding that students in Taiwan expressed a significantly more positive attitude toward science than did students in Australia ($p < .01$). Despite the fact that students in Australia held more favorable perceptions of the learning environment, students in Taiwan had more positive attitudes toward their science class. Those findings prompted the researchers to examine the perceptions of the students in each country more closely as part of the qualitative data collection that is discussed further in this article.

Mixed methods researchers converge, connect or embed the two datasets

### *Qualitative Data*

28 The results of the large-scale quantitative probe led the researchers to generate qualitative data to provide insights into students' perceptions. In the spirit of the interpretive study, data generation and analysis led to examining sociocultural factors that influence the learning environments in different countries. Findings related to the qualitative data are reported below in three parts: cross-cultural viability of the WIHIC questionnaire; teacher and student interviews; and researchers' stories.

Mixed methods researchers analyze qualitative data and report findings

29 *Cross-cultural viability of the WIHIC questionnaire.* Although statistical analysis had established the cross-cultural validity of the WIHIC questionnaire, the researchers wanted to establish the viability of the questionnaire in Australia and Taiwan. Using information collected through interviews with students in Taiwan and Australia, we could determine not only whether students across cultures had interpreted the items of the questionnaire consistently but also the reasons for students' responses to questionnaire items. The researchers therefore were not only in a better position to interpret the quantitative data more accurately, but also to understand students' perceptions and feelings about particular aspects of their classroom environment. During that process, the researchers identified the strong points and pitfalls associated with using a questionnaire framed in a Western context in a different culture.

30 The students' anecdotes were generally consistent with their perceptions as described by the WIHIC questionnaire. Therefore, the questionnaire data appear to provide a basis for measuring students' perceptions of the learning environment in both countries. Overall, the interviews suggest that students interpreted items in ways that were reasonably consistent with other students within the same country.

31 The questionnaire data provided a basis by which we could examine the similarities and differences between learning environments in Australia and Taiwan from the students' perspective. We found that, where statistically significant differences in questionnaire scale means were found, student interviews usually provided a plausible explanation, suggesting further support for the viability of the questionnaire. The inclusion of interview data was vital for making sense of the questionnaire results in both countries.

Analyzing data and reporting results

**Table 1.—Factor Loadings, Internal Consistency Reliability (Cronbach Alpha Coefficient), and Ability to Differentiate Between Classrooms (Analysis of Variance Results)**

| | Factor loading | | | | | | | | | | | | | |
|---|---|---|---|---|---|---|---|---|---|---|---|---|---|---|
| | Student cohesiveness | | Teacher support | | Involvement | | Investigation | | Task orientation | | Cooperation | | Equity | |
| Item no. | Aust | Taiw | Aust | Taiw | Aust | Taiw | Aust | Taiw | Aust | Taiw | Aust | Taiw | Aust | Taiw |
| 1 | .62 | .59 | | | | | | | | | | | | |
| 2 | .47 | .56 | | | | | | | | | | | | |
| 3 | .53 | .68 | | | | | | | | | | | | |
| 4 | .68 | .60 | | | | | | | | | | | | |
| 5 | .60 | .71 | | | | | | | | | | | | |
| 6 | — | — | | | | | | | | | | | | |
| 7 | .64 | .63 | | | | | | | | | | | | |
| 8 | — | .59 | | | | | | | | | | | | |
| 9 | | | .64 | .67 | | | | | | | | | | |
| 10 | | | .68 | .65 | | | | | | | | | | |
| 11 | | | .65 | .75 | | | | | | | | | | |
| 12 | | | .56 | .55 | | | | | | | | | | |
| 13 | | | .63 | .62 | | | | | | | | | | |
| 14 | | | .68 | .70 | | | | | | | | | | |
| 15 | | | .62 | .59 | | | | | | | | | | |
| 16 | | | .43 | — | | | | | | | | | | |
| 17 | | | | | .65 | .53 | | | | | | | | |
| 18 | | | | | .77 | .65 | | | | | | | | |
| 19 | | | | | .46 | — | | | | | | | | |
| 20 | | | | | .58 | .50 | | | | | | | | |
| 21 | | | | | .47 | .41 | | | | | | | | |
| 22 | | | | | .49 | .45 | | | | | | | | |
| 23 | | | | | — | — | | | | | | | | |
| 24 | | | | | — | — | | | | | | | | |
| 25 | | | | | | | .65 | .61 | | | | | | |
| 26 | | | | | | | .58 | .64 | | | | | | |
| 27 | | | | | | | .71 | .70 | | | | | | |
| 28 | | | | | | | .63 | .61 | | | | | | |
| 29 | | | | | | | .64 | .68 | | | | | | |
| 30 | | | | | | | .63 | .66 | | | | | | |
| 31 | | | | | | | .66 | .66 | | | | | | |
| 32 | | | | | | | .61 | .64 | | | | | | |
| 33 | | | | | | | | | .65 | .49 | | | | |
| 34 | | | | | | | | | .58 | .49 | | | | |
| 35 | | | | | | | | | .55 | .59 | | | | |
| 36 | | | | | | | | | .62 | .51 | | | | |
| 37 | | | | | | | | | .71 | .54 | | | | |
| 38 | | | | | | | | | .65 | .58 | | | | |
| 39 | | | | | | | | | .67 | .62 | | | | |
| 40 | | | | | | | | | .63 | .58 | | | | |
| 41 | | | | | | | | | | | .55 | .44 | | |
| 42 | | | | | | | | | | | .59 | .40 | | |
| 43 | | | | | | | | | | | .58 | .53 | | |
| 44 | | | | | | | | | | | .63 | .47 | | |
| 45 | | | | | | | | | | | .65 | .47 | | |
| 46 | | | | | | | | | | | .67 | .54 | | |
| 47 | | | | | | | | | | | .62 | .58 | | |
| 48 | | | | | | | | | | | .52 | .56 | | |
| 49 | | | | | | | | | | | | | .68 | .56 |
| 50 | | | | | | | | | | | | | .70 | .65 |
| 51 | | | | | | | | | | | | | .69 | .67 |
| 52 | | | | | | | | | | | | | .71 | .66 |
| 53 | | | | | | | | | | | | | .72 | .71 |
| 54 | | | | | | | | | | | | | .74 | .58 |
| 55 | | | | | | | | | | | | | .63 | .64 |
| 56 | | | | | | | | | | | | | .68 | .64 |
| Alpha reliability | | | | | | | | | | | | | | |
| Individual | .81 | .86 | .88 | .87 | .84 | .85 | .88 | .90 | .88 | .86 | .89 | .87 | .93 | .90 |
| Class mean | .87 | .91 | .95 | .95 | .88 | .90 | .95 | .96 | .96 | .94 | .93 | .92 | .97 | .95 |
| $Eta^2$ | .11** | .07** | .14** | .34** | .09* | .11** | .15** | .22** | .14** | .36** | .15** | .28** | .15** | .24** |

*Note.* Findings were reported for the What Is Happening In This Class? Questionnaire. Loadings smaller than .4 were omitted. The sample consisted of 1,081 students in 50 classes in Australia and 1,879 students in 50 classes in Taiwan. Aust = Australia; Taiw = Taiwan.
$^*p < .05$. $^{**}p < .01$.

**Table 2.—Mean, Standard Deviation, and *t* Test for Paired Samples for Differences Between Taiwan and Australia in Perceptions of Classroom Environment and Attitude for the Class Mean as the Unit of Analysis**

| | *M* | | *SD* | | |
|---|---|---|---|---|---|
| WIHIC scale | Australia | Taiwan | Australia | Taiwan | *t* |
| Student cohesiveness | 31.61 | 31.60 | 1.33 | 1.54 | 0.06 |
| Teacher support | 24.68 | 24.24 | 2.89 | 2.79 | 0.74 |
| Involvement | 24.76 | 23.04 | 2.09 | 1.89 | 4.60* |
| Investigation | 23.56 | 22.90 | 2.43 | 2.54 | 1.43 |
| Task orientation | 31.75 | 30.98 | 1.80 | 2.24 | 2.10* |
| Cooperation | 30.43 | 29.56 | 1.80 | 2.24 | 2.44* |
| Equity | 31.68 | 30.04 | 2.24 | 2.81 | 3.40* |
| Attitude | 23.59 | 26.43 | 4.41 | 3.67 | –3.55* |

*Note.* WIHIC = What Is Happening In This Class? Questionnaire.
$^*p < .05$.

32 One pitfall that was highlighted through student interviews was that, despite the accuracy of the back translations, the Chinese version of the questionnaire did not always capture the full or literal meaning of the original questionnaire. In some cases, the questionnaire items were outside of the realm of students' experience, as with the item "I discuss ideas in class," because some Taiwanese students had not been involved in discussions in class in the Western sense, and therefore interpreted *discussion* as questioning.

33 After gathering the qualitative data, three important points emerged for the researchers of both countries. First, although the classroom environments were different in the two countries, the scores did not necessarily reflect fully the overall quality of education. Second, when interpreting the data in terms of scales of the WIHIC questionnaire, consideration must be given to whether the scales reflect what is considered to be educationally important in the countries and cultures from which the data were collected. Third, comparisons of quantitative data from different countries should be made with caution because we found that there were some items for which students in one country consistently interpreted items slightly different than did students in another country (as with the Student Cohesiveness Scale).

34 From the student interviews, which were based on items of the WIHIC questionnaire, research methods evolved (including observations and interviews with the participants) that the researchers felt would help them understand socio-cultural factors that influence the learning environment. Generally, the researchers found that the learning environment in each country is influenced by socio-cultural factors and the education system. The following section outlines the differences between the cultures and education systems of the two countries and how they impinge on the learning environment that is created.

35 *Observations, Stories, and Interviews.* This section explores factors that influence the learning environment in Australia and Taiwan. Data were gathered using classroom observations and participant interviews. The observation data are presented in the form of stories (Clandinin & Connelly, 1994) written to portray cultural archetypes of science classrooms in each country. The themes presented in the two stories (one from Taiwan and the other from Australia) take into consideration observations and interviews made over a number of occasions in the respective countries; they aim to provide an authentic paragon with which the reader can identify (Adler & Adler, 1994). Although all aspects of the stories might not be present in any one classroom, none are uncommon in the science classrooms that were observed. The two stories are followed by interpretive commentary (based on interviews with selected students and their teachers from the classrooms observed), as suggested by Geelan (1997). The stories and their subsequent commentaries provide a culturally sensitive basis on which the researcher was able to explain differences and similarities between the learning environments in each country.

36 The first story attempts to represent Australian science classrooms by extracting themes that were familiar over a number of observations in selected classes. That story is followed by interpretive commentary to help place it in context with other science classrooms in Australia.

*A Science Class in Australia*

37 A bite in the faint breeze hints of the winter to come but is contradicted by a wide expanse of cloudless blue sky. The sand dunes that I remember have given way to terra-cotta tiled rooves and dual carriage ways. The school, at ten years old, is relatively new and the neoteric design and facilities reflect this. Rusty brown stains on the walls, caused by minerals in the bore water used to irrigate the lawns and gardens throughout the hot dry summer, look strangely out of place on this modern building.

38 The science teacher, whose class I am here to observe, escorts me through the maze of single-storey buildings. A cacophony of sounds assail us as we walk: students preparing for the next lesson; magpies squabbling over scraps of food; doors banging shut on metal lockers; and the talking,

laughing and screeching of students on their break. Above the din, a student's voice is raised as he shouts to "dob in" a fellow student for taking his ruler. The shout is ignored by the teacher as the ruler is thrust back into the student's hand. Another student falls into step with us and banters light-heartedly with the teacher before moving off to rejoin his mates.

39 The teacher guides me through a door with a conspicuous "Staff Only" sign which leads to the science department. I am led through to the teachers' work area, a hive of activity with a desk for each teacher piled with papers and books. Materials, resources books and files related to teaching science at each age level are visible on bookshelves and in messy piles. A photocopier is placed in a prominent position, not far from a sink on which coffee cups, ingrained with tannin and caffeine, are turned upside down to drain.

40 After a brief introduction to members of the staff, we move through to one of six science laboratories where this teacher's next lesson will be held. The spacious bright room, with large windows along one wall, looks out over neatly manicured grass and pathways that surround the school. There are four rows, each with two long gray benches, with tall stools neatly tucked under them. A bench, meant for student laboratory work, stretches along three walls of the laboratory, and is fitted with sinks and gas connections. Suspended on the wall above the bench are shelves filled with test-tubes, pipettes and beakers. At the front of the class is a bench which has been raised slightly higher than the others. Fitted with a perspex shield, sink and fittings for a Bunsen burner, it is clearly meant for demonstrations. Today, however, it is strewn with teacher's notes, books and an overhead projector.

41 In the few minutes before the lesson starts, the teacher explains that the school has a separate class for high-ability students and that the grade 10 class which I am to observe is randomly selected from the remaining students. The teacher goes on to explain that one science lesson a week has been devoted to a library session, during which small groups of students have the opportunity to research a topic of their choice and prepare a presentation. Rather than devote several lessons to listening to the presentations, the teacher has chosen to start each lesson with one presentation based on this research.

42 The siren wails, reminding me of an air raid warning, and the teacher excuses himself. He steps onto the verandah and waits for the students to settle down before allowing them to pour into the laboratory. Twenty-five students rush to grab stools and move them next to friends. The boys look scruffy and disheveled, dressed in sloppy joes, jeans and sneakers and sporting a range of hair cuts from long unbrushed mops to short, army-style, crew cuts. In contrast, the girls look neat, are fashionably dressed in a variety of designer label sweat shirts, and have freshly brushed hair.

43 After much scraping of chairs on the hard floor and chatter among the students, the teacher draws their attention to the front of the class. Three girls, all of whom appear to be nervous, walk to the front and read their presentations from sheets that act as cue cards. A boy from the audience points out a mistake made by one of the girls during the presentation. The girl looks uncomfortable and turns to the teacher who excuses the error as "mis-read information." The teacher proceeds to turn the boy's point into a problem-solving exercise, taking the heat off the girl and giving other students in the class the opportunity to discuss and resolve the problem amongst themselves.

44 Once resolved, the teacher asks the students to evaluate the group's presentation. The students have a sheet on which they rate each presentation according to objectives that they have pre-determined, such as interest or content. The teacher provides a short reminder about how to complete the sheet before a student near the back calls out to let the teacher know that he doesn't have one. It appears that several students, for a variety of reasons, have not brought their sheets to class. Prepared for just such an event, the teacher lightly chastizes them and hands out duplicates. The students proceed to evaluate the presentation, whilst the girls work as a group and do a self evaluation that will be included in their portfolio.

45 The evaluation is followed by a short, sharp question-and-answer session that is geared towards revising the last lesson. Not all students are on task (with a group of students at the back talking amongst themselves), but the majority are. The subject for this lesson is radio-isotopes, a difficult one for students at this level, but part of the curriculum. The teacher selects students with their hands up to answer the questions, making a point of praising those who answer correctly and encouraging those who don't with "good try" or "close but not quite."

46 The group at the back continues to chatter and is ignored by the teacher until the volume starts to escalate. The teacher stops what he is saying and asks them to keep the noise down just as one member of the group retorts: "He's borrowing paper." The manner of his response borders on rude, but the teacher lets it go without comment. Rather, he turns to write notes on the board for the students to copy. After a bustle of activity and clicking of files, the class is almost silent for the first time as students take down the notes.

47 As the first of the students finish, the teacher explains the activity which is to follow. Students are to become radioactive particles (they must toss a die and, if it is a six, the particle (student) decays. The reaction includes outward groans and none of the students seem overly enthusiastic. As the teacher distributes the dice amongst the students, they start chatting amongst themselves, clicking and tapping the dice, steadily increasing the noise level. Two girls are brushing their hair near the front, putting it back into pony tails. A late arrival walks in and is given a die before sitting down. Ignoring the fact that the other students are not paying attention, the teacher instructs them to toss their dice.

48 I am amazed that anything could be heard over the noise, but 25 dice were promptly tossed. Two students shoot their dice across the floor, claiming it to be an accident when the teacher looks at them. When asked by the teacher to raise their hands if they threw a six, an inordinate number of students respond. Like me, the teacher must wonder about this because he goes on to explain the need for honesty if the activity is to work.

49 The teacher does not record the first throw and instructs students to throw again. This time, two students throw a six, which the teacher records on a table that he has drawn on the board. During subsequent throws, I notice that a boy at the back of the class raises his hand twice. When the teacher realizes that there is a discrepancy in numbers, the boy brazenly yells out: "You counted me twice." The teacher looks annoyed but does not make an issue of it. To make the numbers in his table correct, the teacher asks one of the remaining students to stand out.

50 At the end of the activity, the teacher moves amongst the students, collecting the dice. When he returns to the front of

the class, he explains how to convert the table which they have made into a graph. As he makes up the graph, a student draws his attention to an error that he has made with the scale. Affably, the teacher thanks the student for pointing out his mistake, congratulates him on his powers of observation and adds: "It shows what an incompetent mathematician I am." The mistake is rectified and the graph completed before the teacher goes on to demonstrate how to work out the half-life of an isotope. Whilst most of the students appear to be listening and others are taking notes, I notice that the group of students at the back of the class are passing notes to each other. The teacher starts to talk about the half-life of isotopes and radioactivity and to relate them to the effects of nuclear weapons and its use in the treatment of cancer. As the teacher describes his personal experience with cancer and the effects of Hiroshima, it becomes clear that these real-life examples, and the element of gore in his descriptions, have captured the students' attention. They are not only paying attention but also asking questions and contributing to the discussion, including students in the group at the back of the class.

51 The teacher glances at the clock on the wall and I can almost feel his reluctance to draw the discussion to a close as he asks the students to copy the table and graph into their files. As they do so, he wheels out a video player and turns on a short movie about isotopes. It is complex in nature and appears to be above the level of the students, yet they sit quietly, half watching as they finish their graphs and pack away their books for the next lesson.

52 That story illustrates aspects of Australian science classes that can be considered fairly typical. It describes a lesson in which the teacher uses a variety of teaching methods and moves between whole-class and small-group activities. Although some of the classes that were observed were more teacher centered, the majority of teachers who were interviewed stated that they purposefully moved away from such approaches. Of those teachers, most of them said that they felt it is important to provide opportunities for students to be involved in discussions, group activities, and cooperative work.

53 The story describes the use of an activity to help explain the half-life of an isotope to students. Although interviews revealed a range of factors that prevented teachers from moving away from teacher-centered methods as often as they would like, the teachers agreed generally that doing so was beneficial to the students. According to interviews with teachers in Australia, they have considerable freedom to decide how they would deliver the content of the curriculum. Interviews indicated that the methods by which the content of the curriculum is delivered is left largely to the discretion of the school and, in some cases, individual teachers.

54 The story also describes the science teachers' work area that is filled with books, resources, and a photocopier. According to the teachers who were interviewed, those resources are essential to assist them to design programs and decide how they can best tailor the curriculum to suit the needs of their students. Many teachers design and photocopy worksheets and information sheets and, in one school, the science teachers had cooperatively designed and printed a series of science topic books relevant to the students from their school.

55 The story describes the use of self- and peer assessment in the classroom. Many science classes observed in Western Australia used student portfolios from a variety of sources to build a profile of students. The design of the portfolios and the way in which they were used varied between schools because they were generally designed collaboratively by teachers in the science department.

56 The story describes a question-and-answer session in which the teacher revises a previous lesson. The Australian teachers who were observed generally asked questions to the whole class and selected only those students who raised their hands; the only exception was when the teacher used questioning as a means of classroom control (e.g., when a student was talking at an inappropriate time). Once the students responded to the question, the teacher often thanked them for their answers or any comments they made and, if the answer was wrong, the teacher made remarks such as "good try" or "almost." Teacher interviews revealed that that group of Australian teachers was sensitive to students' difficulties in answering questions in a whole class situation and tried not to put the students' self-esteem at risk.

57 Finally, the story describes a variety of disruptions to the lesson, ranging from discussions between students to talking back to the teacher. With the exception of the higher ability classes, this behavior was not uncommon in the science classrooms observed.

58 The next story develops a cultural archetype on the basis of observations of science classrooms in Taiwan. This story, like the Australian story, develops themes that were common over a number of observations.

*A Science Class in Taiwan*

59 The drive to the school was an experience in itself. Never had I known such traffic. Rivers of motor scooters weaved in, out and around our car as we sped along roads choked with traffic. We are greeted by a huge archway, inscribed with the name of the school, as we enter the school grounds. Iris, my colleague and friend, has come to act as an interpreter, and she clears our entrance to the school with the security guard at the gate. The humidity hits us as we step out of the air-conditioned car and make our way toward the building. The path passes through a lawn, dotted with garden beds and bordered with miniature hedges. Each of these garden beds houses small trees that had been trimmed and clipped over years, to form exotic shapes.

60 I have been informed that protocol dictates that we meet with the principal before observing the classrooms, and so we make our way to her office on the third floor. As we climb the wide staircase, we are greeted by students in neatly pressed uniforms, armed with brooms and dustpans, cleaning their allotted areas.

61 At the office, we are greeted by the principal and seated in large comfortable chairs. Over a cup of tea, we discuss the research project and our reasons for observing the science teacher. I am shown the rather impressive school trophy collection, kept in large glass cabinets behind her desk, before a

student is asked to take us to the classroom where I am to observe a lesson.

62 We climb to the fourth floor and enter the classroom through a door at the back of the room. The teacher hasn't arrived yet and the general chatter and noise of students is deafening. My blonde hair attracts the attention of some of the students, drawing furtive glances and giggles. "Hello lady" shouts a class clown. I reply, sending the class into whoops of laughter. As a Westerner, I am something of a novelty.

63 A synthesised recording of the chimes of Big Ben is blasted through speakers, heralding the start of the next lesson. The teacher's arrival sends students scurrying to sit behind small wooden desks. Each desk has a single shelf underneath on which books and pens have been placed. Bags, satchel like, are draped on the backs of chairs. Emptied of the necessary equipment, the bags still looking ominously full.

64 Prompted by a class leader, seven straight rows of students, with six in each, stand, bow their traditional salute and greet the teacher, out of sinc and in boisterous voices. There is confusion—I am sitting in somebody's seat. After a brief disruption, the students are all facing the teacher, with their books open and eyes forward, ready for the lesson. Iris and I are both perched at the back of the class, with our knees between two students and our chairs touching the wall behind us. It's a tight fit.

65 The teacher smiles a welcome over the heads of the students. Above her hangs the Taiwan flag, below which is a poster depicting the country's founder, Sun Yat Sen, looking benignly at students. Bold characters, peeling slightly through age, placed on either side of the poster, demand that students respect their teacher and treasure wisdom. There are two blackboards in the class, one at the front of the class (that was wiped clean by a student as we waited) and one at the back that is covered in Chinese characters.

66 From behind the podium at the front of the class, the teacher begins the lesson. Her voice, amplified through a microphone worn around her neck, sings out above the noises outside: a jackhammer thumping nearby, a plane passing overhead, the distant hum of traffic, a car horn. She asks a question to the whole class which is followed by an answer, chorused from the class in unison—boys' voices drowning out those of the girls. There are more questions and more answers as the previous lesson is revised thoroughly.

67 Today's lesson will be about ferns and it is clear from the posters and specimens that the teacher has brought in that she is well prepared. Students turn to the correct page in their textbook and I notice that the teacher is referring to her own copy before starting. The teacher begins her lesson in a lively, animated style, her eyes seeming to include each student as she speaks. I am surprised that I am able to follow the lesson with some accuracy, despite not understanding the language. The teacher makes frequent use of the blackboard to illustrate the various parts of the fern and describe their propagation. I notice that most of the students are listening and watching her, although one girl is resting her head on her desk and a boy is staring absently out of the window.

68 A burst of laughter from the students draws my attention to the latest illustration on the board, a rather sketchy drawing that vaguely resembles a fern. The teacher takes it good naturedly and continues to draw a second diagram showing the spores of the fern. At this point, the teacher produces the specimens which she has brought into the class. She explains, drawing examples on the board, and illustrating important facts before giving each one to a student. Each specimen is described at length and the relevant points are outlined in the text. Students turn the pages of the text in unison and some make notes.

69 A student near the front is whispering to her neighbor, who answers with a nod of her head. The teacher looks in their direction briefly but ignores the pair. One of the students is handed a specimen which is examined and touched, providing a moment's distraction. At regular intervals, the teacher asks the students whether they have a question, and waits for a few moments. Invariably there were none, except on this occasion. A student wanted to know whether a fern that he had seen in Singapore had medicinal value. The teacher, deciding that the question was not directly related to the lesson, defers it until the end.

70 The day is hot, sultry, oppressive. Six fans, hanging from a ceiling spotted with mildew and flaking paint, whir ineffectually overhead, barely stirring the sticky air. Students begin to fidget and move around in their seats. I find myself shifting positions to get more comfortable on the wooden slats of the chair and to encourage circulation. Those students who were taking notes at the beginning of the lesson have stopped. To the left of me, there is small group of boys fiddling with their pens—practising the art of flicking them expertly from one finger to another, twirling them as they do.

71 At this point, the teacher produces a poster that has been drawn and colored by hand. The illustration of the canopy is well done and draws oohs and aahs from the students. From her position at the front of the class, the teacher attracts students' attention, this time with a brief story of an experience that she had had climbing the mountains outside Kaohsiung. I notice that the pen flicking stops and the boy, who was looking out of the window, is paying attention to the teacher. The story is brought to an abrupt close when she examines her watch (something I have noticed her do throughout the lesson). The students are instructed to put their books away and given a reminder of tomorrow's test. Several students turn around automatically, to look to the blackboard behind me that lists the tests to be taken over the next week.

72 I had assumed that the lesson had finished but, once the textbooks were out of sight, the teacher called out a number from her book. Random selection of students by their identity numbers was common practice in the classrooms, and I even remember one teacher using the second timer on his digital watch to ensure that the selection was fair. There is a burst of laughter from the other students as the boy who was selected stands up next to his chair. The teacher asks him a question and he responds in a quiet voice. Whilst the teacher gives no outward indication that he is correct, he must have been because he sits down. Looking at her book, she selects another student. There is another burst of laughter as another number is selected and a boy pulls himself to his feet.

73 The boy listens to the question, looking at his feet and rubbing his hands together. I find myself feeling nervous for him, willing him to get the answer right. I needn't have been concerned because his answer, whilst wrong, was merely corrected before he sat down. I continued to watch him after he had sat, but there was no ridicule from his peers and no sidelong glances or shrugs borne out of embarrassment that I would have expected in an Australian class. The process was repeated until the lesson had been covered. Students laughed and cheered when their peers were called, as if part of a game. The students answered the questions in quiet voices (in

contrast to the boisterous ones that had greeted me when I had arrived) and sat down once they had been corrected.

74 When the last of the questions had been answered, the teacher outlined the important points and showed the students on what pages of the textbook they could be found. Raising her voice, to be heard over the din made by the chimes of Big Ben played through the speakers, she winds up the lesson. Once the chimes stop playing, there is relative quiet and the students stand to bow their salute to the teacher, marking the end of the lesson.

75 This story describes a typical junior high school science class in Taiwan and reveals distinct differences between classrooms in the two countries as discussed in the next section.

*Issues Emerging From Interviews, Observations and Stories*

76 Besides the physical differences such as the weather, school structure, and classroom layout, other more subtle differences discussed below could be explained only after interviews with the participants: nature of the curriculum, pressures experienced by teachers, respect for the teacher, questioning techniques, and educational aims.

77 *Nature of the curriculum.* Interviews with teachers and students in both countries indicated that the nature of the curriculum could be a major influence on the learning environment created by teachers in each country. The story of a Taiwanese classroom describes a teacher-centered lesson in which students appear to play a fairly passive role. The classes observed by the researcher in Taiwan were, without exception, teacher centered and, although the roles of the students varied between teachers, there were generally few opportunities for discussions or questions. Interviews with teachers revealed that the teacher-centered approaches were largely a result of the examination-driven nature of the curriculum. An example follows:

> The way we teach is constrained. Students have to do the entrance exam to senior high school and they like to be crammed . . . .The exams, the [content of the] textbook and the amount of homework restrict how much work we can do outside of the textbook. Every aspect of science education is constrained. (Taiwanese teacher, Interview 3, p. 3)

78 The story describes the teacher's battle to fit the required content into each lesson and the desire of the teacher to avoid giving the students additional work. The science curriculum (for both biology and physics) was presented to students in the form of textbooks, and examinations were based on their content. As a result, it was important for teachers to cover all areas. Teachers who were interviewed explained that teacher-centered methods were the most practical way to cover the content in the given time frame and diversions (described in the story as student questions referring to real-life situations) often were not possible given the time constraints. An example follows:

> The textbook is very big and the teacher has to go through each stage. There is too much to teach . . . and there isn't enough time to cover the content of the book. Ideally I would like to give students the chance to learn what is not in the textbook . . . (but I) don't do that . . . because of the shortage of time. (Taiwanese teacher, Interview 3, pp. 2–3)

It appears that the competitive nature of the curriculum encourages teachers to concentrate on developing academic ability as efficiently as possible. Diversions from the teacher-centered methods also were viewed negatively by many parents, teachers, and students as being off task, as in the following example:

> Under the education system that we have in Taiwan, the lecture kind of teaching is the most efficient way to teach students and get a good score. . . . The students' time is already very tight and they work too hard already, so [by teaching in this way] I can do something for them. For example, I don't ask the students to go to the library for information for their study, because it would be another burden on the students. (Taiwanese teacher, Interview 1, p. 6)

79 Rote learning, described in the story as a question-and-answer session that makes use of chorused answers to revise a previous lesson, is frequently used in Taiwan. Many of the lessons observed involved rote learning at some stage; teachers and students believe that such learning prepares students better for the examinations. One teacher, referring to a comment made about moving away from teacher-centered methods, stated that "The students know how the class should be taught . . . and that there will be a problem if the teacher changes this" (Taiwanese teacher, Interview 3, p. 3). Good examination results are of paramount importance to students in Taiwan. If students attain good results, it increases the likelihood of being allocated a position in a *star* school (i.e., a school with outstanding results measured by the number of students who enter a university).

80 In contrast, the Australian teachers who were interviewed generally expressed a desire to use methods in their science classes that were not teacher centered. Their reasons were varied, but they felt that by using a variety of approaches students would be able to better develop a range of abilities in their students. In many cases, the teachers claimed that they were encouraged, through professional development days and by other staff, to use a variety of methods in their teaching.

81 Rote learning was frowned upon by many of the teachers interviewed in Australia; one teacher commented that "developing the students' ability as learners is more important than the acquisition of content knowledge" (Australian teacher, Interview 1, p. 2). In general, the teachers were of the opinion that by incorporating a range of teaching styles they were more likely to cater to the range of learning styles present in their class. In addition, they felt that their students were more likely to understand concepts if they were actively involved in their learning.

82 Interviews indicated that the nature of the curriculum was largely responsible for the type of teaching approaches used in each country. Teachers who were interviewed in Australia indicated that, like Taiwan, the science curriculum in Western Australia is defined by set content that

needs to be covered. However, unlike Taiwan, where the curriculum is examination-driven and presented in the form of a textbook (whose depth and scope left little time for any method of teaching other than teacher centered), the methods by which the Western Australian curriculum are delivered is left largely to the teacher. Consequently, the nature of the curriculum led to different learning environments in each country.

83 *Pressures experienced by teachers.* Interviews with teachers in both countries revealed that pressures, each from different sources, could influence the learning environment created in each country. In Taiwan, interviews revealed that teachers experience pressures from their principal, parents, and other teachers when the test scores of their science classes are displayed for comparisons with other teachers. The principal, eager for schools to maintain or improve their position (according to the number of students who gain access into star schools), pressures teachers to push students toward improving their test results. The homeroom teacher also pressures teachers to ensure that the grades of students in her or his class do not slip and that the teachers improve their performance if their results were lower than those of other teachers, as in the following example:

> The class scores are [posted] in one of the offices and the teachers go there to check their class. . . . They want to see whether they have a good score compared to the other teachers. . . . The score of the class puts the teacher under a lot of pressure [from the home-room teacher] and . . . , if your class score is the lowest, your attitude towards that class can change. (Taiwanese teacher, Interview 1, p. 6)

84 Parents, eager for their students to attend a star school to improve their chances of attending a university, also pressure teachers. In Taiwan, social mobility is available to students of any status through education. Because the expectation of many parents is that their child will attend a university, they exert pressure on students to perform well in examinations. In addition, parents have high expectations of teachers and their ability to obtain high performance from the students, as in the following example:

> [T]he parents' attitudes can act as a constraint [to our teaching] because sometimes, if the teacher is not on task in the classroom, the students will tell their parents and they will go to the school to tell the teacher to teach more content. (Taiwanese teacher, Interview 1, p. 5)

85 Teachers in Australia, however, were under different types of pressures. Many of the Australian teachers who were interviewed felt that pressures that they experienced were more likely to come from the expectations of the school science department, school, and State Department of Education than from the parents or principal. Those teachers generally felt that they were expected to perform tasks over and above classroom teaching, routine lesson planning, assessment and programming tasks, such as tailoring the curriculum to the students' needs or designing and implementing student self-assessment projects.

86 Observations of science classrooms in Australia did not appear to reflect those pressures. The teaching methods and approaches varied widely among teachers; some were highly innovative and creative in their lessons and others (the majority of teachers observed) used more whole class activities and teaching (as described in the first story). Interviews with teachers, however, indicated that the tasks they needed to perform outside of teaching could affect their lessons because less time was available for planning.

87 Apparently the pressures of an examination-driven curriculum experienced by teachers in Taiwan were more likely to create a consistently teacher-centered learning environment. In contrast, the pressures related to the factors experienced by teachers in Australia had a more indirect influence on the learning environment dictated through time available for planning rather than on a particular teaching method or range of methods.

88 *Respect for the teacher.* Classroom observations and interviews suggested that there could be differences in the ways in which students regard their teachers; students in Taiwan had more respect for teachers than did students in Australia. The traditional bow of students at the beginning and end of lessons, described in the story, is considered to be a mark of respect. Interviews with teachers and students in Taiwan indicated that teachers have high status within the community and that they are highly respected by their students. According to Huang (1997), teachers in Taiwan hold a professional status within the community and are respected as experts in their field. Reinforcing their status and professional standing, one of the teachers who was interviewed in Taiwan explained how he intentionally distanced himself from his students

> If I'm too close or friendly, students feel that I am more of a friend than a teacher. So, if I'm too close, they won't feel pressured to study. . . . [By distancing myself], they [the students] won't forget what position they hold or lose respect. (Taiwanese teacher, Interview 1, p. 1)

89 Although the teachers in both countries complained about discipline problems with students, we noted that there was more evidence of disruptive behavior in science classes in Australia (described in the first story as answering back and chatting between friends) than in Taiwan. Unlike teachers in Taiwan who distance themselves from students, teachers in Australia tend to treat students more as equals. In some cases, therefore, Australian students seemed more likely to act in a manner that could be considered disrespectful to the teacher.

90 In Taiwan, the teachers' knowledge was not questioned by any of the students interviewed. They rarely questioned the teaching methods or the lesson content: "I like what the teacher is teaching me. She teaches very well and it is always interesting. So I don't need to question the way she teaches" (Item 63, Taiwanese student F). On the other hand, students whom we interviewed in Australia were more likely to complain about their teacher and the teaching methods.

91 Some Australian students complained that they found sci-

ence lessons boring and said that they would choose to have science taught differently. There were cases (especially for students in lower ability classes) of students viewing science and their science teachers as something to be endured because the subject was compulsory: "I find science confusing and sometimes I don't understand Mr C. Science just isn't interesting" (Item 45, Australian student 4.3). "Sometimes we get to do investigations. . . . Sometimes they're not interesting. I'm not interested in science" (Item 39, Australian student 4.2). Students in both countries, however, claimed that they would prefer science classes to include more experiments and laboratory work.

92 For the classroom in Taiwan described in the second story, there was only one incident of students talking during the lesson. The researcher noted during classroom observations that student disruptions were minimal; brief, whispered discussions with a neighbor were the only signs of disturbance. Students who were interviewed indicated that those discussions generally were related to points that were unclear from the lecture. Although teachers in Taiwan discussed discipline problems with the researcher, those problems appeared to be associated more with inattentiveness than with lesson disruptions.

93 In the classroom in Australia described in the first story, there were several incidences of students talking among themselves, calling out, or answering back to the teacher. The teachers who were interviewed said that a lack of discipline was one of the biggest constraints to their teaching. Those teachers complained that disruptive students often prevented them from being able to teach in ways in which they would ideally like. In some cases, teachers felt that they often found themselves in the role of counselor and spent teaching time sorting out students' problems. One teacher expressed concern at the lack of avenues to which a teacher could turn for assistance with disruptive behavior.

94 The students whom we observed in Australia were more likely to interrupt or to be disrespectful toward the teacher. There appeared to be a larger gap between the status of teachers and students in Taiwan than in Australia. That point is highlighted in the first story, which describes an Australian teacher performing tasks, such as giving out papers, that normally would be undertaken by students in Taiwan. Teachers who were observed in Australia appeared to treat students as equals and, in some cases, that meant that students were more likely to act in a disrespectful manner.

95 *Questioning techniques.* Both stories describe the use of questioning in the classrooms, but it appears that the techniques used were different for the two countries. The question-and-answer session described in Australia depicts a teacher posing questions to the whole class and selecting only students with their hands raised. Interviews with teachers indicated that they were careful not to damage the self-esteem of students and to ensure that their pride among their peers was protected. According to student interviews, many students were reluctant to raise their hands unless they were reasonably sure of the answer, whereas others made a point of never answering questions in class. Students explained that ridicule from peers was possibly the main reason for their reluctance to answer questions: "I usually don't like putting my hand up. . . . If I get the answer wrong, then I get embarrassed [because] other kids in the class could laugh at me" (Australian student A).

96 In contrast, teachers who were observed in Taiwan (described in the second story) selected students randomly using the students' identity numbers (stitched above the pocket on their school shirts) rather than their names. The selected student stood up to answer the question and, if the answer was wrong, the teacher bluntly told him or her. The student then either tried again or sat down and listened to the answer of another student. Interviews with students revealed that they were not uncomfortable with this method of questioning and that questions were used as a means of gauging what students need to know or what they do not understand to enable them to improve and learn. As one student put it, "When he [the teacher] teaches important content, he checks that we understand. So he asks us questions" (Taiwanese student, Interview 2, Item 23).

97 *Educational aims.* A final factor that was considered important to the teacher's creation of the learning environment was the educational aims considered important in each country. In Taiwan, the teachers who were interviewed indicated that education was focused predominantly on the development of the academic ability of students. Social and emotional aspects of a student's development were generally considered to be more the responsibility of the family and wider community than of the school (Stevenson & Stigler, 1992). In contrast, the teachers in Australia considered academic advancement to be one of a number of aspects to be developed in students; they believed that social, emotional, and physical development held equal value. The educational aims held by those Australian teachers were more academically oriented for students at the senior high school level, where the curriculum is more examination driven.

98 The science classrooms described in the stories presented in this section have different learning environments. If the stories are to be considered archetypes for the science classrooms in their respective countries, then they can be used to help explain the differences and similarities. Teachers apparently create learning environments to suit a variety of social and cultural factors within their respective countries. There are different opinions in Australia and Taiwan of what is considered to be the ideal learning environment.

99 Interviews with students and teachers indicated that, although the classroom environments are different in the two countries (as indicated by the mean scale scores of the WIHIC questionnaire), that fact does not necessarily reflect the overall quality of education. Students in Taiwan perceived that the classroom practices assessed by each scale of the WIHIC occurred to a lesser extent than their Australian counterparts did. In a Western sense, that perception could be considered less favorable of the learning environ-

ment, but it has to be considered in terms of the questionnaire and whether the scales reflect what is considered to be educationally, socially, and culturally important in the countries where the data were collected.

Conclusion section

## Discussion

100 The present study has highlighted the importance of cross-national studies to help our understanding not only of classroom environments in other countries, but also of classroom environments in our own country. The study was distinctive because it used multiple research methods to help researchers understand better the different aspects of classroom environments and to examine a broad range of questions.

101 The quantitative data, collected using the What is Happening in This Class? (WIHIC) questionnaire and an attitude scale in the first phase of this study, supported the reliability and validity of both the English and Mandarin versions of all scales. The final 56-item version of the classroom environment questionnaire had 8 items in each of the seven scales. The a priori factor structure was replicated with nearly all of the items loading only on its own factor. Internal consistency (alpha reliability) for two units of analysis and ability to differentiate between classrooms were found to be satisfactory.

Interpreting the research

102 A comparison of scale means between the two countries revealed interesting anomalies that, in the spirit of the interpretive approach, prompted the researchers to determine why differences might occur. The initial data indicated that Australian students consistently perceived their classroom environments more favorably than the students in Taiwan did on all scales, but, in contrast, Taiwanese students had a more positive attitude toward their science classes. To explore those findings in more depth, the researchers took the roles of *bricoleur,* as described by Denzin and Lincoln (1994); they pieced together the data collected using different methodology to gain deeper insights into the learning environments.

103 The quantitative data made an important contribution to the *bricolage* of information built up during the study, but it was limited when used for comparative purposes. We found that students from Australia and Taiwan responded to questionnaire items in ways that were meaningful to their own situations and were influenced by social and cultural factors. Consequently, the interpretation of the data became more meaningful when combined with data gathered using other research methods. That finding provided a precautionary note regarding *imposed etic* (Berry, 1969), experienced when researchers use a questionnaire framed in one cultural context and impose those categories, variables, concepts and constructs on a different culture.

104 The generation and analysis of data collected using classroom observations, interviews with participants, and narrative stories allowed the researcher to (a) explore students' perceptions of the learning environment, (b) identify factors that influence the learning environments in Taiwan and Australia, and (c) make meaningful interpretations that took into account the background, culture, and situation of individuals. By adopting an interpretive approach that enabled the researchers to weave together the data collected from multiple paradigms and research methods, they could examine components that could be influenced by culture such as "situational and contextual factors, . . . [including] social expectations, norms, task definitions and social cues" (Maehr & Nicholls, 1980, p. 8) that otherwise might be overlooked.

105 The learning environments created in each country were influenced by the nature of the curriculum; the more examination-driven curriculum lead to more teacher-centered approaches in the classroom. Consequently, emphases considered important to science education in Western Australia, such as involvement, were not always as important or possible in Taiwan. The pressures experienced by teachers in each country appeared to influence the learning environment and in some respects seemed to be on opposing ends of a pendulum swing. On one hand, there were pressures related to an examination-driven curriculum, whereas, on the other hand, there were pressures related to implementing innovative ideas and tailoring a less prescriptive curriculum to students' needs.

106 The degree of respect that students held for their teacher appeared to influence the classroom environment. In the rowdier environment in Australia, students appeared to be more disruptive in class; that was in contrast to the classes in Taiwan, which were comparatively quiet and free of students' disruptions. There were points, good and bad, to be said for both learning environments; students in Taiwan were less inclined to ask the teacher questions than their Australian counterparts, but the Australian students were more likely to encounter occasions when learning was interrupted by the disruptive behavior of others.

107 Each country has much to learn from the other with regard to the development of a learning environment that fosters positive attitudes and a love of learning. The comparative nature of the present study of learning environments in Taiwan and Australia made possible the examination of similarities and differences between the learning environment and students' perceptions in each country. By comparing the learning environments in two such different cultures, the researchers identified the qualities inherent in each. As such, cross-cultural comparisons of this type have the potential to provide understanding of concepts as seen by those persons within the culture under study, generating new insights (Brislin, 1983; Fraser, 1996; Stigler & Hiebert, 1997) and making possible the inclusion of the social context in which behaviors occur (Bilmes & Boggs, 1979; Tseng & Hsu, 1979). Comparative studies of this nature enable researchers, teachers, and teacher educators to gain better understandings about their own beliefs and social and cultural restraints to their teaching.

## REFERENCES


Adler, P. A., & Adler, P. (1994). Observational techniques. In N. K. Denzin & Y. S. Lincoln (Eds.), *The handbook of qualitative research in education* (pp. 377–402). Newbury Park, CA: Sage.

Berry, J. W. (1969). On cross-cultural comparability. *International Journal of Psychology, 4,* 119–128.

Bilmes, J., & Boggs, S. (1979). Language and communication: The foundations of culture. In A. Marsella, R. Tharp, & T. Ciborowski (Eds.), *Perspectives on cross-cultural psychology* (pp. 47–76). New York: Academic Press.

Brislin, R. (1970). Back translation for cross-cultural research. *Journal of Cross-Cultural Psychology, 1,* 185–216.

Brislin, R. W. (1983). Cross-cultural research in psychology. *Annual Review of Psychology, 34,* 363–400.

Carter, K. (1993). The place of story in teaching and teacher education. *Educational Researcher, 22*(1), 5–12.

Casey, K. (1995). The new narrative research in education. In M. W. Apple (Ed.), *Review of research in education* (Vol. 21, pp. 211–253). Washington, DC: American Educational Research Association.

Cheung, K. C. (1993). The learning environment and its effects on learning: Product and process modeling for science achievement at the sixth form level in Hong Kong. *School Effectiveness and School Improvement, 4,* 242–264.

Chionh, Y. H., & Fraser, B. J. (1998, April). *Validation and use of the 'What is Happening in this Class' (WIHIC) questionnaire in Singapore.* Paper presented at the annual meeting of the American Educational Research Association, San Diego, CA.

Clandinin, D. J., & Connelly, F. M. (1994). Personal experience method. In N. K. Denzin & Y. S. Lincoln (Eds.), *Handbook of qualitative research* (pp. 413–427). Newbury Park, CA: Sage.

Denzin, N. K., & Lincoln, Y. S. (1994). Introduction: Entering the field of qualitative research. In N. K. Denzin & Y. S. Lincoln (Eds.), *Handbook of qualitative research* (pp. 1–17). Newbury Park, CA: Sage.

Feyerabend, P. (1978). *Against method: Outline of an anarchistic theory of knowledge.* London: Verso.

Fraser, B. J. (1981). *Test of science-related attitudes* (TOSRA). Melbourne, Australia: Australian Council for Educational Research.

Fraser, B. J. (1986). *Classroom environment.* London: Croom Helm.

Fraser, B. J. (1990). *Individualised Classroom Environment Questionnaire.* Melbourne, Australia: Australian Council for Educational Research.

Fraser, B. J. (1994). Research on classroom and school climate. In D. Gabel (Ed.), *Handbook of research on science teaching and learning* (pp. 493–541). New York: Macmillan.

Fraser, B. J. (1996, March). *NARST's expansion, internationalization and cross-nationalisation: History in the making.* Presidential address at the annual meeting of the National Association for Research in Science Teaching, St Louis, MO.

Fraser, B. J. (1998). Science learning environments: Assessment, effects and determinants. In B. J. Fraser & K. G. Tobin (Eds.), *The international handbook of science education* (pp. 527–564). Dordrecht, The Netherlands: Kluwer Academic Publishers.

Fraser, B. J. (1999). "Grain sizes" in learning environment research: Combining qualitative and quantitative methods. In H. C. Waxman & H. J. Walberg (Eds.), *New directions for teaching practice and research.* Berkeley, CA: McCutchan.

Fraser, B. J., McRobbie, C. J., & Fisher, D. L. (1996, April). *Development, validation and use of personal and class forms of a new classroom environment instrument.* Paper presented at the annual meeting of the American Educational Research Association, New York.

Fraser, B. J., & Tobin, K. (1991). Combining qualitative and quantitative methods in classroom environment research. In B. J. Fraser & H. J. Walberg (Eds.), *Educational environments: Evaluation, antecedents and consequences* (pp. 271–292). London: Pergamon.

Fraser, B. J., & Walberg, H. J. (Eds.). (1991). *Educational environments: Evaluation, antecedents and consequences.* London: Pergamon.

Geelan, D. R. (1997). Weaving narrative nets to capture school science classrooms. *Research in Science Education, 27,* 553–563.

Goh, S. C., Young, D. J., & Fraser, B. J. (1995). Psychosocial climate and student outcomes in elementary mathematics classrooms: A multilevel analysis. *The Journal of Experimental Education, 64,* 29–40.

Huang, I. (1997). Science education in Asia. *The Interdisciplinary Journal of Study Abroad, 3*(2), 13–24.

Keeves, J. P. (1992). *The IEA study of science III. Changes in science education and achievement: 1970 to 1984.* Oxford: Pergamon.

Keeves, J. P., & Adams D. (1994). Comparative methodology in education. In T. Husén, & T. N. Postlethwaite (Eds.), *The international encyclopedia of education* (2nd ed., pp. 948–958). Oxford: Pergamon.

Khoo, H. S., & Fraser, B. J. (1998). *Using classroom environment dimensions in the evaluation of adult computer courses.* Paper presented at the annual meeting of the National Association for Research in Science Teaching, San Diego, CA.

Kim, H. B., Fisher, D. L., & Fraser, B. J. (in press). Classroom environment and teacher interpersonal behaviour in secondary science classes in Korea. *Research in Science and Technological Education.*

Kuhn, T. S. (1962). *The structure of scientific revolutions* (3rd ed.). Chicago: University of Chicago Press.

Lakatos, I. (1970). Falsification and the methodology of scientific research programs. In I. Lakatos & A. Musgrave (Eds.), *Criticism and the growth of knowledge* (pp. 91–196). New York: Cambridge University Press.

Maehr, M., & Nicholls, J. (1980) Culture and achievement: A second look. In N. Warren (Ed.), *Studies in cross-cultural psychology* (Vol. 2, pp. 221–267). London: Academic Press.

Moos, R. H. (1979). *Evaluating educational environments: Procedures, measures, findings and policy implications.* San Francisco: Jossey-Bass.

Riah, H., & Fraser, B. J. (1998, April). *The learning environment of high school chemistry classes.* Paper presented at the annual meeting of the American Educational Research Association, San Diego, CA.

Schibeci, R. A., Rideng, I. M., & Fraser, B. J. (1987). Effects of classroom environments on science attitudes: A cross-cultural replication in Indonesia. *International Journal of Science Education, 9,* 169–186.

Stevenson, H. W., & Stigler, J. W. (1992). *The learning gap: Why our schools are failing and what we can learn from Japanese and Chinese education.* New York: Summit Books.

Stigler, J. W., & Hiebert, J. (1997). Understanding and improving classroom mathematics instruction: An overview of the TIMSS video study. *Phi Delta Kappan, 79,* 14–21.

Teh, G., & Fraser, B. J. (1994). An evaluation of computer-assisted learning in terms of achievement, attitudes and classroom environment. *Evaluation and Research in Education, 8,* 147–161.

Tobin, K., & Fraser, B. J. (Eds.). (1998). Qualitative and quantitative landscapes of classroom learning environments. In B. J. Fraser & K. G. Tobin (Eds.), *The international handbook of science education* (pp. 623–640). Dordrecht, The Netherlands: Kluwer Academic Publishers.

Tobin, K., Kahle, J. B., & Fraser, B. J. (Eds.). (1990). *Windows into science classes: Problems associated with higher-level cognitive learning.* London: Falmer.

Tseng, W. S., & Hsu, J. (1980). Culture and psychotherapy. In A. Marsella, R. Tharp, & T. Ciborowski (Eds.), *Perspectives on cross-cultural psychology* (pp. 333–345). New York: Academic Press.

van Maanen, J. (1988). *Tales of the field: On writing ethnography.* Chicago: University of Chicago Press.

Walberg, H. J. (Ed.). (1979). *Educational environments and effects: Evaluation, policy and productivity.* Berkeley, CA: McCutchan.

Walberg, H. J., Singh, R., & Rasher, S. P. (1977). Predictive validity of students' perceptions: A cross-cultural replication. *American Educational Research Journal, 14,* 45–49.

Wong, A. F. L., & Fraser, B. J. (1996). Environment-attitude associations in the chemistry laboratory classroom. *Research in Science and Technological Education, 64,* 29–40.

Wong, A. F. L., Young, D. J., & Fraser, B. J. (1997). A multilevel analysis of learning environments and student attitudes. *Educational Psychology, 17,* 449–468.

Wong, N. Y. (1993). Psychosocial environments in the Hong Kong mathematics classroom. *Journal of Mathematical Behavior, 12,* 303–309.

Wong, N. Y. (1996). Students' perceptions of the mathematics classroom in Hong Kong. *Hiroshima Journal of Mathematics Education, 4,* 89–107.

Wubbels, T., & Levy, J. (Eds.). (1993). *Do you know what you look like?: Interpersonal relationships in education.* London: Falmer.

## APPENDIX
### Items in the What is Happening in This Class? Questionnaire

#### Student Cohesiveness

1. I make friendships among students in this class.
2. I know other students in this class.
3. I am friendly to members of this class.
4. Members of the class are my friends.
5. I work well with other class members.
6. I help other class members who are having trouble with their work.
7. Students in this class like me.
8. In this class, I get help from other students.

#### Teacher Support

9. The teacher takes a personal interest in me.
10. The teacher goes out of his/her way to help me.
11. The teacher considers my feelings.
12. The teacher helps me when I have trouble with the work.
13. The teacher talks with me.
14. The teacher is interested in my problems.
15. The teacher moves about the class to talk with me.
16. The teacher's questions help me to understand.

#### Involvement

17. I discuss ideas in class.
18. I give my opinions during class discussions.
19. The teacher asks me questions.
20. My ideas and suggestions are used during classroom discussions.
21. I ask the teacher questions.
22. I explain my ideas to other students.
23. Students discuss with me how to go about solving problems.
24. I am asked to explain how I solve problems.

#### Investigation

25. I carry out investigations to test my ideas.
26. I am asked to think about the evidence for statements.
27. I carry out investigations to answer questions coming from discussions.
28. I explain the meaning of statements, diagrams, and graphs.
29. I carry out investigations to answer questions that puzzle me.
30. I carry out investigations to answer the teacher's questions.
31. I find out answers to questions by doing investigations.
32. I solve problems by using information obtained from my own investigations.

#### Task Orientation

33. Getting a certain amount of work done is important to me.
34. I do as much as I set out to do.
35. I know the goals for this class.
36. I am ready to start this class on time.
37. I know what I am trying to accomplish in this class.
38. I pay attention during this class.
39. I try to understand the work in this class.
40. I know how much work I have to do.

#### Cooperation

41. I cooperate with other students when doing assignment work.
42. I share my books and resources with other students when doing assignments.
43. When I work in groups in this class, there is teamwork.
44. I work with other students on projects in this class.
45. I learn from other students in this class.
46. I work with other students in this class.
47. I cooperate with other students on class activities.
48. Students work with me to achieve class goals.

#### Equity

49. The teacher gives as much attention to my questions as to other students' questions.
50. I get the same amount of help from the teacher as do other students.
51. I have the same amount of say in this class as other students.
52. I am treated the same as other students in this class.
53. I receive the same encouragement from the teacher as other students do.
54. I get the same opportunity to contribute to class discussions as other students.
55. My work receives as much praise as other students' work.
56. I get the same opportunity to answer questions as other students.

---

Items are scored 1, 2, 3, 4, and 5, respectively, for the responses *almost never, seldom, sometimes, often,* and *almost always.*

*Source: Journal of Educational Research,* Vol. 93, Issue 1, pp. 48–62, 1999. Reprinted with permission of the Helen Dwight Reid Educational Foundation. Published by Heldref Publications, 1319 Eighteenth St., NW, Washington, DC 20036-1802. 

# CHAPTER 13 Action Research Designs: Research for Solving Practical Problems

*Throughout this text, we have emphasized formal research conducted to add to our collective knowledge about research problems. Sometimes, however, researchers and practitioners conduct research to solve real problems in local settings. Action research designs are best suited for these situations. Action researchers explore a practical problem with the aim of developing a solution. As both a consumer of research and a practitioner, you need to learn about the process of conducting action research. This chapter introduces two types of action research, reviews their key characteristics, provides steps for planning action research studies, and suggests strategies for evaluating action research studies.*

**BY THE END OF THIS CHAPTER, YOU SHOULD BE ABLE TO:**

- Explain how action research differs from other research approaches.
- Name two different action research designs.
- List key characteristics for each of the action research designs.
- Plan an action research study in response to a problem in your own practice setting.
- Identify the action research design used in a reported study.
- Evaluate the action research design as reported in a research article.

Before reading further, stop and think about some practical problems that you have faced in the past year or that you can imagine facing in your profession in the future. Try to list at least three problems that matter to you.

Perhaps you came up with problems similar to ones that others have faced, such as:

- Children on free and reduced lunch at your school are not able to get enough to eat over the weekends.
- There is a history of alcohol abuse associated with the high school prom each year.
- Students are not making use of the school library.
- Immigrant parents have difficulty participating in parent–teacher conferences.

Each of these problems could call for formal quantitative, qualitative, and mixed methods research studies. You could also gain knowledge about these problems by reading literature reporting related research. Any one of these problems, however, may also be facing you and your community at this moment. You may want to learn about these problems, but you also want to develop a plan and take action to try to bring about a workable solution.

Based on the knowledge you have developed about the research process, you possess the tools to develop such plans using an action research design. Research does not have to be something that someone else does, but can become part of *your* repertoire of skills and strategies that you bring to address problems that are important to you. By identifying a problem, gathering information, acting on that information, and reflecting on what you learn, you can use the process of research to help find solutions to problems. That is the goal of action research.

## What Is Action Research?

Action research has an applied focus. Similar to mixed methods research, action research uses data collection based on either quantitative or qualitative methods or both. However, it differs in that action research addresses a specific, practical issue and seeks to obtain solutions to a problem. Thus, **action research designs** are systematic procedures done by practitioners (e.g., teachers, social workers, nurses) to gather quantitative and qualitative data to improve the ways their particular professional setting operates (e.g., a school), their practice (e.g., their teaching), and their impact on others (e.g., student learning). In some action research, the researcher seeks to address and solve a local, practical problem, such as a classroom issue for a teacher. In other situations, the researcher seeks to empower, transform, and emancipate individuals in educational or other community settings.

## Who Conducts Action Research?

Action research provides an opportunity for educators and other practitioners to reflect on their own practices. Action researchers can be teachers, administrators, specialists, counselors, nurses, social workers, and community leaders, to name a few possibilities. Within school settings, action research offers a means for professional development for teachers and staff and for addressing school-wide problems. In fact, the scope of action research provides a means for teachers in the schools or practitioners in the community to improve their practices for taking action and to do so by participating in research. Action research studies may also include active partnerships among practitioners, university researchers, and community members.

## What Is the Process of Research for Action Research Studies?

Different from the more linear process of other research designs, action research represents a dynamic process for conducting research. Action researchers engage in a dynamic process involving iterations of activities, such as a cycle of activities. The key idea is that the researcher cycles or spirals back and forth among reflection about a problem, data collection, and action. A school-based team, for example, may try several actions after reflecting on the best time for high school classes to begin. Reflecting, collecting data, trying a solution, and spiraling back to reflection are all part of the process of action research, as depicted in Figure 13.1. The process does not follow a linear pattern or a causal sequence from problem to action.

## How Did Action Research Designs Develop?

The social-psychologist Kurt Lewin coined the term action research in the 1930s (Mills, 2007). He developed a process for groups to use to address societal issues. This group process consisted of four steps: planning, acting, observing, and reflecting. Lewin's approach introduced many of the modern ideas of action research: a process of steps, participation, the democratic impulse of involvement, and the contribution to social change (Kemmis, 1994). The development of action research continued in the 1970s with the recognition of the importance of involving practitioners in the solution to their own problems. For example, the Fort Teaching project in England focused on teachers studying their own practices. Researchers and schools also formed inquiry teams in the United States. Another recent development has been the participatory, emancipatory, or community action research approach in which groups assume responsibility for their own emancipation and change (Kemmis & Wilkinson, 1998). Scholars have used ideological foundations such as feminism and critical race theory to develop action-oriented, advocacy means of inquiry.

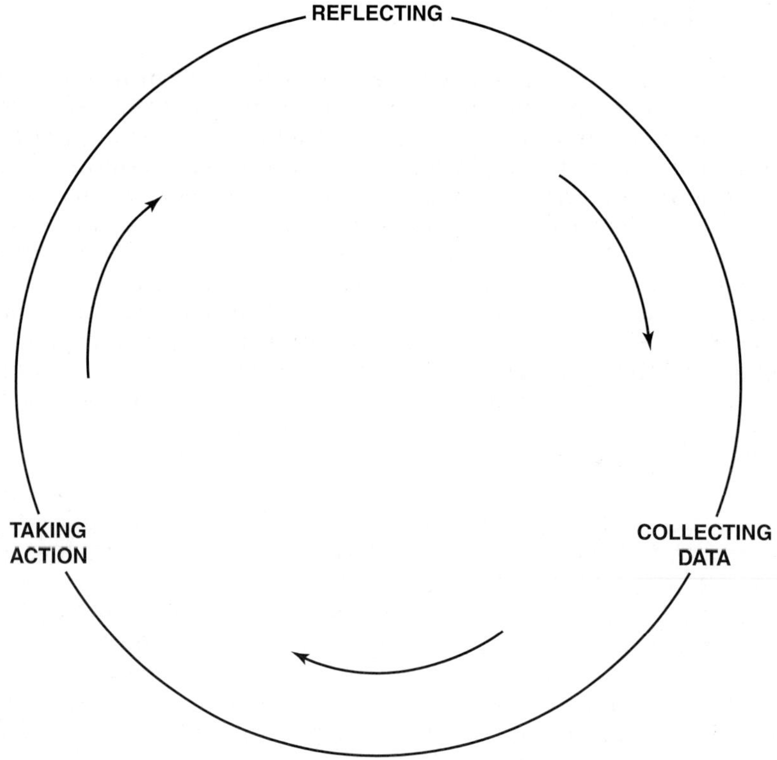


**FIGURE 13.1 The Action Research Process Cycle**
*Source:* Adapted from Stringer (2008).

From these developments, two distinct types of action research have emerged. As summarized in Figure 13.2, these two action research designs are:

- practical action research, and
- participatory action research.

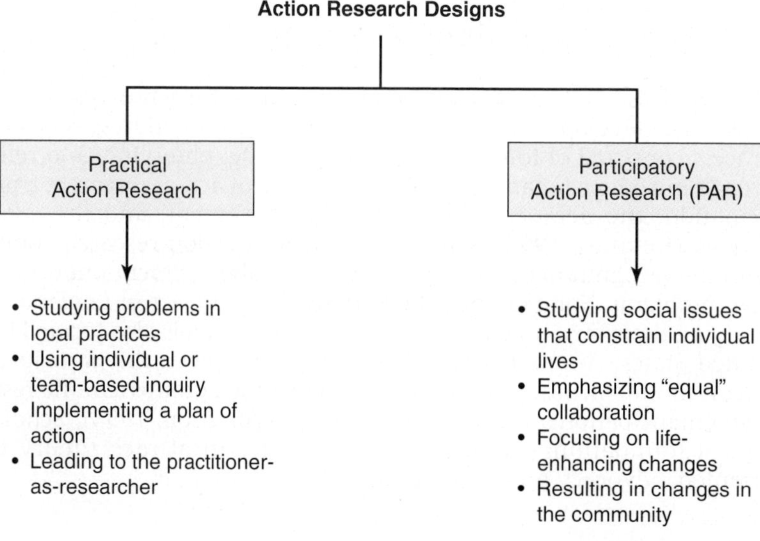


**FIGURE 13.2 Types of Action Research Designs and Their Use**

## What Is the Practical Action Research Design?

*Here's a Tip for Reading Research!*

The two action research designs share many common procedures. The best way to recognize the difference is by considering the intent of the research. Practical action research is used to address a practical problem in one's professional practice. Participatory action research is practical too, but emphasizes emancipation or change in our communities or society.

Teachers seek to research problems in their own classrooms so that they can improve their students' learning and their own professional performance. Teams comprised of teachers, students, counselors, and administrators engage in action research to address common issues, such as escalating violence in school. In these situations, educators seek to enhance the practice of education through the systematic study of a local problem. This form of action research is called practical action research, and its purpose is to research a specific professional situation with a view toward improving practice. **Practical action research** involves a small-scale research project, narrowly focuses on a specific problem or issue, and is undertaken by individual practitioners or teams within a practice setting such as a school or clinic. Examples of practical action research studies include:

- An elementary teacher studies the disruptive behavior of a child in her classroom.
- A team composed of students, teachers, and parents studies the results of implementing a new math program in the junior high.
- A nurse studies her professional development using technology in communicating with patients.

### Practitioners Use Practical Action Research to Solve Local Problems

Teachers and other practitioners choose to engage in action research when they seek to improve specific, local issues by solving a problem. This problem may be the difficulties in documenting learning by pre-kindergarten students (Haigh, 2007), ascertaining whether problem-based learning is superior to the traditional lecture (Dods, 1997), or discovering how literacy in writing emerges for first-grade students (Ceprano & Garan, 1998). Action research calls for practitioners to be researchers. For example, teachers can study concerns in their own schools or classrooms and implement site-based councils or committees in schools to enhance research as an integral part of daily classes and education. In this spirit, educators use action research to test their own theories and explanations about learning, examine the effects of their practices on students, and explore the impact of approaches on parents, colleagues, and administrators within their schools. With an emphasis on self-reflection and learning, practitioners also choose to conduct action research to advance their own professional development.

### Practical Action Researchers Use a Spiral Approach to the Process of Research

There is no set process that practitioners must use when conducting a practical action research study in their setting. Mills (2007), however, advances a model called the dialectic action research spiral. This model, shown in Figure 13.3, provides teachers, social workers, nurses, and other practitioners with a four-step guide for their action research project. Mills emphasizes that it is a model for practitioners to use to study themselves, not a process of conducting research on practitioners. It is a spiral because it includes four stages where investigators cycle back and forth between data collection and a focus, and data collection and analysis and interpretation.

In this procedure, the teacher-researcher (or nurse-researcher or social worker-researcher) identifies an area of focus, such as increasing parent involvement in the elementary classroom. This process involves defining an area of focus, doing reconnaissance (self-reflection and description), reviewing the literature, and writing an action plan to guide the research. Then the teacher-researcher collects data by gathering multiple sources of data (quantitative and qualitative) and by using a variety of inquiry tools, such as interviewing other teachers or sending questionnaires to parents. Data collection also consists of attending to issues of validity, reliability, and ethics, such as provisions for informed consent.

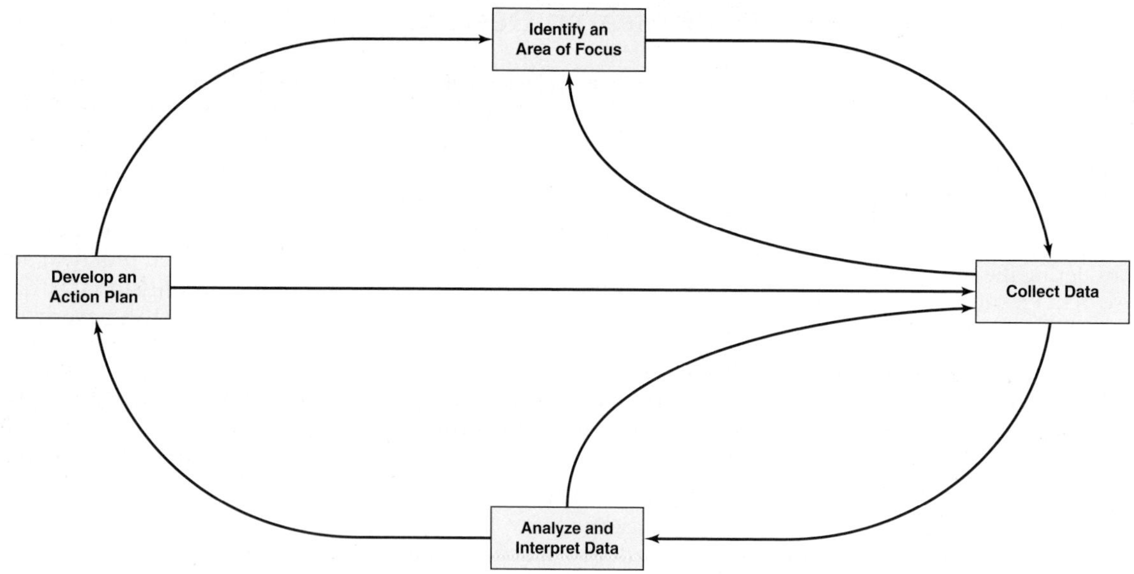


**FIGURE 13.3 Mills' (2007) Dialectic Action Research Spiral**

*Source:* From Geoffrey E. Mills *Action Research: A Guide for the Teacher Researcher,* 3/e. Published by Merrill, an imprint of Pearson Education. 

The teacher-researcher follows this phase with analysis and interpretation. The process includes coding surveys, interviews, and questionnaires; identifying themes; doing an organizational review; engaging in concept mapping (i.e., visualizing the relationship of ideas); analyzing antecedents and consequences; and displaying findings. The teacher-researcher might summarize the strategies described by other teachers alongside the opinions of parents. Interpretation involves extending the analysis by raising questions, connecting findings to personal experiences, seeking the advice of critical friends, and contextualizing the findings in literature and theory.

In the final stage, the teacher-researcher completes an action plan or chart. This chart includes a summary of findings, recommended actions, and the identification of individuals responsible for action and individuals who need to be consulted and informed. Perhaps a few teachers will team to start a new program of sending weekly updates home to parents or one parent will work with the teacher to help communicate goals to all parents. The chart also indicates who will monitor and collect the data, the timeline for data collection, and the resources needed to carry out the action (e.g., cookies and coffee available for an evening parents' meeting at the school).

Overall, this process emphasizes practical action research centered around studying a local problem, engaging in inquiry by an individual practitioner (e.g., teacher-as-researcher) or a team, and focusing on professional development.

## Key Characteristics of a Practical Action Research Study

You can identify a research study using a practical action research design by looking for the term *action research.* Although practical action research can be used in any practice setting (e.g., a health clinic or a state service agency), many examples appear in the education literature. These studies also use the term *teacher inquiry* for this approach. The format of practical action research reports will vary because they are intended to be useful for other practitioners instead of serving as formal reports of research. Nonetheless, these studies will usually include the following characteristics:

- ***The action researcher needs to solve a practical problem.*** The aim of a practical action research study is to address an actual problem in a professional setting. Thus, action researchers study practical issues that will have immediate benefits for practitioners. These issues may be a concern of a single teacher in a classroom or a problem involving many employees in an organization. Action researchers do not undertake this form of research to advance knowledge for knowledge's sake, but to solve an immediate, practical problem.

- ***The action researcher gathers information using a dynamic process.*** Action researchers engage in a dynamic process involving iterations of activities. As illustrated in Figure 13.3, this process includes iterations among reflecting about a problem, collecting quantitative and qualitative information, interpreting this information, and action. A school-based team, for example, may try several actions after reflecting on the best time for high school classes to begin.
- ***The action researcher studies his/her own practices.*** Action researchers study and experiment with their own practices. As they study their own situation, they reflect on what they have learned—a form of self-development—as well as what they can do to improve their practices. Action researchers deliberately experiment with their own practices, monitor the actions and circumstances in which they occur, and then retrospectively reconstruct an interpretation of the action as a basis for future action.
- ***The action researcher uses the information to develop a plan of action.*** At some point in the process, the action researcher formulates an action plan in response to the problem. This plan may be simply presenting the data to important stakeholders, establishing a pilot program, implementing new practices, or establishing an ongoing agenda to explore new practices. This plan may also be shared more broadly in a report or Web site or at a conference to share the lessons learned with other practitioners.

## An Example of a Practical Action Research Study

Dicker (1990) used an action research study to examine her response to being assigned to teach a new communications course that was outside of her teaching expertise in math and drama. She clearly faced a very practical problem in her setting. The author reflects on her experiences and participates with another former teacher of English. She used four sources of data in this project: her own journals (the major source), student journals, comments from a former teacher, and tape recordings. Throughout the study, a dynamic process unfolds, with this teacher trying out an idea, making adjustments, and exploring another idea. A series of mini-plans ensues as this author shares her personal frustrations and successes in teaching an unfamiliar subject in a high school.

### What Do You Think?

Suppose you are reading a collection of research articles related to the problem of students' lack of motivation. Why might the author of one of the reports have decided to use a practical action research design? What characteristics would you expect to find in this study?

### Check Your Understanding

A middle school math teacher may be concerned that her students are not motivated in her pre-algebra class. She decides to implement a practical action research study to focus on developing strategies to improve her students' motivation. We expect that she will gather information, such as talking with other teachers, reviewing papers written about teaching math, and surveying the students about the types of activities they find motivating. She develops a plan to try two different strategies: Having students bring to class examples of math that they find in their every day lives and asking students to work in groups on a math problem that represents a real-world application of math. She also documents the number of questions asked during each class and the percentage of students who complete each activity. Throughout the year she keeps a journal of the activities she tries and how well they worked so she can continue to refine the strategies she uses.

How might you use a practical action research design to address a problem you face?

## What Is Participatory Action Research?

> *Here's a Tip for Reading Research!*
>
> Notice that both practical action research and participatory action research can be abbreviated with the letters "PAR." In published studies, PAR almost always stands for *participatory* action research, and authors often use this shorthand for this design. Therefore, we will also use PAR as we discuss the participatory action research design in this chapter.

Participatory action research has a long history in social inquiry involving communities, industries and corporations, and other organizations outside of education. Rather than a focus on individual teachers solving immediate classroom problems or schools addressing internal issues, **participatory action research** (PAR) has a social and community orientation and an emphasis on research that contributes to emancipation or change in our society. Drawing on the ideological works of the Brazilian Paulo Freire, the German critical theorist Jurgen Habermas, and more recently Australians Stephen Kemmis and Ernest Stringer (Schmuck, 1997), this approach has emerged as an action-oriented, advocacy means of inquiry. Often PAR emphasizes qualitative data collection, but it may also involve quantitative data collection.

### Researchers Use Participatory Action Research to Improve the Quality of People's Lives

Researchers conduct participatory action research when their goal is to improve the quality of people's organizations, communities, and family lives (Stringer, 1999). Although espousing many of the ideas of teacher and school-based practical action research, it differs by incorporating an emancipatory aim of improving and empowering individuals and organizations in educational and other settings. Applied to education, the focus is on improving and empowering individuals in schools, systems of education, and school communities. PAR researchers study issues that relate to a need to address social problems that constrain and repress the lives of students and educators. For example, individuals have engaged in PAR studies to empower parents whose children have been classified as having emotional disabilities to improve family-school relationships (Ditrano & Silverstein, 2006) and to improve economic and educational opportunities of street-life oriented Black men (Payne, 2008).

Researchers also choose to use participatory action research when they have a distinct ideological foundation that shapes the direction of the process of inquiry. This foundation may include principles of ideologies such as feminism, critical race theory, or disability theory. These theories encourage PAR researchers to engage in a process of research that promotes egalitarian and democratic aims. PAR researchers strive for an open, broad-based involvement of participants in their studies by collaborating in decisions as consensual partners and engaging participants as equals to ensure their well-being. For example, in their inquiries researchers emphasize the importance of establishing contacts, identifying stakeholder groups, identifying key people, negotiating the researcher's role, and building a preliminary picture of the field context of the study (Stringer, 1999). The social values of liberation and life-enhancing changes also are important. PAR researchers seek to bring about a new vision for schools, community agencies, youth clubs, and ethnic groups within schools.

### Participatory Action Researchers Use a Social Process Emphasizing Collaboration

While all types of action research utilize a dynamic process, the participatory action research process emphasizes a social process and collaboration among researchers, stakeholders, and participants. Stringer (2008) provides one model for thinking about this action research process within a participatory context. His model portrays the action research process as a helix, which you can see in Figure 13.4. This helix model contains three phases: look, think, and act.

Let's examine more closely the components of the action research process for looking, thinking, and acting. In this model, Stringer (1999, 2008) places emphasis on the importance of looking to build a picture in order to help stakeholders understand issues they are experiencing. The "look" phase consists of collecting data (e.g., through interviews, observation, and documents), recording and analyzing the information, and constructing and reporting to stakeholders about the issue. It may look for injustices or ways in which certain individuals are being oppressed. The "think" phase then

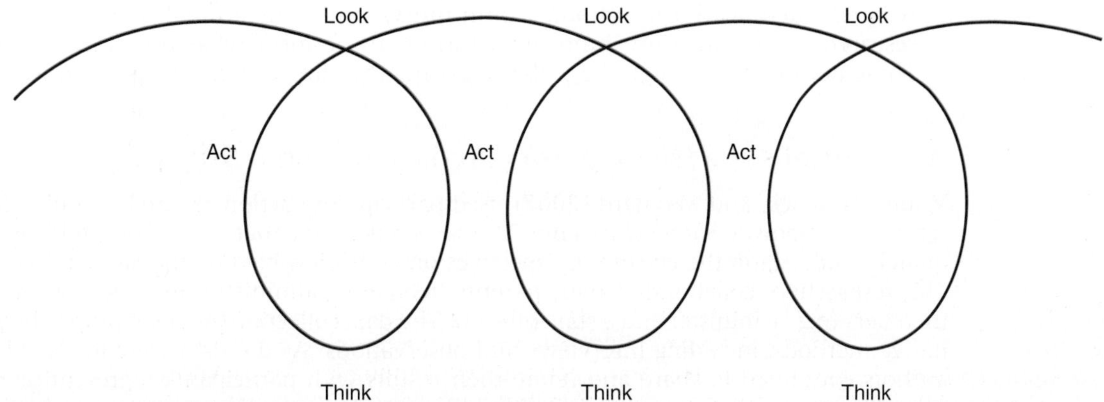


**FIGURE 13.4 Stringer's (2008) Action Research Helix**

*Source:* From Ernie Stringer *Action Research In Education*, 2/e. Published by Merrill, an imprint of Pearson Education. 

moves into interpreting the issues in greater depth and identifying priorities for action in collaboration with stakeholders and participants. In the final phase, the researcher identifies the "act" phase—working with participants to devise solutions to the problems. This involves devising a plan and setting direction, such as objectives, tasks, and persons to carry out the objectives and securing needed resources. It also means implementing the plan, encouraging people to carry it out, and evaluating it in terms of its effect and achievements for improving lives.

## Key Characteristics of a Participatory Action Research Study

You can identify a research study using a participatory action research design by looking for terms such as *participatory action research, critical action research,* or *community-based inquiry*. You can expect to find the following key characteristics when you read a PAR report:

- ***The PAR researcher wants to help individuals free themselves from constraints.*** PAR is emancipatory in that it helps unshackle people from the constraints of irrational and unjust structures that limit self-development and self-determination. These constraints may be found in the media, in language, in work procedures, and in the relationships of power in educational settings. The intent of a study, for example, might be to change the bureaucratic procedures for teachers in schools so that they can better facilitate student learning.
- ***The PAR researcher gathers information using a recursive process.*** PAR is recursive (reflexive or dialectical) and focused on bringing about change in practices. This occurs through spirals of examination, reflection and action. When teachers reflect on their roles in schools, they will try one action and then another, always returning to the central question of what they learned and accomplished because of their actions.
- ***The PAR researcher emphasizes collaboration.*** PAR researchers collaborate with others, often involving participants as co-researchers in the research. These co-researcher participants may be individuals within a school or outside personnel, such as university researchers or professional association groups. This collaboration involves establishing acceptable and cooperative relationships, communicating in a manner that is sincere and appropriate, and including all individuals, groups, and issues. Many aspects of the research process are open to collaboration in a PAR project. During this collaboration, roles may vary and be negotiated, but the concept of interacting is central to the process.
- ***The PAR researcher shares the research to bring about change.*** Although PAR researchers publish in scholarly journals, they are typically more interested in sharing the information locally with individuals who can promote change. PAR researchers report their research with individuals who can immediately use the

results, such as local school, community, and educational personnel. PAR researchers may also use innovative forums to perform what they have learned. These performances might be a play, a poem, a reading of text, slides, or music.

### An Example of a Participatory Action Research Study

Valdez, Dowrick, and Maynard (2007) used participatory action research at one middle school to empower Samoan parents. The researchers felt that the school did not adequately understand the cultural perspectives on education held by the Samoan parents. The researchers collaborated with parents, teachers, administrators, and community members (e.g., a minister and a state official). The data collection included primarily qualitative methods, including interviews and observations. As the data were analyzed, the authors continued to share and refine their results with participants representing each role (parents, teachers, etc.). The findings uncovered many cultural misperceptions that existed in the community, such as perceptions about parents' role in education. From the increased understanding of all stakeholders' perspectives, the school developed new programs and policies that aligned better with the cultural values of all ethnic groups represented at the school thereby reducing barriers against Samoan parents' involvement.

### What Do You Think?

Suppose you are reading a collection of research articles related to the problem of students' lack of motivation. Why might the author of one of the reports have decided to use a PAR design? What characteristics would you expect to find in this study?

#### Check Your Understanding

Perhaps a teacher notices that two students have recently become unmotivated in his high school classes. Through conversations with other teachers and the students, the teacher learns that the students are members of the school's gay, lesbian, bisexual, and transgender (GLBT) community and that other students have recently begun harassing them. The teacher discusses his concerns with the principal and, with her support, they initiate a participatory action research project to improve the culture for all gay and lesbian students at the school. We might expect the report of this study to emphasize collaboration, such as the research team, including the principal, teachers, GLBT and non-GLBT students, and community activists. They might gather information such as surveying all members of the school (staff and students) and interviewing representatives of different groups. Together the research team of adults and adolescents put together an action plan that includes creating a committee on diversity at the school. In addition, the research team may use the results of their research to develop a play that illustrates the injustice of harassment and is performed by the school drama club for the school and members of the community.

How might you use a PAR design in your community?

## How Do You Plan Your Own Action Research Study?

You can now recognize and interpret action research studies you find in the literature. In addition to reading about others' projects, you can design and implement your own action research design. By using an action research approach, you can apply the tools of research to gather information about, reflect on, and take action in response to problems that you want solved in your local setting.

Drawing from numerous books available on conducting action research (e.g., Mills, 2007; Stringer, 2008), we provide eight steps that you can take to conduct your

For practice planning an action research study, go to the *Activities and Applications* section under the topic "Action Research" in MyEducationalResearchLab, located at www.myeducationlab.com. Complete the exercise "Action Research on the High School Science Club."

own action research study. As you read them, remember that action research is a dynamic, flexible process and that no precise blueprint exists for how to proceed. However, these steps in the process can illustrate a general approach for your use.

### Step 1—Determine if Action Research Is Possible in Your Setting and with Your Colleagues

You should consider action research when you want to systematically address problems in your work situation or community and to advance your own professional development. It requires that you have the time to collect and analyze data and to experiment with different options for solving the problem. To help with the process of reflection, you ideally need collaborators with whom to share findings and who can potentially serve as co-researchers on the project. Action research also requires some familiarity with the many types of quantitative and qualitative data collection (like introduced in this book!). You can use these procedures to gather information in order to devise a plan of action.

*Here's a Tip for Applying Research!*

Remember that in an action research study, you will participate in your own research project. You are not studying someone else; instead you are examining and changing your own practices to solve a problem you face.

### Step 2—Specify the Problem You Want to Study

The most important factor in action research is that you need to solve a practical problem. This problem is one that you face in your own practice or in your community (Kemmis & Wilkinson, 1998). After reflection, write down the problem or phrase it as a question to answer. In some situations, action researchers may begin with collecting data, evaluating existing information, or even planning an action to try. Viewing action research as a spiral of activities (recall Figures 13.3 and 13.4) introduces several points in the spiral in which you might begin your action research study.

### Step 3—Locate Resources to Help You Address the Problem

Explore several resources to help study the problem. Literature and existing data may help you formulate a plan of action. You may need to review the literature and determine what others have learned about solving the issue. Asking colleagues for advice helps initiate a study. Teaming with university personnel or knowledgeable people in the community provides a resource base for an action research project. Individuals who have conducted action research projects can also help you during your research study.

### Step 4—Identify Information You Need to Examine the Problem

*Here's a Tip for Applying Research!*

Consider whether statistical procedures may be helpful for the quantitative data that you collect in your project (such as student scores or teacher attitudes). Most colleges and universities have statisticians who are willing and able to assist you with analyzing your data. You can also find free statistics calculators available online, such as from http://graphpad.com.

Plan a strategy for gathering data. This means that you need to decide who can provide data, how many people you will study, your access to individuals, and the rapport and support you can expect to obtain from them. Even if you do not need to obtain formal approvals for research (which you would have to do if you plan to use the research for a graduate research project), you may want to inform your principal and other constituents about your research plans and seek their approval.

Another consideration is what type of data you need to collect. Your choices are to collect quantitative data or qualitative data or both. The choice of data sources depends on the questions, time and resources, availability of individuals, and sources of information. In general, the more sources used, the more you will be able to understand the problem and develop viable action plans. It is wise, however, to limit data collection in your first action research study so that you have a manageable amount of information to analyze.

### Step 5—Implement the Data Collection

Implementing data collection takes time, especially if you gather multiple sources of information. In addition, your participants may have limited time to complete instruments or engage in interviews. Keeping an accurate record of the information collected, organizing it into data files for numeric or theme analysis, and examining the quality of the information are important data collection steps. You should also keep a record of your own actions and reflections throughout the process, as these notes will become another source of useful data.

*Here's a Tip for Applying Research!*

Action research is a great way for you to continue your professional development as it provides a formal process of reflecting on your practice, gathering new information, and changing your practices. This process also takes time and can be challenging. Do not expect to develop a perfect plan on the first attempt. By focusing on the spiral approach, you can continue to learn and improve over time.

### Step 6—Analyze the Data

You may decide to analyze the data yourself or enlist the help of other scholars or data analysts. You might show your results to others to find out how they would interpret the findings. In most situations, descriptive statistics about the trends in the quantitative data (as discussed in Chapter 8) and general themes in the qualitative data (as discussed in Chapter 11) will suffice for your analysis. The major idea is to keep the data analysis manageable so that you can identify useful information in formulating a plan of action.

### Step 7—Develop a Plan for Action

A plan may be an informal statement about the implementation of a new educational practice. It might be a plan to reflect on alternative approaches to addressing the problem, or to share what you have learned with others, such as other teachers, individuals in district offices, or other schools and communities. You might formally write out this plan or present it as an outline. You can develop it yourself or collaborate with school personnel in writing it. The important point is that you now have a strategy for trying out some ideas to help solve your problem.

For practice identifying the steps in an action research study report, go to the *Building Research Skills* section under the topic "Action Research" in MyEducationalResearchLab, located at www.myeducationlab.com. Complete the exercise "Identifying Steps in the Research Process for an Action Research Study" and use the provided feedback to further develop your skills for reading research articles.

### Step 8—Implement the Plan and Reflect

In many action research projects, you will implement your plan of action to see whether it makes a difference. This involves trying out a potential solution to your problem and monitoring whether it has an impact. To determine this difference, you might consult your original objectives or the research question that you sought to answer in the action research project.

You also need to reflect on what you have learned from implementing your plan and sharing it with others. You may need to share it broadly with school colleagues, school committees, university researchers, or policy makers. In some cases, you will not achieve an adequate solution, and you will need to try out another idea and see if it makes a difference. In this way, one action research project often leads to another.

## How Do You Evaluate a Study's Action Research Design?

As the name action research implies, there are two aspects you can consider when evaluating any action research study. First, it is a form of research and therefore the action researcher should use sound procedures for gathering and analyzing qualitative and quantitative information. We have provided quality indicators for these methods already in this book. Second, this research design should result in actions that help to solve real problems. Therefore, you should also emphasize the quality of the actions that result from any action research project. Figure 13.5 provides criteria you can use to assess an author's implementation of an action research design with an emphasis on the features unique to action research.

Use the following criteria to evaluate the quality of the research design in an action research report. For each evaluation item, indicate the following ratings:

+ You rate the item as high quality" for the study.
✓ You rate the item as "ok quality" for the study.
– You rate the item as "low quality" for the study.

In addition to your rating, make notes about each element when you apply these criteria to an actual published study.

| In a high-quality action research report, the author . . . | Application to a Published Study | |
|---|---|---|
| | Your Rating | Your Notes |
| 1. Focuses on an issue in practice or the local community. | | |
| 2. Collects multiple sources of data (often quantitative and qualitative) to help address the problem. | | |
| 3. Collaborates with others during the study to find the best solutions. | | |
| 4. Shows respect for all collaborators so they are equal partners in the action research process. | | |
| 5. Advances a plan of action for trying to solve the problem. | | |
| 6. Reflects on his/her own development as a professional. | | |
| 7. Helps to enhance the lives of participants by solving a problem, empowering them, changing them, or providing them with new understandings. | | |
| 8. Develops a plan recommending changes to practice. | | |
| 9. Reports the research in a way that is understandable and useful to audiences, including other practitioners. | | |

**FIGURE 13.5** Criteria for Evaluating the Quality of a Study's Action Research Design

Keep in mind that although action research has gained support in education and other fields, it is not without critics who are reluctant to view it as a legitimate form of inquiry (Stringer, 1999). Some view it as an informal process of research, conducted by teachers and other practitioners who are not formal academic researchers. The practical aspect of action research also suggests an applied orientation to this form of inquiry with a less than scientific approach. Action researchers typically report results of their studies not to scholarly journals, but to online journals, Web sites, or local school groups. The methods are adapted and changed in response to the practitioners' objectives to understand a practical problem. Hence, the design may not have the rigor and systematic approach found in other designs. Despite these limitations, action research studies are among the best source of information to learn about potential solutions to real problems because they are conducted in real professional settings by real practitioners. Therefore, the results may directly apply to your own setting and practice.

## Reviewing What We've Learned

- Look for action research designs as sets of procedures for using research to solve real problems in professional and community settings.
- Consider teachers, administrators, practitioners, and community members as potential action researchers.
- Note that action research uses a cyclical or spiral approach to conducting research that emphasizes reflection, data gathering, and action.
- Determine the type of action research design as either a practical action research design or a participatory action research design.

- Expect practitioners, such as teachers, administrators, nurses, or counselors, to use action research to solve local problems.
- Understand that practical action research studies are part research and part professional development.
- Expect individuals to collaborate when using action research to free individuals from constraints in their schools and communities.
- Look for action research studies to produce plans for action, materials or performances, and research reports.
- Consider the steps for conducting action research as a model for solving problems in your own setting.
- Assess the use of action research designs by considering whether the key characteristics of the design were implemented and whether the study resulted in local improvements.

## Practicing Your Skills

At this time, read carefully the "action research Internet skills" study starting on p. 345 at the end of this chapter. As you read this article, pay close attention to the elements that illustrate the use of an action research design.

Once you have read the study, assess your knowledge of the content of this chapter by answering the following questions that relate to the action research Internet skills study. Use the answers found in the Appendix to evaluate your progress.

1. What problem did this author want to solve in her local setting?
2. What evidence do you find that the teacher-researcher used a spiral approach to her study?
3. In what ways did the teacher-researcher collaborate with others?
4. What actions did the researcher take as a result of her study?
5. Give three pieces of evidence that this study is a good example of action research.

# The Action Research Internet Skills Study

Let's examine another published research study to apply what you have learned about reading research articles and to evaluate how a practitioner used an action research design (by completing the *Practicing Your Skills* questions listed on the previous page). A formal reference for this study is:

Heil, D. (2005). The internet and student research: Teaching critical evaluation skills. *Teacher Librarian, 33*(2), 26–29.

As you read this article, note the marginal annotations that signal the major sections of a research report, the steps of the research process, and the major characteristics of action research. In addition, use the following walk-through to help you understand how the steps of the research process are described within the major sections of the report.

## The Introduction Section

- Identifying a research problem (paragraph 01)
- Reviewing the literature (paragraphs 02–06)
- Specifying the purpose (paragraph 01)

The author of the action research Internet skills study (Heil, 2005) begins her study by highlighting a problem she faced as the librarian at her school. She needs to understand why students prefer to use the Internet for their research on school projects and how to design a curriculum unit to teach them how to critically evaluate Internet sites. She lists her questions and immediately states her purpose of doing an action research study to answer the questions for her school and eighth-grade students. She provides a small amount of literature review to add justification of the importance of this problem in paragraphs 02–06, but clearly her main motivation for the research is to develop a plan for solving this problem at her school.

## The Method Section

- Selecting a design and collecting data (paragraphs 07–15 and 30–31)

The author selected the action research design (paragraph 01) for her study. She discussed various aspects of this design as part of her methods, including collaborating with other teachers and examining her own practices (paragraphs 07–09). She also describes gathering a variety of quantitative and qualitative data sources from 14 eighth-grade students as part of her study. These included collecting surveys, interviews, open-ended questions on surveys, and worksheets from students (paragraphs 10–15). She used the data to inform her development of the curriculum unit. We also learn in paragraph 35 that she has used a spiral approach by continuing to implement the curriculum and gather data in subsequent school years.

## The Results Section

- Analyzing the data and reporting results (paragraphs 11–31)

Using a more flexible format that will appeal to other practitioners, the author reports her results as she describes the data that she collected. The results include summaries of students' responses in Tables 1 and 2, as well as descriptions of how student perceptions changed to be more realistic and critical with the curriculum (e.g., paragraph 30). She also developed and implemented a specific plan of action, namely the six-steps of the Internet site critical evaluation unit, which is described along with student reactions.

## The Conclusion Section

- Interpreting the research (paragraphs 32–35 and Notes)

The author concluded the report with a brief discussion of the study. Instead of comparing to past studies in the literature, she reflected on her process, what she learned, and how she continues to gather information, reflect and act. She concludes the report by informing readers of how she has continued to study this unit over the years (paragraph 35). This report had many elements of a formal research study, but presented the process in a way that would be useful to practitioners and that emphasized the local setting in which the study was conducted. In addition, by reviewing the *Notes About the Article,* we learn that this work is also being disseminated via a Web site where other practitioners can examine the curricular materials.

*Source:* This article is reprinted from *Teacher Librarian,* Vol. 33, Issue 2, pp. 26–29, 2005. Reprinted with permission of Scarecrow Press.

FEATURE ARTICLE

# the Internet and student research: teaching critical evaluation skills

The action research purpose statement focuses on solving a practical problem

Action researchers use research designs to plan their studies

TO USE THE INTERNET EFFECTIVELY, STUDENTS NEED TO BE TAUGHT CRITICAL-EVALUATION SKILLS THAT THEY CAN APPLY TO EACH WEB SITE THEY USE FOR RESEARCH. THE ACTION RESEARCH REPORT DISCUSSED IN THIS ARTICLE EXEMPLIFIES THE COLLABORATIVE TEAMWORK INVOLVED IN CREATING A CRITICAL-EVALUATION UNIT FOR INTERNET SITES TO BE USED WITH MIDDLE SCHOOL STUDENTS.

Results of the unit show that giving students background information on the Internet and showing Internet site examples to change their previous perceptions increased their understanding of the research tool. Teaching students about ways to evaluate Internet sites gave the students the information they needed to make more informed decisions about how they use the Internet.

Introduction Section

## INTRODUCTION

Identifying a research problem

Specifying a purpose for the research

01 The school year has begun and research projects are underway, but the library shelves are quiet and unused. A quick survey of the computer area shows once again that the students are using the Internet as their first source to locate information. As I watch this scene day after day, I ask these questions: Why do students find the Internet so appealing? Do students know the credibility of sites on the Internet? Do students know how to evaluate sites before using them? Would a unit on how to critically evaluate Internet sites increase the information literacy of the students? I decided to do action research to answer these questions.

by delilah heil

## LITERATURE REVIEW

02 Information literacy is defined as "a set of abilities requiring individuals to recognize when information is needed and have the ability to locate, evaluate, and use effectively the information needed" (Association of College and Research Libraries, 2000, p. 2). An important part of information literacy is the ability to evaluate Internet sources critically and to decide if each source is unbiased, accurate, and written by a qualified person who has specific knowledge on the topic. This ability is crucial to being a good user of resources and to research. However, many Internet users do not realize that "quality control does not exist on the Internet . . . there is a cesspool of waste" (Herring, 2001, Reasons section, para. 3).

03 Internet users "have developed an infatuation with information; any information is good information—the more of it, the better, as long as it is easy to obtain" (Scott & O'Sullivan, 2000, Value of Learning section, para. 6). Students usually choose less reliable commercial sites over educational or government sites for their research even though only one fourth of the commercial sites are suitable for academic purposes (Haycock, 2000). Students avoid more reliable databases and library materials because these sources take more time and involve more steps with fewer results (O'Sullivan & Scott, 2000).

04 The results of a questionnaire study (O'Sullivan & Scott, 2000) about students' preferred use of materials indicated that the majority of the students chose the Internet to conduct research, citing ease of use, speed of use, and the convenience of finding infinite information quickly as the top reasons for their choice. Almost 63% of the students cited the information's depth and variety as being a benefit of the Internet. Only 10% noted downfalls to the Internet, such as bias or inaccurate information. Students' responses also showed that they do not view information on the Internet critically.

05 Watson's research (2001) focused on the grade level at which students would be most receptive to learning Internet critical evaluation skills. The research showed that middle school students are the prime targets for information literacy skill training because they are still actively experimenting with the Internet and have reached a developmental stage where they can better comprehend the reliability of information.

06 These studies indicate a strong need for information literacy instruction on the quality of the material presented on the Internet. Teacher-librarians must teach students that although there is a large quantity of information available

Audiences that may benefit locally



Reviewing the literature

A practical problem that needs to be solved

Action researchers collaborate with others

Action researchers focus on their own practices

on the Internet, the quality of the sites is extremely important when using the Internet as a research tool.

Method Section

## COLLABORATION ASPECTS

07 Collaboration is an important factor in anything teacher-librarians do, but it is particularly important when doing action research. The easiest way to begin collaboration is to publicize what the project entails and see if anyone is interested. Many of the school's teachers were attending an in-school summer workshop with me at the time I publicized the project. The computer teacher commented that the topic fit into her eighth-grade computer class. She was looking for materials to use along with the required textbook lessons and felt that this unit would cover her needs and benefit students. She became a collaborative teaching partner.

08 While discussing the requirements for the research, we decided to use only research topics that were relevant and necessary to the eighth-grade curriculum. Students are required to do so much research for classes that having them work on topics we chose simply to fulfill our needs seemed wasteful. We asked the eighth-grade teachers attending the workshop what research projects they were planning to assign. The geography teacher wanted to assign a research project but could not work lab time into the schedule because all the labs had scheduled classes during her class time. Our research project met her needs, so we became a collaborative team. The final project that each student created would have to meet the requirements of that student's teachers. The collaborative team then decided how to best set up the final project.

09 Other people soon collaborated with us. Former students at the workshop who were teacher helpers heard of our plans. Learning that we needed Internet sites that would make the problem areas clearer to the students, they volunteered to create the teaching models. Using our notes and worksheets, they put their technology expertise to work developing two legitimate-looking sites.

Collecting data

## RESEARCH SITE AND SUBJECT DESCRIPTION

10 The school district is located in a small, rural Midwest community that is in the low to middle socioeconomic group, discerned by the fact that 47% of the students are eligible for free or reduced-price lunches. The school serves 391 students with the following ethnic backgrounds: 98% Caucasian, 2% Native American. Of the total eighth-grade class, 50% of the students participated. These 14 students (8 female and 6 male) were all of Caucasian descent.

TABLE 1

| Internet Use | Yes | No |
|---|---|---|
| Do you use the Internet for pleasure activities such as games? | 10 | 4 |
| Do you use the Internet for e-mail? | 12 | 2 |
| Do you use Internet chat rooms? | 8 | 6 |
| Do you use the Internet to research homework projects? | 14 | 0 |
| Do you use online databases provided by local libraries? | 5 | 9 |
| **Research Use** | | |
| When you are assigned research, which do you use first? | Books 4 | Internet 10 |
| Do you critically evaluate a site before choosing it as a research source? | Yes 2 / No 6 | Don't Know 6 |

Internet and Research Use

## PRE-UNIT DATA COLLECTION DESCRIPTION AND ANALYSIS

11 Students completed a pre-unit survey to determine their Internet use habits, their research habits, and their knowledge of the Internet and critical evaluation skills. Table 1 lists the Internet use statements, the research statements, and the students' responses. The Internet and research use responses showed that about 75% of the students used the Internet for games and for socialization activities such as e-mail. All of the students used the Internet for research projects. The research statement responses showed that 71% of students used the Internet first for research and that 85% of the students either do not choose to or do not know how to critically evaluate the Internet sites.

12 The two students who responded yes to the critical evaluation statement were interviewed further to determine their understanding of critical evaluation. When asked what is involved in critical evaluation of sites, one student responded that looking at the site to see if some of the information matches what is already known and seeing that the site contains the information that is being researched shows critical evaluation skills. The other student responded that checking out the pictures and graphs to see if they contain good information and the site's professional appearance is a method to critically evaluate a site.

13 Do students have adequate perceptions of the Internet? To find out, students were presented statements pertaining to the Internet and asked to rate the statements using a Likert Scale. Table 2 lists the statements and the responses. The responses indicated that 85% of the students had not formed strong opinions about the cost of publishing materials on the Internet. Forty-two percent of the students had not

Action researchers collect quantitative and/or qualitative data

Action researchers analyze quantitative and qualitative data

TABLE 2

| Statement About Internet | Strongly Agree | Agree | Neither Agree nor Disagree | Disagree | Strongly Disagree |
|---|---|---|---|---|---|
| All the information found on the Internet is reliable. | 1 | 1 | 4 | 4 | 4 |
| It is costly to publish materials on the Internet. | 0 | 1 | 12 | 1 | 0 |
| A person must get approval before publishing to the Internet. | 1 | 6 | 6 | 0 | 1 |

Internet Perceptions

Action researchers present quantitative and qualitative results

Analyzing data and reporting results

formed a strong opinion or agreed that information on the Internet is reliable. Ninety-two percent of the students either did not have a strong opinion or agreed that one must have approval before publishing on the Internet. This data presented strong indications that students do not have a good understanding of the Internet.

14 Students also responded to open-ended questions on the survey. The overwhelming response to the question, "What attracts you to the Internet for research?" was that the Internet provides fast access to information on any topic. When asked, "What do you consider to be reasons for not using the Internet?" the responses varied. A few students responded that there were no reasons; others suggested that the unwanted pop-ups and inappropriate sites were reasons to avoid using the Internet.

15 Finally, students completed a worksheet to determine how they select Internet sites. They had to locate one reliable Internet site on the Korean War and then respond to two questions: "In the search list, what number in the list was the site that you chose to use and why?" Six of the 14 students selected the first site and cited the reason for their choice as, "because the first hits in a search are always the best ones." The other 8 students picked from various sections of the list and cited good charts, graphs, information, and that the sites "looked official" as reasons for their choices.

16 Our survey reflected results similar to other researchers' data. It also showed that students would benefit from a unit on how to evaluate Internet sites.

Results Section

## THE INTERNET SITE CRITICAL EVALUATION UNIT

17 The unit involved six critical steps and a great deal of practice and review of the steps. The following is a description of each step as well as observations to students' reactions throughout the process.

18
### Step 1: Get the Students' Attention and Provide Motivation

The collected data showed that students believe the Internet is a reliable source of information, so their perception had to change before they would understand the importance of evaluating sites. To get their attention, we showed them sites that presented information that was contrary to what they had learned. We selected two sites that said the earth is flat. Students agreed that the earth is not flat and realized that everything on the Internet is not accurate. This led students to question the credentials of Internet site creators. Understanding that anyone can post any information to the Internet offered an opportunity to address some of the other misconceptions that became apparent during data collection.

19 We discussed with the students what elements, such as logos and emblems, they thought made a site look credible. We also mentioned the fact that experts who understand how search engines work can cause a site to register in the top 10 hits of a search even if it is not the most applicable. Students began to question how they could determine if a site contains reliable information.

20
### Step 2: Overview of Critical Evaluation Process and Terminology

Using a PowerPoint presentation, we reviewed information and introduced new information, and we gave the students an Internet Evaluation Checklist that showed the essential steps so that they were not distracted by having to take notes.

21
### Step 3: Applying the Process to the Model Internet Sites

Using the Internet Evaluation Checklist, the teaching team guided students through the first model web site. We also reviewed and gave oral quizzes on the step-by-step processes that students had to memorize. Next, the students evaluated the second site on their own, allowing them to work through the process and to find the fun areas embedded in the site. Although these fun areas were also evaluated, they served to lighten the tension and frustration the students were experiencing in their first attempts to critically evaluate Internet sites. During this process the teaching team was deluged with questions showing that the students were attempting to think through and make meaning of the process for themselves. We then reviewed the site and their findings.

22
### Step 4: Group Work

Evaluating Internet sites is hard, time consuming, and often frustrating for beginners. The teaching team divided students into groups of two. The paired students became peer-evaluation partners who worked through the site-evaluation process together and learned from each other. The teaching team changed the group dynamics after two site evaluations.

23 Before starting the evaluation process for each web site, the teaching team gave a specific teaching prompt such as, "You need to know about both sides of the cloning issue for your research. Would this site be a good choice?" Such a question was extremely important where bias could factor into the decision to use or reject a web site. After each group completed one web site evaluation checklist, the entire class reviewed the process and the findings of each group. Students demonstrated where they looked to find information and discussed their decision-making process for using or rejecting a site.

24 Initially, students were frustrated with the process as could be seen from their journal entries and from their in-class comments. They wanted everything they were looking for to be easy to find. They questioned why sites were not all created the same, and why there were no required areas on web sites that would make looking up information easier. After gathering all the information, the students also had great difficulty analyzing all the data and making their own judgment on the sites—a critical part of the process.

25 As students continued to evaluate more sites, the teaching team saw a glimmer of understanding as many of the students delved deeper into web sites, questioning more of what they found. We also noticed, however, that if a site had information that students wanted, they chose to ignore clear signals that the site was inappropriate for research.

26
### Step 5: Introducing Students to Databases on the Internet

The teaching team also made students aware that not all material on the Internet is unreliable and discussed the databases purchased by libraries and institutions that are credible for research purposes. We talked to the students about the purpose of databases and the evaluation process that goes into these publications. The information in the students' journals suggested that they found databases to be more difficult to use than a search engine on the Internet but easier than looking up magazines in the *Reader's Guide to Periodical Literature.*

27 The students questioned why we did not tell them about the usefulness of the databases earlier. We responded that they were so engrossed in the Internet that they would not have given something that seemed harder to use a second glance; many of the students agreed that our



Action researchers make a plan for action

Interpreting the research

Conclusion Section

The action researcher reflects on what has been learned

Action researchers use a spiral, interactive approach

assumption was right. They also agreed that learning how difficult it is to really evaluate information on the Internet made the Internet less appealing for research.

28 **Step 6: Applying the Unit to Real Research** The teaching team gave each student a geography research topic along with the rubrics listing the requirements for both the geography class and the computer class. Students could use library resources, Internet resources, or their geography textbook to complete their research project; however, they had to evaluate at least five Internet sites and find two credible sites to include in the research project. To use an Internet site in their paper they had to critically evaluate it and explain why they chose the site as being usable for research purposes.

29 Initially, students still questioned their abilities to critically evaluate sites. Their journals and class discussion showed that they were frustrated when the teaching team did not have an answer key for the site they selected to use. Later, the majority of students applied much time and effort and asked many questions about sites they wanted to use. They questioned themselves and the teachers more when they found a site that had the information they were looking for but that had questionable evaluation areas. This process showed that they knew what they found was probably not quality material, but they desperately wanted someone to say that it was acceptable to use so they would have their sources.

## POST-UNIT DATA COLLECTION DESCRIPTION AND ANALYSIS

30 When compared with the pre-unit survey, the post-unit student responses for what draws students to the Internet was the same. The students' Internet perceptions, however, had changed to be more realistic and better informed. Responses to the essay questions gave the greatest insight to the change in perception. Students no longer found a great deal of information to be the most valuable part of the Internet. In fact, the two most popular disadvantages they listed to using the Internet were too much information and too much evaluation required of the information.

31 Students were also asked to rank a predetermined list of resource materials in an attempt to find out where the Internet was now ranked. The list included general Internet, subscription databases on the Internet, magazines in the library, encyclopedias, and library books. In the pre-unit survey, 71% of the students selected the Internet as their first choice. Then, 75% of the students selected subscription databases on the Internet and encyclopedias as the top choices, followed by library books and magazines in the library, and last, the general Internet.

## CONCLUSION

32 The Internet site critical-evaluation unit that was designed to help students understand critical-evaluation skills was challenging for the teachers as well as the students. Both the teaching team and the students grappled with the fact that although there are many clues that one can use to evaluate an Internet site, there are no clear-cut answers.

33 The action research process helped me to answer my initial questions. Why do students find the Internet so appealing? Collected data showed that students generally find the Internet appealing because of the large amount of information that the medium contains. Do students know the credibility of sites on the Internet? Survey results showed that students do not have adequate background knowledge of the Internet and how it functions to understand the credibility of sites found on the Internet, and students do not know how to critically evaluate sites. Would a unit on critically evaluating Internet sites benefit students? Results of the unit showed that giving students background information on the Internet and showing Internet site examples to change their previous perceptions increased their understanding of the research tool. Teaching students about ways to evaluate Internet sites gave the students the information they needed to make more informed decisions about how they use the Internet.

34 The process does not end here for me. As a teacher-researcher, I followed up with this group to gather further data on how they are applying the knowledge they gained from this unit. As a teacher-librarian, I find it vital to provide the information contained in this unit to all students across multiple grade levels so that Internet users can make more informed decisions about their choices.

## UPDATE

35 This Internet site critical-evaluation project has been replicated several times since writing this article, and the results have not varied significantly from the results of the initial project. Other teachers are also emphasizing the need to critically evaluate web sites. Over this time I have observed the positive long-term results of the unit, finding that—with a strong emphasis and reminders—as research projects arise in the students' lives, exposure to this information does change the way students perceive and use the Internet.

Notes About the Article

## REFERENCES


Association of College & Research Libraries. (2000). *Information literacy competency standards for higher education.* Retrieved April 15, 2002, from www.ala.org/acrl/ilintro.html

Haycock, K. (2000). Web literacy [Electronic version]. *Teacher Librarian, 27*(5), 34.

Herring, M. Y. (2001). Why the Internet can't replace the library [Electronic version]. *The Education Digest, 67*(1), 46–49.

O'Sullivan, M., & Scott, T. (2000). Teaching Internet information literacy: A collaborative approach (part II) [Electronic version]. *Multimedia Schools, 7*(3), 34–37.

Scott, T. J. & O'Sullivan, M. (2000). The Internet and information literacy: Taking the first step toward technology education in the social studies [Electronic version]. *The Social Studies, 91*(3), 121–126.

Watson, J. (2001). Snapshots of a teen Internet user [Electronic version]. *Educational Media and Technology Yearbook, 26,* 115–124.

Delilah Heil is a teacher-librarian for the Lemmon School District in Lemmon, South Dakota. She provides library services for children in grades K–12 and teaches high school English. Her web site that contains the Critical Evaluation Unit materials discussed in this article can be found at http://dh015.k12.sd.us/. She can be reached at *Delilah.Heil@k12.sd.us.*

Action researchers share their results with other practitioners

Feature articles in *TL* are blind refereed by members of the advisory board. This article was submitted November 2003 and updated and accepted June 2005.

# PART SIX

# Understanding the Conclusions to Research Reports

Throughout Parts I–V, we have used the analogy of a journey to think about research. Think for a moment about what you do at the end of a journey. If you are like many people, you might put together a scrapbook so you can show the pictures and mementos you picked up along the way. At the very least you probably recap what happened on the trip by telling people about it. Perhaps you start by sharing the trip's highlights. These might include the best sights, the tastiest food, or the scariest moment. You might also compare your trip to those you have taken previously or even those taken by others. As you reflect, you will probably think of things that you wish you had done differently, like wishing you had taken a train instead of a bus. If you like to travel, you may also be thinking about where you want to go on your next trip!

These end-of-journey considerations are the same kinds of issues that researchers discuss when they reach the end of their research journeys. This sharing comes in a conclusion section of a research report. Researchers make interpretations of their trip. This section is the fourth and final major section of any research report. You will learn how to recognize and interpret the elements that researchers report in their concluding sections of quantitative, qualitative, mixed methods, and action research reports.

The final chapter is:

- Chapter 14—Interpreting Research: Identifying the Conclusions About a Study

CHAPTER

# 14 Interpreting Research: Identifying the Conclusions About a Study

*A research study ends with statements that convey the authors' conclusions about the study. This "conclusion" appears in the final paragraphs of a research article. Authors use this passage to interpret the procedures and results of the study. A* Conclusion *section is not simply summarizing the study, it has several elements to it: restating the findings in a more general way than the results, relating the findings to the literature, providing personal reflections on the meaning of the study, pointing out limitations of the research, advancing ways that new research can extend the present study, and ending on a positive note of the overall contribution of the research. This is an ideal conclusion, and it is found in good research reports. In this chapter, you will learn how to identify and read the concluding sections that authors write for quantitative, qualitative, mixed methods, and action research studies. You will also learn what information is appended at the back of a study.*

**BY THE END OF THIS CHAPTER, YOU SHOULD BE ABLE TO:**

- Identify the elements that comprise a conclusion section in a research article.
- Describe the differences in conclusion sections among the different approaches to conducting research.
- Identify the types of back matter that goes into research reports.
- Evaluate a high-quality conclusion section.

You might feel like researchers have said all they need to say about any research study once they have reported the introduction, methods, and results. After all, you know why the study is important, what they did, and what they found—what else is there to learn? In actuality, researchers have a number of loose ends to tie up at the end of their reports. You may have already noticed a pattern to the ending of reports from those you have read in this book. This pattern usually includes two features: a conclusion section and back matter after the conclusion.

## How Do Researchers End Their Research Reports?

> For practice identifying the elements of a conclusion section, go to the *Building Research Skills* section under the topic "Evaluating a Research Report" in MyEducationalResearchLab, located at www.myeducationlab.com. Complete the exercise "Interpreting an Article's Conclusion" and use the provided feedback to further develop your skills for reading research articles.

In addition to reporting results, researchers provide their *interpretation* of the results. Authors write these reflections about the study into a conclusion section of the report. In this section (or sections), the authors often return to the original purpose and research questions or hypotheses and discuss in what ways the study answered the questions. They also discuss the strengths and weaknesses of the study to help readers understand what conclusions they can and cannot draw about the results. You can recognize this section by headings such as *Conclusion, Discussion,* and *Implications.* We will examine the elements of this section in more detail in this chapter.

In addition, immediately following the conclusion, authors often share comments or additional information that are related to the article, but not an essential part of the research process. As introduced in Chapter 1, this material is called "back matter." It can be identified under headings such as *Notes, Comments, Acknowledgment, Appendices,* and *References* found at the end of the article. We will also examine elements of the back matter in this chapter.

## What Elements Do Researchers Report in Their Conclusion Section?

Providing interpretation in a conclusion section is an essential step of the process of conducting research. When researchers interpret their studies, they step back from the results and make sense of what was found. **Interpretation** means drawing conclusions about the results and explaining how the results answer the study's research questions.

Authors address a common set of topics when interpreting their research results in a conclusion section. Their interpretation includes the following elements:

- a summary of the major results,
- a discussion relating the results to the literature,
- personal reflections of the researcher about the meaning of the data,
- implications and suggestions for practice,
- limitations of the present study,
- future research needs, and
- the overall significance and contribution of the study.

### A Summary of the Major Results

In the process of interpreting results in a report, researchers first summarize the major findings. This summary is a statement that reviews the major conclusions to each of the research questions or hypotheses. For example, in the quantitative goal orientation study (Self-Brown & Mathews, 2003) from the end of Chapter 5, the authors summarized, "Results from the goal analyses indicated significant differences within and across classroom structure conditions" (paragraph 28). Similarly, the authors of the qualitative classroom management study (Garrahy et al., 2005) from the end of Chapter 10 summarized their findings with statements such as, "Our results provide insights as to how teachers acquired and implemented their knowledge about class management over time" (paragraph 29).

The summary is different than the results: It represents general, rather than specific, conclusions. For example, in quantitative research the specific results include detail about statistical tests, significance levels, and effect sizes. General conclusions state overall whether the hypothesis was rejected or whether the research question was supported or not supported. Likewise, in qualitative research, the specific results include description and theme passages. The intent of the qualitative summary passage often varies, from a restatement of the themes, to answering the research questions, to providing general learnings. Mixed methods and action research studies can include both types of specific results, and the authors also state both types of general conclusions.

> *Here's a Tip for Reading Research!*
>
> As a general rule of thumb, authors will not introduce new results in the conclusion section. This section will only summarize and interpret the results that were reported in the results section of the report.

### Relating the Results to Other Literature

After the summary, interpretation may also contrast and compare results with theories or bodies of literature. The researcher interprets the findings in view of this past research, showing how the findings may support and/or contradict prior studies. This interpretation often includes explanations as to why the results turned out the way they did. These explanations may be based on predictions made from a theory or conceptual framework that guided the development of research questions or hypotheses. For example, returning to the quantitative goal orientation study (Self-Brown & Mathews, 2003) we learn, "Those results [the significant differences among groups] were consistent with the theoretical relationship predicted by Ames (1992c) and the hypothesis in this study that the type of classroom evaluation structure would influence student goal orientation" (paragraph 28).

In addition, these explanations may include discussing the existing literature and indicating how the study results either confirmed or disconfirmed prior studies. The authors of the qualitative classroom management study (Garrahy et al., 2005) compared their findings to past research when they wrote, "Similar to Schempp's (1993) case study of a high school physical education teacher, the elementary teachers in this study most valued knowledge that came from personal practice" (paragraph 30). Thus, you will frequently find past research studies being presented by authors as they interpret their own results.

## The Personal Interpretation of the Researcher

In some studies, researchers will offer their own personal reflections about the results in addition to bringing in prior literature. This is common in qualitative and action research and in some mixed methods research. Because qualitative researchers believe that the researcher's personal views can never be kept separate from interpretations, personal reflections about the meaning of the data are included in the research study. Researchers base these personal interpretations on hunches, insights, and intuition. Because they have been to the field and visited personally at great length with individuals, they are in a good position to reflect and remark on the larger meaning of the data. The two examples that follow illustrate the diversity of personal reflections found in studies that emphasized the qualitative approach.

In the qualitative new teacher study (Clayton, 2007) from the end of Chapter 3, the authors reflected about the meaning of professional development for the three teachers:

> The image of new teacher learning that emerges from this discussion is more appropriately characterized as tilting toward curriculum making in particular moments of space and time. Rather than making absolute shifts from one view of curriculum and teaching to another, these teachers, on occasion, tilt toward curriculum making and all the epistemological and ontological ideas associated with that view. On other occasions, they tilt in different directions that would, on face value, appear to contradict these views. (*paragraph 46*)

The next example shows how researchers can offer personal commentary about new questions that need to be answered. In the discussion at the end of the Internet skills action research study (Heil, 2005) from Chapter 13, the teacher researcher remarked:

> The process does not end here for me. As a teacher-researcher, I followed up with this group to gather further data on how they are applying the knowledge they gained from this unit. As a teacher-librarian, I find it vital to provide the information contained in this unit to all students across multiple grade levels so that Internet users can make more informed decisions about their choices. (*paragraph 34*)

## Implications and Suggestions for Practice

In the process of interpreting results, researchers also present the broader implications of the research for distinct audiences. **Implications** are those suggestions for the importance and usefulness of the study for different audiences. They elaborate on the significance for audiences that were initially identified in the statement of the problem section at the beginning of the study (as we discussed in Chapter 3). In effect, now that the study has been completed, the researcher is in a position to reflect and remark on how the different audiences may benefit from the results.

While researchers may offer implications for different types of audiences, you are probably most interested in the implications and suggestions for practice. Implications for practice include the use of the findings for practice (e.g., in classrooms, in health clinics, or with certain people, such as adults or teenagers). Researchers often suggest the meaning of the results for practice situations. For example, the author of the qualitative parent role study (Auerbach, 2007) from Chapter 1 discussed several implications of the study's results for educators, such as providing information about the college process in multiple languages and having educators recognize that parents can offer support and be involved in ways that the school does not readily notice (see paragraphs 64–65). The authors of the quantitative youth literacy study (Nippold et al., 2005) from Chapter 7 provided eight specific suggestions for activities that may support youth literacy habits, such as organizing book clubs and providing class time for sustained reading (see paragraph 29–31).

## The Limitations of the Present Study

The reality is that no research study is perfect. Researchers provide a critical evaluation of their studies by advancing the limitations or weaknesses of the study that may have affected the results. **Limitations** are potential weaknesses or problems with the study identified by the researcher. Researchers enumerate these weaknesses one by one as part of their study's conclusions. These limitations are useful to other potential researchers who may choose to conduct a similar or replication study. Limitations also help readers judge to what extent the findings can or cannot be generalized to other people and situations. They do not mean that the study is bad; they do, however, inform you about the ways that the results are limited.

In quantitative studies the limitations often relate to inadequate measures of variables, loss or lack of participants, small sample sizes, lack of control of confounding variables, and other factors typically related to data collection and analysis. For example, in the quantitative goal orientation study (Self-Brown & Mathews, 2003), the authors advance the following limitation for their study: "One limitation was that it did not control for teacher expectancies and how these may have influenced students' goal setting" (paragraph 32). Therefore, they noted a variable that was not controlled in their study, but that could have influenced the results. Limitations in qualitative research may address problems in data collection, unanswered questions by participants, or better selection of purposeful sampling of individuals or sites for the study. Mixed methods researchers often discuss quantitative and qualitative limitations. Action researchers tend to focus their limitations in terms of the practicality of the solution over the specific research procedures used.

## Future Research Needs

*Here's a Tip for Reading Research!*

By looking closely at future research sections, researchers often gather useful ideas to assess the current state of research on a topic. After reading through several journal article future research passages, you could make a list of topics presented for further inquiry and see if there is overlap among the topics and what general trends the researchers suggest for future study of a content area.

After stating limitations, researchers advance future research directions. **Future research directions** are suggestions made by the researcher about additional studies that need to be conducted based on the results of the present research. These suggestions are a natural link to the limitations of a study. For example, note how the authors of the quantitative parent involvement study (Deslandes & Bertrand, 2005) from Chapter 1 state a limitation immediately followed by a suggestion for future research in this passage:

> There are limitations of this study that suggest directions for future investigations. First, the sample used in our investigation included only students in Grades 7, 8, and 9, and the subsamples were of various sizes. Future investigations need to expand across the secondary levels. (*paragraph 46*)

These suggestions for future research provide useful direction for researchers who are interested in investigating needed areas of inquiry. For those reading a study, future research directions highlight areas that are unknown and provide boundaries for using the study's information.

## The Overall Significance and Contribution of the Study

The final element that might be included in a conclusion section is a statement about the overall significance and unique contributions of the study. This is typically a brief and final passage to create the effect of leaving a research report on a positive note. Researchers include these passages as strong statements of the conclusions of their studies. When written well, the overall significance provides a wrap-up of what the study accomplished, what new knowledge was generated, and why it is important. For example, see how the authors of the mixed methods learning environment study (Aldridge et al., 1999) from Chapter 12 state the importance of their research in the final paragraph of their report:

> Each country has much to learn from the other with regard to the development of a learning environment that fosters positive attitudes and a love of learning. The comparative nature of the present study of learning environments in Taiwan and Australia made possible the examination of similarities and differences between the learning environment and students' perceptions in each country. (*paragraph 107*)

## What Do You Think?

Examine the following four excerpts taken from a quantitative correlational study about African American adolescents' career decision status (Constantine et al., 2005, pp. 314–316). What elements of interpretation do you find in the excerpts?

**(a)** Findings revealed that African American adolescents who perceived greater career barriers tended to report higher degrees of career indecision. This finding, however, seems somewhat inconsistent with results indicated by some previous researchers. For example, Rollins (2001) reported that African American adolescents perceiving higher degrees of racism reported greater self-efficacy for career decision-making tasks . . .

**(b)** In light of the aforementioned issues, it is important that career counselors first identify the extent to which some African American adolescents perceive certain occupational barriers and then process with these students the potential consequences of harboring these barriers in terms of their current and future educational and career development . . .

**(c)** The study must be tempered in light of several potential limitations. First, generalizability of the findings is cautioned because the study's participants may differ somehow from other African American adolescents residing in a large urban city in the northeastern United States . . .

**(d)** Additional research is needed concerning the career development experiences of African American adolescents. For example, research on the intersections of race, gender, and racial and gender identity in the context of various career development tasks might help to identify and address African American adolescents' perceived career barriers, particularly with regard to stereotypes they might possess about perceived options available to them based on their race and/or gender (Gainor & Lent, 1998; Swanson et al., 1996; Swanson & Woitke, 1997) . . .

### Check Your Understanding

These excerpts each illustrate a different element. In excerpt (a), the authors compare one of their results to a prior study in the literature. In this case they note that the current result is inconsistent with a previous finding. In excerpt (b), the authors offer practical implications of their study by providing suggestions for career counselors. Excerpt (c) is an example of discussing limitations of a research study. The authors note that the findings are limited to the sample studied and may not generalize to a larger population of all African American adolescents. In excerpt (d), the authors make suggestions for future research about the topic of career development with African American adolescents.

## What Is Included in the Back Matter of a Research Report?

Researchers include notes, reference lists, and appendixes as back matter to their research reports. They provide additional information for the reader of a research report that goes beyond a description and analysis of the study.

### Notes

After the conclusion section, the researcher may include notes for the readers. These **notes** provide general information such as how to contact the author, what agency funded the study, or who the author thanks for assisting with the study. Sometimes authors include specific notes that provide additional information about a specific point within the text. These notes are usually indicated by a superscript number (e.g.,[1] or [6]) within the article text. You can then find the text of the note listed by number at the end of the article.

Let's consider an example of the use of notes. The quantitative parent involvement study (Deslandes & Bertrand, 2005) at the end of Chapter 1 provides an example of both general and specific notes. The authors acknowledged their funding source with a general note:

> This research was supported by grants to the first author from the Fonds québécois de la recherche sur la société et la culture (FQRSC) and to both authors from the Centre de Recherche et d'Intervention sur la Réussite Scolaire (CRIRES). *(p. 173)*

They also included specific notes, such as the following comment that provides additional information about the cases involved for one result. This note is indicated with a superscript 2 in paragraph 26 of the article.

> [2.] Merging the 770 parents' file with the students' file totaled 514 cases.

### Reference Lists

Research articles may or may not include Notes, but they will always include a list of references after the conclusion section. Almost without exception, this list will have the heading *References*. In these **reference lists**, researchers provide detailed information about all the sources they used in writing the report. An important idea to remember is that every source cited in the article should appear in this list and every source in the list should be cited somewhere in the article.

The format and ordering of the references in the list will depend on the style used for the report. (Recall the discussion of style manuals in Chapter 4.) In educational research reports, references are usually listed in alphabetical order based on the last names of the first author. Therefore, if you want to see the full reference for "Adams & Johnson, 2004" you know to look near the beginning of the list since the first author's last name begins with the letter A. You may find some reports that list the references in the order in which they appear within the reports' text. In these reports, the references are usually numbered (1, 2, 3, etc.) so readers can identify them. This is common in research reports from the health sciences. All of the studies included in this textbook used an alphabetical listing for the reference lists.

*Here's a Tip for Applying Research!*

You might find good questions to ask when collecting data in your own research project by looking at the appendixes of articles published on the topic. Before using these items, however, you should contact the author and request their approval. You should also be sure to give credit to the source of the items.

### Appendixes

The final feature that you may find at the end of a research report is information in appendixes. Researchers use **appendixes** to provide detailed information to supplement the main report. The most common types of information found in the appendixes of research reports are examples of questions used during data collection and details about or examples of data analysis procedures. For example, the authors of the qualitative classroom management study (Garrahy et al., 2005) at the end of Chapter 10 included two appendixes at the end of their report. Appendix A lists sample questions that were asked during the interviews with teachers. Appendix B provides example quotes for each of the major themes that the authors identified during the data analysis.

## How Are Conclusions and Back Matter Written Differently in Quantitative and Qualitative Research Reports?

*Here's a Tip for Reading Research!*

Authors will often write one (or more) paragraphs per element listed in Figure 14.1. Some will also include subheadings. Use the subheadings to recognize how the information is organized.

You now are familiar with seven elements that are typically included in the conclusion sections and three elements found in the back matter of research studies. Authors use the elements in the conclusions to convey their interpretation of the results of their study. You can understand an article's conclusion by looking for and identifying these elements. It is possible for any research report to include any or all of these elements. There are, however, some general differences between quantitative and qualitative conclusions and back matter.

The elements typically found in quantitative and qualitative conclusions and back matter are listed in Figure 14.1. The order shows the typical order in which authors discuss the topics, but you will find that different authors may use a different order.

Looking at the two lists, you can see that many similarities exist in how researchers interpret their studies. In general terms, they address the same topics. One exception is that qualitative researchers include personal reflections because they are using a subjective approach to conducting research. Quantitative researchers usually do not include any personal reflections because they are using an objective approach to conducting research. Mixed methods researchers and action researchers often use a combination of the elements, depending on whether their study emphasized a quantitative or qualitative approach or used both equally.

There are other differences in the details of the elements as well. For example, quantitative researchers interpret their results in terms of their original predictions or hypotheses. Since qualitative researchers do not make predictions or state hypotheses, they do not make such comparisons. Quantitative and qualitative researchers also report different types of limitations. Quantitative researchers report weaknesses in their studies that limit their ability to explain the trends in a population, the relationship

**FIGURE 14.1 Conclusion Sections and Back Matter in Quantitative and Qualitative Research Reports**

| Quantitative Research | Qualitative Research |
|---|---|
| Conclusion Section<br>■ Summary of major results<br>■ Explanations of results in terms of predictions and prior studies<br>■ Implications and suggestions for practice<br>■ Limitations of the study<br>■ Suggestions for future research<br>■ Overall significance of the study<br><br>Back Matter<br>■ Notes<br>■ References<br>■ Appendixes<br>  ■ E.g., Data collection instruments | Conclusion Section<br>■ Summary of major findings<br>■ Comparison of findings with existing studies<br>■ Personal reflections<br>■ Implications and suggestions for practice<br>■ Limitations of the study<br>■ Suggestions for future research<br>■ Overall significance of the study<br><br>Back Matter<br>■ Notes<br>■ References<br>■ Appendixes<br>  ■ E.g., Interview or observational protocols<br>  ■ Lists of codes and themes |

*Note:* Mixed methods and action research studies use a combination of these two approaches.

among variables, and the reason for differences among groups. Qualitative researchers report weaknesses in their studies that limited their ability to develop a rich exploration or a deep understanding. Mixed methods researchers often discuss both quantitative and qualitative limitations along with those that arose when they attempted to mix the two components. Action researchers tend to focus on personal reflections, implications for practice, and the overall significance of the action plan. These differences relate back to the very reason that researchers choose to use a specific research approach at the beginning of their process of research!

### What Do You Think?

Recall the mixed methods learning environment study (Aldridge et al., 1999) at the end of Chapter 12. Examine the ending of this article found on pages 329–331. Where do you find the conclusion section? What types of back matter did the authors include?

### Check Your Understanding

This article includes three features commonly found at the end of research reports. First, the authors provide a conclusion section. Their conclusion is in a section with the heading: *Discussion* (see paragraphs 100–107). Second, the authors include a list of references that were cited within the article. Third, the authors included the survey questionnaire that was administered to the participants as an Appendix.

## How Do You Evaluate Conclusion and Back Matter Sections?

You have now learned the important elements that go into the interpretation discussions for quantitative, qualitative, mixed methods, and action research studies. When you read the conclusion of a research study, you want to first identify these elements to understand the information presented. You also, however, want to evaluate how well the authors addressed these elements in a given study. Figure 14.2 provides a series of statements you can use to evaluate the conclusion in a research study. As you apply these evaluation criteria to research studies, they will assist you in considering not only if the elements are present, but also whether they are discussed in a rigorous way that is consistent with the quantitative or qualitative approach.

## Reviewing What We've Learned

- Expect the end of a research article to report a conclusion section, notes, a reference list, and appendixes.
- Recognize that researchers interpret their results by reflecting how they address the study's research questions.
- Note that researchers are willing to identify and discuss potential weaknesses in their study. In this way, they recognize that no study is perfect.
- When examining a conclusion section of a research report, look to see if the author has included a general summary of results, a discussion relating the results to the literature, personal reflections about the meaning of results, implications of the results for practice, limitations of the study, suggestions for future research, and the overall significance of the study.

Use the following criteria to evaluate the quality of the conclusion and back matter in a research report. For each evaluation item, indicate the following ratings:

+ You rate the item as "high quality" for the study.
✓ You rate the item as "ok quality" for the study.
– You rate the item as "low quality" for the study.

In addition to your rating, make notes about each element when you apply these criteria to an actual published study.

| **In a high-quality research report, the author . . .** | Application to a Published Study | |
|---|---|---|
| | Your Rating | Your Notes |
| 1. Does not repeat results or introduce new results, but presents a general summary of the results. | | |
| 2. Compares the study's results with prior results published in the literature. | | |
| 3. Incorporates personal views about the results in a qualitative, mixed methods, or action research study and does not present personal reflections about the results in a quantitative study (and some mixed methods studies). | | |
| 4. Mentions implications and suggestions for practice for audiences identified in the introduction. | | |
| 5. Notes several limitations of the present research that are consistent with quantitative and/or qualitative approaches. | | |
| 6. Lists future research studies that are needed based on the results and limitations of the present study. | | |
| 7. Ends the study on a positive note citing the unique contribution of the research. | | |
| 8. Includes useful "back matter" information that is auxiliary to the report. | | |

**FIGURE 14.2 Criteria for Evaluating the Quality of a Study's Conclusion and "Back Matter"**

- Consider whether the back matter is complete with notes, references, and appendixes.
- While conclusions follow a general format, expect some differences in the discussion between quantitative, qualitative, mixed methods, and action research reports.
- Use the criteria to assess the quality of conclusion and back matter sections.

## Practicing Your Skills

Practice using your skills and knowledge of the content of this chapter by answering the following questions. Use the answers in the Appendix to evaluate your progress.

Return to the conclusion section (paragraphs 24–32) of the quantitative youth literacy study at the end of Chapter 7 on pages 203–206. Use this conclusion section to answer the following questions.

1. Consider the authors' interpretation of this study. What good examples do you locate where the authors addressed the following elements?
   - A summary of a major result
   - A discussion relating a result to other literature
   - An implication of the results for practice
2. Consider additional interpretive approaches. What good examples do you locate where the authors addressed the following elements?
   - A limitation of the study
   - A suggestion for future research
   - A statement of the overall significance of the study

APPENDIX

# Suggested Answers to Practicing Your Skills Exercises

## Chapter 1

1. The quantitative parent involvement study is a research study. The authors used language such as "the authors examined" (in the abstract) and "in the present study" (in paragraph 02). Looking just at the abstract, the authors reported that they collected data in the form of "survey responses" and they gave examples of specific "results" and "findings" produced by their data analysis. Therefore, this study met the basic definition of research by having data collection and analysis.
2. The qualitative parent role study is a research study. The author mentions "this qualitative case study" in the abstract, which hints that it is a research study. However, we need to read until paragraph 03 to learn for sure that the author collected data ("3 years of ethnographic data") and analyzed the data to produce findings ("findings suggest that . . ."). Therefore, this study met the basic definition of research by having data collection and analysis.
3. There are six steps in the process reported about any research study. We expect that the authors will report the research problem, literature review, and purpose in the introduction section. In this article, the introduction includes the section with no heading and the second section called "Influences on Parent Involvement." We expect that the research design selection and data collection will be described within the *Method* section. We also expect that the authors will report the findings from the data analysis in the *Results* section and interpret what they found in the conclusion section. In this study, the conclusion section is divided into three sections labeled *Discussion, Implications and Limitations,* and *Conclusions.*
4. These two studies may be important to read to add to your knowledge about parent involvement (e.g., what factors are related to parent involvement and what parent types exist in terms of their involvement). They might also inform your position in a policy debate, such as whether to start a parent involvement program in your local school district. Finally, they also suggest improvements for practice. For example, at the end of the quantitative parent involvement study the authors suggest providing training programs to teachers to help them develop knowledge and skills to initiate first contact with parents. At the end of the qualitative parent role study, the author encourages educators to broaden their definition of how parents may be involved and to recognize a wide variety of perspectives on being involved in the education of one's children.

## Chapter 2

1. Here are some examples of quantitative characteristics found in the quantitative parent involvement study. In this study, the researchers:
   - make a prediction that four factors will influence parent involvement with their adolescents at school and at home;

- ask specific, narrow questions (e.g., what are the relative contributions of parents' self-efficacy to predict parent involvement?);
- collect data from a large number of participants (i.e., 770 parents);
- collect data consisting of numbers, (i.e., scores from parents on an instrument);
- analyze these numbers using mathematical procedures (i.e., statistics); and
- remain invisible (objective) in the written report (i.e., do not mention themselves).

**2.** Here are some examples of qualitative characteristics found in the qualitative parent role study. In this study, the researcher:

- makes no prediction about the parents' roles, but relies on participants to shape what is reported;
- asks broad, general questions (e.g., what do parents think and do?);
- collects data from a small number of participants (i.e., 16 parents);
- collects data consisting of words (i.e., text from participants during interviews);
- analyzes these words by deriving themes or categories (e.g., moral supporters); and
- remains visible, present, and subjective in the written report (i.e., mentions herself).

**3.** An example of applying Figure 2.2 to the quantitative parent involvement study is:

| In a high-quality quantitative research report, the author . . . | Application to a Published Study | |
|---|---|---|
| | **Rating** | **Notes** |
| 1. States a problem that is best addressed by explaining trends or relationships about specific variables. | + | The problem calls for explaining the factors that predict parents' involvement at home and at school (paragraph 02) because little is known about the factors that lead parents to be involved. |
| 2. Uses the literature to indicate the questions that need to be answered. | + | The literature points to specific factors that are expected to predict parent involvement (paragraphs 03–10). |
| 3. Presents the purpose and research questions as statements that relate variables and are very specific. | + | The purpose statement and research questions identify and relate specific variables. Specifically, the authors want to learn whether parents' role construction, self-efficacy, perception of teacher invitations, and perception of adolescent invitations predict parent involvement at home and at school (paragraph 02) for parents of children in grades 7, 8, and 9. |
| 4. Gathers numeric data from a large group of participants. | + | The authors used a correlational research design and collected data in the form of numeric scores from instruments from 770 parents (paragraph 14). |
| 5. Reports numbers using statistical information to describe trends, compare groups, or relate variables. | + | The authors reported extensive statistical information that describes individual variables (e.g., Table 3) and relates multiple variables (e.g., Tables 4–5). |
| 6. Makes an interpretation based on the studies of others using an objective approach. | + | The authors interpret their results compared to other research such as finding that their results are "consistent" with previous studies (paragraph 36). |

**4.** An example of applying Figure 2.3 to the qualitative parent role study is:

| In a high-quality qualitative research report, the author . . . | Application to a Published Study | |
|---|---|---|
| | **Rating** | **Notes** |
| 1. States a problem that is best addressed by exploring participants' views because the variables are not known. | + | The problem calls for exploring parents' beliefs and behaviors because little is known about parent roles in education for marginalized parents or about parents roles in terms of college access (paragraphs 02–03). |
| 2. Uses the literature to describe the problem, but not suggest the specific questions that need to be answered. | + | The literature is used to highlight the deficiencies in current models of parent involvement and the importance of considering parents' perspectives and the contexts in which those perspectives have formed (paragraphs 04–12). |
| 3. Presents the purpose and research questions in an open-ended way so that the researcher is open to participants' views. | + | The purpose statement and research questions are open-ended in order to explore parent roles and what parents think and do (paragraph 03). |
| 4. Gathers text or image data from a few individuals. | + | The author used an ethnographic research design (paragraph 03). The gathered data included interviews with and observations of 16 parents (paragraphs 14–15). |
| 5. Reports words or images and describes the participants' views or identifies themes in their views. | + | The author used text analysis (paragraph 16) to analyze the collected data. She identified three categories (or themes) that describe the different parent roles based on her analysis of the data and used words and quotes to describe each category (e.g., Table 1). |
| 6. Makes an interpretation based on his/her own assessment of the results using a subjective and reflexive approach. | + | The author reflected on her role as the researcher in paragraph 17. She also discussed the larger meaning of the three categories, such as the contexts that shape the different parent roles (paragraphs 55–60) and the meaning of the results for marginalized parents. |

## Chapter 3

1. This first sentence indicates that there is a clear need because there are many new teachers facing difficult situations (environments that are highly politicized with emphasis on test scores). It is an effective hook for anyone interested in issues around new teachers.
2. The research problem mentioned in this study is the "concerns about teacher quality" and how they place pressures on new teachers beyond those that come with simply being a new teacher. The author believes that this problem calls for an exploration that describes in detail how novice teachers learn to teach through curriculum making.
3. The author justifies the importance of the problem in paragraphs 01–02. She uses literature to justify the existence of different pressures on new teachers and to introduce the idea of curriculum making as one possible way of addressing this problem. These justifications are drawn from the existing literature.

4. The author identifies the following deficiency in the existing knowledge in paragraph 02: "little exists that articulates components of curriculum making specifically drawn from empirical data based on novice teachers. Moreover, this gap is exacerbated by a lack of empirical data specifically on the processes of learning to teach through curricular enactment within the context of high-stakes accountability environments." Therefore, this problem is important to study because there is a need to fill a void in and extend existing research.
5. At the end of paragraph 03, the author states the study's findings "suggest some important implications about novice teacher learning." Therefore, although specific audiences are not named, we can assume that audiences include those concerned with new teachers such as education researchers, teachers of preservice teachers, principals, and teachers.
6. Indications for the need for a qualitative study are found at the end of paragraph 02. These include the need to explore participants' perspectives to describe the components of curriculum making, the processes of learning to teach, and the contexts in which these occur.

## Chapter 4

1. To find literature relevant to the increasing incident of teenage pregnancies in high schools, the following search terms might be useful: pregnant OR pregnancy AND "high school."
2. (a) The author is describing a theoretical perspective from the literature that guides her thinking about the study. This perspective does not direct her questions, but informs her thinking about the importance of understanding how individuals' construct their own positions and experiences. (b) The author uses the literature to document what is not known in the literature, namely that we do not know enough about how teachers learn to teach by making curriculum. (c) The author uses literature to justify her methods and procedures for conducting the study.
3. An abstract for the qualitative new teacher study could be written as follows:

### Reference

Clayton, C. D. (2007). Curriculum making as novice professional development: Practical risk taking as learning in high-stakes times. *Journal of Teacher Education, 58*(3), 216–230.

### Research Problem

The author is concerned with the increased challenges that face new teachers in the current high stakes environment. These challenges place pressures on new teachers above and beyond those that come with being a new teacher. Concerns are focused on the quality of new teachers and the ability for the profession to retain quality teachers. There is a gap in what is known about how new teachers learn to teach in the high stakes environment.

### Purpose and Research Questions

The purpose of this qualitative case study was to describe how three novice teachers in an urban setting learn to teach through curriculum making while participating in a professional development program. The study is informed by perspectives of social constructivism. Research questions focus on the teachers' perceptions of curriculum and their role in developing and implementing curricular materials, the challenges and opportunities that arise during their participation, their feelings about the participation, and how they use the experiences.

### Data Collection Procedure

Three teachers participating in the Beginning Teachers' Program were purposefully selected. The sources of data included individual and group interviews, classroom observations, documents from the program sessions, and archival data.

### Findings

For each of the participating teachers, the author presented a description of the teacher and themes that emerged from the teacher's experiences and perceptions. The themes focused on how the teachers' thinking about teaching and teacher practices changed during the curricular activities that were part of the program. These descriptions and themes highlight what happened during the program and the tension areas that emerged, including managing student relationships to curriculum, ownership of curriculum, and sources of classroom knowledge. The findings describe how the teachers changed their conceptions about teaching and teaching practices. The author concludes that the teachers' conceptual change came *after* trying new practices, not before.

## Chapter 5

1. (a) The independent variable is classroom structure. It has three levels (token economy, contingency contract, and control). (b) The dependent variables are number of performance goals and learning goals set for mathematics. (c) The independent variable is a treatment variable because the researcher manipulates the classroom structure that each group receives. (d) An example of a confounding variable is teacher behaviors since each class had a different teacher and it is possible that their behaviors influenced the outcomes.
2. A good purpose statement for this study would be: The purpose of this study is to compare students in a token economy group, contingency contract group, and control group in terms of the number of performance and learning goals set for mathematics by elementary school students in Florida. This statement clearly identifies the major variables, participants, and research site in one sentence. In contrast, the purpose statement provided by the authors does not include signal words such as "the purpose" and does not identify the participants and site.
3. Here are possible examples. Note that the participants and research site are not stated since they are included in the good purpose statement provided in question #2. (a) How does the token economy group compare to the contingency contract group in terms of number of learning goals set? (b) There is no difference between the token economy group and the control group in terms of the number of performance goals set. (c) The contingency contract group will set more learning goals than the token economy group.
4. The central phenomenon is curriculum making.
5. A good purpose statement for this study would be: The purpose of this qualitative case study is to describe the experiences of curriculum making for three new teachers participating in the Beginning Teachers' Program. This statement includes the essential details of the study in one concise statement. The purpose statement in the study does not include the site or mention the use of a qualitative approach.
6. (a) What are the curriculum-making experiences of the new teachers? (b) How do the new teachers think about their teaching?

## Chapter 6

1. The authors of the quantitative parent involvement study used a correlational design. Evidence for the use of this design includes: (a) the study of a single group (parents of secondary-level students around Quebec), (b) no mention of a treatment or intervention, (c) an interest in identifying variables (e.g., parent role construction and self-efficacy) that predict other variables (parent involvement at home and at school), and (d) discussing results in terms of the associations among variables.
2. The purpose of the study was to determine whether certain variables are related to parent involvement at school and at home for parents in the Quebec region. Therefore, a correlational research design does match the study's purpose to assess the relationship among variables for a single group.
3. The authors can claim that certain relationships exist among the measured variables (such as perceptions of academic invitations is useful for predicting parent involvement at home for students in Grade 7) for the studied parents. They cannot make claims that certain variables *cause* parents to be involved based on the results of this study because they did not use experimental procedures. They also can make only limited claims about parents in general because they did not use probability sampling to select participants from all possible parents. The results may apply well to parents within the Quebec setting, however.
4. The authors of the quantitative goal orientation study used a quasi-experimental design. Evidence for the use of this design includes: (a) the study of more than one intact group (two fifth-grade classes and one fourth-grade class), (b) the administration of a different treatment condition to each group (token economy, contingency contract, or control), (c) an interest in testing the impact of the treatment on certain dependent variables (e.g., number of performance and learning goals written), and (d) comparing the groups in terms of the outcome measures.
5. The purpose of the study was to determine whether classroom structure could cause an effect in the number of learning and performance goals set. The best design to determine cause and effect is a true experiment. The authors chose to use a quasi-experiment, probably due to the difficulty of randomly assigning children to groups. They also were not able to control for the teacher because each class had a different teacher. This means that the authors did not control for all possible confounding variables in their quasi-experiment.
6. The authors can make only limited claims about the treatment causing the measured effects because other possible explanations were not well controlled. Since students were not randomly assigned to the groups, the measured differences could have resulted for some other reason. For example, perhaps fourth-graders write different types of goals than fifth-graders or perhaps there were differences among the teaching practices of the classroom teachers. The researchers also can make only limited claims that their results will apply to all fourth- and fifth-graders since only a small number of students participated and they were from only one school.

## Chapter 7

1. The authors collected data from 100 sixth-grade children at a public middle and 100 ninth-grade adolescents enrolled at a high school in a lower middle-income neighborhood in western Oregon. They were selected using a nonprobability strategy. Teachers volunteered to gather data from their students. The sample size was 200 students.
2. The authors used the "Student Questionnaire" to gather data. This questionnaire was designed for this study so we do not have evidence of past scores to ensure its quality. The authors did include the instrument in the Appendix of the article so we can make our own judgments. The questions appear clear and straightforward.
3. The authors discuss ethical procedures, such as notifying parents about the study, assuring that participation is voluntary and the data will be kept confidential, and asking students to indicate their willingness to participate in the study. The

authors also used standard procedures for collecting the data. One of the investigators went to the classroom to gather the data and this person read each question out loud to ensure that students were listening to the directions and completing the form.

4. To make the results more generalizable, the researchers needed to identify a population (such as all sixth- and ninth-grade students in the United States) and then use probability sampling to select participants. Of course, getting a list of all sixth- and ninth-grade students in the United States would be very difficult!
5. The authors cannot claim that grade level causes the difference. Claims of cause and effect should be limited to experimental studies. The authors can simply conclude that a difference exists.

## Chapter 8

1. Tables 1, 2, and 3 all report descriptive information about individual variables. In this example the variables are all individual items from the survey questionnaire. In the tables, the authors report the percentage of students who responded positively to items along with the standard deviation values.
2. The authors report the results of inferential analyses in paragraph 19. The researchers used a hypothesis testing procedure to test for differences by gender for various variables for a sample in order to make conclusions about the population of sixth and ninth grade students.
3. The five steps of hypothesis testing for this result included:
   - Stating a null and alternative hypothesis:

     $H_0$: There is no difference between boys and girls in terms of their preference to read poems during free time.

     $H_A$: Girls prefer to read poems during free time more than boys.
   - Setting the alpha level to .005 (as reported in paragraph 22).
   - Collecting data about free time reading preferences from a sample of sixth and ninth grade students.
   - Computing an $F$ statistic and its associated $p$ value for the sample: $F(1, 196) = 19.57, p < .0001$.
   - Making a decision to reject the null hypothesis because $p$ is less than alpha and concluding that girls do prefer to read poems during free time more than boys. The authors also report the effect size for this difference as "medium," so we can conclude that this result also has some practical significance.
4. The alpha level is the maximum risk that the researchers are willing to take that they incorrectly find a difference. In this particular analysis, the researchers chose to set this level at .006. This means that they are willing to take up to a 0.6% chance of incorrectly rejecting the null hypothesis for this hypothesis test.

## Chapter 9

1. By recognizing the research design in a report, you know what type of purpose the researcher plans to address, what kinds of data collection and analysis to expect, and how the results will be reported. Knowing this information not only helps you to interpret a report, but it also helps you judge the quality of the research study by considering how well it implemented the research design.
2. The researchers probably plan to use the following designs:
   - Case study: The author wants to describe how students bounded by schools in urban contexts describe their teachers and learning practices. This design is the best choice if the author wants to develop description and themes.
   - Grounded theory: The authors want to develop a theory of a process, which is best suited to a grounded theory design.
   - Narrative research: The author wants to use individuals' stories to understand the issue of emerging mathematics teachers' identities. The study of individual stories is best suited to a narrative research design.
3. Although the author mentions using more than one design, the qualitative parent role study demonstrates many characteristics of an ethnographic research design.

Evidence includes: (a) referring to "ethnographic data" in the purpose statement (paragraph 03); (b) focusing on a culture-sharing group (parents of color without college experience participating in the Futures Program over three years); (c) collecting data through extensive fieldwork over three years (paragraph 15); (d) emphasizing of cultural aspects of the group (e.g., "highlighting . . . the cultural logic behind their actions," paragraph 03); (e) describing the shared patterns of what the parents do and think about college access for their children (e.g., Table 1); and (f) discussing the role of the researcher and her personal reflections (e.g., paragraph 17). An ethnographic research design matches the study's purpose of describing the shared patterns of a culture-sharing group.

4. Although the author mentions using strategies from more than one design, the qualitative new teacher study best fits the use of a case study research design. Evidence includes: (a) identifying the study as a "case study" in the abstract and opening of the method section (paragraph 10); (b) studying three teachers bounded by their participation in a program; (c) gathering multiple types of data (paragraph 11); (d) reporting description of the program (paragraphs 07–09) and teachers (paragraphs 15–16); and (e) reporting themes that developed for each case (e.g., Taking another look, Seeing differently, and Encouraging active participation). A case study research design matches the study's purpose of describing an activity (curriculum making) and the contexts in which the activity occurs for cases (three novice teachers).

## Chapter 10

1. The sites in this study included urban, suburban, and rural public elementary schools. The participants included 20 Caucasian elementary physics education teachers. They were purposefully selected to be information-rich participants because the researchers knew them through their professional affiliations and so that they would represent diverse views in terms of teaching experience and school demographics. The researchers noted that they took steps "to maximize the variety of teachers involved in the study" (paragraph 09). This strategy is best described as maximal variation sampling.
2. The researchers collected two types of data: interviews and observations. The interviews included both one-on-one and telephone interviews. The researchers used the interviews to learn the different teacher perspectives about classroom management and the observations to see how the teachers managed their classes. Focusing on interviews fits the purpose of describing what teachers know about management and fits the general grounded theory procedures that were used.
3. The researchers note a few of their procedures. They gained access to potential participants through their prior contacts with elementary physical education teachers. They only used telephone interviews in cases where they already had a good understanding of the teacher and program. Each interview lasted 45-90 minutes. The researchers developed an interview protocol, which is found in the article's appendix. They also audiorecorded each interview.
4. The authors did not provide any information about ethical issues, except noting that the participants "volunteered." We also learn in paragraph 15 that pseudonyms are used for the participating teachers. It would have been better for the authors to include information about gaining permissions. They do inform us as to how they gained access to the participants; that is, through their professional affiliations as university practicum supervisors, committee members, or conference attendees.

## Chapter 11

1. The authors discuss implementing each of the major steps in qualitative data analysis. First, although they did not explicitly state that they transcribed the data, they refer to "each transcription" in paragraph 10 so we know that they did transcribe their data. Second, they explored the data by reading each transcription "numerous times to become intimately familiar with the data" (paragraph 10).

Third, they coded the data developing "personal coding systems" for each member of the research team (paragraph 10). Fourth, they used an iterative process of refining the codes to build major themes as stated in paragraph 12.

2. The authors validated their findings using several validation strategies described in paragraph 13. These strategies included member checking (taking information from the interviews back to the participants for clarification), triangulation of data across different teachers and of findings across multiple researchers, and searching for examples of negative cases that were counter to the emergent findings.
3. The authors reported their results in the form of three major themes: knowledge origin and influences, knowledge evolution, and knowledge content.
4. The authors utilized a variety of narrative elements in these excerpts. Excerpt (a) is an example of citing contrary evidence to convey the complexity of a finding since most participants felt one way (their college program provided them with little knowledge about classroom management), but one participant felt a different way (her college program provided her with extensive knowledge about classroom management). Excerpt (b) is an example of an author including minor themes (out-of-school changes and in-school changes) within a larger theme (knowledge evolution). Excerpt (c) is an example of describing multiple perspectives by listing the different strategies used by the teachers.

## Chapter 12

1. Evidence that this is a good mixed methods research study includes: (a) the use of signal words such as the phrase "multiple research methods" in the title and a "multimethod approach" in the purpose statement (paragraph 09); (b) the rigorous collection and analysis of quantitative data (a questionnaire administered to 2960 students across two countries) and qualitative data (observations and interviews with students and teachers); and (c) explicitly combining the two by using the qualitative results to help explain specific quantitative results.
2. The researcher needed quantitative research to describe the trends in attitudes about science learning and compare those trends in two countries. From these results, however, an anomalous result emerged. The Australian students had more positive perceptions of their classroom environments, but the Taiwanese students had more positive attitudes toward their science classes. Therefore, the quantitative results were inadequate for explaining these trends. The authors needed a second, qualitative phase to explore the reasons behind these differences.
3. This study was conducted in two phases. It started with collecting and analyzing quantitative data and then moved to collecting and analyzing qualitative data. The study appears to prioritize the quantitative data, using extensive quantitative language at the beginning of the article (factors, variables, etc.) and starting with the quantitative phase. Therefore, its notation is:
   QUAN → qual.
4. The authors combined the two datasets by connecting from the quantitative results to the qualitative data collection. In addition, the researchers interpreted what they learned across the two datasets in their conclusion section.

## Chapter 13

1. This teacher librarian faced a problem that students at her middle school want to only conduct research on the Internet, but they do not have the skills to critically evaluate Internet resources.
2. This teacher-researcher used a spiral approach of reflecting, collecting information, and taking action. She began by reflecting on the problem. She gathered information by finding teachers with which to work and collecting information from students about their perceptions of the Internet. She then took action by designing a curriculum unit to promote critical evaluation skills. She continued to gather student reactions and reflect on them as she implemented the unit in steps. She also continued her spiral approach by gathering information and monitoring performance in future years. Finally, she also reflected on what she had learned by engaging in the process.

3. She collaborated with other teachers, including the computer and geography teachers. She also collaborated with teacher helpers who were interested in the project.
4. The primary action plan that resulted from this action research project was a six-step unit to teach critical evaluation skills. She also wrote the article that was ultimately published and shared her action materials via a Web site so other practitioners could use them.
5. Indicators that this is a good action research study include: a focus on a practical issue, the collection of multiple types of information (surveys, interviews, open-ended questions on surveys, and worksheets from students), collaborating with others, advancing a plan for action and implementing this plan, the author's reflection on her own professional development, and sharing her results in a report and through a Web site so other professionals can learn from her efforts.

## Chapter 14

1. The authors of the quantitative youth literacy study interpret their results in the *Discussion*, *Study Limitations*, and *Implications* sections of their conclusion.
   - In paragraph 24, they provide a summary of a major finding in response to their study's purpose: "Fortunately, the results indicate that reading is at least a moderately popular free-time activity for students in the 11- to 15-year age range."
   - In paragraph 24, they compare a major result (interest in reading declines and interest in using email increases) with other literature to show that the result is "consistent" with trends found by other researchers.
   - The authors provide numerous implications of their results for practice in paragraphs 29–31. These implications include strategies that speech-language pathologists (SLPs) can use to promote youth reading habits.
2. The authors of the quantitative youth literacy study also discuss these additional interpretation elements in the conclusion.
   - In paragraph 28, they identify limitations of their study's procedures. For example, the sample was limited because it represented only certain types of students in one area of the country. Another limitation was that the study focused only on one type of reading (during leisure time) and therefore may not accurately describe all trends related to youth reading.
   - The authors suggest future research that is needed in paragraph 28. For example, future research should investigate all types of youth reading and the reading habits of various subgroups, such as those with reading disorders.
   - The final paragraph of the study, paragraph 32, provides a brief overview of the significance of this study.

# GLOSSARY

**Abstract** is a one-paragraph summary of the article's content written by the article's author and placed at the very beginning of the article.

**Action research designs** are systematic procedures done by practitioners to gather quantitative and qualitative data to improve the ways their particular professional setting operates, their practice, and their impact on others.

**Alpha level ($\alpha$)** is the maximum risk that researchers are willing to take during hypothesis testing that they make a mistake when they conclude that they have sufficient evidence that there is a difference between groups or a relationship between variables in the population.

**Analyzing data** consists of the researcher taking the data apart and putting it together to identify patterns or trends within the data.

**Appendixes** appear at the end of a research report and authors use them to provide detailed information (e.g., data collection questions) to supplement the main report.

**Audience** consists of individuals and groups who the authors expect will read and potentially benefit from the information provided in the research article.

**Audiovisual materials** consist of images or sounds that qualitative researchers collect to help them understand the central phenomenon under study.

**Back matter** of an article consists of any notes about the article, a list of references, and appendixes.

**Bracketing** is a process by which a qualitative researcher reflects on his or her own views and experiences related to the study's central phenomenon, describes these perspectives in writing, and then works to set them aside (or bracket them) during the analysis process.

**Case study research designs** are qualitative procedures to explore in depth a program, event, or activity involving individuals within a bounded system.

**Central phenomenon** is the concept or process explored in a qualitative research study.

**Central research question** is the overarching question that the researcher explores in a qualitative research study.

**Central tendency** is a type of descriptive statistic that is a single number that summarizes a collection of scores.

**Close-ended questions** are questions asked in quantitative data collection that include preset options from which the participant can respond.

**Codes** are labels that qualitative researchers use to describe the meaning of a segment of text or an image during data analysis.

**Coding process** is the qualitative analysis process to make sense out of text data where the inquirer divides the data into text or image segments, labels the segments with codes, examines codes for overlap and redundancy, and collapses these codes into broad themes.

**Collecting data** means the researcher selects individuals for a study, obtains their permission to study them, and gathers information by asking them questions or observing their behaviors.

**Conceptual framework** represents a philosophical perspective or a body of knowledge from the literature that the researcher uses to inform a study.

**Conclusion section** is a major section in a research report where the researcher discusses the interpretation of the results and research study.

**Confounding variable** is an attribute or characteristic that the researcher does not directly measure, but that may influence the relationship between the independent and dependent variables.

**Contrary evidence** is information that does not support or confirm the themes and provides contradictory (but realistic) information about a theme in a qualitative data analysis.

**Control variable** is a type of independent variable that is not of central interest to the researcher, but that the researcher measures because it may also influence the dependent variable.

**Correlational research designs** are procedures in quantitative research in which investigators measure the degree of association (or relationship) between two or more variables for a group of individuals.

**Deficiency in knowledge** means that the past literature or experiences of the researchers do not adequately address the research problem.

**Dependent variable** is an attribute or characteristic that is dependent on or influenced by the independent variables. It is the outcome in which the researcher is most interested.

**Describing and developing themes from the data** consists of answering the major research questions and forming an in-depth understanding of the central phenomenon through description and thematic development in qualitative research.

**Description** is a detailed rendering of people, places, or events in a setting in qualitative research.

**Descriptive statistics** are statistical tools that help researchers summarize the overall tendencies in the data, provide an assessment of how varied the scores are, and provide insight into where one score stands in comparison with others.

**Disseminating research** consists of the researcher developing a written report about the study and sharing it with researcher and practitioner audiences.

**Documents** consist of public and private records that qualitative researchers obtain about a site or participants in a study.

**Early stage literature** consists of studies posted to Web sites, papers presented at conferences, professional-association newsletters, drafts of studies available from authors, and student theses and dissertations.

**Effect size** is a means for identifying the practical strength of the conclusions about group differences or about the relationship among variables in a quantitative study.

**E-mail interviews** are a type of qualitative data collection in which the researcher collects open-ended data through interviews with individuals using computers and the Internet.

**Embedded mixed methods design** is a set of procedures for collecting one type of data (quantitative or qualitative) within a larger study that is guided by the other method (qualitative or quantitative), having the secondary dataset address a different question than the primary dataset, and using the secondary dataset to augment the implementation and/or interpretation of the primary method.

**End-of-text references** are the references listed at the end of a research report with the full information about a source in the literature.

**Ethnographic research designs** are qualitative procedures for describing, analyzing, and interpreting a culture-sharing group's shared patterns of behavior, beliefs, and language that develop over time.

**Evaluating research** involves researchers and practitioners assessing the quality of a study using standards advanced by relevant audiences.

**Evidence-based practices** are personal and professional practices that have been shown to be effective through research.

**Experiments** are quantitative research designs that involve the researcher manipulating the conditions experienced by participants. Researchers use experiments to test whether a treatment influences an outcome.

**Explanatory mixed methods design** is a set of procedures that researchers use to first collect and analyze quantitative data and then collect qualitative data to help explain or elaborate on the quantitative results.

**Exploratory mixed methods design** is a set of procedures that researchers use to first collect and analyze qualitative data to explore a topic and then collect quantitative data to help extend or generalize the qualitative results.

**External audit** is a process in which the researcher asks a person outside the project to conduct a thorough review of the study and report back, in writing, the strengths and weaknesses of the project.

**External validity** in quantitative research is the extent to which a researcher can generalize the results from the study sample to a population.

**Fieldnotes** are text (words) recorded by the researcher during an observation in a qualitative study.

**Figure** is a summary of quantitative information presented as a chart, graph, or picture that shows relations among scores or variables.

**Focus group interviews** are a type of qualitative data collection in which the researcher interviews a group of people, asks a small number of general questions, and elicits responses from all individuals in the group.

**Front matter** of an article consists of the title, author information, and an abstract.

**Future research directions** are suggestions made by the researcher in the conclusion section about additional studies that need to be conducted based on the results of the present research.

**Gatekeeper** is an individual who assists in the identification of places to study, has an official or unofficial role at the site, provides entrance to a site, and helps qualitative researchers locate people to study.

**Grounded theory research designs** are systematic, qualitative procedures that researchers use to generate a general explanation (called a *grounded theory*) that explains a process, action, or interaction among people.

**Hypotheses** are statements used only in quantitative research in which the investigator makes a prediction about the outcome of a relationship among variables.

**Hypothesis testing** is a procedure that researchers use to make decisions about quantitative results by comparing an observed value of a sample with a population value to determine whether a difference or relationship exists in the population.

**Identifying a research problem** consists of the researcher specifying an issue to study, developing a justification for studying it, and suggesting the importance of the study for select audiences that will read the report.

**Implications** are suggestions stated in the conclusion section of a report for the importance and usefulness of the study for different audiences.

**Independent variable** is an attribute or characteristic that influences or affects an outcome or dependent variable.

**Inferential statistics** are statistical tools that help researchers compare groups or relate variables and infer results from a sample to a population.

**Instrument** is a tool for measuring, observing, or documenting quantitative data. Examples include demographic forms, performance measures, attitudinal measures, behavioral observation checklists, and factual information.

**Internal validity** in quantitative research is the extent to which a researcher can claim that the independent variable caused an effect in the dependent variable.

**Interpretation** means authors draw conclusions about the results and explain how the results answer the study's research questions in the conclusion section of a research report.

**Interpreting the research** means the researcher explains conclusions drawn about the data and results to provide answers to the research questions, discusses limitations of the study, and suggests implications of the results.

**Interview** is the qualitative data collection process of asking one or more participants general, open-ended questions and recording their answers.

**Interview protocol** is a form designed by qualitative researchers that contains instructions for the process of the interview, the questions to be asked, and space to take notes about the responses from the interviewee.

**Introduction section** is a major section in a research report where the researcher writes about the research problem, literature review, and the study's purpose.

**Journal articles** are polished, short research reports that have been sent to an editor of a journal, accepted for inclusion, and published in a volume of the journal.

**Justifying a research problem** means presenting evidence for the importance of the issue or concern from the literature and/or personal experience.

**Limitations** are potential weaknesses or problems with the study identified by the researcher in the conclusion section of a report.

**Literature map** is a figure or drawing that visually displays the research literature (e.g., studies, books, and summaries) on a topic.

**Literature review** is a written summary of journal articles, books, and other documents that describes the past and current state of information about a topic; organizes the literature into sub-topics; and documents a need for a study.

**Mean** (or average) is the total of the scores divided by the number of scores.

**Member checking** is a process in which the researcher asks one or more participants in the study to check the accuracy of the findings.

**Method section** is a major section in a research report where the researcher describes the selected research design and data collection procedures. This section may also include information about the data analysis procedures.

**Mixed methods research design** is a set of procedures for collecting, analyzing, and "mixing" both quantitative and qualitative methods in a study to understand a research problem.

**Mode** is the score that appears most frequently in a list of scores.

**Multiple perspectives** means that the qualitative researcher provides several viewpoints from different individuals and sources of data as evidence for a theme.

**Narrative discussion** is a written passage presented in the results section of a qualitative report in which authors summarize, in detail, the findings from their data analysis.

**Narrative research designs** are qualitative procedures in which researchers describe the lives of individuals, collect and tell stories about these individuals' lives, write narratives about their experiences, and discuss the meaning of those experiences for the individual.

**Nonparticipant observer** is an observer who visits a site and records notes without becoming involved in the activities of the participants.

**Nonprobability sampling** means that the researcher selects individuals because they are available, convenient, and represent some characteristic the investigator seeks to study.

**Notes** appear at the end of a report and provide general information (such as how to contact the author or what agency funded the study) and additional specific information about a point made within the text.

**Observation** is the process of gathering open-ended, firsthand information in qualitative research by observing people and places at a research site.

**One-on-one interviews** are a type of qualitative data collection in which the researcher asks questions to and records answers from only one participant at a time.

**Open-ended questions** are questions asked in qualitative data collection that allow the participant to create his/her own options for responding.

**Participant observer** is an observational role adopted by researchers when they take part in activities in the setting they observe.

**Participatory action research (PAR)** involves a collaborative research project with a social and community orientation and an emphasis on research that contributes to emancipation or change in our society.

**Peer-reviewed journals** are journals that only publish research reports after they have undergone a review process where experts in the field independently evaluate each study before the journal will publish it as an article. This is the most rigorous type of research publication.

**Percentile rank** of a particular score is the percentage of participants in the distribution with scores at or below a particular score.

**Phenomenological research designs** are qualitative procedures that a researcher uses to understand a single phenomenon by collecting information about and describing essential aspects of the experiences (events, interactions, meanings, etc.,) of several individuals who have experienced the phenomenon.

**Plagiarize** means to represent someone else's ideas and writings as if they were your own, without giving proper credit.

**Population** is a group of individuals or organizations that have the same characteristic and that a quantitative researcher wants to learn about in a study.

**Practical action research** involves a small-scale research project, narrowly focuses on a specific problem or issue, and is undertaken by individual practitioners or teams within a practice setting such as a school or clinic.

**Preliminary exploratory analysis** in qualitative research consists of the researcher exploring the data to obtain a general sense of the data, memoing ideas, thinking about the organization of the data, and considering whether more data are needed.

**Probability sampling** means the researcher selects individuals (or units, such as schools) from the population through a random process so that each individual has a known chance (or probability) of being selected. Examples of probability sampling include random sampling and stratified random sampling.

**Probes** are subquestions under each main question that the researcher asks to elicit more information during a qualitative interview.

**Process of research** consists of seven steps used by researchers when they conduct a research study. The steps include: identifying a research problem, reviewing the literature, specifying a purpose for the research, selecting a research design and collecting data, analyzing data and reporting results, and interpreting the research, and disseminating and evaluating the research.

**Purpose for research** indicates the researcher's major intent or aim for conducting the research study.

**Purposeful sampling** means that researchers intentionally select sites and individuals to learn about or understand the central phenomenon. Examples of purposeful sampling include maximal variation sampling and homogenous sampling.

**Purpose statement** is a statement of one or more sentences that advances the overall direction or focus for the study in a research report.

***p* value** is the probability ($p$) that an inferential statistical result could have been produced by chance if the null hypothesis were true for the population.

**Qualitative research** is a type of research in which the researcher studies a problem that calls for exploration; relies on the views of participants; asks broad, general questions; collects data consisting largely of words (or text) from participants; describes and analyzes these words for themes; and conducts the inquiry in a subjective and reflexive manner.

**Qualitative research designs** are sets of procedures for collecting, analyzing, and reporting text and image data to answer research questions that call for exploring participants' views. Examples include narrative research, phenomenology, grounded theory, case study, and ethnography.

**Quantitative research** is a type of research in which the researcher studies a problem that calls for explanation; decides what to study; asks specific, narrow questions; collects quantifiable data from participants; analyzes these numbers using statistics; and conducts the inquiry in an unbiased, objective manner.

**Quantitative research designs** are sets of procedures for collecting, analyzing, and reporting numeric data to answer research questions that call for explanation. Examples include true experiments, quasi-experiments, single-subject designs, correlational designs, and survey designs.

**Quasi-experiment** is an experimental research design where the researcher assigns existing groups to different conditions of the treatment variable.

**Range of scores** is the difference between the highest and the lowest scores for a variable.

**Reference list** is a list of detailed information about all the sources the author used in writing the report that appears at the end of a research report.

**Relative standing** are statistics that describe one score relative to a group of scores

**Reliable** means that scores from an instrument are stable and consistent.

**Reporting results** involves the researcher representing the data in tables, figures, and pictures to summarize the results found from the data.

**Representative sample** means that the individuals selected for the sample from the wider population are typical of the wider population so that results can be generalized to the population.

**Research** is a process of steps used to collect and analyze information in order to increase our understanding of a topic or issue.

**Research design** is a set of quantitative, qualitative, or combined procedures for collecting, analyzing, and reporting data in a research study.

**Research problem** is an issue, controversy, or concern that guides the need for a study and indicates the importance of a study's topic.

**Research questions** are questions in quantitative or qualitative research that narrow the purpose statement to specific questions that the researcher seeks to answer.

**Results section** is a major section in a research report where the researcher presents the results from analyzing the collected data in a study.

**Reviewing the literature** means that the researcher locates summaries, books, and journal articles on a topic; chooses which literature to include in their review; and then summarizes the literature in the written report.

**Sample** is a subgroup of the population that participates in a research study.

**Sample size** is the number of participants (or organizations) that participate in the study.

**Sampling error** is the difference between the data collected from the sample (sample estimate) and what the researcher would get if data were collected from the whole population (true population score) in quantitative research.

**Sampling strategies** are approaches that researchers use to select individuals or organizations for the samples in research studies.

**Scoring data** means that the researcher assigns a numeric score (or value) to each response category for each question on the instruments used to collect data.

**Selecting a research design** consists of the researcher choosing an overall plan for conducting the study based on the specified purpose.

**Single-item score** is an individual score assigned to each question for each participant in a study.

**Single-subject research** is an experimental research design where the researcher determines the effects of a treatment on a single individual by observing their behavior over a baseline period and during the treatment.

**Specifying the purpose for research** consists of the researcher identifying the major intent or objective for a study and narrowing it into specific research questions or hypotheses.

**Standard deviation** is a measure of how dispersed the data points are about the mean value.

**Statement of the problem** passage conveys the importance of a report by addressing the following five elements: the topic, the research problem, evidence for the importance of the problem, deficiencies in the knowledge about the problem, and the audiences that will benefit from a study of the problem.

**Study-by-study review of the literature** is a literature review written to provide a detailed summary of each study grouped under broad themes.

**Style manuals** present formats for writing research reports by providing a structure for citing references, labeling headings, and constructing tables.

**Summaries** in the literature provide overviews of the literature and research on timely issues written by leading specialists in the field.

**Summed scores** are the scores of an individual added over several items that measure the same variable.

**Survey research designs** are procedures in quantitative research for administering a survey or questionnaire to a small group of people in order to identify trends in attitudes, opinions, behaviors, or characteristics of a large group of people.

**Table** is a summary of quantitative information organized into rows and columns.

**Telephone interviews** are the process of gathering qualitative data from individuals by asking a small number of general questions over the telephone.

**Thematic approach to qualitative research** is a generic approach to conducting qualitative research where researchers collect qualitative data, develop themes as results, and discuss general conclusions from the themes to describe multiple perspectives about a topic.

**Thematic review of the literature** is a literature review written to present the literature in broad categories and to provide the major results from studies rather than the detail of any single study.

**Themes** (also called *categories*) are similar codes aggregated together to form a major idea in the database during qualitative data analysis.

**Theory** explains and predicts the relationship between independent and dependent variables in quantitative research.

**Topic** is the broad subject matter that a researcher wishes to address in a study.

**Transcription** is the process of converting audiotape recordings or fieldnotes into typed text.

**Triangulation** is the process of corroborating evidence from different individuals (e.g., a principal and a student), types of data (e.g., observational fieldnotes and interviews), or methods of data collection (e.g., documents and interviews) in descriptions and themes in qualitative research.

**Triangulation mixed methods design** is a set of procedures that researchers use to simultaneously collect both quantitative and qualitative data, analyze both datasets separately, compare the results from the analysis of both datasets, and make an interpretation as to whether the results support or contradict each other.

**True experiment** is an experimental research design where the researcher randomly assigns individual participants to different conditions of the treatment variable.

**Valid** means that the scores from an instrument make sense, are meaningful, and enable the researcher to draw good conclusions from the sample to the population.

**Validating findings** means that the researcher determines the accurac y or credibility of the findings through strategies such as member checking or triangulation.

**Variability** is a type of descriptive statistic used to indicate the spread of scores in a distribution for a variable.

**Variable** is a characteristic or attribute of an individual or an organization that researchers can measure or observe and that varies among the individuals or organizations studied.

**Within-text references** are references cited in a brief format within the body of the text to provide credit to authors.

**Z score** is a relative standing score that is calculated by converting an original score into a relative score measured in units of standard deviations.

# REFERENCES


Abril, C. R., & Gault, B. M. (2006). The state of music in the elementary school: The principal's perspective. *Journal of Research in Music Education, 54*(1), 6–20.

Aldridge, J. M., Fraser, B. J., & Huang, T. I. (1999). Investigating classroom environments in Taiwan and Australia with multiple research methods. *Journal of Educational Research, 93*(1), 48–62.

Alkin, M. C. (Ed.). (1992). *Encyclopedia of educational research* (6th ed.). New York: Macmillan.

Amatea, E. S., Smith-Adcock, S., & Villares, E. (2006). From family deficit to family strength: Viewing families' contributions to children's learning from a family resilience perspective. *Professional School Counseling, 9*(3), 177–189.

American Psychological Association. (1927–). *Psychological abstracts.* Washington, DC: Author.

American Psychological Association (APA). (2001). *Publication manual of the American Psychological Association* (5th ed.). Washington, DC: Author.

American Psychological Association. (2003). *Ethical principles of psychologists and code of conduct.* Washington, DC: Author.

Anderson, E. S., & Keith, T. Z. (1997). A longitudinal test of a model of academic success for at-risk high school students. *Journal of Educational Research, 90,* 259–266.

Andrews, A. B., Luckey, I., Bolden, E., Whiting-Fickling, J., & Lind, K. A. (2004). Public perceptions about father involvement: Results of a statewide household survey. *Journal of Family Issues, 25*(5), 603–633.

Angrosino, M. V. (1994). On the bus with Vonnie Lee. *Journal of Contemporary Ethnography, 23,* 14–28.

Apthorp, H. S. (2006). Effects of a supplemental vocabulary program in third-grade reading/language arts. *Journal of Educational Research, 100*(2), 67–79.

Asmussen, K. J., & Creswell, J. W. (1995). Campus response to a student gunman. *Journal of Higher Education, 66*(5), 575–591.

Auerbach, S. (2007). From moral supporters to struggling advocates: Reconceptualizing parent roles in education through the experience of working-class families of color. *Urban Education, 42*(3), 250–283.

Baggerly, J., & Osborn, D. (2006). School counselors' career satisfaction and commitment: Correlates and predictors. *Professional School Counseling, 9*(3), 197–205.

Beare, P., Torgerson, C., & Creviston, C. (2008). Increasing verbal behavior of a student who is selectively mute. *Journal of Emotional and Behavioral Disorders.* doi:10.1177/1063426608317356 (published on May 7, 2008).

Bikos, L. H. et al., (2007). A longitudinal, naturalistic inquiry of the adaptation experiences of the female expatriate spouse living in Turkey. *Journal of Career Development, 34,* 28–58.

Bodycott, P., Walker, A., & Lee, J. C. K. (2001). More than heroes and villains: Pre-service teacher beliefs about principals. *Educational Research, 43*(1), 15–31.

Bogdan, R. C., & Biklen. S. K. (1998). *Qualitative research for education: An introduction to theory and methods* (3rd ed.). Boston: Allyn & Bacon.

Brickhouse, N., & Bodner, G. M. (1992). The beginning science teacher: Classroom narratives of convictions and constraints. *Journal of Research in Science Teaching, 29,* 471–485.

Brotherson, S. E., Dollahite, D. C., & Hawkins, A. J. (2005). Generative fathering and the dynamics of connection between fathers and their children. *Fathering, 3*(1), 1–28.

Brown, S. P., Parham, T. A., & Yonker, R. (1996). Influence of a cross-cultural training course on racial identity attitudes of white women and men: Preliminary perspectives. *Journal of Counseling & Development, 74*(5), 510–516.

Bryant, A., & Charmaz, K. (Eds.). (2007). *The handbook of grounded theory.* London: Sage.

Buck, G. A., Leslie-Pelecky, D., & Kirby, S. K. (2002). Bringing female scientists into the elementary classroom: Confronting the strength of elementary students' stereotypical images of scientists. *Journal of Elementary Science Education, 14*(2), 1–9.

Buck, G. A., Plano Clark, V. L., Leslie-Pelecky, D. L., Lu, Y., & Cerda-Lizarraga, P. (2008). Examining the cognitive processes used by adolescent girls and women scientists in identifying science role models: A feminist approach. *Science Education, 92*(4), 688–707.

Campbell, D. T., & Stanley, J. C. (1963). Experimental and quasi-experimental designs for research. In N. L. Gage (Ed.), *Handbook on research in teaching* (pp. 1–80). Chicago: Rand-McNally.

Carrington, S., Templeton, E., & Papinczak, T. (2003). Adolescents with Asperger syndrome and perceptions of friendship. *Focus on Autism and Other Developmental Disabilities, 18*(4), 211–218.

Ceprano, M. A., & Garan, E. M. (1998). Emerging voices in a university pen-pal project: Layers of discovery in action research. *Reading Research and Instruction, 38*(1), 31–56.

Charmaz, K. (2006). *Constructing grounded theory.* London: Sage.

Churchill, S. L., Plano Clark, V. L., Prochaska-Cue, M. K., Creswell, J. W., & Ontai-Grzebik, L. (2007). How rural low-income families have fun: A grounded theory study. *Journal of Leisure Research, 39*(2), 271–294.

Cihak, D. F., Kessler, K., & Alberto, P. A. (2008). Use of a handheld prompting system to transition independently through vocational tasks for students with moderate and severe intellectual disabilities. *Education and Training in Developmental Disabilities, 43*(1), 102–110.

Clandinin, D. J. (Ed.). (2007). *Handbook of narrative inquiry: Mapping a methodology.* Thousand Oaks, CA: Sage.

Clandinin, D. J., & Connelly, F. M. (2000). *Narrative inquiry: Experience and story in qualitative research.* San Francisco: Jossey-Bass.

Clayton, C. D. (2007). Curriculum making as novice professional development: Practical risk taking as learning in high-stakes times. *Journal of Teacher Education, 58*(3), 216–230.

Clemens, P., Hietala, J. R., Rytter, M. J., Schmidt, R. A., & Reese, D. J. (1999). Risk of domestic violence after flood impact: Effects of social support, age, and history of domestic violence. *Applied Behavioral Science Review, 7*(2), 199–206.

Connelly, F. M., & Dukacz, A. S. (1980). Using research findings. In F. M. Connelly, A. S. Dukacz, & F. Quinlan (Eds.). *Curriculum planning for the classroom* (pp. 24–34). Toronto: OISE Press.

Constantine, M. G., Wallace, B. C., & Kindaichi, M. M. (2005). Examining contextual factors in the career decision status of African American adolescents. *Journal of Career Assessment, 13*(3), 307–319.

Corbin, J., & Strauss, A. (2008). *Basics of qualitative research: Techniques and procedures for developing grounded theory* (3rd ed.). Thousand Oaks, CA: Sage.

Cortazzi, M. (1993). *Narrative analysis.* London: The Falmer Press.

Courtney, S., Jha, L. R., & Babchuk, W. A. (1994). Like school? A grounded theory of life in an ABE/GED classroom. *Adult Basic Education, 4,* 172–195.

Craig, C. L. (2004). The dragon in school backyards: The influence of mandated testing on school contexts and educators' narrative knowing. *Teachers College Record, 106*(6), 1229–1257.

Creswell, J. W. (2003). *Research design: Qualitative, quantitative, and mixed method approaches* (2nd ed.) Thousand Oaks, CA: Sage.

Creswell, J. W. (2007). *Qualitative inquiry and research design: Choosing among five approaches* (2nd ed.). Thousand Oaks, CA: Sage.

Creswell J. W. (2008). *Educational research: Planning, conducting, and evaluating qualitative and quantitative research* (3rd ed.). Upper Saddle River, NJ: Pearson Education.

Creswell, J. W., & Brown, M. L. (1992). How chairpersons enhance faculty research: A grounded theory study. *The Review of Higher Education, 16*(1), 41–62.

Creswell, J. W., & Plano Clark, V. L. (2007). *Designing and conducting mixed methods research.* Thousand Oaks, CA: Sage.

Davis, K. D., Winsler, A., & Middleton, M. (2006). Students' perceptions of rewards for academic performance by parents and teachers: Relations with achievement and motivation in college. *Journal of Genetic Psychology, 167*(2), 211–220.

Deslandes, R., & Bertrand, R. (2005). Motivation of parent involvement in secondary-level schooling. *Journal of Educational Research, 98*(3), 164–175.

Dicker, M. (1990). Using action research to navigate an unfamiliar teaching assignment. *Theory into Practice, XXIX,* 203–208.

Ditrano C. J., & Silverstein, L. B. (2006). Listening to parents' voices: Participatory action research in the schools. *Professional Psychology Research and Practice, 37*(4), 359–366.

Dods, R. F. (1997). An action research study of the effectiveness of problem-based learning in promoting the acquisition and retention of knowledge. *Journal for the Education of the Gifted, 20*(4), 423–437.

DuBois, D. L., & Neville, H. A. (1997). Youth mentoring: Investigation of relationship characteristics and perceived benefits. *Journal of Community Psychology, 25*(3), 227–234.

Educational Resources Information Center (U.S.). (1991). *ERIC directory of education-related information centers.* Washington, DC: Author.

Eisner, E. W., & Day, M. D. (Eds.). (2004). *Handbook of research and policy in art education: A project of the National Art Education Association.* Mahwah, NJ: Lawrence Erlbaum Associates.

Epper, R. M. (1997). Coordination and competition in postsecondary distance education. *Journal of Higher Education, 68*(5), 551–587.

Favaro, A., Zanetti, T., Huon, G., & Santonastaso, P. (2005). Engaging teachers in an eating disorder preventive intervention. *International Journal of Eating Disorders, 38*(1), 73–77.

Fetterman, D. M. (1998). *Ethnography: Step by step* (2nd ed.). Thousand Oaks, CA: Sage.

Finders, M. J. (1996). Queens and teen zines: Early adolescent females reading their way toward adulthood. *Anthropology and Education Quarterly, 27*(1), 71–89.

Fothergill, A. (1999). Women's roles in a disaster. *Applied Behavioral Science Review, 7*(2), 125–143.

Fraenkel, J. R., & Wallen, N. E. (2000). *How to design and evaluate research in education* (4th ed.). Boston: McGraw-Hill.

Frankenberger, K. D. (2004). Adolescent egocentrism, risk perceptions, and sensation seeking among smoking and nonsmoking youth. *Journal of Adolescent Research, 19*(5), 576–590.

Garrahy, D. A., Cothran, D. J., & Kulinna, P. H. (2005). Voices from the trenches: An exploration of teachers' management knowledge. *Journal of Educational Research, 99*(1), 56–63.

Glaser, B. G. (1992). *Basics of grounded theory analysis.* Mill Valley, CA: Sociology Press.

Glaser, B., & Strauss, A. (1967). *The discovery of grounded theory.* Chicago: Aldine.

Glesne, C., & Peshkin, A. (1992). *Becoming qualitative researchers: An introduction.* White Plains, NY: Longman.

Greene, J. C. (2007). *Mixed methods in social inquiry.* San Francisco: Jossey-Bass.

Greene, J. C., & Caracelli, V. J. (Eds.). (1997). *Advances in mixed-method evaluation: The challenges and benefits of integrating diverse paradigms: New directions for evaluation, 74.* San Francisco: Jossey-Bass.

Greene, J. C., Caracelli, V. J., & Graham, W. F. (1989). Toward a conceptual framework for mixed-method evaluation designs. *Educational Evaluation and Policy Analysis, 11*(3), 255–274.

Grouws, D. A. (Ed.). (1992). *Handbook of research on mathematics teaching and learning.* New York: Macmillan Publishing Company.

Haigh, K. M. (2007). Exploring learning with teachers and children: An administrator's perspective. *Theory into Practice, 46*(1), 57–64.

Hall, L. A. (2007). Understanding the silence: Struggling readers discuss decisions about reading expository text. *Journal of Educational Research, 100*(3), 132–141.

Harrison, A. (2007). *Relationship-building in an undergraduate leadership program in teacher education.* An unpublished Ph.D. dissertation, University of Nebraska–Lincoln, Lincoln, Nebraska.

Harry, B., Day, M., & Quist, F. (1998). "He can't really play": An ethnographic study of sibling acceptance and interaction. *Journal for the Association of the Severely Handicapped (JASH), 23*(4), 289–299.

Hatch, J. A. (2002). *Doing qualitative research in education settings.* Albany, NY: State University of New York Press.

Heil, D. (2005). The internet and student research: Teaching critical evaluation skills. *Teacher Librarian, 33*(2), 26–29.

Heinlein, L. M., & Shinn, M. (2000). School mobility and student achievement in an urban setting. *Psychology in the Schools, 37*(4), 349–357.

Howard, T. C. (2002). Hearing footsteps in the dark: African American students' descriptions of effective teachers. *Journal of Education for Students Placed at Risk, 7*(4), 425–444.

Huber, J., & Whelan, K. (1999). A marginal story as a place of possibility: Negotiating self on the professional knowledge landscape. *Teaching and Teacher Education, 15,* 381–396.

Huff, R. E., Houskamp, B. M., Watkins, A. V., Stanton, M., & Tavegia, B. (2005). The experiences of parents of gifted African American children: A phenomenological study. *Roeper Review, 27*(4), 215–221.

Hughes-Hassell, S., & Lutz, C. (2006). What do you want to tell us about reading? A survey of the habits and attitudes of urban middle school students toward leisure reading. *Young Adult Library Services, 4*(2), 39–45.

Ivankova, N., & Stick, S. (2007). Students' persistence in a Distributed Doctoral Program in Educational Leadership in Higher Education: A mixed methods study. *Research in Higher Education, 48*(1), 93–135.

Jick, T. D. (1979). Mixing qualitative and quantitative methods: Triangulation in action, *Administrative Science Quarterly, 24,* 602–611.

Jones, J. (1999). *The process of structuring a community-based curriculum in a rural school setting: A grounded theory study.* Unpublished doctoral dissertation, University of Nebraska–Lincoln.

Joint Committee on Standards for Educational Evaluation. (1995). *Program evaluation standards.* Kalamazoo: The Evaluation Center, Western Michigan University.

Judge, S., Puckett, K., & Bell, S. M. (2006). Closing the digital divide: Update from the early childhood longitudinal study. *Journal of Educational Research, 100*(1), 52–60.

Kemmis, S. (1994). Action research. In T. Husen & T. N. Postlethwaite (Eds.), *International encyclopedia of education* (2nd ed., pp. 42–49). Oxford and New York: Pergamon and Elsevier Science.

Kemmis, S., & Wilkinson, M. (1998). Participatory action research and the study of practice. In B. Atweh, S. Kemmis, & P. Weeks (Eds.), *Action research in practice: Partnerships for social justice in education* (pp. 21–36). London: Routledge.

Kerlinger, F. N. (1964). *Foundations of behavioral research.* New York: Holt, Rinehart and Winston.

Kern, P., Wolery, M., & Aldridge, D. (2007). Use of songs to promote independence in morning greeting routines for young children with autism. *Journal of Autism and Developmental Disorders, 37,* 1264–1271.

Kester, V. M. (1994). Factors that affect African-American students' bonding to middle school. *Elementary School Journal, 95*(1), 63–73.

Ketner, C. S., Smith, K. E., & Parnell, M. K. (1997). Relationship between teacher theoretical orientation to reading and endorsement of developmentally appropriate practice. *Journal of Educational Research, 90,* 212–220.

Kim, R. I., & Goldstein, S. B. (2005). Intercultural attitudes predict favorable study abroad expectations of U.S. college students. *Journal of Studies in International Education, 9*(3), 265–278.

Knesting, K., & Waldron, N. (2006). Willing to play the game: How at-risk students persist in school. *Psychology in the Schools, 43*(5), 599–611.

Komives, S. R., Owen, J. E., Longerbeam, S. D., Mainella, F. C., & Osteen, L. (2005). Developing a leadership identity: A grounded theory. *Journal of College Student Development, 46*(6), 593–611.

Lalley, J. P., & Miller, R. H. (2006). Effects of pre-teaching and re-teaching on math achievement and academic self-concept of students with low achievement in math. *Education, 126*(4), 747–755.

Landreman, L. M., Rasmussen, C. J., King, P. M., & Jiang, C. X. (2007). A phenomenological study of the development of university educators' critical consciousness. *Journal of College Student Development, 48*(3), 275–296.

Larson, R. W., & Brown, J. R. (2007). Emotional development in adolescence: What can be learned from a high school theater program? *Child Development, 78*(4), 1083–1099.

Lassetter, J. H., Mandleco, B. L., & Roper, S. O. (2007). Family photographs: Expressions of parents raising children with disabilities. *Qualitative Health Research, 17*(4), 456–467.

LeCompte, M. D., Preissle, J., & Tesch, R. (1993). *Ethnography and qualitative design in educational research* (2nd ed.). San Diego: Academic Press.

Libutti, P. O., & Blandy, S. G. (1995). *Teaching information retrieval and evaluation skills to education students and practitioners: A casebook of applications.* Chicago: Association of College and Research Libraries.

Lincoln, Y. S., & Guba, E. G. (1985). *Naturalistic inquiry.* Newbury Park, CA: Sage.

Liu, E., & Johnson, S. M. (2006). New teachers' experiences of hiring: Late, rushed, and information-poor. *Educational Administration Quarterly, 42*(3), 324–360.

Lloyd, G. M. (2006). Preservice teachers' stories of mathematics classrooms: Explorations of practice through fictional accounts. *Educational Studies in Mathematics, 63,* 57–87.

Luzzo, D. A. (1995). Gender differences in college students' career maturity and perceived barriers in career development. *Journal of Counseling & Development, 73,* 319–322.

Mak, L., & Marshall, S. K. (2004). Perceived mattering in young adults' romantic relationships. *Journal of Social and Personal Relationships, 24*(4), 469–486.

Malecki, C. K., & Demaray, M. K. (2003). Carrying a weapon to school and perceptions of social support in an urban middle school. *Journal of Emotional and Behavioral Disorders, 11*(3), 169–178.

McAllister, G., & Irvine, J. J. (2000). Cross cultural competency and multicultural teacher education. *Review of Educational Research, 70*(1), 3–24.

McCabe, D. L., Butterfield, K. D., & Treviño, L. K. (2006). Academic dishonesty in graduate business programs: Prevalence, causes, and proposed action. *Academy of Management Learning & Education, 5*(3), 294–305.

McCoy, L. P. (2005). Effect of demographic and personal variables on achievement in eighth-grade algebra. *Journal of Educational Research, 98*(3), 131–135.

McVea, K., Harter, L., McEntarffer, R., & Creswell, J. W. (1999). A phenomenological study of student experiences with tobacco use at City High School. *The High School Journal, 82*(4), 209–222.

Merriam, S. B. (1998). *Qualitative research and case study applications in education.* San Francisco: Jossey-Bass.

Miles, M. B., & Huberman, A. M. (1994). *Qualitative data analysis: A sourcebook for new methods* (2nd ed.). Thousand Oaks, CA: Sage.

Miller, D. L., Creswell, J. W., & Olander, L. S. (1998). Writing and retelling multiple ethnographic tales of a soup kitchen for the homeless. *Qualitative Inquiry, 4,* 469–491.

Mills, G. E. (2007). *Action research: A guide for the teacher researcher* (3rd ed.). Upper Saddle River, NJ: Merrill/Prentice Hall.

Milton, J., Watkins, K. E., Studdard, S. S., & Burch, M. (2003). The ever widening gyre: Factors affecting change in adult education graduate programs in the United States. *Adult Education Quarterly, 54*(1), 23–41.

Mishna, F. (2004). A qualitative study of bullying from multiple perspectives. *Children & Schools, 26*(4), 234–247.

Moerer-Urdahl, T., & Creswell, J. W. (2004). Using transcendental phenomenology to explore the "ripple effect" in a leadership mentoring program. *International Journal of Qualitative Methods, 3*(2). Article 2. Retrieved April 26, 2006, from http://www.ualberta.ca/~iiqm/backissues/3_2/pdf/moerer.pdf

Morse, J. M. (1991). Approaches to qualitative-quantitative methodological triangulation. *Nursing Research, 40,* 120–123.

Moustakas, C. (1994). *Phenomenological research methods.* Thousand Oaks, CA: Sage.

Neff, J. M. (1998). From a distance: Teaching writing on interactive television. *Research in the Teaching of English, 33,* 146–157.

Nelson, L. W. (1990). Code-switching in the oral life narratives of African-American women: Challenges to linguistic hegemony. *Journal of Education, 172*(3), 142–155.

Nippold, M. A., Duthie, J. K., & Larsen, J. (2005). Literacy as a leisure activity: Free-time preferences of older children and young adolescents. *Language, Speech, and Hearing Services in Schools, 36,* 93–102.

Niven, D. (2006). A field experiment on the effects of negative campaign mail on voter turnout in a municipal election. *Political Research Quarterly, 59*(2), 203–210.

Oshima, T. C., & Domaleski, C. S. (2006). Academic performance gap between summer-birthday and fall-birthday children in grades k–8. *Journal of Educational Research, 99*(4), 212–217.

Pajak, E. F., & Blasé, J. J. (1984). Teachers in bars: From professional to personal self. *Sociology of Education, 57,* 164–173.

Patton, M. Q. (2002). *Qualitative research and evaluation methods* (3rd ed.). Thousand Oaks, CA: Sage.

Payne, Y. A. (2008). "Street life" as a site of resiliency: How street life oriented Black men frame opportunity in the United States. *Journal of Black Psychology, 34*(1), 3–31.

Plano Clark, V. L., Miller, D. L., Creswell, J. W., McVea, K., McEntarffer, R., Harter, L. M., & Mickelson, W. T. (2002). In conversation: High school students talk to students about tobacco use and prevention strategies. *Qualitative Health Research, 12*(9), 1264–1283.

Preissle, J. (1996). *Jude's juicy journals: Periodicals friendly to qualitative research.* Athens: College of Education, University of Georgia.

Rhoads, R. A. (1995). Whales tales, dog piles, and beer goggles: An ethnographic case study of fraternity life. *Anthropology and Education Quarterly, 26,* 306–323.

Richards, L., & Morse, J. M. (2007). *README FIRST for a user's guide to qualitative methods* (2nd ed.). Thousand Oaks, CA: Sage.

Richie, B. S., Fassinger, R. E., Linn, S. G., & Johnson, J. (1997). Persistence, connection, and passion: A qualitative study of the career development of highly achieving African American-Black and White women. *Journal of Counseling Psychology, 44,* 143–148.

Robinson, D. H., Katayama, A. D., Beth, A., Odom, S., Hsieh, Y., Vanderveen, A. (2006). Increasing text comprehension and graphic note taking using a partial graphic organizer. *Journal of Educational Research, 100*(2), 103–111.

Rushton, S. P. (2004). Using narrative inquiry to understand a student-teacher's practical knowledge while teaching in an inner-city school. *The Urban Review, 36*(1), 61–79.

Russek, B. E., & Weinberg, S. L. (1993). Mixed methods in a study of implementation of technology-based materials in the elementary classroom. *Evaluation and Program Planning, 16,* 131–142.

Schacter, J., & Jo, B. (2005). Learning when school is not in session: A reading summer day-camp intervention to improve the achievement of exiting first-grade students who are economically disadvantaged. *Journal of Research in Reading, 28*(2), 158–169.

Scheib, J. W. (2003). Role stress in the professional life of the school music teacher: A collective case study. *Journal of Research in Music Education, 51*(2), 124–136.

Schmuck, R. A. (1997). *Practical action research for change.* Arlington Heights, IL: IRI/SkyLight Training and Publishing.

Self-Brown, S. R., & Mathews, S., II. (2003). Effects of classroom structure on student achievement goal orientation. *Journal of Education Research, 97*(2), 106–111.

Shadish, W. R., Cook, T. D., & Campbell, D. T. (2002). *Experimental and quasi-experimental designs for generalized causal inference.* Boston: Houghton Mifflin.

Shek, D. T. L. (2007). Perceived parental behavioral control and psychological control in Chinese adolescents in Hong Kong: A replication. *Adolescence, 42*(167), 569–574.

Small, S. P., Brennan-Hunter, A. L., Best, D. G., & Solberg, S. M. (2002). Struggling to understand: The experience of nonsmoking parents with adolescents who smoke. *Qualitative Health Research, 12*(9), 1202–1219.

Sociological Abstracts, Inc. (1953–). *Sociological abstracts.* San Diego: Author.

Spindler, G., & Spindler, L. (1992). Cultural process and ethnography: An anthropological perspective. In M. D. LeCompte, W. L. Millroy, & J. Preissle (Eds.), *The handbook of qualitative research in education* (pp. 53–92). San Diego: Academic Press.

Spradley, J. P. (1980). *Participant observation.* New York: Holt, Rinehart and Winston.

Stake, R. E. (1995). *The art of case study research.* Thousand Oaks, CA: Sage.

Stevens, P. E., & Doerr, B. T. (1997). Trauma of discovery: Women's narratives of being informed they are HIV-infected. *AIDS Care, 9*(5), 523–538.

Strauss, A., & Corbin, J. (1990). *Basics of qualitative research: Grounded theory procedures and techniques.* Newbury Park, CA: Sage.

Strike, K. A., Anderson, M. S., Curren, R., Geel, T. V., Pritchard, I., & Robertson, E. (2002). *Ethical standards of the American Educational Research Association: Cases and Commentary.* Washington, DC: American Educational Research Association.

Stringer, E. T. (1999). *Action research* (2nd ed.). Thousand Oaks, CA: Sage.

Stringer, E. T. (2008). *Action research in education* (2nd ed.). Upper Saddle River, NJ: Merrill/Prentice Hall.

Swidler, S. A. (2000). Notes on a country school tradition: Recitation as an individual strategy. *Journal of Research in Rural Education, 16*(1), 8–21.

Tashakkori, A., & Teddlie, C. (1998). *Mixed methodology: Combining qualitative and quantitative approaches.* Thousand Oaks, CA: Sage.

Tashakkori, A., & Teddlie, C. (Eds.). (2003). *Handbook of mixed methods in social and behavioral research.* Thousand Oaks, CA: Sage.

Tesch, R. (1990). *Qualitative research: Analysis types and software tools.* Bristol, PA: The Falmer Press.

Ting, S. R. (2000). Predicting Asian Americans' academic performance in the first year of college: An approach combining SAT scores and noncognitive variables. *Journal of College Student Development, 41*(4), 442–449.

Unger, M., Faure, M., & Frieg, A. (2006). Strength training in adolescent learners with cerebral palsy: A randomized controlled trial. *Clinical Rehabilitation, 20,* 469–477.

Valdez, M. F., Dowrick, P. W., & Maynard, A. E. (2007). Cultural misperceptions and goals for Samoan children's education in Hawaii: Voices from school, home, and community. *The Urban Review, 39*(1), 67–92.

Van Maanen, J. (1988). *Tales of the field: On writing ethnography.* Chicago: University of Chicago Press.

van Manen, M. (1997). *Researching lived experience: Human science for an action sensitive pedagogy* (2nd ed.). London, Ontario, Canada: The University of Western Ontario.

Vittersø, J., Akselsen, S., Evjemo, B., Julsrud, T. E., Yttri, B., & Bergvik, S. (2003). Impacts of home-based telework on quality of life for employees and their partners: Quantitative and qualitative results from a European survey. *Journal of Happiness Studies, 4,* 201–233.

Vooijs, M. W., & van der Voort, T. H. A. (1993). Learning about television violence: The impact of a critical viewing curriculum on children's attitudinal judgments of crime series. *Journal of Research and Development in Education, 26*(3), 133–142.

Weber, C. J., & Bizer, G. Y. (2006). The effects of immediate forewarning of test difficulty on test performance. *Journal of General Psychology, 133*(3), 277–285.

Wolcott, H. F. (1974). The elementary school principal: Notes from a field study. In G. Spindler (Ed.), *Education and cultural process: Toward an anthropology of education* (pp. 176–204). New York: Holt, Rinehart and Winston.

Wolcott, H. F. (1994). *Transforming qualitative data: Description, analysis, and interpretation.* Thousand Oaks, CA: Sage.

Wolcott, H. F. (1999). *Ethnography: A way of seeing.* Walnut Creek, CA: AltaMira.

Yin, R. K. (2003). *Case study research: Design and methods* (3rd ed.). Thousand Oaks, CA: Sage.

Zhvania, N. (2007). *Approaches to the accountability policy and its consequences on school, teacher and student behavior.* Unpublished manuscript, University of Nebraska–Lincoln.

# NAME INDEX

# SUBJECT INDEX